DATE DUE

DE 8'99			
OC 26 00			
NO 13 00			
AP 3 01			

DEMCO 38-296

MAJOR GENERAL ULYSSES S. GRANT

KENNETH P. WILLIAMS

GRANT RISES IN THE WEST

The First Year, 1861–1862

INTRODUCTION TO THE BISON BOOKS EDITION

BY MARK GRIMSLEY

UNIVERSITY OF NEBRASKA PRESS
LINCOLN

quirements of American National
e of Paper for Printed Library

.... printing indicated by the last digit below:
10   9   8   7   6   5   4   3   2   1

Library of Congress Cataloging-in-Publication Data
Williams, Kenneth P. (Kenneth Powers), 1887–1958.
[Lincoln finds a general. Volume 3]
Grant rises in the West: the first year, 1861–1862 / Kenneth P. Williams;
introduction to the Bison Books edition by Mark Grimsley.
p.   cm.
Originally published as v. 3 of Lincoln finds a general. New York: Macmillan,
1952.
Includes bibliographical references and index.
ISBN 0-8032-9793-9 (pa: alk. paper)
1. Grant, Ulysses S. (Ulysses Simpson), 1822–1885—Military leadership.
2. Command of troops.   3. United States—History—Civil War, 1861–1865—
Campaigns.   4. Southwest, Old—History—Civil War, 1861–1865.
5. Mississippi—History—Civil War, 1861–1865.   I. Title.
E672.W73   1997
973.7'3'092—dc21
97-2249   CIP

Reprinted from the original 1952 edition, titled *Lincoln Finds a General: A
Military Study of the Civil War*, vol. 3, *Grant's First Year in the West*, by the
Macmillan Company, New York. Reprinted by arrangement with Scribner, an
imprint of Simon & Schuster Inc.

To
E. L. W.

INTRODUCTION

Mark Grimsley

The book in your hands was originally the third volume of a work that ran to five volumes—and might have run to seven if cancer had not killed the author in 1958. But although part of a larger set it reads smoothly on its own, especially in tandem with volume 4 in the series, which is also a Bison reprint. Together, these two volumes tell the story of how Ulysses S. Grant rose from obscurity to become the North's foremost general. They also provide a wonderfully clear, detailed account of how the Union high command managed to win some vital early successes in the western theater— and hold on to those gains despite several determined Confederate counterstrokes. Over forty years after its publication, *Lincoln Finds a General* (changed to *Grant Rises in the West* for the Bison Books editions) remains a classic of Civil War history, and its best volumes are the ones that focus most extensively on its central subject: U. S. Grant.

Kenneth P. Williams had immense regard for Grant. "[He] remains unique after two world wars," Williams wrote in the preface to the series; "he is still in many ways the most profitable and the most inspiring of all generals to study. He was a soldier's soldier, a general's general. . . . He was the embodiment of the offensive spirit that leaves the enemy no rest." And, Williams added, he was the general for whom Abraham Lincoln searched three years, a search that Williams called the "chief military problem" faced by the Northern president.[1]

Yet after this preface, and an evocative chapter on the first hours of the Wilderness campaign entitled "A Preview of a General," Grant all but disappeared from the narrative for the first two volumes of *Lincoln Finds a General*. Instead, Williams detailed the commanders who largely failed Lincoln in the eastern theater: Irvin McDowell, John Pope, Ambrose Burnside, Joseph Hooker, and above all, George B. McClellan, whom Williams might have called the "anti-Grant." McClellan has had plenty of critics among Civil War historians, but none more severe, more unyielding, more prosecutorial than K. P. Williams. His contempt for McClellan's overcaution, his disapproval of McClellan's tense relationship with Lincoln, dominated the early volumes. Williams's anti-McClellan mania culminated in a bizarre attempt to rehabilitate McClellan's rival, John Pope, who may have suffered disaster at Second Bull Run but was still okay in Williams's book because, well, at least he was willing to fight.[2]

Happily for Williams, McClellan left the stage just one chapter into volume 2. By the close of that volume, Williams had crisply disposed of Burnside and Hooker and gotten a competent commander, George G. Meade, at last into the saddle of the Army of the Potomac. Gettysburg was fought and won, there were some inconclusive maneuvers in autumn 1863, and the eastern stage was set for Grant's arrival as general in chief.

Only then, having shown the reader in absorbing detail just how badly things could go, was Williams ready at last to tackle the rise of his hero, Grant. But, although subtitled *The First Year, 1861–1862*, this volume is actually a solid account of Federal strategy and operations in the western theater from the war's beginning through the summer of 1862. Only in this way, Williams believed, could he place Lincoln's search for a top commander—and Grant's development as that commander—in proper context.

In doing so, Williams performed an immense service. The cornucopia of works on the military aspects of the Civil War is a byword among historians and publishers. Yet this literary feast has strange omissions. For example, the Confederate high command and strategy have suffered no neglect: Frank E. Vandiver's *Rebel Brass*, Thomas L. Connelly and Archer Jones's *Politics of Command*, and Steven E. Woodworth's two volumes on Jefferson Davis and his generals are only a sampling of works devoted to these subjects. But we have nothing comparable for the Union side. Indeed, *Grant Rises in the West* remains the only detailed treatment of the Union high command so far. Other books—even T. Harry Williams's worthy *Lincoln and His Generals*—are at best overviews. If you want to watch the month-by-month, week-by-week machinations of the North's commanders, you have to consult Kenneth P. Williams.[3]

Williams is worth consulting in any case, because his work displays a lucid writing style and keen powers of analysis. These last derived not only from his vocation as a professor of mathematics (he taught for many years at Indiana University) but also from his service as a World War I infantry officer. Other historians may get lost in anecdotes or hasten to familiar set-piece dramas; Williams unerringly follows the strategic threads as they weave together to form the tapestry of the war. *Grant Rises in the West* is not about the common soldier, though the common soldier makes an occasional appearance. Still less is it about the civilians, white and black, who stood in the path of war. Williams's subject is command: its challenges, its stresses, and above all its endless demand for decisions, decisions, and more decisions. To be sure, the focus on strategic and operational decision making tends to eclipse other aspects of command. There is little in the book about logistics, for example, or the cultivation and motivation of subordinates, or the intersection between military and political affairs that was a prominent (if often unwelcome) concern of high-ranking Civil War commanders. But Williams excels at detailing the strategic decision-making process and the factors that go into it, and if he is sometimes as harsh in his judgments as any armchair general has ever been, it must be admitted that he has reasoned through the decision making more astutely than most and, in so doing, earns his right to judge.

The present volume, *The First Year, 1861–1862*, opens with two biographical chapters on Grant the man, covering his life from childhood through his initial Civil War service as colonel of the Twenty-first Illinois. The narrative then broadens as Williams traces the development of Union strategy in the western theater, a vast region that extended from the Appalachians to the Ozarks. When the war began, Union forces in the western theater faced two main military problems, one defensive, the other offensive. The defensive problem centered on how to hold the vital border states of Missouri and Kentucky. Missouri became the scene of both conventional and guerrilla warfare between Union and secessionist forces; Kentucky, having taken refuge in a dubious neutrality, was treated quite circumspectly by the Union and Confederacy until early September 1861, when a rebel force under Major General Leonidas Polk occupied the town of Columbus, Kentucky, which was located on a high bluff overlooking the Mississippi River. Grant played a significant part in the struggle for the two states. In southeastern Missouri he helped expand the North's control over the region. In Kentucky, his prompt response to Polk's incursion—Grant at once ordered the occupation of the important river towns of Paducah and Smithland, at the mouths of the Tennessee and Cumberland Rivers, respectively—went far to nullify the Confederate advantage and set the stage for later offensive operations.

The second problem facing Union leaders in the West concerned where to strike in order to inflict the most telling blows against the rebellion. One thrust was obvious: the Federal government recognized from the outset that it should seize the Mississippi River in order to divide and isolate the Confederacy. Another evident need was for a strong column to gain control of northwest Arkansas, the region from which rebel forces could most easily menace Missouri. After that, political and military opinion tended to diverge. President Abraham Lincoln looked longingly toward east Tennessee; aware that the region contained perhaps the largest concentration of Unionist sentiment in the Confederacy, he wanted to liberate its people at the earliest possible moment. But although Union General in Chief George B. McClellan agreed with Lincoln, field commanders like Don Carlos Buell demurred, arguing that the dearth of rail connections and good roads made an early advance into east Tennessee impossible. Buell preferred instead to advance southward toward Nashville. He also suggested a joint army-navy thrust up the Tennessee and Cumberland Rivers.

Buell was not the only one to recognize the potential of these rivers as a corridor of invasion. So did Major General Henry W. Halleck, the overall Union commander in Missouri. Grant too grasped the importance of the two rivers. Indeed, to anyone aware of the North's naval advantage and able to read a map, a movement up the Tennessee and Cumberland was obvious.

But it is one thing to identify a promising maneuver, another to execute it. In the end, it was Grant who made the offensive. His objectives were two forts just below the Kentucky state line: Fort Henry on the Tennessee River, Fort Donelson on the Cumberland. The former succumbed with amazing ease. Poorly sited and half-drowned by winter floodwaters, Fort Henry actually surrendered to Union gunboats before Grant's ground forces even reached it. Fort Donelson on the Cumberland River proved tougher to crack, but thanks to Grant's adroit generalship (and an incompetent Confederate defense) this strongpoint capitulated on 16 February 1862, and with it some 12,500 Confederates fell into Union hands. It was the first decisive Northern victory of the war—indeed, one of the most important victories of the entire conflict—and its strategic fruits were vast. The entire Confederate defensive line in the western theater was compromised. Union gunboats ranged up the Tennessee River as far as Muscle Shoals, Alabama. Nashville fell without a fight. Confederate forces at Columbus and Bowling Green, Kentucky, found their positions untenable and withdrew all the way to northern Mississippi. By mid-March, western and central Tennessee were largely in Union hands.

Yet, although Fort Donelson made Grant a hero and won him huge troves of cigars from Northern admirers, the real benefactor was Henry W. Halleck. As Grant's superior he was entitled to some of the credit for the victory and, indeed, he was not shy about taking all of it. "[G]ive me command in the west," Halleck wired McClellan the day after the Confederate surrender.

"I ask this for Forts Henry and Donelson."[4] He soon received what he wanted. Churlishly, however, he turned at once on Grant, hinting broadly to Washington that Grant was being derelict in his duties and might also be drinking. Grant survived this attempted character assassination unscathed, partly because his exploits had won him favor within the War Department and partly because his local Congressman intervened on his behalf, vigorously and effectively. (Curiously for a staunch admirer of Grant, Williams treats the entire episode as a simple if unfortunate misunderstanding on Halleck's part, and he fails to mention Halleck's innuendo about Grant [301–5].)[5]

With Nashville in Union hands and the Confederate army in full retreat from its positions at Columbus and Bowling Green, the key Northern objectives in the West now became the defeat of Confederate forces in northwest Arkansas, the capture of the Mississippi River fortress at Island No. 10, and the seizure of the strategic railroad junction at Corinth, Mississippi. General Samuel R. Curtis accomplished the first goal at the battle of Pea Ridge on 6–8 March 1862. John Pope, after lengthy siege operations, took Island No. 10 on 7 April. Meanwhile, as Buell's army advanced to join it, Grant's army assembled at Pittsburg Landing on the Tennessee River, the obvious jumping-off point for a final offensive against Corinth.

The Confederacy seemed on the ropes, and Grant, like many Northerners, saw the rapid crumbling of the Confederate military posture as indicative of demoralization and an imminent Northern triumph. Believing thus, he elected not to entrench the Pittsburg Landing encampment despite the fact that doctrinally it was the correct thing to do. His green troops already knew how to wield shovels; better to train them to march and fight in preparation for the battle of Corinth ahead. Surely the Confederates would not attack.

But they did. Gathering reinforcements from all over the western theater, General Albert Sidney Johnston unleashed forty thousand rebels against the Union encampment around Shiloh Meeting House on 6 April. The surprise was virtually complete. Grant, who was ten miles away when the attack began, arrived to find thousands of raw Northern volunteers huddled along the bluff at Pittsburg Landing. By day's end the Confederates had shoved Grant's army back almost to the Tennessee River. "[W]e've had the devil's own day, haven't we?" Sherman said to Grant late that night. But Grant refused to be stampeded. "Yes," he replied. "Lick 'em tomorrow, though."[6]

Grant proved correct. Decimated by heavy losses and disorganized by its costly success, the Confederate army could not press home its advantage, particularly after the arrival that evening of heavy reinforcements from Buell's army. The next day, Grant and Buell recaptured the lost encampment and sent the rebels in full retreat toward Corinth.

Williams's treatment of Shiloh exemplifies the strengths and weaknesses of the book. His account of the battle is vivid and accurate; he is sober and careful in his dissection of the command issues involved. Yet he seems deliberately to mute the element of surprise. "Psychologically," he concedes, "the Northern army was badly surprised" (391). But Grant bears scant responsibility for this. Instead, Williams implies that it was somehow a product of the Northern soldiers' mindset. Throughout the book, Grant is the standard by which all other generals are measured. As such, Williams finds it far easier to praise Grant than to assess him critically. Thus, Williams's interpretation smacks at times of tautology: whatever Grant does is great generalship because Grant is a great general.

On the whole, however, this is a minor fault, and it is considerably offset by Williams's fair-minded, balanced appraisal of other western commanders, including the oft-derided Halleck, Buell, and Pope. Moreover, Williams's obvious admiration for Grant did not prevent him from crafting what another Williams—T. Harry Williams—praised as a "picture of Grant . . . as fine as anything we have."[7] Over forty years later, that verdict still stands.

NOTES

1. Kenneth P. Williams, *Lincoln Finds a General: A Military Study of the Civil War*, 5 vols. (New York: Macmillan, 1950–59), 1:ix.

2. For Williams's defense of Pope, see Williams, *Lincoln Finds a General*, 1:356–58.

3. Frank E. Vandiver, *Rebel Brass: The Confederate Command System* (Baton Rouge: Louisiana State University Press, 1956); Thomas L. Connelly and Archer Jones, *The Politics of Command: Factions and Ideas in Confederate Strategy* (Baton Rouge: Louisiana State University Press, 1973); Steven E. Woodworth, *Jefferson Davis and His Generals: The Failure of Confederate Command in the West* (Lawrence: University Press of Kansas, 1990); Woodworth, *Davis and Lee at War* (Lawrence: University Press of Kansas, 1995); T. Harry Williams, *Lincoln and His Generals* (New York: Alfred A. Knopf, 1952).

4. Halleck to McClellan, 17 February 1862, *War of the Rebellion: A Compilation of the Official Records of the Union and Confederate Armies*, 128 vols. (Washington: Government Printing Office, 1880–1901), Series I, 7:628. Hereafter *Official Records*. All citations are to Series I.

5. Bruce Catton is much more critical of Halleck in *Grant Moves South* (Boston: Little, Brown, 1960), 193–208. A dispatch in which Halleck relays a rumor that "Grant has resumed his former bad habits"—a veiled reference to Grant's prewar drinking problem—looms large in Catton's account but is completely overlooked in Williams's. See Halleck to McClellan, 3 March 1862, *Official Records*, 7:680.

6. Quoted in Catton, *Grant Moves South*, 242.

7. T. Harry Williams, review of *Lincoln Finds a General*, vol. 3, *Grant's First Year in the West*, in *Journal of Southern History* 19, no. 2 (June 1953): 244.

CONTENTS

I	*Point Pleasant to Galena*	1
II	*"And Captain Grant"*	10
III	*Ten Weeks of Grant and Frémont*	42
IV	*Belmont*	75
V	*Enter Halleck*	101
VI	*The Year Ends in the West*	130
VII	*An Unplanned Sunday at a Crossroads*	159
VIII	*Telegrams Bring an Order*	178
IX	*Gunboats Take a Fort*	199
X	*Fort Donelson*	229
XI	*Still the Generals Wrangle*	260
XII	*Halleck Gets the West*	283
XIII	*The Armies Gather*	310
XIV	*Shiloh*	345
XV	*Spring Changes into Sultry Summer*	396
	Appendix	441
	Notes	457
	Bibliography	547
	Index	553

ILLUSTRATIONS

Major General Ulysses S. Grant   *Frontispiece*
July 30, 1861 Letter by A. Lincoln   xxvi
following page 266
Major General John A. McClernand
Major General Don Carlos Buell
Commander Henry Walke
Major General Lew Wallace
Major General Benjamin M. Prentiss
Major General William T. Sherman

MAPS

Theater of War, 1861–1865   xxiv
Missouri   20
Vicinity of Ironton   25
Central Missouri   44
The Cairo District   48
Columbus "Demonstration"   79
The Forces Lincoln Planned to Use   110
Western Kentucky and Tennessee   121
Zollicoffer's Move to Mill Springs   134
Battle of Mill Springs, January 19, 1862   173
Forts Henry and Donelson   204
Grant's Isolated Position, February 7, 1862   215
The Investment of Fort Donelson, February 12–16, 1862   236
Grant and Johnston, February 14, 1862   240
The Situation in Eastern Kentucky, February 24, 1862   285
The Missouri-Arkansas Theater   288
Curtis and Van Dorn, March 5, 1862   290
Pope's Operation Against New Madrid, February 24 to
    March 14, 1862   294
The Savannah-Corinth Region   312
Grant's Position at Pittsburg Landing   317
Battle of Shiloh, April 6, 1862, 5:00 A.M.   358
Battle of Shiloh, April 6, 1862, 9:00 A.M.   364
Battle of Shiloh, April 6, 1862, 4:00 P.M.   373

Battle of Shiloh, April 6, 1862, Late Afternoon   375
Battle of Shiloh, April 6, 1862: The Routes of Nelson and Wallace   380
Battle of Shiloh, April 7, 1862, Noon   387
The Tennessee-Alabama Theater   401

PREFACE

THE FIRST two volumes of this work treated the war in the East through 1863. Though important events in the West were referred to, they were not considered in detail, because it was desired to preserve a continuity in the history of the operations of the Army of the Potomac. Western campaigns were mentioned mainly in order to show the remoter problems with which the High Command had to deal while crucial movements and battles were taking place in Virginia, Maryland, and Pennsylvania.

This volume treats the war in the West up to mid-July, 1862, when Halleck was called to Washington to be General in Chief. Though Grant is the central character, all operations are considered, in order to reveal the characteristics of other Federal commanders as well as opposing generals, and to give events in their proper setting. The plan of treatment followed causes the reader to see here Frémont, Pope, and Halleck at times previous to their entry in the earlier volumes. There is a disadvantage in this; but in no other way would it have been possible to keep the desired unity in the treatment of eastern operations. McClellan also enters as General in Chief during the period from November 1, 1861, to March 11, 1862. Since he was simultaneously commander of the Army of the Potomac, one sees his activities in the higher position only when considering the western theater of war.

It is a pleasure to record my appreciation of the encouragement that I have received from many people, and to express my thanks for the helpful answers that have been given to questions I have asked. To some I owe special thanks. Dr. C. Percy Powell of the Manuscript Division of the Library of Congress, and Dr. Neil Franklin of the National Archives, and their assistants, were most helpful when

I sought documents. The Library of Congress kindly furnished prints of Mathew Brady photographs. Mr. James W. Holland, Regional Historian of the National Park Service with headquarters at Richmond, Virginia, formerly Superintendent of the Shiloh National Military Park, and Mr. Albert Dillahunty, Historian at Shiloh, both wrote me at length in answer to my letters, furnishing information carefully gathered from the records. When I visited the park they were generous in their time and assistance. The entire manuscript has been read by my wife, by Professor John M. Hill, and by Colonel Herbert G. Esden. To them and to Mr. Cecil Scott of The Macmillan Company I owe much. I am again also greatly indebted to Major General E. F. Harding, who read most of the chapters and discussed with me some of the questions involved in the campaigns.

K. P. W.

Department of Mathematics
Indiana University
Bloomington
May 6, 1952

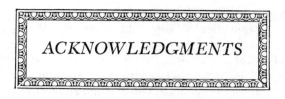

ACKNOWLEDGMENTS

Permission to quote copyrighted material is acknowledged to publishers and authors as follows: Appleton-Century-Crofts, Inc.—*The Rise of U. S. Grant* by A. L. Conger, New York and London, D. Appleton and Company (1913), reprinted by permission of Appleton-Century-Crofts, Inc.; The Bobbs-Merrill Company, Inc.—*The Army of Tennessee* by Stanley Horn, copyright, 1941, by The Bobbs-Merrill Company, Inc.; Thomas Y. Crowell Company—*General Grant's Letters to a Friend* edited by James G. Wilson; Doubleday & Company, Inc.—*The Lincoln Papers* by David C. Mearns, copyright, 1948, by David C. Mearns; Harcourt, Brace and Company, Inc.— *Abraham Lincoln: the War Years,* Vol. I, by Carl Sandburg, copyright, 1939, by Harcourt, Brace and Company, Inc., copyright, 1936, 1937, by Carl Sandburg, *Abraham Lincoln: the War Years,* Vol. II, by Carl Sandburg, copyright 1939, by Harcourt, Brace and Company, Inc., copyright, 1936, 1938 by Carl Sandburg, *Sherman—Fighting Prophet,* by Lloyd Lewis, copyright, 1932, by Harcourt, Brace and Company, Inc.; Harper & Brothers—*An Autobiography* by Lew Wallace, (1906); Houghton Mifflin Company—*Abraham Lincoln, 1809–1858,* by Albert J. Beveridge, copyright, 1928, by Catherine Beveridge; Little, Brown & Company and the Atlantic Monthly Press —*Lincoln's War Cabinet* by Burton J. Hendrick, copyright, 1946, by Burton J. Hendrick; Liveright Publishing Corp.—*Meet General Grant* by W. E. Woodward, copyright, 1946, by William E. Woodward; Longmans, Green & Co., Inc.—*Leonidas Polk* by William Polk, (1915), *Science of War* by Colonel G. F. R. Henderson (1905), *Lincoln's Secretary* by Helen Nicolay, copyright, 1949, by Helen Nicolay; Louisiana State University Press—*Guns on the Western Waters* by H. Allen Gosnel, copyright, 1949, by Louisiana State

University Press; W. W. Norton and Company—*Memoirs of a Volunteer* by John Beatty, copyright, 1946, by W. W. Norton and Company; Prentice-Hall, Inc.—*Thomas: Rock of Chickamauga* by Richard O'Connor, copyright, 1948, by Prentice-Hall, Inc.; G. P. Putnam's Sons—*Ulysses S. Grant* by W. C. Church, (1897), *Letters of Ulysses S. Grant* by Jesse Grant Cramer, copyright, 1913, by Jesse Grant Cramer; Charles Scribner's Sons—*George Washington*, Vol. IV, by Douglas S. Freeman, copyright, 1951, by Charles Scribner's Sons, *General Grant's Last Stand* by Horace Green, copyright, 1936, by Horace Green; The State Company—*Braxton Bragg* by Don C. Seitz (1924).

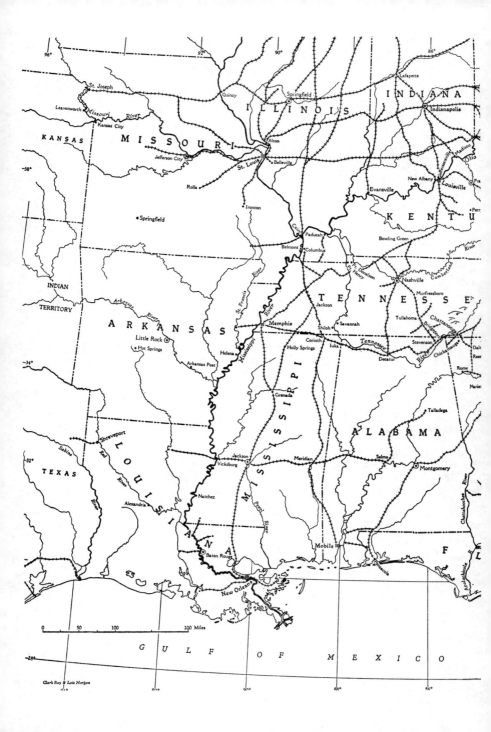

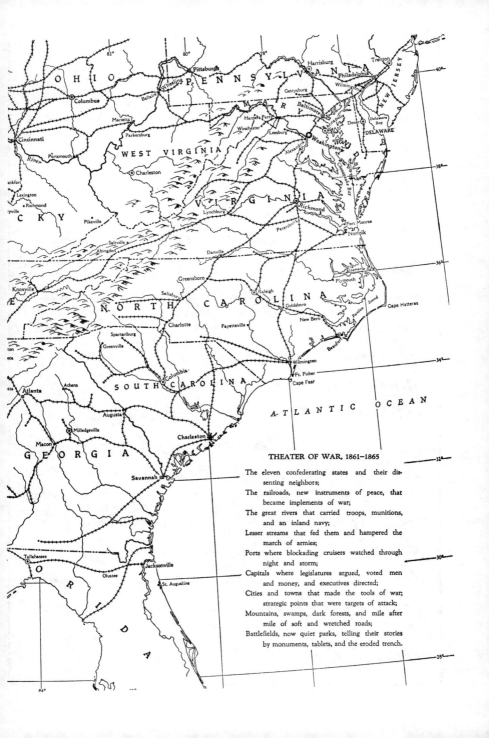

THEATER OF WAR, 1861–1865

The eleven confederating states and their dissenting neighbors;

The railroads, new instruments of peace, that became implements of war;

The great rivers that carried troops, munitions, and an inland navy;

Lesser streams that fed them and hampered the march of armies;

Ports where blockading cruisers watched through night and storm;

Capitals where legislatures argued, voted men and money, and executives directed;

Cities and towns that made the tools of war; strategic points that were targets of attack;

Mountains, swamps, dark forests, and mile after mile of soft and wretched roads;

Battlefields, now quiet parks, telling their stories by monuments, tablets, and the eroded trench.

Executive Mansion
July, 30. 1861

Hon. Sec. of War
My dear Sir:

In addition to those named in my note of yesterday, please send me nominations as Brigadier Generals of Volunteers, for Ulysses S. Grant, John A. McClernand, and Benjamin M. Prentiss, of Illinois; B F. Kelly, and Frederick W. Lander, of Virginia; Joseph Hooker, of California; Edward D. Baker, of Oregon; Siegel, of Missouri; Rufus King, of Wisconsin; and Thomas W. Sherman, of the regular Army—

You perceive I have only the initials for Kelly & Lander; and no part of the Christian names for Hooker & Siegel. Please fill them in, so far as you

have the means, and leave spaces
for me to fill the rest, which I
shall try to do—

And be sure to have the
nominations reach me in time to be
sent to the Senate to-day—

Yours very truly
A. Lincoln

GRANT RISES IN THE WEST

CHAPTER I

POINT PLEASANT TO GALENA

The South will fight. Grant to Rawlins

O N the April Saturday when the news came that Fort Sumter had
been fired upon, Ulysses Grant was living in Galena, Illinois. He was
relatively a newcomer to the town, having only the spring before
joined his brothers Simpson and Orvil as operators of a hardware
and leather goods store owned by their father, Jesse R. Grant, now
retired and living in Covington, Kentucky. Fifteen of the thirty-nine
years of his life had been spent in the Army, and considerable ill-
fortune had been his lot since he started a civilian career at the age
of thirty-two.[1]

A soldier's life had not been his own conception, but that of Jesse,
who saw in it the way for an education and a professional career for
his oldest son. The father himself had not had the advantage of much
formal education, but he was a man of fine mind as well as strong
character, who read much, wrote letters to newspapers, and saw that
Ulysses enjoyed the opportunities afforded by the schools in the
vicinity of Georgetown, Ohio, where in addition to his tannery he
owned a livery stable and a farm. One day—so the story goes—
Jesse Grant saw the local militia company being drilled by Virginia-
born but Georgetown-reared Jacob Ammen, who had graduated from
West Point. An idea came to Grant's mind, and after the company
had been dismissed he questioned Lieutenant Ammen about the
advantages that would come to his own son from an education at

[1]

the Military Academy. While a remark about West Point may have been made to Ulysses by his father, the boy did not know that active steps were being taken to make a soldier out of him, and he was both surprised and displeased when his father, with evident pleasure to himself, told him that he believed he had secured the necessary appointment. Ulysses lost no time, however, in futile protestations but set to work preparing for the entrance examinations that he would have to take. There was, he thought, a fair chance that West Point would be abolished in accordance with the frequent and vehement urgings of some congressmen; if he were not happily rescued from a military career in that fashion, he could resign after graduating and engage in teaching or engineering work, as many officers had done, and Jake Ammen soon would do.

Though he had always been called Ulysses, his name was really Hiram Ulysses Grant, the first name having been given in deference to the desire of his maternal grandfather, John Simpson, owner of six hundred acres of land and a big brick house. It was an easy matter to drop off the first name and use the one that Jesse and Mrs. Simpson preferred, but when Ulysses put his initials, H. U. G., on a trunk in brass-headed tacks, he saw he dare not venture away from home with such a combination. So he decided on an inversion and reported himself at West Point as Ulysses H. Grant, only to be told that no such cadet was expected, though they were looking for a Ulysses S. Grant from Ohio. The congressman who made the appointment had forgotten about the unused name and had supplied Simpson as a matter of course. Ulysses protested without success, continued to sign himself as U. H., and not until he graduated did he accept the fact that he was U. S. Grant. When they noted the initials that the Academy used, other cadets promptly called him Uncle Sam, but soon they were calling him just Sam Grant.

Grant's academic record at the Academy was not impressive, and he stood just below the middle man in the class of thirty-nine who graduated in 1843. In mathematics, however, he achieved so much distinction that he had good prospects of being called back as an instructor if events had not intervened. While he showed no special interest in military tactics or drill, he did in horses and riding. This merely continued an attachment formed at a very early age, for he understood and managed horses so well that when he was only ten he drove passengers to Cincinnati, and a little later he took trips for his father that would keep him away from home for several days. The record in high jumping that Grant set at the Academy stood for twenty-five years; only one other member of his class could handle the horse with which he made the record jump, and no one but Grant for exhibition purposes.

The Fourth Infantry, to which Grant was assigned after graduation, was stationed at Jefferson Barracks, nine miles below St. Louis, and within five weeks after his arrival in late September, the brevet second lieutenant found himself in command of one of its small companies. Thus he early had experience in the most basic of all military positions, that of a captain. In preparation for the assistant professorship at West Point to which he was looking forward, he began to review his mathematics and to carry on other serious reading. His study, however, suffered after he had made a visit to White Haven, the near-by home of the parents of his classmate Fred Dent, for Mrs. Dent and six-year-old Emmy were greatly attracted to the young officer and he became a frequent visitor. In February Emmy's sister Julia, about whom Grant had heard much conversation, came home from St. Louis, where she had remained for the social season after completing a course in a finishing school. Soon Emmy discovered that her lieutenant was in love with her sister, though it required the commotion over the annexation of Texas and the departure in May of the Fourth Infantry for a camp in Louisiana to make Ulysses fully recognize the fact. Before he left he and Julia had become engaged.

For about a year Grant was in the Louisiana camp, and then for eight months near Corpus Christi. On March 11, 1846, his eyes were turned toward the Rio Grande as he marched southward in the last of the four contingents that composed the small army of General Zachary Taylor. Hostilities followed in early May, when the battles of Palo Alto and Resaca de la Palma were fought not far from Taylor's camp. On September 6, when near the end of the grueling three-hundred-mile march to Monterrey, Grant wrote to Julia complaining of the slowness of the war—six months of it and only two battles! "If we have to fight," he said, "I would like to do it all at once and then make friends"—words that years later had the echo, "Let us have peace." After the hard battle at Monterrey, in which he distinguished himself, Grant was transferred to the new army of General Winfield Scott and took part in the latter's bold operations from Vera Cruz to the capture of Mexico City. Most of the time he was regimental quartermaster, but he usually managed to arrange his duties so as to get into active combat, where his personal bravery was as apparent as were his steady reliability and faithfulness to duty as a supply officer. Many a soldier in the Civil War was unknowingly the beneficiary of the fact that he had as a general a former infantryman who had served as a quartermaster.

Ulysses and Julia were married on August 22, 1848, and after that there came assignments to Sackets Harbor, New York, to Detroit, then back to the harbor post on the eastern end of Lake Ontario—with the chance of being called back to the Academy as a teacher growing dimmer every month. In the spring of 1850 Julia returned to Missouri, and in the home of her parents her first child, Frederick Dent Grant, was born on May 30. Two years later, when the Fourth Infantry moved to Governors Island to take ship for California, she went to the home of Jesse Grant, now living in Bethel and serving as the town's first mayor. Jesse had come a long way since he married Hannah Simpson and took her to live at Point Pleasant in the modest cottage overlooking the Ohio, twenty-five miles above Cincinnati, where Ulysses had been born. Then he had only a trade and the determination to prosper. Now he was reported to be worth $100,000, a large amount in the eyes of the people of Bethel.

Grant felt keenly the separation from his family, augmented soon after his departure by the birth of a second son, who was given his own name—as revised by the congressman and the Army. In an effort to make it possible for Julia and his children to join him, he sought to supplement his income by raising cattle, hogs, chickens, and potatoes for the San Francisco market, as well as cutting ice. But the successive ventures were unprofitable when they did not actually lose money. After a year of such disappointments at Fort Vancouver on the Columbia River, he was transferred to Fort Humboldt, near Eureka, California, two hundred and fifty miles north of San Francisco, where two companies of the Fourth Infantry were stationed. It was a drab and lonesome post; in addition the commanding officer was Brevet Colonel Robert C. Buchanan, whose hostility Grant had felt from the time he joined the regiment at Jefferson Barracks, where Buchanan had been senior captain. Eventually there was an incident, about which many and discordant accounts were told, some definitely incorrect. "The Army is as prone to gossip as a New England sewing-society," was Colonel Church's appraisal.[2] All that is certain is that on April 11, 1854, Grant wrote a letter accepting the commission of captain that had arrived several months after the rank had been given him, and another letter tendering his resignation.

Julia had gone to White Haven, and there, on sixty acres of land given to her by her father, Grant started to become a farmer. For upwards of two years they lived first with the Dents and then in a house belonging to an absent brother of Julia, while Grant felled trees, adzed and stacked the logs to season, split shingles, and dug a cellar for a house, which was "raised" with the help of neighbors in the summer of 1856. For cash to provide the necessities of life he cut and sold cordwood in St. Louis. Julia had three slaves, but the single male of the trio had been trained for household duties. Though Grant would later ask permission of Lincoln to make foot soldiers out of proud cavalrymen for whom there were no horses, he probably did not suggest debasing caste-conscious Dan, whom Emmy described as the "most polished piece of human ebony" anyone every saw, by putting an ax into his uncalloused, cultured hands. The farming venture did not succeed—poor seasons, a depression, and Grant's ill health combining to cause successive failures.

After the four years of futility on the farm, where a third son and a daughter were born, there were two discouraging years with ventures in St. Louis, and then Grant resorted to his father. While Ulysses was in West Point, Jesse and a tanner in Bethel had opened a store in Galena, then the metropolis of the Northwest, the partner operating the store while Jesse moved to Bethel and carried on the production of leather. After the amicable dissolution of the partnership Jesse had started a store of his own in the Illinois town, with his sons Simpson and Orvil as managers. Simpson was now in the first stages of tuberculosis, and it was sadly evident that his place would have to be taken by another. It was, however, not the first time that thoughts of going to Galena had been in Ulysses's mind, for in a letter written from Matamoros on June 5, 1846, he had said, after asking Julia if she would be willing to come to Mexico if the Fourth Infantry remained there, "I think it probable though that I shall resign as soon as this war is over and make Galena my home. My father is very anxious to have me do so."

When Grant wrote thus about going to Galena the hard march to Monterrey was close at hand; when he actually went there the crucial election of 1860 was only five months away. The census taker that year counted 9,241 persons in the town where—strangely enough—Julia's father had in 1824 opened the first trading post. But the number of inhabitants alone did not give an indication of the commercial importance or general distinctiveness of Galena. From the near-by mines nearly a billion pounds of lead of unusual purity had been shipped out on the river that bore the town's name and emptied into the Mississippi. Writing a year after the end of the Civil War, one author said, "In but few towns of the country has there been more wealth accumulated. . . . In no place in the West is there dispensed a more refined and generous hospitality." Many nationalities and varied backgrounds were represented in its population, and a hotel with two hundred rooms testified to the constant flow of transients and the need of facilities for public entertainment. In describing the physical aspects of Galena writers used unusual adjectives and likened it to an Alpine city because hills rose abruptly from near the river and houses were perched upon terraces along the winding streets that led to the tops of the hills.[3]

Famous names were associated with Galena's history. Among the early settlers was William S. Hamilton, son of Alexander Hamilton, who became a colonel in the Black Hawk War. His mother, daughter of General Philip Schuyler and member of a prominent New York family, spent the winter of 1838–1839 visiting the son who never married, who wore coarse clothes and went barefooted, but beneath whose rough exterior it was said there was a heart of gold and a cultivated mind. Near the end of the Black Hawk War in 1832, Winfield Scott had marched from the village of Chicago to Galena; the small frame building he used as headquarters may still have been standing when Grant arrived. The town also had its memories of Zachary Taylor, Grant's other respected general, who represented the ultimate in aversion to military trappings, just as Scott did in addiction to parade and show—and bold operations. Some Galenians could likewise talk knowingly about a figure currently exerting influence on Southern action, who before long was much in the headlines—Jefferson Davis. While a lieutenant in the regular army, Davis had been stationed at Fort Winnebago and at Fort Crawford, near Prairie du Chien, Wisconsin, and often sought relief from the boredom of the garrison by visiting Galena.

When Grant arrived at Galena there was excitement about the Republican Convention which was soon to meet in Chicago, and which in early June passed over the much-favored William Seward and, on the third ballot, nominated Lincoln for the Presidency. The town also had many supporters of another citizen of Illinois, Stephen Douglas, the "Little Giant" who had defeated Lincoln for the Senate two years before. The Democratic Convention which had met for ten hot, tempestuous days in April and early May in Charleston, South Carolina, had ended in disruption, but Douglas received on June 22 the nomination of the delegates who had reassembled in Baltimore, while Southern bolters at once put up John C. Breckinridge of Kentucky, then Vice President, as a candidate. Though he had been born in Vermont, Douglas had less hostility to slavery than the Kentucky-born Lincoln, for he had been largely responsible for the repeal of the Missouri Compromise and the passage of the Kansas-Nebraska Act that had made the question of slavery in the territories a flaming issue. His doctrine of "popular sovereignty" was a straddling appeal, halfway between the demand of the South that slavery should be protected in the territories and that of Lincoln that it be barred.

Grant's father and brothers were among the Whigs who had gone enthusiastically into the new Republican party in 1856; but Ulysses had voted for James Buchanan, not because he held the Democratic candidate in much esteem, but because he cared less for the army record of John Frémont, the Republican nominee. In Galena he was exposed to the arguments of Orvil and other ardent Republicans, among them William Reuben Rowley, clerk of the circuit court, who advanced the view that Ulysses had the right to vote on account of a visit to Galena in October, 1859. If he had lined up politically with Orvil and Rowley, an effort to vote might have brought a challenge from fiery John Aaron Rawlins, a former city attorney, who was caring for the legal business of the Grants and vehemently preaching the doctrine of Douglas as the way to national salvation.

Rawlins had begun life in extreme poverty, and at fifteen, as second oldest in a family of eight children, he had to assume heavy responsibilities because drink interfered with the farming activities of his father. It had been his intention to become a preacher; but he shifted to the law, a fortunate change, for the vocabulary he had acquired in driving oxen would have been a handicap to a career in the pulpit. In the legal profession he had been successful in spite of outbursts of colorful language and an indifference about collecting fees. Fearing that, like his father, he might fall a victim of intemperance if he drank at all, Rawlins had become a fervent teetotaler. While Grant could not have foreseen the close association that he was to have with the firm's lawyer when first they met, there was from the start a bond of attachment. As Ulysses watched Simpson sink with tuberculosis, Rawlins saw his young wife, mother of his three children, slipping away with the same malady. On the night that news came of the election of Lincoln there was jubilation among the Republicans assembled in the Grant store; but Rawlins recorded that his new friend, who had been a thoughtful observer of the campaign,[4] remarked to him afterward, "The South will fight."

In his new position Grant worked mostly on the books,[5] though he also went to the front of the store to make sales, often charging, according to one story, either too much or too little. Sometimes he went to a vacant room above the store to play cards and smoke his clay pipe. He also took over the calls that Simpson had made on customers in Wisconsin and Iowa, as well as in Illinois, for the establishment did a wholesale as well as a retail business. It soon became known that the new representative of the Grant firm had been an army officer and was a veteran of the Mexican War; so, as the winter wore on, troubled people came to him to learn his views about the war that was being talked about and feared.

In Prairie du Chien there took place an incident remembered as more significant than the former captain's conversations. A customer of the Grant firm had transferred to a third party the ownership of a stock of goods for which he had not paid. Finding they were locked in a stone building, Grant hired a lawyer, secured a writ of replevin, and with a large and bold-looking deputy sheriff went to get the goods. From behind the barred door there came the threat that anyone entering would be killed. The officer of the law stopped, apparently thinking it was time for negotiation. Grant asked him why he did not deputize some one to go in for him, if afraid to do so himself. Whereupon Boss Brunson said, "Very well, I'll deputize you." So authorized, Grant made a rush at the door, planted a smashing foot against the lock, and in a few seconds had the shotgun out of the hands of the boastful defender. At Grant's orders the man boxed the goods; and presently they were aboard a steamboat bound for Galena. Apparently years of adversity had not lessened the reserve of action that lay beneath Grant's very calm exterior. Here was the same Sam Grant who near Brownsville had tamed a wild horse in a

way that made talk around many campfires; the same Sam Grant who
had taken a gun to the top of a belfry when he might have been out
of the fight doing the work of a quartermaster; the same Sam Grant
who had led storming parties before Mexico City, and of whom James
Longstreet later said, "I had occasion to observe his superb courage
under fire—so remarkable was his bravery that mention was made of
it in the official report, and I heard his colonel say, 'There goes a man
of fire.' "

CHAPTER II

"AND CAPTAIN GRANT"

Been answering your messages since day before yesterday.
Do you receive the answers?   *Lincoln to Frémont*

On the evening of Tuesday, April 16, Galena's two brass bands marched to the courthouse along flag-decked streets. News had come the day before that Fort Sumter had fallen and that Lincoln had called for 75,000 militia.[1] From Washington there also had come the word that Senator Douglas had declared strongly for the Union. That was enough for many of his followers and even for a few who had voted for Breckinridge; but other Democrats were holding back and advising a cautious attitude. Coercion of a sovereign state was an ugly thought. Even the Republicans did not dispute that. But the flag of the nation had been fired upon and had been pulled down from above a fort that belonged to the United States. On that simple fact they took their stand.

John Rawlins was not a man who would ask "What does Douglas say?" before making up his mind at such a time, and he went to the courthouse prepared to speak. According to the story, a friend stopped him at the entrance and told him that a meeting of Black Republicans was not one for a Douglas leader to address. The vehement answer left no room for argument, and, brushing aside the would-be detainer, Rawlins strode up the stairs to the courtroom.

Appropriately Mayor Robert Brand was promptly placed in the chair, and he spoke for compromise and peace. He was for the

President all right, and for the flag, and for the laws, be they right or wrong. But there should be no warring by one part of the country on another; the Republicans should not be allowed to stampede the country into fighting. Galena stories differ as to what happened after Brand's cautionary pronouncement, but a resolution put by Congressman Elihu B. Washburne was carried. Though embellished with many patriotic words it was more than mere rhetoric, for it declared that two military companies should be raised immediately in Galena. It is also certain that Rawlins made an impassioned speech. It was no longer a question of politics, he declared, and he summed up the issue: "It is simply country or no country. I have favored every honorable compromise; but the day for compromise is passed. Only one course is left for us."

Obviously the only course left was war, and at least one of those who heard Rawlins so declare knew about grueling marches, cheerless bivouacs, and hard battles. The story has it that on hearing the news about Fort Sumter Grant said that, having been educated by the government, he should offer his services. Thus he needed no rhetoric to influence him; but he went away from the meeting deeply impressed with the logic, the single-mindedness, and the earnestness of Rawlins. The thirty-year-old Galena lawyer had had no military experience, but he was a man of loyalty, energy, and determination. That much the onetime captain learned that night. As he listened to Rawlins did Grant wonder how long the war would last? Later he would write that on account of the superior resources of the North he thought the conflict would be only a ninety-day affair. That seems almost incredible, for he had seen in the Mexican War the time required to organize, equip, and train volunteer troops. But it will be seen that the statement in his *Memoirs* is confirmed by a letter he presently wrote to his father.

Resolving to raise military companies is one thing; obtaining subscribers to enlistment is another. Two days after the meeting of the 16th another was held, with plans made beforehand to ensure its running smoothly. County Treasurer John E. Smith, a good friend of Washburne and an aide on the staff of Governor Richard Yates, called the meeting to order, and someone promptly said, "I nominate for chairman, Captain Ulysses S. Grant." It was the voice of Smith himself, according to Rawlins, but that of Washburne, according to Augustus Chetlain. Somewhat embarrassed, Grant, unknown personally to many in the assembly, took the chair and the serious business of getting recruits began. Once more Rawlins spoke; but all he could do was urge others to do their duty, for his wife's illness prevented him from leaving home. Galenians understood and did not discount what he said. Washburne also spoke. The first to actually enlist was Chetlain, and when the meeting closed there were twenty names. Though far from being enough for the two units that had been voted, the number warranted a telegram to the governor that Galena would furnish a company.

No one should have expected Grant to enlist, for a man with his experience had no place even as a company commander in the new forces. If not assigned to some important staff duty, he should have a regiment. Nevertheless Grant was through with the store and the Galena company received practically all his attention; he helped complete its recruitment and took over its training, since Chetlain, who was elected captain, had had no military experience. From the governor word came that there were no uniforms for the Galena unit, and it would have to be properly clothed by the town before going to the rendezvous at Springfield. So, as the men drilled with laths under Grant's direction, tailors under his instructions cut uniforms from cloth furnished by a local merchant, with some financing by a local bank.

Though he had no time for the ledgers in the store, Grant found opportunity to write his father-in-law an important letter the day after he had presided at the courthouse meeting. Knowledge of the Southern sympathies of Colonel Dent did not cause Grant to moderate the expression of his own devotion to the government, and he also sought to dispel illusions that Julia's father might be entertaining. "The North," he wrote, "is responding to the President's call in such a manner that the rebels may truly quake. I tell you there is no mistaking the feelings of the people. The Government can call into the field not only 75,000 troops but ten or twenty times 75,000 if it should be necessary and find the means of maintaining them too. It is all a mistake about the northern pocket being so sensitive." Nor did Ulysses spare the owner of White Haven in the matter of his son's sentiments: "I have just received a letter from Fred. He breathes forth the most patriotic sentiments. He is for the old Flag as long as there is a Union of two states fighting under its banner and when they dissolve he will go it alone." As if he feared he might not be doing his old classmate justice, he added, "This is not his language, but it is the idea not so well expressed as he expresses it." [2]

Although his own father needed no admonishing, Grant two days later began a letter to him: "We are now in the midst of trying times when every one must be for or against his country, and show his colors too, by his every act." Any regret that Jesse Grant had felt because Ulysses had not followed him and his other sons into the Republican party would disappear when he read: "Whatever may have been my political opinions before, I have but one sentiment now. That is, we have a Government, and laws and a flag, and they must be sustained." He had not, he explained, yet offered himself, for he did not want to act hastily, and there were more than enough for the "first call of the President." But he had promised to go to Springfield with the Galena company and would offer his services to the governor to help organize the six Illinois regiments. Knowing his father's tendency to speak his mind and realizing that sentiment in Covington was probably hostile, he expressed the thought that Jesse might not be entirely safe. In that case he advised him to move, saying, "I would never stultify my opinion for the sake of a little security." [3]

The industrious tailors soon had the uniforms completed and on the 25th, behind the bands and a flag made according to Grant's directions, the Galena company marched to the station between lines of cheering citizens. Following it, carpet bag in hand, strode the drillmaster, the onetime captain of infantry.[4] In two days he would be thirty-nine years old.

The mustering officer at Camp Yates, which was deep in mud when the Galenians arrived, was Captain John Pope. Son of a prominent Illinois pioneer and judge, he had graduated from West Point in the class next ahead of Grant's, and the two had served together under Taylor in the Mexican War. Pope had come to Springfield from the headquarters of the Department of the West at St. Louis, perhaps with the expectation that he would be made commander of the Illinois brigade. He apparently was friendly enough toward Grant, and he offered to recommend him to the state officials for some sort of an appointment. The story of the next few days is, however, full of contradictions, different people afterward striving for credit in placing Grant's merits before the governor. Prospects could not have been promising at first, for on the 29th he wrote to his sister Mary, "It was my intention to have returned to Galena last evening, but the Governor detained me, and I presume will want me to remain with him until all the troops are called into service, or those to be so called, are fully mustered in and completely organized." [5]

Grant had not exaggerated the response to the President's call. All companies were oversize and many units above the quota had been offered. The legislature was in session and it wisely passed an act providing for the maintenance and discipline of the surplus troops for a month; then if Washington made another call, Illinois would have men ready at hand. "There is no disposition to compromise now," Ulysses wrote to his sister. "Nearly every one is anxious to see the Government fully tested as to its strength, and see if it is not worth saving." Mary, the youngest of Jesse's six children, had been born just a few weeks after Ulysses entered the Military Academy, and though not a student of government, she could easily understand her brother's platform, unencumbered as it was with any abstractions. To her Ulysses also amplified his suggestion about leaving Covington: "If father were younger and Simpson strong and healthy, I would not advise such a course. On the contrary, I would like to see every Union man in the border slave states remain firm at his post. Every such man is equal to an armed volunteer at this time in defence of his country." [6]

Illinois had been short of arms as well as of uniforms. But on the 26th trains brought twenty thousand rifles and muskets with ammunition from the arsenal at St. Louis, thanks to a clever stratagem by Captain Nathaniel Lyon, who had succeeded in loading them on a boat for Alton in spite of the watchfulness of St. Louis secessionists, themselves eager for weapons. Thus Governor Yates's regiments were soon equipped and three of them went without delay to the strategic town of Cairo, while the remainder made ready for departure. When the brigadiership went to Benjamin M. Prentiss, colonel of one of the new regiments, who had been a captain of volunteers in the Mexican War and since then a prominent politician, Pope withdrew to St. Louis. Thereupon the governor made Grant commander of Camp Yates and a mustering officer for the new thirty-day men, with his previous pay of two dollars a day raised to the handsome figure of $4.20. [7]

Still only a helper and an onlooker, Grant wrote to his father on

May 6 that he probably could have had the colonelcy of a regiment, but had been "perfectly sickened at the political wire-pulling for all these commissions, and would not engage in it." He would not, he assured his father, be backward in offering his services, and he commended the new call for troops that had just been made. Julia was, he said, taking "a very sensible view of our present difficulties," and though she would be sorry to see him go, she thought the circumstances might warrant it and would put no obstacle in his way. The response of the North had strengthened his view that the conflict would not be long, and he asserted, "My own opinion is that this war will be but of short duration." So positive was he that he foresaw the possibility of a strange turn of events: "A Northern army may be required in the next ninety days to go South to suppress a negro insurrection. As much as the South have vilified the North, that army would go on such a mission and with the purest motives."

After such prognostications Grant leveled a sally at Gideon J. Pillow, against whom he would first contend in battle. Pillow, a former law partner of James K. Polk, was early given a brigadier's commission in the Mexican War, and after winning the sobriquet "Polk's spy" had aroused merriment among regular officers when he dug a trench on the wrong side of a parapet. Later he caused talk by laying claim to a wound of dubious character which nonetheless brought him a major generalcy from his White House friend. The Tennessean was now in Confederate service and Grant remarked in his letter to Jesse that there was no doubt but that the *valiant* Pillow" had planned an attack on Cairo, but would probably desist on learning that the place was well garrisoned and had a ditch filled with water on the outside of the parapet. He would not go so far— though others might—as to say that Pillow would shoot himself, but he did think Pillow might irritate a little scratch "until he convinced himself that he had been wounded by the enemy." [8]

From the time of the secession of the seven cotton states in late 1860 and early 1861 there had been a strong movement for secession in Missouri, encouraged by the governor, Claiborne F. Jackson. A special convention, called by the legislature, was not the pliant, subservient group the secessionist leaders hoped for, and it voted overwhelmingly against separation. Balked in his first effort, Jackson called the legislature into special session on May 3. Although this

body also refused to vote the state out of the Union, it placed extensive funds at the governor's disposal for the purpose of arming the
state against any emergency, and gave him great power in the matter
of drafting men into service. Jackson appointed ex-Governor Sterling
Price as major general of state forces, and also nine brigadier generals,
who began to organize and arm regiments.

These proceedings were carefully watched by Captain Lyon, Second
United States Infantry, in command at the St. Louis arsenal. On May
10, Lyon, at the head of about 400 regular troops—many newly
enlisted—and some of the loyal "Home Guard" organized by Francis
P. Blair, Jr., descended suddenly on a force of several regiments
assembled by the governor's orders at Camp Jackson in the suburbs
of the city. The camp was broken up, and some 50 officers, including
Brigadier General Daniel M. Frost, and 639 men were marched as
prisoners to the arsenal. In addition, Lyon seized many arms, including cannon, as well as ammunition and equipment, which had been
sent from New Orleans and Baton Rouge in boxes marked "marble."
Part at least of this material had been appropriated by the "sovereign
state" of Louisiana from the United States arsenal in Baton Rouge.[9]

From his confinement in Lyon's arsenal, Frost, a West Point
graduate and a friend of Grant, the next day addressed a letter of
strong protest to Brigadier General William S. Harney, commanding
the Department of the West, who had just returned to St. Louis. The
deeply aggrieved Missouri brigadier pointed out that all the men in
Camp Jackson had taken an oath to defend the constitution of the
United States, and that the national flag was flying over his camp
at the time it was so unexpectedly surrounded by Lyon's force.
While it was true that many of the men, and perhaps entire companies
in the camp, were opposed to secession, Lyon was too well acquainted with the real purposes of the governor and the inclinations
of Frost to be deceived. The prisoners were paroled without delay
and Harney reported to Washington that Lyon's conduct had his
entire approval.[10]

Circumstances made Grant a witness of the departure and trium-
phant return of Lyon's expedition. He had gone to Belleville, Illinois,
to muster a new regiment, and finding that only one or two companies
had reported, he decided to visit St. Louis. He arrived in time to
observe Blair forming his men outside the arsenal, and went up and
introduced himself to this brother of the Postmaster General, whose

extreme Republican views he would not have endorsed a year before. As the hours passed the tension in the city increased and wild rumors spread among the angry crowd when distant shots were heard. There was indeed bloodshed in spite of Frost's surrender without resistance, for on the return march the German Home Guards answered a pistol shot with a volley that killed twenty-eight civilians and wounded an unknown number. When the expedition got back Grant was waiting at the arsenal to congratulate Lyon and Blair upon their achievement.[11]

Two weeks saw the completion of his mustering duties and found Grant back in Galena with his mind made up: he would let the War Department decide where he could best serve. In a letter to the Adjutant General dated April 24 he tendered his services and expressed the view that his age and experience made him "competent to command a Regiment if the President in his judgement should see fit to entrust one to me." [12] He explained what he had been doing to help in Illinois and gave his address as Springfield. There he went on the last day of the month, after writing to his father that during the six days he had been at home he had "felt all the time as if a duty were being neglected that was paramount to any other duty I ever owed." He had been reflecting on what he had done; though he said he was satisfied, he added, "But to stop now would not do." [13]

The expected letter from Washington did not come. Grant's letter, after arriving safely, had been lost, and was not found until several years after the war, when it turned up by accident.[14] His thoughts turned to George B. McClellan, who had come back into service as a major general, with command of the new Department of the Ohio, which included Illinois. McClellan had been a plebe at West Point during Grant's last year, but there had been no familiar association between them. In Mexico, where McClellan had served in the corps of Engineers, their paths had come close together, but again there was no personal contact. An acquaintanceship had, however, been formed at Fort Vancouver, when McClellan reported there in June, 1853, to be properly outfitted for explorations of a railroad route through the Cascade Mountains. As quartermaster at the post, it had been Grant's responsibility to prepare McClellan's party for its venture into the wilds.[15]

The mail having brought him no letter from Washington, Grant went to see his family at Covington, and without delay called at

McClellan's headquarters in Cincinnati, thinking that Little Mac might give him a position on his staff. If three errors in spelling had caused a finicky clerk in Washington to be careless with Grant's letter, his plainness of dress and modesty may have given an unfavorable impression to the unknown person at McClellan's bustling headquarters who told him that the general was out but would be back at any moment. After two hours he left to return the next day, with the same result. Grant's story was that he asked to have the general informed that he had called; McClellan's story in his memoirs was that he missed seeing Grant because he was out of the city.[16]

When no message came to his father's house as a result of the word he had left at headquarters, Grant started back to Springfield. On the way he stopped at Lafayette, Indiana, to see his classmate Joseph J. Reynolds, who had recently advanced from a professorship of engineering at George Washington University in St. Louis to a grocery store in the ambitious town on the banks of the Wabash. Reynolds had become colonel of an Indiana regiment, and it was possible that another regiment from that state was in need of a commander. During Grant's absence from Springfield, however, things had been astir in that place; in particular, the Twenty-first Regiment which he had mustered at Mattoon was in near mutiny against a bragging, strutting, and unmilitary commander. A credible story has it that the troubled governor asked a clerk from the Galena store who happened to be in town, why Ulysses Grant was indifferent to being elected to command one of the eleven thirty-day regiments. The clerk enlightened him: Grant could not reconcile himself to being elected to a military office; but, if he were appointed he would certainly accept. So Yates sent a telegram to Covington, and Jesse Grant forwarded it to Lafayette, whence Grant, finding that there were no vacancies in Indiana regiments, had already departed.[17]

It was on June 16 that Grant sat down in the adjutant's tent of the undisciplined and boisterous Twenty-first at Camp Yates and wrote an order taking command. In later years Aaron Elliott, who had been a private at the time, reminisced, "We could not exactly understand the man. He was very soon called 'the quiet man' . . . and in a very few days he reduced matters in camp to perfect order." [18]

But a hurdle remained, and a serious one. Would these thirty-day men volunteer for three years, to become a part of the force Lincoln had called for on May 3? Enthusiasm for a soldier's life and eagerness to be in battle had already evaporated from many hearts, and only about half of the 1,250 men Grant had mustered on May 15 were now in camp. The test was to come on June 28, and as speakers to his regiment, Grant, upon advice of friends, chose two prominent Democratic congressmen, John A. McClernand and John A. Logan. There could be no question about McClernand, for even Black Republicans praised his stout Union views; but concerning Logan, who came from the southern part of the state, there was some doubt. Grant selected the sure hitter to lead off, and McClernand struck a sharp patriotic note. But Logan made the really dramatic speech with a moving appeal that brought the Twenty-first almost to a man into Federal service for three years. Thinking that their commander should add his share to the oratory, Logan ended by introducing Grant to the regiment; but his response to cries for a speech consisted of five words: "Men, go to your quarters!" [19] Perhaps by that time this was all they expected from "the quiet man."

On July 3, when drill and discipline had reached an encouraging state, Grant was ordered to Quincy with his regiment.[20] Movement by railroad would have been direct and simple, and many officers would have thought it necessary because the regiment had no transportation for its camp equipage. But Grant hired wagons, provided for rations, and started on the ninety-mile march, knowing full well that there would be blistered feet and limping, perspiring soldiers—but a much better regiment when they reached Quincy. Marching is part of an infantryman's business, and Grant had seen soldiers toughened in the cruel march from Matamoros to Monterrey. Whether there were rains while he was on the road seems not to have been recorded, but he probably would not have regretted a hard, soaking shower and a wet field to camp on. Soldiers who grumbled that night would soon be bragging and exaggerating among themselves and in letters home. Upon reaching the Illinois River Grant camped for a few days, waiting for a boat to take him to St. Louis, pursuant to a change of orders. A second change, however, sent him by train to Quincy, with instructions to proceed at once to the relief of another Illinois regiment reported as surrounded by Rebels some distance west of Palmyra, Missouri.[21]

Grant acknowledges that the small operation ahead of him caused him to feel considerable "trepidation." His alarm was not at the prospect of physical danger, as his Mexican record showed; it was at his responsibility as commanding officer. He was, however, not put to the test, for the supposedly besieged regiment straggled into Quincy

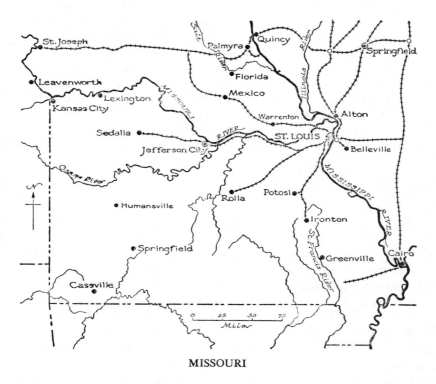

MISSOURI

before he had completed preparations for its relief. "I am inclined to think both sides got frightened and ran away," was his later comment. Whatever may have happened to the Missouri troops in question, there were other secessionists in the state, organized and at times aggressive, and Grant's regiment moved to Palmyra; then after a few days it joined the Fourteenth Illinois under Colonel John M. Palmer, which was guarding workmen rebuilding the railroad bridge over Salt River, about twenty-five miles farther west.

After the completion of the bridge Grant was ordered to move against a hostile force commanded by Colonel Thomas Harris, encamped at Florida, some twenty-five miles away. Again it was necessary to rent wagons and hire drivers, which was a difficult matter in a sparsely settled community. But finally Grant was on the road at the head of his regiment of about a thousand men, with all its equipment, provisions for a week, and ammunition for the anticipated engagement. Of his first march against the enemy he later wrote:

We halted at night on the road and proceeded the next morning at an early hour. Harris had been encamped in a creek bottom for the sake of being near water. The hills on either side of the creek extend to a considerable height, possibly more than a hundred feet. As we approached the brow of the hill from which it was expected we could see Harris' camp, and possibly find his men ready formed to meet us, my heart kept getting higher and higher until it felt to me as though it was in my throat. I would have given anything then to have been back in Illinois, but I had not the moral courage to halt and consider what to do; I kept right on. When we reached a point from which the valley below was in full view I halted. The place where Harris had been encamped a few days before was still there and the marks of a recent encampment were plainly visible, but the troops were gone. My heart resumed its place.

The thought came to Grant that Harris had been as much afraid of him as he had been of Harris. This was a new view of the matter, which he said he never afterward forgot. The evidence of the deserted camp was confirmed by inquiries in the village of Florida. Stories of Grant's collecting transportation for an expedition against him had reached Harris, who without delay retired to a place where he would not be in danger. However, he had not been destroyed; he had only moved, taking his equipment with him. Perhaps on the way back to Salt River the realization came to Grant that rebellions are not put down in that way. He relates that the houses along the road, deserted a few days before, were again occupied, the people greeting the soldiers in a friendly way. Armed men had been feared by the citizens—often with good reason; but Grant's regiment had kept to the road and there had been no pillaging. The expedition brought no battle streamer to the colors of the Twenty-first Illinois, but it disciplined the men a little and made a new soldier of their commander. Not often has an officer learned as much from so small an undertaking.

Grant's next station was Mexico, Missouri, where the Second Missouri, a three-month regiment, had had a skirmish on July 15. As senior colonel, he was in command of all troops in the vicinity, and he brought other regiments up to the discipline and deportment of his own, much to the relief of the community. It was at Mexico that he read in the St. Louis papers that the President had appointed him to a brigadiership upon the recommendation of the Illinois congressmen, who had placed his name first on a list of seven. Senate confirmation followed a few days later. The new general did not know, however, that a list of five prospective United States brigadiers that appeared on August 5 in the *Richmond Daily Enquirer* ended very casually with the words "and Captain Grant."

Lincoln was engaged at the time in the difficult task of creating general officers for the greatly expanded army. As the result of recommendations he made on July 30 and August 1, some twenty-six names appear to have been added to the list of thirty-seven brigadiers commissioned as of May 17. To a country used to a small military establishment it looked like a very large number; and the impression has been common that politics dominated Lincoln's selection. But a study of the roster shows that most of the men were to distinguish themselves. The top thirteen were regular officers then on active duty; the next eleven appointments were to former regulars. Some of the remaining commissions went to men who had been officers in the Mexican War. When one considers that there was no draft, and that the ability to raise three-year regiments and arouse sentiment to back the war was something to be considered, the number of "political" appointments was surprisingly small. Probably that of Governor William Sprague of Rhode Island was most open to challenge, and he declined. Of the former regulars, the Galena leather and hardware dealer stood sixth, just ahead of the Lafayette grocer.[22]

Ranking Grant was one former regular officer whose offer of service on May 8 had not been lost as had Grant's, but had within a week brought appointment as colonel of the newly formed Thirteenth United States Infantry: William Tecumseh Sherman.[23] Likewise ahead of Grant were fiery little Captain Lyon, an infantryman, and Captain Pope, a topographical engineer.

A letter to his father on August 3 gave some interesting observations: The people in the vicinity of Mexico were largely secessionists; though they regretted the breaking up of the Union, they regarded it as a *fait accompli*. The papers spoke of the Federal troops as annihilated by the state troops when there had in fact been no engagement; his own regiment had been reported at least once to have been cut to pieces, although not a shot had been fired at it. He had received the greatest hospitality and attention, but doubted that the residents believed a word he said concerning the strength of the North or the objects of the administration. His nomination as a brigadier had surprised him, as he had asked no one to intercede for him; he had in fact declined an offer of Governor Yates and Senator Lyman Trumbull to write to Washington in support of his tender·of services. There was one thing which evidently pleased him more than his promotion. The regiment he had taken over "in a very disorganized, demoralized and insubordinate condition" now had "a reputation equal to the best"; and upon hearing that he would likely be promoted "the officers, with great unanimity," had requested to be attached to his command. After saying this about himself, he cautioned Jesse not to let it go further.[24]

On the day that Grant was ordered to Quincy, the state of Illinois was transferred to the new Western Department. In deference to the strong desire of many people of the region and the vehement urgings of Montgomery and Frank Blair, and perhaps with some personal belief in the man, Lincoln made John Frémont commander of the department, and appointed him a major general in the regular army, with his commission, like McClellan's, dating from May 14. Frémont had formerly been in the regular army; but he had neither tactical training nor experience of much consequence, having gone directly from civil life into the topographical engineers. He was well-to-do and had spent the winter in France; and it was not until July 1 that he and his ambitious wife, the former Jessie Benton, arrived in New York, where he tarried, to the great annoyance of Lincoln, attending to personal matters. The task that faced him when he finally reached St. Louis on July 25 would have tested the capacity of one far more level-headed and experienced. A state almost in rebellion had to be controlled. Troops for the purpose existed, but many of them were disorganized, undisciplined, and untrained. Arms were lacking, and equipment and supplies had to be procured by contracts with persons often too eager to make money and ready to defraud the government.[25] In addition it was necessary to harmonize the discordant views of two antagonistic groups of Unionists: those who wanted to rid the country of slavery by abrupt means, and those who regarded the preservation of the Union as the primary object. Extremists of the first category were numerous in the large German element in St. Louis, and Grant's letter to his father makes it clear that many secessionists of Missouri clung tenaciously to the idea that emancipation of slaves was the purpose of the administration, in spite of Lincoln's clear pronouncements to the contrary.

Grant's letter to his father also said that troops were being gradually shifted toward the Mississippi, and on August 6 Frémont ordered Pope, who was commanding the North Missouri District, to send the Twenty-first Illinois and some other regiments to St. Louis without delay. Two days later he directed Grant, present at his headquarters, to proceed with his old regiment to Ironton, the terminus of the St. Louis and Iron Mountain Railroad. A concentration of Union forces was being made in this somewhat difficult country because of enemy activity in the vicinity and to the south. Grant was made commander of the district, and the letter of instructions handed to him was extensive and detailed. Ironton was to be made secure by intrenchments, laid out by an engineer officer and constructed with the assistance of two engineer companies which were to be sent presently. Grant was to "scour the country in advance" as well as employ spies to watch the enemy; he was to be prepared for "a sudden movement" with the force under his command; and he was to communicate daily with department headquarters. A locomotive was put at his disposal for running errands and performing other tasks along the railroad—a valuable provision, in keeping with Frémont's firm belief in railroads.[26]

Grant would have liked to buy some books and have a uniform made in St. Louis, but he took no time for such matters. He reached Ironton the same day and at once issued an order taking over command. Frémont's directive of the morning and Grant's order of the afternoon of August 8, 1861, mark the real entry of the future General into the Official Records.[27]

Two years later Lincoln was to write, "General Grant is a copious worker and fighter, but a very meager writer or telegrapher." [28] The daily letters from Ironton prove that the new general was indeed a "copious worker"; but they also completely disprove that he was remiss in reporting to his superiors. Statements such as the humorous one of the President and an unjust charge by General Halleck in March, 1862, which will be discussed later, are perhaps responsible for false ideas about certain aspects of Grant's generalship. The great strategist and relentless fighter of the later years of the war began in 1861 as a very careful and industrious administrator; and nothing proves this fact so well as his own letters, the first of which also shows that he possessed the sense of humor that is desirable, if not necessary, in a general:

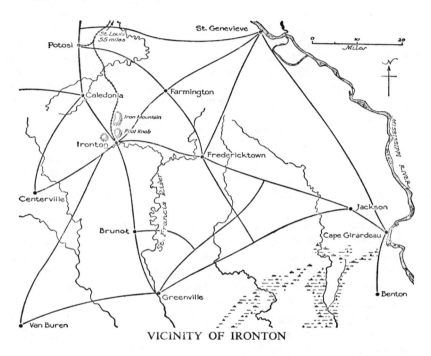

VICINITY OF IRONTON

Headquarters U.S. Forces,
Ironton, Mo., August 9, 1861

Capt. John C. Kelton, Asst. Adjt. Gen., Saint Louis, Mo.:

Sir: Inclosed herewith please find consolidated report of the troops at this place as near as can be given at present. I arrived here yesterday, and assumed command, in pursuance of directions from Maj. Gen. J. C. Frémont. Since that time I have studied the nature of the ground it may become necessary for me to defend, the character of the troops, and the means, &c., to do it with. From all that I have yet learned from spies and loyally-disposed citizens, I am led to believe that there is no force within 30 miles of us that entertain the least idea of attacking this position, unless it should be left so weak as to invite an attack. It is fortunate, too, if this is the case, for many of the officers seem to have so little command over their men, and military duty seems to be done so loosely, that I fear at present our resistance would be in the inverse ratio of the number to resist with. In two days more, however, I expect to have a very different state of affairs and to improve it continuously. Spies are said to be seen every day within a few miles of our camp; marauding parties are infesting the country, pillaging Union men, within 10 miles of here. At present I can spare no force; in fact, have not suitable troops to drive these guerrillas out and afford to Union citizens of this place or neighborhood the protection I feel they should have. Artillery and cavalry are much needed, and the quartermaster's department is yet quite deficient. The number of teams would scarcely suffice for the use of this as a military post without making any forward movement, and the horses of those we have are many of them barefoot and without forage. I have taken steps to remedy those latter defects.

> *U. S. Grant,*
> Brigadier-General [29]

Lacking a staff, Grant had had to go over the entire field of military questions, administration, intelligence of the enemy, training of troops, supply, and logistics, and apparently he had not missed much. How much a believer he was in the possibility of rapid improvement when there are proper directions and firm control is shown by the fact that he wanted only two days for changing discipline radically. Noticeable also is the fact that while he stated that the quartermaster department was deficient, and that there was need for both artillery and cavalry, he actually asked for nothing. Knowing that department headquarters could not pull rabbits out of hats and was buried under heavy problems, he went to work with what he had.

Much of the next day must have been spent in the reforms that Grant said would produce results in two days. He understood the good material with which he had to deal, and he had already demonstrated the effectiveness of his method of training. In the report that he sent on the 10th he stated he still did not believe there was any danger of an immediate attack upon his post, though the enemy reconnoitered to within a few miles of his pickets. Because of the hostile activity he urgently recommended that cavalry and field artillery be sent to him as early as they could be *spared*.[30]

Opposed to Grant was one of the "big names" in the Confederate service, Georgia-born Brigadier General William J. Hardee, who had been commandant of cadets at West Point not many months before Sumter was fired upon. His translation of a French military work became known as "Hardee's Tactics," and it was an official manual for Federals and Confederates alike. Turning his back upon training officers for the United States, he had offered himself to assist in dissolving the Union and was made a brigadier on June 25. Assigned to command in northern Arkansas, he was told "to watch over and protect" not only that part of Arkansas, but "also that part of the State of Missouri contiguous thereto." From Pitman's Ferry, almost on the northern border of Arkansas, where he had set up his headquarters on July 22, the translator of the drill book had already taken up his task in a part of southern Missouri. But he in turn was being watched, and Grant wrote on the 10th: "From information received today, which I am disposed to think reliable, General Hardee is at Greenville, with 2,000 men and six or eight field pieces, with 1,000 more troops thrown forward to Stoney Battery, near Brunot. Of this force one-third is represented to be cavalry, well mounted and equipped." [31]

The master of drill and instructor of cadets had had as many weeks to train his regiments as Grant had had days; and he had artillery and cavalry while Grant had neither. He was only thirty-five miles away, and—as was proper for the writer of the text book—he had a good covering force much nearer. But the Federal commander seemed to feel in no danger. Observing that the region was healthy, Grant did, however, recommend that one or two of the newly raised regiments be sent to him from Jefferson Barracks. That would allow him, he explained, to use his older regiments more freely for scouting duty and leave him free to concentrate on the essential drill of the new men.

Not only was Hardee threatening from the south; a hostile force was trying to get upon Grant's rear, and perhaps while he wrote on the evening of the 10th a raid was made upon Potosi, twenty-five miles north of Ironton and five miles west of the railroad. Grant reported on the 11th: "An attack was made on the Home Guards at Potosi last night, resulting in the wounding of five of them and the shooting and taking of six of the other party, shooting three of their horses, and getting a number of pistols, shot-guns, rifles, etc." Four well-armed prisoners had been brought to him, and the attack had been made by about one hundred and twenty men, commanded by a

Captain White of Fredericktown. Grant reported his counteractivities and announced that he had started to form a staff, having appointed an officer of his old regiment to be his aide. He also stated that he had set up a school to instruct the officers and noncommissioned officers of the Ninth Missouri; their teacher would be an officer he had himself taught, First Lieutenant Vance of the Twenty-first Illinois.[32]

On the 12th Grant could report that he had scouts in from the direction of Brunot, and that they had gone as far as the most advanced positions the Confederate pickets had occupied. "Tomorrow," he said, "I shall have a party in pursuit of them." But he added that the enemy could not be caught without cavalry.[33]

A problem other than military had arisen. Grant had stopped the delivery of six packages of letters, four to points in Arkansas, one to Memphis via Little Rock, and one to Brunot. It was the correct thing to stop the mail; but he knew that the question involved was a political one, and he stated that he was detaining the mail only until he received proper instructions. He added, "I am entirely without orders for my guidance in matters like the above, and without recent acts of Congress which bear upon them." Busy as he was and doing personally work normal to several officers, it is difficult to see how he would have found time to read acts of Congress; but this early manifestation on his part of a clear appreciation of the subordination of the military to the civil and political authorities is important. If he had had higher training such as officers receive today his actions would not have been so notable. But he had been an indifferent student of tactics and other military subjects at West Point, and his experience in the Mexican War contributed little more than to make a good, tough, efficient regimental field soldier. That fundamental military training, added to his common sense, fairness, balance, and ability to project himself into the positions of his subordinates and superiors as well as of the enemy, made it possible for him to meet situations as they arose.

On the same day Grant wrote to his sister Mary. Foreseeing that he would have "precious little time" for writing, he had subscribed to the *Daily St. Louis Democrat* for the family at Covington; but he would try to send two letters a month, even if they had to be written after midnight. In answer to an urgent request for his view about how long the war would be, he wrote that this was a matter on which he had changed his mind so often that he did not know now what to think. After saying that he did not doubt but that the "rebels" would be whipped so badly before the next April that they could not make a stand, he added: "But they are so dogged that there is no telling when they may be subdued." Mary was naturally proud of the general in the family, who had attained his position without seeking anyone's favor or endorsement, and she had been importuning "Ulys" for a photograph. She now received some encouragement, for he ended his letter, "If I get a uniform and get where I can have my daguerreotype taken, your wish in that respect shall be gratified." [34]

On the 12th Frémont directed Grant to send columns to take possession of Centerville and Fredericktown, in order to protect his flanks and keep better control over the general neighborhood. He was also to send, "with all necessary precaution, a moving column on the road to Greenville, whose duty it will be to ascertain the enemy's forces, movements, and intentions." The department commander passed on what information he had about the Potosi affair, adding that he had sent a regiment reenforced by two companies and fifty horsemen to take and hold that important place—an action that would allow Grant to call in the four companies he had sent there after the raid. [35]

The next day—the 13th—Grant reported that he had reliable information that an enemy force of about 3,000 men, mostly mounted, but poorly armed, had passed the night near Fredericktown and that it was their intention to move to Farmington and then strike to destroy the railroad behind him. In addition, he had a credible report that a well-armed force under Hardee himself was advancing upon Ironton from the south. He did not specifically request reenforcements, but stated that he would feel confident of holding his position against the threat of the moment if a battery of artillery and one more infantry regiment were sent to him the next day. He closed his dispatch with the statement, "My impression, from the facts before me, is that if attacked at all, it will be on Thursday, possibly Wednesday." [36] Wednesday, as a matter of fact, was the very next day; but the man who a month before had been so thoroughly frightened over a possible clash with the unknown Harris now spoke of an attack by Hardee in about the same way that he would have referred to a possible rain. In his letter to his sister he had also alluded to the possibility of the enemy attacking, saying, "I have here about 3000 volunteers nearly all infantry, but our position being strong, and our cause a good one, it would trouble a much larger force of the enemy to dislodge us."

Grant, nevertheless, made very careful preparations, and reported the next day:

Today, supposing an attack possible, I had eleven teams, belonging to the Pilot Knob Iron Company, drawn into service, giving a receipt for them. The command was directed to make storehouses of the wagons for their provisions, so that, in case of a move to the support of our pickets becoming necessary, supplies could be moved to them without delay. Every move of the enemy seems to evince a determination to fall upon the railroad at some point north at the same time an attack is made here. I am not fully persuaded that an attack will be made here for the present, but hold my command ready to make the best resistance possible with the means at hand.[37]

After apologizing for failure to make the comment in the proper place in his letter—in connection with the remark that there were eight pieces of artillery at Ironton—he stated, "I have no artillerists, nor officer suitable to take command of a company to drill them as such." Having been a quartermaster and a commissary officer, as well as a line officer of infantry, Grant lone-handed could do much; but he had never been in the artillery and had no knowledge of a gunner's business except what he had possibly obtained as a cadet. To have cannons, but neither gunners nor cannoneers, and no one to turn infantrymen into artillerymen, was something to disturb a commanding officer threatened with attack; and he closed his letter, "I would respectfully recommend the appointment of an ordnance sergeant for this post." For Grant, that was almost table-pounding.

Since the beginning of the war Lincoln had had some very bad weeks. It would have been a relief to him to read the dispatches of the man from Galena, who would be content with copies of recent acts of Congress and one ordnance sergeant; and who, when threatened with attack, took possession of eleven wagons, loaded them up with groceries, and prepared to turn his outpost line into a main line of resistance.

While Grant was holding his command alerted and his eleven wagons ready to march out and give battle to Hardee, a tragicomedy was taking place in St. Louis, with important reactions in Washington. General Frémont, who as an explorer had known danger, hardship, and privation in many and extreme forms, was showing he was unsuited for high military command, for he promptly went to pieces upon receiving word of a severe defeat that had been suffered by his main field force.

In the first part of June, Lyon had set out with an expedition from St. Louis, intending not only to secure southwestern Missouri, but also to proceed all the way to Little Rock. Mid-July found him at Springfield with only about 7,000 men, while reports he received indicated that reenforcements would bring the enemy force in his front to about 30,000. His own troops were badly clothed, poorly fed, and imperfectly supplied with tents, and none had been paid. The three-month men, whose terms of service would shortly expire, were disheartened, and few intended to reenlist. Actually things had been badly handled, for one hundred and ten wagons had been sent to Rolla with considerable amounts of arms, ammunition, and provisions, only to remain there. Wanting to place responsibility on Washington, Lyon wrote to his St. Louis adjutant: "Scott will cripple us if he can. Cannot you stir up this matter and secure us relief? . . . Everything seems to combine against me at this point. Stir up Blair." Lyon's field adjutant was Major John M. Schofield, of whom much would be heard before the war's end, and on July 26 he reported to St. Louis that many men were actually barefooted and unable to march. After speaking of the Federal defeat at Bull Run, news of which had just been received, he engaged in a little prophesying: "I fear this will prevent our getting re-enforcements. If so, the next news will be of our defeat also." [38]

Nevertheless the zealous Lyon advanced; and on August 4 he reported himself twenty-four miles beyond Springfield on the road to Fayetteville, Arkansas. He was in contact with a force of enemy cavalry and had lost four killed and five wounded in a skirmish. Where the main body of the enemy was, he did not know; but, being without supplies and in danger of being cut off by the numerous hostile mounted force, he deemed "it impractical to advance" and intended to fall back. Except for the expiration of the terms of the three-month men he thought he could hold a position near Springfield; but, things being as they were, he would fall back either to St. Louis or to Kansas, most probably upon the former via Rolla, in order to secure reenforcements and supplies. From memory he put down the strength of his four brigades as 5,868, and said the enemy's force would reach 15,000, and might be brought to a total of 20,000 in an effort to cut him off. Though many of the enemy would be "ill-conditioned troops" with such arms as they personally owned, they would be mounted and able to cause him much annoyance. In addition to Missouri state troops Lyon was apprehensive of a regular Confederate force of 4,000 men "well-armed, and prepared for effective service," commanded by Brigadier General Ben McCulloch, a Tennessean who had fought in the Texas war for independence and gained some renown as a commander of rangers in the War with Mexico. The discouraged Lyon ended the last report he was to write: "In fact, I am under the painful necessity of retreating, and can at most only hope to make my retreat good. I am in too great haste to explain at length more fully. I have given timely notice of my danger[s], and can only in the worst emergencies submit to them." [39]

Without being molested in any way, Lyon retired on the 6th to a position near Springfield with the little "Army of the West," which consisted of regiments from Missouri, Kansas, and Iowa, with detachments of regulars. McCulloch followed with his regiments from Missouri, Arkansas, Texas, and Louisiana, and took a position twelve miles away along Wilson's Creek. In spite of his announced intention of retiring—and his statement about not submitting to dangers—the Federal commander quickly made up his mind to risk battle with the greatly superior enemy, but was dissuaded by his subordinates because of the tired condition of his command. Then, a day having been spent in resting and distributing shoes that had arrived from Rolla, he decided on the afternoon of the 9th to march that evening in two columns and attack the enemy early the next morning. [40]

Lyon himself led the stronger column on the right and, having reached the vicinity of the enemy at 1:00 A.M., struck about daylight. Surprise gave the attacking column the initial advantage; but the enemy rallied, and his numbers soon began to have effect. The Federal commander, who had taken three guns at Cerro Gordo, had been breveted a captain at Contreras, and later made a full captain for valor, was in the midst of the blazing battle. Soon he fell, and his adjutant wrote of him:

Early in this engagement, while General Lyon was leading his horse along the line on the left of Captain Totten's battery, and endeavoring to rally our troops, which were at this time in considerable disorder, his horse was killed, and he received a wound in the leg and one in the head. He walked slowly a few paces to the rear and said, "I fear the day is lost." But upon being encouraged that our troops could again be rallied, that the disorder was only temporary, he passed over to the right of the center, where our line seemed to be giving way, obtained another horse, and, swinging his hat in the air, led forward the troops, who promptly rallied around him. A few moments later he was carried from the field dead. His death was known at the time to but very few, and those few seemed to fight with redoubled valor.[41]

Where now was the other column under the command of Colonel Franz Sigel, which consisted of only two regiments, two troops of cavalry, and a battery, and which apparently was supposed to cut off the enemy's retreat? The reports of Schofield and Major Samuel D. Sturgis, who succeeded to the command of the main force, put upon Sigel the responsibility for their not knowing where he was, though his account of the battle indicates he was where he was supposed to be.[42] Arrangement for liaison had evidently not been made and Lyon should have been looking after the coordination of his two columns and not leading one of them in the attack. The battle continued until early afternoon, when, without having achieved any unity of action, both Federal columns made good their retreat to Springfield. Sigel had only one of his six guns, and Sturgis had no ammunition, no arrangement having been made for resupply near the battlefield. To place responsibility for the defeat on Colonel Sigel was most unfair; yet that is virtually what Schofield and Sturgis did. Considering the numbers engaged, the Battle of Wilson's Creek was more sanguinary than that of Bull Run, which had brought disillusionment to the North only three weeks before.[43] It has sometimes been said that in the death of Lyon the North lost one of her most promising officers. Undoubtedly he was brave; but it must be conceded that, having made the ill-advised decision to attack a very superior force, he committed other serious mistakes.

Springfield was at the time remote from railroad and telegraph, so that news of the defeat was much delayed and came as a shock to people who thought that matters were progressing happily for Federal arms in that region. On August 13 the readers of the *New York Tribune* were gratified with the headlines: "Important from Missouri—The Rebels Repulsed Again—They Fly to the Woods— General Lyon Endeavors to Draw Them Out." The dispatches that were the basis of such headings had come from Franklin and Jefferson City, and were dated the 12th. The next day the paper had headlines still more arresting: "Great Battle in Missouri—Defeat of the Rebel Forces—A Splendid Union Victory—General Lyon Killed." All this had been achieved, it was stated, by 8,000 troops against 23,000 "Rebels." Then the headline writer prepared the reader for bad news by informing him that Sigel, who had succeeded to command, had very coolly returned to Rolla. The news dispatch that followed had been filed in St. Louis on the afternoon of the 13th and began bluntly, "Rumors are current in the street, in which some reliance is placed, that Gen. Lyon's command in the South-West has been totally routed by the rebels." Secessionists, the message continued, had received the news the night before, word having been brought to Rolla by a very eager messenger who had killed no fewer than four horses in a mad ride from Springfield. Official dispatches were believed to be in the hands of General Frémont; but, as nothing had been divulged, Union men entertained great apprehension for the safety of their army. All were looking for the evening train from the west, hoping that it would bring information that was reliable, even if it were not cheering.

Horace Greeley's reporter was well informed; Frémont had received the bad news officially in time to wire the Secretary of War on the 13th:

> General Lyon's aide reports engagement, with severe loss on both sides; General Lyon killed; Colonel Sigel, in command, retiring in good order from Springfield toward Rolla. Let the governor of Ohio be ordered forthwith to send me what disposable force he has; also governors of Illinois, Indiana, and Wisconsin. Order the utmost promptitude. The German (Groesbeck's) Thirty-ninth Regiment at Camp Dennison, might be telegraphed directly here. We are badly in want of field artillery, and to this time very few of our small-arms have arrived.[44]

It would not have been a bad message if it had stopped at the end of the first sentence, though the reference to Franz Sigel as a colonel when an order by Frémont the same day described him a brigadier general, indicated a little confusion. Without restraint the excited Frémont proceeded to issue orders to his superior, and telegraphed to Lincoln: "Will the President read my urgent dispatch to the Secretary of War?" [45]

Two messages should have been sufficient to arouse Washington, but either the imaginative Frémont or his devoted wife thought of stirring up the Postmaster General. Though before long they were to rupture their relations with Frank Blair, they were still on good terms with him; so to Montgomery Blair there went a telegram that began, "See instantly my dispatch to the Secretary of War." [46] It closed by telling him that if the report of the battle as brought by Lyon's aide were true, he had no time to lose. One must believe that a staff officer wrote the very calm message that was sent to General Scott's adjutant, reporting that Sigel was coming back not only with his baggage train, but with $250,000 in hard money from the Springfield bank.[47]

Night apparently did little to quiet the general's alarm, and on the 14th he wired Lincoln:

General Grant, commanding at Ironton, attacked yesterday at 6 by a force reported at 13,000. Railroad seized by the enemy at Big River Bridge, on this side of Ironton. The governor of Ohio postponed my urgent request for aid until ordered by you. Will you issue peremptory orders to him and other governors to send me instantly any disposable troops and arms? An artillery company of regulars at Cincinnati, which has been there three months. I have applied for it repeatedly. The enemy is in overpowering force, and we are very weak in men and arms. We have neglected nothing, and will do all that is possible, but not one moment should be lost in giving us any possible aid in fixed artillery and men with arms in their hands. A little immediate relief in good material might prevent great sacrifices.[48]

Frémont may have received a report that Grant had been attacked; he may have merely fabricated. But Greeley's correspondent sent in a far different story when he telegraphed: "It is reported that Gen. Hardee, with a force of 12,000 to 15,000 rebels, is marching on Pilot Knob. The Federal force at that point is about 5,000 with eight pieces of cannon." [49] Apparently he did not know who commanded at Ironton, or that there were no artillerymen there; but he had the correct count of guns.

Washington took its cue and did everything that Frémont had so emphatically suggested. Cameron immediately telegraphed to Governor Dennison of Ohio to get Groesbeck on the way to St. Louis at once, giving him a good supply of artillery and small arms; all other available troops were to follow. To the chief executives of Indiana,

Illinois, and Wisconsin went instructions to do their utmost, and to report their actions. Before the 14th was over, a telegram informed the general of what had been done, and assured him that Dennison had reported that Groesbeck would move promptly.[50]

There had been no necessity for Frémont to call upon Washington for reenforcements, for near at hand under his own orders he had all the reserve strength that was required; and he actually used it promptly and effectively. On the 13th no fewer than five regiments were ordered from St. Louis to the important railroad terminus of Rolla, one hundred and ten miles away, almost doubling the force at that point.[51] Furthermore, the new regiments were free of all three-month men. Two additional regiments were also sent to reenforce Grant and protect his communications.[52] Dispatching reserve regiments from St. Louis of course lessened the means to deal with any turbulent and jubilant Southerners in that city who might take advantage of the occasion for a demonstration or uprising. So with telegrams to the Secretary of War, the Postmaster General, and the President—to say nothing of governors—out of the way, the general wrote a proclamation putting city and county under martial law.[53]

On the 15th the cheering news was out that the defeated Federal army was safely back at Rolla—or soon would be—and some particulars of the battle began to appear. As at Bull Run, there had been good fighting by Federal regiments, and the hundred-and-twenty mile march back to Rolla in about five days with 370 wagons over a road that could not have been good showed that they had other qualities of fine troops. But there had been turmoil on the way between the officers. Though Sigel had had military training and experience in Germany, he showed marked deficiencies as a commander. Schofield wrote that on the morning they were to march from Springfield he found the wagons of Sigel's brigade unloaded at two o'clock and the general himself sound asleep, while all the rest of the command was ready to move. Some regiments in the column, in which there was no rotation of place from day to day, would arrive at the new camping ground in the middle of the day, while others would have to make camp in rugged woods after dark. Many men went without food for twenty-four hours, "and some much longer." Finally part of the command that had breakfasted on what was at hand was detained three hours while beef was killed "for Colonel Sigel's breakfast." Clamor became so great that Sturgis, questioning Sigel's authority, took over command at the end of three days. In spite of everything morale does not seem to have been lost in all units, for a battery commander wrote on the 17th: "My men behaved well, and cannot be convinced that we were not victorious." [54]

Though news from Rolla brought good cheer to the Pathfinder, there came from Washington the words of an exasperated President:

Been answering your messages since day before yesterday. Do you receive the answers? The War Department has notified all the governors you designated to forward all available force, and so telegraphed you. Have you received these messages? Answer immediately.[55]

Frémont's reply was brief: dispatches had come the day before from Blair and Scott, "and today" from the Secretary of War.[56] When subsequently it was learned that Grant had not been attacked, it is probable that the President did not place upon him the responsibility for the false report that his superior had telegraphed; and it is equally probable that Grant was unaware of what seems to be the first report about him that was made to Lincoln.

Hardee not only failed to appear on Wednesday; he did not show up even on Thursday, the 15th. But Grant was not completely disappointed with the authority on tactics, for the Confederate commander was giving him a chance to test the idea that had come to him on the lonesome ride from Florida back to the bridge at Salt River—the enemy too can get frightened. From an officer who was spying for Grant in Greenville, word came that a clergyman had slipped out of Ironton and had reported to Hardee what was going on.[57] The loaded wagons and other preparations that Grant was making to march out and meet the Confederates must have been a main item in the minister's tale. Hardee, upon getting the information, had turned about and started back to Greenville; here was evidence that even the writer of the text book could experience "trepidation." Immediately Grant decided to make a movement on Greenville. The two regiments of reenforcing infantry had arrived, but there still were no cavalry and no artillerymen. This did not hold him back, and in writing to St. Louis about his plans he spoke of following "tomorrow with artillery, should they arrive." His style of waging war was beginning to appear and one gets the first glimpse of the man of Donelson, Shiloh, Vicksburg, and the other great battles and movements that followed, the man who would constantly push things and not turn back.

Grant worked rapidly but thoroughly, never forgetting to inform headquarters as to what he was planning and doing. In haste, just before "the cars" left, he sent word that he would have a column moving against the enemy at Fredericktown "by 12 o'clock probably today"—the 16th. Deficiency in artillery he could not make up; but mobility for his infantry he could give. He reported to Frémont's adjutant that he had already purchased—subject to the department commander's approval—sixteen wagons and sixty-eight mules, and could get more. Furthermore, he knew the quality of his purchases: they were better than those "heretofore employed or found in the service of this command." Believing that government should not be a wastrel even in conducting war, he had sought to save a little money by making a good bargain: if the conditional purchase were validated at once, no rent would have to be paid for the previous use of the wagons and animals. He did not have a single tent for his head-quarters or any stationery for the quartermaster department; but in spite of these deficiencies he promised to "report as often as prac-ticable." [58]

Even as Grant was writing, another messenger arrived with the word that the enemy force was much greater than had previously been represented, and might be 25,000 or 30,000. The spy furnishing the information was an officer in disguise, and one cannot tell what Grant actually thought about the reliability of the report; his letter made no comment, merely indicating that he was going on with his operation unless it was countermanded.

For one thing Grant may deserve a little censure: the minister who had reported to Hardee was back in town, and Grant told Kelton he had ordered his arrest and would forward him to St. Louis if he were caught. In view of the fact that the minister had really done Grant an excellent turn in taking his report to Hardee, to arrest him seems like ingratitude. But there was the possibility that on the next trip the good man might report that Grant had no artillerymen, and that until they arrived his eight guns were as harmless as those on a courthouse lawn.

More important, however, than Grant's reports to St. Louis were his orders for his expedition. Since an order for the entire command was not practicable, he wrote directives for the different regimental commanders. To Colonel P. E. Bland of the Sixth Missouri went the note:

> As soon as the wagon train is all up you may move with your command to the first convenient place for halting overnight. In the morning move cautiously on to about 10 or 12 miles from here, and await orders from me.
> Permit no pressing of horses or other property by your command. The policy meets with my decided disapproval, and must be suppressed.[59]

This is the first operation order in the records from Grant's pen; it shows a commander who knew his own mind, one who could direct a subordinate in a clear and terse way, leaving him with the thought that he was to obey orders, but also with the necessity of making an important decision. The most responsible part in the operation not unnaturally went to Grant's old Twenty-first Illinois, which on the evening of the 16th was twelve miles out on the road to Greenville. To its commander, Colonel J. W. S. Alexander, there went the directive:

> To-morrow morning reconnoiter the ground in advance of you as far as Marble Creek. There make a halt for further orders, unless you should have such information as would make it an undoubted good move to depart from these instructions. Since you left I have learned that Hardee has returned to his position at Greenville, and is much stronger than has been heretofore supposed. Colonel Hacker has been instructed to join you at Marble Creek, if a practicable road is to be found across. Five companies will leave here to-night following you, and, in case of necessity, can re-enforce you by a forced march.[60]

This order is notable in several particulars. Though starting out on his first operation, Alexander was made to face the possibility of one of the most trying decisions that can confront a soldier, that of departing from the instructions of a superior. A commander who acts contrary to orders may find himself in serious difficulty because of disobedience. But Grant wanted subordinates who would unhesitatingly accept responsibility, and he was careful not to give too detailed instructions to a commander he could trust. Important words in his instructions were "information" and "undoubted." Alexander was not to depart from his order on the basis of a rumor or for an illusory purpose. On the other hand he could not protect himself by being cautious; and he would be remiss in halting at Marble Creek if he could go farther advisedly. In addition he was informed that the enemy was much stronger than had been supposed. But after responsibilities had been multiplied the colonel of Grant's old regiment was told that he would not be forgotten; the last sentence of the order said that. If as a result of Grant's direction Alexander should find himself in difficulty, those five companies would be driven relentlessly to his aid.

More than two years later the grizzled, battle-toughened Sherman was to write to Grant that the thing that had always sustained him most was the realization that Grant would be thinking of him, and that if he got into a tight place, Grant would come—"if alive." So in the first operation that he planned, Grant revealed to Alexander that he had given full consideration to the possibilities and had plans to meet emergencies. Nothing could more effectively strengthen a subordinate in the determination to come up to the exacting standard of the first sentence of Army Regulations and "execute with alacrity and good faith" an order which he had received.

It so happened that on August 16 Grant himself was put to an exacting test as a subordinate, for with his own orders for an advance issued, he was directed to send part of a regiment back to St. Louis. Though starting on an operation against an enemy reported as stronger than had been previously believed, he obeyed without question, and did not even express a regret in what he wrote that night to Captain Kelton: "I send this evening three companies of the Ninth Missouri Regiment to St. Louis, in accordance with instructions just received. The late hour of receiving the order, and the distance to the railroad depot, precludes the possibility of sending their baggage to-night. That will follow in the morning, however." [61]

Then Grant brought Kelton up to date on his own operation: "I have now one regiment of troops 12 miles from here, on the Greenville road, and eight companies at or near Fredericktown. This last is a key-point to the railroad north from here, and should be held. To-night four companies move from here towards the position occupied on the Greenville road." To Frémont goes the credit for having directed the seizure of Fredericktown at the same time that he ordered sending a column on the Greenville road. But Grant seems to have enlarged the scope of the Greenville mission, and the description of Fredericktown as "a key-point to the railroad north from here" was his own.

Just how much Grant would have made out of his Greenville operation, and whether he would have hazarded an attack against a stronger enemy after the unhappy outcome of the battle near Springfield, cannot be told. The movement was, however, well started on the 18th, and Grant was preparing to join the leading column the next morning, when the evening train brought General Prentiss with orders to take over the Ironton district. Prentiss had been at Cairo, and it is not clear why Frémont made the shift; there is no evidence that he was dissatisfied with Grant, and he may merely have been confused over the relative ranks of his brigadiers.[62]

Without delay Grant started back to St. Louis, and the movement toward Greenville, which he explained to Prentiss, was canceled. But it had served a useful purpose in Grant's training, and the whole Ironton experience was more important than one would gather from his very brief account of it in his *Memoirs*. He knew that he left behind him a command much different from the undisciplined force he had taken over only ten days before; but it certainly never occurred to him that the letters and directives he had written during his brief stay in the hilly country about Pilot Knob would make excellent study for an officer long after the book by Hardee had lost all except historic and antiquarian interest. There is actually a compelling reason for looking carefully at Grant during those days in mid-August. It has been claimed that Rawlins was the originator or inspirer of some of Grant's most notable acts or operations. Rawlins, however, was not at Ironton; and not often has a commanding general had to depend more upon himself, to the smallest detail. None of the Ironton decisions was momentous; in no one of them was a great issue involved. But they reveal a man; they show his mind; they lay bare his character; they make plain how he reacts. They demonstrate whether he is passive and cautious, or active and bold. Later, when decisions *are* momentous, one can reexamine the decisions made at Ironton and the orders issued to carry them out and consider whether or not they set the pattern for what followed.

CHAPTER III

TEN WEEKS OF GRANT AND FRÉMONT

> As to the needlessness of the movements of troops I am a
> better judge than the newspaper reporters who write about it.
>
> *Grant to his sister*

DURING his trip around the world Grant commented upon the impressive headquarters that McClellan had at Cincinnati, saying that such pomp and ceremony were common at the beginning of the war, and adding that McClellan had three times as many men with "quills behind their ears" as he had found necessary to employ at the headquarters of a much larger command. But apparently he never made any recorded remarks about Frémont's establishment in St. Louis. The country was, however, well informed of its grandeur and also knew that there was a feminine touch in the West, though the Army at the time did not officially have women on its rolls. *Harper's Weekly* was not slow in giving its readers a picture of the large three story house "where the gallant General, assisted by his wife, the famous Jessie, spends eighteen hours a day in the work of the campaign." Doubtless the modest brigadier who had started on a field operation without a tent was amused by the "pomp and ceremony" of his superior's bodyguard, a company of three hundred men "made up of the very best material Kentucky could afford; average height, 5 feet 11½ inches, and measuring 40½ inches around the breast." The near-giants from the Blue-Grass State who were watching over the safety of the great explorer and his helpmate, though uniform in physique, were far from a single pattern in other respects. Their roster in fact showed "a number of lawyers, physicians, musicians, prominent merchants, school-teachers, ministers, three superintendents of Sunday-schools, a noted theatrical performer, and nearly every variety of the mechanical department." Until tattoo was sounded, so the story read, the company spent the evenings singing; then the men went to their tents for religious services, for a notable feature of the organization was a chaplain in every tent.[1]

When the brigadier in civilian clothes reported at the great house behind an impressive wall, he may not have seen General Frémont or his wife. It was the Captain Kelton to whom Grant had directed his correspondence from Ironton, who, signing himself "your obedient servant," transmitted the order from Frémont that took Grant and his aide, Lieutenant Clark B. Lagow, to Jefferson City, one hundred and twenty-five miles from St. Louis.[2] The Pacific Railroad that led to the capital had track extending forty miles beyond, passing through the village of California and reaching triumphantly to the newly built Sedalia. The free population of 2,749 that the census of 1860 gave Jefferson City was momentarily augmented by many refugees who had fled from regions held by secessionists. Numerous Home Guard organizations were in or near the town, as well as some Federal regiments; but the condition of uncertainty was revealed by the fact that the new state government which had been created by the convention in July was functioning in St. Louis.

Grant's new assignment returned him to the command of John Pope, then in charge of the North Missouri District, with headquarters in St. Louis. His first report, addressed to Pope's adjutant on August 22, began:

During yesterday I visited the camps of the different commands about this city, and selected locations for troops yet to arrive. I find a great deficiency in everything for the comfort and efficiency of an army. Most of the troops are without clothing, camp and garrison equipage. Ammunition was down to about ten rounds of cartridges, and for the artillery none is left.[3]

As at Ironton, there were guns but no artillerymen. Grant had not as yet been able to locate the quartermaster or the commissary; but it was clear that their departments were in bad condition. There were no rations to issue; the mules that had been recently received were being carefully guarded, but no effort had been made to put them into teams. There were, however, more pressing matters than the "general looseness prevailing." On the 20th a railroad train "densely filled with Home Guards" had been fired into ten miles west of Jefferson City,[4] and Grant said he had organized an expedition of three hundred and fifty men to scour the country in the vicinity of the incident. The situation in transport and rations being what it was, it would be necessary for the force to live off the country, but he had

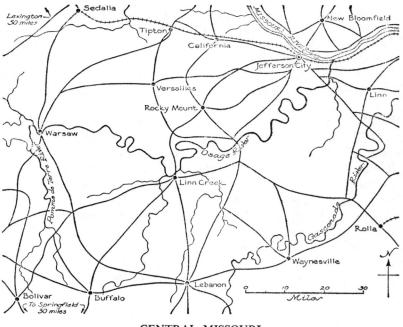

CENTRAL MISSOURI

given "stringent instructions," as to how supplies were to be obtained. The entire nearby country was in a state of ferment and Union men were being driven out and their property appropriated. Grant believed that mounted Home Guards would be the most effective means of dealing with the situation. They could, he said, in most cases mount themselves; when this was impossible, "horses could be obtained from good secessionists who have been aiding and abetting the Southern cause."

The next day Grant wrote, "I am not fortifying here at all. With the picket guard and other duty coming upon the men of this command, there is but little time left for drilling. Drill and discipline are more necessary for the men than fortifications." There was an added reason for not intrenching. No engineer officer was present to give proper directions and Grant himself had no time to devote to the matter; he had, he said "very little disposition to gain a Pillow notoriety" for a branch of the service that he had "forgotten all about." He was still wrestling with figures in an effort to compile an accurate consolidated morning report and have the command in such condition that prompt reports could be made. Thoughts of active operations were also beginning to enter his mind, for, after reporting that there were no published county maps, he said he could learn about the "relative practicability" of roads from persons who were conversant with them.[5]

On the 25th directions came from Frémont for Grant to seize the banks at Lexington and Liberty, the latter place one hundred and fifty miles distant on the other side of the Missouri River. In acknowledging the order Grant said it had been passed on to a colonel "who was under marching orders at the time the instructions came." In the capital, however, there was still confusion because of the continued influx of refugees, and Grant recommended that an officer be sent to get the undisciplined state troops better organized so they could handle the situation. Of McCulloch's activities in the vicinity of Springfield he had no reliable information, though rumors were current that the Tennessean was moving toward Jefferson City. A spy, however, had brought word of the formation of new secessionist companies, some of considerable proportions. After saying that bands were coming from north of the Missouri to augment the Confederate concentration south of the river, Grant showed a touch of vexation: "If I had sufficient force, all that could be stopped." [6]

Two days later a spy came in from Lebanon and another from Springfield with the word that detachments of secessionists were moving north to concentrate at Linn Creek. Home Guards that Grant had sent out on the evening of the 25th to arrest two secessionist captains had returned with their quarry, seized during the night. The captains claimed they "had come in" solely to lay down their arms in accordance with the proclamation of Governor Gamble—the temporary executive chosen in late July by the state convention. But something about their story made Grant doubt that they had "come in in good faith," and he suspected they had intended to return to "Jackson's army." While he was thus not to be easily imposed upon, he was prompt to release persons against whom the case was clearly weak. He freed some men suspected of having fired on the train, who had been brought in by his "posse," declaring that "from all the evidence they were the most innocent men in the county." [7]

Grant again was doing the work of several officers, and experiencing at the same time some added annoyances. Though he was breaking in teams as rapidly as possible so as to make himself mobile, he was handicapped by the fact that the harness which had been sent him was not only entirely too light, but was very inferior in quality. Under the least strain the chains snapped. But this did not prevent him from going on with his preparations for the expedition to Lexington. He had ordered the purchase of new traces for the teams already working and would continue to do this as fast as additional animals were hitched up.

History was, however, to repeat itself: Grant was not to lead the expedition he was preparing. He had sent his last brief dispatch, recommending that someone with proper authority stop the mails from going westward so as to prevent the leakage of news, and he was about to join the regiments which he had concentrated west of the town, when Colonel Jefferson C. Davis unexpectedly appeared upon the scene with an order placing him in command at Jefferson City. Grant immediately explained his plans, and within the hour he was on a train for St. Louis, leaving his aide to give additional information to his successor and to follow the next day with the baggage and horses.[8]

The week in Jefferson City had afforded Grant something more than additional experience in turning confusion into order, preparing troops for a minor operation, and weighing information about the enemy. It had given him an important fact from which to fashion still further his military philosophy. The spy from Springfield had reported that the Confederates had concealed some of their guns after the Battle of Wilson's Creek, and, leaving many of their dead unburied, had started to retreat.[9] Upon learning that the Federals had marched away, they had turned around and entered Springfield, where Ben McCulloch presently proclaimed that he wished to liberate the people who had "been overrun and trampled upon by the mercenary hordes of the North." [10] Here was fresh confirmation of the thought that had come to Grant when as colonel of the Twenty-first Illinois he rode back to Salt River. As the cars carried him away from Missouri's congested little capital he must have wondered what his next assignment would be; but he could also reflect profitably upon the experiences of the week.

The new assignment was to the command of the District of Southeastern Missouri, and it came to Grant in a directive over Frémont's signature which was handed to him on the night of his arrival.[11] The region was one of great strategic importance and North and South alike were striving to gain positions that would control the Mississippi. Both were handicapped by the official attitude of neutrality which Kentucky had sought to maintain. On May 28 Washington had cautiously made the portion of the state within a hundred miles of the Ohio River into the Department of Kentucky, with headquarters "for the present" at Louisville. The commander was to be Colonel Robert Anderson, a native of the state and well known since his trying days at Fort Sumter. Since he soon became ill, the order in reality was a dead letter. Regiments from Kentucky were in both armies and more were forming; but neither Federals nor Confederates had sent forces to seize tempting positions upon the rivers that formed her northern and western boundaries. On August 15 the *Cincinnati Commercial Tribune* published a Washington dispatch of the 8th which said that Anderson, now a brigadier in the regular army, had, against the advice of his physicians, determined to take the field. When warned that he might break down, he had answered that "the Union men of Kentucky were calling on him to lead them, and that he must and would fall in a most glorious cause." Emboldened by the general, the government formed the Department of the Cumberland out of Tennessee and Kentucky; but it refrained from designating a headquarters.[12] As Grant was journeying back to St. Louis, Anderson was making ready to leave Washington for Cincinnati, which was to be a post of observation.

Frémont directed Grant "to proceed forthwith to Cape Girardeau and assume command of the forces at that place." Reports indicated, he said, that 4,000 Confederates were fortifying Benton, Mo., while

1,500 more were camped behind the hills two miles below Commerce. Prentiss had been ordered to march from Ironton toward Cape Girardeau, destroying any hostile detachments he might meet. When he arrived, Grant was to take command of a "combined forward movement."

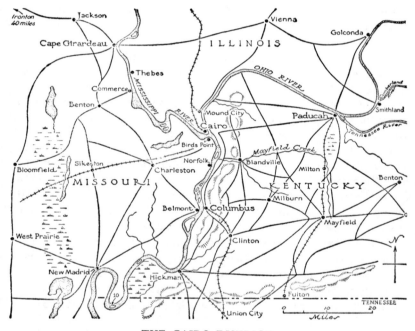

THE CAIRO DISTRICT

Conspicuous in the letter, which sketched several minor moves, was the sentence, "It is intended, in connection with all these movements, to occupy Columbus, Ky., as soon as possible." Such a course could cause the Federals to be the first invaders of Kentucky; but as will be seen presently, Frémont had no scruples about trespassing on the province of the President and no hesitancy in causing him the greatest embarrassment.

From Cape Girardeau Grant wrote on the 30th, "I arrived here at 4:30 o'clock this evening and assumed command of the post." An expedition for Jackson, consisting of thirteen companies of infantry, two guns, and fifty horsemen had left the night before. But the colonel in command, who had already reported that Jackson was free of the enemy, had taken only two days' rations, which seemed insufficient to Grant. Accordingly rations for three additional days were to start at daylight, with the exception of meat, which would have to be procured locally, but in strict accordance with regulations. As at Ironton and Jefferson City, transportation was inadequate; but the thirteen wagons then operating could be supplemented by eight more as soon as harness was received for some captured mules. Frémont had recommended that Grant "do everything to promote the work of fortification commenced at Cairo, Bird's Point, Cape Girardeau, and Ironton." Already the work at Cape Girardeau had been checked and Grant reported it as being pushed with vigor, the Negroes carrying on their part of the work with evident satisfaction.[13]

Though Grant's report of the next day, to which he afterward referred, is not in the records, a letter to his father fills the gap and reveals his own appraisal of his recent activities. Having observed that his son had been moved frequently and had not been given command of a brigade, Jesse Grant thought Ulysses was being discriminated against, and a letter expressing his concern had just arrived. In his prompt answer the general told his father that he was "laboring under an erroneous impression." His assignments had "been complimentary rather than otherwise," though they had indeed kept him "laboriously employed." As if to shut off further paternal complaints, he remarked, "All I fear is that too much may be expected of me." It was true, he said, that he had had four positions within as many weeks, but either something that had been said to him in St. Louis, or his own discernment caused him to remark that he was "probably done shifting commands so often." So much for himself. As for the people of Cape Girardeau: It was generally said that they were secessionists.[14]

As Grant was thus reporting about the Missouri town, deep anxiety for the Blue Grass State was stirring minds north of the Ohio. "I earnestly hope the Government will not lose a moment in preparing for the crisis in Kentucky." Thus read the opening sentence of a telegram that Indiana's Governor Morton sent on August 29 to Thomas A. Scott, Assistant Secretary of War. He wanted arms for troops and artillery for defense "of our river towns." Volunteering was proceeding "with unabated vigor," and the governor stated, "With assurances of good arms we can run our regiments up to forty." Still unable to rest, still doubting whether Washington was awake to the situation, the Hoosier executive said in a second message: "Civil war in Kentucky is inevitable. The advices from my scouts leave no doubt on this subject. A force should be provided ready to march to the support of the Union men at a moment's warning." [15]

Then, as the month changed to September, Robert Anderson took over. To Salmon Chase, Secretary of the Treasury, he telegraphed from Cincinnati: "Just arrived. Hardly time to form an intelligent opinion of the state of affairs in Kentucky. Met several gentlemen of Louisville, who seem to think an invasion from Tennessee immediately threatened." He needed everything in the way of equipment and also "an abundant supply of money." He promised to do everything possible and to report day by day. "Please have as many regiments as possible placed, subject to my orders and within call, in Ohio, Indiana, and Illinois," was a part of the plea of Anderson's strangely addressed message.[16]

While Anderson was telegraphing his wants, Grant was sending to St. Louis good news which he said he believed was reliable. The enemy was giving up—if he had not done so already— all his positions north of the line from Birds Point on the Mississippi to Sikeston, some twenty-five miles to the west. Without delay Grant wrote to Brigadier General McClernand, the former congressman whose eloquence had contributed to bringing the Twenty-first Illinois into three-year service, and who had been in command at Cairo for a few days, suggesting that he have Colonel W. H. L. Wallace "push out to Charleston at once and reconnoiter, without waiting to hear from the column from Ironton." As soon as Prentiss made a junction with Colonel Marsh at Jackson, it was Grant's intention to take command of all the troops personally and move down the river. In his original instructions Frémont had told him that Colonel G. Waagner had been ordered to proceed down the Mississippi under escort of two gunboats and seize Belmont, opposite Columbus, where it was understood some intrenchments were under construction by the Confederates. Belmont, said Grant, should already have been seized if events had moved in accordance with orders.[17]

Again Prentiss appeared unexpectedly, arriving at Cape Girardeau with some cavalry, when Grant believed him to be at Jackson, where indeed he would have been if he had read with due care the order which Frémont had sent him on August 25. Grant directed him to return to Jackson and make ready for the move to Sikeston, while he informed St. Louis that the shortage of transportation had prevented moving adequate provisions to Jackson and that there would be a delay of at least one day in the movement south. The next day Prentiss raised the question of relative rank and ended by positively refusing to obey Grant's order. But in an accommodating spirit he issued an order for his own arrest, and thus cleared the way for Grant to direct Colonel John Cook of the Seventh Illinois to take over the troops at Jackson. Cook was directed to hold himself in readiness for further orders and to send surplus baggage to Cape Girardeau, keeping only what was "strictly required" for the expected movement. Lest Cook be bothered with the question of rank, Grant gave careful instructions about the seniority of his regimental commanders.[18]

Prentiss's refractoriness did not prevent Grant from leaving Cape Girardeau on the morning of September 2, after putting in command the colonel of the Eighth Missouri, to whom were passed the instructions about fortification, with the injunction that the officers overseeing the work should be given all available facilities. It was to strategic Cairo, about which Lincoln had been concerned a month previously, that Grant went to establish the headquarters of his district, which included the southern tip of Illinois. The dispatch reporting his arrival informed Frémont of the Prentiss incident, and said he would forward copies of all orders given the balky general, as well as charges against him. There was also an explanation relative to the command at Jackson, to which Grant had sent thirty thousand rations.[19]

The Prentiss incident—which was reported in the papers—puzzled Grant, and he would have been still more perplexed if he could have seen the message that Frémont had written to Prentiss on August 28, in which he explained carefully his own previous misunderstanding about relative ranks and told Prentiss that Grant was the senior and would be in command when their troops were united. This message may not have reached Prentiss, who was probably confused by the fact that he had been a state brigadier when Grant, a colonel, was mustering troops; but he stood ten places below Grant in Federal ranking. On the 3rd Grant furnished Prentiss a copy of the charges that he had sent to Frémont, and wrote that he had no personal feeling in the matter; if it should be Frémont's wish, he was "perfectly willing to see the charges quashed and the whole matter buried in oblivion." Apparently that is exactly what was done. In the same letter Grant told Prentiss that one of the latter's newspaper correspondents had sent dispatches to Cairo for telegraphing that "were of such a character, and so detrimental to the good of the service" that he had felt it his duty to suppress them.[20] Keeping their stories from the wires is not usually a way to make friends of reporters.

On September 3 Grant also wrote his first letter to Elihu Washburne, from whom he had heard while at Jefferson City. He explained his new assignment and said, "I would be most pleased to have you pay me the visit here, or wherever I may be, that you spoke of paying me there." He referred to Rawlins, to whom he had offered a position on his staff as soon as he was made a brigadier. The Galenian had replied on August 12, expressing his appreciation and accepting the offer. But before he could take the field it was necessary for him to rejoin his wife at her old home in New York state. Grant did not know that Mrs. Rawlins had died on August 30, but he told Washburne he had no idea of withdrawing his offer, if Rawlins was disposed to accept, "no matter how long his absence." An idea of the magnitude of the struggle ahead was dawning on Grant, for he said, "The past would have been a good school of instruction for him in his new duties; the future bids fair to try the backbone of our volunteers." [21]

Grant's report that Sikeston was being abandoned was a little premature, and on the 3rd Frémont challenged it by saying he had word that there was a force of 16,000 men at the place, with artillery and experienced cavalry in firm control of the swampy region. But Brigadier General M. Jeff Thompson, of the secessionist Missouri State Guard, with headquarters near Sikeston, was not hopeful. From spies located wherever there were Federals, Thompson was obtaining abundant information, and on the 2nd he informed Brigadier General Pillow, commanding at strategically situated New Madrid, that Union troops were pouring into Cairo, 8,000 having been reported there the previous Saturday night (August 31). Threatened by the Federal move from Jackson, Thompson wrote on the 3rd that he was falling back the next day and would probably continue his southward movement. "I am afraid your plans have been frustrated," he said to Pillow, "and hope you will now suddenly and unexpectedly change them, and strike a severe blow somewhere." Thompson did not attribute Federal advantage to superiority in numbers, but to mails, telegraphs, steamboats, and railroads. In his judgment only quick and sharp blows could be of any avail against the Unionists.[22]

Better information was not long in reaching Grant and on the 4th he was about as well posted concerning Thompson as was Pillow. A Negro had come in with the story that on September 2nd four regiments of Tennessee and Mississippi troops had left Sikeston, declaring they were going to New Madrid, and then to Memphis. With them went ten or twelve pieces of artillery pulled by horses, a large gun drawn by five yoke of oxen, and a mortar by three yoke. It looked like a case of complete evacuation and Grant said he believed the man had told "a very straight story."[23]

The falling back of the Confederates left the little expedition to Belmont endangered. Colonel Waagner had probably not expected to find much of a town, but he may have had in mind the good meal for which soldiers are always hopeful, and there was a tinge of disappointment in the report he sent at 6:00 P.M. of the 2nd: "I arrived at Belmont at 1.30 p.m. I have not as yet been able to discover any building in the town." Though perhaps poor at finding habitations, the colonel was otherwise observant and reported, "The people resident on the Ohio and Mississippi Rivers have a very great respect for the gunboats." Nevertheless Commander John Rodgers, who had a chance to observe activities at Columbus, advised that Waagner be withdrawn; this Grant did on the 4th, ordering him back to Norfolk.[24]

The movement of the column from Jackson was not resumed, though the reason is not apparent. Colonel Cook was still in command and Grant directed him to keep his force in restraint, allowing "no marauding, insulting of citizens, searching of houses, except [as] you may find it necessary, and then let it be done by persons specially detailed for the purpose." Cook was to keep at least four days' rations on hand and be ready to move without delay, and he was given the injunction, "Should the cavalry horses or mules require shoeing, have it done while you are lying still."[25]

Though Grant of course knew that no Federal troops had been sent into Kentucky and that the administration was acting very circumspectly with regard to the state, he had to believe that Frémont's statement about occupying Columbus reflected instructions from higher authority. He had it in writing that it was intended to seize that place "as soon as possible"; for an officer aggressively minded and prompt in carrying out orders, that was all that was needed. So on September 4 Grant telegraphed Frémont that he could spare infantry, artillery, and cavalry sufficient to seize Columbus Heights. Then he made the prediction that New Madrid would fall within five days. But time was crucial; the move should be made the next night.[26]

New Madrid fall within five days! Certainly Grant had lost no time after reaching Cairo in thinking of positions that might be gained. Why would New Madrid fall? It was not only below Columbus but was on the other bank of the Mississippi; thus it would not be directly threatened by the seizure of the Kentucky town. But from Columbus it would be easy to cross the river and move against the rear of New Madrid. And Gideon Pillow was in command. Even if he had learned on which side of an earthwork the ditch belongs, he would still be the same man. Grant's prediction revealed he knew how important in war is the character of one's opponent.

But the commanding bluffs at Columbus were already in the possession of the Confederates.

On the 2nd Colonel Waagner had reported to Frémont: "At Columbus the rebels fly the secession flag from the top of a lofty pole in the center of the village in defiance of our gunboats." When returning from Belmont with his two gunboats Commander Rodgers had been fired upon by musketry; he had returned the greeting in kind and for good measure had added the fire of "two great guns." It did not look as if Kentucky was neutral. Frémont, who had incurred Presidential disapproval for having compromised the administration in Missouri, gave no instructions to Grant, but reported to the War Department about the attack on the gunboat. The next day—September 5—he telegraphed Lincoln that he thought the enemy intended to throw his main force into West Kentucky and would "immediately occupy Hickman, Columbus, the ground opposite Cairo, and Paducah." Washington, however, was not in the mood to invade Kentucky merely in order to anticipate the Southerners, and the prompt reply that Secretary Cameron sent to Frémont gave no instructions, but merely asked if he would like to have some available Indiana regiments.[27]

Confederate troops under Major General Leonidas Polk, whose

command had been extended on September 2 so as to include operations in Arkansas and Missouri, had occupied Columbus and Hickman the next day. When word of this reached Richmond on the 4th
Secretary Walker telegraphed the general to withdraw his troops from
Kentucky. Polk, a West Point graduate who had resigned from the
Army and entered the ministry, only to exchange the habiliments of
a bishop for those of a general when war broke out, received Richmond's apparently angry note at Union City, Tennessee, close to the
Kentucky border. To President Davis he sent a long dispatch explaining that the enemy had some three or four days before "seated himself
with cannon and intrenched lines opposite the town of Columbus,
Ky., making such demonstrations as left no doubt upon the minds
of any of their intention to seize and forcibly possess said town."
There was an error in fact, for Waagner had reached Belmont only
two days before and apparently had no guns with him; and there was
an error in deduction, for the Union colonel was under instructions
to operate toward Charleston, Missouri. But it is the business of a
general to be suspicious, and one fresh from the pulpit knows how evil
men may be; so Polk said he had thought it proper, under the plenary
power that had been given him, to move some of his regiments into
Kentucky. He believed the effect on the Federals had been wholesome for they had steamed away from Belmont even before he had
fortified his position. However, the ex-bishop, apparently fearing the
Yankees would turn out to be vexatious backsliders, said boldly, "It
is my intention now to continue to occupy and keep this position."
The bishop-general converted the President, who telegraphed back—
still on September 4—"The necessity justifies the action." [28]

Word of Polk's action soon reached Grant. Knowing the strong
secession proclivities of Governor Magoffin, but that Unionists were
three to one in both branches of the Kentucky legislature elected just
one month before, Grant telegraphed to the Speaker of the House of
Representatives at Frankfort on September 5, "I regret to inform you
that Confederate forces in considerable numbers have invaded the
territory of Kentucky, and are occupying and fortifying strong positions at Hickman and Chalk Bluffs." An order publishing the information to his subordinates directed that everything possible be done to
hamper the communications of the Confederates; all ferries, yawls,
flats, and other boats within reach were to be seized at once. To

Frémont all information was sent in telegrams not themselves in the record but referred to in one sent probably in the evening, in which Grant said a detachment had been in Kentucky most of the day to execute preliminary work for the fortifications that had been ordered constructed opposite Cairo. More important was a restatement of Grant's intention for the next day: "I am now nearly ready for Paducah, should not telegram arrive preventing the movement on the strength of the information telegraphed." [29]

Columbus had fallen to the enemy; it must not be so with Paducah, strategically situated at the mouth of the Tennessee River, an obvious invasion route into the South. Grant's prompt reaction was one of the major decisions of the war.

Grant did not allow Frémont too much time to cancel his project, and an hour before midnight he started up the Ohio with the Ninth and Twelfth Illinois regiments of infantry and a four-gun battery. Lest the enemy be forewarned, no one had been allowed to leave Cairo and the telegraph office had been taken over. It had been Grant's intention to be at Paducah near daybreak, but the expedition of two gunboats and three transports was compelled to stop at Mound City while troops were transferred from a broken down vessel to another boat. Had the delay not occurred, it is possible that Confederate Brigadier Lloyd Tilghman and staff, and the newly raised company of volunteers, would have had to board a train for Mayfield without even a sketchy breakfast. Without firing a shot the Federals had possession of the town by 8:30; United States flags began to appear in place of the Confederate emblems which had been flying, but which had disappeared before the boats tied up. Paducahians were expecting the arrival of 3,800 Confederates believed to be only sixteen miles away. Grant accepted this report as correct, but he did not credit the rumor that a large enemy force was coming down the Tennessee. The telegraph office was seized, and a goodly number of complete rations found at the railroad station, as well as two tons of leather, all ready for shipment to the Confederate army, changed allegiance. [30]

After placing his force so as to protect the city, and writing a proclamation to the citizens, in addition to careful instructions for Brigadier General E. A. Paine, [31] who was left in command, Grant departed and was back in Cairo at 4:00 P.M. Awaiting him was a long dispatch from Frémont directing him to seize Paducah if he felt strong enough; if he did not, he was to occupy a position in Illinois, suitable for a battery that could control the Ohio and the mouth of the Tennessee.[32] A short telegram informed Frémont that Paducah was a *fait accompli;* a long letter written the same day gave full details, and ended with an acknowledgement of the efficient aid rendered by McClernand in fitting out the expedition. Additional instructions were sent back to Paine; he was to seize wharf boats for warehouses, and, in case he feared an attack, he was to take all money in the banks and place it on one of the gunboats. As a reenforcement, five companies were hurried up the river without any baggage; but they were to return on the boat that presently would take the Eighth Missouri, summoned the day before from Cape Girardeau for transfer to Paducah. To its commander Grant wrote, "I have selected your regiment and yourself for that post, deeming it of the utmost importance to have troops and a commander that can be expected to do good service." The day's activities were not over; Grant went on to Cape Girardeau, whence on the next day he proceeded to Jackson to see if it were possible to spare any troops from there.[33] He wanted Paducah tied down tight.

Upon returning to Cairo Grant received some pleasing news: Brigadier General Charles F. Smith was being sent to command at Paducah. For this fine officer, who had been Commandant of Cadets when Grant was at West Point, the Cairo general felt an admiration resembling his great esteem for Winfield Scott. Smith, a brevet colonel at the time, had on April 6 been put in command of all troops in Washington, and it was he who on the 23rd alerted Irvin McDowell, then still a major, in a note that contained the memorable words: "Should an attack be made tonight in the direction of the President's Mansion, the Massachusetts troops will promptly move to its defense, leaving the District of Columbia volunteers and Pennsylvania troops for the defense of the Capitol." Smith had just been given his star. Perhaps because Frémont did not wish to subordinate him to Grant, though ostensibly it was to simplify Grant's command problem, he kept Smith directly under his own command. This was not a good arrangement, but Grant and Smith, neither of whom worried about himself in his attachment to duty, were soon to give an example of fine cooperation. Smith was directed to throw up earthworks and prepare to plant guns—Frémont's favorite prescription—but was admonished to make no advance without further orders. To Grant there also came information that sixteen heavy guns had left Pittsburgh for Cairo on two special trains, some of which, along with reenforcements, were to go to Paducah.[34]

No commendation came to Grant for his Paducah action; he received instead over the signature of Frémont's military secretary a sharp reproof for the telegram he had sent to Frankfort on September 5.[35] In being sensitive about Grant's by-passing him merely in the matter of information, and that at a time when hours were important, the department commander was showing himself inconsistent, for he actually requested and continued to receive communications directly from McClernand, about which Grant—McClernand's immediate superior—could not have known.[36] In his *Memoirs* Grant referred with a touch of humor to the admonition Frémont administered to him. No effort at explanation, no expression of wounded sensibilities went to his superior; instead, Grant promptly forwarded important information about the hostile garrison at Columbus, brought in by one of his spies and confirmed by Kentuckians. There were, he said, eighteen regiments at the place, with cavalry and field artillery. Two heavy batteries covered the river, and there were two gunboats, one of which had made bold to come within three miles of Cairo.[37]

The telegraph promptly flashed to the country news of the expedition, the Confederate column that had been narrowly anticipated, the seized rations and leather, and also the text of the proclamation. One especially pleased person must have been Governor Morton, whose alarm had steadily mounted until on September 2 he had wired Washington, "If we lose Kentucky now, God help us." But to Richmond the news was depressing. General Samuel Cooper forgot all about Polk's action and his telegram to General Zollicoffer at Knoxville, "The neutrality of Kentucky has been broken by the occupation of Paducah by Federal forces," looks somewhat like an effort to change the record.[38]

Since no combat was involved, one might dismiss the seizure of Paducah too hastily. The military student is not disposed to search the records to discover whether the Confederates were actually moving on the city. It was possible that they were, and Grant was wise in accepting the reality of the report. He knew that by the time he left Paducah couriers would have met the column with the word of his arrival and information that he had only two regiments and four guns —at most 1,200 men, against the 3,800 the report had mentioned.

Certainly he was eager to get back to Cairo and certainly the boat must have seemed to travel slowly. Then we see a shrewd move: the immediate sending of the five companies as a temporary strengthening of the occupying force. Though they may have debarked with little more than their rifles and overnight kits, they gave General Paine not only more men but a clear indication that his superior could well play all his cards. The fighting power of the Eighth Missouri was increased by an appeal to its pride; and then a search was made for more available men by the general himself. Economy of force, mobility, decisiveness, raising morale of troops, those are prominent topics in the shop talk of officers. They are all well illustrated by the Paducah expedition.

While the Frankfort legislature, encouraged by Grant's action and a visit on the 7th from Robert Anderson,[39] was preparing to compel Governor Magoffin to sign reluctantly a strong Union proclamation,[40] John Frémont was sending Jessie to Washington in an effort to extricate him from a serious self-created difficulty.

Alarmed over the many secessionist bands operating throughout the state, which were strong even in the northeast section, Frémont, on August 30, without consulting Washington, had issued a proclamation taking over "the administrative powers of the State." He drew a line running from Fort Leavenworth on the west, through Jefferson City, Rolla, and Ironton, to Cape Girardeau, and announced that any person taken with arms in his hands north of this line would be tried by a court-martial. Though courts might argue over guilt, they would not have to debate the sentence; Frémont prescribed a firing squad. Then he launched into the troublesome questions of the confiscation of property and slavery. Nothing shows more clearly the difference between Grant and Frémont than their procedures in such matters. While Grant had struck with swiftness at Paducah, he had been cautious at Ironton about detaining mails, and had wanted to act in accordance with laws. Busy though he was, Frémont was inexcusably remiss if he did not know that Congress had dealt with the subject of confiscation in an act of August 6. However, just as nine months later he was to ruin Lincoln's plan for destroying Stonewall Jackson by disobeying an explicit order, so now he acted on his own ideas about the most troublesome and inflammable issues of the war. He declared as confiscated for the public use the real and personal property of all persons who should take up arms against the United States, or who should be "proven to have taken an active part with their enemies in the field." The climax was: "and their slaves, if any they have, are hereby declared freemen." [41]

Lincoln read the pronouncement in the papers with amazement and on September 2 he wrote to Frémont a note beginning, "Two points in your proclamation of August 30 give me some anxiety." He stated that if men were shot there would be retaliation, "and so, man for man, indefinitely." That portion of the proclamation the President set aside by merely saying, "It is, therefore, my order that you allow no man to be shot under the proclamation without first having my approbation or consent." The confiscation of property and the liberation of slaves would, Lincoln said, "alarm our Southern Union friends and turn them against us; perhaps ruin our rather fair prospect for Kentucky." He asked Frémont to modify that portion of his edict and make it conform to the recent act of Congress, a copy of which he sent the general. There was no trace of annoyance in the dispatch, and even its urgency was moderated by the kindly termination, "This letter is written in a spirit of caution and not of censure. I send it by special messenger, in order that it may certainly and speedily reach you." [42]

The Frémonts decided that Jessie should go to Washington as the department commander's representative; but it took more time to get her off than Grant required to prepare his Paducah expedition. In the letter that Frémont wrote to Lincoln on the 8th he related how the idea for his proclamation had come to him during the night; and frankly he said, "I wrote it the next morning and printed it the same day." It was entirely his own idea, for he said, "I did it without consultation or advice with any one, acting solely with my best judgment to serve the country and yourself." After revealing his precipitancy, Frémont said he could not retract on the slavery question, because it would look as if he "had acted without the reflection which the gravity of the point demanded." He had, he said, thought the measure right and necessary, and still believed it to be. He stubbornly told the President that if his pronouncement were to be set aside, he would have to be openly directed to make the correction. With regard to "shooting of men," Frémont also remained adamant, arguing the case as fatuously as he handled the point about slaves. Observing that promptitude is necessary in war, he asserted, "I have

also to ask that you will permit me to carry out upon the spot the provisions of the proclamation in this respect." [43]

A second letter that Mrs. Frémont carried to the President described the military situation. Smith, it was asserted, had been re-
enforced at Paducah, and more troops and guns were to go to him;
he could take Mayfield and Lovelaceville (ten miles east of Blandville), so as to be in the rear of Columbus; Smithland, where the
Cumberland empties into the Ohio, would be seized. Grant was to be
given certain tasks; and a way by which the Federals could strike as
far as Nashville was outlined. This was taking Frémont outside his
department, and he said, "By extending my command to Indiana,
Tennessee, and Kentucky you would enable me to attempt the accomplishment of this all-important result." [44] Frémont's emissary was
to surrender nothing; she was to present near-demands. Lincoln would
read one letter that conceded no error in the administration of the
territory already confided to Frémont; then he would open another
that asked for authority over three more states.

Two years later Lincoln discussed the midnight meeting which he
had had with Jessie Frémont, who, according to a biographer, hastened from her hotel to the White House without taking time to
change her rumpled and travel-stained dress. The substance of his
remarks went into John Hay's diary. Mrs. Frémont had taxed him so
severely that Lincoln had to exercise all the "awkward tact" he possessed to avoid quarreling with her. Nor had the daughter of Missouri's former influential senator hesitated to allow threats to hover
in the background of her attack. Said Lincoln: "She more than once
intimated that if General Frémont should decide to try conclusions
with me, he could set up for himself." [45]

The stormy session was not devoted entirely to the contents of the
two letters that Mrs. Frémont presented. Perhaps her words were
sharpest and her anger keenest over a matter not referred to in either
letter—the bitter war that had replaced the close friendship between
the Blairs and Frémont. Lincoln's secretaries wrote: "The reputation
of General Frémont was the creation of the Blairs. It was at their
solicitation that the President appointed the Pathfinder a major-
general in the regular army and gave him command of the important
department of the Missouri." [46] The first sentence is a gross exaggeration, for Frémont had a standing with the public which he owed in

no way to Francis P. Blair, Sr., or to his sons; and the second sentence needs qualification because he had many other supporters than the Blairs.

Frank Blair, congressman from St. Louis and an organizer of the Home Guards, had, however, not observed Frémont long before he began to doubt his fitness for the position in which he had helped place him. The general's method of dealing with army contracts was a cause of suspicion, and the elaborate fortifications he was building about the city did not appeal to one with Blair's fondness for aggressive action. Reports went to his brother, the Postmaster General, who in turn showed them to Lincoln, with whom he was on very close terms. However, as late as August 24, Montgomery Blair opened his heart in naïve confidence to the general,[47] saying things which, when published, caused him much embarrassment both with the President and fellow cabinet members. A letter that Frank Blair wrote on the 21st fell into the hands of Quartermaster General Meigs, who wrote at length to Frank on the 28th in an effort to disabuse the minds of both Frank Blair and Frémont "of some errors which may give trouble." [48] Thus something in addition to the panicky messages which Frémont had sent after the Battle of Wilson's Creek had raised doubts about the general before everyone was startled by his manifesto of August 30. While Jessie Frémont was journeying to the capital, Montgomery Blair and Montgomery Meigs were hastening to St. Louis to attempt to straighten out the tangled situation. Learning of their trip from the senior Mr. Blair, Mrs. Frémont's anger mounted still higher and from her hotel she wrote a note to Lincoln requesting copies of any letters which had caused him to send the two Montgomerys to St. Louis; the President politely declined to gratify her, but stated that he had not been acting in any hostility toward her husband.[49]

Lincoln's answer to Frémont's letter of the 8th about the proclamation was written soon after the unpleasant midnight interview; it bears the date of September 11 and was sent by mail. He said he very cheerfully ordered "that the said clause of said proclamation be so modified, held, and construed as to conform to and not to transcend the provisions on the same subject contained in the act of Congress" approved on August 6. He directed also that the act in question be published at length with the order he was giving. The man whose wife had implied that he might set up for himself was given very clearly to understand that Congress made the laws of the Republic. But damage had been done that Lincoln could not undo. The radicals had shouted their approval of Frémont's acts, and having had their way for awhile, they now urged with even louder voices that prompt extinction of slavery be the order of the day without reference to its necessity as a war measure. Some conservatives were won over, and on September 22 Lincoln wrote to one of them, emphasizing the effect in Kentucky, whose "Legislature would not budge till the proclamation was modified," and where a whole company of volunteers had thrown down their arms and disbanded. The state seemed as crucial to Lincoln as it did to Governor Morton, and he said: "I think to lose Kentucky is nearly the same as to lose the whole game. Kentucky gone, we cannot hold Missouri, nor, as I think, Maryland. These all against us, and the job on our hands is too large for us. We would as well consent to separation at once, including the surrender of this capital." [50]

Even before Frémont had received Lincoln's note disapproving his proclamation, he had sought to win a feud with Governor Gamble by asking the President not to allow the governor to raise any more regiments "for the present." His wife could hardly have reported about her unsuccessful errand before he tried to settle his quarrel with Frank Blair by putting him in arrest. When one recalls that it was said that a Blair never went into a fight without going in for a funeral, and that the three Blairs always made common cause, John Frémont was very rash. (Montgomery Blair was well known in St. Louis, for he had practiced law there and had won the title of Judge.) The papers spread the battle before the people and in some cases at least got to the root of the matter. After saying one day that Blair had been arrested for using disrespectful language to his superior, the *New York Tribune* corrected the statement the next day by reporting, "This, we believe, is not exactly correct; the real ground of arrest we understand to be that Col. Blair had written letters to the President, and to at least one member of the cabinet, charging General Frémont with inefficiency, and with extravagance in the expenditure of money." Within a few days the same paper questioned the competency of Frémont to arrest Blair. Although the latter had been very active in raising regiments and had worn the uniform of a colonel, he had not accepted a commission, having in fact declined a colonelcy during the last session of Congress. On the other hand,

Frank Blair, congressman from St. Louis, could hardly be expected to discontinue relations with the President and the cabinet. To Frémont's effort to arrest him, Blair replied with formal charges against the general. By the time the compositor had put all the charges and specifications into type, he had set two long columns of closely packed lines three inches long.[51]

Presently Frémont relinquished the St. Louis battlefield to some of his aides and started westward to engage the Confederates, after having, on September 21, made "acting major-generals" out of four brigadiers and the same number of "acting brigadier-generals" out of colonels—another irregular procedure. But before departing he had to report to the Secretary of War the surrender at Lexington of a Federal command of about 2,800 men which had been under siege for a week by a much stronger force under General Price. Said the departing general, "I will send you from the field more details in a few days." In a few hours a reply was back from Winfield Scott, short and pointed: "Your dispatch of this day is received. The President is glad you are hastening to the scene of action. His words are, 'He expects you to repair the disaster at Lexington without loss of time.'" After dispatching orders for the concentration of the divisions of the Army of the West, Frémont left St. Louis, with Major Charles Zagonyi in command of his bodyguard of stalwart and eager Kentuckians.[52]

The charges and reports about Frémont were not being ignored, though the President would take no action without thorough investigation. At 2:30 A.M. on October 11, the Secretary of War and the Adjutant General of the Army, Colonel Lorenzo Thomas, arrived in St. Louis, the latter to take notes that were embodied in a comprehensive report written ten days later. As soon as they had breakfasted the investigators went to Benton Barracks, where Brigadier General Samuel R. Curtis, a regular officer who had brought the Second Iowa Volunteers into service, was in command. Curtis reported that Frémont never consulted him nor told him his plans; while he would feel free to go to General Scott to express opinions, "he would not dare do so to General Frémont." As a summary of Curtis's views, Thomas wrote, "He deemed General Frémont unequal to the command of an army, and said that he was no more bound by law than by the winds." The paymaster in St. Louis was found to be in the greatest difficulty over the irregular appointments that Frémont had made, in number no fewer than two hundred. In Frémont's mind a mere note signed by himself created an officer. Bad irregularities in the matter of contracts were uncovered and Thomas wrote, "It is the expressed belief of many persons that General Frémont has around him in his staff persons directly and indirectly concerned in furnishing supplies." [53]

The investigators did not content themselves with prying into matters at department headquarters; they joined Frémont on the 13th at Tipton, some thirty-five miles west of Jefferson City. An adjutant general can be forgiven a passion for location and strength of troops, and Thomas set down Frémont's five divisions as containing 38,789 men. At Tipton there were, in addition to the staff and bodyguard, parts of two divisions, the rest of the army not yet having joined. The prospects for catching Price did not look very promising, for he had fallen back toward Arkansas with his estimated 20,000, taking with him much plunder and numerous bands of disaffected persons. Rumors were in fact arriving that he was crossing the Osage River, a considerable stream, and Frémont's army was not equipped with transportation for a long pursuit. Such was the report that Lincoln must have had in his hands soon after it was written on October 22. Nor did Thomas fail to give in detail actions that Frémont could have taken to reenforce Lyon before the Battle of Wilson's Creek, as well as the neglected possibilities to relieve Lexington—accessible by water—before its surrender. Perhaps nothing in the report was more irritating to the President than the copy of Frémont's order directing that two hundred copies of his proclamation be sent to Ironton for distribution, issued after Lincoln had annulled most of the manifesto. Along with the report was a detailed description of Frémont's plan for retaking Springfield—which would need no retaking if Price continued his retirement.

Action followed swiftly. On October 24 General Scott issued an order—his last general order—relieving Frémont of command of the Western Department and putting Major General Hunter, then leading one of Frémont's divisions, in his place. It was forwarded through General Curtis, to whom Lincoln wrote a note saying that when he, or the messenger he should send from St. Louis, reached General Frémont, the order was not to be delivered if Frémont had personally fought and won a battle, or was engaged in battle, or was "in the immediate presence of the enemy in expectation of a battle." [54] The courier found the general concentrating his army and believing the enemy was approaching. The courier thought otherwise and delivered the order.

Frémont's growing misconception can be traced in the records. On October 24 Major Zagonyi wrote to him from Springfield, relating how the bodyguards had left their camp near the Pomme de Terre River on October 24 and had fought for the possession of the town. "I have seen battles and cavalry charges before," he said, "but I never imagined that a body of men could endure and accomplish so much in the face of such a fearful disadvantage." Shouting "Frémont and the Union," his men had been irresistible in their onset. Twenty-three of the enemy had been buried while only fifteen of his own men had been killed. His loss in horses had, however, been considerable, and his concluding sentence showed there had been close shooting: "Revolvers are also seriously damaged by the enemy's bullets." But Zagonyi failed to report that a company of Irish Dragoons had reenforced the Body Guards, an omission that brought a strong protest from the physically and mentally wounded dragoon commander.[55]

Frémont himself reached Springfield on the 27th with Sigel's division and was loudly acclaimed by the Unionists who had suffered much during recent weeks. As midnight passed on October 30–31 he wrote his absent division commanders that the enemy was marching upon Springfield and they must make "the utmost exertions" if they were "to reach him in time to aid." A second dispatch told Hunter that the arrival of the divisions was awaited in order to attack, and he must make daily reports of his progress. Fresh dispatches the next day said that more positive information revealed the enemy was then, or soon would be, only a day's march away. The divisions were to move "with the greatest celerity," even if it entailed living "on beef alone." Fearing that his previous messages had not reached Pope, Frémont on November 1 ordered him to make forced marches so as to join "the advanced corps." A dispatch to Hunter the next day said the advance guard of the enemy would be at Wilson's Creek that night and that Union men were flocking in for protection. That Curtis's messenger had also arrived and delivered Scott's order was clearly though indirectly revealed: Hunter was not only to have his division hasten, but was to push on personally "to assume the command." Also on the 2nd Frémont issued an order bidding his men farewell and asking them to give his successor "the same cordial and enthusiastic support" with which they had always encouraged him.[56]

The next day Hunter telegraphed the Adjutant General: "I take command of the department to-day. General Frémont left for the East this morning. I do not think the enemy is in force in our neighborhood. I will telegraph you daily." The dispatch was not put on the wire at Rolla until the 7th, but the newspapers had reported the change of command, and, not wanting any nonsense, McClellan, the new General in Chief, telegraphed Curtis on the 6th to act promptly on all matters in St. Louis until he heard from General Hunter. Special attention was to be given to the arsenal and the telegraph office was to be taken over. At Frémont's headquarters Hunter found considerable correspondence with Price on various questions. After studying it he wrote to Price that he could in no wise recognize certain agreements and could neither issue nor allow to be issued a "joint proclamation" purported to have been signed by Price and Frémont on November 1. All the documents were sent to Washington with a covering letter explaining why Hunter thought it "impolitic in the highest degree to have ratified General Frémont's negotiations." [57]

Hunter found excellent advice with regard to his future operations in a careful document prepared by the President on October 24 and consigned to Curtis for delivery to him after the relief of Frémont. It was one of the longest, most interesting, and significant of Lincoln's written military appraisals. General Scott may not have even known about the document, but the imminence of his retirement and his recent inactivity save the President from the charge of serious infringement on the duties of the General in Chief. Said the President: "The command of the Department of the West having devolved upon you, I propose to offer you a few suggestions. Knowing how hazardous it is to bind down a distant commander in the field to specific lines and operations, as so much always depends on a knowledge of localities and passing events, it is intended, therefore, to leave a considerable margin for the exercise of your judgment and discretion." It looked to Lincoln as if Missouri was being given up by the enemy except in the southeastern portion of the state, and that there was little chance of overtaking Price without the danger of overextending lines of communications. He suggested that the pursuit should be abandoned and that Hunter divide his command "into two corps of observation, one occupying Sedalia and the other Rolla, the present termini of railroad." This would provide an opportunity to "recruit the condition of both corps by re-establishing and improving their discipline and instruction, perfecting their clothing and equipments, and providing less uncomfortable quarters." The President did not think the enemy would return to Missouri from the southwest "before or during the approaching cold weather." If the policy were adopted and if the enemy did not reappear in great force, Hunter would find that he had a surplus of numbers and he could send some of his troops elsewhere, with the possibility always of returning them by railroad in case of need. Lincoln foresaw the continuance of local uprisings for a time; these could be met by detachments and local forces, and they would "ere long tire out of themselves." The dispatch ended: "While, as stated in the beginning of the letter, a large discretion must be and is left with yourself, I feel sure that an indefinite pursuit of Price or an attempt by this long and circuitous route to reach Memphis will be exhaustive beyond endurance, and will end in the loss of the whole force engaged in it." [58]

Hunter's decision came in a message sent on the 11th from south of Warsaw: "In conformity with the views of the President, in which I fully concur, I fall back on Rolla and Sedalia." Price had, he said, left Cassville on the 7th in full retreat for Arkansas, preceded by McCulloch, both men being probably already out of Missouri. His own command was in good order and fine spirits. He asked that a slander about the Germans in his command should be corrected; though an effort had been made to induce them to mutiny when Frémont was removed, they had shown themselves loyal and efficient. In a dispatch sent later in the day from Warsaw Hunter said an enormous amount of army stores and public property was "in the hands of irresponsible, ignorant, and illegally appointed persons," who had given no security, held no commissions, and were accountable to no tribunal. In order to place the department "on a basis of integrity, capacity, and responsibility," he asked that six experienced and reliable officers—ordnance officers, engineers, and quartermasters—be sent to him. A wide-awake telegraph operator thought that

Washington would appreciate a little postscript, so he added that a message had just arrived confirming General Hunter's "former dispatch as to General Price falling back into Arkansas." [59]

Frémont's quarrel with Lincoln over the proclamation, his feud with Frank Blair, and his preparations for departure from St. Louis stopped effective operations in the Cairo area. Grant, however, continued to forward reports of reconnaissances as well as intelligence otherwise obtained. He had a well placed contact in Columbus, for on one occasion he said his information had come "from an official of Major-General Polk." He reported that he was certain that Hardee had crossed into Kentucky with five regiments. When he warned St. Louis that a large force had left Columbus for the interior, he was careful to add that he did not know whether it was bound for Paducah; when he reported that another contingent had crossed to Missouri, he commented that he believed it was for the purpose of harvesting corn. With regard to his own command, Grant wrote on September 10, "All the forces show great alacrity in preparing for any movement that looks as if it was to meet an enemy, and if discipline and drill were equal to their zeal, I should feel great confidence against great odds." A Confederate gunboat, tauntingly named the *Yankee,* had refused to be lured into deep water, but had kept close to shore and the guns of Columbus. But in spite of her aloofness, Unionist Captain Stembel had put a shell into her wheel house, compelling her to maneuver on one engine. "If it were discretionary with me," said Grant in conclusion, "with a little addition to my present force I would take Columbus. Your order will, however, be executed." [60]

Reflections about the war that were not in his letters to headquarters appeared in one to his sister. Mary and her father, stirred doubtless by the seizure of Paducah and eager for news, had just written him. In reply, he said:

What future operations will be, of course, I don't know. I could not write about it in advance if I did. The rebel force numerically is much stronger than ours, but the difference is more than made up by having truth and justice on our side, whilst on the other they are cheered on by falsehood and deception. This war however is formidable and I regret to say cannot end as soon as I anticipated at first. [61]

Near mid-September Rawlins reported at Cairo and Grant gave him the important position of adjutant. His experience as a lawyer, his intelligence, his integrity, and his great zeal made his development rapid. Not only did he study the duties of his office, he studied his commander, and his attachment to Grant was to become only less intense than his devotion to his country. Soon he was probably able to take over a little of the burden of the man who had seldom been able to get to bed before two or three o'clock in the morning; [62] and one can be sure a thrill of pride ran through John Rawlins when he first wrote "By order of Brigadier General Grant" and appended his own name and position.

On October 1 Grant reported: "The packets plying between Saint Louis and Cairo constantly leave freight at points above here intended for the interior. This enables the enemy to supply all his wants." With his letter there went an inventory of goods he had seized two days before at Charleston and brought back. He stated frankly, doubtless with the concurrence of lawyer Rawlins, that he had serious doubts as to whether there was a law authorizing the seizure, but he had no doubt of the propriety of breaking up the trade. He asked for instructions from the commanding general, and in the meantime put an efficient procedure into operation. Boats were designated to follow the steamers from St. Louis, make all the landings they made, and pick up the cargoes they discharged. Some unnamed officer thought it would be simpler to seize the steamers themselves, and he brought one of them into port, an act that caused some complication. Grant, however, persisted, sent lists of the goods picked up by two trailing steamers and asked what should be done with them. This commerce, he observed, not only enabled the enemy to obtain valuable supplies but also "all the information in possession of citizens of Saint Louis." [63]

As early as September 29 Grant observed that it was time to think of providing winter quarters for the garrison at Cairo. Log huts could easily be built, but though they would be cheap, there was no money, and credit was exhausted. Citizens were already muttering, and unless a paymaster arrived soon to pay troops, there would be discontent among the soldiers. The question of the physically unfit and the sick was causing concern, for Cairo was not a healthy place, having been referred to on July 21 by General Lyon's adjutant as "that sickly hole." Grant wrote to Captain McKeever—who was in charge of

Frémont's St. Louis headquarters—that since the general was in the field, he had come to the conclusion that he also could regard himself as commanding an army in the field and therefore, in accordance with Army Regulations, could sign discharges upon a surgeon's statement of disability. This would allow him to accelerate the discharge of those men who "should not be detained a single day." He also requested authority to grant sick leaves and inquired if he could not send officers and men on recruiting duty. The comfort and health of his command would be greatly helped by eight thousand bed-sacks and he hoped they could be furnished him.[64]

As the North's resources and war potential, without authoritative agencies or previous war plans, came to the support of the growing army, the accumulating supplies became a problem, in spite of critical shortages of arms and other important items. Grant had been using a large wharf boat for storage; it saved labor in handling since large quantities of rations were being sent out by boat. But the navy was also developing Cairo as the chief base for the inland fleet that was to come into being. The general who had already conducted one small combined operation and who would soon lead others, solved problems harmoniously with the naval officers, though he had to refer some questions to St. Louis. Grant did not confine himself to reporting deficiencies and making respectful requests; he made trips to get equipment. In asking permission to visit St. Louis and Springfield, he said by way of explanation, "I have frequently reported our deficiency in many necessaries to a complete outfit, and want to give my best efforts to remedy the evil." A short time later he told of a visit to Governor Yates. Though Yates had no artillery or small-arms available at the moment, he thought that by the end of November he might be able to furnish a battery of rifled guns.[65]

At last Grant's uniform had arrived, and he sent his sister a photograph of himself and staff of four officers. "A good looking set, aren't they?" he queried, after identifying the numbered officers. To his father, who evidently had been making suggestions, he sent further remonstrances: "I do not want to be importuned for places. I have none to give and want to be placed under no obligations to any one." After stating that there was no telling when he might have to discipline someone who had done a favor or had been recommended by himself, he said, "I want always to be in a condition to do my duty without partiality, favor, or affection." Mary had been concerned by newspaper criticisms of her brother; this brought the answer, "As to the needlessness of the movements of troops I am a better judge than the newspaper reporters who write about it." [66]

Though the sending of two of his best regiments to the great force that McClellan was accumulating at Washington had left Grant with little more than a weak garrison, he was still thinking about Columbus, and he wrote to Smith that he had a plan to approve or recommend if there were any chance to advance. But so long as he was weak he intended not to be taken at a disadvantage. "Despairing of being immediately re-enforced," he wrote to Colonel Richard Oglesby at Norfolk, "I deem it the better part of valor to be prudent." Then he directed his subordinate to concentrate at Birds Point, selecting his encampments so as to leave "as clear a field for defense as possible." In mid-October Grant, at Frémont's direction, sent a punitive expedition of three infantry regiments, three companies of cavalry, and two guns in pursuit of some enemy detachments which had been committing depredations against the Iron Mountain Railroad. At about the same time he also received what was probably his first dispatch from Sherman, who, because of Anderson's poor health, had been given command at Louisville. Sherman was so worried over a possible strong enemy advance that he had telegraphed directly to Lincoln. Believing that a threat against Columbus by Grant and Smith would prevent such a move, he had requested a demonstration. Grant wrote to Smith that he was ready to cooperate with Sherman to the extent of his limited means, but due to the expedition he had just sent toward Ironton, he could not start with more than 5,000 men. He informed St. Louis that he was communicating with Smith and would aid in any demonstration that seemed feasible. There the matter apparently rested, for, with Frémont absent, McKeever was hardly in a position to make a decision. Demonstrations without the possibility of attacking—which Grant was not strong enough to do—may not have appealed to him too much. But he was alert to the chance of a real blow, and presently he passed on to Smith information he had received from "a strong, unconditional Union man" that a regiment of Confederate cavalry was being formed at Princeton, Kentucky. Though well mounted, the secessionists were short of arms, and Grant outlined a night boat ride up the Cumberland with some cavalry to Eddyville, whence a macadamized road led to Princeton, only twelve miles away. He thought his old teacher might "take steps to secure these fellows." [67]

In September the rumor was abroad in Cairo that the Confederate government had sent General Albert Sidney Johnston to take over-all command in the West. The fifty-eight-year old officer, who had graduated from West Point in 1826 well up in his class, had had a colorful career in and out of the Army and was well known to the whole country. When the military desires of a regiment of Texans that he had commanded had been so well satisfied by the hard march from Matamoros to Camargo that the men voted 318 to 224 in favor of disbanding rather than reenlisting, Johnston remained to serve General Taylor in a volunteer capacity. At the battle of Monterrey he had attracted the approving eye of Colonel Jefferson Davis, while Taylor is reported to have said that Johnston was the best soldier he had ever commanded.[68] He had reentered the regular army in 1849, and after commanding the Second Cavalry on frontier duty in Texas he led the troops employed in the "Mormon War" that broke out in 1857. Johnston was relieved after three winters in Utah Territory, and, having returned to Washington, was, according to his son, favored by General Scott for the position of Quartermaster General.[69] The appointment, however, went to Lieutenant Colonel Joseph E. Johnston, not without its being observed that the appointee had been born in Virginia, the native state of Secretary of War John B. Floyd. In late 1860 Sidney Johnston was given command of the Pacific Department with the rank of Brevet Brigadier General.

Although he had had no part in Scott's culminating campaign in the Mexican War—which did so much to train excellent officers— many persons in the South regarded Johnston as the best of the brigadiers in the United States Army when the Civil War broke out. There was great rejoicing when it was learned that he had resigned, presumably to cast his lot with the seceding states, and again when word arrived that he had evaded Federal efforts to intercept him on his long ride across the hot desert and had reached San Antonio. His son wrote later that Jefferson Davis was wont to remark, "I hoped and expected that I had others who would prove generals, but I knew I had *one,* and that was Sidney Johnston." [70] Since Johnston had been born in Kentucky and had many friends there, it was natural that

Davis, also a native of the Blue Grass State, should send him westward in the hope that he might save the crucial Commonwealth from the machinations of another of its sons—Abraham Lincoln.

In spite of the fact that Grant reported on September 20 that he had no confirmation of the reports about Johnston, that officer had already reached Nashville and the spirit of hopefulness caused by his arrival pervaded the long letter he wrote to Davis on the 16th. Even as he picked up his pen, fresh word, in which he said he had confidence, had come from Columbus: Polk was on the march toward Paducah with 7,500 men. Grant probably could have said that was an exaggeration; but it was Johnston's first day in high command and he was looking at things optimistically. More accurate was his statement that he would seize Bowling Green the next day with 5,000 men and would add supports as needed. Johnston also issued a resounding proclamation in which he said that it was for the people of Kentucky to decide whether they would "join" the United States or the Confederacy, "or maintain a separate existence as an independent and sovereign State." [71] Apparently the general had not reviewed his history or posted himself on recent events; Kentucky had become a state of the Union eleven years before he was born and had never proclaimed that she had seceded. To talk about Kentucky "joining" the United States was enough to make a Northerner explode from anger; it was worse than Grant's sending the picture of himself and staff to his secessionist Aunt Rachel.[72]

Originally Grant had had in front of him Hardee, the expert on tactics; then he had Polk, who perhaps was a little rusty on drill, but knew every word in the prayer book. Now giving orders to the recent commandant of cadets and the ex-bishop was a four-star general,[73] Taylor's and Scott's favorite, and Jeff Davis's presumptive best. It was quite an array of talent to be opposed to the former captain of infantry, who could write a proclamation only half as long as Sidney Johnston's. Nevertheless Grant was looking only for a chance to strike. Soon he would prove the correctness of the statement of Colonel Henderson, the great biographer of Stonewall Jackson: "Grant, like Moltke, was always ready to try conclusions." [74]

CHAPTER IV

BELMONT

We found the Confederates well-armed and brave.
Grant to his wife

OCTOBER, the Midwest's choicest month, was gone. After eight weeks of hard work, Grant had a command that had improved greatly in discipline and military knowledge. He knew that it would respond to his orders, and that officers and men alike would meet the exacting test of battle if he led them well. His return for October 31 gave an aggregate for duty of 11,161 in infantry, cavalry, and artillery. There were five brigades: General McClernand's at Cairo and Mound City; Colonel Oglesby's and Colonel W. H. L. Wallace's at Birds Point; Colonel Plummer's at Cape Girardeau; and Colonel Cook's at Fort Holt, Kentucky. Grant was, however, not prepared for a serious advance, for on the 27th he reported to St. Louis that in addition to deficiencies in the equipment of the different arms, his transportation was inadequate for "any forward movement." If it were not for lack of essential equipment, he and Smith could, he said, take Columbus.[1]

Just how affairs were being directed in the Western Department at this time is a puzzle. After Frémont took the field in late September, Captain Chauncey McKeever exercised authority considerably in excess of that normal for an adjutant, though he seems to have informed his chief as to his actions, while Frémont himself sent directives to Smith and Grant, not all of which, however, seem to have survived.

An unjust and rather amusing description of command arrangements was given by Anna Ella Carroll, who had arrived in St. Louis about the middle of October. She was the pretentious woman who after the war posed as an influential advisor to Lincoln and who presented to Congress claims for compensation for the idea of the Federal advance up the Tennessee River that began in early 1862. In a magazine article published in 1886, that was perhaps a final effort to win popular support for her fantastic claim, Miss Carroll said, "I went to General Fremont's. He was absent on one of his expeditions. His wife was in command in St. Louis." [2] Jessie Frémont undoubtedly had much influence upon her husband, but Miss Carroll exaggerated her importance as definitely as she did her own.

On November 1 McKeever directed Grant to make demonstrations along both sides of the river toward Charleston, Norfolk, and Blandville, and to keep his "columns constantly moving back and forward against these places, without, however, attacking the enemy." [3] He stated that General Smith was being instructed to have his command engage in similar exercise; the two generals were in fact to cooperate in their mock warfare. Demonstrations are essential to military operations, and a commander who never used them would simplify his antagonist's problem very much. But excessive demonstration can spoil the morale of a command and take the edge off its alertness. Grant himself had spoken of the alacrity which his men showed in preparing for any movement that "looked as if it were to meet the enemy"; and it is not likely that he was much pleased at the thought of keeping regiments merely moving "back and forward" along the two sides of the great river. But a new order came before he could begin his exercise in marching.

A directive may have reached McKeever from Frémont, and on November 2—the day Frémont received the order relieving him of command—he wrote to Grant that the troublesome Jeff Thompson was on the St. Francis River, twenty-five miles southeast of Greenville with about 3,000 men. A force was already moving against him from Pilot Knob and Grant was instructed to send troops from Cape Girardeau and Birds Point to assist in driving Thompson into Arkansas. The next day Grant wrote—in the form of a letter—his order for the operation; and like other things from his pen, it is worthy of careful study. He directed Colonel Oglesby, a veteran of the Mexican War, to take three regiments and four companies of infantry, three companies of cavalry, and a section of artillery, put them on steamboats, go up the river to Commerce, Missouri, and then march to Sikeston, using a Mr. Cropper for his guide. Cooperation with the force from Ironton was outlined, and once more instructions were given about care in obtaining supplies from the country. This was indeed the last thought the general left with the colonel, his letter ending, "You are particularly enjoined to allow no foraging by your men. It is demoralizing in the extreme, and is apt to make open enemies where they would not otherwise exist." [4]

Grant, however, significantly changed the mission. Whereas McKeever had spoken merely of "driving Thompson into Arkansas," Grant told Oglesby, "The object of the expedition is to destroy this force," leaving entirely to his subordinate "the manner of doing it." "Pursue the enemy in whatever direction he may go": such was the modified and amplified order that went out of the Cairo headquarters. Grant knew there was risk in what he was ordering and he cautioned Oglesby "not to fall in with an unlooked-for foe too strong" for his command to handle. No time was lost, and on the evening of the same day the little force was on its way. How Lincoln would have liked to see such a message as Grant wrote to Oglesby and such promptness in starting out, and how he would have liked to watch the Eighth, the Eighteenth, and the Twenty-ninth Illinois, with four companies of the Eleventh, the grim looking guns, the young troopers and the wagons, move in smooth, disciplined fashion down to the waiting steamboats! Doubtless a quiet general *did* watch them, and doubtless Colonel Oglesby received words of approval and encouragement—in addition to the carefully written instructions that had been prepared. On this November 3 there were some historic departures other than that of Oglesby's little command. The deposed Frémont set out from Springfield on his long ride to Rolla, while Winfield Scott left the nation's Capital for retirement, George McClellan and a squadron of cavalry braving pitch darkness and a pouring rain to go to the station, where they "saw the old man off."

Grant provided a distracting force for Oglesby's operation; on the 4th he ordered Colonel Plummer to send the Tenth Iowa from Cape Girardeau in the direction of Bloomfield "with a view to attracting the attention of the enemy." [5]

From department headquarters there came on November 5 a telegram stating that the Confederates were sending troops from Columbus by way of White River to reenforce Price's army in southwestern Missouri. Grant was ordered to make a demonstration against Columbus at once in order to stop the imaginary movement to build up the enemy force that Frémont—under whose orders McKeever was still operating—had thought was moving against him in the vicinity of Springfield. Grant's plan was quickly made and he requested Smith to make a threat against Columbus, saying that he was fitting up an expedition of about 3,000 men "to menace Belmont." The next morning he decided to deflect temporarily the direction of Oglesby's column toward New Madrid, and sent to that commander a small reenforcement under Colonel Wallace, who was to take the short cut from Birds Point through Charleston. Because it was hazardous to send Oglesby close to New Madrid, Grant instructed the colonel to communicate with him "at Belmont" when he reached the point nearest to Columbus from which a road led to Belmont; and Wallace, who was the bearer of the new order to Oglesby, was carefully briefed that Oglesby was to halt.[6]

Colonel Conger in his study of Belmont apparently did not read Grant's orders to Oglesby and Wallace carefully. After asserting that Oglesby was "to march past Belmont to New Madrid," he has him in a predicament and suggests that Grant intended to land at Belmont in order to protect him, as well as do a little menacing. The purpose of the change in orders to Oglesby seems, however, clear enough; Grant merely wished to regain control of his western column by having it move to a convenient position, halt, and report; further orders would be in accordance with circumstances.[7] But the words "at Belmont" that he used when telling Oglesby where to address him must remain somewhat enigmatic.

Grant still had some troops to use on the east of the Mississippi and he ordered Colonel Cook to march on the morning of the 7th from Fort Holt to Elliott's Mill (in the direction of Columbus) with two days' rations. He was to return the next day if further instructions did not reach him by 2:00 P.M. of the 8th.[8] The district commander would have essentially everything he commanded away on three missions.

Not much is recorded in history or military books about Belmont, and sometimes the battle is mentioned chiefly to point out the errors and to observe how Grant profited from his mistakes. But the reader should note carefully what has been said about the different

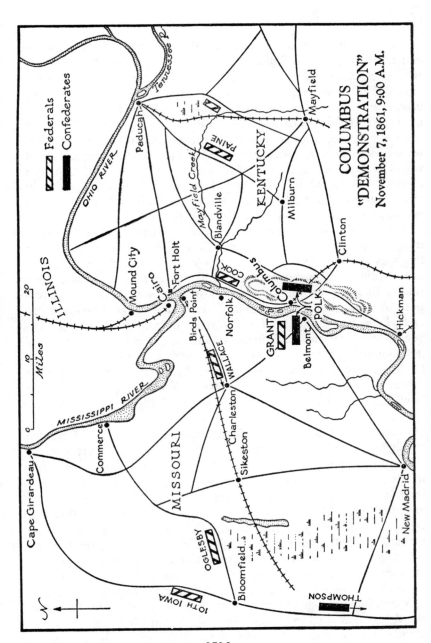

COLUMBUS "DEMONSTRATION"
November 7, 1861, 9:00 A.M.

columns—four of them, not counting the one under Brigadier General Eleazer Paine that Smith was sending (with a detached regiment to protect its left flank); he should study the map carefully, for the positions of those four forces were certainly in Grant's mind as he proceeded with his preparations "to menace Belmont." What about the safety of the Tenth Iowa which Plummer was ordered to send from Cape Girardeau to approach Bloomfield from the north? It would soon enter territory held by Thompson where apparently it would be exposed, as a result of the change in direction of Oglesby's column. That good officer would, however, be in contact with it; and it will be seen that Grant did not forget the Tenth, though no new orders went to the regiment on the 6th.

Actually Grant was placed in a rather intricate situation. With troops dispatched on one assigned mission, he had received another that was definitely more important. We see him hold the first mission in abeyance in a way to mitigate the evil of dispersion. One studies Belmont not only to discover whether Grant was an aggressive, intrepid combat commander who could make soldiers fight, and whether, as he had said a few weeks before, he would not hesitate to encounter superior numbers. One examines it also to discover if Grant has the qualities that give promise of a General in Chief. One need not worry because the word "menace" cannot be pinned down, or fret because it is impossible to determine just what Grant implied when he told Oglesby to send word to him "at Belmont."

Grant himself commanded the Belmont expedition, and on the evening of the 6th his four transports dropped down the river under the cover of the wooden gunboats *Tyler* and *Lexington*.[9] Five regiments, two companies of cavalry and a six-gun battery (four six-pounders and two twelve-pound howitzers), totaling 3,114 officers and men, were aboard. Nine miles below Cairo the expedition tied up against the Kentucky shore; enemy outposts, if alert, would send the news to Polk at Columbus, giving him something to think about before going to bed. Personnel on the transports quieted down early "impressed with the probability of realizing their most ardent wishes";[10] though they were on the left bank of the river, the rumor was running through the boats that they were bound for Belmont. We do not know at what time Grant lay down—if at all—or Commander Henry Walke, who was in the *Tyler* below the transports.

But Fate was watching and ruled that the Federal commander should not sleep long, for the situation changed abruptly at two o'clock, when a special courier arrived by steamboat from Colonel Wallace with a wholly unexpected message: A reliable Union man had reported that the enemy had been crossing troops from Columbus to follow and cut off the force of Colonel Oglesby. This seemed probable to Grant. So in addition to the mission of detaining troops from going to Price, he now had the problem of protecting his western column.

It was an hour heavy with destiny for the United States. Grant faced a quick decision. The decision would show the kind of general that he was; and on that would depend the future of the nation. The stage was appropriate to the importance of the act that was being played: the great river lapping against the vessels; the quiet, darkened boats, barely visible in the moonless night; the sentinels on the decks; some men sleeping easily, others restless; the protecting gunboats with their alert watches peering into the night, waiting for an hour to pass before they would drop down to engage the forts; a mist rising from the broad waters and slowly gathering into fog; and in the lighted cabin of the *Belle Memphis* the general who had read the unexpected message. The very hour was chosen to make the test more searching; for it was one when resolution often wanes. Napoleon was wont to speak of "three-o'clock-in-the-morning courage."

Grant decided that he would change the demonstration into an attack. He would do more than "menace Belmont"; he would throw everything he had into a sharp blow against the enemy regiments reported to have crossed the river. That would keep them from cutting off Oglesby; and it would give his regiments the battle that they wanted, and his battery the opportunity to see what it could do. Rawlins, with eight weeks of schooling behind him, already devoted to his chief, wrote the order. He set down the hour as "2 o'clock a.m."; the decision had been made as quickly as that. Then followed the sentence, "The troops composing the present expedition from this place will move promptly at 6 o'clock this morning." In a slight reorganization of the force, Colonel Henry Dougherty was given command of a small brigade consisting of his own Twenty-second Illinois and the Seventh Iowa; he was to follow McClernand's brigade. At a place beyond the range of enemy guns, to be selected by Commander Walke, the expedition was to debark upon the Missouri shore.[11] It was an adequate order, with no waste of words.

To Colonel Oglesby directions were sent to march toward Belmont, and no explanation seems to fit them well. Just where the order would find him, Grant could not tell, and he could be of no use whatever in the attack that Grant had determined to make that day. Building up a large force near Belmont was certainly not his intention, and the best explanation may be that he foresaw the possibility of defeat by a force whose strength he did not know, after which he would not be able to reembark—though his report counters this. If he contemplated the necessity of extricating himself by road toward Charleston, it would indeed be heartening to have Oglesby on the march to meet him. Though it teases one not to know with certainty what went through Grant's mind in those early hours of November 7 when he decided and worked so fast, an incontrovertible fact marks the general as definitely as his decision to strike shows his inherent offensive spirit. Concentration on the task in his immediate front, formidable though it was, did not cause him to forget Oglesby. Nor did he forget the Tenth Iowa: to Plummer, from whom a report also came, went new instructions with regard to that regiment.[12] It is indeed from the order Grant sent to Plummer that we know of the new directions to Oglesby, for he wrote, "Requiring Colonel Oglesby's command with me, however, I have sent a messenger after it to him in this direction." The sentence—like other parts of the dispatch—has a touch of haste, and the words may not have fitted his thought so very well. Oglesby made no mention of the new order in his report, though he stated that he received at Bloomfield the order "to turn the column in the direction of New Madrid." But the commander of the Tenth Iowa, who had joined Oglesby, stated that after receiving from him the order to march "toward New Madrid," he received a new order to march "towards Belmont"; thus the order got through.[13]

The more we think about it, the more worthy of note is that cabin on the *Belle Memphis* with its oil lamps burning dimly. It was far from what a headquarters should be in a trained staff, but a headquarters at its very best in the chief requisite: the character and mind of the commander. One sees new evidence of the trait that had revealed itself on September 6, when Grant, finding that the regiment from Cape Girardeau had not reached Cairo, immediately had sent five companies to strengthen Paducah in the interim. By no means insignificant is the fact that Grant, tied up at night on the bank of a river near the enemy, received in the early morning hours reports from both Wallace and Plummer Such things do not just happen; they are provided for. Beginning to take clear form was the general-ship that caused Sherman to speak of the confidence he derived from the knowledge that he would not be forgotten. Far less crucial moments than that steamboat scene, far lesser events in our history, have been the subject of an artist's brush.

Turned back by heavy fog after he started down the river at three o'clock, Commander Walke rejoined, received the new orders, and sharp at the appointed hour he led the transports to a point some three miles above Belmont. According to the sailor, Grant had his command "disembarked and under marching orders" at half past eight.[14] Leaving a guard and reserve of five companies near the transports, the Federal commander soon deployed into line of battle well covered by skirmishers, and before long he was heavily engaged with the Confederates who had six regiments in action. Through dense woods Grant forced the enemy back "foot by foot, and from tree to tree" a distance of more than two miles to their encampment on the river bank. In his report he wrote: "Here he [the enemy] had strengthened his position by felling the timber for several hundred yards around his camp, making a sort of abatis. Our men charged through this, driving the enemy under cover of the bank, and many of them into their transports, in quick time, leaving us in possession of everything not exceedingly portable."

From their commanding position at Columbus, the Confederate batteries, which were three times rather ineffectually engaged by the gunboats, took Grant's troops under fire after their own regiments had found shelter close to the river. Federal guns moved to positions near the shore, and the six-pounders opened on the steamers *Prince* and *Charm* which were taking reenforcements across the river, with such effect that Polk reported that Grant had heavy artillery. The report of the captain of the *Charm* described the panic of the Confederates who had sought safety under the river bank and who greeted the arriving reenforcements with cries, "Don't land! Don't land! We are whipped! Go back!" [15]

Considerable booty was in the possession of the Federals; and for an officer who had been a quartermaster it was painful not to be able to cart at least some of it away. In his report Grant noted that, because he had no wagons, he had been compelled to burn the tents, the blankets, and other property; but even with wagons, he probably could not have done much packing, for he was in a precarious position, and time pressed. When the camp was well committed to flames, Grant started back to his transports, the regiments fresh from the jubilant looting that endangers discipline even in a more seasoned command. But he did not go entirely empty handed, for with him went captured horses and prisoners, and no fewer than six enemy guns. Three guns that were being moved by the men and one that was drawn by an inefficient team had to be spiked and abandoned, the enemy later claiming they had recaptured them. To move guns by hand is not easy, and soldiers who undertake to drag pieces two miles through woods over bad roads without horses are real enthusiasts.

Some fighting had to be done in order to reach the transports, for Polk had sent several fresh regiments across the river above Belmont, and they, with reorganized parts of the previously defeated units, all under the command of Pillow, sought to cut the Federals off from their boats. A good charge cleared the route, and Grant's command continued toward the landing, to which the transports had also returned after moving upstream to escape the shells of the longer-range guns on the opposite bank. Rivaling the effort to get the captured guns away in spite of lack of teams were the exertions of Grant's surgeon to save the non-walking wounded. His only vehicles were three springless, anguish-producing quartermaster wagons, but these seem to have been used as effectively as possible. Soon the whole force except Napoleon Bonaparte Buford's Twenty-seventh Illinois, was embarked—the enemy, reenforced by still more regiments, pressing after the Federals, and pouring a heavy fire upon the departing vessels. Grant's statement in his *Memoirs* that he was the last man aboard, and that his horse, apparently understanding the situation, slid down the long bank and trotted across the plank thrown out from the transport, is little more than the repetition of what had been said by a very careful military historian who embellished his work with few personal incidents.[16]

Buford had been ordered to return with the main force, but he had taken the road from Belmont to Charleston and then, in order to avoid shells which the gunboats intended for the Southerners, he had followed a road up the river bank. In his report Grant said: "On his appearance on the river bank a steamer was dropped down, and took his command on board, without his having participated or lost a man in the enemy's attempt to cut us off from our transports." Though he had fought well, and though his name was a good one for a soldier, the colonel of the Twenty-seventh had left his place in column, had not been available for combat, and his absence had naturally given concern to the expedition commander. McClernand's report makes it seem certain that he was responsible for making contact with Buford's regiment and carrying out the rescue described by Grant so briefly.[17]

Thirty-five miles away at Paducah the sound of the guns at Columbus was distinctly heard. Smith knew it was not action provoked by the expedition he had dispatched the day before to demonstrate against that place.[18] It must be Grant. What was his old pupil up to? Being already under orders from McClellan to report direct to Washington, Smith telegraphed about his own operation and ended, "Heavy firing now heard in the direction of Columbus, caused, it is supposed, by General Grant's movements towards Belmont." [19] So, even before the expedition had returned to its base, Washington was warned to expect news of a battle.

Darkness came long before the transports tied up at Cairo. There was much to do that night. There were the wounded, unanticipated in any number in an expedition that had sailed only to demonstrate; there were the prisoners, another unexpected feature. Then, too, a report had to be made, and orders had to be issued to commanders still in the field. To McKeever a five-sentence report was sent that began, "We met the rebels about 9 o'clock this morning two miles and a half from Belmont, and drove them step by step into their camp and across the river." It ended, "Loss heavy on both sides." To Commander Walke, who was holding his gunboats some miles below Cairo, a vessel was dispatched to bring in the Union soldiers and the prisoners he was carrying, with instructions to maintain his position until Colonel Cook was back from his expedition down the left bank. To Oglesby a report of the day's events was sent along with an order to return to Birds Point by way of Charleston—a route that Grant was now certain would not be cut. Plummer was ordered to recall the troops that had been sent from Cape Girardeau.

Probably Grant got greatest pleasure in writing the message that went to Smith. After stating that he had driven the enemy out of Belmont and had destroyed their camp with heavy loss on both sides, Grant relaxed a little and said, "They had eleven regiments against our 3,000 men." When account is taken of the regiments the Confederates had thrown into the pursuit, Grant's estimate was good, and showed he could observe a battlefield with accuracy. But he sent the telegram to Paducah not out of the wish to swagger or boast; he was thinking of the demonstrating column that Smith had sent, and which should be called in. Delicately he said to the honored soldier who was his senior in years and experience, "If you have an opportunity communicate with General Paine our arrival here this evening." [20] The day which had begun at 2 A.M. with a searching decision, which involved a landing of troops, a sharp attack, a retirement and reembarkation under heavy pressure, was rounded out in a way that gives it a good place in military history.

By morning some auditing had been done, and a telegram to St. Louis put the Federal casualties at approximately two hundred and fifty, half of them killed or mortally wounded. McKeever was also told that Confederate prisoners reported that a large force was "prepared to join Price." It is problematical how much credence Grant gave to the statement of the captured men—a statement which incidentally does not seem to be confirmed by the Confederate reports; but he was certainly obligated to pass on to headquarters anything that bore on ideas he knew were there entertained about possible enemy movements. And the belief that reenforcements had gone or were going from Polk to Price was what had initiated the move toward Columbus. To his friend Smith, Grant also sent his much-too-low estimate of his own casualties; but with surprising accuracy he put the enemy losses at between five hundred and six hundred, "including 130 prisoners brought from the field." In both dispatches he asserted, "The victory was complete"; and he dwelt upon the fact that he had started back with all the enemy artillery, but had had to abandon four guns in the woods for want of teams.[21] Failure to say anything to Smith about the statement by enemy prisoners suggests that Grant did not put too much reliance on it, in spite of what he had said to McKeever.

Quick in making decisions and quick in striking, Grant also was

prompt in issuing an order of appreciation to his troops, and November 8 saw the first order of that kind that he composed. Totally un-
embellished with adjectives, it made no boasts about a great victory;
nor did it make any reference whatever to the kindly favors and
blessings of a merciful or approving Providence. In a most matter-of-
fact way the order began, "The general commanding this military
district returns his thanks to the troops under his command at the
battle of Belmont on yesterday." That the fighting had been hard,
he told them in a most effective way; he stated that except for the
battle of Buena Vista it had been his fortune to be in all the battles
fought in Mexico by Generals Scott and Taylor, and that he had
never seen one more hotly contested or one where troops behaved
with more gallantry. "Such courage," he said, "will insure victory
wherever our flag may be borne and protected by such a class of
men." The order closed with an awkward sentence about the sympathy that was due from the country for the men who had fallen.[22]
It is a little surprising to find a soldier such as Conger caviling at the
order and speaking as if its lack of details came from Grant's realization that he could not "delude" soldiers who "had been there" and
well knew that there had been dark moments.[23] Conger appears to
misconstrue the order as much as he does the dispatches that Grant
sent to McKeever and Smith, failing to perceive, for instance, that
the fact that Grant passed on to McKeever the story the prisoners
had told is not conclusive indication of what he thought of it, while
his silence on the subject to Smith may well be such.

Many badly wounded Federals had been left on the field, and
the day after the battle Grant sent a flag of truce with a note to Polk
asking permission to collect the unfortunates and give them medical
assistance.[24] The bearer of the message was fifty-year-old Major
Joseph Dana Webster, Grant's engineer officer, who after sixteen
years in the topographical engineers had resigned from the Army in
the same year as Grant and had become prominent in Chicago. On
the boat there were sixty-four Confederates Grant was offering to
return "unconditionally," since he had no power to make exchanges
and apparently believed a formal procedure might imply recognition
of the Confederacy. Polk's reply graciously extended permission to
minister to the Union wounded and indicated that Grant's representative had conveyed the information the Federal general expected
an equal number of wounded for the disabled men he gave up.[25]

Since recent instructions from Richmond prevented Polk from acting, he wired his Secretary of War, asking if an exception could be made in the case of severely wounded cases, while Grant's officers did some visiting with friendly and courteous Confederates who took it upon themselves to bring a few badly injured aboard. Night came without a telegram from Richmond, and Grant's boat returned to Cairo bearing most of the proffered men, some having been left to compensate for the thirteen Federals taken back by Webster. Other "releases" were to follow.

Polk may have been nettled into speaking in his reply to Grant of the latter's "unimportant affectation of declining to recognize these states as belligerents" partly because Grant had begun his note by referring to the battle of the day before very casually as a "skirmish," a description hardly in harmony with the words he used the same day in his order to his own command. But Grant showed his even-handed admiration for American soldiers, his words being: "skirmish of yesterday in which both sides behaved with so much gallantry."

The 8th had almost gone when Grant interrupted his work to write a letter to his wife. It was an unemotional narrative of the day before; but it fully expressed his gratification with the results, and the confidence in his officers and men that the battle had given him. There was even a tribute to the enemy, in the sentence that stands at the head of this chapter. In describing the retirement, he wrote, "There was no hasty retreating or running away"—a statement supported by the successful reembarkation. Because he had other duties still to perform, Grant had his clerk copy the letter as an addition to some introductory sentences he addressed to his father.[26]

On the 8th the *Chicago Tribune* carried not only an Associated Press dispatch about the battle, but one from its special Cairo correspondent. Readers learned that Grant and McClernand both had behaved gallantly; Grant's horse had been killed, McClernand's had been wounded twice. The reports were mainly factual, leaving untouched the purpose of the expedition, and would have done no harm if the editor of the paper had not soon intruded. The correspondent of the *Chicago Evening Journal,* who did not use the wires but spent a feverish hour writing a story to go by mail, did not do so well. He spoke of the "disastrous yet glorious expedition," having been tricked into such a view by a distorted idea of Grant's purpose. Belmont, he asserted, was believed to be lightly occupied, and, because it was an important place, it had been decided to seize it. But traitors had reported the Federal plans, with the result that the Unionists had been completely frustrated. After indulging without restraint in such fancy, the journalist observed that he had no time to record the "unfounded rumors and reports" that were "floating around," quite as if what he had said had come straight from headquarters. Horace Greeley copied the account in New York; the *Cleveland Herald,* and doubtless other papers, joined in spreading the distorted account.[27]

Grant's letter to his wife stated:

. . . Belmont is entirely covered by the batteries from Columbus and is worth nothing as a military position. It cannot be held without Columbus.

The object of the expedition was to prevent the enemy from sending a force into Missouri to cut off troops I had sent there for a special purpose, and to prevent reinforcing Price.

Little, if anything, in Grant's statement of his purpose would have been of aid to the enemy; and it could have been the basis of a communique that would have given the people of the North a correct understanding of the Belmont battle. But the day of communiques had not yet arrived, and correspondents were free to indulge their fancies and to misrepresent as they chose. Grant had shown some disposition to censor telegraphic dispatches; but he had no control whatever over what was sent by mail.

Although the *Chicago Tribune* would finally become a hearty supporter of Grant, and in accordance with the vitriolic and abusive journalism of the day, would later warn the *New York Herald* that "it must keep its copperhead slime off our Illinois General,"[28] its first editorial comments after Belmont did not help his career. Not suspecting that there might be more to the operation than was apparent to his correspondent, the editor wrote on November 9:

The disastrous termination of the Cairo expedition to Columbus is another severe lesson on the management of this contest with the rebels. Our troops have suffered a bad defeat. Hundreds of men have been killed and wounded, and other hundreds taken prisoners. The loss of the enemy is far lighter than ours. The object of the expedition was not attained.

The rebels have been elated and emboldened while our troops have been depressed, if not discouraged.

The desire to turn the battle into a Federal defeat lingered in the editor's mind and the casualty list that appeared the next day gave rise to the sentence, "It may be said of these victims—'they have fallen, and to what end?'"

Tribune readers were, fortunately, to learn the truth. By the 10th the Cairo correspondent had revised his idea, and wrote that Belmont was not a defeat, but "a decided and valuable victory." Grant's first report was also published on the 14th, and a short editorial correctly stated what his objectives had been. Two days later a long and blistering "letter to the editor" from Cairo, contained the statement: "We accomplished everything we went for. Belmont is taken, is in ashes, and is now abandoned by the enemy." [29] The writer also asserted that Confederate officers stated that their loss in killed and wounded had exceeded that of the Federals. Nor were the *Tribune's* columns the only place where indignation flared against its hastiness in accepting Federal defeats. A dispatch to the *Louisville Journal* from Cairo singled out the Chicago paper as one whose editorials had shown a "determination to embarrass and disparage our army." [30] In spite of all the efforts made at correcting the initial and distorted criticisms, misconception concerning Grant's first battle lingered in the public mind; and unjust charges about Belmont were hurled at him years later when he ran for President.[31]

McClernand, as ambitious as he was brave, used the battle to get in some sly work. He took it upon himself to telegraph on the 6th directly to McClellan about the expedition that was being prepared. On the 8th he sent a fairly long report of the operation, remembering to say when he was two-thirds finished, "General Grant was in chief command," and concluding, "I will report at large by mail." But the scheming general and ex-congressman had a change of plan, probably because of specific instructions from Grant, and his long report of the 12th was properly directed to his immediate superior. In it he managed to give a nice compliment: "Nor should I omit to add that this gallant conduct was stimulated by your presence and inspired by your example." Grant even received one of the impressive *here's* with which the accomplished rhetorician pointed up his great climaxes: "Here your horse was shot under you." McClernand's order thanking his troops—three times as long as Grant's—was also florid, and was something of a preview of the congratulatory order that was later to prove his undoing.[32]

Grant's telegrams about Belmont reached St. Louis at a time of confusion. A colonel of Frémont's, evidently preceding the general with tidings of his approach, was in the city on the 8th, and he prepared a dispatch for Washington, claiming Grant's engagement as a Frémont victory. General Curtis, with a tight hold on the telegraph office, looked askance at a message "improperly addressed and coming from an irregular source"; but after sending a copy to General Hunter he allowed it to go forward along with his own telegram explaining the situation. Frémont was expected momentarily, and a crowd with a strong German cast was assembled to hail him; mixed with it were some of Curtis's officers for the purpose of getting their hands on Frémont's money chests. Though Curtis was not sure whether they would succeed, he concluded his message to Washington with the comforting words, "All quiet." The next morning he wired that he had secured the chests and had sent them away "under a strong escort." But there was more to report than the safety of the money with another reassuring "All quiet." From McKeever, who had gone to Cincinnati at a time that is not apparent, there had come the startling telegram: "General Grant did not follow his instructions. No orders were given to attack Belmont or Columbus." The message was addressed to Frémont; but it is not clear whether it was received before or after the 9th, when he ordered a report made about Grant's attack, which his staff officer had already made the day before. An ex-post-facto order by an officer who has been without a command for a week is a little unusual, though perhaps not surprising from a John Frémont. Curtis dutifully conveyed the substance of McKeever's second sentence to the General in Chief's adjutant, but tactfully suppressed the first.[33]

The ambiguity of Curtis's telegram seems to suggest that McClellan concluded that Grant had acted without, but not contrary to, orders; and perhaps he thought that Frémont sought by his belated order to gain undeserved credit for himself that might lead promptly to a new assignment. The message that the General in Chief sent to Grant on the 10th was cordial but did not so much as refer to the battle, though it directed Grant to report his "wants and wishes."[34] Grant probably never knew of McKeever's sharp charge, which Curtis failed to repeat; [35] and in view of the fact that McClellan was to suggest Grant's arrest on an unfounded charge of not making reports after he captured Fort Donelson, we may well say that Samuel Curtis censored on November 9 with an inspired pencil. On the 14th McClellan did very well indeed by Grant in a general order commending recent Federal successes. Grant's operation got the climactic position: the General in Chief said he had made a daring attack with an inferior force, and noted the destruction of enemy property that had been achieved. Very properly Grant's name was the only one mentioned.[36] This may have chagrined McClernand, but must have helped correct the newspaper accounts that not only failed to make clear who had been the responsible commander, but tended to leave the impression that the undertaking had been a cooperative adventure by the two Illinois brigadiers.

Lincoln's response to the battle was all that it could have been. He knew Grant only as one of the many brigadiers who had been hopefully created during the summer. McClernand, he knew well as a fellow townsman who had solicited a strange favor from him fourteen years before. To him Lincoln wrote on the 10th "not an official but a social letter." Cautiously he said he could not judge of the precise value of the recent battle; but he ended, "Please give my respect and thanks to all." [37]

The President's concluding sentence was a weighty one: "respect and thanks" to those who had fought hard, even while he as yet had no report explaining the objectives of the expedition. Lincoln's judgment after reading revised versions of the battle does not seem to be in the record. But to William T. Sherman, Grant's destruction of the enemy camp was like a little ray of light breaking through the cloud of melancholy, if not despair, that was oppressing him at the moment. When the Secretary of War and Adjutant General Thomas called on him at Louisville in mid-October on their way back to Washington from their St. Louis investigations, he gave them a "gloomy picture of affairs in Kentucky." [38] Sherman saw the younger men of the pivotal border state going over to the secession cause, while the North was being supported by men who may have contributed much to electing in June a nine-to-one Unionist delegation to Congress, but whose age made them of little value in the rough business of fighting. Cameron and Thomas were astonished when they understood him to say that no fewer than 200,000 men would have to come from northern states to clear Kentucky of Confederate troops and make it a secure operational base. Sherman was to later assert that he had been grossly misunderstood; but, unfortunately, the Thomas report was published, increasing the unfriendliness of the press from which Sherman initially suffered.[39] Nor did his spirits rise after his visitors had left; as he studied the new reports that came from Bowling Green, where the chief enemy concentration was, and the other extensive regions of the state under the Confederate flag, his depression increased.

On the very day when Grant was preparing his Belmont expedition Sherman wrote to Thomas his first dispatch in answer to telegraphic instructions from McClellan to make daily reports. In it we have a full statement of his pessimism over his own signature, which cannot misrepresent him. His short closing paragraph began: "Do not conclude, as before, that I exaggerate the facts. They are as stated, and the future looks as black as possible." And then with a touch of the frankness that was to be a part of his greatness, Sherman even suggested that some one replace him: "It would be better if some more sanguine mind were here, for I am forced to order according to my convictions." It seems strange that Belmont should have raised the hope of a general almost in despair; but Sherman said later that it did. He would himself see the mettle of the men who fought Grant's first battle, of whom Dana and Wilson wrote: "Neither officers nor men who participated in that battle were ever known to falter in the hour of danger, but wherever hard work was required or hard blows were to be given, a regiment with 'Belmont' upon its flags was sure to be found." [40]

There were faults in the battle of Belmont; and plenty of fingers have been pointed at them, for it is natural that the first battle in which a famous general commanded should be carefully scrutinized. Conger appraises: "Strategically—in a narrow sense—it was difficult to justify; tactically foolhardy, but psychologically a necessity." Yet, in spite of the fact that he criticizes Grant for accepting as reliable the report—which was false—that Confederates had been crossing at Belmont to cut off Oglesby, Conger ends up with the commendation: "Looking back on it and knowing the exact situation, it is not easy to find a better solution of the problem than Grant's." [41] The operation was in fact a difficult one, being definitely a combined operation. Scott conducted nothing of the sort in Mexico, and there had never been a comparable maneuver. Today it would be carefully prepared, with planners studying photographs of the region to be invaded and working out details. But Grant did not even know where he was going to land or much about the condition of the river banks; nor did he have the least assurance that Commander Walke would be able to prevent enemy reenforcements from crossing the river so as to isolate the battlefield.

Grant's failure to have a good reserve in hand as he attacked has drawn the heaviest fire from his critics; but Conger is altogether in error in asserting that it was not until his first report of the 12th that Grant—in order to meet criticism—called the five companies left at the transports a reserve. In a casual way he spoke in his letter to his wife on the 8th of the "small reserve" that was initially not deployed. Conger's claim that the force was in fact merely a "transport guard" is supported by the statement of Captain Detrick, who commanded them. Obviously, however, steamers guarded by two gunboats and able to back away from the bank were safe against damage or seizure; and the five companies were soon called forward and used as a sort of flank guard—as Conger says. Later, according to Detrick's report, they covered the reembarking of most of the command and went aboard only when ordered to do so; this was certainly excellent service for a reserve. Nevertheless, with his entire force deployed at once, except those five companies, Grant did not have a reserve to meet the contingencies of battle; and the single line shown on the diagram that accompanied his report looks precariously thin. The general himself had to be both support and reserve, going to any place where the battle needed to be directed or reanimated. With the near equality of the contending forces, a regiment held in reserve initially would surely have been thrown into combat before the camp was taken; and after that matters would probably have been about as they were. There was unquestionably a lack of discipline during the destruction of the Confederate camp, and Conger observes that there should have been special details of men to carry out the burning, so that the bulk of the force could be held under arms. This is certainly true. But control, always hard at such a time, becomes more difficult when the second-in-command leads off in good Fourth of July fashion with the shout "Three cheers for the Union!" and records the fact in his report. Grant's *Memoirs* mention the short eulogies upon the Federal cause that some of the higher officers delivered whenever there was the opportunity.[42]

An especially bright spot in the operation was the handling of the battery. The two gunboats were totally unable to prevent the sending of reenforcements across the river and thus maintain the isolation of the defeated regiments and allow their leisurely destruction or capture. The reenforcements had to be turned back by the weapons of the landing force itself, which Captain Taylor got through the woods to the river bank, if there was to be time for the burning of the camp. Taylor, who the next day turned in a report that accounted for all his property—to the last ax, tin cup, and whip—said nothing about this work, but we know of it through the Confederate reports and a statement by McClernand. Taylor in fact was somewhat disappointed with his performance, but pointed out that the density of the woods made maneuvering difficult. Nevertheless his cannoneers caused Polk to believe the Federals had a heavy battery and the four hundred rounds that he reported he fired had a very important part in the battle. Although he left two caissons and a wagon on the field, he reembarked with eight guns instead of the six he had taken ashore; and the twenty horses and the mule that had belonged to Leonidas Polk's command more than replaced the three Federal animals that had been killed.[43] Artillery instructors may well point to the first day of battle of Captain Ezra Taylor, Battery B, First Illinois, as one to emulate.

And what about Jeff Thompson, whose activities had started the rather complex sequence of events that culminated with the first strike on the Mississippi? He escaped. But in spite of this, Colonel Oglesby thought that his own expedition had been very much worth while. After hard marching and the building of some bridges, his advance guard had a slight skirmish with some of Thompson's men, while the advance of the supporting Tenth Iowa drove others back toward Bloomfield. Thompson evacuated the town on the evening of the 6th and sent a message the next morning to Polk that he was safe, being twenty miles ahead of his pursuers. The town authorities sent a request for protection to the commander of the Iowa regiment, and it was there that Oglesby received Grant's order to turn toward New Madrid. The generally good discipline of the Federal troops made a favorable impression on the people and Oglesby wrote: "Four-fifths of the inhabitants are ready to return to the Union whenever the Government can assure them from punishment from the rebel army. The yoke of Jeff. Thompson is a heavy one, and the people are becoming disgusted at his arbitrary sway. The scrip he has substituted for a good currency is totally worthless." Three years later Oglesby was to take off the uniform of a major general to become governor of Illinois, and one can believe that he could judge the sentiments of people better than most officers at the heads of columns. Grant had ordered him to return to Birds Point by the direct road through Charleston; but Oglesby wrote, "To avoid the terrible swamp in front of Bloomfield I returned by Cape Girardeau"—an exercise in discretion that his superior may have noted with satisfaction.[44]

Paine's column from Paducah did well on its outward march, and a patrol got through to the river, returning at 4:00 A.M. of the 8th with the information that Grant's expedition had returned to its base. But the column made a bad record on its homeward course, for there was much lack of discipline and considerable plundering. Every company had read to it an order expressing the surprise and strong disapproval felt by C. F. Smith.[45] Though the words may have cut deep in the minds of men remembering a hard march, a time would come when his regiments would appreciate the general who was preparing them for battle.

Apparently none of the Confederate pickets had sent word about the considerable Federal river expedition that had tied up above Columbus on the evening of November 6, so Polk could go to bed thinking of the tender of resignation he had sent that day to Jefferson Davis.[46] He was not, however, to have a night's sleep without the intrusion of a new problem; for at about the very hour that Grant received the message stating that enemy troops had crossed the river, a courier arrived at Confederate headquarters with the information "of a strong force designed to attack General Thompson's position at Bloomfield and New Madrid." What measures Polk might have taken to succor Thompson cannot be told, for his thoughts were given an entirely new direction soon after daybreak by reports of the debarking of a sizable force on the Missouri shore above Belmont. He did not for a moment share the Cairo reporter's delusion that the Federals had come for the purpose of setting up a camp just across from his headquarters. He could not know that the Union troops had little more than over-night baggage and supplies; but he knew full well that the excellently situated batteries at Columbus made Belmont untenable. He thought the operation on the west of the great river a diversion and a Yankee trick, designed to cause him to send most of his command into Missouri, while other Bluecoats burst upon Columbus from the north and east. He promptly sent four infantry regiments across the river, and presently a fifth, to reenforce the regiment and artillery already there, and he believed that this force should suffice to hold the well protected camp.[47]

The bulk of his command, Polk held in hand to meet the expected attack upon Columbus itself. When he learned that the Union force had a battery, he ordered two more batteries to go to the help of his hard pressed soldiers. The guns got as far as the Missouri shore, and then the annoying and mortifying discovery was made that the steamer had lost her stage planks. The batteries then returned to Kentucky, one of them recrossing the river later, though not in time to be used in the battle. It must have been about noon when Polk, less apprehensive of what lay to the east, began to throw other regiments across the river above Belmont. Incredible as it seems, he apparently did nothing in active reconnaissance, and in his report he was silent about actual contact with Paine's brigade, which had left Paducah at 2:00 P.M. of the 6th and had reached Milburn, twelve miles from Columbus only at 7:00 P.M. of the 7th, after a heavy day's march of twenty-four miles.[48] The column had of course been observed leaving Paducah and had been reported;[49] but when Polk received his first information and just what it was cannot be determined.

Not having received from Sidney Johnston a prompt acknowledgment of a telegram claiming a victory, that he sent on the evening of the 7th, Polk repeated it the next morning. Then he sent an entirely new message in which he said, "Enemy intended to attack both sides, but from some cause failed." In his enthusiasm he could not wait for the news to reach Richmond properly through channels, and he sent directly to Jefferson Davis a dispatch which must have brought that rather solemn man to his feet in a cheering mood. According to Polk the Federals were completely routed, the roads to the transports, which he more than doubled to seven miles, were filled with dead, knapsacks, ammunition, and *guns*. The Confederate battery which had been engaged Polk pronounced "immortalized," though ironically four of its spiked pieces were on the route of the Federal retreat, while the other two were probably being affectionately cleaned by Federal cannoneers in Cairo. Polk stated that General Grant was himself reported as killed—matching a comparable statement made by Grant about Pillow in his telegram of the 8th to McKeever. One can imagine what the good bishop could do in the pulpit if he had for text anything that equaled the evil of the Yankees. His eloquence brought a hearty reply from the Confederate President.[50]

Polk had the same mistaken view as to the Federal intentions when he wrote his long report on the 10th: after speaking of the fear of an attack in his rear "at every moment," he asserted that subsequent information proved that such indeed had "been the enemy's plan." His killed he put at 105, and his wounded at 405.[51] His total casualties of 641 were very close to the upper figure that Grant had given on the 8th, a figure which, however, Grant afterward thought too small.[52] Polk said the Federal losses amounted to at least 1,500 men, and then, with a fondness for unusual fractions that would confound even a mathematician, he said as many as "fourteen-fifteenths" of them must have been killed, wounded, or drowned. Although the regiment-by-regiment report that Grant's medical director made a week later put the Union killed and wounded too low, later revisions gave the total casualties as only 607.[53] The one thousand arms that Polk stated had been gathered up not only tallies with the number of killed and wounded in the battle, but confirms Grant's claim that there was no undue haste in his retreat. Although Grant had quickly sought to keep a balance in the matter of valor, Polk asserted that "the results of the day proved beyond all doubt the superiority of our troops in all the essential characteristics of the soldier." His order to his troops five days after the engagement spoke of "the obstinate resistance offered by a handful of men to an overwhelming force." [54] Not only from prisoners, but from Northern papers Polk must have had a complete identification of the opposing force by November 12; and, allowing for the sickness which was prevalent in the Federal camp as well as his own, he should have known that Grant had just about the number of men that the Yankee papers claimed.

In December, upon rereading his report, Polk discovered some mistakes in grammar, whereupon he telegraphed Adjutant General Cooper, "In my report of the battles of Columbus and Belmont you will find I speak of the enemy in the plural—they, them, &c.

In the copy you are making for Congress will you please do me the favor to change it [sic] to the singular—he, him, &c?" But, alas, on the 9th the message came, "Your telegram of the 7th received too late. Copies of your report had already been sent to Congress." However, the Southern congressmen either did not detect Polk's transgressions, or did not mind, for on the 13th Davis communicated to him a copy of a long resolution of thanks for himself and Brigadier Generals Pillow and Cheatham.[55]

Any chagrin General Polk felt over his slip in grammar was soon forgotten in a real trouble that descended upon him. Gideon Johnson Pillow—stormy petrel of the Mexican War—thought Leonidas Polk merited no praise for the battle of Belmont, and though the Richmond Congress could forgive his confusion over singulars and plurals, Pillow could not forget his uncertainty on November 7. On January 16, 1862, Pillow sent to the Secretary of War his version of the battle. After repeating the fable about being attacked by a greatly superior force, he asserted that he should have been promptly and strongly supported at all hazards and not abandoned to his fate "for four long hours, and until so much blood and so many valuable lives were *sacrificed*." He refused to condone Polk's fears of an attack on Columbus, and he put his finger clearly on the point when he charged that his superior had "the means to have known if any enemy was near except that which my command had engaged." After tendering his resignation (which was not accepted) Pillow concluded his long document with a very pretty compliment for Davis, whom he described as "chosen of God for the work of our national deliverance." The paper was embarrassing to handle, and on January 20 it was referred to Polk himself. And thus did Polk, who doubtless knew about troublesome rectors, learn about cantankerous brigadiers. In an effort to clear himself of Pillow's aspersions, he gathered report after report from his subordinates, until they fill sixty-one pages in the records, as against the thirty-one of Federal documents. On March 12 he wrote to Davis that he had not had a moment he could call his own since he had "received from the War Department a copy of the very extraordinary letter addressed to it by General Pillow."[56]

Polk's son, in an article twenty-five years later, corrected some of his father's statements, saying that most of the fighting had been done by Grant's 3,114 men and 4,000 Confederates, with an additional 1,000 added to the latter before "they took up the pursuit." [57] But he left the question of his father's reconnaissance to the east unanswered and said that Grant failed in his objective. He also seemed disposed to accept Pillow's high figure for the Federal dead.

The two commanders soon met on flag-of-truce boats to discuss exchange of prisoners and other matters. To his wife, Polk wrote on November 15 that Grant—sixteen years his junior—seemed at first grave and ill at ease. But he had succeeded in getting a smile out of the Federal, after which they had conversed pleasantly. "I am favorably impressed with him," said Polk; "he is undoubtedly a man of much force." [58] It is possible that Grant had never seen a bishop, let alone talked with one; but he quickly learned how to deport himself and Polk wrote, "We have now exchanged five or six flags, and he grows more civil and respectful every time." If the two generals could have seen into the future, they might have explored the possibility of trading those two ambitious brigadiers: Gideon Pillow and John McClernand.

CHAPTER V

ENTER HALLECK

> Will you allow me to suggest the consideration of a great move-
> ment by land and water up the Cumberland and Tennessee
> Rivers? *Whittlesley to Halleck*

A VEXING problem throughout the war was that of properly dividing
the country into the departments that were essential for control and
general administration. Shifts of states and parts of states were made
from time to time in accordance with experience and circumstances,
and the departmental history of some of them—notably Virginia—
is impressive. Although the question was especially troublesome in
areas where active operations were in progress, it nevertheless intruded elsewhere. The problem that arose when McClellan landed
on the Peninsula in a department commanded by General Wool has
already been mentioned, and also the way in which it was handled.
Soon after Lee launched the Gettysburg campaign in 1863, the state
of Pennsylvania, which had been in the Middle Department for over
a year, was broken into two departments—those of the Susquehanna
and the Monongahela. This may appear at first to have been unwise;
but the division was entirely for the purpose of local defense, the
mobilization of militia, and the formation of the reserve corps that
Stanton contemplated, but which did not materialize. So far as
command of mobile forces was concerned, all department lines were
obliterated, and Meade was empowered to give orders directly to
all commanders, an arrangement which continued for a few weeks

after Lee had returned to Virginia.[1] Arbitrary boundaries doubtless led at times to confusion and lack of cooperation, but the very frequency of the changes is evidence of a constant effort at adaptation. Problems similar to those of the Civil War existed again in World War II, a fact that should temper one's view toward what was done in the 1860's, when the problem was much more troublesome.

On November 9—eight days after McClellan became General in Chief—the extensive Western Department was divided into the Departments of Kansas and of Missouri. To the latter went not only the states of Missouri, Iowa, Minnesota, Wisconsin, and Arkansas, but also Illinois and the part of Kentucky west of the Cumberland River. Illinois had been in the Western Department since July 3, but all of Kentucky, together with Tennessee, had comprised the Department of the Cumberland, though forces from the Western Department were at Paducah and opposite Cairo. The placing of both banks of the Mississippi below its junction with the Ohio and the lower part of the Tennessee River under a single control was a sound strategical provision and prepared the way for operations that were to follow. Doubtless there was debate as to whether the Cumberland or the Tennessee should be the dividing stream: that the former was chosen was by no means an accident or matter of caprice. The Department of the Cumberland was eliminated and the section of Kentucky east of the Cumberland River and all of Tennessee, as well as Michigan, Ohio, and Indiana, were placed in the Department of the Ohio.[2] That the Tennessee and Cumberland Rivers changed departments as they crossed the Kentucky line probably seemed unimportant at the moment, the state of Tennessee being entirely in Confederate control. Whether the High Command would be sufficiently alert and the department generals sufficiently cooperative to prevent the arrangement from causing operations to halt or fail was a question for the future.

General Hunter, who had taken over command of Frémont's forces only a week before, was given the new Department of Kansas, with headquarters at Fort Leavenworth, while Major General Henry W. Halleck received the vitally important Department of Missouri. In view of Sherman's recent statements it is not strange that command of the Department of the Ohio passed to another officer. Don Carlos Buell, below Sherman but above Grant in the group of brigadiers who were dated back to May 17, and who was currently commanding a division in the Army of the Potomac, was given the command, with Sherman going to a subordinate position in the Department of Missouri.[3]

The telegram that John Frémont sent from St. Louis on November 9 asking for orders,[4] brought him no new assignment. Shortly thereafter he and his devoted wife went to New York, where they were the guests of honor at a dinner given by Henry Ward Beecher, the diners including—according to the *New York Tribune* of December 8—"a large representation from the pulpit." Editor Greeley thought well of Frémont's Missouri record, and the deposed general was complimented by the comment, "The vestibule of the Astor House continues to be thronged with persons anxious to see the 'Pathfinder.' "

Hunter, now nearing sixty, was well known to both the President and the country. On October 20, 1860, he had written to Lincoln from Fort Leavenworth, justifying the liberty he was taking by the gravity of the information he had to communicate. A "lady of high character" who had spent part of the summer visiting friends and relatives in Virginia had informed him "that a number of young men in Virginia had bound themselves, by oaths the most solemn" to cause Lincoln's assassination, should he be elected. The major feared the Republican candidate might laugh at a story which he said did "appear too absurd to repeat," but he nevertheless earnestly asked him to keep certain unpleasant facts in mind. It may have been the postscript, informing Lincoln that they had met in early days in Chicago "and again at the great Whig Convention in Springfield in 1840"—during a period when Hunter was in civilian life—or a suggestion from Colonel E. V. Sumner, who was on duty in St. Louis, that was responsible for Hunter's being one of the four army officers on the train that took the President-elect from Springfield on February 11, 1861. At Buffalo while he was striving to keep a surging crowd under control, his arm had been broken; during the tense situation that followed Fort Sumter, he was in charge of guards at the White House. He headed the list of brigadiers dated back to May 17, and was made a major general of volunteers after the Battle of Bull Run, where he was wounded. Grant, after commenting briefly about the general in a letter to his father, predicted, "Hunter will prove himself a fine officer." [5] The assignment to Fort Leavenworth, where he had formerly been paymaster, was a great disappointment, and—as will be seen—it overtaxed Hunter's patience because of its lack of responsibility and opportunities for combat.

Henry Halleck, well known in California and in professional military circles, was personally a stranger to Lincoln. The scholarly qualities that were the basis of his eminence were displayed at an early age. Finding no pleasure in work on the New York farm where he was born in 1815, he ran away from home and found shelter with his maternal grandmother, who indulged his bent for "book learning" by sending him to Union College. Election to Phi Beta Kappa gave proof of his character and ability. Distinction followed him to West Point, where he not only served as a cadet officer, but graduated third in a class of thirty-one. After a period of duty in New York harbor, he visited Europe in 1845 and was well received in France, where he met some of the higher officers and was permitted to visit fortifications. A report on national defense which he wrote upon his return was published as a Senate document, and it brought him the honor of an invitation to lecture at the Lowell Institute, though Boston and Cambridge audiences had no special interest in military subjects. The request by both regular and militia officers for copies of the lectures led to their publication in 1846 under the title *Elements of Military Art and Science*. Professional knowledge of a high order filled the pages of the young lieutenant of engineers, and much of his treatise remains interesting today. In spite of the fact that he was in service, Halleck approached the subject of preparedness with boldness. His discussion of the role of engineers carries the footnote: "While these pages are passing through the press, Congress has authorized the President to raise *one company* of engineer troops. This number is altogether too small to be of any use in time of war." Nor did the White House escape; after relating how thirty civilians, and only four Military Academy graduates, had been assigned as officers to a new dragoon regiment, with the result that twenty-one of the former either were dismissed or resigned in fear of such action, Halleck blasted "pothouse politicians, and the base hirelings of party." Then he inquired whether politics would "seek to increase that vast patronage of the executive which is already debasing individual morality, and destroying the national character." [6]

The War with Mexico broke out the same year and Halleck was

sent to California on a transport that took seven months for the long trip around the Horn; but the time was not wasted, for he debarked with a translation of Jomini's *Political and Military Life of Napoleon.* He saw a little action in Lower California and was breveted captain for gallantry. Full rank soon followed, and while on duty in San Francisco, he had a prominent part in the design and construction of the Montgomery Block, the largest and most remarkable building of its kind in the country at the time it was built. Completely fireproof, it was reared on a gigantic raft of redwood logs, twenty-two feet thick. "Halleck's Folly," the papers said derisively; but the structure went through an earthquake undamaged, and after sheltering a multitude of distinguished persons, was standing a century later.[7]

In 1854 Halleck resigned from the army because he saw no future in the military profession. Having already completed the necessary study of law, he at once started a legal career, and he was markedly successful in this as well as in his business enterprises. But he did not forget the need of military preparedness, and knowing that the state whose constitution he had helped to frame needed protection, he became major general of the California militia. His pen continued to be busy. He wrote much about the legal aspects of mining, and his treatise on international law was published in the year that the Civil War broke out. This work, which was to be widely used in abridged form as a text, was described by *Harper's Weekly* as "the result of fifteen years' study." Mrs. Halleck was a granddaughter of Alexander Hamilton. One of those who highly recommended "Old Brains" to Lincoln was Winfield Scott Hancock. Scott himself, in the letter to Cameron in which he complained of McClellan's insubordination, spoke of awaiting the arrival of Halleck; his presence would give him "increased confidence in the safety of the Union." [8]

Halleck, who had been given an interim appointment to a major generalship in the regular army, reached the Capital before the situation in southwest Missouri was clarified. On November 6, the *New York Tribune,* after noting that he had been presented the day before to the President and had met with the cabinet, commented, "The Command to which he is destined is not yet made public." The order of the 9th assigning him to Missouri was followed two days later by a long letter of instructions from McClellan, containing doubtless the gist of their conversations.[9]

The major theme was the correction of the deplorable conditions caused by Frémont's administration. Halleck was to reduce "to a point of economy, consistent with the interest and necessities of the State, a system of reckless expenditure and fraud, perhaps unheard of before in the history of the world." He was to examine carefully the illegal commissions that Frémont had lavishly bestowed and was to suspend all pay and allowances to such persons until their cases could be considered and proper appointments be made. If any of the men in question offered trouble, they were to be escorted under guard to some point outside Halleck's department and be given the promise of arrest in case they returned. All outstanding contracts were to be carefully scrutinized, with doubtful cases referred to McClellan's headquarters. In the "political conduct of affairs," the new commander was to try to convince Missourians and their neighbors that the war was solely for "the integrity of the Union," to uphold the power of the National Government, "and to restore to the nation the blessings of peace and good order."

Military matters were disposed of very briefly. The force which Hunter was bringing back from its trek to Springfield was to be located at Rolla and Sedalia, just as Lincoln had suggested in his appraisal on October 24. The remaining troops in the department were to be held "on or near the Mississippi, prepared for such ulterior operations as the public interests may demand." It would be interesting to know what the two major generals said about Grant's attack on Belmont, but McClellan probably did not show Halleck the dispatch he sent Grant on the 10th that ended with the direction: "Communicate fully and often." Frémont had shown his unfitness for command by instructing McClernand to report directly to St. Louis; it was worse for McClellan to instruct Grant to by-pass Halleck. In mid-September Scott had issued an order directed toward stopping irregularities in army correspondence, but McClellan quickly reinstituted such practices, in spite of the fact that on the day he took over from Scott he complained to his wife of the confusion he found at headquarters and assured her it would be speedily ended. The new General in Chief received a rebuff from Grant, though he may not have recognized it. The Cairo commander made a long report to Washington on the 14th; after that he communicated only with St. Louis. His first letter informed Halleck of the report that had gone to the Adjutant General of the Army, and noted that no requisitions had been forwarded.[10] Grant was no more thrown off his balance by improper suggestions from Washington than by actions of the enemy.

McClellan's statement about holding forces on or near the Mississippi for such "operations as the public interests may demand," suggests that on November 11 there was no accepted scheme of operations for the West. There had nevertheless been plans, and while the security of Washington was still a question, Scott was evolving a campaign which he described at length on May 3. Replying to a letter in which McClellan had made some proposals, the General in Chief stated that it was intended to blockade the southern Atlantic and the Gulf ports and make "a powerful movement down the Mississippi to the ocean, with a cordon of posts at proper points." The expedition was to be composed of approximately 60,000 regulars and three-year volunteers, and was not to get under way before November 10, the delay allowing for training of troops and also for the "return of frosts to kill the virus of malignant fevers below Memphis." Scott emphasized that it was intended to halt the expedition and capture obstructing batteries from the land side; he estimated that twelve to twenty steam gunboats would have to precede the transports.[11]

Such was the first plan, and one can be glad that McClellan wrote to Scott, because his reply gives an authentic record of the proposals that were entertained in those early days of war. In a letter to McClellan dated May 21 a new proposal was made. Scott now intended to descend the Mississippi with a small force while a larger one went by land as near the river as possible. At what points, he asked, could the two columns make contact, so that the interior one could be supplied? "Would 80,000 men be sufficient to conquer its way to New Orleans and clear out the Mississippi River to the Gulf?" [12] One must remember that Scott had done wonders in Mexico with a very small command, and that eighty thousand men seemed to him to be a great host. And where was there a general who, with any degree of certainty, could handle that number of men? Although the General in Chief had increased his figure a little since he spoke of 60,000 men, the increase was insignificant when one remembers that, by May 21, Virginia, North Carolina, Tennessee, and Arkansas had—except for certain formalities—cast their lot with the cotton states, increasing greatly the military potential arrayed against the Union. But more men were to be available; for, even before Scott wrote, it had been decided to go far beyond the modest call of May 3, and the mounting strength of the South was met by the great increase of power that western governors, meeting at Cleveland, put at the disposal of the President.[13]

There was a full realization in the South of the importance of the Mississippi; and on August 12 a Confederate captain of ordnance at Memphis sent some discerning appraisals and recommendations to General Polk. His letter began:

If this war should unfortunately be prolonged, the valley of the Mississippi must ultimately become its great theater, for the enemy now working to subjugate the South knows the value of our great artery of commerce and of the prominent cities upon it too well for us to doubt that he will bend all his energies to control them.

Stark and clear were the captain's words: "subjugate," "control." He indeed knew more than guns, harness, caissons, and rifles; he knew some history. Recalling the experience of the colonies in the Revolution, he foresaw that the credit of the Confederacy would ebb with the months. Accordingly, he urged all speed in arming: he wanted three hundred field guns with adequate ammunition and accessories for an army of one hundred thousand men in the West, and he stated that within a week two machines for rifling cannon would be in operation with a daily capacity of six pieces. It must have been encouraging to Polk to learn that a certain firm could make bayonets and gun barrels ready for rifling "in any quantity"; that dies for making rifle locks and nipples were then being made in Memphis and could be produced in large quantities; and that "abundant machinery" was in "readiness for turning its power into any required channel."

Able Captain W. R. Hunt did more than keep track of what the factories in Memphis were doing; he watched events in Washington and studied the temper of the North. Though his words were restrained and his manner properly subordinate, his concluding sentence contained a broad hint:

The spirit animating the United States Congress and people, and the great preparations made for a war upon a grand theater, induce me to urge upon you the importance of a timely and efficient preparation on our part, and the plan of equipping ourselves I have now the honor to submit to your superior judgment.[14]

Just what came of the suggestions cannot be said; but the letter gives the Southern states a higher war potential than is sometimes recognized. Even in towns where new arms were not made, factories were set up for changing flintlocks into percussion weapons and otherwise modernizing them. Nevertheless, in the South even more than in the North, regiments were forced to wait for arms.

When September ended, the strength of the army was several times what Scott could have expected when he wrote his second letter to McClellan. Still there were not 80,000 men available for an operation down the Mississippi; and a memorandum of John Nicolay's shows that on October 2 Lincoln was very depressed in spirit. The financial situation was bad; Kentucky had been successfully invaded by the Confederates; Missouri had virtually been seized. Nicolay added: "October here, and instead of having a force ready to descend the Mississippi, the probability is that the Army of the West will be compelled to defend St. Louis." [15] This put the prospects far too gloomily; for although it was true that the Confederates had done some wishful thinking about the river metropolis, they entirely lacked the potentialities for an offensive.

As a matter of fact, the President's day of heavy melancholy followed shortly after he had written a paper giving in characteristically lucid form an appreciation of the western front, with plans for a new operation.[16] It is not dated, but since it speaks of Paducah being strongly held, it must have been written after September 6, and it must have been written at least two weeks before October 5, because it describes an operation Lincoln wished begun before that date. The document makes no reference to a movement down the Mississippi; nor does it show any concern about St. Louis. Lincoln's thoughts were turned entirely toward East Tennessee, and he set forth a plan to aid the people of that region, who on June 8 had voted 29,127 to 6,117 against separation from the Union.[17] His initial military objective was to seize a point on the strategic Virginia-Tennessee Railroad "near the mountain pass called Cumberland Gap"; this achieved, the liberation of the region would follow.

The paper is not that of the ordinary amateur or armchair strategist; it savors strongly of the professional. Lincoln began by locating all the Federal forces from Cincinnati to Cairo and Birds Point; he suggested the places where troops still training should go, paying attention to economy of force and supply. He pronounced the Ohio probably secure from Louisville to its mouth, in virtue of the gunboats and forces already on the river. He pinpointed Sherman on Muldraugh

Hill, forty miles south of Louisville, with 8,000 men. Then he sketched in the enemy. General Buckner with a force equal to Sherman's was just south of him. In front of the gap at which Lincoln was looking with such covetous eyes—twenty-five miles in front of it—at Bar-

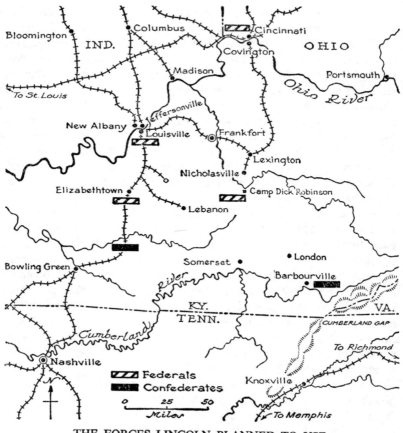

THE FORCES LINCOLN PLANNED TO USE

bourville, Kentucky, was the Confederate Brigadier Felix Zollicoffer with 6,000 to 8,000 men. Seventy-five miles from Zollicoffer in the direction of Lexington, and twenty-five miles from Lexington, was friendly Camp Dick Robinson, where George H. Thomas had 5,000 or 6,000 men. Thomas had been with Patterson in July and had had the brush at Falling Waters with his fellow Virginian, T. J. Jackson. Now a brigadier, away from the state that disapproved his strong attachment to the Union, he was part of the effort to gain Kentucky.

Such were the troops in position. But there were strategic reserves at Louisville and Cincinnati, and others flowing to those points from camps in the rear, and Lincoln sought to bring them into the picture, effectively and where the enemy did not expect them. A real war game for a High Command was what the solitary man was working on; only it was not a game, but stark reality to Lincoln as he thought of the Tennessee Unionists. Both from Covington—across the river from Cincinnati—and from Louisville, a railroad ran to Lexington; he noted not only that they were in Federal hands, but that home guards were watching over them to prevent sabotage. The railroads could be relied upon to do fast, sure work: bridges would not suddenly go out. With Sherman where he was, it was probable that the Confederates would believe Bowling Green to be the Federal target; the Federal general could certainly keep Buckner from going to help Zollicoffer. Lincoln would also wait for his intended move until some pending operations on the Atlantic coast would securely pin the enemy down there; then reenforcements could not come to Knoxville from the East.

When everything was ready, the forces at Cincinnati and Louisville would be moved quickly by rail to Lexington, and thence to Thomas for the venture against the famous gap. As no railroad existed much beyond Lexington, a march of one hundred and twenty miles over ungraveled roads would be necessary; but Lincoln observed: "Union sentiment among the people largely predominates"—an important factor indeed, for it would reduce the strength of the garrisons that would have to be dropped off to keep communications open. He knew well enough that real trouble would begin as the gap was approached, and he wrote: "It is for the military men to decide whether they can find a pass through the mountains at or near the gap which cannot be defended by the enemy with a greatly inferior force, and what is to be done with regard to this."

There was more than a sentimental objective in the operation that Lincoln planned. Beginning with early spring, many trains of troops from the cotton states had moved over the railroad through Knoxville.[18] Cutting it would not only free Unionist residents of that town from the jeers, taunts, and threats heaped upon them by passing

Southern regiments, but compel these to make a long detour through Atlanta, throwing an added burden on Confederate rail lines already taxed. Lincoln did not stress this fact now, but he afterwards implied it clearly, as will be seen. However, he did speak of other possible gains from the movement, and he ended with the statement: "The coast and gap movements made, Generals McClellan and Frémont, in their respective departments, will avail themselves of any advantages the diversions may present." This was vain hope; but the President still had much to learn about his two senior major generals.

What happened to Lincoln's thoughtful paper immediately after its composition is a mystery. Perhaps the discouragement revealed to Nicolay—attributable to no specific, discernible event—caused him to retain it. Surely, however, he continued to think of his plan and, as his spirits revived, believed in its general feasibility; for on October 31—Scott's last day of command—the paper was entered on the books of the Headquarters of the Army. McClellan certainly read it without delay; and its contents, as well as the suggestions for Hunter that Lincoln wrote on October 24, were reflected in the directions that McClellan gave to Halleck and to Buell. One thing is certain: the Mississippi expedition was in abeyance, and that not solely because of its difficulty, but because other targets were being examined and other moves projected.

Halleck arrived in St. Louis on November 18 and assumed command the next day. For headquarters he chose those formerly occupied by Brigadier General Justus McKinstry (who was soon under arrest in connection with contracts), not the pretentious building used by Frémont. Lack of ceremony and display undoubtedly would have made a good impression on many who did not care for Frémont's style; but a general order published on the 20th proved to be one of the season's sensations, providing ammunition for the Pathfinder's friends and bringing upon the new department commander eloquent condemnation in newspapers and in Congress. Addressed to the laudable purpose of preventing information from reaching the enemy, the order directed that fugitive slaves should not be allowed to enter any camp or permitted with troops on the march. Furthermore, such persons then within the lines were to be "immediately excluded therefrom." [19] This was all too hasty, and it overlooked the fact that contrabands were the source of much information about the enemy, though their reports had especially to be carefully appraised. The order had a second part which was generally overlooked in the abuse heaped upon the opening paragraph: Commanding officers were not to allow any unauthorized person to enter or leave the lines, and they were to use "the greatest precaution in the employment of agents and clerks in confidential positions."

Halleck defended General Order No. 3 in a publicized letter replying to one from Frank Blair. He believed the order was necessary and said, "It was a *military* and not a *political* order." He stood ready to carry out orders with regard to fugitive slaves given to him by his superiors and would enforce laws Congress might pass, but he could not make laws. An interpretation of the order that Halleck sent to General Asboth did not mention the safeguarding of intelligence, but said its purpose was to prevent persons in the army "from acting in the capacity of negro-catcher or negro-stealer." The order did not, he said, forbid the proper employment of Negroes, or prohibit giving food and clothing to escaped slaves and caring for them in outside camps when that was "necessary to prevent suffering." [20]

The initial telegram to McClellan on the 20th was what one might expect from a man fresh from a law office and the proof sheets of a work on international law. Halleck had found no authority for martial law; he wanted it, and in the meantime he requested a telegram saying such a document was on the way. Five days later a dispatch from the Adjutant General brought the request of the General in Chief for an explanation of the necessity for martial law in the Missouri department. A brief reply to McClellan said that the authority was vital, but that if it were refused there would be no proclaiming of martial law, however badly the public interest might suffer. A letter the day before to Adjutant General Thomas had already explained matters more fully. Halleck wished to leave normal matters to the civil authorities as much as possible; but in some places there were no regular tribunals. In St. Louis martial law had nominally existed for weeks, but on what basis, Halleck did not know. Commissioners appointed by the President were asking for persons to be brought before them, but the general believed he had no authority to act, though he was certain the President could give it. Again on the 30th Halleck prodded McClellan with a telegram, and wrote at length on the subject, saying that he intended to act strictly under authority and according to instructions, and that the President should relieve him of command if he did not wish to trust him with the requested power.[21]

The table-thumping brought results, and on December 2 the President wrote an impressive document with the full signature "Abraham Lincoln" reserved for important papers, and duly attested by that of the Secretary of State. If Lincoln was in any way amused by the punctiliousness of his new commander, he was probably also glad to know that the free and easy methods of Frémont were definitely at an end. That Halleck was indeed not eager to use the power given him was shown by the fact that Christmas had passed before he issued an order stating that the martial law previously proclaimed would be enforced. At the same time he instituted martial law along all railroads in the state, again saying that it would be enforced. Carefully he explained that his power came from the President, and that it was not intended "to interfere with the jurisdiction of any civil court which is loyal to the Government of the United States and which will aid the military authorities in enforcing order and punishing crimes." [22]

In discussing Halleck's activities for the next month it is best to treat separately western Missouri and the Cairo and Paducah district. Messages were coming constantly from all three places, and in the end what was being done at the junctions of the four great rivers would be the basis for carrying the war to the South; but it was to the West that the new commander had to devote his main attention, while coping with administrative problems near his headquarters.

In his letter to Hunter of October 24, Lincoln had said that Price was apparently retiring toward Arkansas, and McClellan's directive implied that he anticipated no immediate trouble from the commander of the secessionist Missouri State Guard. As late as November 16, a dispatch from St. Louis stated that Price's force and McCulloch's cooperating regular Confederate troops had retreated into Arkansas. The situation changed rapidly, however, and on the day that Halleck took over, McCulloch sent dispatches to Richmond from Springfield, saying that he had marched back some seventy-two miles to that place upon hearing that the Federals were retiring. But after examining the situation, he found that it was inexpedient to attempt a winter campaign, and he was returning to Arkansas. As soon as his troops were in winter quarters he would, if permission were given, come to Rich-

mond to discuss plans for the spring. Price, he said, appeared to be
planning some effort in the direction of the Missouri River.[23]

Price wasted no time. A telegram to Halleck on the 23rd from a
colonel at Sedalia asserted he had reliable information that the former
governor was marching north at the rate of thirty miles a day with a
force estimated at from 33,000 to 50,000, would that very day cross
the Osage River, and was heading straight for Sedalia. The excessive
rate suggested that Price's men were mounted on something fleeter
than Missouri mules. Nevertheless the warning could not be ignored,
and Halleck instructed the colonel to send out reconnaissances. Upon
hearing from him the next day Halleck alerted other forces. Also on
the 23rd he sent Sherman westward on a general inspection tour.
Three days later a telegram came from Sherman at Sedalia, beginning, "Look well to Jefferson City and the North Missouri Railroad.
Price aims at both." Sherman believed that McCulloch would threaten
Rolla while Price crossed the Osage, and he was uneasy about two
detachments sent out from Sedalia. Soon there was a second message
from Sherman, saying that his information about Price and his intentions was good. Apparently somewhat dubious, Halleck on the
27th ordered him not to make any forward movement of troops, but
only to send out reconnoitering parties "in the supposed direction of
the enemy." Main bodies were to be held in position "till more reliable
information is obtained." [24]

A telegram to McClellan on the 27th put administrative matters
in St. Louis badly enough: "Affairs here in complete chaos. Troops
unpaid; without clothing or arms. Many never properly mustered into
service and some utterly demoralized. Hospitals overflowing with
sick. One division of 7,500 has over 2,000 on sick list." Price and
McCulloch were "said to be moving north," but Halleck does not
seem to have been alarmed over the situation. He had alerted his
troops—two small divisions at Rolla, three near Sedalia; all the
telegraph wires were working well, so he was in hourly communication with every commander. Price's force was put at from 15,000
to 23,000; "local rebels" had taken up arms north of the Missouri
and were fortifying themselves in Albany; Prentiss had been ordered
to move against them from Chillicothe.[25]

This same day, John Pope sent from Syracuse—twenty miles east
of Sedalia—a very different estimate of the situation from Sherman's.
Scouts were in from twenty-five miles south of the Osage, and they

had encountered nothing but small parties and guerrillas, probably trying to make their way to their homes north of the Missouri River. Price was reported at Greenfield—thirty-five miles northwest of Springfield—and there was "not the slightest prospect of his attempting to come north." On the 28th Sherman telegraphed that he had ordered forward the divisions of Pope and Thomas J. Turner, and said the cold on the naked prairie was so intense it was necessary to move either forward or back. It was a strange message, and it brought a reply from Schuyler Hamilton (Halleck's brother-in-law) stating that headquarters did not believe that an immediate attack on Sedalia was intended, and directing Sherman to return and report his observations about the condition of troops. When Pope, disturbed over the situation, asked for instructions, the answer was made that Sherman had been recalled, and that the department commander wished the troops left as they were and made as comfortable as possible.[26]

Added to Halleck's troubles now was a mentally upset regular officer, at a time when he was sorely in need of subordinates with professional knowledge. Sensing from her husband's letters that something was amiss, Mrs. Sherman had come to St. Louis to meet him.[27] Halleck gave him a leave of absence, writing to McClellan:

I am satisfied that General S[herman's] physical and mental system is so completely broken by labor and care as to render him for the present entirely unfit for duty. Perhaps a few weeks' rest may restore him. I am satisfied that in his present condition it would be dangerous to give him a command here.

Reports from Sedalia, Halleck said, indicated that "General S was completely 'stampeded,' and was 'stampeding' the army." [28]

A personal letter that Halleck wrote to Sherman was well calculated to speed his recovery.[29]

Reports about Price continued, and they were of the most contradictory character. First he was moving northward, then southward, only to be coming north again. His command was said to be in poor condition, badly disaffected, and breaking up, when, as a matter of fact, in response to a proclamation which he issued on November 26, replacements were coming in to make up for the men who were going home. Price wanted 50,000 men and he went after them with rhetoric: "Are Missourians no longer true to themselves? Are they a timid, time-serving, craven race, fit only for subjection to a despot? Awake, my countrymen, to a sense of what constitutes the dignity and true greatness of a free people." After tossing in a little poetry, the former governor perorated: "Do I hear your shouts? Is that your war-cry which echoes through the land? Are you coming? Fifty thousand men! Missouri shall move to victory with the tread of a giant! Come on, my brave boys, 50,000 heroic, gallant, unconquerable Southern men! We await your coming." [30]

The typesetter may have sighed when he looked at the many pages of copy, and have wished that salvation might come through fewer words; but Missourians in large numbers loved the words of their Virginia-born orator and leader. Soon bands of varying size were marching south to join him. However, the Federals worked hard to intercept them, and among the captures by Pope was a complete brass band. Then, in order to make speed, Pope loaded 2,000 infantry in wagons and sent them with four guns and 500 cavalry toward Lexington to do some more intercepting. A few days later—December 14—he informed Halleck that 4,000 "rebels" had left Lexington, moving south with a large train; he thought he might be able to cut them off and asked for instructions. Halleck told him to make the attempt, and on the 15th Pope took the road with 4,000 cavalry, infantry, and artillery on an expedition that netted 1,300 prisoners, 1,000 stand of arms, 1,000 horses, 65 wagons, and much other equipment. The Federal loss in the brief action that took place just before dusk on a bitterly cold day was 2 killed and 8 wounded. With pride Pope wrote: "The march alone would do credit to old soldiers, and it gives me pleasure to state that it has been performed with cheerfulness and alacrity. The troops reoccupied their camps at Sedalia and Otterville just one week after they marched out of them." Halleck was prompt in congratulating the general and his men for "the brilliant success" of the expedition; he hoped it was the forerunner of still greater achievements.[31]

The major of the Second Missouri Cavalry, reporting about a scouting expedition through Saline County, stated he not only had captured all of a group of twenty-eight men whom he had surprised at cards and breakfast, but had camped for the night on the farm of Claiborne F. Jackson, the unseated secessionist governor. Above the Jackson home the Stars and Stripes had been flown. Evidently friends or neighbors did some talking, for presently other Yankees came and unearthed two tons of powder on the place. Price's mailbags also produced good yields; from them it was learned that McCulloch was back in Arkansas, and that the Missouri guardsmen were roundly abusing him, presumably because he would not march north and join them. But Halleck did not know the magnitude of the quarrel going on among the enemy; nor did he know that Jefferson Davis, who had wanted to supersede both McCulloch and Price with Henry Heth, had paid him a nice compliment in a letter to a congressman: "The Federal forces are not hereafter, as heretofore, to be commanded by path-finders and holiday soldiers, but by men of military education and experience in war." [32]

In view of the situation he was reporting in Missouri, Halleck was probably surprised on December 5 by a telegram from McClellan saying troops were to be sent from his department to Buell. He wrote the next day:

I assure you, General, this cannot be done with safety at present. Some weeks hence I hope to have a large disposable force for other points; but now, destitute as we are of arms, organization, and discipline, it seems to me madness to remove any of our troops from this State.[33]

McClellan replied that it was not his intention to strip his subordinate of troops that could not be spared, and asked, "Can you yet form any idea of the time necessary to prepare an expedition against Columbus or one up the Cumberland and Tennessee rivers in connection with Buell's movements?" What followed this query was bewildering, McClellan stating that he intended to reenforce Hunter so he could move into Indian Territory and northern Texas. "It will require," he said, "some little time to prepare Hunter, but when he moves you might act in concert with him." [34] Halleck now could not tell whether it was to Buell or to Hunter that he was to play second fiddle.

The President was reading the reports from St. Louis, and wrote on the long one of the 19th the indorsement, "An excellent letter." [35] But he added that he was sorry that Halleck was so unfavorably impressed with General Lane. Lane's men, according to Halleck, had been coming from Kansas into Missouri to plunder indiscriminately; he asserted he could conceive of nothing more injudicious than the rumored appointment of the Kansas senator as a general. "It will take," he said, "20,000 men to counteract its effect in this State, and, moreover, it is offering a premium for rascality and robbing generally." [36]

There were few more controversial figures in the war, and not many who caused more annoyance to Lincoln, than James H. Lane. In the Mexican War, he had distinguished himself as a regimental commander, taking his Third Indiana to the succor of Jefferson Davis's "Mississippi Rifles" at a most opportune moment in the battle of Buena Vista.[37] In the spring of 1861 Lincoln had entertained the view that Lane could be really useful to the Northern cause, and sent him forth to raise a brigade in Kansas. According to Nicolay and Hay, the regiments which the senator from the newly admitted state recruited, "contained much of the free and reckless fighting material of the frontier, which had been educated by the Missouri border ruffians to guerrilla methods"; [38] and complaints about their excesses reached Washington long before Halleck directed his blast against their commander. Lane did not accept the brigadier generalship he had worked hard to acquire, because Lincoln would not appoint him to the command of the Department of Kansas, and acceptance would compel him to retire from the Senate.[39] Lincoln's secretaries disapproved of Halleck's outburst against politicians; [40] but when full account is taken of the extremely difficult situation in which he was placed, it is hard to believe he was wrong about the harm that could be wrought by the man of whom Beveridge wrote, "His skill in intrigue was uncanny and his power over audiences like magic." [41]

The file of dispatches from Paducah and Cairo was certainly examined by Halleck without delay. One from Smith,[42] dated October 16, described Fort Henry, a work the Confederates had constructed on the Tennessee River just below the Kentucky border, to bar a route of invasion whose advantages to the Federals was obvious. Just when the first shovels of dirt were thrown is not clearly recorded; but by mid-August work was apparently in progress under the direction of Colonel A. Heiman, slaves from Tennessee and northern Alabama being employed.[43] Smith's manner of reference to it shows that the existence of the work was well known to the Federals, but his dispatch may have been the first official report of a reconnaissance. A few days earlier the little gunboat *Conestoga* had gone up the river, and her captain pronounced the fort "a respectable earthwork, mounting heavy guns, with outworks, and a garrison of probably 1,700 to 1,800 men." Three other sources of information concurred, Smith said, in giving it twenty guns and a garrison of 2,000 men. Not far above it the enemy was constructing three gunboats, to be iron-plated and to carry heavy ordnance. With these and a land column, they were boasting that they would attack Paducah. "The old scheme," Smith commented. He had himself gone up the river that day as far as the "Chain of Rocks," and said he could easily render the gunboats useless by sinking a barge or two loaded with stone.

While in Washington, Halleck may have seen a report that Smith sent to McClellan on November 8, which described not only Fort Henry but also Fort Donelson, a much less developed work on the Cumberland, twelve miles to the east.[44] Although the Cumberland did not reach deep into the South as did the Tennessee, but soon turned back into Kentucky, where it gathered its waters from the western slopes of the mountains that gave it its name, it still was a great threat to the Confederates. It flowed through Nashville, which, like Memphis, had rapidly become a munition center. Not only were weapons being altered there, but percussion caps and powder were coming from its factories and mills in increasing amounts. Also very important were the Cumberland Iron Works, on the river twenty miles below Clarksville, and likewise on the railroad from Memphis to Bowling Green.

On the very day that Smith made his first report on Fort Henry, A. G. Henry of Clarksville, Confederate senator and a friend and defender of Jefferson Davis, wrote to General Sidney Johnston, "It seems to me there is no part of the whole West so exposed as the valley of the Cumberland." [45] If the Confederates could not attack Paducah, there was nothing to prevent the Federals from steaming up the river, and destroying not only the railroad bridge at Clarksville, but the valuable rolling mills. Henry was afraid that the Yankees might appear at any minute, but thanks to his efforts, the situation was rapidly improved.[46] On November 1 he was in much better spirits. He then spoke jubilantly about Fort Henry, and stated that eight barges had been sunk in the Cumberland below Donelson—effectively blocking the channel, an experienced steamboat captain had told him, even if the water should rise ten feet. But there was still more to be cheerful about than that; the man who had been so worried a bare fortnight before now said, "It seems to me the guns of Donelson, if

well manned, would be amply sufficient to defend the river against the
Lincoln gunboats." [47]

But the steamboat captain had been much too optimistic. On
November 7 Henry had to inform General Johnston that a Lincoln

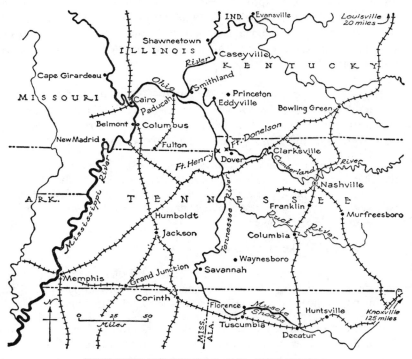

WESTERN KENTUCKY AND TENNESSEE

gunboat had passed the obstruction on a reconnoitering expedition.
As luck would have it, Johnston, before receiving Henry's letter,
wrote to Secretary Benjamin that the Cumberland's channel was
blocked against gunboats not only at Eddyville—thirty-five miles
below Donelson—but also near the state line. Smith, too, had his pen
in hand, and wrote to McClellan that *Conestoga* had just come in
from a run up the Cumberland to Dover, "where the enemy have a
work called Fort Gavock, or Fort MacGavock, or something else,
usually called Fort Gavock." (Lieutenant Colonel R. W. MacGavock,
of a prominent family, was in command of the work, to which the

name Donelson had been definitely fixed.) Smith gave a revised statement about the armament and garrison of Fort Henry—fourteen to sixteen guns and 1,200 men—and reported that a man he had sent up the Tennessee to obtain information about the Confederate gunboats had been captured. He was evidently undisturbed about the prospects, for he concluded, "I mention these things because it is a favorite idea announced on the other side that Paducah is to be attacked from three quarters at once, one quarter being by one or both rivers." [48]

Halleck was probably more surprised—especially if he had seen Smith's letter—at the reports that came to St. Louis of a threat to southern Illinois than he was when he learned that Price was moving northward. On the 22nd he telegraphed to Smith:

It is reported that General Hardee, with 8,000 men, is about to cross the Ohio between the Wabash and Cumberland, to destroy the Ohio and Mississippi and the Illinois Central Railroad. Others say that he is to be re-enforced by General Polk and attack Paducah. Keep me advised of the enemy's movements.[49]

Smith replied the next day:

My last information was that 2,000 men, with three field pieces, were at Princeton, running off hogs—plundering generally. I have sent the gunboat Conestoga to gain information and watch the Ohio.[50]

A letter examined more fully the possibility of an attack on Paducah and described the alarm on the other side of the Cumberland, whence the inhabitants were constantly sending messages that a Confederate force was approaching. Up to the moment nothing had occurred but marauding, and even the recent increase of force appeared to be for sweeping the country of provisions, without any idea of crossing the river. It was all very simple, and Smith said: "They want the means of transportation to do so." Nevertheless, on the last day of the month the general reported sending a part of a regiment to Cave in Rock, Illinois (opposite Caseyville), after receiving a report that some Confederates were planning to seize a steamboat at Caseyville and cross over. Busy *Conestoga* was to start up the Ohio at once to examine the situation, having just returned from a trip up the Tennessee to "look after the rebel gunboat" which was reported as venturing below Fort Henry—on a trial run, Smith thought.[51] Though not apprehensive of attack, he believed it desirable to have another vessel added to the *Conestoga,* which was unarmored but carried four 32-pounders. Watching for hostile gunboats in two rivers and for crossings of a third, was indeed a heavy assignment for a single craft.

Probably on the very day he passed on to Smith the reports coming into his headquarters, Halleck received from outside his department a dispatch so important that it is given in full:

Cincinnati, Ohio, November 20, 1862

Major-General Halleck, Saint Louis:

Sir: Will you allow me to suggest the consideration of a great movement by land and water up the Cumberland and Tennessee Rivers?

1st. Would it not allow of water transportation half way to Nashville?

2d. Would it not necessitate the evacuation of Columbus by threatening their railway communication?

3d. Would it not necessitate the retreat of General Buckner by threatening his railway lines?

4th. Is it not the most passable route into Tennessee?

Yours, respectfully, &c.,

Chas. Whittlesey,
Colonel, and Chief of Engineer Department [52]

Later there was to be much argument about who first thought of a movement up the Tennessee River. The son of Sidney Johnston disposed of the question in excellent fashion in 1887, when he wrote, "It was obvious enough to all the leaders on both sides," not knowing that Grant had made an equally significant comment in a letter to Washburne seventeen years before. Though it seems certain that McClellan did not mention such an operation during his conversations with Halleck in Washington, Halleck had hardly taken over command in St. Louis when the fruits of such a move were compellingly put before him. But what about Forts Henry and Donelson? Whittlesley did not so much as mention them, and they were the crux of the question. Work on them was steadily progressing, as well as on a commanding fort across the Tennessee from Fort Henry, to remedy an error in the location of the latter. Senator Henry had reported it as his "military opinion"—concurred in, he believed, by Johnston's chief engineer—that the defensive potential of Donelson against attack from the land side was excellent, on account of the rugged and wooded nature of the terrain. Properly felled trees, he said, "would protect it against cavalry, the approach of artillery, and almost of infantry." The country between the two forts, being "covered by a heavy forest with undergrowth," also gave a pleasant feeling of security to Sidney Johnston, who wrote to Secretary Benjamin as early as November 8, "It can be defended by a force inferior to the invading force." [53]

But the people of northern Alabama and Mississippi were still apprehensive of visits from the Yankees, and they sent a delegation to Columbus to confer with the generals about the river that flowed for one hundred and fifty miles through the one state and then for a short distance was a boundary between the two. On November 23 the delegation published at Tuscumbia a circular—which it hoped no editor would copy in his paper—giving its rather gloomy findings. The committee of seven had talked with General Pillow (in command at Columbus because of Polk's injury) who had said without hesitation that the Tennessee River was not safe. The committee asked for volunteers—older men, 5,000 of them if possible, with clothing and tents prepared by wives and daughters, and "as many negro men as can be raised"—to go down the river and help in its defense. The enemy, the committee said, was preparing a great expedition by land and water against the Confederates on the Mississippi. The position at Columbus was described as "one of great strength"; but, unless it was properly sustained on its flanks and rear, there could be disaster. Said the committee in conclusion: "Our young men at Columbus are not only enduring the hardships of the camp and meeting gallantly the hazards of the battle, but laboring in the trenches with spades and shovels now, and who are we that we should be exempt from the burdens imposed for the common defense?" [54]

Presently Pillow's ideas were to change—as was their habit—and he would write to Johnston that he believed the enemy was preparing to move up the Tennessee and merely demonstrate against Columbus.[55] Then all the trenches would be nothing more than mute evidence of the weary spading and shoveling that had so impressed the visitors.

Upon receiving Halleck's order taking over command, Grant addressed a report to Captain Kelton, who was back in the place of McKeever, stating that the enemy had at Columbus forty-seven regiments of infantry and cavalry, and more than a hundred heavy guns; an additional 8,000 men were at Camp Beauregard, near Fulton. Both figures were overestimates. Work on the fortifications at Columbus, he wrote, was going forward day and night; a gunboat had arrived two nights before, another was soon expected. The condition of his own command was "bad in every particular except discipline." There was a deficiency in transportation and not a single ambulance; clothing was inferior in quality and lacking in quantity; arms were mostly repaired old flintlocks, some very poor; none of his cavalry was properly armed, eight companies being without any weapons. As funds had been meager, the government's credit was about exhausted. A postscript noted that deficiencies had been reported frequently, and proper requisitions made.[56]

On November 27 Grant reported that the enemy had five hundred Negroes building fortifications at New Madrid. His own cavalry had called at Belmont, but had found no enemy there. On December 1 he wrote, "Bishop Major-General Polk's three gunboats made a Sunday excursion to see us this evening." They had opened fire when half a mile beyond range of the nearest point in Camp Holt and had turned about when their guns were replied to; the Federal gunboats had followed, but had been unable to get within range. Grant made no mention of an expedition to New Madrid planned for December 8, but necessarily called off because of inability to get the gunboats to cooperate. It would be interesting to know what he intended to accomplish, and whether he meant to pass the Columbus batteries at night; but the brief note to McClernand and Wallace postponing the operation, "owing to the inability of the gunboats to co-operate," appears to be the only record that survives. A spy coming from Columbus on the 8th reduced the number of heavy guns to fifty-four but increased the light batteries to ten; infantry and cavalry were reported as before. Wrote Grant: "I believe that I have full means of keeping posted as to what is going on south of this point and will keep you fully informed." Though not a paying subscriber, the general was a reader of the *Memphis Appeal,* and when Mississippi called 10,000 sixty-day state troops to help with the defense of Columbus, he passed the word and the source on to headquarters for what it was worth.[57]

If Grant's plans with regard to New Madrid were shrouded in mystery, a message he sent to headquarters on the 13th is annoyingly inexplicable. Having only five days earlier reported that the enemy had "not the slightest intention of attacking Cairo"—being himself greatly in fear of attack—he now reported that information just in made him expect an attack, probably on Birds Point, the next morning. He was fully prepared for the best defense that his means would allow, let the blow fall where it would; troops were sleeping on their arms with cartridge boxes full, four regiments being on steamers with the gunboats standing by; and every means had been taken to detect the enemy's intention.[58] Though Polk was contemplating no blow against Grant, ambitious thoughts had been stirring in the minds of Gideon Pillow and Commodore George N. Hollins, who commanded the Confederate gunboats. On the 2nd Pillow wrote to Polk urging an attack on Birds Point and Fort Holt, in concert with the gunboats, mainly to destroy the new Federal boats that were nearing completion.[59] He stated that Hollins was confident that they could succeed, and might "possibly take Cairo itself." Polk asked for the views of other subordinates, and two brigade commanders wrote long letters opposing the venture.[60] As a matter of fact, the force of 11,000 to 12,000 men which they estimated could be put into the attack was double Grant's strength at Birds Point and Fort Holt combined, while his strategic reserve at Cairo numbered only 5,000.[61] One of Polk's brigadiers, however, not only emphasized the strong Federal batteries, but spoke of a defending force of 34,500 men, with 20,000 in Cairo itself. The two officers thought the proposal not only foredoomed to failure but was bad psychology: it would anger and stimulate the North, arousing previously lackadaisical persons. Quite possibly the Pillow proposal leaked out and became a lively subject for Columbus gossip; but what led Grant's agent to report a proposed movement ten days later is a mystery.[62]

Halleck may have been surprised to learn that Grant had gone into an all-out alert so soon after his positive statement five days before. A fixed idea, however, had not paralyzed the Cairo commander, and though Halleck could not read the actual orders that Grant issued he could see from his letter that defensive preparations in a distinctly difficult position were excellent: A mobile reserve was ready, with arrangements made to detect quickly the point of attack. Certainly the department commander also noted with satisfaction that Grant did not even hint at reenforcements. Apparently he was not even wishing for his old teacher not many miles up the Ohio.

Promptly after Halleck's arrival Grant reported his frequent, but unsuccessful, efforts to have river traffic controlled in such a way as to prevent supplies from reaching the enemy; and Halleck responded by immediately ordering General Curtis, in local command at St. Louis, to do whatever was practicable. But the trouble persisted, and Grant presently wrote that goods put ashore at Price's Landing by the steamer *Perry* had been moved without delay to Hickman and New Madrid. Included in the cargo were eighty barrels of whisky, a commodity the general said he did not mind having shipped South, if it were not for "a possibility that some barrels marked whisky might contain something more objectionable." Though he did not wish to interfere with the drinking habits of the Southerners, it was different with their diets. Corn meal and beef being abundant, their dinners and suppers were assured; but Grant evidently thought it possible to revise their breakfast menus, for he wrote, "If salt can be kept out, they will have some difficulty in saving their bacon." [63]

Matters were clearly in tight hands at the river junction. "Grant cannot be taken from Cairo," said Halleck in the confidential letter of December 2 that told McClellan of Sherman's condition. The next day he wrote that after full consideration of the correspondence that had passed between Grant and Polk with regard to prisoners taken at Belmont, he had concluded that exchange was the proper thing. Using some plain but awesome words, the learned general wrote in the best academic style: "A prisoner exchanged under the laws of war is not thereby exempted from trial and punishment as a traitor. Treason is a state or civil offense, punishable by the civil courts; the exchange of prisoners of war is only a part of the ordinary *commercia belli*." [64] McClellan of course understood that he was saying exchange of prisoners was not an implied recognition of the Confederacy, which was what Grant seemed to fear.

Halleck would also have been pleased to see Grant's messages to subordinates about tightening discipline still more. Oglesby was directed to investigate immediately property taken at Belmont or elsewhere and illegally held by personnel. Offending officers were to be placed in arrest, and soldiers in confinement for "conduct of such an infamous character." To Colonel Ross, Grant wrote: "One thing I will add: In cases of outrageous marauding I would fully justify shooting the perpetrators down if caught in the act—I mean our men as well as the enemy." [65]

Although Halleck did not hurl Latin at Grant, he did humiliate him in mid-December with some very plain English words for an act of which Grant had been a victim. Some of the prisoners who had been taken in the May raid on Camp Jackson, and who were being released in accordance with an agreement between Frémont and Price, were en route south when Grant received from St. Louis over the signature "W. H. Buel, Colonel," the telegram: "The D. G. Taylor left here at 1 p.m. today. Stop her and send back all the Camp Jackson men. They all have assumed names." Send them back, Grant did, with a message of explanation to headquarters, only to receive on the 19th from Halleck the telegram: "By what authority did you send back exchanged prisoners? They are not under assumed names. All were identified here before exchange." Presently another dispatch arrived saying that no Colonel W. H. Buel was known in St. Louis, and adding, "It is most extraordinary that you should have obeyed a telegram sent by an unknown person and not even purporting to have been given by authority." Grant answered the next day, quoting the sentence and saying, "In justice to myself I must reply to this telegram." Though his words were mild, there was a thrust in them: "I never thought of doubting the authority of a telegram from Saint Louis, supposing that in military matters the telegraph was under such surveillance that no military order could be passed over the wires that was not by authority." Then, noting that orders with regard to prisoners might come from the provost marshal's office or from General Curtis, he said, "I do not know the employés of the former nor the staff of the latter." In closing, he returned to his most effective point: "The fact is I never dreamed of so serious a telegraphic hoax emanating through a large and responsible office like that in Saint Louis." [66]

In these simple but challenging sentences may lie the explanation of Halleck's future attitude toward Grant. He had shown comprehension and sympathy toward Sherman and had been very generous in complimenting Pope; but toward the general in Cairo he reacted bitterly. His answering message would have been excellent if it had stopped with the first two sentences: "The person who sent the telegram about the prisoners has been discovered and placed in confinement. He has no authority whatever." But, unable to admit any responsibility for what had happened, Halleck added the sharp admonition, "You will hereafter be more careful about obeying telegrams from private persons countermanding orders from these headquarters." This completely missed the point that Grant had made about not having a complete roster of responsible officers; and, though professional soldiers may be used to plain words, he had the right to feel harshly and unjustly reproved. So far as St. Louis was concerned, the incident was closed, but two days later a letter went to General Polk. After explaining what had happened, Grant said: "It turned out, however, that the dispatch was a wicked hoax perpetrated by an individual in Saint Louis who has been arrested and will be properly punished. No one regrets the occurrence more than I do." [67] Grant had said his officer could bring an answer; evidently there was none.

Sherman was back in quiet Lancaster, Ohio, resting jangled nerves. St. Louis, with its bitter enmities and its martial law, could not have offered much wholesome relaxation, and the Army did not in those days have troupes of cheerful players to take laughter to tired generals and homesick soldiers. Still, as always, there was cause for smiles in the incongruities that break out in the most serious of matters. Any brigadier should have been put in good humor for a week by a letter that came to Curtis, which, after berating him for the oath of allegiance required of many persons, ended:

Union don't mean war and war don't mean union. The more war the less union. But why reason with crazy men?

Naomi [68]

CHAPTER VI

THE YEAR ENDS IN THE WEST

*He who does something at the head of one regiment will
eclipse him who does nothing at the head of a hundred.*

Lincoln to Hunter

IN ORDER to discover what the High Command was planning for
the West, it is necessary to turn to Louisville, where Don Carlos Buell
assumed command of the Department of the Ohio on November 15.
On the 7th, two days before Buell was formally given the department,
McClellan had written him a letter of instructions, which was not
signed, being apparently superseded by a directive of November 12.[1]
The directive spoke of the fullness of the talks that the two officers
had had upon the subject of Buell's future operations, so that the
new commander must have been aware of the views that McClellan
had expressed in the earlier letter, if indeed he had not read it. At
all events the unsigned letter of November 7 is an unimpeachable
record of the thoughts that McClellan entertained soon after succeeding to Scott's position.

The letter opened by expressing the intention of giving instructions
for Buell's guidance, without fettering him. Political conditions might
be more important in Kentucky at the moment than military ones,
and McClellan said he knew he was speaking for the President when
he wrote, "We are fighting only to preserve the integrity of the Union
and the constitutional authority of the General Government." The
people of Kentucky were to be made to realize that their "domestic

institutions" would in no way be interfered with and would receive "every constitutional protection." Nashville, said McClellan, should probably be the first objective if the East Tennessee situation were not so pressing. He concluded:

> It therefore seems proper that you should remain on the defensive on the line from Louisville to Nashville, while you throw the mass of your forces by rapid marches, by Cumberland Gap or Walker's Gap, on Knoxville, in order to occupy the railroad at that point, and thus enable the loyal citizens of Eastern Tennessee to rise, while you at the same time cut off the railway communication between Eastern Virginia and the Mississippi. It will be prudent to fortify the pass before leaving it in your rear.

The proposal resembles so closely the campaign Lincoln had outlined in the undated memorandum which has already been described, that it is impossible to believe McClellan had not read it. Though the President seemed to recognize a possible difficulty in taking the mountain passes, McClellan revealed no doubt. The war in fact had not been a fortnight old when he wrote to Scott from Cincinnati, suggesting that he be allowed to lead a column from Ohio through the mountains to Richmond, Virginia, saying that he was prepared to meet the difficulties of the mountainous country. It was a conditional move, however, and McClellan said that if Kentucky should become entangled in the conflict, and as many as 80,000 Federal troops should be available, it would be more decisive to cross the Ohio at Cincinnati or Louisville, "march straight on Nashville, and thence act according to circumstances." [2]

Although Nashville had the preference in the two competing programs as early as April 27, and was still favored from a purely military point of view on November 7, it was not mentioned in McClellan's final letter of November 12. This is a fact of interest and significance in what was presently to develop. Knoxville was the target finally fixed upon, and McClellan spoke of "the necessity of entering Eastern Tennessee as soon as it can be done with reasonable chances of success." Continuing, he said he *hoped* that Buell would, "with the least possible delay, organize a column for that purpose, sufficiently guarding at the same time the main avenues by which the rebels may invade Kentucky." He came very close to nullifying everything he had said when he assured his subordinate that he was "perfectly free to change the plans of operations," if it should turn out that the *suggestions* made were "founded on erroneous data." The word "suggestions" seems weak, but the General in Chief did not go so far as to say that Buell might substitute something for the East Tennessee operation if he merely *chose* to do so. In spite of that, Buell seems to have come to the West thinking that McClellan—whom he addressed in official correspondence as "My dear Friend"—had left him practically a free hand.

The situation in the general vicinity of Cumberland Gap had changed significantly since Lincoln outlined a movement on Knoxville. On October 21 Zollicoffer had somewhat imprudently attacked a Federal force under Albin Schoepf in a strong position on Rockcastle River. Each commander reported the other as having 7,000 men; but Thomas, under whom Schoepf was serving, said the Northerners mustered 5,000, and the Confederate gave his own strength as 5,400. Zollicoffer retreated to Cumberland Ford, ten miles north of the Gap, through a hilly country which he reported as almost barren of supplies. On the 29th he wrote that the road to the Gap would soon be almost impassable; but November 2 saw him in position at the pass, writing to the Secretary of War that the enemy was advancing in large force. The three eight-inch howitzers and the two Parrott guns which General Johnston had sent to him were, said Zollicoffer, sufficient for only one of the three passes he had to watch, and he wanted some additional eight-inchers. Two days later Richmond sent three more. To Johnston's adjutant Zollicoffer telegraphed that there was reason to believe the Federals were advancing by a route to the west that would bring them to unfortified gaps near Jamestown and Jacksboro. Toward the latter place he was moving most of his infantry and would start a six-pounder battery and his Parrott guns the next day. No Yankees having shown up in the vicinity, Zollicoffer informed Richmond two days later that he thought the enemy move was a feint; but he sent word to Johnston that the generally strong Union sentiment of the Kentuckians in front of him made it difficult to tell just what was going on.

In spite of his difficulty in getting information, Zollicoffer was willing to hazard a guess to headquarters at Bowling Green: "I am now inclined to suspect that the enemy will make no forward movement toward East Tennessee, but will retire from this line to give support to a concentrated movement in General Buckner's front. We have vague news to this effect from citizens, communicated through our cavalry scouts on the Barboursville road." Like Lincoln, the former newspaper owner and congressman was impressed with the railroad facilities at the disposal of the Federals; and, referring to the enemy reserves, he said it would be possible to "glide them around" one way to fall upon him, and "glide them around" the other way and hit Buckner. Zollicoffer had had no military experience, and his battlefield record was limited to a duel in which he had balanced a wound in his pistol hand by clipping his antagonist's head. Now in the difficult position of guarding mountain passes and watching a population eager to rise in the defense of the Union from which he himself had opposed secession, he showed he had strategical as well as dueling acumen, though his language was sometimes more picturesque than military. In view of the situation, he suggested that he fortify Cumberland Gap as strongly as possible, leave a minimum force there, fortify or thoroughly blockade the passes near Jacksboro as well as byways west of that place, and then concentrate in the open country near Jamestown, with a view to advancing toward Danville, Kentucky. He would then be in a country less sterile than the "Wilderness of Kentucky" that now lay in his front, whose barrenness he may have exaggerated; and he could not, he said, be in a region more hostile. After stating that he had authorized the construction of huts to shelter the garrison at the gap, he closed his able letter with a sentence eloquent in its restraint: "The late cold, rainy weather has been severe upon those who are thinly clad." [3]

On the 6th word came to Zollicoffer that 6,000 Federals were advancing on Jamestown; and he at once prepared to march with five regiments of infantry, a battery, and some cavalry, totaling about 3,500 men, through Clinton toward Wartburg and Jamestown.[4] Two days later he wrote from Jacksboro that a reliable citizen from Huntsville, Tennessee, reported that the enemy was sending a column from Williamsburg in addition to the one from Monticello.[5] Hastening southward the same day along a good road at the base of the mountain, he encountered a messenger just as he was turning westward on the road from Knoxville to Wartburg, and received a dispatch with more cheering news. The Federals were not advancing from Monticello; they only had a camp of unknown strength five miles east of that point. The Confederate commander halted his weary column and sent the good news to Richmond and also to General Johnston. He stated he would return to Jacksboro and completely blockade the two wagon roads through the mountains in that vicinity. This work would, he thought, require a week or ten days; when it was completed he would advance by the Jamestown route.[6] It was probably

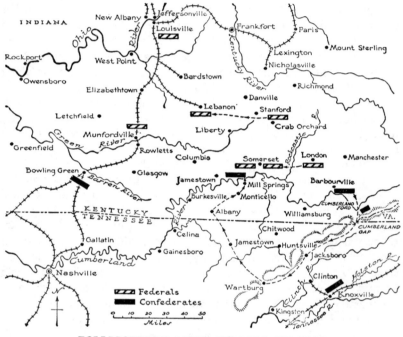

ZOLLICOFFER'S MOVE TO MILL SPRINGS

while carrying out his blockading that he received a message from Johnston approving his proposed fortification of Cumberland Gap and the movement of his main force westward.[7]

What did the Federals know about Zollicoffer's moves and the situation at Cumberland Gap? Immediately after administering the sharp repulse to the Southerners on October 21 Schoepf seemed eager to press forward, and thought it practical to do so, according to a dispatch two days later to Thomas. He believed the intervening forces of Zollicoffer could be scattered; and after "turning the Gap"—a significant form of statement—he could, he asserted, get and hold possession of it. He thought even more than that was possible, for he might be able to lay hold of "the great railroad from Richmond, Va., and Manassas to Memphis and the South." Categorically he asked his superior, "Shall I do it?" After suggesting that reenforcements be sent forward so as to sustain him in case he failed, the Marylander stated that he was credibly informed that supplies could be obtained for his present force—or even for a larger one—along the route of advance to the Gap. This opinion, Schoepf said, was shared by Horace Maynard of Tennessee. Maynard, a strong Union congressman, with Senator Andrew Johnson was pressing hard upon the administration for a relief expedition to his home region. As the families of both men were precariously situated in East Tennessee, they were likely to minimize, if not ignore, the difficulties of the operation they so vigorously urged. Thomas's answer to Schoepf is missing; but Schoepf referred to it in a letter of the 25th, and it is clear that Thomas directed that two Ohio regiments move a short distance toward London, though he recalled the First Kentucky to Crab Orchard. Moreover, in a message on the 23rd congratulating his subordinate on his recent success, he wrote, "I cannot determine yet whether we shall be able to advance until I can find out more about forwarding of clothing and ammunition." Schoepf's enthusiasm had apparently dwindled; perhaps because he had learned that the sustenance problem would be difficult for both men and animals in case of an advance. After requesting two companies of Kentucky cavalry, he said that he thought it would be "prudent" for the detachment "to bring with them as much corn as they can find transportation for, that being a scarce article in this neighborhood." [8] If Zollicoffer's statements were correct, even bacon and eggs would not have been plentiful. But soldiers have the habit of turning up in barren country with morale-building items such as chickens, and the truth was probably somewhere between the report of Zollicoffer and the early one of Schoepf.

On the last day of October, General Sherman—who, in spite of the scarcity of transportation, had three weeks before urged upon Thomas "an advance movement in the direction of the Cumberland" —stated that he did not believe there was a chance to invade East Tennessee on account of the nearness of winter and the impassability of the roads.[9] Nevertheless an advance was begun, and presently Thomas was at Crab Orchard, about seventy miles from the coveted pass. At London, approximately a halfway point, was acting Brigadier

General S. P. Carter, a former navy lieutenant and a devoted Unionist from East Tennessee, with two regiments from that region and one from Kentucky, all eager to press forward, and willing to make great exertions and endure hardships. On the day that McClellan gave the letter of instructions to Buell, Carter wrote to Thomas that he had word that Zollicoffer had left Jacksboro on the 6th with five regiments, moving in the direction of Knoxville. He stated further—correctly—that there was only one Confederate regiment and a part of another guarding Cumberland Gap; he said he believed the point might be seized with little difficulty. Undoubtedly the converted sailor had good sources of information, and it is safe to assume that he learned of Zollicoffer's return to block the Jacksboro passes. He wrote that he wanted powder, balls, and caps not only for his own men but for the East Tennesseans, to whom he had already sent one such consignment. He concluded: "We thank you, general, for your assurance that as soon as you can you will move towards East Tennessee. Our men and officers have entire confidence in you and shall be most happy to see you in our midst. . . . I am persuaded you will do what is right and proper." [10] George Thomas must indeed have had a way with him, for an Annapolis graduate, even when temporarily wearing the habiliment of a soldier, is not ordinarily that enthusiastic about a West Pointer.

Everything, however, was to change, and that very quickly. On November 11 the signs of the near-breakdown which, as we have seen, brought Sherman a grant of leave before the end of the month, were beginning to be manifest. He wired Thomas to fall back because there was a *rumor* that Buckner was moving toward Lexington. He also said that if it were true that the enemy forces at the Gap had been increased to 20,000—as had been reported to him—it would be madness to try anything in that direction. The next day the alarmed general wrote, "I am convinced from many facts that A. Sidney Johnston is making herculean efforts to strike a great blow in Kentucky; that he designs to move from Bowling Green on Lexington, Louisville, and Cincinnati." [11]

What were the actual "facts"? Practically nothing that Sherman said was accurate, and he gave himself away in his last sentence: "We find it impossible to penetrate their designs, except I know their force is very large [which was not the case] and they have pressed in all the wagons from several counties, for which they could have no other use than what I name." It apparently did not occur to him that his opponent might wish only to make himself mobile so that he could retreat at need; and he seemingly believed that Johnston was blessed with full and accurate knowledge about himself. Yet only four days earlier Johnston had written to Secretary Benjamin about the "extreme difficulty" he had in obtaining reliable information about the Federals; and he had asked that $5,000 be deposited to his credit in a Nashville bank for secret service.[12]

Sherman directed Thomas to prepare to fall back to Danville, leaving his Tennessee regiments in a "kind of ambush near Rockcastle River"; and he gave a code sentence for starting the withdrawal if his fears were confirmed. To Sherman's telegram of the 11th, which reached him on the 12th, Thomas replied: "I will give orders at once for a retrograde movement, but I am sure the enemy are not moving between us. All my information indicates they are moving south." Sherman may have been somewhat chagrined by his subordinate's communication—brought to him by an officer courier—and on the 13th he admitted that he had detected no signs of an enemy advance but had inferred the "fact" from "the current belief among secessionists" in Louisville. The doubting Thomas reported that Colonel T. E. Bramlette, who was at Somerset, did not—on the 11th—think the enemy had any intention whatever of advancing. He also forwarded Carter's letter with the information about the Gap, remarking that other sources of information previously found reliable confirmed its statements. This merely strengthened Sherman's belief that the Confederates were preparing to throw everything into a push on Louisville. If the Gap was strongly occupied by the enemy, it was madness to move toward it; if weakly held, things were generally ominous. It was a case of "Heads, I win; tails, you lose." On the 14th Thomas's telegraph instrument clicked out four words, "Your application is granted." That was the signal for him to start to retreat. But two days later, before any movement had begun, a message came from Sherman saying that Buell had arrived and taken command. Thomas was to remain at Crab Orchard, pending instructions from the new department commander.[13]

Was there still a chance for East Tennessee?

One cannot tell just when word first reached Federal commanders in Kentucky that the Unionists in East Tennessee had struck boldly at their enemies. General Thomas had been awaiting just such a report, for on October 27 the Reverend William Blount Carter, a brother of the general and now a captain in one of his regiments and a good enough organizer to be a bishop, had written from Kingston, thirty miles southwest of Knoxville, a letter that foretold the blow that he had set forth to direct. Since the long message was probably not written in code it must have been carried to the Federal officer by a devoted and faithful courier. Carter said he was nearing the railroad (Tennessee and Georgia) and would make a desperate attempt to destroy all the bridges; he firmly believed he would be successful. He continued:

This whole country is in a wretched condition; a perfect despotism reigns here. The Union men of East Tennessee are longing and praying for the hour when they can break their fetters. The loyalty of our people increases with the oppressions they have to bear. Men and women weep for joy when I merely hint to them that the day of our deliverance is at hand. I have not seen a secession flag since I entered the State. I beg you to hasten on to our help, as we are about to create a great diversion in General McClellan's favor. It seems to me, if you would ask it, he would spare you at once 5,000 or 10,000 well-drilled troops. Will you not ask for more help? [14]

On November 15 the *New York Tribune* gave its readers arresting headlines about the rising in East Tennessee and the burning of five railroad bridges, based on a Nashville dispatch of the 12th and messages from Richmond and Lynchburg dated the 9th. On the 16th General Carter wrote to Thomas that his brother was back and reported the destruction of six and probably eight bridges, from near the Virginia line to below Chattanooga.[15] Tracks and telegraph wires had also been destroyed, and on the 9th Johnston informed Polk that it was necessary to send messages to Richmond by way of New Orleans.[16] Captain Carter reported that the consternation among the secessionists of East Tennessee was very great, and he had it from reliable sources that there were only 15,000 Confederates in Bowling Green, many of whom were badly armed and poorly organized. He put Zollicoffer's command at 8,000, with 1,000 unarmed and 1,500 sick. After transmitting his brother's report General Carter wrote:

General, if it be possible, do urge the commanding general to give us some additional force and let us advance into East Tennessee; now is the time. And such a people as are those who live in East Tennessee deserve and should be relieved and protected. You know the importance of this

move, and will, I hope, use all your influence to effect it. Our men will
go forward with a shout to relieve their native land.

Also on the 16th the Adjutant General in Washington wrote to
Buell that McClellan had that day telegraphed orders for four more
regiments to join him from West Virginia, and he said: "With these,
superadded to the re-enforcements of which you were advised by
telegraph on the 14th instant, the major-general commanding in-
structs me to say that he expects you will be able to organize a proper
force for immediate operations in the direction of Cumberland
Gap." [17]

But Buell had other ideas.

At five in the afternoon of the 17th, a captain from Buell's headquarters arrived at Crab Orchard and instructed Thomas to move
his command in the direction of Columbia, which was halfway to the
enemy's main position at Bowling Green. There was of course no
excuse for a verbal order, and Thomas was careful to make a written
record in the letter he wrote to his superior that evening. Naturally
a misunderstanding resulted, and Thomas, believing that Carter was
to remain at London, wrote him immediately to that effect. To Buell,
however, he recommended that Carter be withdrawn on account of
the extreme difficulty of supplying him during the winter. Two days
later Buell's chief of staff—Colonel James B. Fry—informed Thomas
that the order was intended to cover his entire command. The maintenance of a supply depot at Crab Orchard—which Thomas had
deprecated—would therefore not be necessary, and he was to move
upon a line for which Louisville and not Cincinnati would be the main
depot.[18]

On the 21st Thomas, leaving many sick at Crab Orchard under
the protection of a regiment, was on the march with his two remaining
regiments—four other such units and two batteries of his division
being already in the vicinity of Columbia and Lebanon. Bad roads
prevented him moving directly to Liberty where Buell had instructed
him to go and await further orders, and he accordingly routed himself
through Danville. Carter was under marching orders to follow over
the road to Crab Orchard, which Thomas reported as being in
"wretched condition." But, for a reason not entirely clear, Buell
changed his mind, and on the evening of the 22nd, issued a short
order that was in Thomas's hands early the next morning: Carter

was to stay at London if he had not already begun to move. The sailor-general had acknowledged Thomas's order to move with considerable regret, hinting that he might have a real command problem on his hands by writing: "Although this brigade has a great dread of the Blue-grass country, and are most desirous of driving the rebels from East Tennessee in the quickest possible time, I trust there will be no difficulty in moving them to any point where there is a prospect of meeting our common enemy." [19]

In directing Carter to remain, Thomas took care to tell him that the previous marching order "was based upon orders from department headquarters" [20]—but overlooked the fact that he had recommended it. Carter made haste to reply:

The order to remain was received with general satisfaction.

The rebel force at Cumberland Gap is, from the best information I can obtain, so small, that I think we will meet with but little opposition in case it is determined to advance by that pass.

Our desires are to get to East Tennessee as soon as possible, in order that our loyal friends there may be relieved. Many of them have been lying out in the woods to escape their enemies, but as the season advances they will be driven to their houses, and be forced into the rebel ranks or carried to prison. Let us up and help them now, when it will require so little to accomplish this desirable and necessary end.[21]

Then Carter urged that the long-awaited paymaster be pushed forward without the delay of a single day. Little there was, even for an enterprising soldier, to purchase in the vicinity of London. The money was to go into East Tennessee, and presently Carter was urging that the paymaster bring gold. He also asked for arms to equip the recruits that were coming to join his regiments. But the Tennesseans wanted something more than gold and muskets. They wanted regimental colors—silken flags of the United States with spread eagles on the staffs to carry over the mountain passes.[22]

On November 22 Buell wrote at length to McClellan about what he was doing. Some forty or fifty fragments of Kentucky regiments were being consolidated into about twenty-two, and would be mustered as soon as possible; about 10,000 arms were needed to equip them. There were a number of things the new department commander did not like; after delineating them, he said, "I mention these little items to show you what sort of organization and subordination has existed in these remote parts." (One would hardly suspect that the general had been born in Ohio.) Buell was studying the country and the enemy, and he assured the General in Chief, "I shall be prepared to do anything you think best after you hear what I propose to do, and I shall do nothing that you are not willing to assent to." And Buell had just spoken of peculiar subordination!

General Sherman, in conformity with the much advertised and surprising statement he had made to the Secretary of War, had told Buell that 200,000 men would be required to accomplish anything. But the new commander stated that he was willing to attempt something with a much smaller force. He thought it important that Halleck should strike at the time he struck, and then he said very deftly, "I think you will agree that his blow should await my preparation." He reported that the enemy was fortifying strongly at Bowling Green, where he could probably concentrate 20,000 to 25,000 men within three or four hours. Calmly he added, "As for his attacking, though I do not intend to be unprepared for him, yet I should almost as soon expect to see the Army of the Potomac marching up the road." The letter ended smugly, "If you have any unoccupied brigadiers—not my seniors(?)—send six or eight, even though they should be no better than marked poles." [23]

The next day Buell passed on to McClellan an unconfirmed report that Zollicoffer had crossed the Cumberland at Gainesboro, Tennessee, probably on the way to Bowling Green. However, the most important statement in his telegram was: "I have a letter from the Adjutant-General. Have you seen cause to curtail my discretion?" [24] Plainly he had not taken the movement on East Tennessee very seriously.

Two days later the General in Chief wrote, still pressing strongly for such a move and saying, "If there are causes which render this course impossible, we must submit to the necessity; but I still feel sure that a movement on Knoxville is absolutely necessary, if it is possible to effect it." Categorically he then made the important statement that not only political but strategical considerations rendered "a prompt movement on Eastern Tennessee imperative," the non-political part of the objective being the cutting of communications between it and the Mississippi Valley. In order that Buell might have sufficient strength, he had already ordered eight regiments to him from West Virginia, three from Ohio, and all available ones from

Indiana. In addition he intended to order to Kentucky early the next week two divisions from Missouri and some regiments from Illinois.[25] Halleck's protest that such a stripping of his department at the time would be dangerous has already been noted.

Perhaps before reading this letter, Buell received on November 27 a telegram from his "dear friend":

General: What is the reason for the concentration of troops at Louisville? I urge movement at once on Eastern Tennessee, unless it is impossible. No letter from you for several days. Reply. I still trust to your judgment, though urging my own views.[26]

It was not a steady message, and in spite of its peremptory beginning, Buell could reason from the concluding sentence that his judgment was being trusted not only in the matter of practicability of operations but in the choice of strategic objectives. His long reply of the same day explained that he preferred Lebanon to Lexington as a point of departure, and it could be easily supplied from Louisville. At the Kentucky city all things were under his eye, while he did not know what could be done from Cincinnati. Furthermore, the wagon road to Cumberland Gap through Somerset—which was a waypoint the two generals had chosen during their Washington talks—was just as short. However, he had begun to think of an operation toward Nashville, turning Buckner out of his Bowling Green position by marching through Glasgow and Gallatin. This operation could be either in conjunction with the one against East Tennessee, or quite independent of it. Then came a new and very important suggestion. In connection with the Nashville thrust there should be "two flotilla columns up the Tennessee and Cumberland, so as at least to land and unite near the State line, and cut off communications between Bowling Green and Columbus, and perhaps run directly into Nashville." A strong demonstration should be made simultaneously via the Mississippi against Columbus. Buell did not take the trouble to elaborate details, but said merely, "You can imagine them all."[27]

This letter makes it certain that the possibility of an operation up the Tennessee and the Cumberland had not been discussed by McClellan and Buell, and that the latter had acquired the idea after coming to his new station, where it may have been current. But his letter, like Whittlesey's concise message to Halleck on the 20th, made no reference to Forts Henry and Donelson, and he had referred rather casually on the 22nd to "some weak batteries on the Cumberland and Tennessee."

Two days later the letter was in Washington and threw McClellan into such an ecstasy that he telegraphed: "Your letter received. I fully approve of your course and agree in your views." [28] Still enthusiastic, he wrote that night, as if repentant for having ever doubted: "I now feel sure that I have a 'lieutenant' in whom I can fully rely. Your views are right. You have seized the true strategic base, and from Lebanon can move where you will." He enjoined Buell to keep up the hearts of the Tennesseans and make them feel that they were not being deserted but would be sustained, and directed, "Be sure to maintain their ardor, for it will avail you much in the future." Then his thoughts turned toward Nashville; and after asserting that as a general thing he was a believer in masses, he expressed the view that it might be possible to attempt two movements, one on East Tennessee, "with say 15,000 men," while the "strong attack" which Buell had proposed should be made against Nashville "with, say, 50,000 men." [29]

Back McClellan then wobbled to the mountains. He asserted that the Union friends in East Tennessee should be protected at all hazards, reaching something like a climax in the words: "First secure that; then, if you possess the means, carry Nashville." Visions of gunboat flotillas returned, and he assured Buell he would give him an ample number, and moreover he would place C. F. Smith under his orders. The real humor in the letter came near the end when he told his subordinate to let him know a little before he was ready to move, "so that we may move simultaneously." There were other "heavy blows" to be struck, but he did not think everything could be prepared for the "grand blows" in less than a month or six weeks. Said McClellan: "Unless circumstances render it necessary, do not strike until I too am ready." Suspecting perhaps that he would spend the winter comfortably in Washington, he added, "Should I be delayed, I will not ask you to wait for me."

The letter ended with the sentence, "I will at once take the necessary steps to carry out your views as to the rivers." More than six weeks were to pass before the roar of heavy guns echoed along the rivers; but it seems unquestionable that Buell deserves the credit for getting a movement up the Tennessee and the Cumberland definitely accepted by the High Command. It was, however, a meaningless acceptance, for when the blow was struck, it was without order or suggestion from Washington.

On December 3 McClellan was in great distress because of two letters from General Carter which Congressman Horace Maynard had placed in the President's hand. They were dated November 21 and 25. The second letter stated that all Carter's men were elated at the order to remain at London and hoped that unless there were pressing necessity there would be no new instructions to move to central Kentucky. "Will help ever come? I do not mean contingent aid, but special and direct," he wrote. The letters were sent to McClellan with characteristic indorsements: "Please read and consider this letter. A. L." McClellan forwarded them to Buell, saying with regard to the East Tennesseans, "Please send, then, with the least possible delay, troops enough to protect these men." It was more than sympathy for the Unionists that controlled McClellan, for he wrote, "I still feel sure that the best strategical move in this case will be that dictated by the simple feelings of humanity." It was proper for Lincoln to give no order; but the case is not so clear for McClellan, in spite of the fact that some deference had to be given to the subordinate nearer the scene of action. He later showed himself unequal to resolute decision and action as an army field commander; so now he may have been merely weakening before the grave responsibilities of a General in Chief. At least, instead of directing his subordinate, he sought to cajole him, by telling him that by seizing and retaining East Tennessee he would win brighter laurels than any he himself expected to gain. Having expressed his "utmost confidence and firmest friendship," McClellan added the postscript, "This letter has been dictated by no doubt as to your movements and intentions, but only by my feelings for the Union men of Eastern Tennessee." [30]

Two days later, still thinking of the move on Nashville, McClellan asked Buell as to the number of gunboats as well as the strength in land forces he would need for the southward thrust. He had that day ordered to Buell two fully armed cavalry regiments from Camp Dennison in Ohio, and would send more infantry from the Northwest, though the latter would obviously be a case of robbing Peter to pay Paul, and a protest from Halleck could have been anticipated. He was telling the East Tennesseans to rest quiet: Buell would take care of them and never desert them. His letter ended: "By all means hold

Somerset and London. Better intrench both; still better, the crossing of the river nearest these points." On the same day the General in Chief wired that he had telegraphed Halleck for information as to his gunboats and disposable troops; as soon as a reply was received, he would arrange details. Very much in earnest he seemed to be, for he directed: "Send me draught of water in Cumberland to Nashville and in Tennessee River." [31]

A reply to some of McClellan's queries went forward on the 10th. Inability to predict enemy reaction made it impossible, Buell said, to give details as to the river expeditions; probably no fewer than 10,000 men should ascend both streams, going as rapidly as possible to Fort Henry and Dover, where the first resistance would probably be encountered. Civilians were reporting Henry as strong, though he had not been able to learn the number of its guns, and seemed still more uncertain of the defenses on the Cumberland. He was, however, perfectly willing to coach his friend as to what Halleck—from whose department troops had been promised him—should do below Cairo: "The demonstration on Columbus and the Mississippi should at least be on such a scale that it can be converted into a real attack if they destroy anything; better still if it can attack in any event." [32]

It is doubtful whether Buell at this time seriously contemplated an effort in the direction of East Tennessee, though it was not until a month later that he unmasked to Lincoln so unmistakably as to draw from McClellan—who saw the letter—a statement of hurt surprise. For that length of time he engaged successfully in ambiguities. To a dispatch from Senator Andrew Johnson and Congressman Maynard, sent on the 7th after interviews with Lincoln and McClellan, he replied, "I assure you I recognize no more imperative duty and crave no higher honor than that of rescuing our loyal friends in Tennessee, whose sufferings and heroism I think I can appreciate." But he wrote on the 10th to McClellan that he thought the constancy of the East Tennesseans would "sustain them until the hour of deliverance," and said bluntly, "I have no fear of their being crushed." [33]

An operation like the one McClellan wished would undoubtedly have been difficult; but Buell, in spite of bad roads that would have been encountered and the supply problem involved, had not yet pronounced it impossible. Carter, who was informed of what had been done to block the various gaps, reported on November 28 that the unoccupied passes south of Williamsburg were obstructed only by rocks and felled trees; he believed an entry into the valley could be made through them. Zollicoffer spoke of roads that could not be traversed by an army train; but he himself requisitioned packsaddles, so that if he returned to the mountains he would have some freedom of movement. Buell may have been indifferent to East Tennessee in part because cutting the important East-West railroad at Knoxville would result in no great immediate advantage to himself. A movement on Nashville would be quite different, and from time to time he said enough about East Tennessee to make McClellan believe he also intended to do something in that direction. The irony of it all was that Sidney Johnston was not deceived. On November 27 he wrote to Secretary Benjamin that "two persons of respectability" from Louisville, entirely unknown to each other, gave information that made him believe the Federal force intended for East Tennesse was to be combined with that in his immediate front. Already he had so notified Major General George B. Crittenden at Morristown, about forty miles northeast of Knoxville, hoping that as a result he could send some of his force to Nashville.[34]

On the 9th Carter arrived at Somerset—thirty miles west of London—having moved as quickly as possible in response to a call from Schoepf, who seemed to be threatened by the appearance of Zollicoffer at near-by Mill Springs on the Cumberland. The Confederate commander not only had pulled Carter out of his position, but had reached what he reported as a fertile and well stocked region, with a gristmill and a sawmill, where he intended to "hut-up" for the winter. Actually he crossed the river, constructed what he reported as a strong position, and promised Johnston he would attempt to keep the enemy at Somerset and Columbia from uniting. The Tennessean's position was however precarious. Carter promptly reported that he could be captured if the Federal force at Somerset moved into his rear, and said by way of stimulus to Thomas, whose division headquarters were at Lebanon, "Unless there is a prospect of doing something very soon, I wish to return to my position in front of Cumberland Gap." On the 15th Thomas informed Buell that Schoepf thought Zollicoffer could be captured through joint action by himself and the brigade of Brigadier General J. T. Boyle, which was at Columbia. Apparently Buell was not interested; and on the 17th he wrote to McClellan: "Zollicoffer is either retiring across the Cumberland or is prepared to

do it at the approach of any superior force. Any formidable demonstrations against him would only harass my troops and derange my
plans. I am letting him alone for the present." Perhaps he recalled
how McClellan had allowed Joe Johnston to keep his outposts on
Munson's Hill, whence they could look across the Potomac into
Washington itself. But some action was to take place in the direction
of Bowling Green, and when the Thirty-second Indiana repulsed an
attack by a superior force at Rowletts Station Buell wrote very
happily, "The little affair in front of Munfordville was really one of
the handsomest things of the season." [35] It was the only action of the
season in his department—and the enemy caused it.

The people of East Tennessee were left to pay for the blow they
had struck not only to assist the Federal column they believed was
approaching, but to provide a diversion for McClellan himself. On
December 10, the day Buell wrote about the East Tennesseans being
sustained by their constancy, Brigadier General W. H. Carroll, who
had been called hastily from Memphis to Knoxville after the Union
uprising, telegraphed to Benjamin that a bridgeburner had been sentenced to be hanged the next day at noon. Following the grim announcement came the words: "Requires the approval of the President.
Please telegraph." The reply was brief: "Execute the sentence of your
court-martial on the bridge-burners. The law does not require any
approval by the President, but he entirely approves my order to hang
every bridge-burner you can catch and convict." Already without the
comfort of any Presidential approval two men had been "sustained"
by their necks; in all, five were so to perish. Many persons were put
in jail; some were transported to Tuscaloosa, Alabama.[36]

The discouraged Maynard complained to Thomas that the Federals were further from East Tennessee than when he had left Kentucky six weeks before. Bitterly he wrote: "There is shameful wrong
somewhere; I have not yet satisfied myself where. That movement so
far has been disgraceful to the country and to all concerned." [37]

In Missouri, Kentucky, and Tennessee, where neighbor was arrayed
against neighbor, brother against brother, and fathers sometimes
fighting sons, the fateful year was coming to a tangled end.

From New Orleans, Claiborne Jackson was reciting at length the
exploits of Sterling Price and urging that the major general of the
Missouri State Guards receive high Confederate command. To Price,

Jackson wrote that Davis undoubtedly wished the chief command beyond the Mississippi to go to Henry Heth, a West Pointer. But there was compensation to the Missourian for the lack of esteem in which he was held in Richmond: he enjoyed a high place in the affections of the Crescent City. He was told: "Six young ladies are now raising a subscription to purchase a sword for you, and in order that as many as possible may have a hand in it they allow no one to give over $1. You may therefore look out for a beautiful present from the young ladies of New Orleans." [38]

On December 20 Sidney Johnston, in something of a panic, telegraphed that large numbers of Federals were crossing the Green River; but the combined efforts of Davis, Benjamin, and Cooper could not reconcile his statement with other information that they had. The next day was cold and cloudy, and Johnston wrote hopefully that the fine weather of the past weeks was ending. Snow and rain seemed likely; bad roads would be on his side; a little rise in the Barren River would give him a good defensive line. Shortly afterward a letter from Benjamin told him that the requested $5,000 secret service money was in a Nashville bank awaiting his order. But nothing could be done in answer to his cry for arms. At romantic Nassau in the Bahamas there was indeed an "immensely valuable" cargo of very nice British weapons, and powder too; but unhappily a "Yankee gunboat" was cruising around outside. Accordingly the War Secretary said it would be necessary for the general to place his trust in a just cause and such means as were at hand. But even the means at hand were to be lessened, for Unionists with matches were busy in Nashville, as they had been in East Tennessee, and a large ordnance storehouse burned with all its equipment and records.[39]

In a long letter of the 24th to the governor of Mississippi asking for more troops, Johnston seemed to be a little optimistic in spite of everything and—if the Federals did not attack—held out the promise: "The North, embarrassed at home and menaced with war by England, will shrink, foiled, from the conflict, and the freedom of the South will be forever established." Christmas Day brought a further swell of contingent hopefulness, and he wrote to the governor of Tennessee, "If well re-enforced now, Tennessee, the valley of the Mississippi, and the Confederacy is safe." The same thought was transmitted to Richmond in the words: "The contest here must be relinquished for the winter by the enemy or a decisive blow soon struck; to make the latter is their true policy." But he still wanted a little Christmas present from Richmond and telegraphed about the promised brigade of Brigadier General John B. Floyd: "Let nothing prevent Floyd's brigade from coming here immediately." He would have done better to suggest that Floyd himself remain in his native state and not try his hand at warfare in the West. Some Virginia regiments would be a valuable addition to Johnston's force—54,004 present for duty out of an aggregate present of 68,368 and a present and absent of 91,988—but Floyd himself was not a military asset.[40]

As the month drew to a close there were some 2,000 Confederates in the gap through which so many pioneers had passed, never dreaming that it would one day be fortified against the movement eastward of soldiers of the United States. In Knoxville was General Carroll with an unarmed regiment and ten guns; a newly raised regiment was also there. Seven independent companies were scouring the country "collecting arms, and suppressing insurrections, etc." But East Tennessee was a powder keg, and Maine-born Colonel Danville Leadbetter wrote to Benjamin, "Notwithstanding the favorable aspect of things generally in East Tennessee the country is held by a slight tenure, and the approach of an enemy would lead to prompt insurrection of an aggravated character." The Unionists had champions among the supporters of the Confederacy who sent letters to President Davis asking for a milder policy, and an envoy to explain a confused and inaccurately reported situation. It was asserted that behind the wholesale arrests and unjust deportations there often lay personal feuds or the wish to settle an old grudge. Even Benjamin, uncompromising toward saboteurs, spoke up for the famous Parson Brownlow. The fiery editor of the *Knoxville Whig,* who could defend slavery by Holy Writ but thought the Union was of almost Divine origin, had seen his paper suppressed in October. In concealment in the mountains before the bridgeburning, he had surrendered himself under the promise of protection, stoutly asserting his innocence of all acts of sabotage; but he was put into jail and threatened with a court-martial. Against this Benjamin vigorously protested, declaring he would have to ask Davis for Brownlow's pardon if promises were not made good. From a crowded jail Brownlow himself was writing to the Confederate President as the year neared its end.[41]

The holiday spirit apparently also affected Buell. In a long letter to the Adjutant General about the over-all situation he stated that Unionist sentiment was strong in Kentucky, and was not confined to older people as had been previously reported. As evidence, he cited the fact that 20,000 troops, of the best material in the state, were being organized. Evidently he did not believe that Zollicoffer's eloquent proclamation to the people of southeastern Kentucky, asking, "How long will Kentuckians close their eyes to the contemplated ruin of their present structure of society?" had had much effect. Nor did he seem to be depressed by the fact that the Richmond Congress had voted Missouri and Kentucky into the Confederacy without their having proclaimed they had seceded. Buell—who reported 57,000 effectives out of a total of 70,000 men—stated that he intended to return Carter's brigade from Somerset to the vicinity of Cumberland Gap. But nothing aggressive was expected of it, for he frankly said, "The plan which I propose for the troops here is one of defense on the east and of invasion on the south." [42] This was a reversal of McClellan's original instructions; nor did it harmonize with his later letters.

Buell forgot his statement to the Adjutant General when he received McClellan's dispatch of the 29th from a sickbed, asking, "Can you tell me about when and in what force you will be in Eastern Tennessee?" An answer by telegraph was requested, and the department commander, undaunted by what he had said six days before to Lorenzo Thomas, replied: "I intend a column of 12,000 men, with three batteries for East Tennessee; but as I have telegraphed you, it is impossible to fix a time for it to be there, so much depends on the circumstances which may arise in the mean time." However, he assured McClellan that the first column would be followed by others, and added that the operation promised "great results," because it would attack the enemy in the rear.[43]

Buell did, nevertheless, appear to be about to make some move, for on the 29th he also sent a map to George Thomas—who a week before had told Schoepf he did not know his chief's plans—and directed him to carry out an operation against Zollicoffer that they had discussed at Lebanon a few days before.[44]

To sober and serious Henry Halleck there came on Christmas Day a cheering message from John Pope at Otterville: "Price in full retreat for Arkansas; says it is by order from Richmond. Passed Humansville on Saturday." The dispatch confirmed one which had arrived the day before, and it looked as if Price must be south of Springfield. Halleck broke into General Sigel's holiday by wiring him at Rolla: "Get all your troops ready for the field. The cavalry as soon as possible." And he ended a long letter to McClellan on the 26th, "If I receive arms in time to carry out my present plans in Missouri I think I shall be able to strongly re-enforce Cairo and Paducah for ulterior operations by the early part of February." [45] This was a very important pronouncement, and the prospective date is one to remember.

Though Halleck had made good progress in his month of command, he had new and vexing troubles in a wave of bridgeburning and other sabotage that had just broken out. On the 23rd he informed commanding officers at fourteen places that it was reported that there would be concerted attempts to destroy railroads and telegraph lines. "Shoot down every one making the attempt," was the grim climax. His letter of the 26th to McClellan enclosed a general order that he had published on the 22nd: Anyone caught in the act of burning a bridge or destroying a railroad or telegraph, was to be shot, and anyone accused of the crime was to be arrested, tried by a military commission, and, if found guilty, condemned to death. Towns and counties were to pay for repairs unless it could be shown that the superior force of the perpetrators had made it impossible to prevent the sabotage. It was an order that not all commanders would relish carrying out, and the general soon had to face the consequences of his order. On the 26th a dispatch from Palmyra stated that two bridge spans one hundred and fifty feet long had been burned on Christmas night. A force was in pursuit, but the officer reporting already had on hand thirty-three bridgeburners and accomplices and queried: "What shall I do with them? Have witnesses against them here." Halleck answered the next day with an order appointing a military commission to start work at Palmyra on the 30th. [46]

Also on December 26 General Sherman, who had returned from leave and had been placed in command at Benton Barracks with strict instructions, handed in a report about the troops he was preparing for the field. The tone was good; evidently he was a rested man. Of a battery he wrote: "I will cause it to be pushed in drill. The men have no swords or pistols, but these are not essential." [47] He had been saved once by a comprehending superior; now it would be up to him to show the stuff that was really in him.

Just before Christmas, Grant's command was extended, apparently at the suggestion of McClellan, to include not only the part of Kentucky west of the Cumberland, but also part of southern Illinois. In the enlarged District of Cairo he had—besides Smith's force at Paducah—14,374 men present for duty and twelve guns.[48] Being now in control of smuggler-infested Cave in Rock, Illinois, and officially a neighbor of Buell, Grant wrote to the Louisville commander, offering cooperation in general, and particularly in breaking up the illicit traffic across the Ohio. "Respectfully" he requested a copy of any orders that Buell had issued on the subject; but the records show no reply. Word from Columbus continued to reach him, however, and he wrote in a long letter to headquarters on the 29th, "I have had a man in Columbus last week who succeeded in completing a map of the enemy's works, which I have every reason to believe is as accurate as it is possible to get before Columbus falls into our possession." [49]

On December 30 Rawlins found time to write a very long and important letter. It was an answer to one of the 21st from Congressman Washburne, who was much disturbed by reports that Grant was intemperate. Rawlins said that he had found Grant "a strict abstinence man" when he himself reached Cairo, and he had been told by men who knew Grant well that such had been his habit for the past five or six years. He spoke of a few occasions when Grant had drunk with visitors or friends; *"but in no instance* did he drink enough to manifest it to any one who did not see him drink." At a dinner on a train given by the president of the Illinois Central Railroad, he had taken about half a glass of champagne, the fact of his drinking being "remarked simply because of his usual total abstinence." The amazing amount of work that he turned out "without the intervention of aides, or assistants" was a refutation of charges that had been made. That Grant had enemies would, said Rawlins, be doubted by no one who knew the efforts he had made "to guard against and ferret out frauds in his district." Rawlins referred Washburne to an inspector McClellan had sent to the district and remarked that the area of Grant's command had been about doubled soon after two general officers had visited Cairo in behalf of General Halleck. After going into the entire subject as it was personally known to him, he concluded by solemnly pledging himself to ask to be relieved of duty with Grant, or to resign his commission, in case his chief should "become an intemperate man." [50]

To General James Wilson, who was later to serve under Grant

as engineer officer and as a hard-fighting cavalry general, the letter of John Rawlins spoke for itself and required no comment.[51]

The month of December brought the Washington government face to face with the gravest possible decision. It began with public opinion in the United States and England thoroughly aroused over the *Trent* affair and the possibility of war between the two countries seemed to increase almost daily. If Britain should become a belligerent it was almost certain that France would follow; and, with the world's greatest navy and one of its finest armies actively supporting the Confederacy, the future of the nation would be very doubtful.

Soon after Captain Charles Wilkes of the United States Navy had caused the international crisis by removing Confederate Commissioners John Slidell and James M. Mason and their secretaries from the British packet *Trent,* a member of Lincoln's cabinet did an extraordinary thing that created a domestic crisis with a persisting aftermath. The report of the Secretary of War for the ebbing year would naturally be an important document; and in view of the revelations about War Department contracts made by a Congressional committee a difficult challenge faced Simon Cameron. He met it by inserting in his report sentences that would make a counterissue; then, without showing it to the President, he had it printed and sent copies to the postmasters in larger cities with instructions to release them to the press as soon as Lincoln should present his own message to Congress. Sensing something wrong, the public printer placed a copy of the document in the President's hands,[52] and he, upon reading it, was surprised to find near the end a paragraph suggesting the use of Negro troops. Cameron had not previously been arrayed with the radicals, and it is plain that his proposal and the means he employed to get it before the public were an effort to rally to his support the zealots who were still shouting for Frémont. He had badly transgressed in the matter of fundamental policy, and Lincoln directed that the pamphlets be recalled by telegraph. The story, however, of what had happened, with the inevitable distortions and inaccuracies that accompany so dramatic an incident, was told in Washington dispatches, and the original report was also published in the papers.[53] That there would be a new Secretary of War was evident; but the Pennsylvania politician and fixer was allowed to retain his rather uncomfortable position for about six weeks.

With the military, the political, and the foreign situations what they were, the preparation of a message to Congress was not a simple task. Of the *Trent* affair Lincoln said not a word; and he handled the slavery question conservatively and cautiously. The message brought strong commendation from Horace Greeley—who, Lincoln said, supported him only about half the time with his one-ton words; [54] but he thought it necessary to remind the President that in certain basic particulars he was inferior to President Davis at Richmond. Noting that Davis had recently sent a message to the "rival conclave" in Richmond, Greeley recorded that he was "quite commonly presumed to be the abler of the two," was certainly the better grammarian, and could "use the English language with decided perspicuity and force." Then Greeley dropped some block-busters for the benefit of Lincoln. Davis's message had been "truculent, sanguinary, demoniac," while Lincoln was not moved even by such an "unseemly display of rage and malignity to use harsh inculpations." Commending Lincoln's message of the 3rd for its brevity, and asserting that it would be universally and intently read, Greeley quoted the part dealing with slaves and slavery and said, "The spirit of this is admirable, and will command general approval." [55] Two days later a long editorial set forth in strong terms his contention that the sole real objective of the war was the maintenance of the Union and the authority of its government, and stated emphatically that there should be no question of arming fugitive slaves until all white volunteers were effectively equipped. "We lack evidence," he wrote, "that the material exists for Black regiments of Unionists, any more than of Indians, that would be worth their cost." [56]

In spite, however, of the mildness of Lincoln's statements, and the volleys of Greeley against Cameron's ill-timed proposal, the Confederates made full use of all that was given them to lessen Union sentiment in the border states, and the outright Northern radicals took Cameron into their fold as one who would make war according to their formula.

The month wore on, and at ten o'clock on Christmas Day the cabinet assembled to decide upon an answer to the final British note, which, though courteous in tone, admitted of nothing but an unequivocal "Yes" or "No" to the demand for the surrender of Mason and Slidell. Of the seven cabinet members, only Blair and Seward favored giving the men up when the discussion began. The President's position has been disputed. It was not easy to surrender two prisoners whom people in the North regarded as they did the Confederate Commissioners. At two o'clock the disagreeing men adjourned to eat their Christmas dinners and think alone about the problem. Actually it was not just a matter of expediently swallowing pride and honor, for Captain Wilkes had delivered into Lincoln's power something far more valuable than two ardent and upper-level secessionists. Though in taking them from the British packet he had violated a principle for which the United States had always stood, England in protesting the act had repudiated a position to which she had held steadily, and which had been one of the chief causes of the War of 1812. Seward had been abusing and baiting England and had seemed eager for an excuse for war; but he saw that compliance with her demand would embarrass and humiliate her. The masterful reply that he had written, and that the cabinet accepted the next day, spoke effectively not only to the British but to the aroused American public, which had to be convinced not only of the rightness but of the logic of the momentous decision. After explaining in smooth words how certain principles had been "laid down for us in 1804, by James Madison, when Secretary of State in the administration of Thomas Jefferson, in instructions given to James Monroe, our Minister to England," he wrote, quite as if there had never been the least thought of war: "The four persons in question are now held in military custody at Fort Warren in the State of Massachusetts. They will be cheerfully liberated. Your lordship will please indicate a time and place for receiving them." By strict adherence to principle a significant victory had been won, and every Englishman had a chance to reflect whether the preparations of the British fleet for war, the movement of troops to embarkation points, and the country's sharp demand harmonized with its historic practice. It was not strange that Mason and Slidell failed to receive an ovation as great heroes, or that British officialdom was very cool to them.[57]

In the North approval of the final decision was mingled in some minds with humiliation; in the South there had to be an outward show of approval, for open condemnation was obviously out of the question. While a smile on the face of a Northerner would have looked like sympathy for an enemy, one on the countenance of a thoughtful Southerner was certainly a mask; for Commissioners Mason and Slidell could do their cause most good when securely locked in a bleak Yankee jail. From Slidell's own dearly beloved New Orleans, Claiborne Jackson wrote to Sterling Price that Lincoln had "backed down"; and he certainly was not rejoicing over the release of the commissioners when he added, "just what everybody here thought the cowardly scamp would do." [58]

The foreign crisis had been met, but troubles aplenty remained for the President. The General in Chief was ill; and though Lincoln knew one item of the western program he apparently had not been informed of the contemplated cooperation between Buell and Halleck. On this subject he telegraphed both generals on December 31, his message to the St. Louis commander reading: "General McClellan is sick. Are General Buell and yourself in concert? When he moves on Bowling Green, what hinders it being re-enforced from Columbus? A simultaneous movement by you on Columbus might prevent it." [59] Seeing the great advantage for his own forces in the railroads from Cincinnati and Louisville to Lexington, Lincoln realized also the strategical possibilities for the enemy in the fast, all-weather rail route from Columbus to Bowling Green. A railway could not have been devised to strengthen better the Confederate line of defense, and already Johnston had been counting upon it. When he was apprehensive of an attack on December 18 he wired to Polk to send 5,000 of his best infantry by rail at once; and Polk—also in line with the President's thought of immobilizing the Columbus troops by a threat —objected to doing this because he himself expected an attack.[60] Lincoln, one notes, said nothing about a movement in the direction of Knoxville, or about one up the Tennessee and Cumberland rivers. Although he was expecting the first operation to be made, there was no reason for mentioning it. Failure to refer to the rivers, is, however, significant, and indicates that on the last day of the year he had no thought of a movement up the Tennessee River.

Lack of plans for the great army then encamped about Washington and uncertainty about any program whatever for united action by the forces in the Departments of the Missouri and Ohio, would have been military trouble enough for the President. But he also had a badly disaffected commander in the Department of Kansas. On December 23 Hunter had written to him a letter which began:

I am deeply mortified, humiliated, insulted and disgraced. You did me the honor to select me as a Major General and I am confident you intended I should have a Major General's command. Yet strange as it may appear I am sent here into banishment, with not three thousand effective men under my command, while one of the Brigadiers, General Buell, is in command of near one hundred thousand in Kentucky. The only sin I have committed is my carrying out your views in relation to the retrograde movement from Springfield.[61]

He referred to correspondence with McClellan, who, he wrote, had explained that it was thought best that there should be in Missouri a commander not previously identified with the situation there; but McClellan had done nothing to explain why a brigadier received the assignment to the Department of the Ohio, rather than himself.

Unquestionably Hunter had a valid grievance; but his reference to his "only sin" was not happy, especially after he had written that he was in full agreement with the views that Lincoln had expressed as to the use of the troops that Frémont had taken to Springfield. Nor was he justified in concluding with a near-demand for an explanation of why he had not been sent to Kentucky, if political considerations made it inexpedient for him to remain in Missouri.

Replying on the last day of the year, Lincoln did not dip his pen into the bottle of mild ink that Seward had used in writing to his "lordship" the British Ambassador, but began, "Yours of the 23d is received, and I am constrained to say it is difficult to answer so ugly a letter in good temper." He admitted losing confidence in Hunter on account of "the flood of grumbling dispatches and letters" from him; but he did not do very well in explaining what the general wished to have explained. He asserted that he had thought and still thought the command assigned to Hunter was as responsible and as honorable as that given to Buell—a contention that is difficult to support. His statement that he knew "General McClellan expected more important results from it" does not agree with what McClellan wrote to Buell —though that may be neither here nor there. Poetry came to the assistance of the struggling President, and he quoted, "Act well your part; there all the honor lies." He concluded with a little original preachment cut to the occasion: "He who does something at the head of one regiment will eclipse him who does nothing at the head of a hundred."[62] As a platitudinous military maxim it may have had value; as a prophecy it was not too bad, for both McClellan and Buell would be on the benches before ten months had passed, and Hunter would still be in the field. Lincoln may have had in mind that Buell had done nothing yet in the direction of East Tennessee. If so, he is not to be criticized for also rapping incidentally the sick McClellan, commanding nearly two hundred regiments in the Army of the Potomac.[63]

Thus did tragic 1861 merge into uncertain 1862, while the serene Ohio poured into the majestic Mississippi waters in which were mingled those of the Cumberland and the Tennessee.

CHAPTER VII

AN UNPLANNED SUNDAY
AT A CROSSROADS

Alacrity, daring, courageous spirit, and patriotic zeal on all occasions and under every circumstance are expected from the Army of the United States.   *Stanton*

A MONTH was to pass before Commodore Foote with four new ironclads and the faithful *Tyler, Lexington,* and *Conestoga* led Grant's transports up the Tennessee against Fort Henry. However eager we may be to see the gunboats knock out the fort and the army take Fort Donelson, we cannot pass over January, 1862, with cursory remarks. Within the month George Thomas would fight and win a minor though important battle not far from Somerset, in which the brave and energetic Zollicoffer would be killed. In western Kentucky an important demonstration by Grant would throw his troops into the field on bad roads and in disagreeable weather and give all elements of the command, from the general and his staff down through his subordinates and their staffs to the lowest private, experience in advanced maneuver that was practiced so extensively in World War II before troops were committed to hard operations—only it was more realistic because a real enemy was near at hand.

January also was of great importance to the High Command. With a sick General in Chief and a Secretary of War who would soon be replaced, Lincoln had to play a personal part for a number of days in the problem of war plans. The telegrams to Halleck and Buell on

December 31 were followed with brief ones the next day, informing each that he was writing to the other that night. The letter to Halleck began: "General McClellan is not dangerously ill, as I hope, but would better not to be disturbed with business. I am very anxious that, in case of General Buell's moving toward Nashville, the enemy shall not be greatly re-enforced, and I think there is danger he will be from Columbus." The President believed that a feigned attack on the latter place from "up-river" would either prevent what he feared "or compensate for it by throwing Columbus" into Federal hands. He had written to Buell, he said, and he wanted the two generals to "communicate and act in concert." He was careful to state that everything was subject to their judgment, and he said, "You and he will understand better than I how to do it." But the closing sentence, "Please do not lose time in this matter," revealed a feeling of urgency that could not escape Halleck.[1]

Answering the short message of the 31st, Buell telegraphed that he had no arrangement with Halleck, but McClellan "would make suitable disposition for concerted action." There was nothing, he asserted, to keep Columbus from reenforcing Bowling Green unless it were itself attacked. Lincoln's second dispatch having probably arrived, he wired at eleven o'clock on the night of January 1 that he had telegraphed Halleck with a view to concert of action and was momentarily expecting a reply. Before hearing from Louisville, however, the St. Louis commander had wired Washington: "I have never received a word from General Buell. I am not ready to co-operate with him. Hope to do so in a few weeks. Have written fully on this subject to Major-General McClellan. Too much haste will ruin everything." [2]

So the year began with messages that could not have been very encouraging to the President; but he had started the two western generals working directly with each other. On the 2nd Halleck informed Buell that all his troops were in the field, except those at Cairo and Paducah, and these were, he said, "barely sufficient to threaten Columbus, etc." Though in a few weeks he hoped to render Buell very material assistance, a withdrawal of any of his troops from Missouri was at the time "almost impossible." "Write me fully," was the cordial ending. The genuineness of his desire to cooperate was shown by his forwarding some information that had come in from C. F. Smith about the reenforcement of Bowling Green.

Then presently he broke down department lines and told Buell to make direct contact with Smith.[3]

Buell responded to Halleck's gesture by writing at length on the 3rd. The enemy, he stated, probably had 80,000 men, and their railroad facilities gave them the possibility of making a concentration within a few hours. The center of their defensive line was where the railroad crossed the Cumberland and Tennessee rivers, and Buell said, "The attack upon the center should be by two gunboat expeditions, with, I should say, 20,000 men on the two rivers." Breaking the railroad was set down as the real objective, but although Buell referred to Fort Henry and a battery at Dover he did not elaborate on their strength, probably because he did not know too much about them. Whatever was done, "should be done speedily, within a few days," for the task would "become more difficult every day." "Please let me hear from you at once," was Buell's friendly ending.[4]

Although he ended his message to Lincoln with an abrupt warning of the danger of haste, Halleck had made a good start toward getting his home front under control. His first general order of the year, issued on New Year's Day, sought to instruct officers about the difference between courts-martial and military commissions. Only the latter could consider offenses by civilians, and treason "as a distinct offense" was not triable even by a commission, for it is "defined by the Constitution, and must be tried by courts duly constituted by law." Nevertheless "certain acts of a treasonable character," such as spying, were punishable by military authorities, and guerrillas should be punished as Napoleon had punished them in Spain and Scott in Mexico. Although the proceedings of all military commissions were to be sent to him for possible revision, Halleck was in no way appeasing, and he wrote to a citizen of St. Louis who believed that sufficient overtures had not been made to Sterling Price: "The time for conciliation, I am sorry to say, has passed. Nothing but the military power can put down the rebellion and save Union men in this State. It is useless now to try any other remedy." [5]

The health of his command was just as essential for offensive operations as equipment and discipline; and the wide circle of Halleck's concern is indicated by a long report addressed to him on January 3 by the president of the Sanitary Commission in St. Louis. This not only traced the great progress that had been made in the condition of troops and the facilities for hospitalization, but spoke of the fine response to appeals for articles the government did not furnish, which would promote the comfort and morale of the sick and the convalescing. From Massachusetts alone more than one hundred and fifty boxes of supplies had been received.[6]

Lincoln himself broke matters open by a short telegram to Buell on the 4th: "Have arms gone forward for East Tennessee? Please tell me the progress and condition of the movement in that direction. Answer." Evasion was no longer possible, and the next day Buell telegraphed candidly and at length. Arms, he said, could go into East Tennessee only under the protection of an army, and plans contemplated the movement of a division from Lebanon, while a brigade simultaneously operated on the Cumberland Gap route. Transportation was a serious difficulty, and the arms—"foreign ones, requiring repairs"—had arrived little more than a week before, and were then being put in order by the ordnance officer. Then Buell said that while he earnestly wished to carry out the operation, his judgment had "from the first been decidedly against it, if it should render at all doubtful the success of a movement against the great power of the rebellion in the West." This power, he said, was mainly arrayed on the line from Columbus to Bowling Green, and it could "speedily be concentrated at any point of that line which is attacked singly." [7]

On the 6th Lincoln replied at length by letter, expressing both disappointment and distress. He had shown Buell's dispatch to McClellan, who would also write. Then he continued:

I am not competent to criticize your views, and therefore what I offer is merely in justification of myself. Of the two, I would rather have a point on the railroad south of Cumberland Gap than Nashville—first, because it cuts a great artery of the enemy's communications, which Nashville does not; and secondly, because it is in the midst of loyal people, who would rally around it, while Nashville is not. Again, I cannot see why the movement on East Tennessee would not be a diversion in your favor rather than a disadvantage, assuming that a movement toward Nashville is the main object.

There was more to it than that, and the President said: "But my distress is that our friends in East Tennessee are being hanged and driven to despair, and even now I fear are thinking of taking rebel arms for the sake of personal protection. In this we lose the most valuable stake we have in the South." Lincoln had, he explained, sent his dispatch of the 4th with the knowledge of Senator Andrew Johnson and Representative Maynard. They would be "upon" him for an answer, and he could not "safely" show them Buell's dispatch, lest they despair, "possibly resign, to go and save their families somehow or die with them." Yet, in spite of the intensity of his feeling, Lincoln refrained from dictation to his general and he concluded, "I do not intend this to be an order in any sense, but merely, as intimated before, to show you the grounds of my anxiety." [8]

McClellan agreed with Lincoln, and wrote to Buell in a letter marked "Confidential": "I was extremely sorry to learn from your telegram to the President that you had *from the beginning attached little or no importance* to a movement in East Tennessee. I had not so understood your views, and it develops a radical difference between your views and my own, which I deeply regret." His ideas were in fact more emphatic than the President's, and he regarded the cutting of the railway in East Tennessee as a matter "of absolute necessity," while Bowling Green and Nashville were of "very secondary importance" at the moment. The movement that he was contemplating for the Army of the Potomac could not be made until Buell's troops were "solidly established in the eastern part of Tennessee." "If that is not possible," he continued, "a complete and prejudicial change in my own plans at once becomes necessary." All this increases the mystery as to the actual intentions McClellan had for the great army he himself commanded. A few weeks before, he had merely told Buell not to delay his advance because of any slowness in the Army of the Potomac. Now it was definitely a question of "You first." After noting that Halleck could not properly support a movement up the Cumberland in the near future, McClellan asked, "Why not make the movement [into East Tennessee] independent of and without waiting for that?" [9]

On the same day Halleck was confirming McClellan's statement; after explaining to Buell his situation in detail he repeated that probably in a few weeks he could help a move up the rivers, and he suggested that an advance on Bowling Green be postponed if cooperation were necessary. He might have said more, for there had been considerable delay in the building of the ironclad gunboats on which so much depended, in spite of work "night and day and Sundays." At the moment Halleck could not have told when they would be finished and accepted. In addition, crews were lacking.[10]

On this letter-writing day Grant also put an important sentence into the record. After informing Kelton that fresh word from Columbus indicated the garrison had been reduced probably to thirty regiments, that the Confederates had stretched a chain across the Mississippi, and that there were torpedoes (mines) in the river both above and below Columbus, he said in conclusion: "If it meets with the approval of the general commanding the department, I would be pleased to visit headquarters on business connected with this command." What was the business? In his *Memoirs* Grant said he wished to discuss with Halleck a movement up the Tennessee.[11] It was four months to the day since he had seized Paducah; and, with his knowledge of the reconnaissances that the *Conestoga* had been making of Fort Henry, there is no reason whatever to doubt the statement.

Now, however, as a result of the predicament into which Buell had got himself, confusion was to be confounded. Though the morning of the 8th brought a note from Halleck, it was written before the receipt of Grant's request to visit St. Louis, and it directed him to make a major demonstration. After having written that it would be a few weeks before he could support a movement on Bowling Green, Halleck decided on the 6th that he could at least create a diversion. Taking at face value Buell's statement that whatever was done should be done "speedily, within a few days," he lost no time in directing Grant to make a threat in the direction of Mayfield and Murray that would give the impression that Dover was the objective. Deception was to be employed to the limit, and Halleck said, "Make a great fuss about moving all your forces towards Nashville, and let it be so reported by the newspapers." Grant's own men were to be fooled, and no member of his staff was to know what was really planned. Halleck promised to send reenforcements and told his subordinate to spread abroad the word that 20,000 or 30,000 more men were coming from Missouri. The object of the move was clearly stated: it was to prevent the dispatch of reenforcements to Buckner at Bowling Green. Quite as if he thought that Buell was all but ready to move, Halleck wired him on the 7th: "Designate a day for a demonstration. I can do nothing more. See my letter of yesterday." [12]

The President was in distress. Accepting the thought that nothing could be done in the direction of East Tennessee, and that the Army of the Potomac would continue in idleness, he telegraphed to Buell on the 7th: "Please name as early a day as you safely can on or before which you can be ready to move southward in concert with Major-General Halleck. Delay is ruining us, and it is indispensable for me to have something definite. I send a like dispatch to Major-General Halleck." In St. Louis the hours wore on, and at midnight Halleck telegraphed to Lincoln: "I have asked General Buell to designate a day for a demonstration to assist him. It is all I can do till I get arms. I have no arms. I have sent two unarmed regiments to assist in the feint. I wrote you yesterday and will write again to-night." [13] Already it was practically "tomorrow." When did Halleck's work day end? Apparently exhaustion or some other pressing duty in connection with troubled Missouri intruded, for the promised letter appears not to have been written.

Grant went into high speed at once and reported on the night of the 8th that Foote would cooperate with three gunboats, while two more would go up the Tennessee as convoy for an infantry battalion and two guns. Smith would march on Mayfield, where the cavalry from Cairo and two infantry regiments would probably join him. He saw clearly the difficulty of making a threat at Dover but said that Smith would maneuver to make it appear that Murray and probably Dover were "the points in greatest danger." No instructions for the column from Cairo had been prepared, but he would go with it; and he might have to deviate from any plan that could be set down at the moment. The continuous rains of the past week promised heavy roads, but he thought the adverse conditions would "operate worse" on the enemy, in case "he should come out to meet us." It might have cheered Lincoln to know he had a general who could reason in that way; and he certainly would have liked the ending: "This movement will be commenced to-morrow, and every effort made to carry out your design." [14]

Halleck could not have expected such promptness, but "General Weather" was to intervene. The next morning there was a dense fog, and—the river not having yet responded to the rains—a steamer had grounded at Dogtooth Bend, twenty miles above Cairo, and had swung around, completely blocking the narrow channel. This would prevent the arrival of reenforcements, and Grant reported that his movement would be deferred a day, to January 10. When that day came Halleck wired Buell that troops at Cairo and Paducah were ready to start (Grant's return for that day showed a total of 20,679 present for duty in six stations, and eighteen field guns), asked again for a day to be set for Grant's demonstration, and requested that it be delayed as long as possible, so that he might use more troops. A message to Grant told him to wait for another dispatch. The wire brought no response from Louisville, and the impatient Halleck telegraphed Grant on Saturday the 11th: "I can hear nothing from Buell, so fix your own time for the advance. Three regiments will go down on Monday." [15] Perhaps he should have prodded Buell with another message; but at least he was not seeking an excuse to keep his men idling even in bad weather.

Buell had won the case for a move toward Nashville—the President's telegram of the 7th showed that; but he may have felt a little guilty when he read on the 12th McClellan's letter of the 6th. He telegraphed: "I have received your letter, and will at once devote all my efforts to your views. Will write tonight." It was already eleven o'clock, and the long letter he wrote to McClellan was dated the 13th. He had not meant that his dispatch to the President should imply that he attached "little importance to the movement on East Tennessee." After noting that his recent activities had drawn the enemy's attention away from East Tennessee as a threatened point, and thus were really all to the good, Buell said, "As I told you in my dispatch, I shall now devote myself to it, contenting myself, as far as Bowling Green is concerned, with holding it in check and concealing my design as long as possible." A move toward Knoxville was certainly not a thing to contemplate with pleasure, and a postscript to the letter expressed Buell's view regarding some unnamed colonel who would enter East Tennessee with 5,000 men and three batteries, supplied by pack mules, and end the war while the rest of the armies looked on.[16]

Buell forgot about his colleague in St. Louis or, if he thought of him, believed he would make no move until he himself set a day for Grant's demonstration. For this he deserves a black mark: obviously he should have released Halleck from standing by and striving to increase the effectiveness of his demonstration—especially since he knew Halleck had also received a telegram from Lincoln beseeching action. Grant was in fact already on his way when he received his chief's instructions of the 10th to await further word. He then put on a restraining hand, but when the three regiments from

St. Louis did not appear as promised—because of ice in the river—
he resumed without them.[17]

The telegram from the penitent Buell caused Lincoln some regret,
and he wrote that he would blame him if he carried out ideas he
disapproved. Buell would realize, said the President, his duty in
regard to the views of McClellan better than himself. Then Lincoln
sketched his thinking about the war and indulged in some strategical
pronouncements. East Tennessee clearly posed a hard problem, and
he expressed anxiety because the line there was "so long and over so
bad a road." Although a concurrent move toward Bowling Green
was clearly approved, East Tennessee was still the ardently desired
target.[18] It is notable that Lincoln again said nothing about a move
up the Tennessee or Cumberland; in fact, if Columbus should become
a prize, it would be taken as the result of a movement directly against
it. An indorsement indicates that a copy of the letter went to
Halleck—an important fact, showing that in mid-January he still
had no "up-the-Tennessee" instructions from the White House.

Buell's telegram raised no regrets in McClellan's mind, and the
General in Chief, who expected to be in the saddle again in a few
days, wrote:

You have no idea of the pressure brought to bear here upon the Government for a forward movement. It is so strong that it seems absolutely
necessary to make the advance on Eastern Tennessee at once. I incline
to this as a first step for many reasons. Your possession of the railroad
there will surely prevent the main army in my front from being re-
enforced and may force Johnston to detach. Its political effect will be
very great.[19]

There is no reason to believe that McClellan did not feel deeply
and earnestly about the East Tennesseans, or to doubt that he desired
their prompt liberation. Nevertheless he was certainly influenced by
his own problem as commander of the Army of the Potomac. Joe
Johnston at Manassas, with a force greatly exaggerated by the
Pinkerton agents, obviously disturbed him. Some day he would have
to fight a battle himself; and that was a different matter from planning high strategy, and ordering a subordinate to move to the attack.
The problem that faced him as General in Chief was not simple; but
an objective for Buell should have been based solely on military and
political considerations, without too much personal solicitude for the
commander of the Army of the Potomac.

McClellan's early thought of strengthening Buell at Halleck's expense still persisted. Actually, however, Buell suggested that some new cavalry regiments, scheduled to come to him, should instead be sent to Paducah and Cairo. Quoting his telegram, the Adjutant General asked Halleck, "Does it meet your views?" Grant also apprised Halleck of what was going on when he reported that Colonel T. H. Cavanaugh, in command of a cavalry regiment at Shawneetown, had been ordered to Springfield to organize a cavalry brigade for service with Buell. He had given the colonel a leave of absence, but had told him his regiment could not be moved without an order from the department commander. Cavanaugh had professed a "decided preference" for duty where he was; but Grant said he gave the preference no attention; the colonel should go where ordered.[20]

In addition to being threatened with the loss of troops from his department at a time when he was trying to build up for operations, Halleck had to intervene to save General Smith. Originally McClellan seemed to be favorable toward Smith; and he had responded to Buell's November suggestion about a move up the Tennessee and Cumberland by saying he would place Smith under him. Then presently he inquired, "Would not C. F. Smith be a good man to command that part of the expedition?" Buell's reply expressed no enthusiasm: "I have not seen Smith for seven years, and am afraid to judge him. I have never rated him as highly as some men." Smith was a rigid disciplinarian, and this had brought the inevitable consequence, for in mid-January Halleck wrote to Lorenzo Thomas about newspaper criticism and agitation to replace him. He had sent two generals and a colonel to Paducah to investigate, and they had reported that the fault in the controversies between Smith and subordinates lay with the latter—an opinion Halleck said he understood was shared by Grant. McClellan, in spite of his earlier apparent regard for Smith, had intruded; but Halleck, unyielding and unruffled, wrote: "I was not aware that any formal report of this matter was expected of me or I should have reported some time ago. That part of General McClellan's orders to place General Grant in command of the district was executed, but the part relating to the withdrawal of General Smith was suspended."[21]

On January 14 Halleck affixed his name to General Order No. 20, a long and grim document that summarized the cases of men tried by the Palmyra commission for treason and bridgeburning. Sentences of six men found guilty of treason were set aside, the charges being pronounced "not triable by a military commission." Approval was, however, given to death by shooting meted out to eight bridgeburners. But Halleck had no zest for taking life, and he left the date of the execution to be fixed later, apparently hoping that sabotage would be stopped without resorting to firing squads. There was to be no foolery in the confinement of the sentenced men, and he ordered, "Any one attempting to escape will be instantly shot down." [22]

Even as Halleck was reviewing the commission's work, disturbing reports came from scouts and spies in the southwest, and Halleck wrote to McClellan that it appeared that Price's retreat was "a ruse, intended to deceive us." Another letter also dated the 14th concluded, "Unless Price is driven from the State, insurrections will continually occur in all the central and northern counties, so as to prevent the withdrawal of our troops." [23]

Then, with Grant starting forth on his demonstration and orders on the way for Curtis to move from Rolla against Price, with his 12,000 infantry and his thirty-five to forty guns, General Halleck blushingly took to his bed with a favorite ailment of common soldiers —measles.

Buell's repentance seems to have been sincere; at least his instructions to George Thomas soon indicated that an advance on Bowling Green had been abandoned, with a plan for East Tennessee the order of the day. His letter of December 29 had directed an operation that either would deal a severe blow to Zollicoffer at Beech Grove on the Cumberland across from Mill Springs, or would alarm the Confederate general and cause him to retire. The operation was to be carried out in concert with Albin Schoepf's brigade at Somerset. It would please Schoepf, who was greatly annoyed because the enemy he had defeated at Rockcastle River was having a comfortable time in a region of comparative plenty, within easy reach of the Tennessee capital. He reported—perhaps exaggerating—the large amount of "bacon, wheat, corn, etc." stored on the farm of a Captain West south of the Cumberland, and said "their main transportation train at Mill Springs, consisting of 1,000 wagons, horses, mules, and cattle, is certainly an object of acquisition." He also sent a detailed sketch to Thomas and explained how a battery emplaced at "point A" on a high hill that commanded both Mill Springs and Beech Grove, would render Zollicoffer's position untenable.[24]

J. T. Boyle, the Federal brigadier at Columbia, was just as offended at Zollicoffer's comfort. He reported that a boat had passed Burkesville the day before, laden with men, cannon, and small arms, as well as clothing, and brought up the possibility of breaking up such traffic. Then he became a bit sarcastic: "If we delay much longer the enemy will have time to bring his re-enforcements from Texas and Louisiana." Lacking cannon, Boyle's men had to rely on "rifles to take off the men from the boats," which was certainly a tedious and inefficient way of dealing with the situation. The vindictive Federal asserted, "With one piece of artillery the boats could be torn to atoms or sunk." [25]

But it was not easy to get a gun to Burkesville or to put a battery at point A. On January 13, Thomas, en route to Somerset, began a letter to Buell: "After two days of the hardest work I have reached this place, 16 miles from Columbia, with the advance brigade of my division; the provision and ammunition train, with a portion of our brigade, is still in the rear, and will probably not reach here to-night." The usually quiet-spoken Virginian may have been saying things about what was marked a "good road" on the map Buell had sent him, which he pronounced the worst road he had ever seen—the recent rains having turned it into "a continuous quagmire" all the way from Columbia. Nor did he have the consolation that the worst was over, for his scouts reported that the shortest road to the enemy—still seventeen miles away—was "much worse than the roads" he had yet seen. Since Thomas had had a visit from Buell just before receiving the order of December 29, he must have known that his chief was contemplating a move against Sidney Johnston. So, after noting that Schoepf had sufficient force to stalemate Zollicoffer, he suggested that he himself proceed at once to Jamestown and thence to Burkesville, from where he could aid an operation aimed at Bowling Green.[26]

Buell, chagrined perhaps at the adverse report about the "good road," acted on the 16th to make Somerset more accessible. He ordered Brigadier General T. J. Wood at Bardstown—well known for its old inn, its distilleries, and its cathedral with canvases by great masters—to pick up a brigade at Lebanon, hasten to Danville, and start building a corduroy road sixteen feet wide toward Somerset, with the 1,000 axes, picks, shovels, and spades that would arrive the next day. The soldier so unceremoniously turned into a road-builder was told that construction would also start at once from the other end. The next day Buell informed Thomas about the road building, and optimistically said it should be finished in a few days. He stated that it was not sufficient to hold Zollicoffer in check; his force was to be captured or dispersed. Without the least intimation of his recent promises to Washington, Buell dashed any hopes that Thomas might be entertaining for a move on Bowling Green, and probably surprised him by closing his letter, "You could not march to Burkesville, and it is not desirable that you should be there." [27]

So Thomas struggled on through the mud, and the 17th found him at Logan's Crossroads, ten miles north of Beech Grove and eight miles west of Somerset. With him were parts of two brigades, a battery, and a battalion of cavalry, while another battery and four regiments were in the rear, "detained by the almost impassable condition of the road." He intended to remain in the position until his rear regiments caught up; but he directed Schoepf, who had ridden out to meet him, to make good their temporary absence by sending the Twelfth Kentucky and the First and Second Tennessee regiments from Somerset.[28] Thomas may not have fully decided just what his future action would be. He was saved all trouble of decision by an attack early on the morning of the 19th by Major General G. B. Crittenden—who had recently superseded Zollicoffer—delivered in the mistaken belief that the badly swollen Fishing Creek would prevent any of Schoepf's command from joining that of Thomas.

The new Confederate commander—acting in conformity with the views of his subordinates—marched out of Beech Grove at midnight with two brigades of eight regiments, six guns, and something over a battalion of horse.[29] A Southern brigadier probably understated the fact when he wrote in his report: "The night was dark and gloomy; a cold rain was constantly descending, rendering the march extremely difficult and unpleasant." [30] Slowly over the almost impassable road, with infantrymen aiding the progress of the guns through the mud, the column made its way toward the camp of sleeping Federals. The uncertain daylight of a gloomy Sunday morning had come when they encountered some Federal cavalry and then infantry pickets. Exhausted though they were by their hours of heavy marching, the Confederates enjoyed the advantage of surprise and the exhilarating effect of early success as they forced the Union outguards back toward the picket reserve.

The battle that followed was not a large one, but it was sharp and led to a decisive result. Since it has always been claimed by some, recently with new vigor, that Thomas was discriminated against be-because of his Virginian birth,* and that his real merits were never fully recognized, this first of the two battles in which he was the responsible commander will be considered in detail.

A courier from Colonel Frank Wolford's First Kentucky Cavalry, which in accordance with Thomas's orders, began exploring at day-light toward Mill Springs, carried the word of the enemy advance to Colonel Mahlon D. Manson, commanding the Second Brigade. The Tenth Indiana, commanded by Lieutenant Colonel William C. Kise, had two picket companies forward on the road, and at 6:30 a messenger also reached him. Then immediately the firing of Kise's outpost announced the opening of the engagement. "The long roll quickly brought the Tenth Regiment into ranks," wrote Kise, who at once sent a third company to join the two already in advance. Presently he followed with the remainder of his regiment on explicit orders from Manson. Whether it was Manson's own decision to turn the outpost line into the main line of resistance, or whether it was in accordance with previous instructions from Thomas, cannot be said with certainty; but it looks as if the credit belongs to Manson. "A regiment of rebels were advancing in line of battle and their treason-able colors were seen flaunting in the breeze," wrote Kise. "The firing continued without cessation for one hour, during which time we engaged three of the enemy's regiments and held them at bay," was his proud but official claim.[31]

Then help came from the Fourth Kentucky, commanded by Colonel Speed S. Fry, whom Manson personally waked up, ordering him to "form his regiment and proceed toward the enemy." The other regiment of the Second Brigade—Tenth Kentucky—being too far away to help, Manson rode to report to the commanding general. Thomas's official account states that he directed Manson to hold the enemy in check while he got the rest of the troops up, adding that they were on the march within ten minutes of receiving orders. But Manson himself took action to see that his own brigade received

* See Appendix II.

help without loss of time, for Colonel Robert L. McCook, commanding the Third Brigade, which also had at hand only two regiments—
Ninth Ohio and Second Minnesota—reported that he was informed
of the enemy attack shortly before seven o'clock by Manson, and that
he had his brigade deployed and moving to the support of Manson's
two regiments when he received the first orders from Thomas.

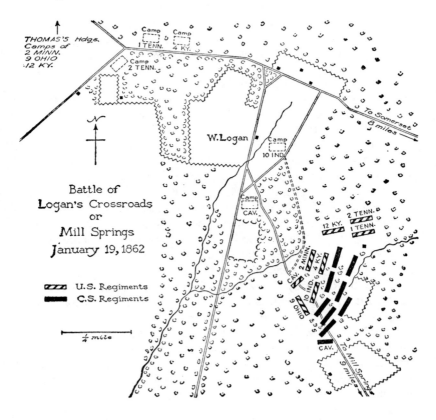

There are other conflicts in the reports. Fry asserts that, in the
absence of specific orders, he decided where to put his regiment into
line, while Manson indicates that he was back from his courier work
in time to find the Kentucky regiment on the road, and that he ordered it to take position on the left of the Tenth Indiana. Most difficult of all to understand is Thomas's statement that when he arrived

on the field he found the Hoosier regiment "in front of their encampment, apparently awaiting orders, and ordered them forward to support of the Fourth Kentucky, which was the only entire regiment
then engaged." If Kise and Manson are right in saying that the
Indiana regiment alone bore the brunt of the attack for an hour, then
Thomas was slow in getting into the new uniform in which one
admirer says he appeared.[32] Kise in fact states that Thomas moved
him from the right of the Fourth Kentucky to meet a threat that was
developing on its left, only presently to order him back to his original
position, where he was soon again heavily engaged. What finally
broke the enemy was a bayonet charge by the Ninth Ohio, which hit
the Confederates on the left flank and caused their entire line to give
way and retreat—in Thomas's words—"in the utmost disorder and
confusion." McCook says that he himself sized up the situation and
gave the order that was carried out "with alacrity and vociferous
cheering"; but it has been claimed that the telling stroke was the
result of an order by Thomas, though his report indicates he had
nothing to do with it.[33] According to Manson's account, Kise took the
cue from McCook and had his men emulate the Buckeyes with
a little bayonet work. The four infantry regiments and Wolford's
cavalry, which the Kentuckian said he dismounted to help the Tenth
Indiana—after he had returned from advancing two miles to the
south—were the only Federal regiments really engaged.

Where, then, were the First and Second Tennessee regiments and
the Twelfth Kentucky that Acting Brigadier Carter, long eager for a
fight, had brought from Somerset over heavy roads, leaving their
wagons beyond flooded Fishing Creek, and that had been camped
nearer the scene of action than the brigade of McCook? Manson apparently paid them no visit; but Carter wrote, "Notwithstanding their
uncomfortable condition for forty-eight hours, they formed in line of
battle on Sunday morning with alacrity to meet the enemy." Unduly
precautious perhaps, Thomas gave Carter the task of guarding the
road from Somerset, but from a position that would support the rest
of the line if need be. Thus it may be said that Carter's men were
initially a reserve. When a threat developed on the Union left they
were moved forward, and took a position echeloned to the rear and
left of the Second Minnesota, which was the leftmost of the four
engaged regiments. They did no more, however, than take a few
prisoners and suffered no casualties.[34] If Thomas had had anything

to do with the bayonet charge of the Ninth Ohio, one can ask why
he did not throw into the fight at the same time three regiments which
seemed to be eager for battle. It would seem that one can excuse
Thomas for neglecting an opportunity only by saying he did not
know it existed.

Fairly early in the action Zollicoffer—whose brigade led the enemy
column—fell with a bullet through his breast from the pistol of the
straight-shooting Kentucky Colonel Fry.[35] Though there may have
been some demoralization afterward in his own regiments, it was not
communicated to the brigade of General Carroll; and there was some
sharp fighting in the battle, with the contestants separated only by a
rail fence. Thomas, who had achieved distinction in the artillery in
Mexico before he was enticed into the cavalry, made efforts to get
his batteries into advantageous positions; but the guns did not seem
to contribute much except noise to either side of the battle.

Quickly Thomas got his regiments in hand with refilled cartridge
boxes, and started after the retreating enemy. From a commanding
position he shelled the Confederate Beech Grove position with two
guns; then, having been reenforced by three more regiments under
Schoepf as well as the Tenth Kentucky, he prepared to attack at daybreak. Empty trenches were found when the advance was made soon
after daylight, Crittenden having abandoned his dangerous position
and crossed the river during the night. Burning his steamboats and
ferry boats to prevent pursuit, he did not tarry at Mill Springs, but
led his tired men toward Tennessee, dispatching a message to Johnston from Monticello. Nothing was said of Zollicoffer's untimely
death, nor of overwhelming enemy numbers. His objective was given
as Celina, or some other point on the Cumberland, whence he could
communicate with Nashville; prospective hunger was hinted at in the
doleful ending, "The country is entirely destitute of provisions." [36]

The equipment and stores that fell into Thomas's hands were varied
and extensive, including 12 guns, 1,000 horses and mules, and some
150 wagons. At least a half dozen regimental colors as well as all the
orders and papers of the fallen Zollicoffer were taken. While the
Federal loss of 39 killed and 207 wounded came from only five regiments, the 125 killed, 308 wounded, and 95 missing of the Confederates came from eight. Thomas's men had not been eating very
well as they struggled through the mud, and the enemy had struck
before they had had breakfast. Their empty stomachs were soon filled,

however, with the cooked rations from the haversacks that the re-treating enemy left behind. Some of the Northerners were afraid of poison, but such pains as they felt came from nothing worse than cold bacon and sullen corn pone. Thomas reported that he had seized sufficient food to meet his needs for three days.[37]

The Battle of Logan's Crossroads—also called the Battle of Mill Springs—was a definite Federal victory, and many accounts of it appeared in Northern papers; it made good reading, of which the North had not had too much. Though the part Thomas actually played on the battlefield is naturally open to some doubt, with the possibility of a Stonewall Jackson stroke by Carter's regiments troubling one a little, the effective pursuit clearly and unequivocally belongs to Thomas; and the congratulatory order he issued to his troops the next day was commendably modest and restrained.[38] Manson and McCook were certainly alert and knew they were there to fight; within two months they and Fry had battle-won stars of brigadiers.

Buell sped the news of victory to Washington on the 20th, and two days later he repeated Thomas's first report with its impressive list of booty.[39] The President must have felt that at last a significant step had been taken in the much desired advance on East Tennessee, while Edwin Stanton, the week-old Secretary of War, had a chance to show his rhetorical power in a congratulatory order. After stating that the purpose of the war was "to attack, pursue, and destroy a rebellious enemy,"—with a reference to traitors thrown in for good measure—he declared, "Alacrity, daring, courageous spirit, and patri-otic zeal on all occasions and under every circumstance are expected from the Army of the United States." He ended by saying that the people would "rejoice to honor every soldier and officer who proves his courage by charging with the bayonet and storming intrenchments, or in the blaze of the enemy's fire."[40] His failure to mention Thomas by name has been called a deliberate slight to the Virginia-born gen-eral, but the charge is weakened by the fact that Lincoln's own later announcement after Gettysburg did not name General Meade.[41] It has also been urged that Thomas deserved promotion, and was held back by suspicion—in spite of three earlier promotions.[42] With the depart-ment commander only a brigadier general, a minor engagement was not enough to justify advancement of a subordinate over his head. No major generals had been appointed since August, when Hunter was promoted and Halleck commissioned; the High Command was evidently waiting for some outstanding performance. Thomas had been saved the necessity of making an attack, and had done little more than profit from a gross enemy blunder. He had not demonstrated the capacity of real generalship—to wage aggressive, relentless offensive action over a period longer than the daylight hours of a winter day.

Not a single, cheering thought could Sidney Johnston salvage from the battle to pass on to Richmond. On January 22 he repeated a message just received from one of Crittenden's staff, which with commendable frankness reported the abandonment of everything and added, "The command is in full retreat towards Knoxville." Now, however, the failure of the attack was ascribed to the Federals' "superior numbers," and the disorderly retreat to the death of Zollicoffer.[43] Crittenden's long report of February 13 indulged in still greater exaggeration, asserting that there were twenty-seven regiments of Federal infantry at Beech Grove, against his nine across the river at Mill Springs.[44] In reality there were twelve. The discomfited general—son of Kentucky's well known governor and senator, and brother of a Union brigadier general—asked for a court of inquiry.[45] Johnston availed himself of the latitude in dealing with the general that was given him by the Confederate Secretary of War, and he did not pay much attention to the reports that reached Richmond charging the defeat to Crittenden's intemperance.[46] In July, however, a court of inquiry was appointed to investigate new charges of intoxication, and presently Crittenden was just a colonel, in which rank he finished the war.[47]

In post-bellum Kentucky Confederate officers were held in high esteem; a record of defeats in bouts with spirituous liquor was not too great a blemish on respectability, and "Colonel" was just about as good as "General." Thus George Crittenden, West Point graduate and a practicer for a time at the legal bar, did not suffer too much for his misadventures, and received the honorable and responsible position of state librarian.

CHAPTER VIII

TELEGRAMS BRING AN ORDER

With permission, I will take Fort Henry, on the Tennessee, and establish and hold a large camp there.   *Grant to Halleck*

Wᴴɪʟᴇ Thomas was routing Crittenden, Halleck was completing his victory over the measles. The 20th of January found him back at his desk, explaining to McClellan his absence, as well as that of some of his staff, who were still sick. The long letter is one of the month's most important documents, and its contents may have occupied the general's mind as he lay in bed. Curtis, near Rolla, was being reenforced, and would, Halleck said, open a campaign against Price with about 15,000 men. Winter and the roads would make the operation difficult, but the enemy would be beaten or driven from the state. Concentration was difficult, because troops were necessary in a number of counties in order to discourage bands of secessionists and aid Union men in organizing the state militia. Ice in the river had allowed only three of the five regiments ordered to Cairo to make the trip; but it was hoped that some additional units could be moved from the northern part of Missouri to increase the force at the great river junction. Probably because he was just reaching the point where he could think of major action outside the state, Halleck wrote out his ideas more fully than he had ever done before. With regard to fundamental strategy he said:

The idea of moving down the Mississippi by steam is, in my opinion, impracticable, or at least premature. It is not a proper line of operations, at least now. A much more feasible plan is to move up the Cumberland and Tennessee, making Nashville the first objective point. This would turn Columbus and force the abandonment of Bowling Green.

Halleck said he had carefully studied the defenses of Columbus. They were very strong, and the place could not be taken "without an immense siege train and a terrible loss of life"; but it could "be turned, paralyzed, and forced to surrender." The line of the Cumberland and the Tennessee was "the great central line of the Western theater of war," and he stressed the importance of the "two good navigable rivers extending far into the interior of the theater of operations." An operation up them should, however, not be attempted without 60,000 effective men. Of Buell's force and plans, he was ignorant. If that general were strong enough, he might accomplish what was desired by a move directly upon Nashville; but Halleck himself condemned the use of two convergent columns. "Under any circumstances it is bad strategy," wrote the author of the *Elements,* "because it requires a double force to accomplish a single object."

Operations west of the Mississippi were considered, with the purpose of seeing which might lead to valuable results and be economical, and which merely costly, with no good accomplishments, though taking essential strength from other places. How high up in the command hierarchy he was hitting when he pronounced a reported move from Leavenworth on western Arkansas and Texas, "contrary to every military rule," he may not have known—nor cared. He asserted it was certainly not a military operation; and he doubtless was aiming at his favorite target, Senator James Lane, when he added, "It may, however, be intended to gratify some political partisan."

Halleck hoped that the force at Cairo and Paducah, "about 15,000," could be doubled by the middle or last of February. Then, if 30,000 or 40,000 more men could be secured from other sources, there would be sufficient strength to hold Cairo and Fort Holt securely, and make up an operating column for the Cumberland and Tennessee. New Madrid disturbed him somewhat. It could be taken by Curtis from the direction of Springfield; but, so long as the Confederates held Columbus, Federal tenure of it would be precarious.

Though the suggestions were hastily written, they were "the result of much anxious inquiry and mature deliberation." The plan, if carried out, would produce important results; and Halleck also considered it to be feasible.[1] It is idle to debate whether he was consciously using ideas that Colonel Whittlesey had set down two months to a day before. That letter doubtless had brought the Cumberland and Tennessee first to Halleck's attention almost upon his arrival in St. Louis; but certain it is that no person with military perception, located in that region, would have been long in thinking of them. Halleck's letter shows that he had explored the entire problem as a responsible general.

Halleck's disapproving reference to an operation down the Mississippi is no sure indication that he believed such a plan was accepted in Washington, for McClellan had written about the Cumberland and the Tennessee. Without doubt there was irresponsible talk, and the public believed a Mississippi movement was in the making; but what newspaper correspondents thought and various gossips believed had nothing to do with real war plans. It is not at all impossible that Grant, a subordinate commander, believed that a Mississippi movement was in favor; certain it is that Rawlins had thought so a month before, for he mentioned it in his letter to Washburne.[2] But Halleck's letter to McClellan shows that western strategy was still undecided on January 20, and that he expected it would be determined upon by the General in Chief with the aid of his own on-the-scene and competent reflections.

A subject very different from high planning, yet connected with the basic question of troop morale, then intruded through a brief note from Lincoln: "This will introduce Gov. G. Koerner, of Illinois, who is my personal friend, and who calls on you at my particular request. Please open the sealed letter he will hand you before he leaves you and confer with him as to its contents." The letter began:

The Germans are true and patriotic, and so far as they have got cross in Missouri it is upon mistake and misunderstanding. Without a knowledge of its contents Governor Koerner, of Illinois, will hand you this letter. He is an educated and talented German gentleman, as true a man as lives. With his assistance you can set everything right with the Germans. I write this without his knowledge, asking him at the same time, by letter, to deliver it.

Lincoln believed that Halleck should have the assistance of Koerner in handling the German element in his command, and if agreeable to the general, he was prepared to turn the former lieutenant governor into a brigadier. He did not intend that Koerner should go into the field—though he had more military knowledge than some army officers—and he wished merely to make it possible for Koerner to give his time as "an efficient, zealous, and unselfish assistant to you." [3] Halleck was ready with an answer: "I nominated Governor K. some time ago for appointment as aide-de-camp, with the rank of colonel, the highest authorized by law as a staff office." He was willing, however, to receive him as a brigadier, and would try to make the best use of him. At the same time he clearly believed that "cross" was not the best description for the Germans, and he was specific as to the trouble: they grumbled for want of overdue pay, and were "continually tampered with by designing politicians in and out of service in order to serve particular ends." A part of the story was the alleged ill-treatment of General Sigel, which Halleck asserted was without the slightest foundation. Difficulties were being met satisfactorily, and any yielding by the government would only create new ones "and give rise to new demands." His concluding sentence was hard to rebut: "Being a German myself by descent, I know something of the German character, and I am confident that in a few weeks, if the Government does not interfere, I can reduce these disaffected elements to order and discipline." [4] Halleck had his way, and "Governor K.," instead of being given a mission of appeasing "cross" Missouri Germans, was presently dispatched to Spain to counter English and French intrigues directed toward bringing about joint recognition of the Confederacy.

From Cairo Captain A. S. Baxter, who had become quartermaster after Grant had put Captain Hatch in arrest, sent Halleck's assistant quartermaster a very dismal tale:

What does Government intend to do? This department has been neglected in every way. No funds; no nothing, and don't seem as though we ever would get anything. . . . Laborers have not been paid a dime for six or seven months; don't care whether they work or not. If they do, don't take any interest in anything. Government owes everybody and everything, from small petty amounts to large. Liabilities more plenty than Confederate scrip and worth less. Regiment after regiment arriving daily. Nothing to supply them with, and no funds to buy or men to work. No transportation for ourselves or any one else.

To tell you the truth we are on our last legs, and I have made my last appeal in behalf of Government unless it's to a higher power, for it will kill any man and every man at the head of departments here the way we are now working. . . . The general commanding and myself have done our best to bring about better results, but our wants are not supplied or even noticed.[5]

The letter was forwarded to McClellan, "for his perusal," Halleck stating in his indorsement that it described conditions general throughout his department; unless funds were soon provided, it would be impossible to organize an expedition from Cairo.

Though Halleck could pass on to Washington the letter from the son of a Vermont chief justice with the thought that its picturesque "no nothing" and "don't care" might be more effective than his own proper grammar, he had to take time to instruct Sterling Price in fundamental law—just as he had been instructing his own subordinates. From a camp near Springfield the Missourian had complained on January 12 that men he had sent forth with explicit instructions "to destroy railroads, culverts, and bridges, by tearing them up, burning, &c.," had been arrested "for alleged crimes." More than that, he understood that, if convicted, they would be "viewed as lawful subjects for capital punishment." Patiently and at length Halleck explained that, so long as Price's men came in "the garb of soldiers and duly organized and enrolled as legitimate belligerents" to carry on destruction "as a military act," the Federals would try to kill them "in open warfare" and, if they captured them, would "treat them as prisoners of war." It was, however, an entirely different matter to send out saboteurs in civilian clothes who did not operate openly as a military force; and he thundered: "You cannot give immunity to crime." But even then he had not finished with Price, for presently there appeared at Federal headquarters a man who pulled from his pocket a stick with a dirty handkerchief attached and offered a duplicate of the letter Halleck had already answered. Then to Price, who once had made the state reverberate with an eloquent proclamation, a letter had to be written explaining the decorum of flags of truce.[6]

There was one subject on which Halleck might have lectured Price but did not: evils of strong drink. The Union commander at Sedalia had reported the observations of two spies who had "humbugged Price completely," going safely through all his camps where they "saw everything." There were "no discipline, no roll-calls, no sentinels, nor pickets to prevent passing in and out of Springfield," and things were bad all the way to the top. After saying that one of the Missourian's brigadiers was "drunk all the time," the report added, "Price also drinking too much." [7] But this was hardly contrary to the rules or usages of war, and Halleck passed over it.

It was being remarked in St. Louis that Sherman—once a department commander—was in a subordinate position, with younger officers in the responsible positions. Halleck explained to McClellan on January 22 that Sherman had returned from leave "greatly improved," but still in his opinion not "entirely in condition to take the field." In the camp of instruction to which he had been assigned he had rendered "most excellent service," while at the same time his health had "gradually improved." Soon he would be ready for the field, and Halleck said, "I should be very sorry to lose his services here, but will oppose no obstacle to the wishes of himself or friends if a transfer be desired.[8] As he signed the letter Halleck could not foresee the bitter telegram that would come to him from Sherman three years later. Sherman knew nothing of Halleck's letter; but he was fully aware of the understanding treatment he had received. Gratitude, however, was forgotten when he later considered himself unjustly affronted.

On the evening of the 20th Grant was back in Cairo, notifying St. Louis that the last of the troops would arrive the next morning.[9] While he was in the field, reports of his operations had gone to headquarters; and his orders show that he forgot nothing. When high water prevented Colonel Cook from crossing Mayfield Creek so that he had to embark at a point on the Mississippi, a note to Captain D. D. Porter requested that a gunboat drop down the river to cover the embarkation and protect the transport.[10] Grant's letter on the night of his return reported recent information from Columbus, and said that two men just in from New Orleans asserted that public confidence in ultimate success was fast on the wane in the South. Of the discomfort of the cold rains and the icy and miry roads over which his men had marched, he had nothing to say, but commented, "The expedition, if it had no other effect, served as a fine reconnaissance." Though he had not received an official report from Smith, he knew he had gone up the Tennessee and landed two and a half miles below Fort Henry. As soon as he heard from Smith he would, he said, "prepare a report of the entire expedition, unless the general commanding department shall see fit to permit me to visit headquarters, as I have before desired."

What was working in Grant's mind was revealed. That evening he had issued a circular "calling upon the company and regimental commanders for a list of river and sea-faring men of their respective commands" who were willing to transfer to gunboat service. Men were absolutely necessary before the boats, then nearly completed, could be used. He would make gunboatmen out of willing soldiers, provided of course that the department commander approved. This much is certain: he wanted to go somewhere, and wanted an escort of gunboats.

In accordance with his chief's instructions, Grant had told big stories before beginning his demonstration; and a Cairo dispatch of the 13th informed the country that 25,000 men were on their way from St. Louis. Journalists were reported as being ready to join the general and staff at a moment's notice. Then the puzzled correspondent wrote: "But the expedition. When it is to go, where it is to go, or whether it is to go anywhere, are mysteries which the journalistic vision fails to penetrate." However, he was not too far wrong when he wrote the movement might be merely a feint to draw troops from Bowling Green or southwestern Missouri. When it was all over, the correspondent for the *New York Times* summed up: "The grand expedition has returned, and the whole thing looks like an immense humbug." [11]

The enemy was as bewildered as the correspondents. On the 18th Johnston reported that Fort Henry was being attacked, and he sent a call for a regiment at Tuscumbia, Alabama; the next day he informed Secretary Benjamin: "The movements of the enemy indicate his intention to turn General Polk's right by the Memphis and Ohio Railroad. Their preparations to attack General Polk in front and on his flank seem to be of immense magnitude." Fear continued to mount, and General Tilghman, commanding at Forts Henry and Donelson, reported on the 21st that Smith would attack one of the forts, or possibly both. Then suddenly the Federals returned home. Polk at Columbus heard that Grant, still very talkative, had said he gave up "because the support he expected from Saint Louis was prevented from reaching him by the ice." Thus in Polk's mind it had not been a mere feint, but a frustrated operation. More digging was in order, and Polk closed his dispatch, "I am continuing to strengthen the defenses of this post." [12]

The trained eye of C. F. Smith had had a look at Fort Henry from near at hand, and, without waiting to reach home, he wrote to Grant's adjutant, "The appearance of the work corresponds, as far as could be discovered, with the rough sketch that General Grant has seen in my quarters at Paducah." History would be much more vivid if we knew the words interchanged between the two brigadiers as they viewed the drawing of the work with which the enemy had sought to block the Tennessee; but their general tenor can be imagined. Now Smith wrote: "I think two iron-clad gunboats would make short work of Fort Henry. There is no masked battery at the foot of the island [just below the fort], as was supposed, or, if so, it is now under water." [13]

On the 22nd Grant had Halleck's reply, a curt enough sentence at the end of a short dispatch: "You have permission to visit head-quarters." [14] Fortunately a letter to his sister the next day, Thursday, reveals more clearly than official letters how his thoughts were running. "You have seen through the papers," said he, "notice of my return from the great expedition into Kentucky." Mary would catch the irony; but, so that she might not think him cautious or timid, he explained how "no attack was allowable." He observed that he now had a larger force than General Scott had ever commanded prior to the "present difficulties," and he hoped it would be his "good fortune to retain so important a command for at least one battle." No part of the entire army was in his view better prepared "to contest a battle" than that in his district, and he was sure he had the confidence of officers and men. "This," he added, "is all important, especially so with new troops. I go tonight to Saint Louis to see General Halleck; will be back on Sunday morning." He was counting on the discretion of his family when he said, "I expect but little quiet from this on and if you receive but short, unsatisfactory letters hereafter you need not be surprised." The letter ended with references to his wife and children, whom Mary might expect to see "about the 1st of February." [15] The wish to command in battle, officers and men with confidence in him, a visit to headquarters, hasty letters in the future, wife and children going to his parents: the pattern is clear.

No reply is to be found for Baxter's letter describing the critical quartermaster situation at Cairo; but it would seem that no hopes were entertained for improvement from action in St. Louis. Baxter had plainly indicated that he might have to appeal to higher authority, as many supply officers have done since his time, and on January 23

Grant sent him to Washington with a letter of introduction to Congressman Washburne. Satisfied that he at last had "an efficient and faithful servant of the Government" in Captain Baxter, Grant hoped that he might do "something for the relief of this much distressed portion of our Army." Having found the right man, he wanted to keep him, and suggested promotion. He also had in mind the unfavorable reports about himself which had reached Washburne; and he wrote, "Captain Baxter can tell you of the great abuses in his Department here and the efforts I have put forth to correct them, and consequently the number of secret enemies necessarily made." [16]

The cold, terse permission from Halleck may have been merely the matter-of-fact answer of one soldier to another; but, coming so soon after the near-censure for a minor slip, Grant had little reason to expect anything but brusque formality from the officer he had known "but slightly in the old army." Actually the meeting of the two men was a dismal and historic failure, for which Grant seems to have been prepared to take some secondary responsibility years later when he wrote in his *Memoirs:* "I was received with so little cordiality that I perhaps stated the object of my visit with less clearness than I might have done, and I had not uttered many sentences before I was cut short as if my plan was preposterous." [17] The ascent of the Tennessee, which was what he proposed, would, of course take him out of his district and into Buell's department if he did no more than attack Fort Henry; but *carte blanche* in such an overstepping of boundaries had been given to Halleck, or at least implied. The latter seems, however, to have lacked the candor and friendliness even to tell the subordinate who had been serving him well that he had recently written to McClellan that the Tennessee and Cumberland constituted the correct line of operations in the West. In spite of this, Halleck may have been more impressed than his scholarly visage indicated; and it is possible that his dispatch of the 24th asking Smith for detailed information about the country south of Paducah and Smithland as far as Forts Henry and Donelson,[18] was a result of Grant's suggestion. It is not certain that Smith's prediction of the morning of the 23rd from near Fort Henry, as to what two gunboats might do to that important work, had reached Grant before he set out for St. Louis.[19] But even if he had been able to reenforce his views with

Smith's, the ultimately responsible superior cannot be blamed for the desire to have some extra checking done.

"Very much crestfallen," is the description in Grant's *Memoirs* of his state of mind on his return to his headquarters, where he found that the pontoon bridge at Paducah had gone in the great rush of waters after the heavy rains, eleven of the boats having been rescued at Cairo.[20] But it is improbable that he discovered at once that McClernand had taken advantage of his brief absence to write a long report of the recent expedition, to which he subscribed himself as "Commanding District of Cairo." [21] It was more than a brazen act, for McClernand was in no position to make a well rounded report— if indeed he wished to—and he made only the scantiest reference to Smith.

Lincoln had been out of the command picture since January 7, when he telegraphed Buell and Halleck that delay was ruinous and he must have something definite; but he reentered almost dramatically on the 27th, when he wrote his full signature to the much criticized "President's General War Order No. 1." [22] This document decreed February 22 as the "day for a general movement of the land and naval forces of the United States against the insurgent forces." No one was directed to strike for East Tennessee, not, certainly, because that was a less ardently desired objective than formerly, but because the recent battle at Logan's Crossroads made it appear that George Thomas was well started toward Knoxville. On the other hand, the inclusion of "the army near Munfordville," and "the army and flotilla at Cairo" among the forces specifically instructed to be ready, indicated clearly that a blow was to be struck against the Bowling Green and Columbus line. Apparently the President thought his soldiers might march a little faster and strike a little harder on Washington's Birthday than on some ordinary day, and his earnestness was further shown by a brief note to Stanton: "The Secretary of War will enter this order in his Department, and execute it to the best of his ability." [23]

The Secretary was not a procrastinator, and on the same day he wrote a "most confidential" note to Ohio's radical-minded Senator Wade, chairman of the new Committee on the Conduct of the War. Whispered Stanton: "An order has this day been made by the President requiring *all the armies* in the field to place themselves in fighting order immediately, and to commence operations by a certain specific day." The success of the movements would depend in a great measure upon the control of the railroad and telegraph lines, and the immediate passage of a bill upon this subject pending in the Senate would have great influence on the war; he therefore asked Wade to "communicate confidentially with the loyal and honest members of both houses and have action—immediate action." [24]

Stanton did not trust even Benjamin Wade with the knowledge of the President's D-day, but he probably unintentionally twisted things a little when he said activity was to commence "by" instead of "on" a specific day. Lincoln's order was not executed; when the date set arrived, he had himself annulled it for the Army of the Potomac and the flag of the Union was already flying from Forts Henry and Donelson—but not as the result of any order from the White House.

On the day Lincoln signed his general war order, Buell wrote a long letter to Lorenzo Thomas saying that there was altogether too much mud for George Thomas to continue to East Tennessee. So bad were the roads and so hard the supply problem that part of the force at Somerset had been on half-rations for several days.[25] But the column that was to follow the Cumberland Gap route was in motion; in fact he had ordered Carter back to that line the day before, instructing him to seize the gap with four of his best regiments and fortify himself strongly in the position.[26] That Buell was working wholeheartedly, in spite of what he himself thought of the possibilities, is shown by his inquiry of General Thomas a few days later:

What now is the condition of the roads? How soon could you march, and how long do you suppose it would take you to reach Knoxville? Are your supplies accumulating in sufficient quantity for a start? How is the road in advance likely to be affected by the passage of successive trains? What dependence can you place in supplies along it, particularly forage? Do you hear of any organization of a force there? Where is Crittenden? Are the fugitives getting together again? What progress has been made in improving the road to Somerset? Please answer at once.[27]

Here was the same clear-thinking officer who had given such important instructions to Major Robert Anderson on December 10, 1860, about possible moving from Fort Moultrie to Fort Sumter.

If Grant's spirits were drooping when he returned to Cairo, they revived quickly. Now he certainly had Smith's report on Fort Henry and the chance to talk to Foote about it. He reopened his case with a one-sentence telegram in which he said exactly what he could do:

Cairo, January 28, 1862

Maj. Gen. H. W. Halleck
Saint Louis, Mo.:
  With permission, I will take Fort Henry, on the Tennessee, and establish and hold a large camp there.

U. S. Grant,
Brigadier General [28]

Not much longer was the telegram that went from Foote: "Commanding General Grant and myself are of opinion that Fort Henry, on the Tennessee River, can be carried with four iron-clad gunboats and troops to permanently occupy. Have we your authority to move for that purpose when ready?" [29] Foote cornered Halleck with an unevadable question; but it was Grant who made a statement unweakened by the word "opinion." Did the soldier and the sailor actually consort together in writing the historic dispatches that paved the way for swift action in the West? [30] We wish we knew the answer, just as we should like to know who clicked off the messages at Cairo, who copied them down as the telegraph instrument rattled them out at St. Louis, which one Halleck read first—and what sort of a look spread over his serious face. Each missing detail is a part of a great drama that can be reconstructed as one fancies. But the messages are there, imperishable: the message of the soldier, the message of the sailor.

The next day Grant sent a longer dispatch stressing the importance of quick action, for the enemy would assuredly strengthen his position. After noting that it would be easy to operate from Fort Henry either on the Cumberland, only twelve miles distant, or against Memphis or Columbus, he said: "It will besides, have a moral effect upon our troops to advance them toward the rebel States." Other results were certainly in his mind, for he concluded: "The advantages of this move are as perceptible to the general commanding as to myself, therefore further statements are unnecessary." [31]

Halleck now had the issue squarely before him, and he faced perhaps the most important decision in his military career. He had recently told the General in Chief that the movement up the Tennessee and the Cumberland ought not to begin until there were 60,000 effectives on hand. Dare he say "Go ahead" when Grant had only about a quarter of that number, and rapid build-up had not yet been arranged? He knew the man in Cairo would move fast; his promptness in getting the recent demonstration started had shown that. Could he supply and support Grant properly? Even the river could give trouble, as its freezing during the demonstration had proved. Only a few miles below Cairo, sensitive point on the line of communications through which reenforcing troops as well as supplies must move, was Columbus; and Halleck must have looked at it with doubt and apprehension. The enemy gunboats had always been cautious; but he could not have been certain of their full number and capacity, or have known what additional naval strength the Confederates had at Memphis and below. Would the force at Columbus react by marching to the Ohio River and capture Fort Holt, whose guns could demolish transports? If the operation failed, the responsibility would all be his, in spite of Grant's positive assertion as to what he would do.

Halleck decided boldly, and on the 29th he wired Foote, "I am waiting for General Smith's report on road from Smithland to Fort Henry. As soon as that is received will give order. Meantime, have everything ready." It was Wednesday, and the eager commodore at once wrote that he would be "ready with four ironclad boats early on Saturday." He and Lieutenant Phelps had been consulting with Grant, and they were of the unanimous opinion that the Tennessee would soon fall, and that the movement should start not later than Monday. There was a postscript: "The roads are said to be good from Paducah to Fort Henry, even at this season." [32]

A Confederate soldier in far-off Virginia now entered the story, to strengthen Halleck's resolve, if indeed he had not influenced his original decision, though his message to Cairo looks as if he had acted solely on the appeals of Grant and Foote. On the 29th McClellan sent to both Halleck and Buell the important telegram:

A deserter just in from the rebels says that Beauregard had not left Centreville four days ago, but that as he was going on picket he heard officers say that Beauregard was under order to go to Kentucky with fifteen regiments from the [Confederate] Army of the Potomac.[33]

Buell's reply the next day said the message had "just" been received. Halleck's acknowledgment unfortunately is not so specific; but nevertheless it was not sent until the 30th. A week later he wrote to Buell that he had had no idea of starting any movement before

the 15th or 20th of February until he received the telegram about
Beauregard.[34] If literally accepted this would mean that McClellan's
message had arrived before he wired Foote to get ready. He was,
however, at that time trying to appease Buell and get some support
from him, and it is entirely possible that he exaggerated, as he did
in reporting to Grant what McClellan had said about Beauregard.
In any case he had as yet issued no order, and had probably not
received Foote's letter of the day before.

Whatever may have been the facts as to the telegram, Stanton was
taking important action without knowledge of the crucial messages
that were passing between Cairo and St. Louis, but solely because of
the President's War Order of two days before. Though Thomas A.
Scott was a close friend of Simon Cameron, who had reluctantly
given up the War portfolio to become minister to Russia, he continued to serve under the new Secretary, a Washington dispatch of
January 22 informing the public that he would have charge of railroad
transportation—an excellent assignment, because he was a railroad
executive.[35] On the 29th Stanton gave Scott a directive that began:
"For the purpose of efficient organization of this department, ascer-
taining and organizing the requisite forces and means for combined
active operation, you are requested to proceed from this city. . . ." [36]
Scott's first point of call was to be Pittsburgh, where he was to inspect
the arsenal and also get data requisite for the possible movement
of troops from Washington to the West.[37] Thence he was to go to
Columbus, Indianapolis, and Springfield, to learn about the condition
of units being raised and the time when they would be ready for the
field, giving "particular attention to the quartermaster and commissary
departments, and to whatever concerns the equipment, subsistence,
and transport of the troops." Visits to St. Louis, Cairo, Paducah, and
Louisville were prescribed, and a thorough investigation into supply
establishments at Cincinnati was the last duty set down. At each place
Scott's arrival was to be reported by telegraph, a full report was to be
made by mail, and he was not to resume his journey until so directed
by wire.

McClellan should have been embarrassed by the report of the
deserter from Joe Johnston's army. Although Thomas's recent victory
and Grant's demonstration, which had been considered an abortive
operation, might well have made the Confederates wish to strengthen
their forces in the West, did they dare subtract substantially from

the army which was holding back McClellan's own much greater force? McClellan the General in Chief did not so much as intimate that he would order McClellan the commander of the Army of the Potomac to see that the enemy did no detaching from his eastern front in order to hamper Federal operations in the West. Halleck on his part took no chances, but assumed—as will be seen presently from his order to Grant—that the victor of Fort Sumter and First Bull Run was already on the way toward Kentucky with fifteen doughty regiments from Virginia. (There is a possibility of a misreading of McClellan's message, in spite of its shortness.) So on January 30 he telegraphed McClellan:

> Your telegraph respecting Beauregard is received. General Grant and Commodore Foote will be ordered to immediately advance, and to reduce and hold Fort Henry, on the Tennessee River, and also to cut the railroad between Dover and Paris. The roads are in such condition as to render all movements exceedingly slow and difficult.[38]

It is important to note McClellan's action with regard to this crucial message. On January 29 he had said in answering Halleck's long letter of the 20th: "I like your views as to the future. They fully agree with my own ideas from the beginning which has [sic] ever been against a movement in force down the Mississippi." [39] Plainly enough Halleck had stated that the Tennessee and the Cumberland gave the true line of operations in the West; and, because the taking of Fort Henry would be the first essential step, it was clear that his dispatch of the 30th indicated a significant turn in the war in the West. Not knowing that Grant and Foote wanted to attack and had asked permission to do so, McClellan could well have felt some concern at what looked like hasty action: it was only ten days since Halleck had said he could do nothing until the middle of February.

The dispatch from St. Louis may have arrived on the 31st when McClellan was busily engaged composing his long and previously described letter to Stanton setting forth the advantages of a campaign up the Peninsula, in contrast to the expected difficulties of an operation against Manassas. Important though it was, the telegram could not have been read very carefully, for in a short note to Lincoln on February 1, McClellan said that Halleck had wired—in reply to his dispatch about the deserter—"that he would at once order movement up the Cumberland River." The General in Chief got the rivers mixed up and said nothing about Fort Henry! But he sent the dispatch to Stanton, so the War Secretary was properly informed.[40] Stanton, however, seems not to have informed Thomas Scott that an important operation was about to start in the West. Since Halleck's concluding sentence gave little promise of immediate results, Stanton probably thought it unnecessary to alter his instructions to his assistant.

Where now was Captain Baxter, Grant's quartermaster? On the 30th McClellan had sent his gloomy letter to the Secretary of War with the indorsement: "I know the fact that in the spring [April and May] there was a great deficiency of funds at Cairo. The public interests require as prompt action as possible in this case." This was quite sufficient to put the responsibility up to Stanton when Halleck's telegram of the 30th came to his hands. Just how Baxter operated is not clear; but he got funds somewhere.[41]

In Cairo it was snowing. Using a barrelhead as a desk, William Reuben Rowley, former clerk of the circuit court at Galena, who had tried to make a Lincoln voter out of Grant, was reporting on the weather and other things to Washburne. He wanted to transfer to Grant's staff; his own colonel was favorable, and the general had said he "would be more than glad" to have him. But permission for Grant to have an additional aide would have to be given by the War Department, and Rowley thought that Washburne could manage that detail. He had had an excellent opportunity to learn the truth or falsity of stories in circulation about Grant, which he supposed had reached Washburne. The persons who were circulating such stories were misinformed, or lying; and he assured Washburne that he would have no cause to regret having had Grant made a brigadier. Outside, the weather was not encouraging. There was the snow; it was "blowing like blazes"; roads were impassable; and there seemed to be little chance of doing anything "for some time to come unless there is a great improvement in the weather." [42]

But on that day one of the most important dispatches of the war arrived at the river junction:

Saint Louis, January 30, 1862

Brig. Gen. U. S. Grant,
Cairo, Ill.:

Make your preparations to take and hold Fort Henry. I will send you written instructions by mail.

H. W. Halleck,
Major-General [43]

The letter of instructions bore the same date, and it too must be pronounced excellent, especially because the department commander had little time to check carefully and revise. All of Grant's available force from Smithland, Paducah, Cairo, Fort Holt, Birds Point, etc., was to be thrown into the operation, with only sufficient garrisons left to hold those places "against an attack from Columbus." Fort Henry was to be taken and held at all hazards. Halleck was sending his chief engineer officer, Lieutenant Colonel James B. McPherson; and a substantial addition that excellent soldier would prove to be. Apparently the St. Louis commander had doubts about the gunboats being able to handle Fort Henry, and contemplated an investment. Once the fort was shut in, cavalry was to be pushed forward to break the railroad from Paris to Dover; the bridges were to be rendered impassable, but not completely destroyed. Grant was told: "A telegram from Washington says that Beauregard left Manassas four days ago with fifteen regiments for the line of Columbus and Bowling Green." That line had, therefore, to be cut quickly, and the department commander ordered: "You will move with the least delay possible." Knowing the importance of fast communications, Halleck told Grant to extend the telegraph line from Paducah up to Fort Henry as rapidly as possible, and said in closing, "Wires and operators will be sent from Saint Louis." [44]

There still was work to do. A second letter to Grant directed him to organize his command as he saw fit, changing it also from time to time as seemed best for the public service, "without the slightest regard to political influence or to the orders and instructions" he might already have received. Foreseeing the pressure that would be brought upon Grant as new regiments arrived, Halleck said he was not to let "political applications about brigades and divisions" trouble him "a particle"—such applications and arrangements were "sheer nonsense." Tucked in with all this was the direction for Grant to supply new troops obtained from Illinois "the best" he could.[45]

Copies of the two letters to Grant were forwarded at once to McClellan, with a covering letter in which Halleck again looked ahead. Noting that Fort Henry and Dover were in Tennessee, he said, "I respectfully suggest that that State be added to this department." [46] From the copy of the letter of instructions to Grant, McClellan could see the twisted reading that Halleck had given to his telegram about the deserter; but he still was not informed that Grant and Foote had underwritten the capture of Fort Henry. Certainly this highly important information should have been communicated to Washington.

Buell was apprised of what Halleck was doing by a short dispatch: "I have ordered an advance of our troops on Fort Henry and Dover. It will be made immediately." [47] Actually Dover had not been included in Grant's mission; but here is very good evidence that Halleck foresaw that Donelson must be taken. Buell doubtless guessed that his colleague's action had been provoked by the telegram about the deserter, but he could hardly have imagined that Halleck had told Grant that fifteen regiments had already left Virginia for the West. Not many days had passed since he had ordered a big demonstration without waiting for word from Buell as to when he wished it made; now it looked as if he had taken very precipitate action on the unconfirmed word of a deserter not cross-examined by himself. Almost anything might happen if higher commanders did such things, and there may have been a touch of resignation in the message:

Louisville, Ky., January 30, 1862
General Halleck:
Please let me know your plan and force and the time, &c.
Buell [48]

After recovering from the shock, the Louisville general wrote to McClellan: "I protest against such prompt proceedings, as though I had nothing to do but command 'Commence firing' when he starts off." But he was not too angry, for his long letter ended, "However he telegraphs me tonight that co-operation is not essential now." [49]

On the 30th James Shields, one-time challenger of Lincoln to a duel, who had "come at the call of the President to throw" himself into the cause, wrote to Stanton: "In compliance with your flattering suggestion of last evening, I beg leave to present a few general views on the best mode of conducting military operations against the rebel army and government of the South." He canvassed the whole field and sketched, in the East, a movement up the Peninsula, one against Manassas, and one that would turn Manassas; in the West, the Cumberland was to be used, and Memphis was to fall before May. Said Shields: "I have commenced elaborating a plan of campaign for Kentucky which may result in turning Columbus and Bowling Green and rendering both these positions useless. But without more local knowledge than I possess I would not venture to recommend it for action." [50] Of interest in itself, Shields's letter is more important as an indication that Stanton, on the day that he dispatched Thomas Scott westward, was reaching for some plan, not bending his efforts toward carrying out one already fixed upon.

Grant did no broadcasting this time. Secrecy was now his aim, and he wrote to Halleck on the 31st, Friday: "I am quietly making preparations for a move, without as yet having created suspicion even that a movement is to be made. Awaiting your instructions, which we expect in the morning, I have not made definite plans as to my movements, but expect to start Sunday evening, taking 15,000 men." To Smith there went a rather long message about the operation. After enjoining secrecy Grant apologized: "I am well aware, however, that this caution is entirely unnecessary to you." [51]

Meanwhile President Lincoln was trying to extricate himself from the difficulties and embarrassments that came from his too hasty involvement with Senator Lane. He wrote to Stanton that what was being noised about as the "Lane Expedition" from Fort Leavenworth should be as much as had been promised at the Adjutant General's office under McClellan's supervision, *"and not any more."* He had never intended that it should be *"a great, exhausting affair,* but a snug, sober column of 10,000 or 15,000." Lane had often been told that he was to be under Hunter, and had "assented to it as often as told." However, the trouble was not over; and at the moment a touching address signed with the awe-inspiring names and the "marks" of the head chiefs of the Creeks and the Seminoles, was on the way to Washington. They lamented the fact that there seemed to be doubt "whether the great war chief, General Lane," was to lead the proposed expedition to their country. Their people would be sad if he did not come; but, if he did, they would follow wherever he led, and would "sweep the rebels before them like a terrible fire on the dry prairie." Eloquently they concluded, "We beg our Great Father and our great war chief, General McClellan, that they will listen to the prayers of their children." [52]

The mention of McClellan's name gave Lincoln a way out, though John Hay may have sighed over the drabness of his language in comparison with that of chiefs who signed with marks, when he wrote the indorsement: "My Dear Sir: The President directs me to send you the inclosed, with his respectful salutations."

Even 10,000 men would have been a "snug" addition for the Tennessee operation, especially if Beauregard arrived with the Manassas regiments. Although in the end Hunter would indeed release troops to Halleck, all Halleck could tell Grant at the moment was that a few more regiments would soon be on their way to join him. His troubles were by no means ended by his decision; and, even as he worked on the question of supporting Grant, he had a new and serious situation to meet. The discontent that had been simmering, especially among the German units, ever since the removal of Frémont seemed about to boil; and on February 2 Halleck wrote a long and confidential letter to McClellan telling of disloyal meetings and of officers who left their commands and came to the city "to stir up mutiny and insurrection." "I have succeeded in introducing police officers into some of these meetings, and their reports are conclusive as to the existence of this plot," said the department commander. General Sigel was pronounced "the instrument rather than the head" of the revolutionists, and Halleck gave the assurance: "I am fully posted in the matter and am prepared for them, but I must have the support of the Government, and the President should make no appointment of these foreign officers without consulting you." To Buell, Halleck wrote a little gloomily. The new mortar boats were a failure; it remained to be determined whether the gunboats were worth half their cost; it would take time to prepare troops to advance much south of Fort Henry.[53]

The final message from Cairo came. Grant was leaving there, in addition to all his sick, eight regiments of infantry, six companies of cavalry, and two of artillery. The last sentence was arresting: "More troops should be here soon if a change of commander is expected at Columbus." [54] Field soldier par excellence, indifferent reader of military books, Grant was putting in practice a cardinal principle: "It's not the number of enemy regiments that counts; it's who commands them." Worded as if to avoid reflection on anyone, the sentence was hardly complimentary to Major General Leonidas Polk.

The next dispatch was short:

Paducah, February 3, 1862

Major-General Halleck,
Saint Louis:
Will be off up the Tennessee at 6 o'clock. Command, twenty-three regiments in all.

U. S. Grant,
Brigadier-General [55]

In Washington no one knew that H-hour was coming with the fall of night. In Richmond there was no thought of the impending blow. Some time on this day, as the new gunboats waited and the transports gathered at Paducah, Secretary Benjamin was writing at length to G. W. Johnson, Confederate Governor of Kentucky, who was conducting a modest government-in-exile at Bowling Green. He was transmitting a call for 46,000 men—about fifty-eight regiments— to serve for the period of the war. Being something of a realist, the Secretary spoke of the "peculiar circumstances" in which Kentucky was placed, and noted the difficulties which embarrassed her authorities; he hoped, nevertheless, that Johnson would spare no pains to have his troops "ready for the field as promptly as possible." Jefferson Davis had paved the way for Benjamin with a proclamation on January 23, promising amnesty to all misguided Kentuckians who had joined the Union forces, and who now, seeing the error of their ways, wanted to change their allegiance. If they would only apply for pardon, take an oath, and promise to obey the laws of the Confederate States, their treason would be forgiven. The new levies that Johnson was to raise would not have to bear the burden alone, and Benjamin's letter concluded:

They will be joined by large re-enforcements from your sister States, and it is confidently believed that but a short period will elapse ere the soil of Kentucky will be freed from the oppression of the invader, and your whole people will be enabled to unite in a common effort for securing the blessings of peace and independence.[56]

The brave words could hardly have started on their journey when Foote told the captain of the *Essex* to proceed.

After nine months of war a General was on his way.

CHAPTER IX

GUNBOATS TAKE A FORT

There is not in the whole field of operations a point at which every man you can raise can be employed with more effect or with the prospect of as important results.

Buell to Halleck

McCLERNAND led the advance up the swollen river. Any instructions for debarkation he may have received seem not to be in the record; but according to his report he landed at 4:30 A.M. of the 4th at Itra Landing, eight miles below Fort Henry.[1] This was too far from the target to suit Grant, who wanted, if possible, to debark south of the short, but flooded, Panther Creek, which flows into the Tennessee from the east. To determine the range of the hostile guns, he went up the river in the *Essex* with Captain Porter, accompanied by two other gunboats, in what appeared to the enemy to be an attack. When approximately two miles from the fort, the gunboats opened fire. Although most of the answering shots fell short, a rifled gun threw shells beyond the mouth of the creek and put one squarely into the *Essex*. With the crew at battle stations the shell struck a good place from the Federal standpoint; for, after knocking things about in the pantry and passing through the officers' quarters, it stopped in the steerage.[2] Had the Confederate commander been aware of Grant's presence on one of the ships and of the reason for his run up the river, he probably would have kept his long-range gun out of action.

[199]

Grant, knowing now that his opponent had such an effective weapon, could plan accordingly.

McClernand's troops were soon ordered aboard again and taken to a point three miles below Fort Henry.[3] Though Panther Creek lay in their front, they were out of range of enemy fire; McClernand christened the place "Camp Halleck." Grant's report to St. Louis was headed, "Near Fort Henry"; it told how matters stood, noted that the transports had gone back to bring up Smith's division, and concluded: "I expect all the troops by 10 a.m. to-morrow. Enemy are represented as having re-enforced rapidly the last few days. General L. Tilghman commands Fort Henry." [4] He had already written many good reports, but this was his first from the field, with orders to make an attack.

A young seaman on the flagship recorded that Grant, accompanied by Smith and McClernand, held a conference with Foote in the cabin of the *Cincinnati*—the flagship—on the afternoon of the 5th. While it was in progress the *Conestoga* brought one of the previously reported torpedoes for the fleet commander's inspection. Five feet long and a foot and a half in diameter, with a rod to hold it in position on the river bottom, and another with prongs to engage a passing vessel and trip a detonating mechanism, it was a novel weapon.[5] Observing the torpedo on the fantail of the boat after the conference, Grant asked that it be taken apart so that he might see how it worked. With wrench, chisels, and hammer the ship's armorer was soon engaged in the delicate and unusual task. Upon the loosening of a nut the malicious object emitted an ominous hissing sound. Wrote Eliot Callender:

Believing that the hour for evening prayer had arrived, two of the army officers threw themselves face downward upon the deck. Admiral Foote, with the agility of a cat, sprang up the ship's ladder, followed with commendable enthusiasm by General Grant. Reaching the top, and realizing that the danger, if any, had passed, the Admiral turned around to General Grant, who was displaying more energy than grace in his first efforts on a ship's ladder, and said with his quiet smile, "General, why this haste?" "That the Navy may not get ahead of us," as quietly responded the General as he turned around to come down.[6]

The laughter was probably less embarrassing to Grant than the nonarrival of the remaining troops when they were expected. As messages from Halleck agreed with the local reports that the enemy was being reenforced, no time was to be lost. Accordingly at 11:00

P.M. of the 5th, Grant issued his order, and it is notable that he anticipated modern practice by calling it "Field Orders, No. 1." [7]

Not being certain that all his force would be on hand at a time to make an earlier movement practicable, Grant set 11:00 A.M. of the 6th as the hour for McClernand's command—the First Division— to move to a position across the road from Fort Henry to Fort Donelson and Dover. "It will be," the order ran, "the special duty of this command to prevent all re-enforcements to Fort Henry or escape from it, also to be held in readiness to charge and take Fort Henry by storm promptly on the receipt of orders."

West of the river, where Smith was camped with the part of the Second Division that had arrived, the situation was obscure, for adequate reconnaissance had been impossible. Of course it was known that the enemy was constructing Fort Heiman on the hill that dominated Henry, and this key point had to be taken. Smith was directed to get all the information he could and secure guides; starting at 11:00 A.M., he was to march with two brigades "and take and occupy the heights commanding Fort Henry." With him was to go such artillery as could be made available and as he believed necessary to protect the hills he was to seize. After taking the position, any troops not needed to hold it were to be sent to the transports, which would carry them across the river to join the First Division. Smith's Third Brigade was to move directly along the east bank of the Tennessee as fast as could be "securely done," and be ready either for an assault or for a move to the support of the First Division.

Bread and meat for two days were to be in the men's haversacks, and Smith was to send a company to Foote "armed with rifles" to act "as sharpshooters on board the gunboats." [8]

Such were the contents of a memorable order. The task given to Smith was a little complex; but he could well be trusted to act with judgment and resourcefulness. Another detail should be noted. Lieutenant Colonel McPherson, the capable regular engineer that Halleck had sent Grant for the operation, was employed in a significant way: the First Division was to move under his "guidance." Of course McPherson could not give orders to McClernand, but the latter probably got the point.

Early on the morning of the 5th, Thomas Scott arrived at Indianapolis, after visits to Pittsburgh, Columbus, Cleveland, and Detroit on which he had made long reports to his chief. Soon he read a telegram that had come to Governor Morton from Halleck asking about possible reenforcements for the move that had started up the Tennessee. Plainly surprised by the news, Scott at once wired to Stanton for instructions as to forwarding regiments in Ohio, Indiana, and Michigan. Halleck's telegram of January 30 to McClellan saying he was ordering the move, had certainly brought no notification to the Assistant Secretary, although Stanton had been informed. Before the day ended Scott himself received a message from Halleck saying he wished all possible infantry regiments sent to Cairo "to re-enforce the column now moving up the Tennessee River." He desired, he said, to cut the enemy's line before the arrival of Beauregard.[9]

McClellan, Buell, and Grant also had dispatches on the 5th from Halleck. The General in Chief was told the gunboats had only temporary crews, but enlistment of regular personnel was under way. Later, relying upon information whose origin is not clear, Halleck wired that it was reported that 10,000 men had left Bowling Green by railroad to reenforce Fort Henry. To a request for a demonstration against Bowling Green, Buell replied that he could not make one: any moves he made must be real ones; he had to repair the railroad as he advanced, and it would probably be twelve days before he could be in front of Bowling Green. In a later message he told Halleck he would send a brigade if necessary. After inquiring if the move was only up the Tennessee, he enjoined, "You must not fail." In a rather long letter Buell repeated that his progress toward Bowling Green would be slow, but left no doubt as to the value of Halleck's undertaking: "There is not in the whole field of operations a point at which every man you can raise can be employed with more effect or with the prospect of as important results." That his thoughts were tinged with some apprehension was shown by a sentence in a dispatch to McClellan, "I hope General Halleck has weighed his work well." [10]

In a telegram to Grant through the commanding officer at Paducah, Halleck had the 10,000 men from Bowling Green actually on the way; as he also did in the message sent that night to Thomas Scott. But he also gave Grant the very important information that a reenforcing regiment had left St. Louis that day; another would follow on the morrow, and a third within a few days.[11] The all important build-up had been started.

The Confederates were alert, and used for intelligence purposes not only the customary pickets but, on the west side of the river, "Captain Padgett's spy company." On the 4th Tilghman telegraphed to General Polk that the Federals were landing troops in large numbers within three miles of the fort; eight gunboats (there were seven) and nine transports were reported. The fort that the Confederate general had to defend was favorably located at a bend in the river, so that its guns could fire effectively at approaching vessels from the moment they passed the island near Panther Creek. Thus it had the first requisite of a good position. But it was not set high, and six of its seventeen guns were at the moment submerged. Remembering this fact, and recalling the commanding hills upon the west bank, Tilghman wrote in his long report of February 12, "The history of military engineering records no parallel to this case." That was the afterthought of a prisoner, who on the morning of the 5th had telegraphed to Johnston's adjutant, "If you can re-enforce strongly and quickly we have a glorious chance to overwhelm the enemy." Apparently thinking that the Federal commander would do things leisurely, he added, "Enemy said to be entrenching below." His own plans were "to concentrate closely in and under Henry." [12]

It rained hard during the night. But rain neither caused discomfort to the sailors snug in sheltered bunks or hammocks, nor made their going harder the next day. Thus Commander Walke, skipper of the new ironclad *Carondelet,* could write that the day of battle dawned "mild and cheering." [13] With smiles the navy men noted the light breeze; it would clear away the smoke from the guns; firing could be more rapid and more accurate.

Promptly on time the turning columns started over the watery, muddy roads, while the gunboats broke their moorings and moved against the heavy current. Like Grant, Foote had two divisions: the four ironclads abreast, followed by the three vulnerable wooden vessels. Though the crews were hastily improvised and left much to be desired according to the standard of a professional officer, Walke wrote, "The captains of our guns were men-of-war's men, good shots, and had their men well drilled." Tilghman's report stressed that the Federals had fifty-four guns against his defending eleven, forgetting that many of Foote's were as useless as those of his own that were under water. Only the bow guns, of which there were twelve in the first division, had value in the Federal attack on the fort. The gunboats carried the heavier metal, but the six-inch rifle in the fort had already demonstrated its effectiveness. "The flagship will, of course, open the fire first," wrote Foote on the 2nd; and there was to be no firing without correct sights; otherwise ammunition would only be wasted, and the enemy encouraged by wild and harmless shooting.[14]

At 1,700 yards the flagship opened; the other vessels at once

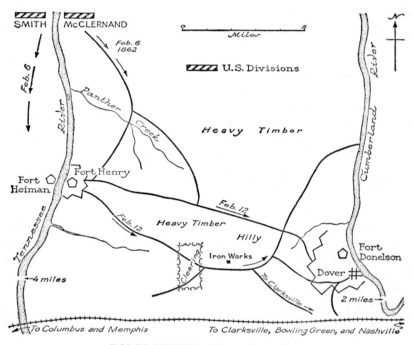

FORTS HENRY AND DONELSON

joined in, and the fort replied. Slowly the range was closed to 600 yards as the din of heavy battle resounded through the flooded woods and quickened the steps of the toiling soldiers. Officers and gunners on the boats could see their shells throwing up the dirt near the embrasures of the fort, while they hoped for direct hits on enemy guns. The pounding on their own casemates, the breaking of iron plates, the penetration of the twenty-four inches of oak in front of them, all testified to the skill of their adversaries, who had the advantage of having recorded the ranges to different points on the river bank. Admiringly Walke wrote that the enemy fire was "as good, if not better, than ours."

A shot through the boiler of the *Essex* put her out of the fight, scalding twenty-eight officers and men, some fatally; she drifted down the river, taking four important guns out of the contest. For something like an hour and a half the battle raged; smokeless embrasures showed the enemy was being hurt; then the attackers saw his flag come down. When the gunboats reached the fort Foote sent two officers ashore to raise a different flag and tell Tilghman he would see him on his flagship.[15] Feelings of exultation of the Federals, who had not seen the awful interior of the *Essex,* disappeared when they viewed the wreckage within the fort. Two guns, including the rifled piece, had burst, disabling their entire crews; two others had been struck almost simultaneously by enemy projectiles, and their crews had been put out of action by flying fragments or bursting shells. In all, seven guns were destroyed or made unusable.[16] The number of prisoners taken by the Federals was not great: seventy-eight, with sixteen additional sick in a hospital boat. Having been early informed of the approach of the investing force, Tilghman had evacuated his two brigades of five regiments, his two field batteries, and his cavalry. In all, something over 2,500 men with seven or eight guns were hastening over the muddy road toward Fort Donelson.

Walke, who had served Grant so well at Belmont and afterward, wrote:

General Grant, with his staff, rode into the fort about 3 o'clock on the same day, and relieved me of the command. The general and staff then accompanied me on board the *Carondelet* (anchored near the fort), where he complimented the officers of the flotilla in the highest terms for the gallant manner in which they had captured Fort Henry. He had expected his troops to take part in a land attack, but the heavy rains had made the direct roads to the fort almost impassable.[17]

The operation had been complex, presenting difficulties of command and control: two main columns unable to support each other, a smaller one moving close to the river, and the naval attack. There was no chance of capturing the Confederate garrison by better coordination or timing, for Tilghman was well informed of the approach of McClernand's column and would presumably have marched away if the gunboats had not attacked at all.[18] Though the Navy's guns had brought down the enemy flag, the decisive factor was the imminence of investment. Had the Confederate general not lowered his flag, but merely withdrawn his men from their guns, Foote could have done little but tie up his gunboats and await the infantry. He did not know how many enemy soldiers were in the fort ready for interior defense, and he had available as a landing force only part of a single rifle company.

Apparently the command post was where it should have been: back near the transports.[19] Though the sudden cessation of the cannonading could mean but one thing to the commanding general, one would like to know what messages from the advancing columns had come to Grant, who, once they had started, could do nothing but await developments. If Smith and McPherson sent back orderlies, while Grant had couriers with the river column, control was as good as could be expected.

While the battle raged, the wooden gunboats, in accordance with orders, kept to the left of the river, and did not shorten the range. After the fort surrendered they set out at once to execute orders given on the 2nd to Lieutenant Commander S. Ledyard Phelps, to break the railroad and then "proceed as far up the river as the stage of water will admit and capture the enemy's gunboats and other vessels which might prove available to the enemy." Back to Cairo steamed the flag officer with the *Cincinnati* and the *St. Louis,* followed by the badly damaged *Essex* with her many casualties. On the flagship one man had been killed, two guns had been disabled, and other damage done by the thirty-one hits she had taken; the *St. Louis,* though struck seven times, had no casualties. Foote, in reporting his losses the next day, said the armored gunboats had stood up well under the heavy pounding on their casemates.[20]

Grant's report to Halleck was brief:

Fort Henry is ours. The gunboats silenced the batteries before the investment was completed. I think the garrison must have commenced the retreat last night. Our cavalry followed, finding two guns abandoned in the retreat.

I shall take and destroy Fort Donelson on the 8th and return to Fort Henry.[21]

The first sentence was more rhetorical than Grant's usual style; the conjecture in the third was wrong, though the thought was natural, because he believed the garrison stronger than it was. But the next statement could have been more impressive if he had waited for the final report from the cavalry, for all the enemy guns were taken, as well as some prisoners. The assertion about Fort Donelson is puzzling, for Grant's instructions from Halleck did not mention capturing it, but only cutting the railroad between Columbus and Dover in addition to taking Fort Henry. Perhaps it was an adroitly phrased suggestion, meaning: "I will take Fort Donelson. You need not order it."

A longer report went to Captain Kelton, and with it a copy of the field order. Though apparently chagrined over the escape of the garrison, Grant said, "I do not now believe, however, that the result would have been more satisfactory." Does this mean he thought he would get the Fort Henry men later? Of Fort Donelson he spoke with confidence, saying that after capturing it he would "regard it more in the light of an advance guard than as a permanent post." With reference to his plan of operation he explained briefly: "Owing to the intolerable state of the roads no transportation will be taken to Fort Donelson and but little artillery, and that with double teams." [22] How did he mean to take the fort with only a few guns? With three gunboats up the river and three returned to their base, the Navy could do little if anything to help him. He must have counted on confusion in command, deteriorated morale, and perhaps a weaker garrison than he had before assumed. But this much is sure: he was not asking for more troops before he undertook the venture.

If "Operation Henry" were staged today, one may be sure a planner would arrange beforehand for the handling of soldiers' mail. But Ulysses Grant started up the Tennessee without apparently giving a thought to letters to and from his men. However, he took care of the important matter on the day that Fort Henry fell, and an order put A. H. Markland, "special U. S. mail agent" in "charge of all mail matter from and to the troops composing the present expedition." Priority was to be given to mail, which as well as persons connected with the service, was to be handled by all boats the government was using, and without charge. [23]

The 7th was to be a busy day in St. Louis and Washington, as well as on the Tennessee River. Borrowing Grant's first sentence, but maintaining impressive rhetoric to the end, Halleck, who had thought the enemy would make a "desperate stand," wired the General in Chief: "Fort Henry is ours. The flag of the Union is re-established on the soil of Tennessee. It will never be removed." McClellan's adjutant at once sent congratulations and said his chief desired Fort Henry held at all hazards. The message ended, "Will give further instructions to-day about further movements." Quickly Halleck came back with a longer dispatch that allayed all doubts by beginning with a firm promise of the retention of the captured work.[24]

There was much more in Halleck's dispatch. Believing that Johnston would not accept complacently the loss of so important a place, he pictured possible enemy reaction. Though he may not have known much about the Confederate strength at Bowling Green when he boldly ordered Grant's advance, a long intelligence summary that McClellan sent him on the 1st had probably arrived before the 7th. An operative who had been in and around Bowling Green on the 15th of January gave the enemy a possible sixty regiments in that general locality. Here was a really sizable force. Because Buell was unable to immobilize it by even a serious threat, as much of his force as possible should be sent to the Tennessee and the Cumberland, Halleck said; then the enemy would have to give up Bowling Green or be completely paralyzed. Judging that Sidney Johnston would act with decision and boldness, Halleck added, "He ought to concentrate at Dover, and attempt to retake Fort Henry. It is the only way he can restore an equilibrium." In this vital moment of the war Halleck did not pound the table, but ended his message with a note of persuasive earnestness: "If you agree with me, send me everything you can spare from General Buell's command or elsewhere. We must hold our ground and cut the enemy's lines. I am sending everything I can rake and scrape together from Missouri." Buell, thrown off balance, had wired McClellan at midnight, "This whole move, right in its strategical bearing, but commenced by Halleck without proper appreciation—preparation or concert—has now become of vast magnitude." After citing the probable enemy strength he pronounced the operation "hazardous." [25]

A few months later, as we have seen in the story of the war in the East, the roles of the two men were reversed, and Halleck sought to get Franklin's and Sumner's corps of McClellan's army to Centerville in time to help John Pope. But even positive orders were not sufficient to bring this about; and McClellan's actions were such that

Lincoln made the strong charge that he did not want Pope to win. Now we have the chance to see how McClellan measured up to his responsibilities and opportunities as General in Chief, and whether he would make a bold decision that might sacrifice Buell a little in order to exploit fully the great opportunity that Halleck, Foote, and Grant had created on the Tennessee. When Buell wrote on the 5th that there was no place where men could be employed "with the prospect of as important results," he was seeing clearly; and his offer of a brigade was all that could be expected at the moment. He said at the same time that, if the bridges over the Cumberland and Tennessee could be destroyed and Halleck could maintain himself, "Bowling Green will speedily fall and Columbus soon follow." Now Grant had Fort Henry and the Tennessee bridge was out, and Buell, who had said it might take him twelve days to place troops in front of Bowling Green, was put to the test. Would he do all that he could to aid a bold operation that had begun propitiously but had elements of danger, or would he hold back in order to salvage as much as possible of his own plans?

Evening came—7:15—before the promised telegram was sent from Washington. After congratulating Halleck and saying his operation had "caused the utmost satisfaction" in the Capital, the General in Chief hedged in the matter of instructions. He advised against a dash on Columbus, adding that it was better to devote everything toward turning the position. This was a perfectly safe suggestion. More impressive was the sentence, "The bridges at Tuscumbia and Decatur should be at all hazards destroyed at once"; but Foote had already thought of that. McClellan suggested rather than ordered: "Either Buell or yourself should soon go to the scene of operations. Why not have Buell take the line of Tennessee and operate on Nashville, while your troops turn Columbus? Those two points gained, a combined movement on Memphis will be next in order." The ending was: "Thank Grant, Foote, and their commands for me." Commendation even stronger than McClellan's came to Halleck from Stanton, "Your energy and ability receive the strongest commendation of this Department. You have my perfect confidence and may rely upon the utmost support in your undertaking." [26]

Not knowing that the *Conestoga, Tyler,* and *Lexington* were already steaming up the river to do all the damage that they could, Halleck addressed to Grant "or" Foote the telegram, "Push the gunboats up the river to cut the railroad bridges. Troops to sustain the gunboats can follow in transports." So far as the records show, no thanks went to Grant, though on the 9th Halleck responded immediately to Foote's official report with a telegram of congratulations for his "brilliant victory." Grant had hinted a little for a compliment when he ended his letter to Kelton, "Hoping that what has been done will meet the approval of the major-general commanding the department, I remain, etc." But, as will be seen, Halleck was contemplating a change of field commander and perhaps refrained from commendation for that reason; it would look strange to remove a man after saying to him, "Well done." Better than any message of mere thanks, however, was one from Halleck's chief of staff, Brigadier General George W. Cullum, who had been sent to Cairo to expedite reenforcements and give orders in Halleck's name. It had an easy and friendly tone, and after speaking of Grant's "very important operations," it told the field soldier of several regiments either en route, or soon moving to him.[27] Sending Cullum to Cairo was a command arrangement of great importance, and Halleck deserves full credit for it. Not every general would have given up his number-one assistant at such a critical time, even though it would keep many vexing details from reaching his St. Louis headquarters.

The wires were working fast, and in another dispatch on the same day Halleck told McClellan that gunboats and cavalry had been ordered up the Tennessee to destroy the near-by bridges, that Columbus was very strong, and that "Fort Donelson will probably be taken to-morrow." A telegram to Buell repeated the glad refrain "Fort Henry is ours," and said Grant expected to take Donelson the next day. Congratulations came back promptly, with the cheering information that a brigade was being sent from Green River to go up the Tennessee; boats would start that night to pick up the regiments. To a message from McClellan, Buell replied: "I hope General Grant will not require further re-enforcements. I will go, if necessary." If availability and time were not involved, it might have been better to send Grant troops from the vicinity of Louisville, for taking them from Green River would weaken the threat on Bowling Green. Unfortunately Buell was not able to send a field battery with the infantry.[28]

How things stood at department headquarters in St. Louis at the end of this important day, Halleck put down in a letter to Buell:

My telegrams of to-day are so full that I have very little to add in answer to your letter of the 5th. You say you regret that we could not have consulted on this move earlier. So do I, most sincerely. I had no idea of commencing the movement before the 15th or 20th instant till I received General McClellan's telegram about the re-enforcement sent to Tennessee or Kentucky with Beauregard. Although not ready, I deemed it important to move instantly. I believe I was right. We must hold. Fort Henry must be held at all hazards. I am sending there every man I can get hold of, without regard to the consequences of abandoning posts in this State. If the rebels rise, I will put them down afterwards. Grant's force is small—only 15,000. Eight thousand more are on the way to re-enforce him. If we can sustain ourselves and advance up the Cumberland or Tennessee, Bowling Green must be abandoned. I suppose the mud there, as it is here, is too deep for movements outside of railroads and river.[29]

There is reason to believe, as has been indicated previously, that Halleck actually made at least a tentative decision solely upon the urgings of Grant and Foote, before he had received McClellan's message about the deserter. Be this as it may, the words "advance up the Cumberland or Tennessee" leave no doubt about his wishing to exploit the opportunity of the moment.

In addition to telegrams and letters, a very important person had arrived in Louisville. Having received no replies to his messages to Washington, Scott remained in Indianapolis (where he found contracts were made in accordance with law, though the commissary had an indebtedness of nearly $2,000,000) until the morning of the 6th. Then he changed his prescribed itinerary and went to Louisville, so that he could—as he wrote to Stanton—"lay before General Buell all the data in relation to military organization in Ohio, Indiana and Michigan, in order to enable him the more effectually to aid General Halleck in the Tennessee River movement." The next day he wrote a "private and confidential" letter in his own hand expressing some concern about the Tennessee River move:

Buell is in great trouble fearing that Halleck may be forced to retire after having possession of Fort Henry. We must have absolute and entire concert of action by these two departments. Think it over and devise some plan by which it shall be done. Buell is very desirous that it should be so and I will endeavor to impress it upon General Halleck tomorrow after I get to St. Louis.

Stanton pointed up the letter with the crisp indorsement, "Buell's fear that Halleck will get hurt." [30]

In another report the same day Scott stated that an operation into East Tennessee was now out of the question; he said also that Buell did not encourage the construction of the contemplated railroad toward Knoxville. After his two days with the Louisville commander he was enthusiastic about him and said: "In General Buell we have *a great officer.*" Not all the people of the region shared the view, and on the very day that Scott wrote, Greeley's paper contained a Cincinnati dispatch of the 3rd that spoke of the "inefficiency and uselessness of Gen. Buell." Solely at his door, said the news item, rested the responsibility for the chance the enemy had had to fortify Bowling Green.[31]

Correspondents who had been passing their time tediously at Cairo, perplexed or disgusted at Grant's recent demonstration, at last had the chance to send exciting telegrams and letters. Unsatisfied with the mere surrender of an important fort, the reporter for the *Boston Journal* invented a dialogue between Foote and Tilghman. Forgetting that the mere hauling down of a flag is a signal of surrender, the newsman had the Confederate commander ask for terms, so that the sturdy sailor could thunder impressively: "Unconditional." Nor was that sufficient; a little argument about the Constitution was served up as a garnish for the historic occasion. Unfortunately, in order to brag about their competent flag officer, Northerners put into his mouth a retort to Tilghman that was unchivalrous and out of character.[32]

Some accounts, however, were accurate, and the *New York Tribune* reporter, correcting an earlier dispatch, said that only eight guns, not fourteen, were taken from the Confederates as they retreated toward Fort Donelson. Much emphasis was put upon the amount of booty that was taken in the fort and at the bridge, and it was said to be worth a million dollars, a figure which looked impressive at that time. Unable to appreciate properly a first-rate achievement that still left enemy armies without a scratch, Horace Greeley editorialized on the 8th: "A few more events such as the capture of Fort Henry, and the war will be substantially at an end." Still gloating on the 14th, he told of a letter found at Fort Henry, which had been written by a Paducah spy, and which had six pages of minute descriptions of gunboats, armaments, and such things but "did not give the strength of our land forces, because, thanks to the prompt and rapid movement of Gen. Grant, nobody in Paducah could learn it."

The governor of Tennessee sped the news of the disaster to Richmond on the 7th,[33] and in a room in the Covington Hotel in Bowling Green Generals Johnston, Beauregard, and Hardee met to make a momentous decision. Beauregard had arrived three days before; though not even a squad of soldiers was with him, but only a few staff officers, crowds had cheered the hero of Sumter and Manassas on the long ride from Virginia through Knoxville and Chattanooga. He was to report to Johnston for assignment to personal command at Columbus, apparently as an immediate overseer of General Polk.[34] The Confederacy had a number of four-star generals, and three were hardly needed at the moment in Virginia to oppose McClellan, even though one was Adjutant General. With the shift of Beauregard, the deployment of the South's top-ranking generals was: Cooper in Richmond, Lee directing matters on the Atlantic coast, Joe Johnston at Manassas, Sidney Johnston and Beauregard in the West. Sidney Johnston had had many adverse conditions to deal with—none perhaps more baffling than Halleck's in Missouri—but the location of his headquarters at Bowling Green challenges Jefferson Davis's high opinion of him. Why was he there? Unity of command in the West was an element of strength that the Confederacy possessed against the greater power of the North, and when Johnston set up his headquarters at Bowling Green he was endangering it. He was likely to become little more than a local troop commander, assuming duties that the competent Hardee was perfectly able to discharge.

After a day's delay in Nashville for presentation to Tennessee's cordial legislators, Beauregard arrived on the evening of the 4th, and met Johnston for the first time.[35] There were things a plenty for the generals to talk about: the number of troops, and the various positions they occupied; equipment and supplies; the recent defeat at Mill Springs; the strange marching around in the mud that Grant had recently done in western Kentucky; the large command that Buell had, and what he seemed to be meditating. Though there were dark spots in the picture, there was also an encouraging fact: McClellan, who had been imposed upon by wooden guns and a weak outpost on Munson's Hill, in addition to drilling his own great army about Washington, was trying to unify remote operations. That was equivalent to cutting down the Federal forces to a marked degree, while the railroad from Bowling Green to Columbus multiplied the possible effectiveness of the weaker Confederates.

After a first evening possibly passed in leisurely discussion, the two generals learned the next day that they had war at their doorstep. However, the messages from Colonel Heiman and General Tilghman were optimistic, and on the 6th there came to hand Tilghman's dispatch of 11:00 A.M. of the 5th, with its very hopeful words about overwhelming the Federals.[36] The move that Tilghman described was precisely the one that Halleck told McClellan the enemy should make. Did Johnston, with two of the South's best generals at his side, actually have the great opportunity that Tilghman pictured—a chance to strike Grant from the east and south at the same time? What forces did he have available for such a counterstroke?

According to Johnston's own return, he had at the end of January 28,000 men in and about Bowling Green, organized into fifty regiments of infantry and cavalry, and twelve batteries; Polk at Columbus had in addition to 2,000 garrison troops some twenty-five regiments, raising the total to about 17,000 men; at Paris there were 1,100 cavalrymen, and 5,000 men occupied Forts Henry and Donelson.[37] A railroad with rolling stock at hand, and two rivers with steamers available, gave Johnston unusual facilities for rapid concentration. Buell could be dismissed as a present threat to Bowling Green, so only a relatively small Confederate force was needed there; and a demonstration by Polk against Cairo and Paducah might hold back Federal reenforcements from the small column that had struck Fort Henry. Strategic reserves in the usual sense, Johnston may not have had; but no one can say that there were not possibilities in the situation worth careful consideration.

Alfred Roman, later a staff officer of Beauregard's, wrote in the 1880's a long account of that general's military operations in which he stated that Beauregard urged an attack on Grant, and continued to advise it after word came on the 7th of the loss of Fort Henry and the escape of most of its garrison to Fort Donelson. It would have been possible, he wrote, for Johnston to throw 27,000 men against Grant's 15,000 by the 10th of February at the latest.[38] Roman noted the favorable disposition of the Confederate troops along the railroad between Bowling Green and Clarksville and said there was adequate transportation; but he passed over other considerations, and we may question the optimistic date he set down with such confidence.[39] Then too we must remember that it may have been a case of an officer bristling with boldness when he was not himself responsible for any failure. Johnston doubtless recalled how de-

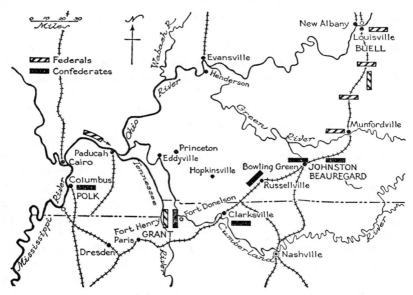

GRANT'S ISOLATED POSITION, FEBRUARY 7, 1862

plorably things had turned out for the Confederates when Crittenden marched out from his intrenchments in the first hours of a wet Sunday morning, hoping to defeat Thomas's regiments before they had had their breakfast. And if we recall the touch of alarm and the talk of falling back behind the Rappahannock that was in Beauregard's message to Jefferson Davis reporting McDowell's advance on Centerville, we can question whether the Louisiana general would have followed a bold rather than a prudent course if he had been the responsible commander. All that we know with certainty are the decisions that were made and recorded in a memorandum signed by Beauregard and Hardee, which says nothing about any proposed but rejected course of action.[40] The document appears to be the work of three gloomy men, united in the belief that the bottom was about

out of the tub. If their views were not in actual agreement, Johnston did not report correctly when he ended a long message to Benjamin the next day with the sentence, "Generals Beauregard and Hardee are equally with myself impressed with the necessity of withdrawing our force from this line at once." [41]

Although Johnston had previously written that Donelson would be very difficult to attack from the land side, the memorandum declared the fort not long tenable.[42] Preparations were to begin at once to remove the army at Bowling Green to Nashville, behind the Cumberland, "a strong point some miles below the city being fortified forthwith, to defend the river from the passage of gunboats and transports." Eyes went beyond the capital of Tennessee: "From Nashville, should any further retrograde movement become necessary, it will be made to Stevenson, and thence according to circumstances." Columbus was likewise pronounced no longer capable of being held, and withdrawal from there, except for a small garrison, was to be to Humboldt, then "if necessary" to Grand Junction, perhaps to Grenada, and if need be, to Jackson, Mississippi. It was seen clearly that the possession of the Tennessee River by the Federals divided Johnston's force east of the Mississippi into two parts that would have to fall back many miles before they could cooperate, if the enemy moved with speed. An effort to keep a grip upon the Mississippi, was, however, to be made; and, with the aid of Commodore George N. Hollins's gunboats, Island No. 10 and Fort Pillow were to be "defended to the last extremity." A "bold stand" by the gunboats at Memphis was also envisaged.

There was a deadly seductive element in the situation that confronted the Confederates, and the Beauregard-Hardee memorandum is disappointingly silent upon the important question of whether additional troops would be put into Fort Donelson, and, if so, to what extent and with what precise mission. Constructed to bar a river, the work could become a fatal trap; men put into it while the Federals were building up their strength might never get out except as prisoners. Everything would depend upon the general who would command within the fort and the one who would throw the investing line. It was clear, however, that Donelson must be held for a time, and it should have been apparent to Johnston that the management of that position would test his generalship.

Before and since the conference in the Bowling Green hotel generals have planned withdrawals, and sometimes on a vaster scale. But on that February 7 there was something unusual. Brigadier Lloyd Tilghman, whose capture the Confederates were lamenting, was writing to Johnston's adjutant: "Through the courtesy of Brig. Gen. U. S. Grant, commanding Federal forces, I am permitted to communicate with you in relation to the result of the action between the fort under my command at this place and the Federal gunboats on yesterday." After describing the battle and testifying to the gallantry of his officers and men, he concluded, "I also take pleasure in acknowledging the courtesy and consideration shown by Brig. Gen. U. S. Grant and Commander Foote and the officers of their command." One of the Confederate officers who for several days was to be on the same boat with Grant and ate at his table, not only wrote in later years that his captor impressed him "as a modest, amiable, kindhearted but resolute man," but recorded an incident that showed Grant's ability to handle a delicate situation with much tact.[43] At the first opportunity, Ulysses Grant showed officers who once had worn the blue that surrender to him would involve no personal humiliation, but considerate, respectful, and understanding treatment.

McClernand likewise was doing some writing. After telling Foote that he had "taken the liberty of giving the late Fort Henry the new and more appropriate name of Fort Foote," he said, "Please pardon the liberty I have taken without first securing your concurrence, as I am hardly disposed to do, considering the liberty which you took in capturing the fort yesterday without my cooperation." The order changing the name of the work, which McClernand said in his report he had "formally issued," was not to prove effective; history has properly preserved the name the builders gave to it—though whom it honored is not definitely known.[44]

The 8th did not see Grant's columns on the way to Donelson. The falling river had responded to the recent rains, and he wrote to Cullum, "I contemplated taking Fort Donelson to-day with infantry and cavalry alone, but all my troops may be kept busily engaged in saving what we now have from the rapidly-rising waters."[45] How many defenders would have confronted Grant that day at Donelson is hard to determine. During the night, Ohio-born Bushrod Johnson, who had taught in Tennessee after resigning from the United States

Army and was now a Confederate brigadier, had arrived and taken command; the force he found totaled about eleven regiments. Brigadier General John Floyd, now at Clarksville, was sending more men into the trap, even while Johnston, unbalanced by the naval accomplishment at Fort Henry, was reporting the intended abandonment of Bowling Green and asserting to Secretary Benjamin that the gunboats would probably repeat their performance and take Donelson without any assistance from Federal troops. At Russellville, Grant's old friend Simon Buckner was entraining his regiments to go to Clarksville, so that they too might get inside Donelson.[46] Grant's statement about taking the fort on the 8th seems overbold; but taking it would not have been as hard on that day as it was several days later, nor the harvest of prisoners as great.

While Grant was writing to Cullum, his sole remaining gunboat, the *Carondelet,* dispatched the day before to break up the railroad at the bridge which defending Confederates had saved on the 6th,[47] came into sight; and he laid down his pen, to resume presently and report success. Since he was to be severely disciplined later for not making reports, the ending of his letter is interesting: "The steamer which will carry this will leave in a very short time, so that I will not be able to send any additional report to General Halleck. I would be obliged, therefore, if you would send this, or a copy, or such portion of it as you think might interest the general commanding the department."

As Grant complained about the encircling water, and Buell telegraphed to McClellan, "I am concentrating and preparing, but will not decide definitely yet," Halleck was reporting to the Secretary of War that he was handicapped by too many brigadiers with commissions from the same day. He gave no fewer than eight names, including Sherman, Pope, Grant, Curtis, Sigel, and McClernand, each of whom was, he said, "unwilling to serve under the other." He had a solution: "If Brig. Gen. E. A. Hitchcock could be made a major-general of volunteers and assigned to this department it would satisfy all and reconcile all differences." How he intended to use the one-time instructor and Commandant of Cadets at West Point was made clear: "If it can be done there should be no delay, as an experienced officer of high rank is wanted immediately on the Tennessee line." Stanton replied that he concurred in the suggestion and would urge its adoption on the President.[48]

Then McClellan's dispatch to Halleck that Buell or he should go to the scene of action arrived, and at noon the Missouri commander replied, "I shall go to Fort Henry on Monday or Tuesday." (It was then Saturday.) With the enemy on both his flanks, Halleck said he could not advance without more troops. If Buell could not move on Bowling Green, all troops not needed to hold the Green River should be sent to the Cumberland to use a water route to Nashville. That was Halleck's proposition. Some days would be required to repair the damaged gunboats; thus, he argued, there was time.[49]

After deliberating further on the General in Chief's message, Halleck later in the day wrote out a rather elaborate proposal for unity of command in the West. Create, said he, a "Western Division," to include an augmented Department of the Missouri, the Department of the Ohio, and a new Department of the Mississippi. Commanders for the departments: Hunter, Buell, Hitchcock. Over-all commander for the new division: himself. Whatever we may think of Halleck's motives—he asserted he did not really desire a larger command— it must be conceded that his proposal would have met the difficulties in command then developing. His growing opinion of Sherman was shown in the closing sentences: "If General Hitchcock cannot be appointed, General Sherman could take the Department of the Mississippi. His health is greatly improved." [50]

Since Thomas Scott had already urged Secretary Stanton to work out a plan to harmonize operations in the West, Halleck's definite proposal would seem to have been made at a propitious moment. But it is doubtful if the Secretary was informed of it by McClellan. Though it would have greatly lessened his problems as General in Chief, the latter probably disliked the subordination of Buell to Halleck.

Halleck did not go to Fort Henry as he planned. He was ill-prepared to jump suddenly into command of troops in the field, and his work at headquarters was far from finished. When appointment presently came to Ethan Allen Hitchcock, that high-minded, scholarly soldier said "No" on the Tennessee proposition, protesting in his famous diary against being put over the head of Grant, who was obviously doing all he could.[51]

Though planning to supersede Grant, Halleck did not hesitate to give him a hard assignment: "If possible, destroy the bridge at Clarksville. It is of vital importance, and should be attempted at all hazards."

How Grant could accomplish the mission before he took Donelson, is hard to see; after that it probably would not be desirable. But the heavy task was balanced by instructions to do some obvious things— such as strengthening Henry against land attack—and by the injunction, "Impress slaves of secessionists in vicinity to work on fortifications." Presently Halleck would learn from the general on the spot that there were no Negroes in the locality.[52]

Then came Sunday. While mechanics hammered his boats back into shape, Foote preached to the Cairo Presbyterians, an admiring correspondent writing that the flag officer was as much at home in the pulpit as he had been on the *Cincinnati* during the recent battle. When a niece in Cleveland learned that the text was, "Let not your heart be troubled: ye believe in God, believe also in me," she wrote to her father that it should have been, "Let not your heart be troubled: ye believe in God, believe also in the gunboats." [53] But though ready to fill an empty pulpit, Foote said "No" when Cullum, at Halleck's direction, asked him to have three gunboats run the batteries at Donelson and destroy the bridge at Clarksville.[54]

While Foote was bidding the Presbyterians to cheer up and contemplate the world to come, Grant was admonishing and promising punishment in this world. One order told regimental officers to stay off the steamboats and live in camps with their troops. Another began: "The pilfering and marauding disposition shown by some of the men of this command has determined the general commanding to make an example of some one, to fully show his disapprobation of such conduct." There was to be no escape, for the order said, "Every offense will be traced back to a responsible party." If the really guilty person could not be located, the brigade or regimental commander would be punished. But Grant appealed to something above fear: "In an enemy's country, where so much more could be done by a manly and humane policy to advance the cause which we all have so deeply at heart, it is astonishing that men can be found so wanton as to destroy, pillage, and burn indiscriminately, without inquiry." [55]

Although the gunboats did not make the desired pilgrimage to Clarksville, Halleck was able to indulge in a little Sunday optimism. He told Cullum of two new regiments that were about to start down the river. To the report that McClellan was showing signs of adopting the St. Louis plan in its entirety he annexed a sharp warning: "If so, look out for lively times." The chief of staff on his part sent his miscellany of information: The *Essex* would have to go to St. Louis to have her boiler repaired; mortar boats were being tested; an Indiana regiment had just arrived with 900 men but only 400 arms; it could be equipped with renovated muskets turned in by another regiment that had just received British Enfields. For some months the unsavory Knights of the Golden Circle had been forming their secret lodges and were being watched; a provost marshal captain had reported to him a "gang of K.G.C." in Randolph County, Illinois.[56]

The day brought to Fort Donelson another new commander—Grant's old adversary at Belmont, Gideon Pillow. Ten days later Pillow wrote officially: "Deep gloom was hanging over the command, and the troops were greatly depressed and demoralized by the circumstances attending the surrender of Fort Henry and the manner of retiring from that place." Some discounting should be done; but the last part of the assertion was probably substantially correct. The new commander reorganized the thirteen regiments into five brigades, and appealed to "the courage and fidelity of brave officers and men under his command to maintain the post." Then he exhorted: "Drive back the ruthless invader from our soil and again raise the Confederate flag over Fort Henry." Even McClernand could not have waxed more eloquent than Pillow in his peroration: "Our battle cry, 'Liberty or death.'"[57]

From near at hand Grant took another look at Donelson and wrote to Mary: "Our men had a little engagement with the enemy's pickets, killing five of them, wounding a number, and expressively speaking, 'gobbling' up some twenty-four more." He announced an important military doctrine just as expressively when he spoke of his intention to keep "the ball moving as lively as possible." After asserting that he believed he could carry on a successful campaign, he explained, "I do not speak boastfully but utter a presentiment." Apparently some of the gobbled-up men had given up-to-the-minute news about the situation in the fort, for he ended: "G. J. Pillow commands at Fort Donelson. I hope to give him a tug before you receive this." Perhaps as Grant wrote, Halleck was reading a telegram in which Buell said he was planning "the rescue of your column, if it should come to that."[58]

Monday brought back the *Conestoga, Tyler,* and *Lexington* from their trip up the river, and Commander Phelps began a very interesting document as he waited to get them through the damaged draw on the bridge above Fort Henry. No fewer than six Confederate boats had been destroyed, either by the Federals or by their owners; a vessel laden with "submarine batteries" (mines) had been blown up with dramatic effect; at Cerro Gordo, Tennessee, he had found and captured the *Eastport,* two hundred and eighty feet long, one of the fastest steamboats on the Mississippi, which was being converted into an ironclad gunboat. She was one of the mystery vessels of which the Federal sailors had been hearing.

While the *Tyler* stood guard over this handsome prize, the other two boats proceeded to Florence, Alabama, at the foot of famous Muscle Shoals. There a deputation of frightened citizens waited upon Phelps, praying that their wives and daughters might not be molested, or their handsome railroad bridge destroyed. A message was sent to the ladies that the Yankees were "neither ruffians nor savages"; the bridge, being on a short spur from Tuscumbia, was left untouched. Only the shoals kept Phelps from going the forty remaining miles to Decatur, where the bridge carried the main railroad from Memphis to Chattanooga and points east.

When Phelps returned to Cerro Gordo he learned from the commander of the *Tyler* that loyal Tennesseans who had enlisted reported that six or seven hundred badly armed men, some of them "pressed," were encamped not far away. Returning up the river to Savannah, he landed 130 riflemen and a 12-pounder howitzer to attack the enemy camp. He found the place hastily abandoned; but equipment and supplies were captured, and also a large mailbag containing letters with military information. At Cerro Gordo the *Eastport* was taken in tow, as well as another vessel loaded with 250,000 feet of the choicest ship and building timber and "all the machinery, spikes, plating, nails, etc., belonging to the rebel gunboat." A third boat laden with timber sprang a leak and had to be abandoned; but the *Eastport* was before long a Federal ram, and because of her speed, superior to other vessels in the Union service. In addition to much material booty, Phelps also garnered papers that told the official history of the Confederate "floating preparations on the Mississippi, Cumberland, and Tennessee." But he thought his destructions and seizures were not the only important result of his expedition, and he wrote:

We have met with the most gratifying proofs of loyalty everywhere across Tennessee, and in the portions of Mississippi and Alabama we visited most affecting instances greeted us almost hourly. Men, women, and children several times gathered in crowds of hundreds, shouted their welcome, and hailed their national flag with an enthusiasm there was no mistaking. It was genuine and heartfelt. These people braved everything to go to the river bank where a sight of their flag might once more be enjoyed, and they have experienced, as they related, every possible form of persecution. Tears flowed freely down the cheeks of men as well as of women, and there were those who fought under the Stars and Stripes at Monterey who in this manner testified to their joy.[59]

Such feelings were not universal by any means, and whole communities fled to the woods at the approach of the gunboats. These were, Phelps explained, places "where the fleeing steamers in advance had spread tales of our coming with fire-brands, burning, destroying, ravishing, and plundering." That there was a basis for such reports, Grant's hard order of the 9th clearly and sadly shows beyond a doubt. For the good behavior of his own men Phelps received credit in the South; and a Memphis dispatch to Richmond, listing the heavy loss of ships and public property, ended, "They took 20,000 pounds of salt pork from Florence, but refused to touch private property, not even cotton." No mention was made of unmolested wives and daughters, or the unharmed bridge. The safety of the latter was, however, duly reported in other telegrams, and readers of the papers may have assumed that silence on some questions meant the Yankees had been happily and surprisingly well behaved.[60]

The gunboat thrust of one hundred and fifty miles had a touch of blitzkrieg: it cut the Confederates in Tennessee into two parts, quite as von Rundstedt sundered the Allies in May, 1940, and American armored columns cut the Germans in twain in August four years later. Although troops would not follow for several weeks, the waters of the Tennessee had become an unhampered highway for the Federal gunboats.

Still enthusiastic, Halleck wired to McClellan that various informants told him troops could not move by road in Kentucky until well into April. By that time he could be in the heart of Tennessee. "Give us the means," he said, "and we are certain to give the enemy a telling blow." Then he played a high card: "We have just taken Poplar Bluff and Doniphan, capturing Major Jennings and 29 men of the rebel army." When McClellan saw that the St. Louis commander had troops only ten miles from Arkansas he might reward him with something more than words—or so perhaps thought Halleck. Hesitant as McClellan was to venture forth with the great Army of the Potomac, and urging a water route to Richmond, he was really not in a good position to argue with Halleck. But he could easily forget this, while Buell, though disliking mud, worried that Paducah might be attacked from Columbus and his troops endangered if he sailed up the Cumberland.[61]

Something appears to have been going on behind Halleck's back, for at 9:00 A.M. of this day—February 10—Buell telegraphed McClellan: "Just received your dispatch. Would like to see you, but would it not attract the enemy's attention too much?" What exactly had the General in Chief said in the apparently lost telegram? A high-level conference between McClellan, Halleck, and Buell would undoubtedly have been much in order at the time; but one can doubt whether Little Mac would have liked to sit at a table with Old Brains at this particular juncture, although Halleck's extensive proposal of the 8th had not yet reached him.[62] With practically no censorship existing, it is likely that the newspapers would have featured a trip by the General in Chief to Louisville. But what did it matter, when the West was already a scene of action?

Clarksville was becoming almost an obsession to Halleck, and he told Grant: "If possible destroy the bridge at Clarksville. Run any risk to accomplish this. . . . Large reenforcements will soon join you." Grant may have seen the illusory nature of the bridge, so long as the enemy had steamers on the river to take troops to Dover. If gunboats could have run the batteries of the fort, it would have been another matter. But on that point Halleck had relaxed, wiring Cullum that, while he was straining every nerve to send troops to take Dover and Clarksville, all he wanted from Foote was a couple of gunboats to precede the transports up the Cumberland. As if to appease the sailor, Halleck concluded, "Show him this."[63]

Grant also had changed his ideas about the gunboats; he wanted some when he struck at Donelson. Though the Navy had stolen Thursday's show, there was no need to put on an all-army operation to balance the account; and he wrote to Foote, "I feel that there should be no delay in this matter, and yet I do not feel justified in going without some of your gunboats to co-operate." Could not two boats be sent at once from Cairo to the Cumberland, towed perhaps by steamers, and with army artillerymen if necessary? Eager to keep things moving, he concluded: "Please let me know your determination in this matter, and start as soon as you like. I will be ready to co-operate at any moment." The Senate having failed to confirm Smith's promotion to brigadier, Grant sent a telegram to Washburne urging him to get a reconsideration. The words, "We can't spare him now," brought confirmation four days later.[64]

Without waiting for a reply from Foote, Grant issued instructions that evening to Walke to proceed with the *Carondelet* to Donelson, the *Tyler, Lexington,* and *Conestoga* following later. In a message to Foote, Walke covered himself by saying that he was "acting upon your general instructions, repeated at Fort Henry," but he hoped the fleet commander would overtake him or send him new orders. Certainly the two services were working in complete and wholehearted harmony, and Walke explained, "General Grant desires that I should be at Fort Donelson as soon as I can get there." [65]

For his own troops the general issued a warning order. With the exception of garrisons for Forts Henry and Heiman, troops were to be in readiness to march early on the 12th; no tents or baggage except what could be personally carried; forty rounds of ammunition and two days' rations upon each man; wagons with three more days of food were to follow, but were not to "impede the progress of the main column." From reenforcing regiments that had arrived, a brigade was added to each division, McClernand being raised to three brigades, Smith to four.[66]

On February 11 things were coming to a head. Halleck telegraphed to Cullum and Foote: "Push ahead boldly and quickly. I will give you plenty of support in a few days. Time now is everything for us. Don't delay one instant." Flattery was mixed with the extra urging given to the sailor: "You have gained great distinction by your capture of Fort Henry. Everybody recognizes your services. Make your name famous in history by the capture of Fort Donelson and Clarksville. . . . Act quickly, even though only half ready. Troops will soon be ready to support you." It was probably more with thought of the eager soldier up the Tennessee than of medals for his own chest that Foote telegraphed Halleck, "I am ready with three gunboats to proceed up the Cumberland and shall leave here for that purpose in two hours—8:30 p.m." Personnel troubles as well as ship repairs were plaguing him; thirty men had run away from a steamer to avoid transfer to a gunboat. Repeating a request previously made, Foote wired the Navy Department, "I trust that the 600 sea-faring men will immediately be sent to me." Since Cullum was in close contact with Foote and was not far from Paducah, Halleck gave him the task of coordination, telling him not to allow any troops up the Cumberland unless preceded by gunboats. The answer was that three gunboats were leaving Cairo that night, and one armored gunboat had already gone to the Cumberland from the Tennessee, with three unarmored to follow.[67] Halleck could keep his situation map well up to date.

John Pope at Jefferson City was being partially stripped of his command. A telegram told him that trains would be leaving to bring two of his regiments and a battery to St. Louis; they must be ready to start immediately. Though Henry Halleck had no reservoir of charm to employ when occasion required, he knew explanations to subordinates were helpful, and he said: "We have stirring times in Kentucky and Tennessee, and want every man we can get." Buell, however, was apparently not kept up to the minute, for he was informed that three or four gunboats would be ready to ascend the Cumberland the last of the week, with more following. After assuring him that Paducah was perfectly safe, Halleck said, "Can't you come with all your available forces and command the column up the Cumberland? I shall go to the Tennessee this week." [68]

Thomas Scott had arrived at Cairo the night before from St. Louis, and was surveying the scene. Only a few days earlier, no less a person than Anthony Trollope had unpacked there the appurtenances of a cultured traveler and the unfinished manuscript in which he was describing the domestic warfare of the Americans. He wrote: "As Cairo is of all towns in America the most desolate, so is its hotel the most forlorn and wretched"; but Scott, habituated only to the comforts of the American seaboard, was not too shaken by the inadequacies of the St. Charles Hotel. He wrote to his chief enthusiastically about Foote; and he said to Halleck after alluding to Walke's success up the Tennessee, "Victory seems to crown all our efforts." Nevertheless he was suffering from doubts, for he inquired: "Is General Grant strong enough and quite ready for the Cumberland and Donelson movement? Position is said to be strong, and we should be strong enough to be very certain of success." [69]

All such things are important for an understanding of the background of great events. But what counted most on the 11th of February, 1862, was taking place up the Tennessee River; and it has been described by Lew Wallace. In September he had reported at Paducah with the new Eleventh Indiana, which replaced the regiment of ninety-day men he had commanded in the East. Presently he was a one-star general commanding a brigade; and, perhaps as a reward for a fruitful cavalry reconnaissance toward Camp Beauregard in late December, Smith put his brigade behind the advance guard in the movement against Fort Heiman.[70] The article that Wallace wrote afterward about Fort Donelson needs no discounting because of bias for Grant. Although he always sought to be fair and just to Grant, Wallace could not dissociate him from the damage done to his own military reputation by a disputed incident in the Battle of Shiloh. Recollections of events long past are always to be suspected, and especially when set down by a writer of fiction; but any embellishment by Wallace of the striking incidents in his vivid story was probably not too extensive.

According to Wallace, a staff officer visited each division and brigade commander on the morning of the 11th and gave the verbal message: "General Grant sends his compliments, and requests to see you this afternoon on his boat." What took place on the *New Uncle Sam* could be called a council of war "only by grace," because it turned out to be merely a friendly, informal gathering where the commanding general smoked "but never said a word." Wallace conjectured that the man who in battle, as in camp, spoke "in a conversational tone," and appeared "to see everything that went on, and was always intent on business" was framing in his mind the order he would issue that night. Each summoned officer left when it suited his fancy; but all knew they would march against Donelson the next day.[71]

The written order that followed did not give the time of starting; it said only that the movement would be made "tomorrow." But the artillery and the bulk of the infantry on the east of the Tennessee had been moved to high ground away from the river to facilitate an early start. The roads and the formation of the columns were prescribed. That something more than the capture of a fort so as to open a river was in Grant's mind was indicated by the sentence, "One brigade of the Second Division should be thrown into Dover to cut off all retreat by the river, if found practicable to do so." It may not as a rule be a good thing to put "if practicable" into an order, for it offers a chance of escape for an irresolute subordinate; but this was a direction for C. F. Smith. Grant did not know how many Confederates were within Donelson's intrenchments, but it did not seem to matter; and his order ended: "The force of the enemy being so variously reported, it is impossible to give exact details of attack, but the necessary orders will be given on the field." [72]

CHAPTER X

FORT DONELSON

I feel every confidence of success and the best feeling prevails among the men.   *Grant to Halleck*

Lincoln had planned aggressive moves for Washington's Birthday.
But it was on his own birthday that twenty-five infantry regiments,
seven batteries, and some cavalry made the historic march against
twenty-eight to thirty regiments and six batteries in a strongly prepared position. "We start this morning for Fort Donelson in heavy
force," was the beginning of Grant's short dispatch to Halleck as
15,000 men turned their faces to the target ten miles away. Two regiments from St. Louis and the brigade from Buell that had arrived
the night before were being sent around by water. That would expedite departure and keep extra wear off roads; but it involved some
risk, for no one knew anything of landing conditions on the flooded
Cumberland or could tell when the departing regiments might be
available for a line of battle. The optimistic commander may have
expected he would have good news to communicate when he concluded, "I hope to send you a dispatch from Fort Donelson to-
morrow." [1]
It was a sunny morning, "cool and invigorating," and behind the
advance guard of a brigade that had camped five miles out, the march
went smoothly, with the troops in good spirits. The two roads that
reconnaissance had uncovered led through a very rolling country,
heavily timbered, with few habitations. McPherson, thirty-three-year-

[229]

old Ohioan, top graduate in his West Point class, and already a key man on Grant's staff, recorded that no road blocks delayed the columns, because the Federal cavalry had scoured the country "continuously and effectively." As Donelson was approached, the terrain grew more rugged and the road, according to one correspondent, "ran through ravines and hollows, and over high hills," where there was no point from which one could "see any distance before or behind him." Near noon the columns converged and deployed, McClernand on the right, Smith on the left, a formation which seems to indicate a departure from earlier plans which envisaged the possibility of Smith's getting a brigade into Dover. But matters were working well, for the sound of cannonading came from the east. It was Walke testing the aim of the *Carondelet's* gunners on Donelson's embrasures, and announcing his arrival in accordance with Grant's request. The advance was continued cautiously in line of battle, with careful exploration to the front and flanks, until the outer intrenchments that covered the fort proper were sighted. Reconnaissance was pushed, and some skirmishing took place; prisoners taken put the garrison at from 20,000 to 25,000 and said that Generals Floyd, Pillow, Buckner, and Johnson were in the fort. In this they both exaggerated and anticipated.[2]

While Grant started the investment, Buell and Halleck were busy with more telegrams, Buell saying he would decide on his ultimate movements the moment he learned something of Halleck's position on the Tennessee. Part of his command was advancing on Bowling Green; the rest was being prepared either to follow or to use the river. He stated that he was apprehensive about forming a junction with Halleck by way of the Cumberland. Halleck encouraged him by saying that the gunboats had cleaned up the Tennessee as far as Florence, and an expedition of three gunboats had started from Cairo for the Cumberland the night before. No fewer than "40,000 rebels" were reported at Dover and Clarksville. Then he twitted: "If so, they have all come from Bowling Green." The gibe seemed to cause a partial decision in Louisville, for Buell replied that he would use a river, but he did not know yet which river. Furthermore, it would take at least ten days to transfer his troops. Still timorous about the Cumberland, he asked why it was necessary to use that stream; he also wished to know where his troops would land, where form a juncture with those of Grant, and by whom they would be commanded. Halleck replied that Grant had already invested Donelson from the land side, but had not been able to take any siege artillery, half the land being under water. Sending troops by the Cumberland had been a military necessity; there had been some risk, Halleck admitted, but it could not be avoided.[3]

In the evening Buell reported to McClellan that he would advance up the Tennessee or Cumberland with a part of his force, leaving the rest to operate against Bowling Green. The movement to the Tennessee, though difficult, promised great results. With the enemy at Columbus, he thought Paducah insecure, and he warned McClellan that he should be prepared to throw in strong reenforcements at any time, for the Federals were divided, and the enemy was strongly fortified at many points. While Buell was still saying in new words that Halleck's enterprise was hazardous, Halleck himself seemed cheerful and he repeated a telegram that Phelps had sent about his dash up the Tennessee to Florence, which ended, "Found the Union sentiment strong." [4]

Correspondents at Fort Henry had already sent news about Phelps, and it was headlined throughout the North. Greeley editorialized: "Old men, young children, youths, women, and maidens, turned out to greet the flag they had so long known only in dishonor and under insult. They wept tears of exultation, and brought gifts of their substance to the friends who represented the Government they love." After lauding Burnside's success at Roanoke and noting that reenforcements were moving to Hunter at Leavenworth for his anticipated operation, he continued: "The cause of the Union now marches on in every section of the country. Every blow tells fearfully against the rebellion. The rebels themselves are panic-stricken, or despondent. It now requires no very far-reaching prophet to predict the end of this struggle." [5]

However, the gloom that had taken hold of the Confederate commanders after the quick fall of Fort Henry began to disappear as the battle was studied more carefully, and cheerfulness touched with optimism was returning. On the 10th the engineer officer in Fort Donelson told of defensive preparations and expressed confidence in a successful resistance against a land assault; it would be harder to cope with a water attack, but he hoped for success there also. Pillow wrote from Donelson to General Floyd at Clarksville: "Upon one thing you may rest assured, viz, that I will never surrender the position, and with God's help I mean to maintain it." Sidney Johnston was so reassured by news from Floyd about the serious injury the Federal gunboats had received at Henry that he telegraphed back on the 11th, "If [at] the long range we could do so much damage, with the necessary short range on the Cumberland [we] should destroy their boats." But he passed the responsibility of ordering more regiments into Donelson, telling Floyd to take command of all troops and use his judgment.[6]

"The enemy are all around my position and within distance to close in with me in ten minutes' march," Pillow telegraphed on the 12th after Grant had started the investment. He spoke of the twenty shells the *Conestoga* had thrown into the fort, to which he had not replied, and he predicted a battle in the morning, accompanied by a gunboat attack. As to the outcome he spoke with caution: "Feel sanguine of victory, though I am not fully ready. I have done all that it was possible to do, and think I will drive back the enemy." Johnston, however he may have appraised Pillow's resolution, seems to have made up his mind; he directed Floyd to leave a small force at Clarksville and take the remainder to Donelson, that night, if possible. The die seemed cast for a fight to the finish.[7]

Having signaled his presence without an acknowledging shot from the enemy, Walke "dropped down the river a few miles and anchored for the night, waiting General Grant's arrival." As the *Carondelet* steamed back up the stream in the morning with men at battle stations a courier from Grant hailed her from the bank and delivered this note to Walke:

I arrived here yesterday and succeeded in getting positions almost entirely investing the enemy's works. Most of our batteries are now established, and the remainder soon will be. If you will advance with your gunboats at 10 o'clock a.m., we will be ready to take advantage of every diversion in our favor.[8]

Obviously the general thought Walke had at least the three old wooden gunboats in addition to the *Carondelet*. Though alone, Walke stood up the stream; and one hundred and thirty-nine shells with fuses cut to ten and fifteen seconds were his answer to Grant's request. This time the enemy was activated, and—according to Walke—opened with all his batteries. His shooting was, however, not too good, and the *Carondelet* received only two hits: one of them from a 128-pound solid shot, that ended in the engineroom after doing some minor damage and causing splinter wounds to half a dozen men. Then Walke broke off the engagement and dropped back to his anchorage, thinking perhaps that his four bow guns were an insufficient match for the armament of the fort.[9]

One sentence was all that Grant's brief report about Fort Donelson gave to February 13: "Owing to the non-arrival of the gunboats and re-enforcements sent by water, no attack was made, but the investment was extended to the flanks of the enemy and drawn closer to his works, with skirmishing all day." It was understatement for, though there had been no general attack, there had been two local ones. On the right, McClernand with several regiments made an ill-advised assault that ran not only into heavy musketry but into cruel artillery crossfires; and he failed to capture the enemy battery that had been annoying him. One of Smith's brigades actually carried a strong position and remained in it until called back. The noise of the fighting was sufficiently heavy to bring Walke back up the river to give the fort an additional forty-five shells.[10]

Disappointed over the nonarrival of the regiments that had gone around by water, Grant ordered Wallace at Fort Henry to bring up two of those left to hold the Tennessee. But even as he was weakening that position he evidently received some report of a threatened attack upon it from Columbus, which he met by asking Halleck to send future reenforcements to Henry. If not needed there, they could march across and join him. One gunboat should, he also said, be kept at Fort Henry.[11]

But a rumor had reached Halleck that Columbus was preparing to strike at Cairo; and after telling Cullum that a regiment and a battery were leaving St. Louis, with two more regiments to follow shortly, he directed, "Stop them, if you fear an attack and want them." The situation being what it was, it was not strange that he said to Foote, "It is of vital importance that Fort Donelson be reduced immediately," or that he made a strong appeal to Buell. Telling the Louisville general of the impending attack on Donelson by land and water, he asked if a cavalry demonstration could not be made against Bowling Green. "A mere feint might help," he explained. Once more he sought to entice Buell to come and take command of the Cumberland operation; in return, he would transfer Sherman—ordered that day to Paducah—to the Tennessee column. That Halleck still regarded Grant as a temporary commander is indicated by a letter to Hunter in which he said it had not been decided who would take immediate command on the Cumberland and the Tennessee.[12]

For two days the wires westward seem to have been untroubled by the General in Chief. But on the evening of the 13th they carried short telegrams to both Louisville and St. Louis. Characteristically McClellan wanted full details as to Buell's strength (facts which, that general presently told him, had been given in his last regular return). Then came sentences of alarm, caused perhaps by Buell's own messages: "Watch Fort Donelson closely. I am not too certain as to the result there." A telegram instructing Halleck to suspend the movement of any troops to Kansas, and saying he would send "next week" six hundred sailors for the gunboats, contained the same thought: "I am anxious about Fort Donelson." Also as the day was waning, Walke received a second message from Grant: four more gunboats on the way from Cairo would probably arrive that night. Not habitually a writer of postscripts, Grant used one this time: "We are doing well on the land side. How are you?" [13] And McClellan was anxious about him!

Daybreak of February 13 had brought Floyd to the beleaguered fort as new commander, and just before Walke opened fire, he telegraphed Johnston at Nashville that Federal gunboats were advancing. He seemed less sure of the water than of the ground, for he said, "Our field defenses are good, I think we can sustain ourselves against the land forces." Johnston's message that night to Richmond quoted the last telegram of the day from Floyd. Stirringly it began, "The day is closed, and we have maintained ourselves fully by land and water." But there was not much zest for the predicted battle: "We will endeavor to hold our position if we are capable of doing so." Grant seems to have been well posted on what was going on within the enemy lines; he reported to Halleck that Floyd had arrived with 4,000 men. Four brigadiers against four brigadiers it now was, for Grant said Buckner, Johnson, and Pillow were also reported to be inside the fort. The enemy had been driven into his works at all points, but a heavy abatis all around prevented carrying the place by storm. He closed with cheerful words: "I feel every confidence of success and the best feeling prevails among the men." [14]

That night the Confederates in their rifle pits and gun emplacements, and the Federals in the encircling lines, were thinking less about the experiences of the day or the real battle still to come than about their cruel momentary suffering. At dusk it had begun to rain; then the temperature fell rapidly and violently, and the rain changed to sleet and snow. Many of the Union soldiers had lost or thrown away their overcoats and blankets as they forced their way through the thick brush, and now, half frozen, they huddled together in the cheerless woods.

"Last night was very severe upon the troops. . . . This morning the thermometer indicated 20° below freezing." Thus Grant reported to Halleck on the morning of February 14. But something more than snow and cold had come during the night: five gunboats and twelve transports, which would "materially strengthen" him. He had failed to reach the river and cut off enemy reenforcements "in consequence of the high water and deep sloughs." "Any force sent for such a purpose would be entirely away from support from the main body," he explained.[15]

Foote, although he did not feel that everything was in proper readiness, yielded to Grant's urgings for a prompt attack; and it was decided that, near two o'clock, he would move up, silence the water batteries, pass the fort, take position opposite Dover, and shell the enemy out of their intrenchments near the river, while the army threw its right forward, took possession of that part of the hostile works, cut the Confederates off from the bulk of their supplies, and forced them back against the Federal center and left.[16] Such was the scheme of maneuver planned, presumably, in Foote's comfortable flagship *St. Louis* as the bitter wind benumbed the men in the opposing lines of battle.

Many of Grant's men on that cold morning had no breakfast. They had consumed the rations for two days with which they had started from Fort Henry, and supply was becoming a critical problem. The wagons that had followed the marching column were forced through the woods to the welcoming regiments; but few vehicles and animals had come with the reenforcing troops, because all available transport space had been used for men. It perhaps was not war as the most careful planners would have had it, but many commanders in the Federal army could have benefited by watching Grant in his headquarters as he gave instructions to his staff, or by riding with him as he straightened out difficulties and encouraged his men, or by hearing him urge an attack against the flag officer's wishes. Action was the surest way to get the soldiers' minds off their discomforts; yet it took the courage of an unyielding man to go forward without delay.

Toward noon Wallace arrived with two regiments and a battery. These were given to Smith, apparently to replace Colonel John

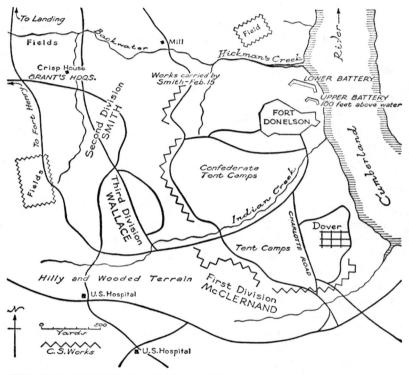

THE INVESTMENT OF FORT DONELSON, FEBRUARY 12–16, 1862

McArthur's brigade, which he had husbanded at first as a reserve, but which was put into the line on McClernand's left. Wallace was stepped up to command of the Third Division, formed from regiments that had just arrived; it was put into the center of the line so as to allow McClernand to continue the thrust toward the right.

As the day was ending, McArthur—apparently on McClernand's order—was shifted to the extreme right flank; and he wrote in his report: "Encamped for the night without instructions, and, as I regret to add, without adequate knowledge of the nature of the ground in front and on our right." According to McClernand, the move brought the end of his line within four or five hundred yards of a creek which was impassable because of backwater.[17] How much personal attention Grant was able to give to the First Division cannot be determined; but this much seems certain: he had no general reserve, and McClernand had none for his rather tenuous line; and the right flank was insecure because the flooded stream had not been reached.

Though the naval attack of which so much was expected came near succeeding, it ended in complete failure. At three o'clock Foote advanced with his four ironclads; chains, lumber, and bags of coal covered their upper decks to give protection from the plunging fire of the enemy guns placed high above the main water battery. Behind the ironclads—one thousand yards behind—came the ubiquitous *Tyler* and *Conestoga*. At something over a mile Foote opened fire and steadily closed the range—to four hundred yards according to himself, or two hundred yards according to the enemy. The battle began auspiciously enough for the Federals, and Floyd wired Johnston: "The fort cannot hold out twenty minutes. Our river batteries working admirable. Four gun-boats advancing abreast." [18]

The closing of the range was, however, Foote's undoing, for by that maneuver he surrendered the superiority of his weapons, and his fire became less accurate. "Their fire was more destructive to our works at 2 miles than at 200 yards. They overfired us from that distance," wrote B. G. Bidwell, the only officer in Donelson's heavy battery who was to escape capture. At Fort Henry fortune had favored Foote by the bursting of the Confederates' only rifled gun; and at Donelson the sole rifled piece—one that threw a good 128-pound projectile—was soon out of action because a hasty or excited gunner left a cleaning wire in the vent. But the eight 32-pounders and the 10-inch Columbiad in the water battery hammered away at the ironclads, whose crews were standing steadily to their guns. Foote wrote that the fight would have been over in his favor in fifteen more minutes, for the enemy fire was slackening and the men could be seen running from the defending batteries. But he did not get those minutes, because the pilothouse of the flagship was shot away and the tiller ropes of the *Louisville* were broken, causing those two vessels to drift down the river out of control. Soon they were followed by the *Pittsburg* and the *Carondelet,* "also greatly damaged" by shots "between wind and water." Though a gun had burst with the usual frightful effect on the *Carondelet,* she still was in action at a distance when Floyd telegraphed triumphantly: "The fort holds out. Three gun-boats have retired. Only one firing now." [19]

It was a disappointing day, but Grant's message to Cullum gave no indication of it. He began by saying he hoped that the transportation belonging to the troops that had arrived would be sent "as rapidly as possible," for it was "almost impossible to get supplies from the landing" to where the troops were. There would also soon be a shortage of artillery ammunition, but he had instructed his ordnance officer to keep a close watch and take steps to avoid a deficiency. Not a word was said about the failure of the gunboat attack; but a significant change of plans was indicated by the statement, "Appearances indicate now that we will have a protracted siege here." It would have to be Andrew Foote who would report the naval failure, not Ulysses Grant.

No one likes a siege, and Grant explained: "The ground is very broken, and the fallen timber extending far out from the breastworks, I fear the result of an attempt to carry the place by storm with raw troops." Again he reassured: "I feel great confidence, however, in ultimately reducing the place." He was not satisfied with extending his right only to the then impassable stream, for the river obviously would fall. Even as he wrote, his chief of staff was making a reconnaissance with a view to "sending a force above the town of Dover to occupy the river bank." The message ended, "Please inform General Halleck of the substance of this." [20]

From May 24, 1861, when he wrote to the Adjutant General in Washington tendering his services, to April 9, 1865, when he sent a two-sentence dispatch to Stanton announcing Lee's surrender, Grant wrote a multitude of messages. Many of them were remarkable, but the dispatch to Cullum of February 14, 1862, with its quiet words, its simple, friendly sentences that described the situation with clarity and brevity, that told of difficulties but left the reader with no fears, was one of the best.

That night Lieutenant John Wilkins of the Eleventh Indiana, just arrived from Fort Henry, wrote in his diary: "There was severe fighting yesterday and to-day and our troops have been roughly handled with heavy loss. . . . It is very cold and we have but few rations and are suffering severely." He described the hilly, dense country and recorded: "So we labor under great difficulties and disadvantages but feel confident of success." He had heard the heavy guns "booming on the River," and said the fleet had been "repulsed with heavy loss and several boats disabled." His prophecy was grim: "Tomorrow will be a bloody day." [21]

In Richmond hopes must have begun to rise with the reading of Johnston's dispatch that quoted "the latest from General Pillow at Fort Donelson": "We have just had the fiercest fight on record between our guns and six gunboats, which lasted two hours. They came within 200 yards of our batteries. We drove them back, damaged two of them badly, and crippled a third very badly. No damage done to our battery and not a man killed." [22]

The picture was also changed in front of Bowling Green, where Brigadier General Ormsby M. Mitchel, a Kentucky-born West Point graduate who had become a well known astronomer, was leading the Federals. Pressing his advance more rapidly than Buell seems to have directed or expected, he had arrived at the Barren River at noon, too late to save the railroad bridge but in time to emplace some guns on one of the dozen hills fortified by the Confederates, and shell the station, where enemy troops were seen entraining. Buell's mind was some three-fourths made up to go to the Cumberland as Halleck had been urging; now he would have to reconsider everything. [23]

From Woodburn, ten miles south of Bowling Green, Hardee reported to Johnston at 10:00 P.M. that, though the Federal fire from the hill had made him abandon the depot, he had left the town in perfect order. He would move on as rapidly as possible and he requested a train to be at Franklin at 5:00 A.M. to take his sick and the extra baggage. A helpful telegrapher at Nashville added the indorsement, "The operator at Franklin informs me there are three empty trains there." [24]

The Confederate retreat had started, but the Federal commanders could not tell whether the enemy would try to hold behind the Cumberland River in the vicinity of Nashville—a city they would abandon only reluctantly.

After a day in Paducah Thomas Scott was back in Cairo, where he found a letter from Halleck that expressed regret at Scott's departure from St. Louis before they could go over plans of operations. Halleck enclosed a draft of a letter that he thought might be

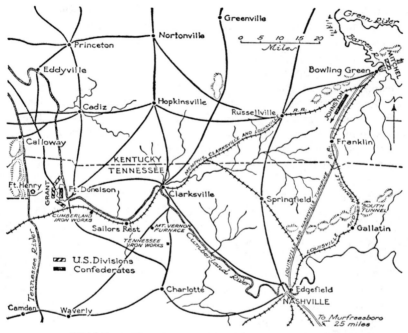

GRANT AND JOHNSTON, FEBRUARY 14, 1862

used as a basis for a letter to Stanton, but Scott forwarded it just as he received it. Conscious that the matter was urgent, he telegraphed his chief that Halleck strongly recommended, as Buell had done, the sending of his disciplined troops from the East. "If you give him the number stated," said Scott, "he is willing to stake his military reputation on complete success in that region [farther south than Fort Donelson] before the 10th of April. I hope you will decide to forward." Scott thought the situation was somewhat hazardous at the moment and stated in a letter that if the enemy had effective gunboats and transports at Columbus, they could take Cairo without much trouble. The disturbing thing was that it was rumored in

Paducah that four pilots and steamboat captains had left Columbus to take charge of some ironclad gunboats at Memphis and New Orleans. "Our military heads must be careful," wrote the apprehensive Assistant Secretary, "to not reduce military posts in this quarter too low or we may lose a few of them." [25]

The anxiety about Fort Donelson that McClellan had expressed the day before had, on the other hand, seemingly disappeared, and he sent a very optimistic message to Halleck. He had just received the latter's "gratifying" report that Curtis had entered Springfield, and he was "in hourly expectation of having similar news in regard to Fort Donelson." After thus nicely complimenting Halleck he dealt him a blow by remarking, "Your proposition in regard to the formation of a Western Division has one fatal obstacle, viz, that the proposed commander of the new Department of Missouri ranks you." [26] True it was that Hunter had been made a major general six days before Halleck; but the commission was a temporary one in the volunteers, while Halleck's was in the regular army. In urging the point McClellan was not on very solid ground; for he had acquiesced, if he had not been responsible, when his good friend Buell, a brigadier, received a more important department than Hunter, much to the chagrin of the latter. Before many months he would learn that an order by the President could put even George McClellan under Henry Halleck.

After thus intimating that he was himself keeping control of matters in the West, McClellan said he would "be glad to hear in detail as to the troops" Halleck had "in the Tennessee and Cumberland Rivers." It was of course quite impossible to keep the General in Chief minutely informed of the changing situation on the rivers; nor was there any likelihood that he would reach an important decision on the basis of information received from Buell and Halleck, and issue a decisive order. Doubtless he thought he would, for he was very optimistic. Having disposed of Halleck's ambitions, he ended: "Burnside has been very successful. All seems to go well." But a late-afternoon telegram from the St. Louis commander was calculated to bring back his uncertainties. There were no horses, Halleck said, for some of the batteries that had gone up the rivers. But he asked for something more than animals: "Can't you spare some troops from the Potomac? I am not strong enough if the enemy concentrates on me." [27] This was a repetition of the warning Buell had given. Actually, troops from the Potomac could not arrive in time for any emergency at Fort Donelson, and Buell, furthermore, had an ample number much nearer at hand. But the suggestion that the Army of the Potomac was not doing anything—tactfully phrased though it was—could hardly have given pleasure to McClellan.

Probably the story of the gunboat battle had not yet reached Johnston when he telegraphed Floyd, "If you lose the fort, bring your troops to Nashville, if possible." [28] He was not facing the grim reality very clearly, for the only instructions that could have had much meaning for the local commander would have been a clear authorization to *abandon* the fort and save his command, if he thought necessary. That was the extremity to which Floyd believed he was reduced, for in spite of his victory of the afternoon over the gunboats, the meaning of Grant's thrust toward the river on the Confederate left was clear. He summoned his subordinates into a council of war and proposed that they attack the Federal right, throw it back, and (to use the words of his report) "pass our people into the open country lying southward towards Nashville." The proposition was unanimously approved; plans were prepared to execute it, and troops were formed and moved to positions for an early start. It would be a difficult operation, in case the Federals fought hard enough to necessitate the committal of most of the Confederate regiments to heavy action before actual retirement started. Whether even Buckner and Bushrod Johnson, former regular officers, realized the difficulty fully is questionable. Johnson wrote that plans were made "for every contingency"; but there was not time for full briefing and for the perfecting of command and control arrangements. Initially there would be the advantage of surprise; but the woods would break up formations, and if hard counterattacks were made by the Federals it would not be easy to get started for the coveted "open country lying southward." [29]

Beauregard, who had been ill for several days while at Bowling Green, was writing from Nashville to one of his Fort Sumter aides, now a Confederate congressman: "I am taking the helm when the ship is already in the breakers and with but few sailors to man it. . . . The loss of Fort Donelson (God grant it may not fall) would be followed by consequences too lamentable to be now alluded to." [30] It looks as if Beauregard as well as Johnston, in spite of the declaration in the memorandum of the 7th, had revived the hope that the position on the Cumberland could be maintained; and he may have concurred in sending the reenforcements that were even at the moment making plans to escape.

It would be pleasant to record that Flag Officer Foote was as much at ease in the saddle as in the pulpit, and that after an early, warm, and ample breakfast, he boarded a horse and laid his course over the frozen and snowy woodland road to the Crisp house, to confer with the army commander. But the shell that had mortally wounded the pilot of the *St. Louis* had damaged the fleet commander's foot, so that he sent a note to Grant early on the 15th explaining his inability to go to see him, and requesting the general to come to his flagship.[31] This Grant did without delay, writing later in his *Memoirs,* that he "had no idea that there would be any engagement on land unless I brought it on myself." In forming such a judgment he must have been influenced by the thought that an enemy who had declined to attack on the 13th, when superiority of numbers was probably on his side, would not take the risk after the arrival of reenforcements had definitely turned the scales in favor of the investing force. So, after directing that the division commanders be informed of his absence and instructed not to bring on an engagement, but to maintain their positions, he rode away to see the naval commander, meeting en route the Twentieth Ohio. It had arrived the night before and was marching to join Wallace's division.[32] In command of the regiment was the Colonel Whittlesey who on November 20 had written Halleck suggesting a strong movement up the Tennessee and Cumberland.

In the conference it was decided that Foote should return to Cairo with two of the disabled ironclads, leaving the other two to protect the transports, "and with all dispatch prepare the mortar boats and *Benton,* with other boats, to make an effectual attack upon Fort Donelson." The sailor had clearly suffered an injury to his pride as well as to his person, for his letter describing the conference told the Secretary of the Navy that the enemy must have brought twenty guns to bear on him, while he could use only twelve. He spoke of the "unequal fight"—unequal because he got too close—and, like a defeated ball player who takes satisfaction in the fact that his opponents have used their best pitcher, he concluded, "I am informed that the rebel batteries were served with the best gunners from Columbus"

—a statement quite disproved by the Confederate reports.[33] In view of his injured extremity one can forgive the slip.

It was probably nearing one o'clock when Grant got back. On the way a member of his staff informed him that a heavy battle had been raging on the right of the line, some seven miles away from the conference boat, and that McClernand's division had been scattered and was in full retreat. This was an exaggeration; but the situation was bad enough, for McClernand had been waging an unequal contest against the enemy assault that had begun at an early hour. Messengers sent to Grant's headquarters for reenforcements brought back word that he was conferring with Foote; so there was nothing that the commander of the First Division could do but fight with his own troops and Thayer's brigade, that Wallace, responding to the crisis, sent him at a very opportune moment. Fight McClernand certainly did, yielding as little ground as possible, and as slowly as he could. Pillow, handling the main Confederate effort, reported that the Federals "contested the field most stubbornly," and said it was two hours before he could make any decided advance.[34]

One cannot be certain as to the exact sequence of events, and Grant put no hour upon this dispatch to Foote:

> If all the gunboats that can will immediately make their appearance to the enemy it may secure us a victory. Otherwise all may be defeated. A terrible conflict ensued in my absence, which has demoralized a portion of my command, and I think the enemy much more so. If the gunboats do not show themselves, it will reassure the enemy and still further demoralize our troops. I must order a charge to save appearances. I do not expect the gunboats to go into action, but to make appearance and throw a few shells at long range.[35]

The flag officer had already departed in a transport, but Commander Benjamin M. Dove, ranking naval officer, wrote him the next day, "At 2:30 p.m. yesterday, shortly after your departure, I received the enclosed dispatch (No. 1) from General Grant." [36] The ship's time should have been accurate; so without much doubt Grant's hour of writing was about 1:30. But the uncertain point is whether he had already been to the right of his line and, if so, what instructions he had given. No decision can be made that is not in conflict with McClernand's or Wallace's report, or with the account of the battle which Wallace wrote twenty-five years later.[37] The dispatch to Foote makes it look as if Grant placed more hope in the few shells from the gunboats than in the charge which he meant to order. But the important thing is that he was thinking of victory, and, seeing beyond the demoralization in his own lines, sensed confusion on the part of the enemy. His thoughts took in the entire battlefield and every fighting resource at his command. Surely this was the beginning of Grant's faith that in a battle there can come a very fateful moment when each side is exhausted and near the breaking point, and coldly impartial victory waits with a smile for him who can summon strength for another blow.

Conger cautions his readers not to think that any field commander whatever might have made Grant's decision, emphasizing that "on the ground and at the time it was by no means easy." Though picturesque details which Wallace put into his later story cannot be accepted, we can pay heed to his statement, "In every great man's career there is a crisis exactly similar to that which now overtook General Grant, and it cannot be better described than as a crucial test of his nature." Had Grant made the decision that a mediocre person would have made, "it is very probable his history would have been then and there concluded." [38]

With the message to Foote on its way, Grant seems to have gone to Smith, who had been doing no more than keep up annoyance of the enemy "by skirmishing and slow artillery fire." Perhaps there was some discussion of the situation; one knows for sure only that Smith reported that toward 3 o'clock ("probably before 2 p.m.," in the view of Conger) he "received the general's personal order to assault the enemy's right a half mile or more from my habitual position." Leading troops in an attack was not a novelty for C. F. Smith, thrice brevetted for bravery in Mexico. Within a short time he was with Colonel Lauman at the head of an attacking brigade, organized in column of regiments to give it great driving power. The Second Iowa was leading, and Smith wrote, "The regiment was ordered to rely on the bayonet and not to fire a shot until the enemy's ranks were broken." The heavy attack the enemy had made against the Federal right caused Grant to tell Smith that he might not find too much resistance; but the terrain was difficult, the steep hillside being covered with obstructions that held the attackers under the fire of the riflemen in the trenches. The regiment's loss was heavy; but soon the Union colors were on the intrenchments, and the enemy was pursued toward the inner works of the fortress proper, where, stiffened by reenforcements, he rallied. Behind the Iowa regiment came the Fifty-second Indiana, which, "from the nature of the ground and want of tactical knowledge," became confused and put some volleys into the ranks of their Hawkeye friends. But another Indiana regiment—the Twenty-fifth—did not blunder, and it effectively covered the Second Iowa, when, with cartridges nearly expended, it retired to the outer line of works. The position was strengthened by bringing up some guns, and there the sixty-year-old Smith stayed; his unfinished report, written a few weeks later, and a month before he died, ended eloquently: "The night was cold, but without the cruel storm." [39]

Cheers carried the news of the success on the left to the regiments that had been so severely engaged upon the right. There Grant had gone to order McClernand and Wallace to take the offensive and recover the ground that had been lost in the morning.[40] According to Wallace's report, McClernand asked him to take command of the assault. The column of attack which he prepared was headed by the Eighth Missouri and the Eleventh Indiana, and Lieutenant Wilkins, who began his diary entry for the day, "Woke up this morning almost buried in snow," closed by saying: "The two regiments are stripping for the fight and we will soon be in the bloody fray. The boys are very enthusiastic and I have no doubt we will soon regain our lost ground." Resuming the next day, he wrote, "We felt that our superior drill and discipline would make success a certainty. General Wallace rode down the line and said, 'You have been wanting a fight—you have got it. Hell's before you.'" [41]

Over ground where lay many dead and wounded from the First Division as well as from enemy regiments, the attack proceeded. "Words cannot do justice to his courage and coolness," was Wallace's tribute to Colonel Morgan L. Smith of the Eighth Missouri, who was in direct command of his own regiment and the Eleventh Indiana. After an hour's hard fighting the enemy gave way and was pursued for something like a mile, close up to his works. Wallace wrote that an order reached him through Webster to retire because a new plan of operations for the next day was being considered, but that he did not carry it out because he was satisfied Grant did not know the extent of the success that had been achieved. He did not say how far he was to retire, and McClernand recorded only that Webster brought an "order to press upon the enemy at all points." Of the wretched night Wilkins wrote: "The cold was extreme, and we did not dare build a fire—nothing to eat since daylight. The wounded on the field were so numerous that but few could be taken care of, and their cries and groans during that awful night I shall never forget." [42]

The statement in Grant's *Memoirs* that the enemy had fallen back "within his intrenchments and was there when I got on the field" [43] is inconsistent with reports. Though the task of getting the Confederates back into their trenches was much facilitated by orders of their generals, Grant was of course entirely unaware of such directions when he ordered assaults by his own troops; and he seems to have gone too far in accepting statements he may have heard later. The eighty casualties suffered by Morgan Smith's two regiments showed that they had a vital part in the retirement of the enemy.

And the gunboats, whose shells Grant seemed to think might have a magical effect, what did they do? Recognizing the urgency of the situation, Commander Dove did not depart with the *Pittsburg* as he was about to do, but ordered the *St. Louis* to attack the fort; and he himself followed in the *Louisville*. After the *St. Louis* had thrown a few shells into the fort the two boats returned about dark to their anchorage.[44] Rather nonchalantly Confederate Bidwell recorded: "Nothing of interest occurred again until Saturday evening late. One boat came above the point and fired several shots, but did no damage." [45] Two years later Wallace testified in a naval investigation: "While my division was engaged, the guns of the fleet opened fire again. I recollect yet the positive pleasure the sounds gave me." [46] How much moral effect the shells from the *St. Louis* had, cannot be said; but it is certain that there was smooth and harmonious coordination of Army and Navy on the Cumberland on that turbulent February day. Grant's appeal and the response strengthened an important team and brought into the battle everything that was available.

Did the Confederate commanders miss a real chance to escape? Conger's reply to an "absurd" criticism of Pillow made by "Ropes and other theorists" merely uses a soldier's appreciation of the disorganized condition of Pillow's command after several hours of hard fighting.[47] Certainly many Confederates could have escaped if Pillow had shouted at the proper moment: "Every man for himself! Run like the blazes for Clarksville!" Smaller units might have been marched away in some order. But one should not criticize the Confederate general for failure to handle the situation in such a fashion. Pillow did not have what was needed for a general retirement: a good coherent force not yet severely engaged, well commanded and ready to hold open the door that had finally been forced back. In the two hours of hard fighting that Pillow said were needed merely to unlock the door, lies part of the explanation of failure.

It is true that after Floyd had gone back to inspect his right, Pillow ordered Buckner, who had been moved from the right and had not been completely engaged, back into his original position. But even to Floyd, who had not planned the move, it did not look entirely unfortunate, for Buckner reached the position that was held by two regiments from the inner works in time to stiffen the defense and halt Smith's advance. Floyd's implication that it was not until night that he planned his march away, and then only if things could be held as stable as they were when he went to inspect the right, helps exonerate Pillow of having been responsible for failure of the Confederates to make good their intention to escape.[48]

Certainly in the absence of the Federal commander from the field luck smiled on the Southerners. Had Grant been present, there is little doubt that he would have quickly judged that the enemy's right had been weakened; and, if he had ordered Smith to assault early, the entire Confederate effort would have been at once imperiled. Among the Federals and Confederates, on any of their farflung fronts, there may have been no officer better fitted than C. F. Smith to develop and exploit such an opportunity as that afforded by the weakened Confederate right. Lauman, leading the brigade that spearheaded the afternoon attack, carried scars from Belmont; and in the storming column was the Seventh Iowa, one of the three battle-tested regiments with which Grant marched to Donelson.

While volleys of musketry echoed through the woods about Fort Donelson, the telegraph instruments were chattering in Washington, St. Louis, and Louisville in the great battle of the generals. Their outbursts had no more effect upon the issue on the Cumberland than the twilight shells from the *St. Louis,* but what they said is an essential part of the record of three important men.

"General Grant cannot any longer be in danger," said Buell in a dispatch that reached the Capital at 4:00 A.M. He believed Grant had 30,000 men, but he failed to repeat what he had told Halleck: some of the eight new regiments he had ordered up the Tennessee from Ohio and Indiana had not understood that they were really wanted. Since he had ninety-two regiments of infantry in Kentucky, his sacrifice in sending promptly a brigade to help with the river operation had not been great. Halleck, too, opened the day optimistically: "Everything looks well. Grant says we can keep them in till mortar boats arrive. Commodore Foote will immediately return from Cairo with two more gunboats. Troops are moving very rapidly to Fort Donelson." [49]

Actually, Grant himself seems to have said nothing about the mortar boats, the craft in which Lincoln had taken a peculiar personal interest, but about which Halleck had expressed a doubt whether they were worth their cost. When he first learned of them, Anthony Trollope, whose comments on Cairo have been noted, went into raptures: "The grandeur of the idea is almost sublime." He seemed to think the thirty-eight craft being built could easily obliterate a city. But after he witnessed some tests that revealed leaking hulls, he conjectured the novel craft would do "very little evil to the enemy," and he added that his "admiration was given to the smartness of the contractor who had secured to himself the job of building them." Navy men also were uncertain, and an officer in the Bureau of Ordnance and Hydrography wrote to Foote as late as January 27, "I have carefully studied the plans of the mortar rafts, and quite agree with you that they will be shaken to pieces by the mortars." Nevertheless six had been equipped with 13-inch mortars and were being towed toward the Cumberland, while Sherman—new commander at Paducah—reported dolefully: "I don't think the mortar boats can be brought upstream; the current is too strong. Left Lyford last night hard at work, but making no progress." [50] It looked as if Grant might have "to keep them in" a long time if the issue depended upon the new instrument of warfare.

At eleven o'clock Halleck reported, "The siege and bombardment of Donelson are progressing satisfactorily"; but alarming messages must have arrived very soon afterward, for he telegraphed in mid-afternoon that the enemy garrison in the fort amounted to 30,000, and that the troops from completely evacuated Bowling Green were concentrating on the Cumberland. "I must have more troops," he insisted. "It is a military necessity." To Buell he reported the shift of hostile forces, and four unsuccessful sorties by the enemy from Donelson. Unless he received more assistance the attack might fail.

This brought the answer that Nelson's division of twelve regiments and three batteries would embark the next day. Halleck breathed more easily: "Your telegram about division relieves me greatly." But he was thinking beyond the present battle, and he told Buell that his proposed move on Nashville from Bowling Green was "not good strategy." It would be better for him to help take and hold Donelson and Clarksville, and then move by the Tennessee to Florence. This would cause the abandonment of Nashville, after the pattern of Bowling Green. Like a book on strategy, Halleck asserted, "All we want is troops in mass." But he did not have sufficient force to make the new strategic move and watch Columbus at the same time. "Come and help me," he pleaded, "and all will be right. We can clear Tennessee as we have cleared Kentucky." [51]

In the evening McClellan wired Halleck: "Have telegraphed to Buell to help you by advancing beyond Bowling Green on Nashville; or, if that be too slow, via Cumberland." At the very moment —eight o'clock—Halleck was telegraphing the General in Chief that the proposed move on Nashville was "bad strategy," and was urging the move to Florence and Decatur. "Give me the forces required, and I will insure complete success," he promised. As if to guarantee that he would keep his word, he concluded, "Price is still in retreat, with General Curtis in pursuit." [52]

An hour before this message arrived, McClellan wired Buell that the move on Nashville was "exactly right," and aid should go to Grant only if he were in dire straits: Nashville gained, Donelson would be given up. Thus Halleck's message calling that move "bad strategy" placed him in a tight spot. "Your idea is in some respects good," he conceded at eleven o'clock; but immediate possession of Nashville was "very important" and could be most quickly attained by the move he had directed. Nor did he admit that the capture of Decatur would cause the enemy to yield Nashville; a threat to occupy Stevenson would also be required. He was not convinced that Buell's movement was "bad strategy," for it would "relieve the pressure upon Grant and lead to results of first importance." A quick decision at Donelson was clearly not in his mind when he said, "Enable Grant to hold his own, and I will see that Buell relieves him." Could it be that the General in Chief was trying to get a share of the credit of victory on the Cumberland for his favorite? He was still uncertain, and concluded: "I am arranging to talk with Buell and yourself over the wires tomorrow morning, and would be glad to have you at the telegraph office when all is ready. Buell will also be in Louisville office, and we can come to a full understanding." [53]

Halleck had already stated his views, and why was it necessary to make Buell cross the river to the telegraph in Jeffersonville to repeat what he had said? But McClellan did not tell Halleck that he had wired directly to Grant only an hour before: "Telegraph in full the state of affairs with you." [54] Not only was he bypassing the department commander; he was reaching for the unattainable: an up-to-the-minute and complete picture of the situation on a distant active front.

Buell also was working late, and telegraphed about midnight to McClellan:

It will take a week to repair the railroad to Bowling Green. No formidable advance can be made until that is done; but I expect my demonstration at an advance to weaken their hold on Clarksville and Donelson unless they can drive Halleck out absolutely, and if they can do it at all they can do it without any great delay. I cannot get as definite information from him as I would like. . . . [55]

A week to reach Bowling Green! Buell seemed to be running a race with the mortar boats. His predicament was partly the result of changing his decision to use the Cumberland or Tennessee, and then reverting to the overland route when he heard that Bowling Green had been abandoned. Still, like all commanding generals, Buell had many troubles, and he wrote to McClellan, "We are certainly busy now." Although his attention was directed chiefly toward Nashville and the Cumberland, he had not entirely forgotten East Tennessee, and he reported, "Carter's column, consisting of six regiments of infantry, one battery (six pieces), and five companies of cavalry at London, should in a few days be advancing on Cumberland Gap." The brigade of James A. Garfield, then at Pikeville, was preparing to drive Brigadier General Humphrey Marshall's "thinned ranks away from the headwaters of [the] Kentucky River at Whitesburg." Garfield reported that there was a shift of sentiment in the region, and Buell wrote: "Large parties of deserters from Marshall's ranks are returning in penitence and destitution to their homes." Marshall, in a long letter to General Cooper from Gladesville (Glade Spring), Virginia, portrayed the same facts in very different colors: "There are neighborhoods between this and Piketon as unsound as any part of Northwest Virginia. They must be thrown behind declared lines, and indeed if the able-bodied men do not enlist they should be drafted or compelled to go south of the railroad. The enemy must not find guides and spies here as he did in Kentucky, or he will have all advantages, and will advance with confidence if not success." At the moment mountain campaigning was more difficult even than usual, for the snow was six inches deep and still "falling rapidly." [56]

Slowly the telegraph line was being extended from Cairo. Now it was at Smithland, and George Cullum wrote Grant it would be rapidly pushed to his headquarters. Sherman was taking over the District of Cairo, Grant being given the "new Military District of West Tennessee." "Go on as you have commenced in your glorious work," urged Cullum. After predicting he would hear of the fall of Donelson the next day, he said bluntly, "You are in the great strategic line." Breaking off to read Grant's letter of the day before, which had just arrived, the older general thought Grant might be too optimistic, and cautioned: "Don't be rash; for, having the place invested, you can afford to have a little patience." Every bit of transportation that Cullum could lay hands on had been ordered forward. But the desired artillery ammunition was not on hand, and hardly any ordnance stores, though an urgent telegram had gone to Halleck. Steamboats, too, were getting scarce, and Engineer Cullum, scolding like a quartermaster, told Grant he must get them back promptly, or he would have no ammunition, food, or forage.[57]

Though Sherman had entered a zone of combat and would soon be a fighting general, he was as yet only a reporter and coordinator. "If troops can reach Grant sooner, turn them all up the Tennessee. Consult him on this immediately," Halleck directed. He was keeping an eye on Sherman, and, having read one of his reports, he cautioned, "Telegrams about movements should be in cipher." [58]

In the White House there was anxiety. A Washington dispatch of February 11 had read: "The President is not receiving visitors, nor attending to much public business to-day, owing to the severe illness of his son, William, to whom he is giving his utmost constant attention." Now a second son was ill, and the storm that had brought snow and bitter cold to the hills about Fort Donelson and the mountains to the east had lashed the ocean into fury, so that there was also great concern about General Burnside's and Commodore Goldsborough's situation on the North Carolina coast. But militarily it was the aspect of affairs upon the Cumberland that caused hours of troubled waiting, and Lincoln's thoughts upon the critical Saturday are revealed in identical telegrams he sent the next day to Buell and Halleck. They contained no orders, did not even ask for information, but gave his analysis, characteristically expressed. Fort Donelson was a certain thing, "unless Grant shall be overwhelmed from outside"; Columbus would "not get at Grant, but the force from Bowling Green will." It was not safe, the President added, to assume that the enemy would not expose Nashville to Buell, for a small force could break the railroad and keep Buell out of the city for twenty days. In the meantime troops would be brought from Nashville, perhaps from Manassas. Probably because he knew McClellan would not use the Army of the Potomac to prevent such a move, Lincoln asked if cavalry from the upper Cumberland could not make a dash and cut the railroad at Knoxville. He wondered also if in the midst of a bombardment of Fort Donelson a gunboat might not run the batteries and destroy the Clarksville bridge. Some of the President's thinking may have been based upon an exaggerated idea of the enemy force originally at Bowling Green; but his concluding sentence left no doubt that he believed the issue hung in doubtful balance: "Our success or failure at Fort Donelson is vastly important, and I beg you to put your soul in the effort." [59]

With telegraphic communications open virtually to the battlefield, Richmond was better posted than Washington. In addition to the defeat of the Yankee gunboats the day before, a victory on land seemed to have been won; for Johnston's message of 5:15 P.M., though it could bring the battle of the 15th up only to one o'clock, reported the capture of two hundred men and four guns, and pictured the bitterness of the fighting: "Our arms were successful, the field having been carried inch by inch, with severe loss on both sides." [60]

With Smith in possession of a commanding section of the outer works and his men encouraged by the feeling of victory, Grant had no intention of going on with a siege, and made preparations during the night of the 15th for an early attack in the morning. Nor was the Navy forgotten; at 8:30 Dove received a message from the general informing him of the situation and asking cooperation by the gunboats.[61] As they waited through the cold night, thoughtful officers and soldiers had a chance to think of how swift and complete can be the change of prospects on a field of battle; it was a thought that their commander also could use in the future. Day had hardly dawned when a bugle on the right of the Confederate lines attracted attention to the inner citadel.[62] Probably not many recognized the "parley" call, but all knew the meaning of the white flag that was seen. A note came through for Grant, signed by Buckner, who had become the Fort Donelson commander in a historic post-midnight conference at Pillow's headquarters in a house at Dover.

Realizing that the Federal assault against the Confederate right would be renewed by his old friend Grant, and that he would not be able to stand against it, Buckner advised capitulation. Though Floyd only two hours before had reported the hard battle not as a frustrated effort to escape, but merely as the result of a decision to attack—and with favorable results [63]—he had to admit the force of Buckner's arguments. But John B. Floyd was personally in a difficult position, for Northern feeling was bitter against him, on account of some of his acts as Secretary of War during the critical months of 1860. The Yankees might think up something very unpleasant if they got their hands on him, and he had no intention of becoming a prisoner. Four weeks later Major Gus A. Henry, Jr., of Pillow's staff wrote:

General Floyd then spoke out, and said that he would not surrender the command or himself.

General Buckner remarked that, if placed in command, he would surrender the command and share its fate.

General Floyd then said, "General Buckner, if I place you in command, will you allow me to get out as much of my brigade as I can?"

General Buckner replied, "I will, provided you do so before the enemy receives my proposition for capitulation."

General Floyd then turned to General Pillow and said, "I turn the command over, sir."

General Pillow replied promptly, "I pass it."

General Buckner said, "I assume it. Give me pen, ink and paper, and send for a bugler." [64]

Thus it came about that Kentucky-born Simon Buckner, one-time teacher of ethics and of military science at West Point, latterly a purchaser of Chicago real estate, wrote to the recent merchant of Galena. But some elements of the garrison escaped before the bugler raised his trumpet to his lips. A raft from the other bank of the river bore Gideon Jonathan Pillow to safety, and a steamer arriving opportunely from upriver ferried over Floyd and parts of the four regiments he had brought from western Virginia. Only to that extent did the last hours of darkness cover a Dunkirk in miniature. There were, however, many men 'who got away on the western bank, and Colonel Nathan B. Forrest showed a talent in retreat, and gave a fine demonstration of leadership by taking his cavalry regiment and two hundred other mounted men up the river road through water that was saddle-skirt deep and icy cold. He was the last to get out, for within fifteen minutes the Federals held the road, forcing Overton's cavalry to return to the Confederate lines.[65]

Buckner's message proposed "the appointment of commissioners to agree upon terms of capitulation of the forces and post under my command," and suggested an armistice until noon. At Monterrey, Grant had seen easy-going but hard-fighting Zachary Taylor appoint commissioners and then allow the entire Mexican garrison to march away with arms and six cannon. Though Taylor was in a difficult position and unable to care for prisoners, even liberals thought he had gone pretty far in the matter of the guns. At Vera Cruz a tougher soldier, "Old Fuss and Feathers" Scott, had likewise appointed commissioners, and though he had ships to evacuate prisoners, he had paroled the defeated Mexicans and had set some entirely free as a gesture of good will in an effort to turn the Mexican people against President-General Santa Anna. But Grant wanted no bickering or bartering, and wrote without delay the most famous of his many messages:

> Headquarters Army in the Field
> Camp near Fort Donelson, February 16, 1862
>
> Sir:
> Yours of this date, proposing armistice and appointment of commissioners to settle terms of capitulation, is just received. No terms except unconditional and immediate surrender can be accepted. I propose to move immediately upon your works.
> I am, sir, very respectfully, your obedient servant,
>
> *U. S. Grant,*
> Brigadier-General, Commanding

General S. B. Buckner,
Confederate Army [66]

It was a hard-looking note to send to the old friend who had assisted him when he arrived in New York short of funds on his way home from California.[67] But Grant knew he would see Buckner, and famous messages he later wrote to Lee did not conclude as did his demand on Buckner. As a commander, Buckner had to concentrate on the words "unconditional and immediate surrender," and the threat in the next grim sentence. At best, the concluding words must have seemed an unnecessary formality; at worst, a mere pretension. After speaking of "the brilliant success of the Confederate arms yesterday," Buckner said in his reply that he could do nothing but "accept the ungenerous and unchivalrous terms which you propose." In the position in which the two men were placed there was literal truth in Buckner's ending, "I am, sir, your obedient servant." [68]

Commander Dove was determined that the gunboats should give more than token assistance in the expected battle. Finding that the condition of the *Carondelet*'s wounded was such that they could not be moved and her guns could not be used, he transferred the injured of the *Louisville* and the *St. Louis* to a transport and "got underway, steaming up toward the batteries of Fort Donelson, both vessels cleared for action." But he found two white flags atop the upper fort; and when he raised a similar emblem from a tug and landed he was met by a major who offered him his sword. This he declined. Taking the major aboard the tug, he went up the river in search of Grant. At Buckner's headquarters in Dover he found Lew Wallace and some of his staff eating corn bread and drinking coffee with the Confederate general and other officers, according to the third of Wallace's accounts. Buckner had sent a message to Bushrod Johnson, commanding his left, telling him that he had dispatched a note to Grant through the right of the lines. He directed that hostilities cease during the correspondence, and told Johnson to send a flag to the enemy posts in his front and acquaint them with the facts. Wallace reported that he was getting ready to storm the position before him about breakfast time when a white flag appeared. Sending word to Grant that the place had surrendered, he hastened without formality into town, counting apparently on Southern hospitality for food. "General Grant," wrote Commander Dove the same day, "arrived about half an hour afterwards." Wallace, by his own account, had been munching and talking thrice that long when his superior rode up.[69]

The prompt dispatch of a message of victory would have been in order, and it might have saved Halleck some concern, though it would have deprived us of the fine report he made to Washington, which began: "Hard fighting at Fort Donelson on Thursday, Friday, and Saturday. At 5 p.m. yesterday we carried the upper fort, where the Union flag was flying last night." He ended: "Unless we can take Fort Donelson very soon we shall have the whole force of the enemy on us. Fort Donelson is the turning point of the war, and we must take it at whatever sacrifice. Our men are in excellent spirits and fight bravely." [70]

Perhaps Grant wished to wait until he could report the full fruits of victory. There were, of course, many things to do, for success had brought new problems. His order providing for the occupation of the surrendered fort ended with a strong injunction against "pillaging and appropriating public property to private purposes"—but in this he was whistling into the wind. The possibility of enemy reaction from Columbus was not overlooked, and Wallace was hurried back to Fort Henry with two brigades, two batteries, and some cavalry. The prisoners were prepared for immediate shipment North, and were allowed all the clothing, blankets, and private property they could carry on their persons; commissioned officers were permitted to keep their sidearms. Rapacity of the Northern soldiers, and the desire for booty, nullified this provision to a considerable degree, Buckner writing in his report, "I regret to state, however, that, notwithstanding the earnest efforts of General Grant and many of his officers to prevent it, our camps have been a scene of almost indiscriminate pillage by Federal troops." Armed prisoners being a novelty to George Cullum, he took up swords and pistols at Cairo, sending them to Camp Douglas, Chicago, to await Halleck's instructions. [71]

The 16th must have been well spent before the *Conestoga* started to Cairo with this message for Halleck:

We have taken Fort Donelson and from 12,000 to 15,000 prisoners, including Generals Buckner and Bushrod Johnson; also about 20,000 stand of arms, 48 pieces of artillery, 17 heavy guns, from 2,000 to 4,000 horses, and quantities of commissary stores. [72]

Cullum and the commissary officers would not miss the concluding words. Grant had temporarily solved his food problem.

On the same day Grant directed to Cullum a short official report on his operations since the 12th.[73] He did not have means, he said, of determining his casualties accurately, but they could not "fall far short of 1,200." It was a gross underestimate, for of the 27,000 Federals finally in the investing lines, 2,608 were killed or wounded, as against a probable 2,000 of the possible 21,000 men the enemy had in the fort.[74] By using boats at Dover to evacuate wounded and 224 Federal prisoners, Floyd spoiled the chance for an accurate determination of his casualties—and increased the number of uninjured Confederates captured, by depriving himself of shipping. Grant's killed in the hard fighting of that cold Saturday were probably just a little under McDowell's on the hot Sunday at First Bull Run. But the lives were the price of a heartening victory and not of a discouraging defeat.

Bushrod Johnson, academy classmate of Sherman, sought to relieve the tedium of being a prisoner by taking a little stroll. Encountering no inquisitive Union pickets, and recalling that he had not given his parole or made other promises, he kept on, as luck would have it, walking south. Though he had never been a teacher of ethics, only of matter-of-fact subjects like physics, chemistry, mathematics, and engineering, conscience troubled him, and he referred his case to his superior, General Pillow. The thought of Gideon Pillow as a referee on conscience is a little droll. He was busy on his own case, trying to explain to Jefferson Davis the catastrophe on the Cumberland and his own escape upon the raft, and had to leave Johnson to struggle alone with his problem of right and wrong.[75]

Buckner went North a prisoner; but before he left he learned that the last word of the unconditional surrender note was genuine, for Grant followed him into his cabin on the steamer and offered him his purse. The last meeting of the two men would be years later at Mt. McGregor, overlooking another river, the one that flowed past the Academy where they had been cadets together. Only a few tortured days remained for Grant. Unable to speak, the suffering General wrote on a slip of paper: "General Buckner—Fort Donelson—will be here on the next train. He is come up especially to pay his respects." [76] Once more Grant wrote notes to Buckner, seated near him that July day on the veranda overlooking the Hudson. People throughout the country knew the General was fighting heroically to finish his *Memoirs,* and they watched the battle against time almost as anxiously as Lincoln had watched the battle on the Cumberland twenty-three years before. Buckner's visit helped replace some of the bitterness of war with sincere good will. Within a month the Confederate general would again be in New York, to have a place of honor at Grant's funeral, with Joe Johnston, Sheridan, Sherman, ex-Presidents Arthur and Hayes, and President Cleveland.

CHAPTER XI

STILL THE GENERALS WRANGLE

Shoes and other clothing are beginning to be wanting to some extent. I am ready for any move the general commanding may order.

Grant to Halleck

Aт тен the next morning—Monday the 17th—St. Louis still did not have the big news, and Halleck sent an alarming telegram to McClellan: "It is said that Beauregard is preparing to move from Columbus either on Paducah or Fort Henry. Do send me more troops. It is the crisis of the war in the West." Then, using an argument similar to the President's, whose message had probably arrived, he stated that a large number of boats had been collected at Nashville; in them the entire force from Bowling Green could "come down in a day, attack Grant in the rear, and return to Nashville" before Buell could get half way there. If Buell must move by land, why not send him to Clarksville? Halleck's words were grave: "I can do no more for Grant at present. I must stop the transports at Cairo to observe Beauregard. We are certainly in peril." [1]

Then the *Carondelet,* which had started before the *Conestoga,* feeling her way through a fog with whistle blowing, arrived at Cairo, and the "glorious intelligence" that the "Union flag floats over Fort Donelson" was put on the wires, while the guns of Fort Cairo roared in a national salute. It was "Grant's late post," said proud George Washington Cullum in a message to McClellan. An hour after noon the jubilant Halleck telegraphed the General in Chief: "Make Buell,

Grant, and Pope major-generals of volunteers, and give me command in the West. I ask this in return for Forts Henry and Donelson." Though Halleck thought too quickly about himself, it is true that unity of command was sorely needed in the West, and now was the time to insist upon it. If prompt congratulations had gone to Grant at once, the record would be better. Halleck had quickly commended other commanders for small achievements and a sentence of appreciation would have made an appropriate beginning for the dispatch he sent Grant directing that 500 sick and wounded be sent to Cincinnati. Federals and Confederates were "to be treated exactly alike," and boats were to be "fitted up as comfortable as possible for our men and the rebels." Grant, struggling with the problems created by his victory, informed Cullum that he was forwarding prisoners. "It is a much less job," he said, "to take them than to keep them." There had, he reported, been a great deal of plundering in spite of all his precautions.[2]

At last the administration had what it was awaiting: a significant victory. John Nicolay recorded how quickly it acted: "Tonight the Secretary of War brought over the nomination of General Grant to be Major General of Volunteers, which the President signed at once." [3]

Though still disturbed about Beauregard, Halleck had the desire for continued action. After directing Sherman to report the force at Paducah and to keep a bright eye open for a move from Columbus by the well-advertised Sumter-Manassas hero, he said, "I am not satisfied with present success. We must now prepare for a still more important movement." In conformity with this thought, Cullum was directed to report on the suitability of Commerce, Missouri, as a depot for an advance against New Madrid.[4]

Eastward a special messenger was hurrying with a dispatch too secret to trust to mail or express or even to telegraph in cipher, in which Thomas Scott urged upon Stanton further aggressive action. He had returned to St. Louis the night before, having come by way of Springfield, only to find that the governor and other high officials, anxious on account of the many Illinois regiments at Donelson, had left for department headquarters. His return had been in accordance with a wish that Halleck had expressed in the letter he had sent Scott at Cairo. Although the Assistant Secretary had approved heartily of the plan of operations which Halleck outlined, and had urged it on Stanton, he was a little suspicious of the general himself, believing he might be wishing to "outgeneral" Buell. This fear disappeared after he returned to St. Louis and had a long confidential talk with Halleck, and on the 17th he reported the general's views and aims as "thoroughly patriotic and honorable." In detail Scott set forth Halleck's plan for the West, which included not only the over-all command, but asked for 50,000 well disciplined infantry and artillery from the Army of the Potomac. They would be used in the main column of advance operating up the Tennessee, and would make it possible to return to Missouri regiments sent to Grant. Thoroughly converted to the proposal, Scott said, "With this organization as set forth, there can be no such thing as fail. Can it be done and done promptly?"

Scott wished the courier to bring back orders after a program had been decided upon, and asked that the safe receipt of his own dispatch be signaled by telegraph. A postscript stated that Halleck had read and approved the letter, and ended with the sentence: "He desires that General Grant be promoted to the rank of Major General for meritorious services and that he shall be assigned to duty with him in the movements of the center column—he believes his promotion would have a good effect upon all Brigadiers in service—stimulating them to unusual efforts for distinction." It would seem that Halleck was not completely lacking in appreciation of Grant's achievement, but Grant certainly never saw this statement that went to Washington. In the body of his letter Scott said Halleck wished Buell made a major general because in the reorganization he proposed, the Louisville general would continue to be a department commander.[5]

Since the Navy had no one comparable to the Army's General in Chief, Foote reported by telegraph directly to the Secretary of the Navy. His foot was painful but not dangerous, and he would soon join the eight mortar boats then en route, with which he hoped to attack Clarksville. "The trophies of war are immense and the particulars will soon be given," said the flag officer. Strait-laced Gideon Welles, who according to Hendrick could hardly mention Stanton's name "without expressing contempt for his character and distrust for his every action," probably did not make haste to communicate to his brother Secretary Foote's statement, "The army has behaved gloriously." [6]

The soldiers in blue at Donelson listened that day to an order expressing their commanding general's great pleasure in congratulating them for the triumph gained by their valor on the 13th, 14th, and 15th. Coldly impersonal and detached, it did not use the word "Your" any more than it did the pronoun "I." Referring to the troops, Grant said: "For four successive nights, without shelter, during the most inclement weather known in this latitude, they faced an enemy in large force in a position chosen by himself," to which "all the safeguards suggested by science were added." No allusion was made to the hard contest of the 15th, but the men were told they had borne everything without a murmur, prepared at all times to receive an attack, with continuous skirmishing by day, ultimately "forcing the enemy to surrender without condition." It was not claimed that the enemy was dealt a crushing blow from which he could not recover, but merely that the victory was "great in breaking down rebellion," and that it had "secured the greatest number of prisoners of war taken in one battle on this continent." At the end there was a prediction: "Fort Donelson will hereafter be marked in capitals on the maps of our united country, and the men who fought the battle will live in the memory of a grateful people." [7]

The news going to Richmond was despondent. Leroy P. Walker, the Confederacy's first Secretary of War, telegraphed from Tuscumbia to Secretary Benjamin, "Better lose the seaboard than this line. The Memphis and Charleston Road is the vertebrae of the Confederacy, and there are no troops for its defense." [8] He would have felt still gloomier if he could have seen the map showing Halleck's proposed objectives that Scott's courier was taking to Washington. Seizing the road near its end would, however, not be as paralyzing as strangling it at Knoxville, as Lincoln wished, for that would cut off from the East—except by a more roundabout way—not only Memphis, but also Nashville, Chattanooga and northwest Georgia. The river route was, however, open and fast, while the road to Knoxville was heavy with mud and barred by mountains.

The next day Halleck put pressure directly on Buell, asking if he could not march on Clarksville and then go up the river to Nashville. Thinking of might-have-beens and talking as if he had been the field commander, he said: "Had the enemy thrown his forces rapidly down the river he could have crushed me at Fort Donelson, and have returned to Nashville before you could have reached that place." Buell replied that he agreed they should be closer together, but the trouble was that the common dirt road from Bowling Green to Clarksville was currently impassable. He might move light if he were sure Halleck could get Clarksville and give him supplies upon his arrival. "What do you think," queried Buell, "if I can get away, of our meeting at Smithland personally, and going up to Grant to study the ground?" [9]

Halleck's alarm about Cairo continued to mount, and he telegraphed Buell that he had recommended a major generalcy for him and told him to come to the Cumberland and take command. There the battle of the West was to be fought, and Buell, said Halleck, should be in immediate command. "Say that you will come," he urged, "and I will have everything there for you. Beauregard threatens to attack either Cairo or Paducah. I must be ready for him." The victory at Donelson was ascribed to the regiments that Hunter had sent: "Honor to him. We came within an ace of being defeated. . . . A retreat at one time seemed almost inevitable." "Help me, I beg you," implored Halleck. "Throw all your troops in the direction of the Cumberland." But the distraught message had a very prophetic ending: "There will be no battle at Nashville." [10]

For two weeks Halleck had certainly borne a heavy burden, and he was beginning to break under the fear of enemy counterattacks. Buell contributed to his further collapse by transmitting a report that Mitchel sent from Bowling Green: "We have reliable information that the enemy has fallen back from Clarksville and was concentrating heavy force at Nashville, and justifying the railroad engineers' reports that four days since a fleet of fifteen boats passed Memphis, ascending the river." [11] The dispatch did not say the boats were loaded; they might be empties, intended to evacuate the Columbus garrison. But as Halleck had stretched McClellan's report about the deserter's story, so he magnified this one. To Cullum—who the day before had written with regard to Beauregard's threat, "For our defense I think we have a force that will give the little Frenchman a warm reception" [12]—he telegraphed:

Act in my name, and assume command over any and all. A large force passed Memphis four days ago—fifteen steamboats loaded with troops, to re-enforce Columbus. Look out for an attack on Cairo or Paducah. Get ready immediately. Use my name in any order you issue. We must be ready for them. I am collecting and sending every man I can find. [13]

In preparing a reception for "the little Frenchman," Halleck did not forget the gunboats, and a message went to Grant, bidding him send all but one of them back to Cairo, after they had destroyed the Clarksville bridge. But sometime on this troubled day Halleck got off a short and cheery message to the General in Chief: "The flag of the Union is floating in Arkansas. . . . The Army of the Southwest is doing its duty nobly." [14]

The observations of astronomer Mitchel about Nashville were inaccurate, for from that place Hardee telegraphed to Jefferson Davis that the army was continuing its retreat to Murfreesboro, where Johnston had already gone. At Iuka, a town on the railroad that Walker likened to a backbone, the local Confederate commander was having domestic trouble, and he issued a circular denouncing his men for stealing chickens, killing hogs, and robbing gardens. They reminded him of Yankees: "Such conduct is disgraceful in itself, unworthy of Southern soldiers and only equaled by the marauding hordes that are invading our soil." [15]

Northerners, unaware of Halleck's fears, not knowing that the Bowling Green Confederates would not stop at Nashville, and never dreaming that Dixie soldiers could enjoy secessionist chickens not rightly come by, went on with their rejoicing. The Senate by unanimous consent dispensed with referring to its military committee Lincoln's recommendation of Grant's promotion, and at once confirmed him a major general of volunteers, appropriately dating the appointment from the 16th. Now he was number ten on the list of generals.[16] Stanton and Lincoln had settled the question as to who would command if Buell went to the Cumberland. The War Secretary was also bringing pressure on McClellan to share some more men with the Navy. While the latter was telegraphing Buell, "What news have you? What of Nashville and Clarksville?" Stanton was writing him that 600 soldiers that had been sent to man the Cairo flotilla were not enough. No fewer than 800 additional should be sent "immediately." [17]

The dreaded Beauregard was not at Columbus devising evil against Halleck. He had in fact got only as far as Jackson, Tennessee, whence he sent a message to Richmond saying that his health was "too feeble to authorize" him to assume command at Columbus, though he would "advise with General Polk." [18] Halleck had not, however, been a victim only of his imagination, for Polk had planned a demonstration against Paducah and Birds Point for the 16th, which Johnston had canceled, pending the arrival of Beauregard.[19] The sick general expressed to the Confederate Adjutant General the belief that Columbus would meet the same fate as Fort Donelson, and unless withdrawn before it was too late its whole garrison would be lost.

Although the 19th brought Beauregard a message from Secretary Benjamin directing the evacuation of Columbus, it was a day when fears seemed to vie with cheery optimism for possession of Halleck's mind. In a dispatch to Cullum he now had the fifteen steamers at Columbus loaded with Confederate troops from New Orleans, and he directed, "If necessary, countermand, in the name of the Secretary of War all orders issued by General Buell or any one else about troops halting or returning to Kentucky." Toward his superior, his approach was a little different, and he told McClellan that all the steamers at Columbus had steam up, ready for a move "probably on Cairo." He wanted more troops and said he and Buell together could paralyze the line between Nashville and Columbus. To Scott, who had gone to Louisville, he telegraphed, "If General Buell will come down and help me with all possible haste we can end the war in the West in less than a month," and he wired Buell he would meet him at any place he appointed. But Halleck sent one dispatch worthy of a cool-minded lawyer, when, in answer to McClellan's statement that Hunter ranked him and that that fact was fatal to Halleck's proposal about the West, he said, "It was decided in the Mexican War that regulars ranked volunteers without regard to dates. This decision, if sustained, makes everything right for the Western Division." He was going a little far, however, when he added, "Give it to me, and I will split secession in twain in one month." [20]

Thanks, general and particular, for past victories appeared. A rather rhetorical order by Halleck congratulated "Flag-Officer Foote, Brigadier-General Grant, and the brave officers and men under their command, on the recent brilliant victories on the Tennessee and Cumberland." The war was, the order said, "not yet ended," but Halleck asserted that troops were being concentrated from all directions, and there soon would be an army that would be irresistible. His eloquence aroused, he did not stop there, but added: "The times and places have been determined on. Victory and glory await the brave." He showed he knew it was as important to win individuals

MAJOR GENERAL JOHN A. McCLERNAND

MAJOR GENERAL DON CARLOS BUELL

CAPTAIN HENRY WALKE

MAJOR GENERAL LEW WALLACE

BRIGADIER GENERAL BENJAMIN M. PRENTISS

MAJOR GENERAL WILLIAM T. SHERMAN

as to cheer on the men with muskets, and a telegram to Hunter was more than profuse in its thanks to him, while the people of Iowa were given cause for pride by a telegram to their governor: "The Second Iowa Infantry proved themselves the bravest of the brave. They had the honor of heading the column which entered Fort Donelson." McClellan was told that it was the coolness and bravery of Charles F. Smith that had turned the tide of battle at Fort Donelson. "Make him a major-general. You can't get a better one. Honor him for this victory and the whole country will applaud," said the St. Louis general. But still no personal message went to Grant, such as was sent to Foote when his official report about Fort Henry reached St. Louis on the 9th.[21]

In an atmosphere of calm and sureness, work was progressing at Fort Donelson. A letter had come from Sherman, which unfortunately is lost, though Grant's reply is preserved. Grant asked that reenforcements come up the Cumberland and said he would take Clarksville on the 21st and Nashville on March 1, provided it met the approval of General Halleck. Then in his first of the many fine and easy letters that went from the senior in rank to the senior in age, Grant said:

I feel under many obligations to you for the kind tone of your letter, and hope that, should an opportunity occur, you will win for yourself the promotion which you are kind enough to say belongs to me. I care nothing for promotion so long as our arms are successful and no political appointments are made.[22]

Into a progress report to Cullum Grant slipped a hint: "If it is the desire of the general commanding department, I can have Nashville on Saturday week." There had, he reported, been "no distinction in the treatment of Federal and Confederate sick and wounded," and he thought the prisoners had appreciated the generally considerate treatment accorded them. Union people were coming in; some secessionists were leaving the country; others were expressing a willingness to "take the oath," if assured of protection. Though there were shortages of some items, notably coffee, there was plenty of food, and so much rice that they would not "want any more during the war." As to the prisoners: "I think I will send you the tail of the elephant to-night or in the morning at furthest." [23]

Scott, striving to understand Halleck's long message to Buell of the day before, wired for some explanations, saying it was Buell's desire to meet his views fully. Buell himself wrote calmly, thanking Halleck for his "friendly offices," and asking clear questions. His information indicated that the enemy was concentrating at Nashville, but he had countermanded the order for troops that had reached Smithland to return to him, and had directed the officer in command to take instructions from Halleck.[24]

In Bowling Green, which Mitchel had reached after "incredible labor, in rain and mud," things were temporarily in repose. Though a million dollars worth of stores had been destroyed by the enemy—according to Colonel John Beatty—there was enough pork, salt beef, and other necessaries to last the division a month. And the diarist found not only pen, ink, and paper conveniently at hand, but also cigars to smoke as he did his writing. The shrewd campaigner recorded on the 18th: "The weather is turning warm again. The men are quartered in houses. I room at the hotel. This sort of life, however pleasant it may be, has a demoralizing effect upon the soldier." There were also deficiencies, and the next day Beatty, in bed while his servant dried his clothes and boots, wrote, "I am badly off for clothing; my coat is out at the elbows and my pantaloons are in a revolutionary condition, the seat having seceded." [25]

Coming so soon after the Confederate defeat at Mill Springs, the loss of Forts Henry and Donelson had done much damage to Sidney Johnston's prestige. On this February 19, ex-Secretary Walker, not knowing that Beauregard lay sick in Jackson, ended a long letter to the officer who had been sent from the East to bolster matters in the West:

My dear general, I have an abiding confidence in your courage, ability, fortitude, and luck. The whole country looks up to you as a forlorn hope. Your name is a tower of strength, and I believe that God has destined you as the special instrument in His hands to work out our salvation.

May His omniscience direct and His infinite goodness preserve you, is the earnest prayer of your friend.[26]

McClellan did well in appraising the situation in the West, and near mid-morning of the 20th he telegraphed Halleck, "I doubt purpose of rebels to attack Cairo. More probably intend abandoning Columbus. Have too few troops at New Orleans to spare any." That was excellent; but making a decision was another matter. Replying to Halleck's panicky statement that he might have to withdraw troops from Donelson to save Cairo, the most that McClellan could say was, "Do not withdraw troops from Donelson until I hear from Buell to-day." Buell, to whom McClellan telegraphed Halleck's fear as well as his own belief, had gone to Bowling Green, and was forty miles from the end of the telegraph. But at 7:00 P.M. his chief of staff wired the situation to Washington: Mitchel at Bowling Green with 10,000 "fighting men," a brigade thrust forward toward Nashville; McCook's division of 15,000 fighting men not far away; Thomas at Bardstown, eight or nine days' march behind; Wood's division of raw troops at Munfordville, three or four days away; Nelson's division at Smithland, available to Halleck. Buell did not think, said Colonel Fry, that he could advance on Nashville in force without the railroad; it was being repaired as rapidly as possible, and more rolling stock had been ordered. As to Columbus: Buell "hardly thought an advance from that point probable," unless the enemy had more gunboats than he believed.[27] When night came, McClellan still had to face the uncertainty of the situation.

But McClellan had a greater worry than doubt whether the Columbus Confederates were or were not a threat to Cairo. With action in the West from Cumberland Gap to northwest Arkansas, and Halleck, Buell, and Scott calling for some of the men in the idle Army of the Potomac, the General in Chief was in a major predicament. He met the situation by making statements that he must have known were not true. To Halleck he said, "In less than two weeks I shall move the Army of the Potomac, and hope to be in Richmond soon after you are in Nashville. . . . We will have a desperate battle on this line." After asking Buell, "How soon can you be in front of Nashville, and in what force? What news of the rebels?," he asserted. "If the force in [the] West can take Nashville or even hold its own for the present, I hope to have Richmond and Norfolk in from three to four weeks." In a message to Scott he indulged in no optimistic forecasts, but said simply, "At present no troops will move from [the] East. Ample occupation for them here. Rebels hold firm at Manassas Junction." [28]

Rationality was returning to Halleck, and he wired Scott—who was with Buell miles beyond the end of the telegraph line—"I mean that Buell should move on Clarksville with his present column; there unite his Kentucky army and move up the Cumberland, while I act on the Tennessee. We should then be able to co-operate." He also turned to psychological warfare by commuting to confinement the death sentences still hanging over the eight convicted bridgeburners. This would foster the "rapidly-increasing loyalty of citizens of Missouri, who for a time forgot their duty to their flag and country." But it was only a provisional mitigation, and the lives of the eight were turned into a means to secure safety and order in the future, for Halleck said: "If rebel spies again destroy railroads and telegraph lines, and thus render it necessary for us to make severe examples, the original sentences against these men will be carried into execution." Though he showed clemency toward the saboteurs, Halleck did not relax in his bid for a unified command, and in the evening he wired McClellan: "I must have command of the armies in the West. Hesitation and delay are losing us the golden opportunity. Lay this before the President and Secretary of War. May I assume command? Answer quickly." It was a pincer operation that was being applied to the General in Chief, for the letter carried by Scott's courier would urge the case directly upon the War Secretary. Nor did Halleck delay in plans for operations entirely under his own control, for he informed Cullum that Commerce had been selected as a base for Pope in an advance against New Madrid.[29]

The partisans of the General in Chief were trying to counter the criticism of his inaction in the East by giving him major credit for victories in the West. It was claimed that he had not only planned everything strategically, but that, seated at one telegraph instrument, while Buell and Halleck listened to the clicking sounders in Louisville and St. Louis, he "made all the orders and dispositions of force to perfect the victory and pursue the enemy." "The battle was fought," continued the *New York Times,* "we may say, almost under the eye of Gen. McClellan. So remarkable an achievement has seldom adorned science." This, retorted Horace Greeley, was merely an instance of the "sort of humbug which has of late become quite common," and he pointed out some slips in chronology on the part of the rival paper, and noted the absence of a telegraph line to Fort Donelson.[30] The victory was, said the *Tribune*'s Washington correspondent, all a result of officers exercising "their own discretion, under the emphatic orders of Secretary Stanton to find and fight the enemy." [31] This too was hardly the truth, and the Secretary himself put the matter right in a letter to Greeley, published on the 20th:

I cannot suffer undue merit to be ascribed to my official action. The glory of the recent victories belongs to the gallant officers and men that fought the battle. No share of it belongs to me. . . . What, under the blessings of Providence, I conceive to be the true organization of victory and military combination to end this war, was declared in a few words by Gen. Grant's message to Gen. Buckner—*"I propose to move immediately upon your works."*

George Cullum was in no doubt as to where credit was due, and that night he wrote to Grant, "I have received with the highest gratification your reports and letters from Fort Donelson, so gallantly captured under your brilliant leadership." Then followed important shop talk: about the prisoners; about the shipping of blankets (very few of these on hand), overcoats, wagons, and other things; about the care of the sick and wounded by doctors and nurses who had freely and generously offered their services. All this would please a conscientious and sympathetic field commander quite as much as the repeated congratulations and assurance of "continued esteem" with which the hard-working fifty-three year old Cairo brigadier closed his letter.[32]

Midnight of February 20–21 had hardly passed when the wire crackled with McClellan's sharp reply to Halleck's near-ultimatum:

Buell at Bowling Green knows more of the state of affairs than you at Saint Louis. Until I hear from him I cannot see necessity of giving you entire command.

I expect to hear from Buell in a few minutes. I do not yet see that Buell cannot control his own line. I shall not lay your request before the Secretary until I hear definitely from Buell.[33]

Still out of bed at 1:00 A.M. and thinking that he would make a decision of some consequence if he only knew more, McClellan sent a brisk dispatch to Buell, and a similar one to St. Louis. He wanted, he declared, a telegram at least once a day, giving the positions of Buell's troops and those of the enemy, as well as "the state of affairs." Unless he had such information he could not tell whether it was "necessary or not to suspend or abandon" his own plans. (And only a few hours before he had told Buell he expected to be in Richmond and Norfolk in three or four weeks, provided only that troops in the West could hold their own!) "Neither Halleck nor yourself," said the General in Chief reproachfully, "give me as much detailed information as is necessary for me. This is the critical period, and I must be constantly informed of the condition of your affairs." [34]

McClellan was demanding the unreasonable. Colonel Fry's report about Buell's army was as good as he could expect; but he seemed to believe his subordinates could give up-to-the minute locations of even enemy units. Later in the day he asked, "What is Thomas' division doing at Bardstown?" To this Buell might have replied: "At Bardstown, Thomas is doing as much as the Army of the Potomac is doing at Washington. Some of his men are admiring the Van Dycks and canvases by other masters, presented by Louis Philippe to the old cathedral; others are gathered in the historic inn where the unhappy exiled prince once lived, discussing the vicissitudes of life and enjoying the product of the renowned distilleries of the old frontier town."

Perhaps recalling how rapidly he had marched on Beverly the preceding July, McClellan said, "Rapid movements are now necessary"; then he harangued: "I repeat, both Halleck and yourself keep me too much in the dark. Your reports are not sufficiently numerous or explicit." To Halleck he telegraphed, "What more have you from Columbus? You do not report either often or fully enough. Unless you keep me fully advised, you must not expect me to abandon my own plans for yours." [35]

Soberly, and much to the point, Halleck wrote to McClellan. After explaining that for two weeks he had been too busy to write and could do nothing but telegraph, he said:

Our successes on the Tennessee and Cumberland and in the Southwest, together with the stringent measures taken here, have completely crushed out the rebellion in this city and State; no more insurrections, bridge-burnings and hoisting of rebel flags. This enables me to rapidly increase my force in Tennessee. Nashville and Columbus must soon fall.

Clinging firmly to his ideas, he said that if Buell had been sent to the Cumberland both places would have been evacuated already, and added, "I cannot possibly be mistaken in the strategy of the campaign." The necessity of keeping forces at Cairo and Paducah to watch Columbus had made it impossible "to act with promptness and efficiency on the Tennessee and Cumberland." The enemy had made a great mistake in not striking at Grant. Continuing, Halleck said, "They have lost the golden opportunity, and I believe they will fall back from Nashville, without a battle, either on Decatur or Memphis. I certainly should if I were in Johnston's place. If he should not, and General Buell should take the line of the Cumberland, so as to co-operate with me on the Tennessee, the enemy would be cut off and forced to surrender." The reasoning here is not very convincing, for though the Cumberland gave a route to Nashville, it is not apparent how its use would cause the quick surrender of troops there if the city were organized for defense.

In good temper Halleck took up the question of reports, but said bluntly: "Certainly you do not expect to get information from me which I cannot obtain myself." [36] He put too much stress on the bad results of the Frémont regime, and did not point out that commanders in contact with the enemy have something more to do than make constant and detailed reports. Halleck himself should have known the general situation with regard to Grant, who had reported he was starting up the Tennessee with twenty-three regiments. Halleck knew what regiments had followed.

Though Halleck was too optimistic about the Missouri situation, his prediction with regard to Nashville was quickly borne out by news received the same day, and he telegraphed to Scott that advices from Clarksville—taken the day before by Foote—indicated that Johnston had fallen back on Columbia—forty miles south of Nashville—and that there was "very little preparation for a stand at Nashville." Then he coaxed: "General Grant and Commodore Foote say the road is now open and are impatient. Can't you come down to the Cumberland and divide the responsibility with me? If so, I will immediately prepare to go ahead. I am tired of waiting for action in Washington. They will not understand the case. It is as plain as daylight to me." [37] It was an irregular request, but Halleck of course did not know that Stanton had reprimanded Scott two weeks before because he unjustly believed that his assistant had been giving orders to generals.[38]

Since the hours of writing and receipt of telegrams are not generally on the messages, it is often not possible to determine just what caused what. But sometime on the troubled 21st Halleck had the satisfaction of reading this message from Stanton:

Your plan of organization has been transmitted to me by Mr. Scott and strikes me very favorably, but on account of the domestic affliction of the President I have not yet been able to submit it to him. The brilliant results of the energetic action in the West fills [sic] the Nation with joy.[39]

An acknowledgment was certainly in order, if not indeed called for, and it is not giving Halleck too much benefit of doubt to believe that it was after he had the Secretary's telegram that he abandoned indirection and telegraphed:

One whole week has been lost already by hesitation and delay. There was, and I think there still is, a golden opportunity to strike a fatal blow, but I can't do it unless I can control Buell's army. I am perfectly willing to act as General McClellan dictates or to take any amount of responsibility. To succeed we must be prompt. I have explained everything to General McClellan and Assistant Secretary Scott. There is not a moment to be lost. Give me the authority, and I will be responsible for results.[40]

Halleck may have been blushing a little over his recent fright about Cairo when he informed McClellan that a scout from Columbus reported that on the night of the 18th "immense cheering at [the] railroad station" was "said to be for Beauregard." Nineteen steamers were on the river, but now he said there were "no preparations either for advance or retreat." Perhaps a feeling of humiliation caused him unconsciously to weaken his bid for extended command, when he reported that Curtis had taken Bentonville, Arkansas, "with wagons and baggage and a large flag which was floating on the courthouse." Instead of letting it go at that, Halleck asked whether Curtis should proceed to Fayetteville or stop and hold the mountain passes, while 4,000 men were sent from Ironton and Doniphan to take Pocahontas and Jacksonport and destroy enemy supplies. He preferred the second plan but Curtis advised an advance on Fayetteville. A general who would ask that question about operations in his own department—except as a gesture of amity—was perhaps not too good a bet for enlarged responsibility. But by evening McClellan, now promising that by "to-morrow" he would hear definitely what Buell could do, was in a conciliatory humor and replied, "I think you are entirely right in not wishing to push Curtis beyond Bentonville. No necessity for anything more than a party of cavalry at Fayetteville. The true line of advance into Arkansas is by Pocahontas and Jacksonport; there you seriously threaten Memphis." And thus the number two man of the West Point class of '46 agreed with the number three of 1839. The General in Chief could well afford to show his gracious, friendly side, for he had gone over Halleck's head and given instructions directly to Cullum. In a dispatch that carried the same hour as the sharp one to St. Louis he said that two or four gunboats and a few mortar boats would secure the evacuation of Columbus, and he pronounced the Navy's report that it would take ten days to repair gunboats and get mortars ready as "inadmissible." They must be ready by Monday—it was then Friday—if Cullum had to take the matter in charge himself.[41]

The letter carried by Scott's courier had only now—February 21—been placed in Secretary Stanton's hands, and he made haste to answer: "The activity of General Halleck and his vigor have made a very strong impression upon the public mind and ought to stimulate the action of every other commanding officer. All my efforts will be directed towards sending troops to him and to General Buell, but how far they will be concurred in by General McClellan, time will show." [42] Unknown to Stanton, the answer was already in the dispatch the General in Chief had sent to Scott.

With reenforcements arriving largely in separate regiments, Grant had had a partially improvised organization at Fort Donelson. On the 21st he recast his command—now twice the size of the force with which he had marched from Fort Henry—into four divisions, each with three four-regiment brigades. The eight batteries plus a battalion of artillery, and the cavalry units were variously distributed. As some of the brigades—all of which were commanded by colonels—had organic guns and cavalry, they constituted potential well-rounded task forces. Smith alone had a battalion of divisional guns, while Grant as army commander had no artillery or mounted units under his direct control.[43] The new division commander was Brigadier General Stephen A. Hurlbut, whose long report as special emissary to Charleston had been instrumental in making Lincoln decide that honorable compromise was no longer possible. Though Hurlbut can be regarded as a political appointee, he was to render excellent service, and he did not try to capitalize on his acquaintance with the President.

The delicate problem of occupying a town of some size in one of the seceded states now faced Grant for the first time, and it was Smith whom he sent to Clarksville, with as much of his division as was equipped with transportation, to "occupy ground about the forts on the north bank of the river." Once more he showed reluctance in telling Smith what should be done: "I have no special directions to give that will not suggest themselves to you, such as keeping the men from going into private houses and annoying citizens generally." He did add that by calling upon the mayor, Smith could secure "a large quantity of army stores" that were reported to be in the town.[44]

After informing Cullum of the occupation of Clarksville, Grant said: "It is my impression that by following up our success Nashville would be an easy conquest; but I only throw this out as a suggestion, based simply upon information from people who have no sympathy with us." After commenting that some of his men were suffering for lack of blankets and overcoats, he closed his letter with sentences fit for the notebook of a general: "Shoes and other clothing are beginning to be wanting to some extent. I am ready for any move the general commanding may order." [45]

Then came the day which Lincoln had designated in late January for a general advance against the enemy, and which he had proclaimed only a few days before as an appropriate time for the people to "assemble in their customary places for public solemnities" and hear the first President's "Immortal Farewell Address." A victory unanticipated when he wrote his War Order had been won, but soon afterward there had come great personal sorrow. The Senate, after passing a resolution of sympathy in the death of his son two days before, had adjourned, to meet later in joint session with the House. Above the Speaker's chair was a large picture of Washington; above that was an impressive eagle with the nation's flag; the stars on the flag were of gold; and there were stars for the eleven states not represented that day upon the floor. Foreign ambassadors were present, but not England's Lord Lyons. Army and Navy officers were resplendent in dress uniforms, and John W. Forney, Senate secretary, read the well known words of the Farewell Address. Seated among the military was the handsome General in Chief; and as he rose to leave there came from the gallery a call for three McClellan cheers. As if fearing that some paper might use the incident for another eulogy, Greeley's correspondent forehandedly reported that the cheers "were given principally from the locality where the call was made." [46]

In spite of mourning in the White House, the urgency of the situation in the West caused Stanton to lay before the Chief Executive both Halleck's telegram of the day before and the papers received from Scott. The result was a message to Halleck saying that after "full consideration of the subject" the President did "not think any change in the organization of the Army or the military departments" was advisable at the moment. But he desired and expected that Halleck and Buell would cooperate fully and zealously with each other, and he "would be glad to know whether there had been any failure of co-operation in any particular." [47] The sorrow of the moment may have left Lincoln with no desire for a clash with McClellan; then too he may have already been contemplating removing him from the High Command.

Restricted to a cabin in the *Conestoga* by his injury and restrained from action by superiors, Foote wrote to Grant from Paducah, saying that Cullum had reported Halleck was "waiting for instructions from the War Department and Kentucky, and directs that everything remains *in statu quo*." He asked his Army colleague to "please hold on to" the gunboats and the mortar boats; then if the signal came for Nashville they were well started, while if the answer were negative they could be sent to Cairo, with the exception of the single gunboat allowed to Grant. The message ended: "With hearty congratulations for your well-earned major-generalship." Having thus felicitated, Foote got back to business in a postscript: "Please have a barge of coal at Clarksville." [48]

Although Grant and Foote had been tugging on the leash since the 21st, it would be several days before Yankee soldiers would assemble in the square before Tennessee's stately capitol on the hill overlooking the Cumberland. On the 23rd Buell was thirty-seven miles away, writing that he was pushing forward with Mitchel's division stripped of its baggage; his pickets were at the very moment already before the city and he would have been there himself had not heavy rains washed out the roads. Wrote Beatty: "The day pleasant and sunshiny. The feet of the men badly blistered, and the regiment limps along in wretched style; made fifteen miles." But Buell promised that tomorrow would see him at his goal, and that the next day and the following would bring up most of his army, part of which was going around by water. Then the ludicrousness of the command situation intruded, for Buell, twenty-eight miles away from the end of the telegraph at Bowling Green, advised McClellan in far-off Washington that "positive instructions be given in regard to the disposition of General Halleck's troops until the work nearest at hand is disposed of." Though the statement looks as if Buell thought he might encounter enemy opposition at the Cumberland, he ended his message, "It appears pretty well established that the enemy have mostly retired from Nashville, with the determination of making a stand at Murfreesborough. They have burned the bridge at Nashville." [49]

It was Grant who really knew what was going on in Nashville, for on the evening of the 23rd he went to Clarksville, arriving shortly after "quite a delegation of citizens" had returned to their homes. "Ostensibly," he reported to Cullum, they had come to bring surgeons to tend their wounded, but the general suspected that what they actually wished was an assurance that their property would be protected. The Nashvillians had said that Johnston had fallen back to Murfreesboro, after destroying bridges, commissary stores and such artillery as could not be taken away. The troops, Grant added, had wanted to destroy the city, but had been restrained by the citizens and a speech by Pillow.[50]

The next morning Nelson's division of Buell's army, which had gone around by water, arrived at Clarksville. On one of the leading boats was Colonel Jacob Ammen, the Jake Ammen of Georgetown, who may have been responsible for giving Jesse Grant the desire to send his son Ulysses to West Point. After teaching mathematics in Kentucky and Indiana for several years, he had returned to Ohio to become a civil engineer. Ammen was back in uniform soon after the outbreak of the war, and on this February day he met his "old friend and brave soldier General C. F. Smith," and recorded in his diary, "We both forgot that we are getting old, and met as young lieutenants in the Regular Army." [51]

Though Grant did not hesitate to order Nelson to proceed with his division of 6,000 men under convoy of the *Carondelet,* he handled the move with care. Upon reaching Nashville Nelson was to make immediate contact with Buell, and if the latter were not within two days' march of the city, Nelson was not to debark, but was to drop back down the river a few miles.[52] A boat ride had undoubted advantages, and Nelson's men would arrive without blistered feet. But there was the possibility of an ambush, and Ammen wrote:

The river is high, the night dark, and the rebels may have batteries on the banks as they had below. We proceed slowly and with caution; one gunboat in advance, just before the Diana. The boats run against trees in the dark; no serious injury. On we go, and would not be surprised to receive a shot from shore.

Nothing untoward occurred, and dawn found the little expedition tying up about a mile below what was obviously one of Nashville's defending batteries. Nelson sent Ammen ashore with some companies to make a reconnaissance. A deserted work was found—Fort Zolli-coffer—which only a short time before had mounted twelve heavy and four light guns; now they were spiked and dismounted, the carriages still smoldering. Reassured, the expedition proceeded to the city, five miles above, and soon the Tenth Brigade was in the Nashville square, with other troops occupying the suburbs. Nelson hastened to meet Buell, leaving to Ammen the honor of receiving the mayor, who, properly provided with credentials, also went forth to see the Federal commander. Toward evening Mitchel's division began to cross, and the occupying troops moved to the fair grounds, east of the city. "Hard to believe all they say," wrote Ammen about the statements of professing Unionists. But there was no cause for skepticism over the tons of salt pork, flour, and forage, or the "manufactory for small-arms" that were quickly taken over.[53]

It was an embarrassment to Buell, who had been hesitant about forming a junction with Grant by the Cumberland, to find that Nelson had already secured the city which McClellan had been saving for him. Brigadier General William Nelson was a Kentuckian and, according to Nicolay and Hay, "possessed the social gifts, the free manners, the impulsive temperament peculiar to the South." He also was a graduate of Annapolis and so could be expected to do especially well when once he got his soldiers on boats. Spurred on by bands, Buell's own column had been pushing down the famous Louisville-Nashville turnpike, Beatty writing, "The bass drum sounds like distant thunder, and the wind of Hughes, the fifer, is inexhaustible; he can blow five miles at a stretch." The column of 9,000 arrived opposite the city that night, but Buell wrote two days later that he had not intended to cross until he "could do so in sufficient force to run no great hazard." Then he had to record that Nelson had arrived during the night and landed before he "was aware of it." He had considered withdrawing him to the north of the river, but had decided against so doing "lest it should embolden the enemy and have a bad effect on the people." So he joined the division on the south bank of the river.[54]

Once on the same side of the Cumberland with Sidney Johnston, with no bridge connecting him to the north bank and a paucity of fuel for boats, Buell became a victim of alarm suggestive of Halleck's recent panic. He hurried four boats down to Clarksville and wrote to Smith, "The landing of a portion of our troops, contrary to my intention, on the south side of the river has compelled me to hold this side at every hazard." He requested Smith "to come forward with all the available force" under his command, and added, "So important do I consider the occasion that I think it necessary to give this communication all the force of orders." Buell believed, he concluded, that his own force would probably be sufficient to relieve Smith in five or six days. Wrote Grant in his *Memoirs:* "General Smith said this order was nonsense. But I told him it was best to obey it." [55]

For the first time Buell was experiencing the feeling of a commanding general in the presence of the enemy. And ironically it was due to Halleck's pleas and Grant's order sending Nelson on up the river. During the night he seemed to hear the tramp, tramp, tramp of Johnston's men hastening back to the city from which they had recently hurried. Still uneasy the next day—the 26th—he wrote to McClellan, "Our force is too small, and offers a strong inducement to the enemy only 30 miles distant, with some 30,000 men, to assume the offensive; but I have deemed it necessary to take the risk." (Did Buell think that the enemy would have an accurate count of Nelson's and Mitchel's divisions and know with precision the time schedule of the arrival of the rest of the invading army, and did he believe Johnston on first reports would completely recast plans he must have made for his future action?) After telling McClellan that he had sent steamers to bring reenforcements from Clarksville, and that other troops were marching as rapidly as possible, he said, "but it must be two or three days before we will be able to show much force." Allowing time for Confederate scouts in Nashville to make estimates, get word to Murfreesboro, and time for new decisions by the enemy and a thirty-mile march, it would be three or four days before Johnston could reappear in front of the city. Buell put March 13 as the date for the probable arrival of Thomas—who was to come by water—

but on the 23rd Fry indicated to the General in Chief that Thomas would embark at Louisville in two days, and he said it was only forty hours by water to Nashville.[56]

When Grant reported on the 25th the arrival of Buell at Nashville, he said to Cullum, "I shall go to Nashville immediately after the arrival of the next mail, should there be no orders to prevent it." (This harmless-looking intention was to cost Grant much.) Two spies from the Eighth Missouri that he had sent to Memphis were back, and he sketched the news: Beauregard had been sick at Decatur, but had gone on to Columbus; there were 12,000 men at Memphis; orders had been issued for the abandonment of Columbus. He was sending Memphis papers for Halleck and he confided, "I am growing anxious to know what the next move is going to be." To Sherman he wrote, "I do not know what work General Halleck intends me to do next." He was getting his command in hand, so there would be no delay when orders came, and he asked if Sherman could return to him a detachment of his troops that was no longer needed at Henderson, Kentucky.[57]

"I have been in the city since an early hour this morning," Grant wrote to Buell from Nashville on the 27th, "anxious and expecting to see you. When I first arrived I understood that you were to be over to-day, but it is now growing too late for me to remain longer." Smith, Grant said, would arrive that evening with a probable 2,000 men, and he would send more if needed; but his own impression was that the enemy was not far north of the Tennessee line. He requested the return of Smith's command if it were unnecessary for Buell's security and gave the reason: "I am in daily expectation of orders that will require all my available force." [58]

Years later Grant wrote that he met Buell on his return to the boat, and what he said of the latter's concern for the city and his own belief that Nashville was not in danger accords with the official record. Their last meeting seems to have been in St. Louis, during Grant's lean years of farming. The note he wrote this February day to the officer who had graduated from West Point two years before himself was the first in which Grant signed himself "Major-General"; it would not be the last in which he spoke of an expected meeting with Buell. He had not, however, twiddled his thumbs; he had paid his respects to the widow of President James K. Polk, who had promoted the Mexican War, which he himself as a lieutenant had strongly condemned. Mrs. Polk had been described by a dazzled English lady as far surpassing the three queens she had seen, not only in beauty, but in regal bearing. She had frowned on card playing and had stopped dancing in the White House because it led to "unseemly juxtaposition," but she had served excellent food and wines at her dinners, which her ability as a conversationalist made still more enjoyable. But on this winter day she did not reveal all her capabilities, and a Northern correspondent wrote that the "well-preserved lady of perhaps 50 years of age" received the Union general and members of his staff "courteously, but with a polished coldness that indicated sufficiently in which direction her sympathies lay." [59]

CHAPTER XII

HALLECK GETS THE WEST

Your friendship for individuals has influenced your judgment.
Halleck to McClellan

Although Halleck may well have believed that the death of the President's son had had some part in the decision that Stanton telegraphed about his proposal for unified command, he still did not accept it meekly. He was very frank in the reply he sent on the 24th: "If it is thought that the present arrangement is best for the public service, I have nothing to say. I have done my duty in making the suggestions, and leave it to my superiors to adopt or reject them." [1] It was a message that could well keep the question active in the minds of Stanton and Lincoln.

Subordinates were also annoying Halleck, and after telling Cullum that the local Cairo commander had no blanks because he had requisitioned none, he said: "There is a screw loose in that command. It had better be fixed pretty soon, or the command will hear from me." Foote was on the list of offenders: "Tell Flag-Officer Foote not to move till I give him further orders. The sending of steamers to General Buell was all wrong. It disconcerted my plans." In the general bombardment George Cullum himself got a fragment: "You should not have done it without my orders. . . . You are too fast at Cairo. Consult me before you order any other movement." Halleck knew what he was doing, for he had just received word that Nashville had been abandoned, and while McClellan still talked about Halleck's cooperating with Buell to the full extent of his power "to secure Nashville beyond a doubt," the St. Louis general seemingly made up his mind to anticipate and play his own cards. To Cullum he said he could now withdraw the forces he had been holding on the Cumberland "to await Buell's movements." "All O.K.; and now for a decisive movement," said Old Brains.[2] So after all he was not mad clear through.

As rapid a move up the Tennessee as possible was Halleck's desire; but McClellan's thought was different, and he wrote this same day: "The next move should be either a direct march in force upon the rear of Memphis or else first upon the communications and rear of Columbus, depending entirely on the strength and movements of the rebels." In the meantime "it would be well to amuse the garrison at Columbus" with mortars and gunboats as soon as they could be spared from the Tennessee and Cumberland. Strangest of all, McClellan was indulging in the fancy of an operation by Buell against Chattanooga; and it had precedence over one up the Tennessee, for he wrote, "It may be better to occupy Corinth instead of Decatur after Chattanooga is firmly in our possession." In a dispatch to Buell that bore the same hour as the one to Halleck he not only put Chattanooga as the next objective after Nashville, but engaged in another fancy: "Cannot Garfield reach the Virginia and Tennessee Railway at Abingdon? We must not lose sight of Eastern Tennessee." [3]

There would have been no finer prize than Chattanooga; but it was one hundred and forty miles from Nashville, and they were not all easy miles, for the pike reached only a little past Murfreesboro, and beyond lay mountains and a great river. Cautious as Buell had been about venturing through Paducah and occupying Nashville, one can only surmise as to any move he would have made against the key city at the foot of Lookout Mountain. The very next day McClellan's ardor had cooled, and he said to Halleck that if the enemy concentrated at Murfreesboro the "next movement must be made with great caution." A few days later, however, he would tell Buell to give Halleck all the assistance he could, and say, quite as if nothing difficult were involved, "and Chattanooga is a very important point to gain." [4]

A move on Abingdon was as visionary at the moment as one on Chattanooga, even if a flood on Washington's Birthday had not caused havoc to Garfield's expedition. High-water records disap-

peared when the Big Sandy—already swollen—rose in one day to
sixty feet above low-water mark. "The citizens here have suffered
fearfully," wrote Garfield from Pikeville on the 24th. From his own
surviving supplies he was forced to succor the people of the vicinity;
and he was fearful of losses in the depots he had built on the river in

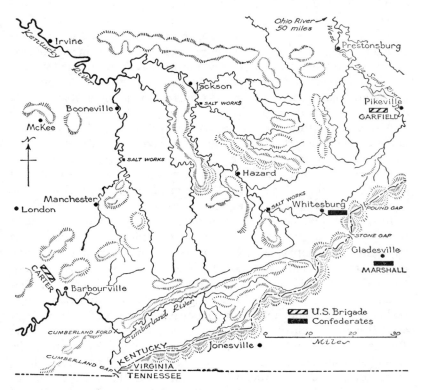

THE SITUATION IN EASTERN KENTUCKY, FEBRUARY 24, 1862

his rear. Though he had not recently encountered any of Marshall's
troops he had information that the mountain gap in his front was held
by a "considerable force." In view of his battle with the flood he
might have smiled at the ending of another dispatch from McClellan
to Buell: "What is Garfield doing?" Buell, who had not yet received
Garfield's letter about the flood, told McClellan of Garfield's projected move: "It will bring him down towards Cumberland Gap, and

I will then unite him with Carter, who in the mean time will, I hope, have gained some advantage at the Gap." The joining of the two forces could well look wise, for Marshall seemed to be permanently driven out of eastern Kentucky. Either Chattanooga or Knoxville was the place to cut the great railroad, and one point was sufficient if it could be held. In thinking of Abingdon, McClellan saw too many things—a fault typical of poor generals, according to Napoleon. The rains had of course also given Carter much trouble, and from Cumberland Ford he wrote, "Never before have I seen roads in such a condition, and unless there comes a favorable change soon in the weather, it will be impossible to transport supplies to our force." Already the thirty-three hundred stomachs for which he was responsible felt the annoyance of short rations.[5]

Aware of the threat toward Knoxville, Johnston had said to Benjamin on February 14, "I hope you will send a suitable commander for East Tennessee from the East." The man selected certainly looked equal to the situation, for he was the one whose timely and dramatic arrival at Manassas had done much to give Bull Run to the Confederates: E. Kirby Smith, now a major general.[6]

In spite of the fact that his own dispatch of the 18th had brought from Richmond an order to abandon Columbus, Beauregard was indulging great hopes for a brilliant counterstroke that would take the war to the enemy. On the 21st special couriers carried a "confidential circular" from Jackson to the governors of Tennessee, Alabama, Mississippi, and Louisiana requesting troops, and saying that he believed he could hold his rear and "take the field with at least 40,000 men, march on Paducah, seize and close the mouths of the Tennessee and Cumberland Rivers"; then, if aided by gunboats he "could also successfully assail Cairo, and threaten, if not indeed take, Saint Louis itself." In order to get a striking force, Beauregard appealed to Major General Earl Van Dorn, who since January 10 had been commanding the trans-Mississippi district of Johnston's large department. Arguing as he had in the circular to the governors, he asked Van Dorn to bring 10,000 men and join the St. Louis venture. Copies of the circular and the letter were sent to Cooper in Richmond, and the break-up of Johnston's department was virtually requested. If the "little Frenchman" was attempting an unsoldierly coup, it must be said for him that Johnston had come close to inviting some maneuvering when he voluntarily reduced himself to commander of a column that was marching away from the region most threatened at the moment. In a letter from Murfreesboro, he himself used language that almost recognized Beauregard as an independent commander. Having on the 23rd reorganized the regiments from Bowling Green into a corps under his own "immediate command," Johnston wrote to Benjamin that he would move "towards the left [right] bank of the Tennessee, crossing the river near Decatur, in order to enable me to co-operate or unite with General Beauregard for the defense of Memphis and the Mississippi." [7]

Nothing of course came from Beauregard's dream, and another strike by Union gunboats under Lieutenant William Gwin forced attention to the south. Gwin went as far as Eastport, Mississippi, pausing at Clifton, Tennessee, to load up a thousand sacks and a hundred barrels of flour as well as some six thousand bushels of wheat, which seemed to him too much food for a little town. That Corinth was an objective point was shown by the closing sentence of an indorsement Cullum wrote on Gwin's report, "Leaving the Tennessee at Hammond [Hamburg], a good road, 18 miles long, leads direct to Corinth." On the same day—February 24—Beauregard awakened to reality and ordered Brigadier General Daniel Ruggles, commanding at Corinth, to do six specific things, one of which was to hold Hamburg "in strict observation from Corinth." To Ruggles also came a report about the guards at the five bridges on the railroad between Corinth and Memphis. With all thoughts of visiting St. Louis gone from his mind, Beauregard ordered Polk to hasten work on the defense of New Madrid and Island No. 10, and make necessary preparations for the rapid evacuation of Columbus. Where, he asked, would be a good place to gather together the balance of the forces between the Tennessee and Mississippi "for ulterior operations?" [8]

Halleck likewise was thinking of the future, and he directed George H. Smith to go to the Tennessee and Cumberland without delay, "prepared with workmen and material to repair or construct a [telegraph] line from Fort Henry to Florence, Ala., and thence in the direction of Memphis." [9]

In northwestern Arkansas the Federal thrust had also come to a halt. Curtis's army of 12,000 men and fifty guns, organized in four small divisions under Brigadier Generals Franz Sigel and Alexander

Asboth, and Colonels Jefferson C. Davis and Eugene A. Carr, was three hundred and twenty miles from St. Louis and two hundred and ten from its base at Rolla. In the vicinity of Cross Hollow, just north of Pea Ridge, where Curtis reported enemy cantonments "better than ours at Benton Barracks," the army had halted. Supply was difficult, and though the quartermaster, Captain Philip H. Sheridan, soon had mills grinding grain at Cassville, it was necessary to spread out to live. Cavalry strikes were made as far away as Huntsville and Fayette-

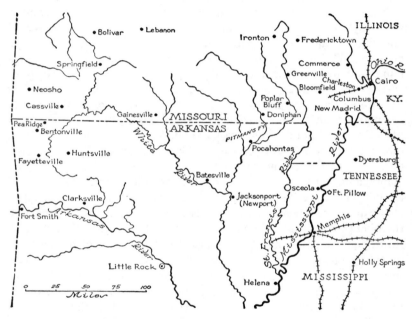

THE MISSOURI–ARKANSAS THEATER

ville, but those advanced places could not be held. Since it had been necessary to leave garrisons at points in his rear, Curtis requested not only replacement clothing for the men he had, but additional troops. Replied Halleck, "Pants will be sent, but cannot now send more troops or horses." However, Hunter would march from Leavenworth with a column of 5,000 men to give support to Curtis's right.[10]

Although it had been stopped, the Federal advance had upset the ambitious plans of the recently arrived Van Dorn. The Mississippian had been in the class ahead of Grant at the Military Academy and seemed as much intended for a soldier's life as his classmate, James Longstreet. Two brevets and a wound in Mexico, and four wounds from battles with the Comanche Indians were a part of his combat record. Even before Beauregard wrote to him, he had been thinking covetously about St. Louis, for he wrote to Price on February 7 from Jacksonport, Arkansas, enumerating prospective forces to the number of 45,000 men, and saying, "With these, can we not hope to take Saint Louis by rapid marches and assault?" A week later in a letter from Pocahontas he went into more detail, and added that after the great Missouri city was captured "we should fortify opposite, on the Illinois side." Beauregard, when he began a week later to envision steaming up the Mississippi, overlooked that optimistic flourish, and said nothing about planting the new flag on the soil of Lincoln's home state. But even as Van Dorn wrote, Sterling Price was falling back very rapidly from Springfield.[11]

On the 26th Van Dorn reported to Johnston that the Federals were near the Missouri line with 35,000 to 40,000 men, while Confederates to the number of about 20,000 under Price and McCulloch were at Cross Hollow. If Brigadier General Albert Pike would join him with his regiments of Indians, Van Dorn would have 26,000 men, and he said, "I leave this evening to go to the army, and will give battle; of course, if it does not take place before I arrive. I have no doubt of the result. If I succeed I shall push on." March 3 had come before he joined Price and McCulloch, who had fallen back before Curtis; and without delay he set out to attack the invaders in their position behind Sugar Creek. Pike and the Indians joined him on the march, bringing the command to 16,000 men; though this was much below the figure Van Dorn had expected, he was still superior in numbers to the Federals. In his report he wrote that he did not think Curtis entertained any suspicions of his advance, and he spoke of his "strong hopes of our effecting a complete surprise and attacking the enemy before the large detachments encamped at various points in the surrounding country could rejoin the main body." [12] He was luxuriating in the dream of every commander, that of gobbling up the enemy piece by piece.

Though Curtis was engaged in a propaganda war, urging the people of Arkansas to disband their companies and lay down their arms, and telling them that a surrender to the flag of the Union was only a return to their natural allegiance, he still had cavalry patrols and spies at work. On March 1 he reported: "The enemy's cavalry is crowding my flanks and attacking my foraging parties. . . . My express comes in regularly, but rebel bands are numerous in the country." Three days later he said the enemy had been reenforced by the Indians and he admitted that his position could be easily turned. "A little would help me," was his restrained request for aid, as he promised that he would be "on the alert, holding as securely

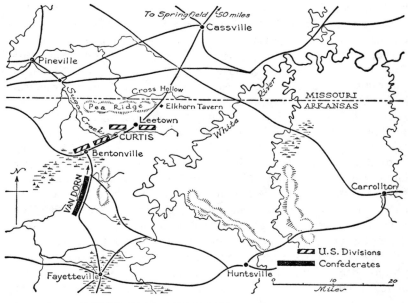

CURTIS AND VAN DORN, MARCH 5, 1862

as possible." The next day was cold and blustery, a day fulfilling the tradition of the month, with enough snow falling to cover the ground. Toward two o'clock, as Curtis was writing, not apprehensive of immediate attack, scouts and fugitive citizens brought word of the rapid approach of the enemy, and a deserter added that the Confederates claimed they mustered 20,000 men. Without delay Curtis had a courier on the way to Sigel ordering him back from the position he held with two divisions at Bentonville. Taking the road at two in the morning, Sigel got away, though his rearguard—"admirably handled," according to Van Dorn—was engaged several times during the day. When night came the Federal command was together, snugly and strongly posted behind Sugar Creek.[13]

Deprived of the relished chance of consuming his enemy in small bites, Van Dorn declined to attack breastworks protected by felled trees, and, availing himself of roads well known to Price and McCulloch, led his column under cover of darkness around the Federal right. But his march was discovered, and Curtis skillfully reversed his front, his right becoming his left, and his left his right. Not wanting to resign the initiative to his ambitious foe, he formed a special force under Colonel Peter J. Osterhaus, consisting of cavalry, artillery, and infantry, and gave him the mission of attacking in the direction where he estimated the enemy center would be found. It was nearly noon of the 7th when the battle began in earnest; and in the center and on the Federal right it was bitterly contested. The death about midafternoon of McCulloch and Colonel James McIntosh, who commanded one of the Indian regiments, caused the Confederate center to weaken; but Carr on the right of the Union battle line was roughly handled.[14]

When night gave the commanders opportunity to appraise the situation, Curtis found he had two divisions that had hardly been engaged. But with the enemy in his rear the supply situation was not good, and Asboth wrote him at 2:00 A.M. recommending "a decided concentrated movement, with the view of cutting our way through the enemy where you may deem it more advisable, and save by this if not the whole at least the greater part of our surrounded army." It looks as if this counsel of despair was accepted to some extent, for, in his final, long and somewhat rhetorical report, Curtis said he redisposed his force so as "to bring all four of my divisions to face a position which had been held in check all the previous day by one." What his actual feelings were cannot be told, though he wrote in his report, "I rested, certain of final success on the coming day." [15]

Earl Van Dorn on his part discovered in the darkness that when you get in the enemy's rear you leave him in your own; and he was mortified by having an ordnance officer tell him he could not find the ammunition wagons. Apparently they had gone off to Bentonville with the subsistence trains. Thus the Confederate general had little to feed his hungry men, his "beaten out" artillery horses, or his guns;

and one need hardly question his statement, "It was therefore with no little anxiety that I awaited the dawn of day." When daylight revealed the Federals "in a new and strong position, offering battle," Van Dorn—according to his report—made his "dispositions at once to accept the gage." And soon the battle had begun again. That the Federal batteries were well handled cannot be doubted; but while the Unionists proudly attributed the retirement of enemy guns to their own good shooting, Van Dorn claimed it was due to the exhaustion of his ammunition. Without much delay he decided to withdraw; and after getting part of his troops on the road and others in position as a covering force he gave the order to march. He pronounced the work of the covering troops "done very steadily," adding that no attempt being made by the enemy to follow, he encamped about midafternoon some ten miles from the field of battle.[16]

The neat withdrawal of Van Dorn is amply confirmed by Curtis's report. After saying that "no force could then have withstood the converging line and concentrated cross-fire of our gallant troops," he added, "Finally our firing ceased. The enemy had suddenly vanished." Sigel pursued a small force in the direction of Cassville but lost contact with it; and several hours passed before Curtis learned that the main Confederate column, after entering Cross Timber Hollow, "had turned short to the right, following obscure ravines which led into the Huntsville road in a due south direction." So ended the strange battle of Pea Ridge, or Elkhorn Tavern, of which there are accurate figures for Federal losses, but only estimates for the Confederates. The next day Curtis complained to Van Dorn that the Indians had indulged in tomahawking and scalping, Van Dorn replying that he hoped this was an error, his Indians "having for many years been regarded as civilized people." Answering charge with countercharge, he said it had been reported to him that some of his men had "been murdered in cold blood by their captors, who were alleged to be Germans." He hoped that perpetrators of atrocities would in the future "be brought to justice, whether German or Choctaw." [17]

On the 9th a long telegraphic report went to St. Louis while, from a point fourteen miles west of Fayetteville, Van Dorn sent a short message to Sidney Johnston, routing it through Hog Eye. He had, he said, "gone entirely around the enemy," and though he did not know where his train was, he believed it was safe. Without delay,

Halleck telegraphed Curtis: "I congratulate you and your command on the glorious victory just gained. You have proved yourselves as brave in battle as enduring of fatigue and hardship. A grateful country will honor you for both." "Our cavalry in pursuit of the flying enemy," was the ending of the dispatch that sped the news to Washington. Johnston may have had difficulty locating Hog Eye, as well as making out just what Van Dorn had done, before his longer report was received. But Halleck did not write off the Southern general because his hasty encircling tour was unorthodox, for he wired Curtis on the 13th: "Be careful to keep your main force together and well in hand. Ascertain the enemy's movements by throwing out cavalry. Be careful of Van Dorn. He is a vigilant and energetic officer, and will be certain to strike any exposed point." [18] That was about as nice a compliment as a soldier could expect from an enemy commander.

On the day that Halleck learned of the fall of Fort Donelson he not only told Cullum to report on the suitability of Commerce as a base for an advance against New Madrid; he directed him to send to that point troops not needed on the Tennessee and Cumberland. Two days later Cullum wrote, "My spy came in this afternoon from Commerce." Then he gave an abundance of pertinent information: wood near; plenty of water; no hay, but 10,000 bushels of corn three to eight miles away; no horses or cattle, such having all been stolen; the road from Benton good except possibly for two miles of embankment over swamps near New Madrid. February 20 brought from Halleck the telegram: "Commerce is selected as the depot for General Pope's command. He will immediately go there to receive his troops which you do not require for the defense of Cairo." Pope arrived on the evening of the 22nd and two days later pushed a brigade of four Indiana regiments under Colonel J. R. Slack to Benton; his order stressed tight discipline, vigilance, "and all the usual precautions common to a force in the presence of an enemy." On the 25th Halleck directed: "Move on your advance guard and working parties to repair the roads. Your force will be at least 10,000 in a few days. The movement must be prompt, as it is reported that the enemy is preparing to evacuate Columbus." Cavalry and batteries were going down the river for the new striking force.[19]

The build-up worked smoothly; and on the 27th Pope issued a

fine order, with none of the silly bombast that weakened his first orders a few months later in the East and caused the resentment of Federal officers and the scorn of Southerners. Here was John Pope

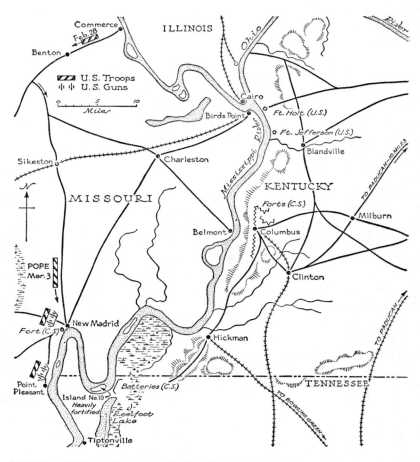

POPE'S OPERATION AGAINST NEW MADRID, FEBRUARY 24 TO MARCH 14, 1862

at his best. His first division, Brigadier General Schuyler Hamilton commanding, was to march at eight the next morning, the second division under Brigadier General John M. Palmer following one day later. The order directed that the men be informed that they were marching to meet the enemy within a few days; but the war was to be only against armed forces, and patrols were to receive "positive instructions to shoot down any person belonging to the army engaged in depredations or outrages upon the people of the country." To Pope's dispatch that he was marching the next morning Halleck replied that additional wagons were being sent as rapidly as possible. "Move on as fast as possible," he enjoined, "a reserve will sustain you. . . . The object must be accomplished if it requires 50,000 men." Push on Pope did, his march covered by cavalry under Colonel Gordon Granger, whose booming voice and fondness for hunting and good eating seemed to mark him as intended for horseback soldiering.[20]

Pope was hardly started when Halleck ordered a thrust into eastern Arkansas to destroy enemy stores at Pitman's Ferry, Pocahontas, Jacksonport, and Batesville. Brigadier General Frederick Steele, close friend and former classmate of Grant, was to be in command; and he was to employ troops already in southwestern Missouri west of the St. Francis River, with additions to bring his force up to 5,000 men. If he succeeded in his primary mission and the country was sufficiently open, he was to proceed to Helena and cut the steamboat communication with Memphis, though it was probable, said Halleck, that Memphis would already have been turned from the east. "On an expedition of this kind," continued the department commander in the long letter he handed to Steele, "you can carry with you but very few supplies except small stores." Subsistence above what was taken from enemy depots would be purchased locally; when cash ran out there would be forcible requisition. The success of the expedition depending upon speed, the train would consist partly of wagons, and partly of pack mules. "Keep the objects of your expedition a profound secret," cautioned Halleck. "Do not communicate it even to officers of your staff. Give it out at first that you are to move on New Madrid, and after you pass that place that Pocahontas is to be the only object, and so on as you advance." Since the purposes of expeditions frequently leaked out through guides, Steele was to watch his very closely "and permit none to escape." In order to baffle persons who might lay hands on messages, special code words were assigned, Jacksonport being "Nashville," Batesville "Saint Louis," and Helena "Salem." [21] Even if the operation did not fulfill its purpose, it would cover Pope's flank and give the enemy more to ponder over. It would likewise produce officers and troops trained in mobility and resourcefulness.

The last days of the Columbus fortress had come. "Light visible all the evening in the direction of Columbus," Cullum telegraphed on March 1. It was the illumination from burning barracks. The next day Polk wired to Richmond: "The work is done. Columbus gone. Self and staff move in half an hour. Everything secured." A violent thunderstorm that silenced Sherman's telegraph prevented him from informing Halleck immediately of the report just received that Columbus had been evacuated the day before; but at eight in the evening he wrote the news, and also that the enemy knew of Pope's projected advance from Commerce. Sherman had already sent a cavalry force to take posession of the abandoned town—if indeed it were abandoned—and he himself went to Cairo. "Attack Columbus as soon as possible. Say to Commodore Foote that time now is everything," was the order that Halleck sent to Cullum on the 3rd. Before daybreak the next morning, six gunboats, four mortar boats, and three transports with troops and eager reporters dropped down the river. Covered by guns ready to open fire, Sherman and Captain Phelps, with some thirty soldiers, made a dash in a tug toward the silent water batteries. No enemy was found; but a correspondent wrote, "Roaming through the town, their horses faring sumptuously upon forage left behind by the Rebels, and themselves comfortably quartered in the deserted houses, we found four companies of the 2nd Illinois Cavalry." [22]

Polk had done well indeed in getting men, guns, ammunition, and stores away from Columbus. But he exaggerated when he said "everything" was secured, for Cullum reported the capture of considerable ordnance stores, part of the great chain which had once been stretched across the river, and a large supply of torpedoes. Both in stories and in pictures the Northern press told about the "infernal machines" that were found in great number, not only in the river, but in the earthworks surrounding the city. The ground mines could be electrically exploded from caverns, and one reporter wrote: "The result may be imagined. Whole regiments could thus be blown up and sent to eternity without even a chance to escape." Foote and Cullum also indulged in superlatives in their efforts to describe the strength of the "Gibraltar of the West." The position, whose abandonment Polk thought was a mistake, was indeed strong, and its guns had numbered one hundred and forty.[23]

Much of the armament and many of the 17,000 men at Columbus had gone to Island No. 10 and New Madrid, where an S turn in the Mississippi gave a singularly strong defensive position. On February 26 Beauregard—still at Jackson—had telegraphed Polk, "New Madrid all important. In my opinion must be watched and held at all costs." Troops could be sent from Fort Pillow (on the east bank of the river, eighty miles below), and if Polk was satisfied that the enemy was planning to move against it, the position was to be "re-enforced at once to all possible extent from Columbus." The same day Polk informed the New Madrid commander, Colonel E. W. Gantt, that he was sending men as well as additional ammunition for his heavy guns; gunboats also would be sent. "Your position is a strong one, which you have well studied," said Polk encouragingly, "and I have no doubt of the vigor and efficiency of your defence. Keep me informed." [24]

On March 1 Pope's advance guard had an encounter with some of Jeff Thompson's men in their swampy lair south of Sikeston, three guns falling to a charge of the Seventh Illinois Cavalry. So unusual were they that Pope described them in his message that night to Halleck: "The pieces of artillery are of small caliber, breech-loading, beautifully rifled, and handsomely mounted on four wheels, drawn by two horses each. They have an ingenious repeating apparatus at the breech, and were undoubtedly made for service in this swampy, low region." [25] With contact mines in the Tennessee and the Mississippi, infernal machines buried in the ground about their forts, ready to be detonated by electricity, and rifled, repeating cannon designed for swamp warfare, it looked as if the Southerners were bringing warfare up to date. In addition to the guns, Pope got some timely information from Thompson's men: the enemy was rapidly evacuating Columbus and occupying Island No. 10.

"Arrived before this place with my whole force at 1 p.m.," wrote Pope from two miles north of New Madrid on March 3. Skirmishers had been pushed into the town, and a part of it had been occupied, the defending garrison, which he estimated at 5,000, keeping out of sight in their works. He could take the place with some loss, but could not hold it on account of six enemy gunboats, for so high was the river that the guns of the Confederate fleet could sweep the land for a distance of a mile. "If the gunboats leave here I take the works," said John Pope. That night the river rose a little higher and the guns of the gunboats looked still more maliciously "into every part of the intrenchments at very short distances." In order to draw some of the boats off and block the river to the enemy, the Federal commander sent 2,500 infantry with artillery and cavalry to Point Pleasant, nine miles below, on the night of the 4th. He asked for heavier guns and, by saying it would be easy for gunboats to shell the enemy troops out of Island No. 10 and pass down to New Madrid, suggested that the Navy get into the operation.[26]

Even as Pope wrote, Cullum was closing the dispatch to Halleck in which he announced the occupation of Columbus: "I urged upon Flag-Officer Foote the importance of immediately attacking the batteries of Island No. 10 and New Madrid, but that gallant commodore, after consulting with his brave officers, was of the opinion that two or three days of repairs to the gunboats was indispensable." Fort Donelson had clearly given the sailors a wholesome respect for heavy land guns, and the next day Cullum had to report that the pilots refused to go into the pilothouses because the plating was off, or so badly damaged as to be useless. Attacking downstream presented a difficult problem, for the boats did not have sufficient reverse power to maintain station, and it looked as if all they could do would be to tie up to the river bank and protect the mortar boats from hostile craft, while the mortars did some high-angle firing. Halleck understood the difficulty and told Cullum on the 7th that he did not wish the gunboats exposed; but he said that since it looked as if he could get no cooperation out of Foote, he would order Pope back. He even directed Cullum to procure transportation to take him up the Tennessee.[27]

Then word came that Pope could handle the situation. The force at Point Pleasant had closed the river to enemy steamboats coming up from below, and had repelled attacks of gunboats under Commodore Hollins. For some reason Pope's dispatch saying he could hold Point Pleasant took three days to reach Halleck, but it dissuaded him from withdrawing the New Madrid expedition. Siege guns, which Pope wrote would let him settle the affair without help from gunboats, were forwarded to Cairo and shipped to the railhead at Sikeston, reaching him in record time. Some were sent on to Point Pleasant and others placed in position before the forts at New Madrid. A heavy bombardment was carried on throughout the 13th, the enemy replying vigorously with his heavy batteries and his gunboats. The next morning revealed a white flag on the hostile works, the Confederates having withdrawn to Island No. 10 during a furious thunderstorm that had started about midnight.

"Nothing except the men escaped, and they only with what they wore," wrote Pope in a long report the same day. Thirty-seven guns, with quantities of ammunition of the best quality and much equipment and supplies of all sorts, were obtained. Burning candles were found in some of the tents, and uneaten suppers on the tables of officers' messes. Pope said he could now send cavalry to Steele, asked as to further operations, and gave the assurance, "I shall reconnoiter Island No. 10 to-day." Before night he had moved the twenty-five heavy guns of the captured fort so as to command the river.[28]

Though small, the operation had been skillful; and Pope had shown he could meet emergencies and act decisively. Shortage of transportation had made it necessary to leave baggage behind, but it was brought up as rapidly as possible, and the operation went forward without delay. Colonel Joseph B. Plummer, a regular army officer from Massachusetts, was in command at Point Pleasant. On the 9th, Pope could tell him not only that 10,000 pounds of coffee and tents were on the way to him, and six wagons were returning to Sikeston for knapsacks; he could also tell him that his commission as a brigadier had been confirmed. Appropriately it dated from October 22, 1861, in recognition of an efficient expedition Plummer had conducted against Ironton and Fredericktown from Cape Girardeau, about which Grant had written him a warm, congratulatory letter.[29]

On the day that New Madrid fell Halleck telegraphed Pope: "I congratulate you and your command on the success which has crowned your toils and exposure. You have given the final blow to the rebellion in Missouri and proved yourselves worthy members of the brave Army of the West." The message that sped the news to Washington concluded: "This was the last stronghold of the enemy in this State. There is no rebel flag now flying in Missouri." [30]

Halleck was indulging in some exaggeration, for there was still plenty of strong secession sentiment throughout Missouri, and guerrilla bands again appeared as spring drew near.

An order which he had issued on Washington's Birthday, to be read at the head of every regiment, sought to win over the people of Tennessee and other southern states:

Let us show to our fellow-citizens of these States that we come merely to crush out rebellion and to restore to them peace and the benefits of the Constitution and the Union, of which they have been deprived by selfish and unprincipled leaders. They have been told that we come to oppress and to plunder. By our acts we will undeceive them. We will prove to them that we come to restore, not to violate, the Constitution and laws.

A few days later he made a further gesture in the same direction by condemning an order of Brigadier General Paine that a Confederate cavalryman be hanged for each of five Union men who had been murdered near Bloomfield, Missouri: "It is contrary to the rules of civilized war, and if its spirit should be adopted the whole country would be covered with blood." The next day—February 27—he reiterated the same thesis under severe provocation, for word had come that poisoned food left by enemy troops in Mud Town, Arkansas, had brought death to one Federal officer and several soldiers, and severe suffering to others. The guilty were to be hanged, and their officers, "although not themselves the advisers or abettors of crime," were, if captured, to be sent to his headquarters in irons, for the laws of war made it "their duty to prevent such barbarities." But still no punishment of the innocent: "The laws of war forbid this." [31]

The withdrawal of troops to carry out active operations gave quiescent groups their chance, and on the last day of February Halleck directed the commanding officer at Jefferson City to move against a strong band at Osceola. The next day General John Schofield, commanding the state militia, reported that the secession bands in Johnson and Henry counties were so strong that it was "impossible for the militia to organize for their own defense." And so it went in various places until March 11, when the commanding officer at Lebanon reported that a district commander of guerrillas had been captured "with his written authority from Price to raise guerrilla bands." This was too much and it brought from Halleck an order stating that Price should know he was following "a course contrary to the rules of civilized warfare, and that every man who enlists in such an organization forfeits his life and becomes an outlaw." He warned: "Their lives shall atone for the barbarity of their general." [32]

Though there were plenty of aggressively minded Southern sym-
pathizers throughout the state, the fall of New Madrid left no place
where the rump secessionist legislature could meet under the Dixie
flag and the protection of Confederate soldiers. The state having been
proclaimed a member of the Confederacy by the Richmond Congress,
a resolution of thanks was certainly in order, and the aspiring legislators had intended to convene in New Madrid on the very day that
John Pope appeared before the town.[33]

Halleck's four months of command at St. Louis had been a period
of notable accomplishment. His *Elements* revealed a broad knowledge
that few officers possess, and not many commanders have to deal with
the varied and baffling problems that confronted him, and solve them
with so few competent assistants. His burden could not have been
much less than Cullum's, who wrote after he had been at Cairo for
a fortnight: "It is mighty hard to play everything from corporal to
general and to perform the functions of several staff departments
almost unaided, as I have done the past two weeks. I hardly get time
to eat very much or to sleep." But there was no spirit of complaint
and Cullum said he was ready for any amount of duty if it would
"crown the great and masterly work" that his chief had "so propitiously initiated." [34] He was also having to function as censor, and
correspondents who apparently thought he should give higher priority
to clearing their dispatches than to getting wagons, artillery ammunition, and troops to Grant, were sniping at him. George Washington
Cullum—who got up from a sick bed to make the trip to Columbus—
not only had a name to inspire devotion, but had a chief who was
himself an example of faithfulness and diligence.

From a purely military point of view, Halleck's record was spotted
by his near-panic for a couple of days over a possible attack on Cairo.
As a superior, his record has the bad blemish of unjust treatment of
Grant. There has been some tendency to explain his attitude as
jealousy toward an able subordinate; but here one encounters not
only Lincoln's statement to John Hay, already quoted, that Halleck
was "wholly for the service" but the stubborn fact that after having
been Grant's superior for two and a half years, he served him loyally
for the last year of the war. Halleck, within a month of coming to
the West, before Grant had done anything that could arouse jealousy,
had administered a sharp reproof to him in connection with the return

of prisoners; and he was snappish when Grant gave a good explanation of his action. Then, after curtly authorizing Grant to visit St. Louis, Halleck showed an inexcusable lack of cordiality in receiving him and dealt brusquely with his proposal, in spite of the fact that he was on record as approving the project Grant presented. The promptness and heartiness of Halleck's congratulations to both Curtis and Pope make it impossible to feel that his failure to send a message to Grant after his far greater achievement at Donelson was mere thoughtlessness. On the other side of the picture is the statement in Scott's letter to Stanton that Halleck wished Grant promoted—a statement worded to imply praise, and which Scott said the general had read and approved.

Grant's *Memoirs* offer nonreceipt of orders, because an operator of Confederate sympathies was at the end of the telegraph, as the reason for the severe disciplinary action to which he was to be subjected. There is indeed evidence that Grant failed to receive an important order to move back to Fort Henry from Donelson, for on March 1 Halleck addressed a dispatch to him at Henry that began, "Transports will be sent to you as soon as possible to move your columns up the Tennessee River." The same day he telegraphed Cullum: "Who sent Smith's division to Nashville? I ordered them across to the Tennessee, where they are wanted immediately. What is the reason that no one down there can obey my orders? Send all spare transports to General Grant up the Tennessee." Sensing that something was amiss, Cullum wrote to Grant, "Evidently the general supposes you on the Tennessee," and quoted the telegram he had received, omitting, however, the next to the last sentence.[35]

On the 3rd McClellan received a telegram which, after briefly describing the situation at New Madrid and Columbus, said:

I have had no communication with General Grant for more than a week. He left his command without my authority and went to Nashville. His army seems to be as much demoralized by the victory of Fort Donelson as was that of the Potomac by the defeat of Bull Run. It is hard to censure a successful general immediately after a victory, but I think he richly deserves it. I can get no returns, no reports, no information of any kind from him. Satisfied with his victory, he sits down and enjoys it without any regard to the future. I am worn-out and tired with this neglect and inefficiency. C. F. Smith is almost the only officer equal to the emergency.[36]

These are harsh sentences, so harsh indeed as to arouse a question as to their justice in the mind of a careful reader who knows they were written at the end of a busy day. McClellan had little time left as over-all commander, and it would be pleasant to record that he handled wisely this new responsibility of high command. He had been associated with Grant for a month at Fort Vancouver when Grant was fitting up McClellan's surveying party. Thus he knew of Grant's habitual care and thoroughness. One of McClellan's first acts as General in Chief had been a commendation in orders of Grant's "daring attack" at Belmont; and he had directed that Grant's Cairo district be enlarged at the time he asked for the recall of Smith. Did he now hark back to some minor incident in Oregon? Or was he influenced by the sentence "There is no return yet from Grant," with which Halleck—in an uncomplaining tone—had ended a message on February 27? [37] Or did he recall the unanswered telegram he himself had sent to Grant on February 15—which, ironically, Grant was to read the day McClellan read Halleck's indictment? One cannot tell. Magnifying, however, rather than discounting Halleck's accusation, the General in Chief replied:

Your dispatch of last evening received. The future success of our cause demands that proceedings such as Grant's should at once be checked. Generals must observe discipline as well as private soldiers. Do not hesitate to arrest him at once if the good of the service requires it, and place C. F. Smith in command. You are at liberty to regard this as a positive order if it will smooth your way.

I appreciate the difficulties you have to encounter, and will be glad to relieve you from trouble as far as possible.[38]

Halleck replied the next day that he did not think it advisable to arrest Grant "at present," but he had put Smith in command. He bluntly wired Grant:

You will place Maj. Gen. C. F. Smith in command of expedition, and remain yourself at Fort Henry. Why do you not obey my orders to report strength and positions of your command? [39]

There was no delay by Grant in calling Smith from Fort Donelson or in embarking Wallace with his division and 300,000 rations. In the correspondence with Halleck that followed, he showed up well indeed. "I am not aware," he wrote, "of ever having disobeyed any order from headquarters—certainly never intended such a thing. I have reported almost daily the condition of my command and reported every position occupied." He noted that he had immediately forwarded a copy of Buell's order calling Smith to Nashville. If Halleck had been inadequately informed, it might have been because Cullum thought his reports of insufficient importance to forward except in "telegraphic synopsis." But Grant, though most respectful, was not meek; and when Halleck spoke of his many requests for strength returns, and of his embarrassment at not being able to supply them to Washington, Grant not only said he had never received the requests, but turned the question back: "You had a better chance of knowing my strength whilst surrounding Fort Donelson than I had. Troops were reporting daily, by your order, and immediately assigned to brigades." Believing that enemies between himself and Halleck must be trying to impair his usefulness, he asked to be relieved from further duty in the department. No enemies were between them, replied Halleck; adding that McClellan was out of all patience, he directed Grant to telegraph his strength in general terms. Back went as fine a report as could be made, with the exact number of men present for duty by branch and location (including 25,506 embarked, and 5,740 at the landing awaiting transportation) and a reminder that a return showing locations had been mailed three days before from Paducah. That Grant's energy never relaxed and his drive never lessened during these dark days is shown by a telegram of the 11th to Cullum: "Nine regiments ready to embark and no transportation for them. Send ten steamers immediately." [40]

A dispatch that Halleck had sent the day before brought word that the thrust up the Tennessee could be strengthened by the release of reserves kept in hand to sustain Curtis, and which were not needed because of the victory at Pea Ridge. Now it could be a major drive and not merely a strong expedition to cut the railroad from Chattanooga to Memphis and return, as had been originally intended.[41] The message ended by telling Grant to "be ready yourself to take the general command." This was cheering; but simultaneously there came a communication from department headquarters dated the 6th that enclosed an anonymous letter about irregularities connected with property taken at Fort Henry that had been received by Judge David Davis, "president of the Western Investigating Commission." In a short reply Grant said, "There is such a disposition to find fault with me that I again ask to be relieved from further duty until I can be placed right in the estimation of those higher in authority." [42] Halleck's answer of the 13th that saved Grant, and to a considerable extent saves Halleck, reads:

You cannot be relieved from your command. There is no good reason for it. I am certain that all which the authorities at Washington ask is that you enforce discipline and punish the disorderly. The power is in your hands; use it, and you will be sustained by all above you. Instead of relieving you, I wish you as soon as your new army is in the field to assume the immediate command and lead it on to new victories. [43]

Rowley, acknowledging notice of his appointment as captain and aide to Grant, wrote to Washburne on the 13th: "We are lying at Fort Henry owing, I believe, to the petty jealousies of some interested parties, but from the appearances we are emerging from under the cloud." He would have written more if he had not been pressed for time, and one wishes there were a fuller contemporary analysis by one of Grant's staff. Grant was a field soldier in every sense, and nothing could have pleased him more than the prospect of again being with his advancing men. He wrote on the 15th to Halleck's adjutant, "I will have consolidated returns ready to mail to-morrow morning, and will then leave for the scene of action, or where the troops are." Then the quartermaster in him spoke up: His stock of rations and ammunition was good, but coal and forage were being consumed at a great rate. The unusual stage of water for the last two weeks had "washed away all the wood for steamboat purposes," and reliance had to be entirely on coal. To Halleck himself he reported that mules and harness were arriving rapidly from Cincinnati, "but as yet no wagons." Rain was falling at the moment, just as it had been doing for forty-eight hours; the weather was cold, and the roads impassable. But what did such things matter? He was going to the front, where the enemy was reported to have 50,000 to 60,000 men. [44]

On the day that Grant was so reporting, the misunderstanding was being officially ended in a long letter from Halleck to Adjutant General Thomas, who had written on the 10th that the President wanted a full report of Grant's absence without leave after the capture of Fort Donelson. Halleck's full explanation gave Grant complete exoneration, though it contained the needless and somewhat condescending statement that the trip to Nashville had been made in "praiseworthy though mistaken zeal for the public service." [45]

A week from the day when McClellan told Halleck not to hesitate to arrest Grant, and before Grant had been restored to command, McClellan ceased to be General in Chief. Although he wrote later that the order of the 11th that came to him while he was on the march to Centerville was entirely unexpected, it could not have been surprising to the general public. A Washington correspondent clearly indicated that some important change was imminent when he wrote on the 3rd, "The town listens with delight to a rumor that President Lincoln has declared his purpose to take the actual command of the Army, and suppress the Rebellion in Virginia without delay." A brief telegram from Stanton to Halleck on the 7th intimated that something was about to happen: "Please send to me the limits of a military department that would place all the Western operations you deem expedient under your command." [46] Said the general in reply:

The Departments of the Ohio and the Missouri should be under one general head. If not, all south of the Cumberland should be added to this department. If I can have the general command of the two, I would leave General Buell in the particular command of his present department and army. The Department of Kansas has less connection with present operations, and could be left as it is.[47]

The last sentence certainly shows that Halleck did not merely wish to increase his domain to the greatest possible extent. However, in spite of what he said about Buell, he was provoked through and through because of failure to have more of Buell's troops than the original brigade sent to him, for his thrust up the Tennessee to secure strategically situated Corinth. On the 6th he had telegraphed Buell: "News down the Tennessee that Beauregard has 20,000 men at Corinth and is rapidly fortifying it. Smith will not probably be strong enough to attack it. It is a great misfortune to lose that point. I shall re-enforce Smith as rapidly as possible." He asked that a division be sent around by water, explaining that it could be supplied by water and get along with a small number of wagons. A telegram to Scott, who had returned to the comforts of Cairo, repeated the report that Beauregard was fortifying Corinth, and said, "If so, he will make a Manassas of it. It is his best point to cover Memphis and Chattanooga. What a mistake Buell did not send forces to move with us up the Tennessee, so as to seize that point. Smith has gone to do it, but I fear it is too late and that he is too weak." Then he struck hard:

"I cannot make Buell understand the importance of strategic points till it is too late." Still provoked the next day, he said to Scott, "Buell should move immediately, and not come in too late, as he did at Donelson." [48]

Not only was Halleck trying to get some of Buell's troops up the Tennessee; he was trying to get them there without serving notice on the enemy. Thus, after issuing an order about trade, he directed that steamers be loaded with goods for Nashville, and when frustrated in this on the 8th by an order of Secretary Chase, he explained to Stanton:

The opening of trade to Nashville was a military ruse, to get steamboats up the Cumberland for the movement of troops, without the enemy's suspecting the object. If sent up empty, the object could not have been concealed. The regulations made with this intent will of course give way to those sent by the Secretary of the Treasury.[49]

On the evening of the 10th Halleck wrote a dispatch to McClellan which would add to the blow in the order Lincoln must have been then preparing. After stating that he intended to go to the Tennessee in a few days, he said, "That is now the great strategic line of the Western campaign, and I am surprised that General Buell should hesitate to re-enforce me. He was too late at Fort Donelson, as Hunter has been in Arkansas." Then he made an attack on McClellan that can hardly be pronounced unfair, though he seemed to forget that he might soon have Buell under his command and had told Stanton that Kansas was irrelevant: "I am obliged to make my calculations independent of both. Believe me, general, you make a serious mistake in having three independent commands in the West. There never will and never can be any co-operation at the critical time; all military history proves it. You will regret your decision against me on this point. Your friendship for individuals has influenced your judgment." [50]

The ground having been cut from under him the next day, McClellan could not reply officially; but he made deferred payment in his memoirs: "Of all men whom I have encountered in high position Halleck was the most hopelessly stupid. It was more difficult to get an idea through his head than can be conceived by any one who never made the attempt. I do not think he ever had a correct military idea from beginning to end." With the passing of years,

McClellan must have forgotten that he had replied to Halleck's long letter of January 20, 1862, about future operations in the West: "I like your views as to the future." [51]

In the President's order that came promptly by wire, Halleck received the new Department of the Mississippi, consisting of his own department and Hunter's, and that part of Buell's lying west of a north-and-south line through Knoxville. Hunter was relieved of his command for a new assignment, and Halleck was directed to "place some other officer at Fort Leavenworth." Cordial messages passed between Halleck and Buell, and Curtis was put in command of Kansas troops in his vicinity by an order that ended, "You will see that they are kept under discipline and will punish any attempt at jayhawking." James H. Lane—whom Halleck considered as the prince of jayhawkers—having failed "to harmonize" with Hunter, had recently returned to Washington to resume his duties as senator, so that Halleck could concentrate on the Tennessee with the hope that the western part of his enlarged department might be more tranquil. (In early May the Department of Kansas was re-created.) Though Buell was subordinated to Halleck, White House regard for him was unimpaired, for Stanton wired Scott, "The President is much pleased with the cautious vigor of General Buell, and relies upon that to guard, above all things, against any mishap by premature and unsupported movements, and expects cordial concert of action between him and General Halleck." [52] "Cautious vigor"! Lincoln would later have reason to consider which quality predominated.

A concluding comment on McClellan as General in Chief seems superfluous; but it may be recalled that the man who was constantly demanding strength returns from Halleck and Buell, himself gave a misleading one when he departed for the Peninsula toward the end of March, and that Lincoln subsequently wrote to him about the baffling character of the figures he gave.

So the war of telegrams was ended. Both McClellan and Halleck had worked hard, often laboring with the pen into the early hours of morning in the quiet of a sleepy headquarters. But neither of them had known the feel of night settling over a great forest, had heard the shots of startled sentinels, had seen morning faintly touch the east and wondered if the gathering light would bring the crash of an enemy attack. Neither had read a message from an alarmed subordinate or listened to the story of a frightened soldier. Neither had seen his regiments giving way before the volleys of a yelling enemy; or heard the cries and moans of thirsty, suffering wounded; or seen the very quiet dead. Neither knew what it was to make the irrevocable decision for the morrow as night at last took over from a seemingly endless day.

CHAPTER XIII

THE ARMIES GATHER

Have out an advance guard and flankers, but march pretty
brisk.   *Sherman to Colonel Hildebrand*

"I HAVE just arrived, and although sick for the last two weeks,
begin to feel better at the thought of again being along with the
troops." Thus Grant began a short note to Sherman on the evening
of March 17, 1862.[1] He was at Savannah, an unpretentious town
near the east bank of the Tennessee, twenty-five miles from Corinth,
key railroad point in northern Mississippi and the objective of the
Federal thrust. Sherman with the new Fifth Division of Grant's
army, was still afloat at Pittsburg Landing,* nine miles upstream on
the opposite bank. The restored army commander had at once taken
over from Smith, who was already troubled by the injury to one of
his legs received earlier in the month when he had jumped into a
yawl.[2] At the time the hurt seemed trivial, but it was to cause the
fine soldier's death before April ended.

At Savannah Grant found some troops already debarked and others
still aboard the mighty gathering of steamers. Without delay he
ordered the troops to Sherman, with the exception of McClernand's
division. New regiments never before in his army were present; and

---

* The place was known both as Pittsburg and as Pittsburg Landing, and it
is referred to in both ways here. Before the coming of the railroads it had been
a shipping point of some importance. Only two or three log buildings remained.

these, he told Sherman, he was also sending. "Organize them into brigades, and attach them to divisions as you deem best," was the direction which showed Sherman he had the full confidence of the new two-star general whom he had ranked so shortly before, and who had been a plebe at West Point when he himself had been about to graduate.

With a letter to St. Louis headquarters went a long report from Sherman about his effort on the 14th to cut the Memphis and Charleston railroad, in which he had been frustrated by "the pouring rain and snow-storm," which had rendered streams impassable and had almost isolated the two brigades he had thrown forward after debarking higher up the Tennessee. Within twenty-four hours the river had risen fifteen feet, submerging the landing at Pittsburg, which the day before had been ten feet above water. Grant reported that a scout sent out by Smith had just returned with the information that the enemy was very strong from Chickasaw all the way to Corinth—150,000 men in all, with a third of the total at Corinth, where Sidney Johnston was said to be. "The number is of course very much exaggerated, and Johnston being there was very much against my expectations," Grant commented. Only a few roads could be traveled because of the flooded condition of the country, and all were "most impassable for artillery." But he was optimistic, and added, "A few dry days, however, would remedy this, and it is certainly time to look for a change of weather." Steamers would be returned as rapidly as possible, Grant told headquarters. Only one complaint slipped into his report, sent only a few minutes after his arrival: "It is with great difficulty that quartermasters at Paducah and Cairo can be impressed with the magnitude of our wants in coal and forage." The corn that could be procured locally was sufficient for only a few days; and it was "respectfully suggested" that his own quartermaster should have funds to pay for such supplies as he could buy.[3] The problem of maintaining a force well advanced in enemy territory had begun to develop in all its fullness.

Not until the 19th was Grant able to get away from his headquarters for a look at the Pittsburg position. Meanwhile a letter of the 17th informed Halleck that he felt satisfied the enemy did not number 40,000 at the moment, and told him that the debarkation points at Pittsburg and Crumps Landing on the west bank—about halfway to Pittsburg—were the only ones then practicable. They had been selected by Smith, in whose judgment he had "full faith." [4] He had foreseen that a new and a tighter headquarters organization would be essential when he went deeper into enemy country, and had issued an order two days before he reached Savannah that began, "The necessity of order and regularity about headquarters, especially in keeping the records, makes it necessary to assign particular duties to each member of the staff." [5]

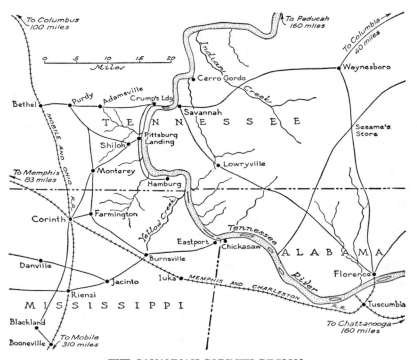

THE SAVANNAH-CORINTH REGION

Today, officers receive systematic training in command and staff work; and tables set forth the allotment of officers and specifically assign their duties. Grant, entirely lacking anything like modern indoctrination, had to work things out largely for himself, keeping the number of officers he used within legal or prescribed bounds, except as he might augment his staff by attaching officers—at the cost of crippling combat regiments. He assigned specific duties to six officers, without mentioning McPherson, who had been sent up the river with General Smith. Colonel Webster, his chief of staff—and engineer, in the absence of McPherson—was made "the adviser of the general commanding," and was to give attention to any duties not otherwise properly covered. The day before he issued his staff order Grant had, in a letter to Stanton, pronounced Webster and Colonel Morgan L. Smith "old soldiers and men of decided merit"; he had "no hesitation in fully indorsing them as in every way qualified for the position of brigadier." [6] That he had something more than a field army to look after was shown by the assignment given to Captain J. P. Hawkins, who had recently reported: he was to have "general superintendence over the quartermaster's department for the entire military district." Colonel Conger, after scrutinizing Grant's staff order against a background of modern ideas, pronounced everything "well covered" except "Operations and Intelligence"; and these in a way would come under the general duties set down for Webster—whose talents were ably demonstrated by notable achievements in civil life. [7]

There was plenty for Grant and all his staff to do on March 18 at the town of Savannah. In his letter to Halleck he did more than report narrowly about what daylight had revealed. He said that enemy cavalry parties all over the state were impressing men into service. Refugees were coming in at Savannah and other river points; some were enlisting, but others were asking "transportation to a safe retreat North." And in addition to this melancholy problem of war there were matters left over from the capture of Henry and Donelson. Steamers were, Grant said, commanded "in whole or in part by secessionists," so that there was "no certainty of honest shipments being made." He was hinting at least at some laxity on his own part when he admitted, "I have found that there was much truth in the report that captured stores were carried off from Fort Henry improperly." Today a staff might take over completely at the rear assembly point, leaving the commander free to go quickly to the advanced position and chat with a front-line soldier here and there; but it would probably deprive us of a letter such as Grant personally wrote that day to his next superior—a great loss for anyone studying the qualities of the general.

"Troops now being in the field, encampments will conform as near as possible to Army Regulations," was the beginning of a short order issued on the 18th. Regimental officers would live in tents; brigade commanders would not be allowed to occupy houses at the expense of the United States, nor at all, unless contiguous to their commands; an improvement of discipline in parts of the command was demanded; division commanders would see that the order was strictly enforced.[8] Nothing was said about security, but the regulations dwelt at considerable length on pickets, grand guards, and other outposts.

Before Grant went to his forward position on the 19th he received—and acknowledged in a message of the 18th to be telegraphed from Fort Henry—an important dispatch Halleck had sent on the 16th. Believing the enemy to be in "strong force," Halleck said his instructions against bringing on an engagement "must be strictly obeyed." Buell was moving for a junction of forces, and he himself hoped to send 10,000 or 15,000 more men from Missouri in a few days. "We must strike no blow until we are strong enough to admit no doubt of the result," cautioned the over-all commander.[9] Grant, before setting out for Pittsburg, should also have received a message of the 18th from Sherman's adjutant, to which the general had added a postscript at 4:00 P.M. saying he was just back from a reconnaissance halfway to Corinth and Purdy. "All right," was Sherman's laconic comment. Approving some things his adjutant had said and disapproving others, he concluded: "Magnificent plain for camping and drilling, and a military point of great strength. The enemy has felt us twice, at great loss and demoralization; will report at length this evening; am now much worn out." [10] It was indeed a new Sherman—optimistic almost to the point of gayety, even when saturated with fatigue.

The next day Sherman debarked his troops and joined Hurlbut's division, which had just gone ashore. Assuming the number that really belonged to McClernand's division, Sherman's order began: "The First Division will occupy the front of this camp." Positions for the four brigades were assigned, and it was stipulated: "Each brigade must encamp looking west, so that when the regiments are on their regimental parades the brigades will be in line of battle. The interval between regiments must not exceed 22 paces. Convenience of water may be considered, but must not control the position of the camp." The cavalry and artillery were not required to be in line, but were to be "stationed as the nature of the ground may admit." [11] Assuredly it was not the order of a man apprehensive of attack; nor was it that of one who entirely dismissed the possibility. Three brigades—actually facing south rather than west—were close together near Shiloh Church, on the road to Corinth, the most likely route of enemy advance; the fourth on the Hamburg road was some distance to the left. A post of honor Sherman had indeed chosen for the previously unengaged regiments of his division: nine from Ohio, two from Illinois, and one from Iowa. If trouble came they would have the chance to show their mettle to the regiments that had fought at Donelson. "Green men out in front," is one way to train troops rapidly—though perhaps not the conventional procedure.

One would like to know more details of Grant's first day at Pittsburg Landing. It was a busy place, with transports discharging troops, guns, wagons, animals, and full camping equipment, under the great handicap of flooded banks and poor roads. He must have seen Sherman pitching his tents, and heard directly about the overland effort on the night of the 16th to reach the coveted railroad to Memphis—if he had not seen Sherman's report, directed to Smith, written on the night of the 17th.[12] The skirmishing that had taken place had convinced Sherman that the railroad could not be reached "without a considerable engagement," which was banned by Halleck's explicit order. Of all this Grant said nothing in the dispatch he sent to St. Louis on his return to Savannah, though he stated that the testimony of his own eyes was that the only practicable landings were Crumps and Pittsburg. Other persons had told him there was nothing better between Pittsburg and Eastport. But he cautioned that what he said applied only "to the present stage of water." While he was with Sherman, information had arrived that the enemy could not have more than 20,000 men at Corinth, though he also had "troops scattered at all stations and important points." That should have seemed to Halleck to be fair confirmation of the 40,000 estimate Grant had made the day before. Sherman's informant had said some heavy artillery had arrived at Corinth two days previously; but he had seen no signs of fortification. "Buell seems to be the party most expected by the rebels," Grant said in closing. "They estimate his strength all the way from 20,000 to 150,000." [13]

The Pittsburg position had not been secured without a fight. Toward the end of February, Beauregard had sent a battery there in the hope that it could dominate the river from the high bluff.

Maybe he thought the guns would keep the Yankees from another visit to Florence, where Commander Phelps had a few weeks before refrained from destroying the bridge. Lieutenant Gwin at Savannah with the wooden *Tyler* and *Lexington* and some men of the Thirty-second Illinois—a regiment of sharpshooters—learning of what was going on, steamed upstream on March 1, and at twelve hundred yards received the fire of some six guns, one of which, Gwin and Lieutenant Shirk, commanding the *Lexington,* were sure, was rifled. Their own guns silenced those of the Southerners, and under the cover of grape and canister they landed four boatloads of sailors and soldiers. The Navy hail of bullets drove away the enemy battery and the infantry regiment supporting it; but the Confederates pressed back upon the Federals when they returned to their boats after destroying under heavy musketry fire a house at the battery position. A soldier and a sailor were killed, and there were a few wounded and missing. The *Tyler,* according to Gwin, was "perfectly riddled with balls." [14]

A few days later Gwin returned, found the battery gone, and advanced more than a mile inland before he encountered enemy pickets. From reports he picked up he put the enemy killed at twenty and the wounded at a hundred—doubtless an exaggeration—and correctly identified the infantry regiment as from Louisiana. The withdrawal of the battery gave the affair the color of a Federal success; but the imaginative Beauregard found grounds for warmly congratulating the regiment that had been engaged. On the 8th, the commanding general of the First Corps of the Second Grand Division of the Army of the Mississippi Valley—an impressive title indeed—issued at Corinth an order that carried Beauregard's thanks to the Eighteenth Louisiana and its colonel "for the brilliant success in their first encounter with the enemy at Pittsburg, Tennessee." It was, hoped the victor of Manassas, "only the forerunner of still more gallant deeds on the part of the regiment." [15]

Lick, Owl, and Snake were the names of three creeks that in a general way bounded the area near Pittsburg from which the Confederate battery had withdrawn, and which was destined to become a great battlefield. Lick Creek, after rising in a swamp and flowing northeastwardly for some eleven miles, emptied into the Tennessee above (south of) the landing. Owl, paralleling Lick at a distance of three to five miles, emptied into the larger Snake Creek,

which poured their combined waters into the river three miles below
the mouth of Lick. The land between the creeks and the river was
a rolling plateau eighty to a hundred feet above the normal river

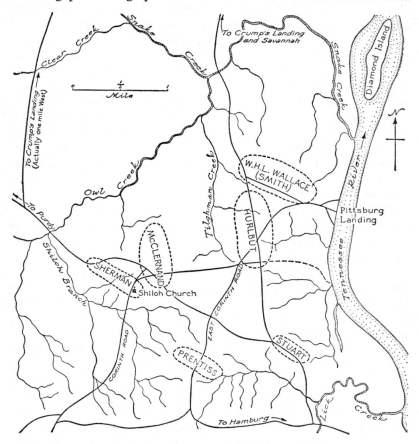

GRANT'S POSITION AT PITTSBURG LANDING

The area was a rolling plateau eighty to a hundred feet above the river,
rising abruptly at the landing. Though wooded in general, it included about
a dozen fields of eighty acres each. Stuart commanded a brigade of Sherman's
division. Lew Wallace's division was at Crump's Landing.

level. It was generally covered with timber; in places there was dense
undergrowth, while some dozen open fields of about eighty acres
each were in the area. The river front between Lick and Snake creeks

was cut by sloughs and ravines, which at the time were covered by backwater, as were also the lower reaches of the two streams.[16]

A road that kept far enough back from the river to avoid the sloughs connected Pittsburg with Hamburg Landing, six miles upstream, and another road—called the River Road though it also was some distance from the river—crossed Snake Creek just below where it received Owl Creek, and led to Crumps, five miles below Pittsburg. From Pittsburg a road led past Shiloh Church and through the hamlet of Monterey to Corinth, twenty-three miles or so away. A mile and a half from the landing, the East Corinth Road turned off sharply toward the left and rejoined the main road six miles beyond; and three miles from the landing, just before the church was reached, the main road intersected one that came from Hamburg and, after crossing Owl Creek, led to Purdy, about twelve miles away. Crisscrossing the area in a confusing way were many secondary roads, some of them little better than trails.

With its woods and clearings, and its streams to furnish water, the enclosed area gave adequate and in many ways favorable room for the assembling of an army—quite as Sherman said. The flanks were well protected, and the only directions from which a hostile force could approach were Corinth and Purdy. Except along the ridges the area would be soft and difficult so long as the rain fell. While the region above the landing was safe from inundation, the steep roads to the bluff would vex the drivers of guns, caissons, and loaded wagons, especially when heavy with mud.

The occupation of Crumps Landing, which was due west of Savannah because of a bend in the river, was necessary for proper protection of the many steamers on the Tennessee. All the ironclad gunboats were being used in the operation against Island No. 10, begun immediately after the fall of New Madrid, and as there were rumors of small enemy gunboats in Duck River and higher up the Tennessee,[17] the *Tyler* and the *Lexington* could not give undivided attention to the river banks. A hostile field battery opposite Savannah could have caused much damage, and wisely Lew Wallace's division was put ashore at Crumps. Its mission, however, was not mere passive defense, and on the 13th, in accordance with orders from Smith, Wallace struck toward Purdy to break the Mobile and Ohio Railroad that ran through Bethel some four miles beyond. Interrupting this line would handicap the Confederate concentration at Corinth, but it would not prevent it, for troops at Jackson would still have the route by way of Grand Junction, while from Humboldt yet a third, though considerably longer rail line was open by way of Memphis. Hampering the enemy's plans even when you cannot spoil them, being a part of war, Smith picked out the Corinth-Jackson line as a target.

Wallace moved with most of his division, for enemy forces were reported at Purdy and Bethel, and between them. The Federal commander in fact picked up word that the Confederates had set out from Bethel to seize Crumps, and had been forestalled by his own occupation of that position. Stationing his infantry so as to hold the enemy in check, he sent the third battalion of the Fifth Ohio Cavalry to the railroad. Its commander came back with the report that he had destroyed a bridge and trestlework at each end for a distance of a hundred and fifty feet; in addition he had torn up some track, bent the rails and thrown them into a creek. "Altogether, he deserves great credit for the energy, courage, and perseverance he manifested," was Wallace's hearty summing up for Major Charles S. Hayes.[18]

But the very next day no less a person than Braxton Bragg reported to Beauregard that the railroad had been completely repaired and would henceforth be carefully guarded. Bragg, about whom dispute has been sharp, a West Point classmate of Joe Hooker and John Sedgwick, has been mentioned in connection with the brief accounts given of his invasion of Kentucky and his part in western battles in 1863. He now comes into the fuller story of the West, after having been in command on the Florida and Alabama coast. On February 28, Beauregard, still suffering from an operation on his throat, wired General Cooper that he was in despair about his condition, and urged that Bragg be sent to Jackson at once. "I will," he said, "when well enough, serve under him rather than not have him here." The question was referred to Bragg himself for decision, and within a few days the two-starred general set out, taking to Corinth some 10,000 well drilled and reliable troops from Pensacola and Mobile, and thus joined the array of top Confederate talent that was opposed to Grant.[19]

Grant had served with Bragg in the Mexican War from Palo Alto and Resaca de la Palma to Monterrey where Bragg's battery had pounded masonry walls from close range and had showered the enemy effectively with canister. One of the most notable character sketches in Grant's *Memoirs* is of Bragg: a man of the highest character and correct habits, with remarkable intelligence and broad information, professional and other, but "possessed of irascible temper" and "naturally disputatious." While zealously watching that his superiors did not infringe on his prerogatives, Bragg kept his eye wide open for minor negligences of subordinates. The character of the famous soldier from North Carolina was in part revealed in a letter he wrote Beauregard on the 15th from Bethel, in which, after noting the necessity of watching in many directions, he said, "Our task is a most difficult one, especially with the mob we have, miscalled soldiers." But the letter was not all so pessimistic; he noted also that, with the country so flooded, people assured him that no enemy force of any size could move against Bethel, and he was accordingly returning the troops at Bethel to a position east of Corinth, where his whole force had arrived from the Gulf coast, except two regiments he had left at Pensacola.[20]

Bragg himself tarried at Bethel, and the next day the desires of a competent and restless artilleryman were stirring within him. He reported to Brigadier General Daniel Ruggles, who had recently reached Corinth with 5,000 men from New Orleans, that troops were coming down from Humboldt. Information was so conflicting that he thought it impossible to make a military movement, though he was "anxious and decided to strike a blow" as soon as it could be done "consistent with any sense of security." He was glad to hear that General Johnston was joining them and was so confident as to say, "With his force we certainly ought to crush any force the enemy can now bring." Back at Corinth two days later Bragg had a different story to tell, and wrote a long letter of discouragement to Beauregard. The disorganized and demoralized condition of the Confederate forces "right and left" gave him great concern. Some discipline remained in the troops he had brought from the Gulf; but there was none whatever in the others. The entire country seemed paralyzed. Nothing was brought in for sale, and supplies were obtained with the utmost difficulty. Unrestrained pillage and plunder by the Southern troops had done much to produce this state of affairs, and it reconciled the people to the approach of the Federals, "who certainly do them less harm." The whole railroad system was "utterly deranged and confused." Wood and water stations were abandoned; employees refused to work because they were not paid; engineers and conductors either were worn out or, being Northern men, abandoned their positions or managed to retard and obstruct operations. Confederate troops so monopolized the eating and sleeping houses that the railroaders were unable to live. "These are distressing facts it is useless to conceal," said Bragg, "and all owing to a want of system and discipline." Even the maps seemed to be demoralized, and Bragg reported he could not even find a place that Beauregard had pronounced strategic. "May it not have changed name or lost its place on the maps in these railroad days?" he queried. The melancholy tale ended: "In the present condition of this army, without transportation, supplies, discipline, or organization, no move toward the enemy can be made. We can only try and keep him in check whilst we labor to correct these radical defects." [21]

Grant's statement that Johnston's presence at Corinth was "very much" against his expectations, raises several questions. Where did he think the top Confederate commander in the West was? Did he believe he was where he should be, or elsewhere? Had he formed his judgment of his adversary? These questions cannot be answered, but certainly Grant must have been assessing his opponent.

On March 5 Johnston telegraphed Benjamin that he had just arrived at Huntsville, Alabama, having a week before sent his plans to Richmond by an officer courier. "The forces are *en route* and in good order," he now reported. The column was marching on Decatur and Corinth, and its advance would reach Decatur in three days. Floyd with 2,500 men had been sent to Chattanooga. Hardee had been left at Shelbyville with a brigade of infantry and two regiments and a battalion of cavalry to load and forward pork.[22] Just why so good a field commander as Hardee had been assigned a commissary's duty, is difficult to see. He could well have been in command of the column, while Johnston was preparing to go without delay to the place he had announced as his objective. If Johnston were indeed to be the real and not just the paper commander in the West, it was high time for him to be engaged in concentrating and organizing all his forces, rather than looking after the remnant left from the shattered eastern half of the original Confederate defensive line. Beauregard, to whom he had virtually yielded autonomy over troops west of the Tennessee, was sick, and he knew that command would devolve upon Bragg. Decisions relative to the troops withdrawn from Columbus, those at New Madrid, Island Number 10, and Fort Pillow on the Mississsippi and also relative to Van Dorn's command west of the great river, all properly fell to Sidney Johnston, and he should have been busy with them.

On the very day that Johnston reported about the march of the column he was personally directing, Beauregard at Jackson was issuing a proclamation: "Soldiers: I assume this day the command of the Army of the Mississippi, for the defense of our homes and liberties, and to resist the subjugation, spoliation, and dishonor of our people. Our mothers and wives, our sisters and children, expect us to do our duty even to the sacrifice of our lives." After saying that anyone in the army unequal to the task, should "transfer his arms and equipments at once to braver, firmer hands, and return to his home," the convalescent general ended: "Our cause is as just and sacred as ever animated men to take up arms, and if we are true to it and to ourselves, with the continued protection of the Almighty, we must and shall triumph." [23]

Still at Huntsville two days later, Johnston reported to Davis that the general condition of his troops was good and effective. Though some of his men had been disheartened by the fall of Donelson, their tone was now restored. He had no fears of an enemy movement through Tennessee toward Chattanooga, but west Tennessee was threatened by heavy forces. In spite of the fact that nothing held his attention away from the menaced region, Johnston did not go forward. On the 11th he reported to Benjamin from Decatur that his troops were crossing the Tennessee line and advancing on Tuscumbia. The enemy was said to have about 12,000 men at Savannah, with thirty or forty more transports expected, and it was supposed that Buell would "concentrate [his] main force there to co-operate with Grant." To Beauregard he wrote encouragingly: "The force here is in good condition and fine spirits. They are anxious to meet the enemy." Though apparently certain as to the enemy's intentions, Johnston still was not exercising full command, and contented himself with sending Beauregard a cipher—a simple transposition affair that could be broken in a few minutes by anyone familiar with the repetitious nature of the letter *e*.[24]

However uncertain we may be of Grant's views of Johnston, there is no doubt about how Southerners then regarded the general in whom they had recently placed great hopes. Even the best of generals will of course suffer from a disaster such as came to the Confederates through the opening of two routes of invasion and the loss of many men and much material. Says Horn: "Public confidence in General Johnston was so far gone that some new recruits made it a condition of enlistment that they should not be called on to serve under him. The papers forgot that just a few weeks ago they had been heaping unstinted praise on him as 'possessing all the qualities of a wise, discreet and brave general.' " [25]

Of the many who demanded summary action from President Davis, few could have been more bitter than Congressman E. M. Bruce of Kentucky. Writing from Atlanta on March 11, he stated he had been with and near Johnston's army ever since that general had assumed command. He still admired him as a man, but pronounced the harsh verdict that Johnston's "errors of omission, commission, and delay" had been "greater than [those of] any general who ever preceded him in any country." One dash of the enemy had cost the South 12,000 men and the Mississippi Valley. Such being the almost unanimous judgment of officers, soldiers, and citizens, it would never be possible for Johnston to reorganize and reenforce his army with any confidence, and it was time for the President to make good on the promise he had made publicly "to take the field whenever it should become necessary." If ever there was a time, it was now. If conditions prevented that, Bruce implored Davis "for God's sake" to give immediate command to Beauregard, Bragg, or Breckinridge, or all would be irretrievably lost. "Save us while it is yet time," was his despairing plea.[26]

Keenly aware though he was of the severity of the criticisms leveled against him, Johnston kept his poise and said in a long letter to Davis on the 18th, "Day after to-morrow, unless the enemy interrupts me, my force will be with Bragg, and my army nearly 50,000 strong. This must be destroyed before the enemy can attain his object,"—which was a somewhat passive way of putting things. The President's reply was one that well could bolster a field commander:

My confidence in you has never wavered, and I hope the public will soon give me credit for judgment rather than continue to arraign me for obstinacy. You have done wonderfully well, and now I breathe easier in the assurance that you will be able to make a junction of the two armies. If you can meet the division of the enemy moving from the Tennessee before it can make a junction with that advancing from Nashville the future will be brighter.

Here was a suggestion for an offensive stroke. The President also said he hoped the people of the Southwest would "rally *en masse* with their private arms," and thus aid in opposing the "vast army" that threatened "the destruction of our country." [27]

Then the general who had furnished a cipher to Beauregard was told that the Richmond President was sending him a dictionary to use to encipher his letters and telegrams. Every message so written would have the telltale repetition of the letters L, M, and R, that would show at once that a three-column dictionary had been used. Already Johnston had given highly secret instructions about the burning of the bridge at Florence if the enemy appeared.[28] Now he should have sent out quiet directions that all three-column dictionaries should be buried. The people of Dixie would indeed have thought the Yankees barbarians if in addition to the bad manners they had frequently shown, they had begun to ransack libraries.

Within a few weeks General Mitchel was to make an enciphered message from Beauregard to Richmond quickly yield its secret.

On the important day of March 19 this message went from Grant to Buell:

Feeling a little anxious to learn your whereabouts and as much as possible of your present movements, I send two scouts, Breckinridge and Carson, to you. Any information you will send by them I will be glad to learn. I am massing troops at Pittsburg, Tenn. There is every reason to suppose that the rebels have a large force at Corinth, Miss., and many at other points on the road toward Decatur.[29]

And what was Buell doing in the matter of making a junction with the force on the Tennessee? His move was an important part of the campaign, and upon it one's judgment with regard to Buell must depend to no small degree.

"I believe you cannot be too promptly nor too strongly established on the Tennessee. I shall advance in a few days, as soon as our transportation is ready," Buell had said to Halleck on March 10. That was while he still exercised independent command, and his words looked promising. Halleck strove to lessen Buell's sensitiveness to being subordinated and said in a message of the 13th, "The new arrangement of departments will not interfere with your command. You will continue in command of the same army and district of country as heretofore, so far as I am concerned." And instead of asking for details in the fashion of McClellan he requested a report of Buell's strength and position "in general terms." Buell replied by telegram the same day that he was writing at length, and gave such information of the enemy as he had: Decatur their main point, with forces also at Huntsville, Corinth, Jackson, and Humboldt; Pensacola and Mobile stripped of troops; Bragg at Memphis. A long letter the next day gave some particulars of Buell's 71,233 effectives: Carter with his five infantry regiments, some cavalry, and a battery held up at Cumberland Ford by high water and difficulty of supply; Garfield's command of about equal size—but with no guns—in the valley of the Big Sandy and on the headwaters of the Kentucky (part of it under orders to move to Bardstown); and 50,000 effectives about Nashville.[30]

Buell's letter did not arrive until the 26th. Had Halleck received it at once he might have thought there was some obliqueness in Buell's saying he was concentrating "to operate against the enemy in front," which suggested that he was setting up in business for himself. But even without the letter Halleck on the 16th adopted the style of a commander and wired: "Move your forces by land to the Tennessee as rapidly as possible. . . . Grant's army is concentrating at Savannah. You must direct your march on that point, so the enemy cannot get between us. . . ." He then replied to a message of Buell about Beauregard's activities *west* of the Tennessee, showing vexation: "I fully understand these movements. Move on, as ordered to-day, to re-enforce Smith. Savannah is now the strategic point. Don't fail to carry out my instructions. I know that I am right." [31]

Between Nashville and Savannah there stretched one hundred and twenty miles, more than a third of them along the turnpike through Franklin to Columbia on the south bank of Duck River—a stream that could easily hamper the march of Buell's army if there were no bridge. At Green River, then at the Barren, and finally at the Cumberland, Buell had found destroyed bridges, and every stratagem and resource at his command should have been used to keep the Columbia bridge from being blown or burned.

Twenty-five years later, Buell wrote that the movement toward Savannah "was commenced on the night of the 15th of March by a rapid march of cavalry to secure the bridges in advance, which were then still guarded by the enemy." Even a small force of Confederates covering the Columbia bridge, with mounted patrols toward Franklin and on the roads to the east, could have made certain of the destruction of the structure in spite of the best planning by the Federals. Only if good information had been secured from spies at Columbia and a stealthy effort had been made to reach the bridge not directly from the north, but with a column that threatened Shelbyville, could there have been much hope of success. "When the cavalry reached Columbia the bridge over Duck River was found in flames, and the river at flood stage," wrote Buell. History had merely repeated itself. On February 14 Mitchel had written to him from the north bank of the Barren before Bowling Green that from the reports of scouts he had thought there "was a chance to save the turnpike bridge," and he had accordingly thrown his advance guard forward by forced marches; but he had to confess, "We are a little late to save the bridge; it was burned this morning at daylight." [32]

Later in the war the destruction of the Columbia bridge would not have been very serious, for a new one could have been built without much delay. But one must ask, Why did not Buell use his twenty days in Nashville to build some pontoons, adapt wagons to carry them, and train an infantry regiment in their use? A few days later he wrote to Halleck that he had ordered such a bridge, and a light stern-wheeler to take it to the Tennessee, steamer and bridge to cost $12,000 and to be ready in ten days.[33] Taking a bridge to the Tennessee was like carrying coals to Newcastle, for Grant had steamers that could ferry troops, and Halleck was making ready to send a pontoon train.[34] Buell's engineer must have been remiss in not foreseeing the need of pontoons en route; and McClellan, the General in Chief, though making sure that the Army of the Potomac was properly equipped before it ventured away from Washington, let his good friend start overland from Louisville for Nashville during the rainy season without one of the essentials of campaigning.

Brigadier General Alexander McD. McCook, an Ohio West Point graduate of the class of '52, commanded Buell's leading division, the Second. On the 18th Buell sent him a message that showed urgency, though it was weakened by a qualification: "Use all possible industry and energy so as to move forward steadily and as rapidly as you can without forcing your march or straggling." Forcing a march is often the hallmark of a real general. Can one imagine Stonewall Jackson telling a subordinate not to force a march, when starting to join another column already deep in enemy territory? "Force the march, but allow no straggling—or be arrested," would more likely have been Stonewall's direction. But Buell of course had his problems. Some were of a political nature, for Andrew Johnson had arrived as military governor and Parson Brownlow had come in from East Tennessee. In addition there was the question of supplies. The railroad from Louisville was not in good working order, and the Cumberland had been falling so rapidly that he had had to call on Halleck for diving boats to remove obstructions the enemy had sunk in the river. Nevertheless he was making progress, and he told McCook the railroad would be open to Franklin the next day and to Columbia in a few days more, while supplies would be waiting at Savannah. He directed that a courier be sent forward to the Tennessee; he should be intelligent and discreet, "so as to avoid the necessity of sending written intelligence, that might be cut off and reach the enemy." [35]

When informing Halleck on the 19th of the mishap at Columbia, Buell said he might "be delayed there for four or five days," adding that he would go forward himself "in two or three days." [36] He was carrying the telegraph line forward, and asked that it be started from Savannah to meet him. Also he wanted large supplies of forage thrown up the Tennessee, for none was procurable in the country. All that he asked for was done; [37] but he fell badly behind his own time table. Little at a time, it was extended, until it doubled his worst prediction of five days.

As he planned his advance, Buell had to provide for the safety of the region behind him, especially for that of Nashville. He had also to give thought to East Tennessee. On the 10th he had received from Lincoln one of the two dispatches the President seems to have sent personally during the entire operation that was developing. It had come through in record time, having been written the same day— the last day of McClellan's career as General in Chief, when there was much excitement in Washington over the withdrawal of the Confederates from the lower Potomac as well as Manassas. It was characteristic: "The evidence is very strong that the enemy in front of us here is breaking up and moving off. General McClellan is after him. Some part of the force may be destined to meet you. Look out and be prepared. I telegraphed Halleck, asking him to assist you, if needed." Though the description of McClellan's march to Centerville was too hopeful, it looked as if the President's surmise about a shift of hostile forces westward might be correct, for Buell told Halleck on the 15th that Brownlow had brought word that E. Kirby Smith was at Knoxville with eighteen regiments from Manassas and had seven others at Cumberland Gap. A week later he informed Stanton that Garfield, having completed the expulsion of Marshall from eastern Kentucky, was being moved with three of his regiments to Bardstown to join Carter's force operating against the gap, Garfield to take command. The same day—March 23—Buell reported to Halleck the arrival of Grant's message, and commented, "It contains no information of importance." [38] What more could Grant have said than he did? Buell had only recently cautioned McCook about trusting too much to paper, and the couriers from Savannah had tongues as well as pockets.

About bedtime on the 19th Grant received a message from the department commander that seemed to open the way for aggressive action. Not knowing for certain where Grant was, Halleck had addressed it to him or the "Commanding Officer at Fort Henry." It was reported, he said, that the enemy had moved from Corinth; then he directed, "If so, General Smith should immediately destroy railroad connection at Corinth." Overlooking the proviso, Grant at once replied: "Immediate preparations will be made to execute your perfectly feasible order. I will go in person, leaving General McClernand in command here." [39]

Though it was eleven o'clock, there was doubtless some planning that night; but orders were not written until the next day. Smith was told: "Hold all the command at Pittsburg subject to marching orders at any time. Troops will march with three days' rations in haversacks and seven in wagons." Every wagon was to carry five days' grain for its own team, while a forage train would take an equal amount for other animals. Baggage was to be cut down "to make the transportation on hand carry the supplies indicated." The order that alerted Wallace at Crumps specifically said "no tents," and limited other baggage to "what the men can carry." McClernand was directed to prepare immediately to move two brigades to Pittsburg, the other brigade to follow as soon as new troops could replace it as a guard for Savannah. At first Grant hoped to be off for Corinth on the 22nd; but his report to St. Louis at the end of the 20th said he could not start before the 23rd or 24th, because of slowness in debarking under the adverse conditions at Pittsburg; again he said he would go himself if an order did not prevent. Optimistically believing that Buell might be speedy, he wrote: "I sent yesterday two scouts to find General Buell. They will probably be back tomorrow." Remembering the orders under which he was operating, he assured his superior:

I will take no risk at Corinth under the instructions I now have. If a battle on anything like equal terms seems to be inevitable, I shall find it out in time to make a movement upon some other point of the railroad, or at least seem to [ful]fill the object of the expedition without a battle, and thus save the demoralizing effect of a retreat upon the troops.

It is very clear that Grant wanted his orders changed to give greater freedom of action. Having said that a deserter just in reported that the enemy at Corinth was in something of a panic and did not want to fight, he ended, "I am very much in hopes of receiving further instructions by mail." [40]

But Grant's eagerness was of no avail, for Halleck wired on the 20th:

Your telegrams of yesterday just received. I do not fully understand you. By all means keep your forces together until you connect with General Buell, who is now at Columbia, and will move on Waynesborough with three divisions. Don't let the enemy draw you into an engagement now. Wait till you are properly fortified and receive orders.[41]

Caution there undoubtedly is in this dispatch; but Halleck had reason to believe that Buell would arrive in a week, and if, after having so heartily urged that general to join him on the Tennessee and forego other moves, he now let Grant settle the Corinth situation alone it would look as if he had manipulated to keep Buell in a secondary role and give his army nothing but hard marching, without any chance for battle streamers.

Grant had to reply that it would be impossible to move "with any celerity," if artillery were taken, while Corinth could not be captured "without meeting a large force, say 30,000"; but he still invited a change of orders: "A general engagement would be inevitable; therefore I will wait a few days for further instructions." A longer dispatch to Halleck spoke once more of enemy morale: "The temper of the rebel troops is such that there is but little doubt but that Corinth will fall much more easily than Donelson did when we do move." One thing there was on the adverse side. Most of the impressed men from Tennessee were being sent to the Gulf coast while better trained soldiers were brought northward to replace them. He had "certain information" that thirteen trains, each with twenty cars of soldiers, had arrived at Corinth. They were of course Bragg's men, but they had come earlier than Grant thought; and he gave no indication that their "disputatious" general was in the vicinity, though Halleck, on the basis of a dispatch from Buell, had reported to Stanton on the 14th that Bragg was in Memphis.[42]

Though no change of orders came, a change of weather did. "Weather here cold, with some snow," Grant reported on the 22nd, after saying that Sherman's division would be advanced "to prevent rebels from fortifying Pea Ridge." The next day he directed Smith to carry out his idea of occupying and partially fortifying that position, and added fretfully, "I do not hear one word from Saint Louis." The enemy was "gathering strength at Corinth quite as rapidly" as he was, and the sooner he could attack the easier would be the "task of taking the place." To hit the enemy before he built up, rather than delay for the arrival of reenforcements, seemed to be his theory. As at Donelson, he was looking at the opposing general: "If Ruggles is in command, it would assuredly be a good time to attack." [43]

Crisp orders that Sherman wrote the same day—March 23—sent two brigades the following morning on a reconnaissance toward Pea Ridge and the village of Monterey, halfway to Corinth. They were to advance to a point Sherman had previously explored, and await him there. "Let the cavalry bring up the rear, out of sight of any enemy's picket you may encounter. Have out an advance guard and flankers, but march pretty brisk. . . . If you encounter scouts, do not pursue, but keep steadily on the road," he told one brigade commander. "Start early, so as to reach the point indicated by 8 a.m. . . . The point of rendezvous is a shoemaker's named Heath, where we left a wounded man on our first expedition," he said to the other. Three days' rations in haversacks, blankets, India-rubber blankets, and forty rounds of ammunition were to go, but seemingly nothing with wheels. It looks as if Sherman remained out overnight, for Johnston, in reporting to Davis on the 25th that he had arrived the day before at Corinth, stated: "The enemy is advancing today from Pittsburg toward Corinth." That the Confederates got the halfway point was indicated by the statement: "Monterey, 11 miles in front, was occupied to-day by a small force of cavalry and two regiments of infantry." Rather unenlighteningly Sherman wrote in his "Diary of Events," "On the 24th made a strong reconnaissance of Pea Ridge, 10 miles toward Corinth." [44]

On the day of Johnston's report to Davis that he had united his forces, Grant sent two maps to Halleck.[45] One showed the Savannah-Purdy-Corinth-Eastport quadrangle, with the roads and railroads, and the elevated ground at Pea Ridge. The other map, of the camp site, revealed that McClernand was facing west toward Purdy rather than toward Corinth, and contained no indication of intrenchments. The brief accompanying note stated, "General Wallace is six miles below, with a good road out, enabling them to form a junction with the main column, when a move is made, six or seven miles before reaching Corinth." [46] The Federal commander was still thinking of how to strike the enemy, and not of how to fend off a blow.

Grant's failure to intrench his camp has been severely criticized. Among the soldiers who have recently written on the campaign, General Fuller and Captain Liddell Hart are unequivocal in their reproaches.[47] Colonel Conger on the other hand did not condemn, and probably saw more clearly than they why Grant did not dig in. Eager as Grant was to march on Corinth and himself attack a position partially prepared, he would not mind if the enemy brought the battle to him, and would do nothing that would discourage Johnston from doing so. "In other words," writes Conger, "Grant had no business being at Shiloh at all if he was afraid of fighting Johnston on equal terms." [48] It is worth remembering that the Confederates had recently twice carried the battle to the Federals in surprise attacks in the West only to suffer severe defeats. George Thomas had beaten the march-weary regiments of Crittenden in a stand-up fight without really committing to battle three of his seven infantry regiments. Grant, though unexpectedly attacked in February by the Donelson garrison, was able to profit from the confusion and mistakes of the enemy, as well as the hard fighting of his own men, and when night came held a choice piece of the Confederates' defensive works. After the contest of the day the intrenchments they had left became something of a lure, while Grant's men, with no such enticement, had pressed closer to the retreating foe. The previous fall when Grant wrote to Colonel Oglesby—who was occupying an exposed position—that the better part of valor was to be prudent, he did not specifically tell him to intrench—only to select his "encampment with a view of having as clear a field for defense as possible." [49]

Nor did Halleck's directive of March 20—"Don't let the enemy draw you into an engagement now. Wait till you are properly fortified and receive orders"—categorically order Grant to intrench. It might be interpreted as meaning "Make no move on Corinth until ordered, but securely intrench your present position at once," but that is not what it says. "Properly fortified" are very flexible words, especially for an officer daily hoping to be allowed to advance, and confident of his ability to fight successfully in the open. In Halleck's book Grant could have read, "Intrenchments, though inert masses, must therefore be regarded as most valuable and important accessories in the defense of a position." [50] This he of course knew; but he also knew that trenches could lessen the chance as well as the will to maneuver and strike back. "We must learn to use other weapons than the pick and the spade. Our armies must be disciplined and learn to fight." Thus wrote John Adams in condemnation of the habit of the soldiers at the beginning of the Revolution to surround themselves with ditches. [51] Without the expenditure of a great deal of time at the expense of important drill of newly arrived men, any trenches that Grant might have built could have been broken at some point without much trouble, and the rest of the line then taken in reverse. Troops forced from intrenchments may think they have lost an essential element of defense and not make another stand.

Though providing cover is now taken more as a matter of course than in the first days of the Civil War when Taylor's and Scott's campaigns in the Mexican War were fresh in mind, the lesson of the Maginot Line and the Siegfried Line will not soon be forgotten, and there never has been greater emphasis than now on the doctrine of "fire and movement" and the necessity of flexible defense in depth. Fire and movement were what Grant, Smith, and Sherman believed in at that time, to the practical exclusion of everything else except steadiness and the will to fight in soldiers and leadership in officers. That generals had something to learn is not surprising; nor does it reflect on them: generals are always having to profit from experience, especially from that of the early engagements of a war. But every regiment that stood up well in the coming battle of Shiloh was more reliable for having done so without the benefit of earthworks; every regiment that broke had an example to emulate in the future and a record to amend.

Grant's real error may have been in not providing better for outposting and patrolling, and in acceptance at face value of reports of deteriorated enemy morale. Having failed to secure Pea Ridge, some covering position between it and his camp was in order. Lacking this there should have been mounted reconnaissance well beyond the outpost line of the divisions. As he had retained no cavalry under his direct control, security measures rested in his subordinates, especially Sherman, except for general directions he gave. Though what Bragg wrote to Beauregard about morale confirmed reports that reached Grant, Johnston spoke of his men as being eager for battle; and Grant should have been less confident about the deteriorated spirit of the enemy. Confident, he certainly was; and on the 22nd he wrote to Washburne: "A severe contest may be looked for in this quarter before many weeks, but of the result feel no alarm." Two days later Rowley told the congressman, "The gen'l is in fine spirits and confident of our ability to 'go in and thrash them as soon as the weather and orders will permit.' " Surprise and rude shock were indeed ahead of him; but the son of General Polk wrote later that the main key to Grant's success was that "he never lent ear to his own fears without intuitively balancing them with what he felt must be those of his opponent." [52]

In addition to predicting the future, Rowley went into the recent past, explaining to Washburne in detail an incident about the return of slaves after the capture of Fort Donelson, which the newspapers had distorted badly. Grant in his letter had been content to say: "So long as I hold a commission in the army I have no views of my own to carry out. Whatever may be the orders of my superiors and law I will execute." As to his difficulty with Halleck, Grant wrote that he had sent frequent reports during and after the Donelson operation, and summed up: "Not getting these, General Halleck very justly became dissatisfied, and was, as I have since learned, sending me daily reprimands. Not receiving them, they lost their sting. When one did reach me, not seeing the justice of it, I retorted, and asked to be relieved." [53] Grant's oversimplification was in a way that favored Halleck.

"The condition of arms, clothing, and subsistence is good. Drill improving," recorded Sherman in his diary. He too was in the best of spirits and wrote to Brigadier General William Strong, now commanding at Cairo: "I hope we may meet in Memphis. Here we are on its latitude, and you have its longitude. Draw our parallels, and we breakfast at the 'Gayoso,' whither let us God speed, and then rejoice once more at the progress of our cause." Whatever Sherman might say later, he wrote on this March 24, 1862: "Most assuredly our cause has received a tremendous lift since we paced the piazza at Benton Barracks, and Halleck has been the directing genius. I wish him all honor and glory; and in my heart I yield to whomsoever has merit and talents to devote to so worthy a cause." [54]

Though Grant had not been able to attack Ruggles, he found a way to annoy the enemy on the day Sherman was eulogizing Halleck, by sending an expedition to bring in Confederate bacon. From Clifton, some miles down the river, citizens whose hearts were not in the cause of Jefferson Davis had brought the information that there was a big supply of army pork near their town. Grant told the major commanding the expedition that he was not going in order to fight, and that "nothing could be gained by a small victory, which would cost us a single man." If the enemy were found in strength he was to return for more men. Three days later the expedition was back with 100,000 to 120,000 pounds of pork, which Grant reported was "in good shape," and had been issued to his troops. Seven days after he sent his scouts to Buell he informed headquarters they had returned. "The three divisions coming this way are yet on east side of Duck River, detained bridge building," was his comment. From Fort Henry came word that a man from Memphis reported alarm in the river city. All energies were being devoted toward building up the force at Corinth; regiments were even coming from Virginia. [55]

On the 26th Benjamin Prentiss, who had relieved Grant at Ironton and had argued the question of seniority at Cape Girardeau, reported for duty; newly arriving regiments were assigned to him to be made into the Sixth Division. After inspecting troops the next day Grant reported, "The health of the troops is materially improving under the influence of a genial sun which has blessed us for a few days past." But a complication was developing. On the 21st the Senate had confirmed as major generals the nine officers Lincoln had nominated on the 3rd. On the list were Smith, McClernand, and Wallace—also Buell and Pope. Grant, getting only the fact of promotion of Smith and McClernand, and not knowing who was the senior, wrote he would as a result have to move his own headquarters to Pittsburgh. But he would not go until he heard again from Buell and was informed just what Halleck wished done with his command when it arrived.[56]

As the invasion reached into the Southland, cotton became a problem and gave Grant something new to think about in the fine big Cherry mansion on the bluff overlooking the river at Savannah, something in addition to his army at Pittsburg and Crumps, the new regiments coming up the river, the storage of supplies, messages from Buell, preparations for camping him, the telegraph line being run toward Nashville, refugee slaves, the enemy at Corinth, and caches of meat his men might relish. He wrote to Halleck that he had allowed forty bales of cotton to be shipped to Louisville, most of it belonging to a strong Union man who already had lost forty bales in flames kindled by the Confederates, with prospects of losing more, because most of what he owned was west of the river. "I could not give all the protection to this species of property that seems needful," he explained. If he had done wrong in allowing the shipment the matter could, he said, be righted at Louisville, for the *John Raine* that had the cotton aboard would not arrive there before his letter reached St. Louis.[57] Confederate generals had problems that did not harass the Federals; but they were free from some of the difficulties that beset Union commanders, which could lead to strong attacks from the Northern press when questions touched on the political and economic aspects of the war. Even when decisions had been made by the government in Washington, there would often be the problem of interpreting and enforcing regulations that themselves had a divisive effect on the Northern public.

Although his cotton action apparently did not get Grant into trouble, the last days of March nonetheless brought another stiff reprimand from Halleck. A telegram from New Albany, Indiana, had informed the department commander that two hundred sick and wounded from Wallace's division had been landed there, where no hospital facilities existed. It certainly was exasperating, though Halleck might have recalled that some of the orders he had sent Grant in the days following the capture of Donelson had not been delivered, and he thundered: "By whose order were these sent to New Albany? I ordered them to be sent to Cincinnati. . . . It is impossible for me to have proper provision for the sick and wounded when no regard is paid to my orders and where each one assumes to act upon his own authority." Then he exploded on another matter: "Again, colonels of regiments in your command have been giving furloughs on surgeons' certificates for sixty and ninety days, and in many cases to men who were not sick at all. Of 180 who arrived here a few days ago a medical board decided that more than three-quarters were fit for duty and should be returned to their regiments." After saying that there seemed to be collusion between officers and men, and that furloughs should be given only by Grant himself "after a proper examination by a trustworthy medical officer," he ended, "If this abuse of the furlough system is not promptly checked half of the army will be on furlough." [58]

Grant again kept calm under stinging words. In the matter of the sick, he had, he said, never received any order about Cincinnati; nor had he sent any men to New Albany. He had only sent them down the river, thinking they would be properly disposed of at Paducah. On the subject of furloughs, his orders to regimental commanders were "most stringent," while steamboats were forbidden to carry any soldiers or citizens without a pass approved by him. Having so written, he thought the matter over. Orders might not be enough. He visited boats and later the same day reported to Halleck that he had found violations of his orders, and already had a number of officers in arrest. "I acknowledge the justness of your rebuke in this respect, although I thought all proper measures had been taken to prevent such abuse, and will see that no such violation occurs in [the] future," was his frank admission. Then he assumed the offensive, ending in a way that could make the department commander feel he had allowed colonels to go up the Tennessee who were unfit for command. The Twenty-first Missouri, Grant said, had kept up a fire at the river banks, sometimes using citizens for targets. Charges had been preferred against the colonel, and the court was at the moment "in session trying him." [59]

"Beautiful—warm. The whole army is being reviewed by divisions," wrote Lieutenant Wilkins in his diary on the 27th. That day his own brigade had been reviewed by Lew Wallace before the other two brigades—and one can be certain that alert eyes were watching to see if ranks were straight and rifles carried properly. After apologizing a little for a battalion of the Fifth Ohio Cavalry—which looked pretty well, considering that it was new—his chest swelled: "Next in order came our Regiment and I never saw them march better: it was splendid." Then came a battery in fine condition and marching well, followed by the Eighth Missouri, which always made a good show. It was so hot and sultry that the men suffered. The entry ended: "General Buell's army is moving to form a junction with this army and are said to be within 30 miles. The Rebel army at Corinth is reported to be 50,000 strong, but thought to be new men and no severe fighting is anticipated."

Such was the camp gossip while one deserter was telling Grant there were seventy-five regiments at Corinth—which would put the force at about 40,000—though others asserted the enemy strength was double that number. All united, however, in saying the Confederate discontent was great, rations meager, and many men ready to desert. Cotton was being burned as if in despair. Grant's command, on the other hand, was improving, for the water now was good and the sun continued "genial." On the last day of the month an order transferred district headquarters to Pittsburg, leaving a rear office at Savannah where all official communications could "be left by troops having easier access with that point than Pittsburg." [60]

It appeared too as if Buell were coming, for on the 31st Grant wrote to McCook, "The two cavalrymen sent by you have arrived. I have been looking for your column anxiously for several days, so as to report it to headquarters of the department, and thinking some move may depend on your arrival." The good news was sent to headquarters the day it came in, and with it the information that the armored gunboat that had just arrived had been ordered up the river with the two old boats, to liquidate the enemy batteries at Chickasaw and Eastport. Sherman—whom Grant seemed eager to have fired at by way of full initiation into his army—was going with a regiment of foot, two companies of horse, and a section of guns. He was to fight no real battle, but was to take or destroy the hostile batteries if they were unsupported. [61] As he waited Grant was trying to bring in something more substantial than secession bacon.

Buell, who had personally reached the vicinity of Columbia on the 26th, was indeed on the near side of Duck River with some 30,000 men. The bridge was completed on March 29, and the day before he wrote Halleck that he had "studied pretty much every contingency"; one of his decisions was to give the impatient Nelson permission to ford the river without waiting for the finishing touches to the bridge. Years later the accomplished General Force, then waiting at Crumps Landing in command of the Twentieth Ohio, wrote, "Nelson having secured the advance, his eagerness gave an impetus to the entire column." [62]

Meanwhile, Sidney Johnston had found Beauregard, Polk, and Bragg waiting for him at Corinth and the four went into conference at once, Beauregard then returning to Jackson. Van Dorn was ordered to move from Arkansas to Memphis, and Johnston issued an order on the 29th taking command "of the Armies of Kentucky and of the Mississippi, now united, and which in military operations will be known as the Army of the Mississippi." Polk got the First Corps; Bragg, the Second; Hardee, the Third. An infantry reserve was given to Crittenden—who was presently arrested and succeeded by Breckinridge. Brigades were to have about 2,500 men and a six-gun battery; divisions, to have two or more brigades and some cavalry. The field command was offered to Beauregard, Johnston suggesting that he himself remain in general command of the department; but finally he took the field army, Beauregard being made second in command. Bragg, in addition to his corps position was made army chief of staff —a bad arrangement. In all, there were sixteen brigades, consisting of seventy-one regiments and eight battalions (which shows that one of Grant's informants had accurate information indeed). There were plenty of stars at Corinth: two full generals, four major generals, and sixteen brigadiers. The corps, the army cavalry—not much, but some —and the second in command made the Confederate force better organized for combat than Grant's with its four major generals (including the ailing Smith) and six brigadiers, but no officer between the army commander and the leaders of the six divisions, with their eighteen brigades of seventy-four infantry regiments.[63] If Grant had had two more good major generals he could have grouped his divisions into corps—following the pattern Lincoln had recently ordered McClellan to adopt in the Army of the Potomac—and would have had a force much better adapted to the vicissitudes of battle.

Halleck was allowed to handle his new department unannoyed by orders from Washington; but he kept the Secretary of War informed as to the general situation and his plans, while passing on information about the enemy received from Grant and Buell. When he learned that troops were coming to Corinth from the south, he queried if attacks might not be made on Savannah and Mobile by Generals Benjamin Butler and T. W. Sherman. As was to be expected, Andrew Johnson, the new military governor of Tennessee—who had been made a brigadier general before he was hurried to the West—thought that Buell had marched away leaving Nashville inadequately protected, and he sent a complaining telegram to Stanton. The latter referred the question to Halleck, who did no more than tell Buell that under no conditions must the security of the city be neglected. To Buell, however, Stanton telegraphed directly on March 30 saying that the War Department could not make decisions with respect to operations in the East if it did not have certain information without delay. What plans were being made for Brigadier General George W. Morgan, who had taken over Garfield's command when Buell ordered Garfield to join his main army? Was it intended to occupy a point on the Virginia and Tennessee Railroad, and if so, where and when? "Time is urgent," Stanton repeated the next day. While the answer Buell sent from Columbia was necessarily rather indefinite, the War Secretary could see that Morgan would at least be a threat to worry the enemy and pin down forces in the Knoxville region.[64]

Although Stanton did not interfere with the western generals, he intruded during the last days of March into the Navy's normal province by ordering a new weapon for the western waters. A civilian engineer, Charles Ellet, Jr., had been advocating high-speed rams as a good means of dealing with enemy gunboats. "However, for a long time he could persuade no one in Washington of the merits of his idea," writes a recent naval historian, who continues:

Finally the performance of the *Merrimac*, in addition to other factors, convinced the War Department. It and not the Navy told him to go ahead and put together a fleet according to his specifications. This relationship pleased him; he feared, and rightly, that his novel and extreme tactics would be hampered by the orthodox and conservative minds of the Navy leaders that he would meet even at the front. He was given a commission of colonel.[65]

So on March 27 Stanton gave Ellet his mission: "You will please proceed immediately to Pittsburgh, Cincinnati, and New Albany and take measures to provide steam rams for defense against iron-clad vessels on the Western waters." It was to be hurry-up work, involving the purchase and reconstruction of fast tugs and steamers, strengthened to withstand the shock of collision. Three places were to get the work "so as to avoid the imputation of local favoritism, and also to bring out the whole mechanical energy of the Ohio Valley." Already the Board of Trade of Cincinnati had been asked to give assistance. "Report daily to me," enjoined the Secretary, who lost no time in explaining the new project to Halleck, of whom he queried, "Can you not have something of the kind speedily prepared at Saint Louis also?" [66]

The rams were to carry no guns; and, though they were hardly suicide vessels, they were no place for cautious men. Frankly Ellet wrote to Stanton, "The men must take service with a full knowledge of the dangerous nature of the duty—the enemy's fire being the least of the dangers." One big bump was all a ram might live to enjoy, and there was no telling what would happen when it came. Replied the War Secretary: "The crew is of great importance. I will give honorable reward, and also prize-money, for successful courage, in large and liberal measure." [67]

Thus in addition to paying for the gunboats and furnishing men for them, the Army started to build its own fleet to serve under a colonel. The action was hardly calculated to cause Welles to make laudatory entries about Stanton in the famous diary; but the Navy Secretary would a few months later work adroitly to take over the peculiar craft whose construction had been due to the approval and energy of his rival.[68]

During March the papers of the North gave no prominence to the gathering of troops near the Mississippi line. It was a month of exciting headlines and fervent editorials; news had to be dramatic to get a favored place. Stories of Columbus —"Gibraltar of the West"— secured without a shot or a drop of blood, ran through several days. Presently there came word of Pea Ridge, and the reputation of Samuel Curtis began to rise. Repeated stories of the battle appeared, with talk of Elkhorn Tavern, accounts of the death of Ben Mc-Culloch, and reports of the barbarities of the Indians. Eyes also were on the East, and much was written about the historic battle between the *Monitor* and the *Merrimac*, which had revived spirits filled with gloom by the havoc the Confederate ironclad had wrought upon the Federal ships at Hampton Roads.

While the great naval battle was still fresh in people's minds there came news of the capture of New Madrid; and John Pope took his place in the public mind as a general of promise. On the same day Burnside scored his notable success at New Bern, North Carolina. Four days later the Senate gave him the stars of a major general, and on the 20th the *New York Times* eulogized, "If anything were wanting to perfect the claims of Gen. Burnside to public respect and admiration, it would be supplied by his official narrative of the victory of Newbern." Belatedly in the middle of the month came word of a battle on February 21 at Valverde, New Mexico, that made less pleasant reading in the North, for a Federal force of about a brigade under Colonel Edward R. S. Canby was routed by Confederate Brigadier General Henry Hopkins Sibley. The battle was fought on the banks of the Rio Grande, a short distance north of Fort Craig and a hundred miles south of Albuquerque. The contest had gone favorably for the Union troops until nearly three o'clock, when Canby arrived on the field and took over command from Colonel Benjamin S. Roberts. Fierce charges by storming parties of reorganized Confederates upon the two regular batteries which had been doing excellent service resulted in fighting of an epic character by both sides. But the guns were taken, and a New Mexico regiment broke and fled, while some dozen regular companies and a regiment of Colorado volunteers recrossed the river in tolerable order. Canby's retirement to his fort left no doubt as to who had won, and some troops that Halleck had been intending to send up the Tennessee were held back for possible dispatch to New Mexico. Although it was asserted by some that the Federals would have won if Canby had remained at the fort, the claim was disputed by others. The government at least did not seem to hold him personally responsible for the defeat, and he was soon made a brigadier general. In the end he held New Mexico, Sibley retiring after abandoning practically all his equipment and losing half of his original invading force of about 4,000 men.[69]

Also a little slow in arriving was the news that, on the very morning that Pope captured New Madrid and Burnside attacked at New Bern, Colonel James Carter had put to rout an enemy force in East Tennessee after leading his reenforced Second Tennessee in single file over Big Creek Gap, near Jacksboro. At the cost of one man wounded, Carter's force killed, wounded, or captured twenty-five of the enemy, secured eighty-six horses and seven mules, and destroyed equipment and supplies he could not carry away. Then, moving to Jacksboro, he added 11,000 pounds of bacon as well as a saltpeter plant to his record of destruction. Though nothing more than a raid, the operation irritated the enemy, increased his uneasiness about the region where Union sentiment was strong, and showed that the gaps could be penetrated, by small, bold forces. Carter reported that the "unbounded enthusiasm" of the inhabitants for his men was tangibly expressed: "Everything they had was freely tendered to us. We found forage and provisions abundant on the route after we left Boston" (near Williamsburg, Kentucky).[70] Almost simultaneously the *New York Times* reported a "brilliant affair" in which Garfield had driven the enemy through Pound Gap: "The rebels abandoned everything. . . . Nobody was hurt on our side." [71] On March 20 it also had big headlines: "More Important Captures in Florida— Surrender of Fort Marion, St. Augustine and Jacksonville—Flight of the Rebel Troops Without Firing a Gun—The Old Flag Run Up in St. Augustine by the Town Authorities—Affairs at Port Royal and Below Savannah."

The Capital itself was the source of exciting news when the enemy unexpectedly withdrew his batteries from the lower Potomac as well as from Manassas. On the 11th Lincoln released to the *National Intelligencer* his order of that day removing McClellan as General in Chief and giving Halleck the enlarged western command. Printed the next morning, it quickly spread throughout the country; along with it appeared the War Order of January 27. Though the order had not been responsible for any operation, it showed that the President had become impatient at inaction, and it gave the foundation for recent gossip that he had been taking an active hand in military moves.

Prominence was also given to the order of the day that Mc-Clellan issued at Fairfax on the 14th, and it set off anew the hot debate about him. The general admitted to his men that he had kept them inactive a long time; but it was not without a purpose: other armies had first to "move and accomplish certain results. I have held you back that you might give the death-blow to the rebellion that has distracted our once happy country. The patience you have shown, and your confidence in your General, are worth a dozen victories." Said the admiring *Harper's Weekly*, "M'Clellan, like Napoleon, is a believer in the efficacy of military eloquence"; and it referred to the "dastardly and atrocious attacks" upon the general that had been conducted by "one or two despicable newspapers" of the city. Having asserted that nothing Napoleon ever said in his orders showed more genius than McClellan's address, the editorial tapered off with more sense: "If he can fight as well as he writes, the Army of the Potomac will win imperishable glory." "Will he move, and will he win?" asked the "despicable" *Tribune.*[72]

Though Pea Ridge in far-off Arkansas was definitely the battle of the month, the defeat administered to Jackson by Shields at Kernstown on the 23rd was a heartening event. While there had been some seventy-five "skirmishes," "engagements," and "actions" in Virginia since the war's beginning, here was a real battle that the Federals had won. Not yet had Jackson shown his great stature as a general; nevertheless he already was "Stonewall," and the setback he received might presage good fortune for the strong and well appointed army that was being embarked to sail to the vicinity of Fort Monroe.

From London came word that the capture of Fort Donelson had caused a sharp change in British opinion and a rise in United States securities. But there was something even more important than that. Earl Russell, the Foreign Minister, had ruled that the blockade of the South was effective, as the *New York Times* put it, in spite of "all the representations of Jeff's London Commissioners—Yancey, Rost and Mann—touching the inefficiency and consequent illegality of the blockade." And the *London Times,* usually unfriendly to the North, said in approval:

If breaking a blockade could vitiate it, the greatest wrong would be in a fair way to create the greatest right. It is not well to encourage doctrines which lead people to acts of violence or fraud in order to build upon them a claim of right and justice. . . . There *are symptoms that the Civil War cannot very long be protracted.* Let its last embers burn down to the last spark without being trodden out by our feet.[73]

In addition to a false report that Island No. 10 had been captured, one was published that Yancey had been intercepted on the way home from his futile foreign mission. With several battle victories and other notable achievements during March, it would indeed have rounded out the month in fine style, if a Union cruiser had seized this eloquent planter and leader of the Alabama bar. (Northern Democrats, like the Republicans, thought ill of him, for they could recall how uncompromising he had been at the fateful Charleston convention of April, 1860, in his demand for a slave code and how taunting he had been in his suggestion that instead of treating slavery as an inherited evil they should boldly pronounce it a positive good. Sober-minded Northerners had reason to believe that there might have been no Confederate States of America if there had not been a William Lowndes Yancey.) Though there was not to be the satisfaction of bringing him into Boston or New York, word came from New Orleans that he had said in a speech upon arrival there that no help could be hoped for from England or France. Stop cultivating cotton, he advised, as a measure of retaliation.[74]

To homes in Illinois, Iowa, Ohio, Missouri, Indiana, Nebraska, Kentucky, Michigan, Wisconsin, Minnesota, and even Pittsburgh, Pennsylvania, letters were coming from Grant's camps and Buell's regiments as they fretted near Columbia. It was distinctly a western army that was poised to take the war into Mississippi, and dispatches from up the Tennessee, though they might not carry big headlines, came close to the hearts of people in cities, in towns, and on the farms. Beauregard's order to his soldiers had been printed in the North as well as in the South. He, too, resembled Napoleon in his belief in military eloquence. But no rhetorical exhortations had come from the pens of Grant or Buell. Correspondents had told of the seizure of the secession bacon, which had been consumed without the benefit of Southern recipes and unfortified with grits. Other reporters were writing of the fine bridge over Duck River being built by the Thirty-second Indiana and the Forty-ninth Ohio, and remarking that certain other Hoosiers had been drummed out of camp for indulging too freely in Tennessee chickens.[75] On the 28th the *Chicago Tribune* carried a Cairo dispatch saying a man just in from Pittsburg and Savannah, Tennessee, put the enemy force at Corinth at 70,000. Everyone knew that a great battle was not far off.

On the last day of March the rolls of the Federal armies recorded a grand total of 637,126 men.[76] Though uncertainty exists as to the exact, over-all Confederate strength at every stage of the war, it could not have been far from 400,000 at this date.[77] The difference is indeed considerable, though not disproportionate to the relative difficulties of invaders and defenders, and gives no sound basis for speaking of Northern hordes.

And at Pittsburg Landing the genial sun had brought the peach trees into bloom.

CHAPTER XIV

SHILOH

The distant rear of an army engaged in battle is not the best place from which to judge correctly what is going on in front.

Grant

"I WANT you to start about midnight as strong a party as you can mount to go out the Corinth road about 6 miles, and there turn to the left or south, to drive any of the enemy's pickets toward Greer's." It was Sherman who was writing; it was April 2; the officer he was addressing was Colonel William H. H. Taylor, commanding the Fifth Ohio Cavalry. Sherman explained that he was sending an infantry regiment to the house of farmer Greer, to be the bag into which the blue horsemen would drive unwary outposts of the Confederates. But Taylor's game was not to be just men in gray uniforms. This was enemy territory and he was to "bring in every suspicious person." If no party was encountered, Taylor was to return when the sun was "an hour high." There was to be no loitering: "The movements must be rapid. I send an aide to explain." [1]

Sherman reported the same day about his expedition of the day before to discover the situation at Chickasaw, in accordance with Grant's order of the last day of March. With a section of Minnesota guns, two battalions of Ohio infantry, and one hundred and fifty troopers from Taylor's regiment, he had gone upstream in two transports, following three hundred yards behind the armored *Cairo*— which had arrived from downriver only at midnight—and the *Tyler* and the *Lexington*. No answer coming from the shells the *Cairo* threw into the enemy emplacements near the mouth of Indian Creek and near Chickasaw, Sherman went ashore, to find abandoned batteries, one of which made use of an old Indian mound. After this personal inspection he attached little importance to Chickasaw as a military position; but he reported that the landing at Eastport, though recently under water, was now the best he had seen: "The levee is clear of trees or snags, and a hundred boats could land there without confusion. The soil is of sand and gravel and very firm." More than that, the road back from the landing was hard. So much for the potentialities of the place. As to the enemy, he had gleaned very little. Infantry scouts sent out by Colonel Hildebrand had found hostile cavalrymen watching the road to Iuka two miles back of Eastport: but Sherman could get no information about the enemy at this place.[2]

Also on this day Sherman was preparing an order for a review and inspection of his division by the army commander. While brigades would not attempt to dress upon one another, they would form a general line "looking toward Corinth, or the enemy." Regiments would be correctly aligned upon their colors, and brigades "after presenting arms will stand at the shoulder while General Grant passes the lines." Colors would salute, and bands play him by.[3] Few army commanders have cared so little for show and military pomp as Ulysses Grant; and it was only because he knew the importance of reviewing his new divisions that he devoted time to it. Now Sherman's regiments and brigades would have the chance to vie with one another, could get more of a division feeling, and could see not only their own immediate officers, but also the commanding general of the army—a most important person for a soldier to know by sight. Grant might be neglecting intrenchments, but he was not failing to build in his men an esprit de corps that would help in a hard stand-up fight. "I find the men in excellent condition, and as a general thing well clothed," he reported to St. Louis.[4]

At midnight Taylor was off with four hundred of his troopers; but the darkness of the night and the lack of guides caused him to halt after he had gone four miles. Starting again at daylight he struck a nine-man enemy picket, which his advance guard charged, wounding one and capturing a private of the First Alabama Cavalry. After procuring a guide a start was made for Greer's house, where, it had been learned, there was an enemy cavalry picket of fifteen men. They had, however, been warned by a man whom Taylor earlier had sought to impress as a guide, but who had posed as a doctor and pleaded ignorance of the country, also want of a horse. When encountered mounted near Greer's the doctor was taken into custody and sent back with the Alabama private for questioning. Taylor ended his report with an accurate picture of the enemy at the moment: three infantry regiments, one of cavalry, and a battery at Monterey, with cavalry in force just beyond Lick Creek.[5]

Learning that there were no batteries at Eastport or Chickasaw, Grant sent Colonel Webster back for more information on the morning of the 3rd; and the colonel advised against use of any point higher up than Hamburg as a debarking place for troops, mainly because gunboats could not accompany them if the river continued to fall. In the covering letter to St. Louis Grant said, "There will be no great difficulty in going any place with the army now concentrated here, but a battle will necessarily ensue at any point on the railroads touched." From Corinth there was nothing reliable, except that the force was "large and increasing." A dispatch was "just in" from the operator at the end of the telegraph line advancing toward Buell. Nelson had arrived within sight and would probably reach Savannah on Saturday (it was then Thursday). Some sort of advance party, however, came in that very day, for Grant informed Nelson: "Your advance has arrived here. All difficulties in our neighborhood will be remedied before your arrival." [6]

Twenty-five miles away in Corinth, Johnston's telegrapher was sending a message to Jefferson Davis:

General Buell 132 R 5—166 L 26—250 M 20—250 R g—239 M 32—111 M 28—Columbia 43 M 6—Clifton 252 M 6—218 M 26—Mitchell 32 R 22—124 R 32—276 R 27—248 M 1—250 R 9—59 R 17—108 M 20—109 R 16—175 R 6ed—109 R 18 . . . .[7]

When Davis got out his dictionary and deciphered the dispatch he read:

General Buell is in motion, 30,000 strong, rapidly from Columbia by Clifton to Savannah; Mitchel behind him with 10,000. Confederate forces, 40,000, ordered forward to offer battle near Pittsburg. Division from Bethel, main body from Corinth, reserve from Burnsville converge to-morrow near Monterey on Pittsburg. Beauregard second in command; Polk, left; Hardee, center; Bragg, right wing; Breckinridge, reserve. Hope engagement before Buell can form junction.[8]

The inspection and review of Prentiss's division which had been scheduled for the 4th was called off, for, however important it was for the army commander to see these newly arrived regiments and for them to see him, there were more pressing things. Word from Lew Wallace of reports confirming the reenforcement of the enemy at Purdy put Grant definitely on the alert, and he took actions that suggest his prompt and decisive steps on December 13 when he heard that the Confederates were planning an attack on Fort Holt or Birds Point. Wallace stated there were now eight regiments of infantry and twelve hundred cavalry at Purdy, and an equal if not larger force at Bethel. What it foreboded he did not know; but he asked Grant to send at once the two batteries that had been assigned his division in the order of the 2nd reallocating artillery and cavalry.[9] Thinking that the enemy might indeed be planning a blow to destroy the Federal supplies at Crumps Landing, Grant went well beyond the request of Wallace in providing against an attack from the direction of Purdy.

Not far from the bridge over Snake Creek on the river road was the camp of the Second Division, now commanded by W. H. L. Wallace, newly wearing the stars of a brigadier, well won at Donelson. Grant personally wrote him, directing him to have the two batteries sent to the Indiana general, and adding, "It is believed that the enemy are re-enforcing at Purdy, and it may be necessary to re-enforce General Wallace to avoid his being attacked by a superior force. Should you find danger of this sort, re-enforce him at once with your entire division." [10] Unequivocal responsibility was thus put on the commander of the division belonging to the absent Smith.

Nor did the matter rest there. Grant informed Sherman of the situation and of the order alerting the Second Division, saying specifically that, although he did not expect an attack, it was "best to be prepared." The preparations were certainly ample, for he told Sherman—the only professionally trained division commander he now had—"I would direct, therefore, that you advise your advance guards to keep a sharp lookout for any movement in that direction, and should such a thing be attempted, give all the support of your division and General Hurlbut's, if necessary." This was more than an order to be prepared to move; it was an order to appraise a contingent situation and act. Badly crippled because he had no general officers between himself and his division commanders—at a time when he had to operate at two headquarters—Grant was taking steps to see that his army could act promptly even if he were not on the field. In the final sentence to Sherman one feels the friendly esteem and reliance he was beginning to have for that officer: "I will return to Pittsburg at an early hour to-morrow, and will ride out to your camp." [11]

But Grant went back that very night, for hardly had he finished a letter to department headquarters when notes came from Mc-Clernand's and Sherman's adjutants saying that their outposts had been attacked, apparently in considerable force. "I immediately went up, but found all quiet," he wrote the next day. In the skirmish which brought him to the scene, several companies of the Seventieth and Seventy-second Ohio infantry regiments and some cavalry had been engaged. The enemy force which had molested them while drilling was driven back and pursued until it retired upon a larger body. In addition to some killed and wounded, each side lost about ten prisoners.[12]

A severe storm came on while the enemy was being followed, and it was still raining hard when Grant returned to Pittsburg, with nothing "visible to the eye except as it was revealed by the frequent flashes of lightning." W. H. L. Wallace and McPherson, whom he met returning from the front, informed him that everything was quiet, but on the way back to the boat his horse slipped and fell on his leg. Though the soft ground saved the rider to a considerable extent, Grant's ankle was sufficiently injured to make it necessary to cut off his boot. Thus the Union general, who already had his most experienced and tested division commander on a sickbed, was himself to be physically handicapped, and for a few days would find it necessary to use crutches when not on horseback.[13]

The suspicious events of Thursday and Friday were by no means passed over by William Tecumseh Sherman, for on Friday the 4th he wrote an order that began:

In case of alarm, night or day, regiments and brigades should form promptly on their parade grounds and await orders. Of course, if attacked, the immediate commanders present must give the necessary orders for defense.[14]

Then followed instructions for the most advanced pickets in event of an attack and a mild reproof for a regiment that "to-day went out in gray flannel shirts, which at a distance of 100 yards resemble the secession uniform." Mistakes could hardly have led more quickly to corrective measures, for the order ended, "These conclusions were illustrated by the events of to-day." The second sentence of the order shows that Sherman's subordinates were not to stand and wait when emergencies arose; they were to appraise and act. The note received that day from Grant had given him a good model, if he really needed it.

An aide of General Beauregard made an important comment about the 5th: "Soon after light the clouds began to break." Grant's injury was sufficient to keep him at Savannah, but at an early hour a note went to Sherman. Regrettably it is lost, though it is safe to assume it explained his not going to Pittsburg and spoke of the affair of the afternoon before, for in his immediate reply Sherman said: "I have no doubt that nothing will occur to-day more than some picket firing. The enemy is saucy, but got the worst of it yesterday, and will not press our pickets far. I will not be drawn out far unless with certainty of advantage, and I do not apprehend anything like an attack on our position." Clearly Sherman was living on a day-to-day basis and was predicting nothing about the morrow. Another note to Grant said, "All is quiet along my lines now." There was enemy cavalry in his front, and probably two infantry regiments and a battery two miles out. The ending was important: "I will send you 10 prisoners of war and a report of last night's affair in a few minutes." [15]

A thorough questioning of the prisoners would have been very much in order and could have turned up startling information; but the staff officer who might have been the most effective interrogator —Colonel McPherson—had been sent with a party to Hamburg to discover the suitability of the place as a location for Buell's command. Preparations for Buell were certainly receiving attention from the army commander, and Ammen, who arrived near noon and went into camp with his brigade just south of town, wrote that Grant and Nelson came to his tent about three o'clock. "General Grant declined to dismount," wrote Ammen in his diary, "as he had an engagement." [16] The reluctance was perhaps due to Grant's injury, but he may well have said he did not expect to be seriously attacked and it would be necessary to go to Corinth for a general battle, although we cannot accept Ammen's quotation marks as indicating Grant's precise words. Diaries of colonels and generals— especially one written as colorfully as Ammen's—are interesting, but they may lack reliability. (Ammen's entry for April 5 is fairly long; that for the 6th covers four large pages, and certainly was not written on that day.)

But there is no doubting the message that came to Grant from Buell on Saturday the 5th, written the day before at a camp three miles west of Waynesboro:

> I shall be in Savannah myself to-morrow with one, perhaps two, divisions. Can I meet you there? Have you any information for me that should affect my movements? What of your enemy and your relative positions; what force at Florence or Corinth? We will require forage as soon as we arrive and provisions in two or three days after. Has a steamer arrived with a bridge for me.[17]

It was not mere eagerness to be on hand that was getting Buell over the road; it was also solicitude for stomachs. Actually he must have asked Halleck previously for permission to stop at Waynesboro, probably for a possible move on Florence, since that place was in his mind as he wrote his message on April 4, as it had been on March 28 when he terminated a dispatch to Halleck with the question, "Is the bridge at Florence destroyed?" and made a similar query of Grant.[18] In view of his past experience with bridges it was hardly worth asking. But Buell had won his point with regard to Waynesboro, and perhaps even as Grant was reading his dispatch, Halleck telegraphed Buell: "You are right about concentrating at Waynesborough. Future movements must depend upon those of the enemy. I shall not be able to leave here till the first of next week. I will write to you to-day, via Fort Henry and Savannah." And in a short message he told Grant: "General Buell's force will concentrate at Waynesborough. You will act in concert, but he will exercise his separate command, unless the enemy should attack you. In that case you are authorized to take the general command." [19]

Halleck's decision to turn the initiative over to the Confederates is surprising in view of his recent sound statement, "We must be ready to attack the enemy as soon as the roads are passable." Ammen recorded that there were small Union flags on some houses at Waynesboro, while the sound of "Yankee Doodle" made the women weep for joy. But eating there would have been a problem, and rations and forage would have had to be hauled thirty miles over poor roads. Worse than that, Buell's army would have been beyond good supporting distance of Grant at Pittsburg. Perhaps Grant's optimism and low estimate of enemy morale had influenced Halleck; but on March 30 Grant had written him that most of the half-dozen recent deserters had said the number of Confederates at Corinth was "usually represented at 80,000 men," while Buell had written him on the 24th that intercepted letters said reenforcements were constantly arriving at Corinth and that they expected "to have 80,000 or 100,000 men." And on the very day that Halleck told Buell to stop at Waynesboro he had telegraphed to Stanton: "Want every man we can get. We have in front of us a large part of the Manassas army. It is probable that the great battle of the war will be fought in Southwest Tennessee." [20]

It cannot be said with certainty that Buell would have tarried in Waynesboro waiting for Halleck's decision while his men tried to find chickens and other articles to buy with the $400,000 the paymaster had given them just before they left Columbia,[21] if his forage wagons had not been nearly empty. But it is possible that he might have.

Conger may be correct in writing that Grant "seems carelessly" not to have noted that Buell's message was dated the day before, and Grant's report to Halleck that Buell would arrive that day, which was in a dispatch sent earlier on Saturday, could have reflected previous information. Grant, however, lost no time in answering the questions of the approaching general: "Your dispatch just received. I will be there to meet you to-morrow. The enemy at and near Corinth are probably from 60,000 to 80,000. Information not reliable. Have abundance of rations here and some forage. More arriving daily. Pontoon bridge arrived to-day." It was good shop talk for generals and shows how well the supply services at St. Louis and in the War Department were working. But one wishes the hours were on the messages.[22]

In a letter to St. Louis—which repeated information sent in a telegram—Grant reported about the skirmish of the day before, about the prisoners lost and taken, and about the enemy having infantry, three guns, and cavalry—"how much cannot of course be estimated." Then he said:

I have scarcely the faintest idea of an attack (general one) being made upon us, but will be prepared should such a thing take place. General Nelson's division has arrived. The other two of General Buell's column will arrive to-morrow and next day. It is my present intention to send them to Hamburg, some 4 miles above Pittsburg, when they all get here. From that point to Corinth the road is good, and a junction can be formed with the troops from Pittsburg at almost any point.

The word "scarcely," rather than "not," and the qualifying parenthesis in the first sentence, are to be carefully noted. Though forward movement was his chief concern, Grant said that McPherson had gone to Hamburg not only "to lay out the position of the camps if advisable to occupy that place," but "to examine the defensibility of the ground." [23]

While Grant, apparently expecting Buell to arrive the next day, was going about his headquarters on crutches that night, Buell was preparing to sleep in a tent in Nelson's camp. In later years he recalled: "I did not see General Grant that evening—probably because he was at Pittsburg Landing when I arrived, but he had made an appointment to meet me the next day." [24] It would not have been at all out of place for Buell to send a note to headquarters, telling of his arrival, saying when he would report the next morning, or asking as to Grant's pleasure. After all, Grant was the senior. Exactly there lay the rub, for in this same article Buell said he did not look upon Grant as his commander.[25] Yet Army Regulations, after listing ranks from lieutenant general to corporal, stated clearly enough, "And in each grade by date of commission or appointment," while the 62nd Article of War stated rather quaintly:

If, upon marches, guards, or in quarters, different corps of the army shall happen to join, or do duty together, the officer highest in rank of the line of the army, marine corps, or militia, by commission, there on duty or in quarters, shall command the whole, and give orders for what is needful to the service, unless otherwise specially directed by the President of the United States, according to the nature of the case.

Halleck's statement to Grant about taking general command in case of attack was premised on Buell's stopping at Waynesboro; he could not take away the full responsibility of a commander imposed on Grant by law after Buell had reached Savannah. Buell had not hesitated to order Smith to Nashville in late February—though he ranked him only in the dates of their commission—when Smith was fifty miles away and in the army of a senior general.

Two miles or so beyond the Federal pickets, the Confederates, deployed in lines of battle, were sleeping—some soundly, some fitfully—upon their arms. The order that brought them there, and the preliminaries to its issuance are of much interest, the order being one of the controversial documents of the war. According to Colonel Thomas Jordan (an 1840 graduate of West Point, and a captain of infantry when he resigned from the Federal army the preceding May), who drafted the order, the decision to attack was the result not of the strong hint from Davis in his letter of March 26 to Johnston, but of a suggestion by Beauregard, whose adjutant Jordan had been since Manassas days. At the bottom of a telegram that reached Corinth about 10:00 P.M. on April 2, decribing some maneuvers by Lew Wallace toward Bethel, Beauregard wrote, as Jordan recalled later, "Now is the time to advance upon Pittsburg Landing." Jordan thereupon took the indorsed telegram to General Johnston, and went with him to Bragg's room just across the street, where the contentiously disposed Bragg received them "in dishabille." Bragg agreed that the moment to act had come but Johnston put forward many objections. Colonel Jordan, however, had the answers—not, he explained of his own contriving, but because of careful briefing by his chief. He wrote later:

General Johnston at last assented to the undertaking. Thereupon I turned to a table in General Bragg's chamber, and wrote a circular order to the three corps commanders, Major-Generals Polk, Bragg, and Hardee, directing that each should hold his corps under arms by 6 a.m., on the 3d of April, ready to march, with one hundred rounds of ammunition; three days' cooked provisions per man in their haversacks, with two more to be transported in wagons.

Bragg and Hardee had receipted for their copies of the order by 1:40; and Jordan had Breckinridge summoned to a telegraph office and directed him to assemble the 6,400 troops between Corinth and Iuka, which were to constitute the reserve. Of the "hypercriticised" directive Jordan wrote, "As I framed the order, I had before me Napoleon's order for the battle of Waterloo, and in attention to ante-battle details, took those of such soldiers as Napoleon and Soult for model." Called to breakfast before he could finish his work,

Jordan returned to his models and his writing, to join, before he had finished it, a conference of Johnston, Beauregard, Polk, Bragg, and Hardee. There everything was gone over orally with a map, the confirmatory written order to follow later.[26] Thus, except for the absence of the commander of the reserve, the operation was launched in the most approved modern manner.

Though the instructions Jordan wrote may have been according to Napoleon in some respects, they did not harmonize well with the order in battle that Johnston described in his telegram to Davis; and from that fact there later came much dispute. Instead of being assigned to sectors, the corps were put one behind the other, front to rear: Hardee, Bragg, Polk. Since Hardee had in reality only a three-brigade division, a brigade—or more if needed—from Bragg's corps was to form on his right, so as to give him a line that would reach from Owl Creek to Lick Creek.[27] Such deployment in column of corps instead of line of corps was certain to cause a serious mingling of units; and not only the army commander but every corps commander would have his attention spread over the entire battle front. In having his army divided into corps, with an able general in command of each, Johnston had an advantage over Grant that was worth a superiority of many regiments; but it was being cast aside in a faulty order. No army of comparable size in the Civil War marched to battle with a potentially tighter command arrangement— or a worse plan of attack.

In an address to his soldiers, Johnston said: "I have put you in motion to offer battle to the invaders of your country. With the resolution and disciplined valor becoming men fighting, as you are, for all worth living or dying for, you can but march to a decisive victory over agrarian mercenaries, sent to subjugate and despoil you of your liberties, property, and honor. . . . The eyes and hopes of 8,000,000 of people rest upon you. . . . With such incentives to brave deeds and with the trust that God is with us your generals will lead you confidently to the combat, assured of success." [28] And the battle order ended grimly: "The fire should be slow, always at a distinct mark. It is expected that much and effective work will be done with the bayonet."

The Confederates intended to be rough.

Though the order said nothing about the hour of attack, it had been hoped that the troops would be in position on Friday night, so as to strike early on Saturday the 5th. But the march did not go well. Hardee's troops had covered many miles since they left Bowling Green, and Bragg had spoken well of the discipline of the regiments he had brought from the Gulf; yet Beauregard wrote in his report that the men "for the most part, were unused to marching." Bragg, though commending the high spirits and eagerness for victory of his soldiers, said they could not march, and added, "A very large proportion of the rank and file had never performed a day's labor." The roads, narrow, and traversing a densely wooded country, became almost impassable after the heavy storm of the 4th, and so filled with water were the creeks and ravines that movement at night was impossible. Thus it came to pass, said Beauregard, that the army did not reach "the immediate vicinity of the enemy, until late Saturday afternoon." Wrote Jacob Thompson, late Secretary of the Interior to James Buchanan, now a colonel and an admiring aide of Beauregard, "About this time General Hardee came forward and pressed you to ride along his line, that the men might be satisfied that you were actually in the field." But many of the men in the second line wanted satisfaction of another sort, and Bragg recorded: "Having been ordered to march with five days' rations, they were found hungry and destitute at the end of three days. . . . In this condition we passed the night, and at dawn of day prepared to move." [29]

What occurred "at dawn of day" may have been a surprise to Johnston, though perhaps not to Beauregard. At a historic council of war held on Saturday night Beauregard had urged calling off the venture, because—he later said—he "could not believe the enemy was still ignorant of our near presence with an aggressive intention." Furthermore there were the empty stomachs. If the army returned to Corinth the Federals might injudiciously follow, giving "a probable opening to the retrieval of the present lost opportunity." But Johnston replied that it was "better to make the venture," and expressed the hope that the enemy would still be found unready for a sudden onslaught, in spite of the day's delay. Bragg's post-bellum statement that there was a second conference early the next morning is supported by a statement in that honest general's report on April 20, 1862: "The enemy did not give us time to discuss the question of attack, for soon after dawn he commenced a rapid musketry fire on our pickets." [30] Thus the attackers were themselves the first attacked.

That Johnston did not take the Federal outposts by surprise, was due to the alertness and enterprise of Colonel Everett Peabody, commanding the First Brigade of Prentiss's division, which was in position east of Sherman, and astride the eastern branch of the road from Pittsburg Landing to Corinth. Peabody, like Colonel T. Lyle Dickey of the Fourth Illinois Cavalry, which had replaced the Fifth Ohio in Sherman's division, felt that trouble might be gathering in the woods to the south. Front-line commanders, with their thoughts not led astray by incorrect deductions as to enemy purposes and morale, and not bothered by a multitude of problems, will sometimes think more accurately than their chiefs about what may be happening just beyond their lines. So it was before the battle of Shiloh; so it has been since. With a premonition of battle and of his own death in it, Peabody sent his brigade officer of the day, Major James E. Powell, out on a reconnaissance at 3:00 A.M. of the 6th, with B, H, and E companies of the Twenty-fifth Missouri, which had received its sailing orders from St. Louis only two weeks before.[31]

Quietly through the dark woods Powell led his little command along a narrow road, past fields belonging to farmers Rhea and Seay, over Shiloh Creek, and to the branch of the Corinth road that ran past the unpretentious little church. Turning to the left, Powell went on with his three companies just before the sun, as Jacob Thompson wrote, "arose in cheering brilliancy" in a sky that "was without a cloud." [32] But he was soon accosted. From Powell we have no report as to what took place, for he, like Peabody, was to die this day. But Major A. B. Hardcastle, commanding the Third Mississippi Infantry Battalion, made a report that leaves no doubt as to just where or how the great battle of Shiloh really began.

Wrote Hardcastle: "About dawn the cavalry vedettes fired three shots, wheeled, and galloped back." Powell evidently deployed after flushing the horsemen and pressed forward, and, according to the Confederate officer, he was allowed to come to within about ninety yards before the Southern infantry pickets opened on him and in turn fell back. Still pressing forward, Powell started his fire on Hardcastle's battalion at a distance of two hundred yards. "We fought the enemy an hour or more without giving an inch," proudly wrote the Mississippi major. But at 6:30, after having four men killed and nineteen wounded, Hardcastle fell back upon his brigade. Before the heavy advancing Confederate line of battle, Powell retired, carrying his wounded with him. He was met by Colonel David Moore, who at Peabody's order had moved out with a reenforcing party of five companies of the Twenty-first Missouri. Moore ordered all of Powell's wounded who could do so to take their place in line, sent for his remaining five companies, and with his regiment advanced toward the enemy. For thirty minutes, he reported, he maintained a position

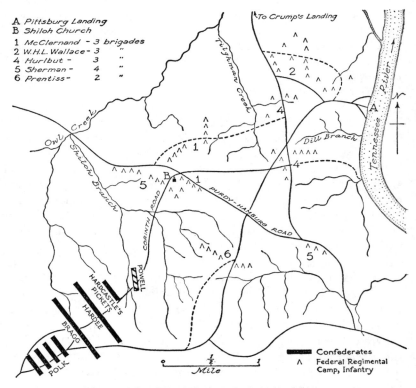

A *Pittsburg Landing*
B *Shiloh Church*

1 *McClernand* - *3 brigades*
2 *W.H.L. Wallace* - 3 "
4 *Hurlbut* - 3 "
5 *Sherman* - 4 "
6 *Prentiss* - 2 "

■■■■ Confederates
∧ Federal Regimental
   Camp, Infantry

BATTLE OF SHILOH, APRIL 6, 1862, 5:00 A.M.

Major Powell, reconnoitering with three companies from Prentiss's Division, attacked and drove in Confederate pickets. Hardee had four brigades in line; Bragg, five; Polk, four in column; Breckinridge followed Polk with three brigades in column.

against four or five regiments, in the meantime communicating word of the enemy advance to General Prentiss.[33]

It was men of the Twenty-first Missouri, one recalls, who had amused themselves by firing at the landscape as they came up the

Tennessee. Now their rifles were used against more menacing targets.

Just about the hour that Major Powell set forth on reconnaissance with his three companies, one of Grant's aides, Captain William S. Hillyer, debarked at Savannah from the mail boat out of Cairo and wakened Rawlins. Rawlins, unable to fall asleep again, got up at daylight, and went to the general's office to examine the mail and begin preparations to close the rear headquarters, which Buell's arrival made no longer necessary, and which were to be moved that day. Presently Grant came down stairs and read his mail as he waited for breakfast, talking the while with Brigadier General John Cook, who had returned from leave during the night. About six breakfast was announced; and, as the officers were eating, Private Edward N. Trembly of the First Illinois Artillery, on detached duty at headquarters, reported there was firing up the river. "Breakfast was left unfinished," wrote Rawlins in an official report to Grant dated a year later, "and, accompanied by your staff officers, you went immediately on board the steamer *Tigress,* then lying at the Landing." [34] On the headquarters boat "steam was continually kept up," but before casting off Grant dictated to Rawlins this message for Nelson: "An attack having been made on our forces, you will move your entire command to the river opposite Pittsburg. You can obtain a guide easily in the village." [35] To Buell, who would listen to the gunfire as he breakfasted with Nelson, and to whom alone Grant would have written if he had supposed he had arrived, Grant himself wrote:

Heavy firing is heard up the river, indicating plainly that an attack has been made upon our most advanced positions. I have been looking for this, but did not believe the attack could be made before Monday or Tuesday. This necessitates my joining the forces up the river instead of meeting you to-day, as I had contemplated. I have directed General Nelson to move to the river with his division. He can march to opposite Pittsburg.[36]

The second sentence strikes one with some surprise. The hedging Grant had done in his letter the day before to Halleck does much, however, to acquit him of now claiming he had expected what not long before he had said would not occur. It was only a general attack that he had ruled out—and that too with a touch of qualification. Any attack would of course begin on the most advanced positions;

but the implication seems to be that Grant thought there might be nothing more than action resembling that of the past two days, which had been sufficiently heavy for him to report to St. Louis. Buell would later say that this view persisted in Savannah throughout the morning. Ordering Nelson forward at once resembled the precautionary action that Grant had taken when warned by Lew Wallace of the possibility of an attack from Purdy.

In spite of having stated that he had "scarcely the faintest idea" of a general attack, Grant had told his superior that he would be prepared if one came. It was indeed too late on April 6 to do things that belonged to full preparation; but there was now no failure to make ready to use all force available, if it should be needed. After writing to Buell, it would seem that Grant dictated to Hillyer this note to Brigadier General Thomas J. Wood: "You will move your command with the utmost dispatch to the river at this point, where steamboats will be in waiting to transport you to Pittsburg." [37] He could not know that most of Wood's division was eighteen hard miles away, and he may have thought Wood, not Crittenden, was next behind Nelson and would soon be arriving. Then the *Tigress* cast off.

At Crumps Landing stood Lew Wallace, who had anticipated that the army commander would soon be passing. Already he had ordered his First Brigade at the landing, and the Third Brigade camped at Adamsville, six miles out on the Purdy road, to close on the Second, halfway between at Stoney Lonesome. Before the month was over Grant indorsed on Wallace's report, "I directed this division at about 8 o'clock a.m. to be held in readiness to move at a moment's warning in any direction it might be ordered." A year later Wallace wrote: "About 9 o'clock General Grant passed up the river. Instead of an order to march, he merely left me a direction *to hold myself in readiness for orders.*" In his *Autobiography* Wallace put the time at "about half after eight o'clock." Thus there is substantially complete agreement as to the hour and the general tenor of the order.[38]

Continuing upstream, the *Tigress* met the *Warner,* with a messenger from the other Wallace to inform Grant that a battle had begun. It was unnecessary to tell by word of mouth what musketry and gunfire was now proclaiming. Still it was an important act, and James McPherson may really have been responsible; for very significantly this one professional soldier on Grant's staff had slept that night and the night before at Wallace's headquarters. The Second Division was in a supporting position for the Pittsburg force; and, though Grant himself was nine miles away, with this division was a staff officer who knew his chief's mind. Had not Grant met Wallace and McPherson returning from the front in the hard rain on the night of the 4th and received from them a report about the situation? Wrote Rowley, one of the impatient passengers on the *Tigress:* "The Warner rounded to and followed us back to Pittsburg Landing." [39]

While orderlies looked to the horses, checking saddles and bridles, one can be sure instructions were given; not many, but important ones. On reaching the field at Donelson, Grant had found some regiments with no ammunition. Nothing would be more important in this contest than the maintenance of fire power, nothing count so much in holding on until Nelson and other parts of Buell's army arrived, if—as the mounting noise of battle indicated—it should turn out that it was an all-out attack by Johnston. Colonel G. G. Pride, a volunteer aide on Grant's staff, took such prompt charge of the ammunition problem as to compel belief that he had been instructed before the *Tigress* ran up to the landing.[40] Going from a steamboat to a battlefield was becoming standard procedure for Grant: Belmont, Donelson, Shiloh. But there was no partiality as to rivers; first the Mississippi, then the Cumberland, now the Tennessee.

It is not strange that the sequence and the times of the actions that Grant took on reaching Pittsburg are uncertain. Perhaps his first act was to order the Twenty-third Missouri, which had just arrived, to march at once to Prentiss's division. A few months later the lieutenant colonel of the regiment recalled the time as 7:00 A.M. Though it must have been later, his statement has importance in the mooted question of hours. At the top of the bluff Grant found the Fifteenth Iowa. It, too, had just debarked and was with the Sixteenth Iowa, which Prentiss had sent back to get the ammunition it should have had when it reached his camp the day before. These regiments Grant ordered, through an aide, to form a line to keep stragglers from the river, and to act as a reserve. For beginners the task was a grim one, involving as it did threatening to shoot men wearing their own uniform; but the colonel of the Fifteenth stated that even a battery was put in position to command the road leading from the field of battle.[41]

About a half-mile from the river Grant met W. H. L. Wallace. "From him," wrote Rawlins, "you ascertained the particulars of the attack and how matters stood up to that time." Then the Federal commander made his big decision from which there could be no turning back: It was an all-out attack from the direction of Corinth; there would not be a secondary blow of any consequence from Purdy upon Crumps Landing. Rawlins was sent back to the river to dispatch Captain Baxter for Lew Wallace. Being a paper-minded quartermaster, Baxter wanted it in black and white, so Rawlins dictated the order to him, saying afterward that Baxter left on the *Tigress* about nine o'clock. According to Lew Wallace it was "exactly 11:30 a.m." when Baxter gave him an unsigned message, with the statement that it was from Grant. The very graphic account in his *Autobiography* relates that his adjutant put the order under his sword belt, forgot about it, and lost it, although this does not agree entirely with what the adjutant himself said just a few years after the event. Wallace's memory of the substance of the order was quite different from what Rawlins recalled on April 1, 1863. According to Rawlins, the general was to move to Pittsburg Landing by the road nearest the river, form in rear of the camp of the Second Division, and await further orders. According to Wallace, neither Pittsburg Landing nor a road was mentioned; he was to "form junction with the right of the army," make a line of battle perpendicular to the river, and—as he wrote in his *Autobiography*—"be governed by circumstances." The claim is not very plausible. Not only was Grant's right flank secure, but Owl Creek, which protected him, also covered the enemy's left, so that Wallace could perform neither a defensive nor a counterattacking role from Sherman's right. At the hour when Grant gave his order the place for a reserve was somewhere behind the center of the Union line. Much argument would have been saved later if the order had been written at Grant's dictation and a copy had been kept; but since Rawlins's reconstruction of it is in accord with the obvious demand of the moment, and since Wallace did not preserve a paper he acknowledged receiving, the case inclines against him.[42]

Having formed an estimate of the situation, Grant sent a second message to Nelson. Written by Captain Clark B. Lagow, another aide, it read: "I am directed by Major-General Grant to say to you that you will hurry up your command as fast as possible. The boats will be in readiness to transport all troops of your command across the

river. All looks well, but it is necessary for you to push forward
as fast as possible." ⁴³

During the four hours that had elapsed since the gray-clad vedettes
fired their warning shots and galloped back to Hardee's line before
Powell's advancing companies, the first great battle of the war had
begun. It has sometimes been criticized as not being in harmony
with the rules and ideas of the day about a well conducted battle.
It was in fact a modern battle, for it consisted of a number of separate
battles—some have said a hundred.

The reader should keep the command situation in mind as he
appraises the separate combats: In the attacking Confederate army
there are two full generals, and a third (Bragg) who will later be
one; and there are two who will become lieutenant generals. There
are these five distinguished soldiers to coordinate and direct the three
corps and the reserve of Johnston's army, with its four actual and
two virtual additional divisions. These men have the initiative, and
the night before, after their sixteen brigades were in position, they
have met and discussed their battle plans. All are on the field early
on the 6th to direct their men from the firing of the first shot.

The line that easily forced Powell back, and then Moore—himself
seriously wounded—after his sharp half-hour fight a mile in front
of Sherman's position, did not move rapidly. The ground was wet
and spongy, and behind the infantry brigades the batteries were following. Bragg's men in places caught up with Hardee's, and inter-
mingling of units began. Johnston soon commenced to lead smaller
commands personally. This would have been censurable if he had
not had Beauregard as second in command. Under the circumstances it was the best thing he could do, for as an inspirer and leader
of men he was outstanding. Though the mixing of units that resulted
from the faulty deployment could not be entirely corrected, command
arrangement was improved as the conflict developed, by having the
corps commanders take charge of sectors, in the order, left to right,
Hardee, Polk, Bragg, Breckinridge. Thus some of the potential advantages the Confederates had were realized, though no credit goes
to Johnston or Beauregard; the corps commanders themselves seemed
to have worked it out.⁴⁴

On the other side there is only Grant, with no other officer of professional training and high rank to give sole attention to coordi-

nating division action. And his first view is not of men fighting bravely but of stragglers, and men gone mad with fear, telling, according to Colonel Hugh T. Reid of the Fifteenth Iowa, "the Bull Run story": their regiment is cut to pieces; they are the sole survivors. The first thing required by an army commander has been provided:

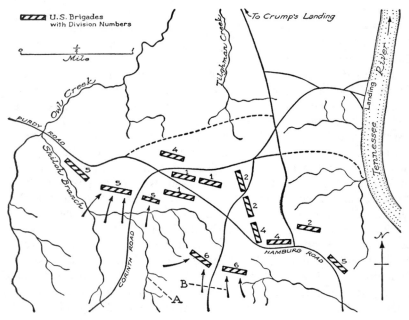

BATTLE OF SHILOH, APRIL 6, 1862, 9:00 A.M.

After being forced from advanced positions at A and B, Prentiss deployed his two brigades just behind his camps. Sherman occupied his original line of battle in front of his camps. The arrows show the direction of the Confederate attacks.

A reserve has been formed. It is small; but it will have to do, and Grant expects two divisions before long. As it awaits his call it is not idle, but seeks to stop the stragglers and turn them back toward the battle. Grant knows his army has gone into action smoothly without him. We do not know the instructions he had given his division commanders as he talked with them on preceding days. But there are the notes he wrote to W. H. L. Wallace and Sherman just two days before. It is immaterial that they directed action in case of an attack from

Purdy; the important thing is that they ordered instant cooperation.

The Fourth Division—near the river—and the Second were in ranks not long after firing was heard, and went into position rapidly upon receiving calls from Sherman and Prentiss. Notable it is that the Eighty-first Ohio and the Fourteenth Missouri were sent from the Second Division to cover the bridge over Snake Creek by which Lew Wallace should come. In a way, these regiments were reserve units, and before the day was over the Eighty-first Ohio was called up for combat, and was put into an important position by Grant himself.[45] Though cooperation between division commanders was to be of the highest order, reflecting credit both on them and the army commander who had given them the spirit of acting together, Grant would have been much better off if he had had a good general to direct Sherman's and McClernand's divisions, and another those of Prentiss, Hurlbut, and W. H. L. Wallace. Then he would have had two, not five, persons to deal with while he gave thought to the use of the expected divisions of Wallace and Nelson.

"General Grant visited my division in person about 10 a.m. when the battle raged fiercest," wrote Sherman in a private letter so important as to be given in the Official Records.[46] It was a historic moment. Grant had been much touched when Sherman offered to come up to Donelson from Paducah, waiving his seniority. In the three weeks just past they had come to understand one another; and, though Sherman was junior to McClernand and Lew Wallace, it was upon him that Grant placed his greatest reliance. Now as they observed each other in this moment of heavy battle there was forged a trust, friendship, and admiration that was to endure as long as both lived, and was to suffer no blot of pettiness. It was to be the intimate esteem of one great soldier for another, not the mere confidence of an able general in a great subordinate, or of a first-rate general for a superior whom he recognized as his better. On this 6th of April there was, according to Sherman, first some "general conversation." Then Grant "remarked" that Sherman was doing right in resisting the advance of the enemy as stubbornly as possible. This led Sherman to express concern as to ammunition. Ammunition, said Grant, had been provided for.

Sherman had already done much to save the battle. His division had been formed by 7:00 A.M. on its prearranged line of battle in front of his camp, the brigades in order from left to right being those of Hildebrand, Buckland, McDowell (all colonels). One of the first casualties was Sherman's orderly, who was killed by a burst of fire aimed evidently at the general, who had gone to the left of his line. A gap between his left and Prentiss's right was not yet filled in, and the Ohio regiment that ended his line, after firing two volleys had disintegrated as an organization. Its colonel had gone into a panic, and was later cashiered for cowardice. The officers of two companies rallied their men and joined other organizations, and much of the rest of the regiment was reformed later in the day under their lieutenant colonel and supported a battery creditably.[47]

It was Brigadier General P. R. Cleburne of Hardee's corps who was assailing Sherman's left and center with a five regiment brigade and a battalion of artillery. The quality of Sherman's fighting is shown by Cleburne's report, which said of his enemy: "Everywhere his musketry and artillery at short range swept the open spaces between the tents in his front with an iron storm that threatened certain destruction to every living thing that would dare to cross them." Bravely, however, the Sixth Mississippi and the Twenty-third Tennessee got within striking distance and charged the line of tents. Said Cleburne, "Under the terrible fire much confusion followed, and a quick and bloody repulse was the consequence." The brigade commander stated that only half the Tennessee regiment and sixty men from Mississippi could be re-formed for further use, and Hardee wrote that of four hundred and twenty-five men in the Sixth Mississippi, three hundred were killed or wounded.[48] Yet Sherman was later to read accounts of how his camp was easily overrun by the Confederates in their first dash!

The position of the Fifth Division was not easy to attack, for it was on a crest that overlooked the wet and bushy valley of Shiloh Creek and its eastern branch (Oak Creek). But the Confederate generals were determined to drive back the Federal right, and the regiments and guns of Brigadier Patton Anderson were brought up from Bragg's corps to make a new effort. The rifles and artillery of Buckland's brigade, however, quickly drove them back. Then Anderson's brave regiments tried it singly, to be stopped again; then they came on by battalions, and were once more driven back. A call was thereupon made on General Polk, all of whose brigades had already been drawn into the battle except those of Colonel R. M. Russell and

Brigadier General Bushrod Johnson. Johnson wrote that his men "came immediately under a heavy fire of the enemy's artillery and infantry, which took such fatal effect as to cause a momentary wavering in the ranks." In one regiment order was restored by the commander "with drawn pistol." Twice the lines of another regiment—reduced to half its original numbers—"were broken from the unsteadiness of the men under fire," when Johnson sought to lead them to the support of a battery. Soon the battery, with its captain's leg broken and half its men disabled, was maintaining only a token fire with a single piece. Such, however, was the stubborn valor of the attackers that re-formed ranks carried Sherman's center and left and threw back a brigade that McClernand had put in on the left of Sherman. Bushrod Johnson was severely wounded; and when Lew Wallace saw the ground in front of where Buckland had fought, he called it "a pavement of dead men." [49]

Jesse Hildebrand's brigade had now, according to Sherman, "substantially disappeared from the field," the redoubtable colonel remaining to help wherever he could. Although McDowell had virtually been unengaged, he was ordered to fall back onto a new line along the Purdy-Hamburg road. The loaded wagons of his brigade as they moved to the rear and a battery whose personnel bolted when their captain was shot as they began to unlimber, caused so much interference that another line still more retired had to be chosen. The time was 10:30, and Sherman wrote: "We held this position for four long hours, sometimes gaining and at other times losing ground, General McClernand and myself acting in perfect concert and struggling to maintain this line." [50]

Upon Sherman's request McClernand had promptly moved to fill the gap between the Fifth and Sixth Divisions. Doubtless Grant saw him after leaving Sherman, for not long afterward McClernand's engineer officer delivered to the Fifteenth and Sixteenth Iowa an order in Grant's name to support the First Division. But that officer led them away from the battle, and it was a member of Grant's staff who caught the Iowa regiments and redirected them to the fight. [51] Now Grant's only reserve was in the battle, except the regiments guarding the important bridge, which might be summoned in a pinch. But Lew Wallace would soon be on hand—or so Grant thought.

After leaving McClernand the army commander probably went to W. H. L. Wallace, but what was said we do not know, for Wallace was to be mortally wounded. When Grant reached the new Sixth Division much had happened. The wounded Colonel Moore, bringing back the small command that had fought a mile in front of Shiloh Church, had joined the rest of Peabody's brigade a half-mile south of Prentiss's camp. There a still harder delaying action took place. "The enemy's fire was terrific and told with terrible effect," wrote Colonel R. G. Shaver, who commanded the brigade of four Arkansas regiments, one regular Confederate regiment, and two batteries that attacked Peabody. Shaver's men were repulsed and thrown back, to be rallied personally by General Johnston, who ordered a new attack. Before this assault Peabody recoiled and retired to his place on the right of Prentiss's real line of battle. Other brigades joined the attacking Southerners, and Prentiss fell back to his line of tents, through which he was driven about nine o'clock, with loss of guns and with considerable demoralization. But it was not only on the Federal side that organizations gave way. The major commanding an Arkansas unit wrote that a regiment from Tennessee "broke and ran back, hallooing 'Retreat, retreat,' which being mistaken by our men for orders of their commander, a retreat was made by them and some confusion ensued." After returning to the battle the Tennesseans repeated their act, and the exasperated major who had crossed the Mississippi to help save the Volunteer State from the Yankees, wrote, "They were in such haste to get behind us that they ran over and trampled in the mud our brave color-bearer." [52]

Not far to the rear of his camp, on the summit of a slope covered by a dense thicket, Prentiss had formed a new line with four rallied regiments, joined presently by the Twenty-third Missouri which Grant had sent from the landing. Two other regiments Prentiss gave as a reserve to Hurlbut on his left.[53] Such was the way in which Grant's division commanders worked in the absence of corps commanders. Along part of Prentiss's front ran an old, washed-out road, where his men could lie down and fire. A feature of utter insignificance when Sunday dawned, by nightfall "the sunken road" was a part of history. There probably was a weakening of the battle as the Confederates regaled themselves in the conquered camps, filling empty stomachs with the ample food they found. It was of course a shocking hour for soldiers to breakfast, but the Yankees would not have reproached the uninvited guests. "Take all the time you want," would have been their heartfelt blessing, as they made ready to meet new assaults by their brave, hard-fighting, well led foe.

". . . and I received my final orders, which were to maintain that position at all hazards," wrote Prentiss. The order came personally from Grant, who reached the position after the relocated Sixth Division had already hurled back one assault. Evidently Grant did not question the necessity of the backward moves by Prentiss, who, writing his report six months later, after a period of captivity, remembered with pride that after he had explained the disposition of his entire force Grant gave "his commendation." [54] One sees more of the battlefield general. He has talked casually with Sherman, then told him he was doing what was correct and that ammunition was on the way; he has ordered two reserve regiments to McClernand; now he commends Prentiss, though he has fallen back; then he gives him the hardest of orders. That order did much to save the battle; the order and the manner in which Prentiss—who once had questioned an order from Grant—carried it out. Hold the position, Prentiss did, though not without valiant aid from Wallace on his right and Hurlbut on his left, holding it after Hurlbut's command and part of Wallace's had retired, yielding it finally as a prisoner.

It would have been natural for Grant to go from Prentiss to Hurlbut; but of that, or of a visit to Stuart on the extreme left, there is no evidence except the general's statement in the *Memoirs,* "I was with each of the division commanders that day, several times." It must have been about noon when Grant met McPherson, who wrote that he first saw his chief with W. H. L. Wallace. Grant told him of his order to Lew Wallace, and McPherson wrote, "At about 12 m., General Wallace not having arrived, General Grant became very anxious, as the tide of battle was setting against us, and shortly after dispatched Captain Rowley, one of his aides, to hasten up General Wallace." [55]

Nelson likewise was overdue, and Grant sought to hurry him, addressing a note "Comdg. Officer Advance Forces, Near Pittsburg, Tenn." so that it would be read by whoever might be in the lead:

The attack on my forces has been very spirited from early this morning. The appearance of fresh troops on the field now would have a powerful effect both by inspiring our men and disheartening the enemy.

If you will get upon the field, leaving all your baggage on the east bank of the river, it will be a move to our advantage, and possibly save the day to us. The rebel force is estimated at over 100,000 men. My headquarters will be in a log building on top of the hill, where you will be furnished a staff officer to guide you to your place on the field.[56]

There is certainly urgency in this message. But nothing in it suggests panic, though that has been claimed.[57] The possibility of losing the day is clearly seen; and the day was indeed lost—though it ended with good prospects for the morrow. The overestimation of the enemy is notable, the figure given being even in excess of the 80,000 men Grant gave the day before as an upper limit for Johnston's strength. Actually the Confederate general had marched with about 40,000 "effectives," so that his force was only comfortably greater than the 37,000 Federals "present for duty" at Pittsburg.[58] As in his message to Foote reporting the crisis he found at Donelson, Grant stressed morale. It was not merely a question of numbers. Reenforcements would inspire the Federals already engaged and dishearten the enemy. The calm, concluding sentence is in a way the most important one in the message. Nelson, or whoever commanded, was told where to report and assured that a battle mission would be ready for him.

In his postwar article Buell stated that a passing boat delivered the message to him while he was going up to Pittsburg, where he met Grant on the *Tigress* about 1:00 P.M. Grant, he said, was obviously relieved by his arrival as "indicating the near approach of succor." But Buell did not record how he explained the fact that Nelson had not yet marched. In his official report Nelson said it was 1:30 P.M. when he left Savannah on an order from Grant "reiterated by General Buell in person." Ammen wrote that for several hours it was thought boats might come for them, and that cavalry was sent out to hunt for a road. Buell's report mentions the order Grant had left for Nelson to march to a point opposite Pittsburg and leaves the impression that, with the exception of Nelson's artillery, there was no notable delay in its execution. But, in his later article, he made no reference to Grant's order, and the reader is allowed to believe that all action originated with Buell because "the firing continued and increased in volume." Both Ammen's diary and Buell's article stress the fact that C. F. Smith, upon whom they called, felt certain that only another hard attack on the Federal outposts was in progress. In the report of General Wood one finds an interesting sentence. It was about noon when he received an order to press on rapidly with forty rounds of ammunition and three days' rations on the troops, but without his baggage. While he was making arrangements to execute the order, a new one came, bidding him to march rapidly but to take his wagons. But something more would slow him down than wagons, for he commented, "An intimation also accompanied the order that the enemy had not made a substantial attack, but simply a forced reconnaissance." [59]

Grim as things looked, Grant could have taken cheer had he been able to know what was going on in the enemy's lines. All of Johnston's reserve was in action. Breckinridge's First Brigade, commanded by Colonel Robert P. Trabue, was committed to battle by 9:30 A.M. The Second Brigade must have been thrown against the Federal left before noon, its commander writing, "We were led by General A. S. Johnston, who told us a few more charges and the day was ours." Not long afterward the last brigade was in combat, and after that the Confederates had no power to control the battle with fresh troops, or to deliver a really decisive blow. Roman's picture of Johnston's line in the early afternoon shows much mingling of corps; on the extreme left were two brigades of the Second Corps, and two more of that corps were on the far right. While perhaps fewer men had fled the battle than on the Union side, many were not in their proper places. Roman wrote, "Straggling also began early in the day, a great many men being engaged in the plunder of the captured camps, while numbers made their way to the rear." Successful though they had been up to that hour, a heavy price had been paid; and an operation officer who had an up-to-the-minute map showing the position of all brigades, and who knew of the plunderers and stragglers, could not have been too hopeful, especially if an intelligence officer had told him that Lew Wallace's veteran division was not yet in action on the Union side. Then a great loss occurred. Johnston was wounded shortly after two, though not, as was frequently said, while leading a charge. In a few moments he had bled to death. For the fierce earnestness of some of the attacks and the will to advance of the Southern soldiers he surely deserves much credit. But the general direction of the battle did not suffer when he fell, for he had been giving little over-all supervision, and Beauregard quickly took over full command responsibilities. [60]

And still Lew Wallace, with whom Grant could have struck back, had not come, and at 2:30 McPherson was sent to look for him. With him went Rawlins and two orderlies; thus two roads could be scouted if need be. The heavy assaults on the Federal line continued, each of the four Confederate corps commanders controlling on the average four brigades. On the left of Prentiss, Stuart, Hurlbut, and one brigade of the Second Division were driven back. On the right a part of W. H. L. Wallace's division gave ground, Wallace himself being mortally wounded. Prentiss, in faithful obedience to Grant's order, stood fast, with some seven regiments of his own and the Second Division, and pieces of others. He retired his flanks, and prepared to make an all-around fight with his 2,500 men. Grant's *Memoirs* state that the last time he was with Prentiss "the General was as cool as if expecting victory." At 3:00 P.M. Grant was again with Sherman, and during a lull that followed, Sherman and McClernand, "on consultation, selected a new line of defense, with its right covering the bridge by which General Wallace had to approach." In falling back to the new position, they gathered in such scattered forces as they could find; an enemy cavalry regiment that charged them was "handsomely repulsed." "General McClernand's division made a fine charge on the enemy, and drove him back into the ravines to our front and right. I had a clear field about 200 yards wide in my immediate front, and contented myself with keeping the enemy's infantry at that distance during the rest of the day," wrote Sherman. Of a quality with his fighting were his words: "In this position we rested for the night." [61]

It would have been better for the Confederates to contain Prentiss as economically as possible, and move to attack the new Federal lines; but they had assembled a giant battery of some sixty guns to break the stubbornly fighting Second and Sixth Divisions even before the force remaining in the "Hornets' Nest" had been isolated, and Prentiss and his men were a magnet that attracted all Confederate units that were near. It would have required better control and fuller understanding of the entire situation to have it otherwise. Many separate assaults—as many, apparently, as twelve—had been made by the Confederates along this part of the line, and a dozen of their regiments had been so badly shattered that their organization was gone. After such rude rebuffs, it was a tempting prize indeed that was presented to them, and they poured shell and musketry fire into the surrounded men. The Federals fought back; but resistance was obviously futile, and ammunition was running out. Wrote Force, "Prentiss, having never swerved from the position he was ordered to hold, having lost everything but honor, surrendered the little band."

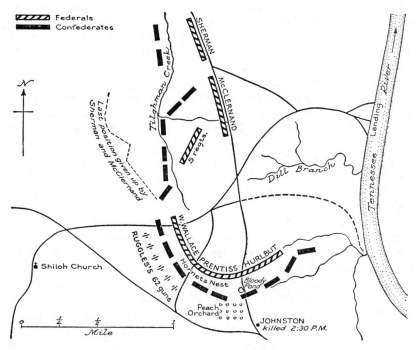

BATTLE OF SHILOH, APRIL 6, 1862, 4:00 P.M.

There were about 2,200 men, including many wounded who were made prisoners; the hour was about 5:30.[62]

But one prize the enemy did not get, and that was the Fifth Ohio Battery, which, according to Force, "had all day long been reaping bloody harvests among the lines of assailants that strove to approach." Before the trap had closed, the battery commander, Captain A. Hickenlooper, had limbered his four guns under a storm of enemy fire, and withdrawn to report to Sherman for further duty.[63]

Guns were to play a decisive part in the final fight of the day. Grant's chief of staff, Colonel Webster, had been a captain in the engineers when he resigned from the army in 1854, but was now nominal commander of the First Illinois Field Artillery. On April 3 he had almost implored his chief to have the remaining batteries of the regiment brought from St. Louis "in time to connect the name of that regiment with a decisive victory." To bring happiness to his colonel-gunner, Grant had made the request of Halleck; and now on April 6 he gave Webster the chance to help achieve the victory of a grim last stand. Just what his instructions were is, of course, not known; but Ezra Taylor, who had so skillfully commanded the six-gun battery that fought with Grant at Belmont, and who now wore a major's leaves and was the proud chief of artillery for Sherman's division, wrote in his report that he was instructed by "General U. S. Grant and Colonel Webster" to take any Illinois batteries or parts thereof and use them where he thought best.[64] That gives a clue to the thinking of the new colonel of artillery and the general who, though he had been brought up in the infantry, had helped serve a howitzer from a belfry during the battles before Mexico City.

So now, as the battle raged about the little body of water which from that Sunday has been known as Bloody Pond, and the great assemblage of Confederate guns hammered relentlessly at the Hornets' Nest, Webster gathered batteries and guns from here and there and put them in an advantageous position for the defense of the landing. Just above this key place a wide and deep ravine opened into the river. For a distance it was full of backwater and quite impassable; then for a half-mile it was still deep, abrupt, and wet, though traversable by infantry. On the good, high ground over-looking this obstacle Webster put his guns, including three of a four-gun battery of the Fourth Division that had fired one hundred and ninety-four rounds per piece. In all, Webster assembled fifty guns, some of them moderately heavy siege weapons.[65]

Hurlbut took position so as to support the great mass of metal, calling in the brigade of Colonel James C. Veatch, which had fought throughout the day with McClernand. At Grant's express command he gathered up all available fragments of broken regiments, and he said in his report, "Many gallant soldiers and brave officers rallied steadily on the new line." In all Hurlbut had about 4,000 men, including many from the three regiments of the wounded Stuart, whose successor in command had been ordered to the guns by Grant in

person. On the right Hurlbut touched the left of McClernand, who
in turn touched Sherman, the line bending at the place of junction

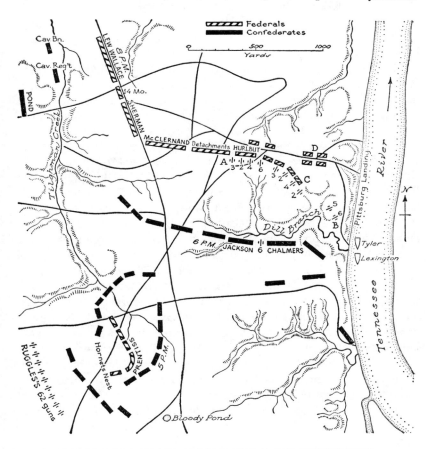

BATTLE OF SHILOH, APRIL 6, 1862, LATE AFTERNOON

In addition to Prentiss, four regiments of the Second Division are shown
in the Hornets' Nest. Webster's batteries: AB. Numerals give the number of
guns. Positions of two additional batteries are not known. Ammen's three
regiments (from Buell's army): C, D. Other regiments on the Federal left
were from Grant's army.

so that Sherman faced generally toward the west. Sherman wrote in
1864 that Grant visited him about five o'clock on Sunday afternoon.
They appraised the situation, taking into account Lew Wallace's

fresh division and knowing that Buell was "near at hand." It was decided that "the enemy had expended the furor of his attack," and Grant, according to Sherman, then ordered him "to get all things ready, and at daylight the next day to assume the offensive." Being in character for Grant, this may be quite true, even though it goes beyond what Sherman wrote in his report.[66]

The Navy's guns were waiting to come effectively into the battle. When Lieutenant Shirk, commanding the *Lexington,* which was tied up at Crumps Landing, heard the firing early in the morning, he at once stood up the river and reported to his senior, Commander Gwin of the *Tyler.* (The *Cairo* had recently left, all ironclads being required in the operations at Island No. 10.) Later, in order to be on hand if Wallace needed him, Shirk dropped back to Crumps; but when he found that the Third Division had left for the main army, he returned to Pittsburg. Impatiently the two sailors waited for a mission; but no message came from Grant. Under modern procedure the Navy would have had liaison personnel with the army commander, to keep posted on the situation, advise him as to what the guns afloat could do, report targets to the ship commanders, and direct fire. But there was no danger that the *Tyler* and *Lexington,* which had covered Grant's reembarking at Belmont, would be an unused battle resource in an hour of crisis; the spirit of support was too deep and strong for that. At 1:25 P.M. Gwin sent an officer ashore to request that he be allowed to fire; from Hurlbut there came back directions that would prevent injury to friendly troops in a delicate firing mission. At 2:50 the gunboats, near which enemy shells were falling, opened and silenced enemy batteries on the extreme Confederate right. Dropping down to Pittsburg at 3:50, Gwin sent one of his gunners ashore to communicate with Grant. "His response was," said the sailor in his report, "to use my own judgment in the matter." [67]

As soon as Prentiss had surrendered, Bragg burned with the desire to push on and seize the landing. If he had had 5,000 fresh troops, well led and determined, and willing to pay a good stiff price, he might have done it. This was indeed just the time for the reserve "to complete a victory." But Breckinridge's three brigades having been put in the battle hours before, and badly used, all Bragg had with which to make a final bid were the brigades of Chalmers and

Jackson, from his own corps. One of Jackson's regiments had been detailed to guard prisoners from the Hornets' Nest, and it is not likely that the two brigades together mustered many more than 2,000 men at this moment. (Prisoners can become a white elephant, and some Confederate units, already badly used, lost their fighting edge upon hearing the report that the entire Federal army had surrendered.) That was all Bragg had with which to advance over difficult terrain and assault Webster's great battery, supported not only by the eager guns of the *Tyler* and the *Lexington,* but by Hurlbut's 4,000 men, the hard core of the stout hearts from many regiments.

In his report (which Grant honored with the brief comment, "This is a fair, candid report, assuming none too much for officers or men of the division"), Stephen Hurlbut wrote, "In a short time the enemy appeared on the crest of the ridge, led by the Eighteenth Louisiana, but were cut to pieces by the steady and murderous fire of our artillery." His praise was not only for the guns of Webster, who was now having perhaps his finest hour, but also for those of Gwin, hurling their greater shells into the enemy. Gwin, in his report, spoke of his fire being "in conjunction with our artillery on shore"; but Shirk did not, and from a letter that Foote sent a few days later to Secretary Welles one would almost think the guns of the *Tyler* and the *Lexington* alone had stopped the enemy. What could have been a more pleasant thought to Gideon Welles than to have his two wooden gunboats save Stanton's army? He would in fact shortly write to Foote that the successful efforts of the gunboats in checking the enemy and repelling their advance was "felt and acknowledged by the country." [68]

Confederate reports give a clear and unquestionable account of what happened. Wrote Brigadier General James R. Chalmers: "This was the sixth fight in which we had been engaged during the day, and my men were too much exhausted to storm the batteries on the hill, but they were brought off in good order, formed in line of battle, and slept on the battle field, where I remained with them." The Alabamians under Brigadier General John K. Jackson were out of ammunition; yet, with nothing to use but the bayonet, their commander said they "advanced under a heavy fire from light batteries, siege pieces, and gunboats." After passing through a ravine "they arrived near the crest of the opposite hill upon which the enemy's batteries were, but could not be urged farther without support. Sheltering themselves against the precipitous sides of the ravine, they remained under fire for some time." [69] Writers who have talked of the "Lost Opportunity" that Beauregard let slip, and have criticized him severely for ordering his brigades to fall back about six o'clock on this historic, bloody Sunday, have shown little appreciation of the real condition of his command after its long day of brave but costly fighting.[70] The candid statements of the officers who made the last effort to win not just a day, but a battle, are his vindication.

Some of Buell's troops were at last on hand. Leading the advance from Savannah was the brigade of Jake Ammen; and, as he seems to have been responsible in a way for Ulysses Grant's being a soldier, it is captivating to think of him as appearing on the scene with succor at a very crucial moment. History has few incidents like that, and one might embellish it a little—but not too much. After a march of three and a half hours over a road that for three miles was good and firm and then led through recently flooded land, Ammen arrived opposite Pittsburg about 5:00 P.M. The pontoons had been brought up the river; but, even if Buell had had men who knew how to lay them, a bridge at any safe place would have obstructed river traffic. Thus the troops had to be ferried over, and they were interfered with by the great swarm of refugees about the landing. The comments which Buell made subsequently caused Grant to write in his *Memoirs* that Buell would have found a similar condition if he had come in from behind the Confederates. The rear of an army engaged in battle is not, he observed, "the best place from which to judge correctly what is going on in front." [71]

Eight companies of the Thirty-sixth Indiana—some four hundred men—at the head of Ammen's brigade were at Grant's order put in to support the six guns of McAllister and Stone that formed part of Webster's great battery. An outburst by the enemy which to Hurlbut and his men probably seemed like a Fourth of July celebration, looked quite different to the generals new to battle. It occurred in connection with the firing of a battery Chalmers had succeeded in getting into position to support his men, which Webster's guns appear to have knocked to pieces in a few minutes. The *Lexington*'s log speaks of an affair that started at 6:00 and ended at 6:10 P.M., and Force makes the significant comment, "Chalmers had not ended his useless attempt when the boats bearing Ammen's brigade of Nelson's division of Buell's army crossed the river and landed." Though

Ammen's regimental commanders did not pretend to any great achievement, Buell's report and his postwar article make it appear as if all of Ammen's brigade was engaged in stopping the Confederates. But Colonel William Grose of the Thirty-sixth Indiana wrote, "It is truthful and right to say here that *no part of Buell's Army except the 36th took any part whatever in that Sunday* evening fight at the Landing," and his regiment fired only a few rounds. Though Grant naturally used the newcomers, it does not follow that the situation could not otherwise have been easily taken care of. Parts of four of Grant's regiments were in fact in position well to the left behind Webster's guns, and Grose said that Major Belknap of the Fifteenth Iowa took position on his flank with a small detachment. But the two Confederate brigade commanders who made the last effort told clearly enough what stopped them: Webster and the gunboats together with the bad terrain.[72]

Night was near at hand when the head of the Third Division began to cross the bridge over Snake Creek—five hours overdue. Rowley had encountered the rear of Wallace's column on the road Grant may have intended the division to follow in an advance on Corinth, that struck the Hamburg-Purdy road two miles west of Owl Creek, where Sherman's right had rested in the morning. The entire division was at a halt, sitting by the roadside, some men with their arms stacked; Wallace, who was at the head of the column, said—according to Rowley—that the road was the only one he knew. His cavalry was called in, and he countermarched, instead of reversing his column and marching rear in front to save time. Rowley wrote that Wallace insisted that he remain to act as guide; but Wallace's *Autobiography* states that Rowley left after saying he knew of no short cuts. Just as the column was veering off to the right to shorten the route to the bridge, McPherson and Rawlins were encountered. All three of Grant's staff officers declared a year later that the marching was slow, Rowley adding that it resembled "more a reconnaissance in the face of an enemy than a forced march to relieve a hard-pressed army." "Execrable roads" was the 1868 explanation of Wallace's former adjutant, and another officer added his corroboration. Before the bridge was reached, some citizens—according to Rowley—reported that it was in Confederate hands; thereupon the column was halted while McPherson and Rawlins went ahead with the cavalry to reconnoiter, to send back presently an "all-clear" message. But when the column arrived at the bridge there came the fear that the enemy intervened between it and the Union army, and an appeal was made—according to Rawlins—to McPherson as to what should be

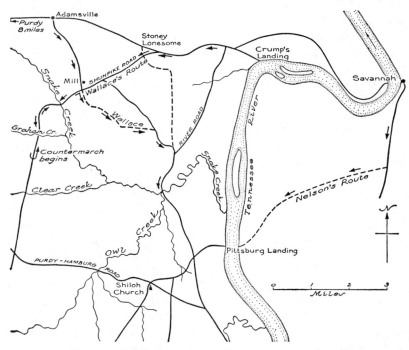

BATTLE OF SHILOH, APRIL 6, 1862: THE ROUTES OF
NELSON AND WALLACE

done. "Fight our way through until communication can be had with General Grant," was the reply, to which Wallace agreed with the words, "That is my purpose." [73]

The colonel of the Twenty-fourth Indiana thus described the arrival of the long expected division: "Under the direction of Colonel Smith, commanding the brigade, skirmishers were thrown out, and my regiment rapidly marched forward in line of battle before some tents, supposed to be occupied by the enemy. On being challenged, however, they proved to be Birge's sharpshooters, and we were received with cheers instead of bullets." [74]

At last they were there, in line of battle behind a stream, facing north, their left connecting with Sherman's right. Six thousand men, they were, under three excellent brigade commanders, Morgan Smith, John Thayer, Charles Whittlesey. Can one doubt that Grant would have known how to use them if they had been on hand when the tempo of the enemy attack slackened about 2:00 P.M.?

Buell had come; night had come; Wallace had come. So also had come the rain, though probably no one noticed when clouds first began to invade a sky which in the morning had been without a blemish. Wrote Hurlbut: "About dark the firing ceased. I advanced my division 100 yards to the front, threw out pickets, and officers and men bivouacked in a heavy storm of rain." The Twenty-fourth Ohio, of Ammen's brigade, was thrown deeper into the forest, its commander writing that he was "ordered by General Grant to advance into the woods a short distance, to ascertain, if possible, the position of the enemy's lines." Buell called on Sherman and later very graciously wrote that perhaps Sherman never showed to greater credit than he did that night. With "such bread and meat as could be gathered from the neighboring camps"—only those of the Second Division were now within the Union lines—Sherman's men rested in the rain in good spirits "and determined to redeem on Monday the losses of Sunday." [75]

The sailors were on the alert, and the log of the *Lexington* records: "Stood down the river; everything quiet. Stood up the river and arrived at Pittsburg at 10. At 10:15 two transports came up with troops; 4 boats arrived with troops." They were Crittenden's division, which moved out to join that of Nelson, whose remaining two brigades had been ferried over by nine o'clock. At 1:00 A.M. the *Lexington* took over firing from the *Tyler,* throwing shells every fifteen minutes in order to disturb and harass the Confederates, many of whom were seeking shelter in the captured Federal camps. [76]

Although the *Tigress* had dry cabins and comfortable bunks, Grant remained with his soldiers, lying down close to a tree. Especially under battle conditions it is imperative that army commanders get rest and sleep, for their minds must function clearly and they must be equal to physical strain. But Grant's mind was made up, and his constitution was a sturdy one. The swollen ankle and the soaking rain, however, kept sleep away, and growing restive after midnight he went back to the log house under the river bank, only to find that the surgeons had taken over. The general returned to his tree.[77]

Beauregard, who slept that night in Sherman's tent near Shiloh Church, wrote later that several corps and division commanders reporting to him expressed the belief that everything possible that day had been accomplished. His message to Richmond told of the death of Johnston, of heavy losses on both sides, and claimed "a complete victory." That was not badly out of accord with the situation of the moment; but, like the early dispatches that had told of McDowell's initial success at Bull Run, it would cause premature rejoicing and make later news all the more bitter. The final day of battle is the telling one, and Beauregard made no reference to what might take place on the morrow. He was discreet, even though he had some cause for optimism. His report mentioned a dispatch during the day from Corinth with news that Buell had been delayed; but according to Jordan's postwar article it stated that Buell was directing his column toward Decatur. This discrepancy is of little consequence. More important is Jordan's statement that Prentiss, who was bedded down that night between Jordan and Jacob Thompson—the latter an old friend of the defender of the Hornets' Nest—had, when shown the message which was causing much hopefulness among the Confederates, said in effect, "Wait and see." [78]

Colonel Preston Pond, Jr., commanding a brigade of Bragg's corps, did not require the testimony of Prentiss to know that the Federals were being reenforced. Beauregard's order to retire had not reached him, and he was bivouacked a half-mile west of Sherman. Soon after the sound of firing had stopped and the rain had taken over, Pond heard cheering from near the landing, and his men responded, "thinking it to be from their friends." But hopes faded when the cheers from the river gave way to the sound of a band playing "Hail Columbia." [79]

Of the important fact that one of Grant's veteran divisions had been absent throughout the day, Beauregard seems to have been ignorant, although its march was observed by a cavalry detachment. Even truthful, hard-fighting Benjamin Prentiss may not have been in possession of this information.

At seven o'clock on Monday—about the time that sailors breakfast after an eventful Sunday—Gwin got a note from Grant: the gunboats were to fire no more—the army was attacking.[80]

Grant did not assume all-out command of Buell's army, even though he had given instructions to some of the first arriving regiments the night before. Nor did Buell rise to the occasion and insist that Grant exercise what was not only his right but his duty under law. Buell, rivaling C. F. Smith with three brevets in Mexico, was to command his fine divisions well that day, cooperating effectively with Grant; but his later remark about not considering Grant as his commander is much against him. Excellent soldier that he was in many ways, he had faults that led to his departure from active command before the year was over; and he seems to have used the battle of Shiloh not only to try to brighten his own record, but to challenge the generalship of other officers who went on to great accomplishments.[81]

Confined to a small area into which some troops had come at night, and where other commands were badly intermingled, it was not easy to mount a rapid offensive—and the rain did not help matters. Wrote Sherman: "At daylight on Monday I received General Grant's orders to advance and recapture our original camps." He first sought to gather in some of his scattered units, especially Stuart's brigade. (Stuart wrote later that his own wound kept him from doing "more than to make an effort to excite the enthusiasm of the men and lead them to the field when they were ordered forward into action.") The enemy having broken contact, it was not difficult at first to advance; and presently Sherman was at the extreme right of McClernand's old camp, where he ran into artillery fire and halted, "patiently waiting for the sound of General Buell's advance upon the main Corinth road." Wallace also moved to the west, then south, upon Grant's order, after driving off a battery supported by a mounted regiment which Pond had left not far beyond Tilghman Creek when he discovered the isolation of his brigade and discreetly retired. McClernand likewise received orders for a forward movement, and Hurlbut a little later. The Fourteenth Wisconsin and the Fifteenth Michigan, which belonged to Grant's army and had arrived during the night, attached themselves to Buell's command, the former to Crittenden's division, and the latter to McCook's, which began debarking as daylight came.[82]

At 5:00 A.M. Nelson advanced, as small, miscellaneous enemy elements came to life and retired without opposition. Halted by Buell, he waited for Crittenden to form on his right. Next to Crittenden the division of McCook took position. When finally Nelson resumed his advance, the enemy fragments in his front had been welded into a compact, fighting group, supported by batteries. Nelson, whose guns had been left at Savannah because of the state of the road, was stopped short until Buell sent him a regular battery from Crittenden's division. Its guns did excellent service, and the brigade of Colonel William B. Hazen, in Nelson's center, charged, handsomely capturing a battery and driving back supporting infantry. Then Hazen's regiments received the fire of two remaining batteries and some sharply attacking Southern infantry, and his men streamed back in confusion, leaving a gap in Nelson's line.[83]

By ten o'clock the noise of battle told Sherman that Buell was advancing, and he himself again moved forward, Taylor helping with three well handled guns. He reached a point on the Corinth road where he "saw for the first time the well-ordered and compact columns of General Buell's Kentucky forces, whose soldierly movements at once gave confidence" to his own "newer and less-disciplined forces." At some of Buell's regiments he could look with the pride of a former commander—for they had been under him when he was in Kentucky the previous fall. To one organization new to combat Sherman paid a special compliment: "Here I saw Willich's regiment advance upon a point of water-oaks and thicket, behind which I knew the enemy was in great strength, and enter it in beautiful style. Then arose the severest musketry fire I ever heard, which lasted some twenty minutes, when this splendid regiment fell back." [84]

Converging toward Shiloh Church were not only McCook and Sherman, with Wallace farther to the right, but also McClernand and Hurlbut. The Fourth Division did not get under way until eight, its commander saying he had time to get some crackers for his men. At nine Grant personally ordered Hurlbut to the support of McClernand, and he went forward with one of his brigades and a battery under the close guidance of Captain Rowley.[85]

The contest that now raged about Shiloh Church had at times a fury surpassing that of the day before. The fresh troops of Buell, well trained and disciplined, were having a great effect, and a battlefield has not often had a more striking instance of cool deliberateness than that exhibited by Colonel August Willich of the Twenty-second Indiana. Believing that his men had been shaken by being fired into by their friends, and that, in one of their charges, they had started firing at too great a distance, he stopped them "and practiced them in the manual of arms, which they executed as if on the parade ground." It was effective treatment, and Willich said they responded with "deliberate and effective fire." Yet Sherman, who spoke of his men as "less-disciplined" than Buell's, exacted of them a great test of steadfastness, when on one of the occasions when ammunition ran out he appealed to regiments to stay in line because retirement would have a bad effect; and in his report he commended two regiments "for thus holding their ground under a heavy fire, although their cartridge boxes were empty." [86]

McClernand as well as Sherman (and likewise Wallace) paid tribute to Buell's troops, telling how Brigadier General Lovell H. Rousseau of McCook's division came to his aid when he would have been forced to retire. But Veatch of Hurlbut's division repaid the favor when on McCook's call he moved to fill a gap on the left of that general. And elsewhere Grant's men were also bringing timely aid to the divisions of Buell. At least four regiments of Smith's old Second Division and some fragments of others, under Colonel James M. Tuttle, followed Buell as a reserve. The Second Iowa, at Tuttle's command, made a fine bayonet charge for Nelson and broke the enemy; the Seventh Iowa stormed and captured a battery for Crittenden; the Thirteenth did good service for McCook later in the day. In addition, the Fortieth Illinois from Sherman's division moved to Ammen's flank when he at one time was forced back. The two newly arrived regiments of Grant's army that were actually assimilated into Buell's divisions appear to have been picked out for unduly heavy work. The twenty-two killed in the Fifteenth Michigan that fought with Rousseau were not much under the twenty-eight killed in the three remaining regiments and three battalions of regulars in the brigade. The Fourteenth Wisconsin, fighting with Crittenden, was to have a total of killed surpassed by only two regiments of the twenty-seven regiments and three battalions that Buell put into action. Neither Buell nor his subordinates, however, mentioned in their reports the assistance given them by units of Grant's army, though Ammen recalled in his diary that Nelson and Buell were "brave and noble." [87]

The Confederate reports make clear who was delivering the decisive Federal blow. Wrote Jacob Thompson only two days later: "The battle raged furiously for four hours, and the enemy was completely silenced on the right and in the center. About 11:30 o'clock it was apparent that the enemy's main attack was on our left, and our forces began to yield ground to the vigor of his attack." [88] Though some of Grant's troops were present on the Federal left and center, none of Buell's were with the Union right. Even the heavy column of McCook, pressing on the enemy's left center, was not working unassisted by Grant's troops.

About noon Beauregard, who could not have had many more than 20,000 men in line that morning, with his ranks "perceptibly thinned under the unceasing, withering fire of the enemy," began to prepare for retirement. In defense, his men had fought with a stubbornness that matched their valor in the attack of the day before, and the management of the shattered units by Beauregard, Hardee, Bragg, Polk, and Breckinridge elicits high praise indeed. It would be hard to single out the units deserving the greatest commendation, for the reports are full of testimony of the highest soldierly behavior. The colonel of the Seventh Arkansas told how his "wearied and almost famished men" formed ranks and marched to heavy combat before they had procured anything to eat. Major General Cheatham chose for honorable mention the Germans and Irish in three Tennessee regiments whose "gallantry and steady courage in behalf of their adopted country equaled that of the native standing for his home." Cleburne's brigade, which had entered action on Sunday with 2,750 men, started the fight on Monday with about a third that number, and after hard usage had shrunk to fifty-eight. Confusion in command naturally showed itself, and Pond told of a succession of five orders he received, which resulted in his brigade—not very heavily engaged the day before—marching first here, then there—until at last it got into Monday's battle. But in an engagement where control had become so difficult, and the organization was all previously untested in action, such an incident is not to be stressed as criticism, though it is instructive from the standpoint of field command. In the end there was weakening; and Thompson, after speaking of the impossibility of rallying commands except to a limited extent, wrote, "The fire and animation had left our troops." [89]

Grant, actively directing the battle on the right, still kept a grip on matters at Pittsburg Landing, where Shirk could hear cheering all along the line as well as heavy firing, as he devoted himself "to acts of mercy, picking up the wounded who had found their way to the river and conveying them to the hospital boats." General Wood, who had marched normally with his division on Sunday after word came that the engagement was essentially only an affair of outposts, received in the evening a new order and a very different report about

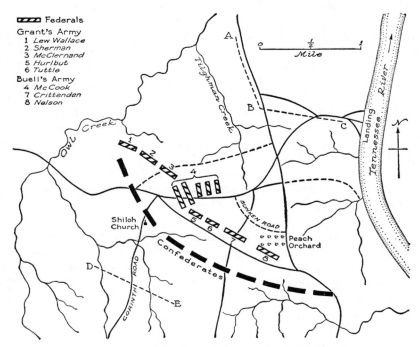

BATTLE OF SHILOH, APRIL 7, 1862, NOON

The Federal line of departure was ABC. From 3:00 P.M. to 5:00 the Confederates covered their withdrawal from positions along DE. A newly arrived regiment of Grant's army was with Crittenden's division, and one with Nelson. Wood's division of Buell's army arrived and was deployed by 2:00 P.M. The numbers have no divisional significance.

the battle. The blinding storm compelled him to halt his column for a while; but his leading brigade, after embarking at Savannah, landed at Pittsburg about noon. Colonel George D. Wagner, its commander, recorded that he was "immediately ordered by General Grant to reenforce the left wing of the army, which was then being hotly pressed by the enemy." When Wood himself debarked soon afterward with the other brigade—that of James A. Garfield, fresh from eastern Kentucky—he received an order from Grant to march where "the firing seemed to be hottest." [90]

There Grant was himself. No longer was he only a commander of divisions. He was once more the leader of fighting soldiers, the lieutenant of the Fourth United States Infantry, only grown a little older. The battle clearly was won, and he could forget he was an army commander and be a little rash. Whether he led a charge has been disputed. Wrote Force: "The lines were pressed closer and the fire was hotter than ever. General Grant called two regiments, and in person led them in a charge in McCook's front, and broke the enemy's line." Buell doubted that there really was a charge; but Rousseau wrote that two regiments, one of which he identified, moved at Grant's order "in double-quick time" against the enemy, and said this ended the fighting of the day. Veatch recorded that Grant ordered him to charge, which he said he did, his men exhibiting great spirit and moving "in a manner worthy of the highest admiration." He followed the enemy until he got in advance of other troops and was "ordered to fall back by General Buell." [91]

Why was there no immediate and effective pursuit? The question has been long and warmly debated. General Fuller notes the simple explanation: while a pursuit by a fresh force well in hand may be easy, one by a command that has been heavily engaged is very difficult.[92] Grant had not made adequate preparations for pursuit, and one by his own army was out of the question. Wood's division of Buell's army might have been kept in hand for the purpose, and Wood said Wagner did engage in "a vigorous pursuit." He lamented the fact that shortage of boats at Savannah had caused him to leave his artillery, whose usefulness and efficiency he could not doubt.[93] Cooperating armies instead of a single, tightly commanded force, and lack of experienced operation officers to plan ahead as the battle of the moment went forward, were having an effect.

Grant knew perfectly what was needed and, to some extent, planned correctly, for he wrote that night to Buell:

When I left the field this evening my intention was to occupy the most advanced position possible for the night, with the infantry engaged through the day, and follow up our success with cavalry and fresh troops expected to arrive during my last absence on the field. The great fatigue of our men, they having been engaged in two days' fight, or subject to a march yesterday and fight to-day, would preclude the idea of making any advance to-night without the arrival of the expected re-enforcements.[94]

With a touch of surprise Confederate commanders spoke in their reports of a lack of pursuit. While some of them were inexperienced and did not realize that it might not be hard to break contact with tired enemy troops, Beauregard could have recalled Bull Run. Did Grant exaggerate "the great fatigue" of the Union troops? A captain in a regular regiment, one of those who had been "subject to a march yesterday and fight to-day," wrote in a long letter to his mother:

We chased them one-quarter mile, when we halted, formed line, stacked arms, and threw ourselves on the ground and rested. Oh, mother, how tired I was, now the excitement of the action was over. I got some liquor which set me up. The dead and wounded lay in piles. I gave water to some poor wounded men, and then sought food in an abandoned camp near us. Pickled pigs' feet, almonds, and cigars rewarded me.[95]

Though Grant's message to Buell made no mention of the heavy rain, he spoke of it in his report, as did Beauregard, who lamented it as a handicap to his retreat. But it also increased the difficulty of pursuit, and the next day the Southern commander wrote to Breckinridge that a forward move by the Federals could not "be supported by artillery in the present state of the roads." Well did Beauregard know that pursuing infantry without guns could be checked by a rear-guard battery or two. In considering the possibility of pursuit, it is hard to avoid thinking of the actual strength of the Confederate army; but the important thing is how Grant and Buell estimated it. Though Grant may have revised in his mind the exaggerated figure he gave the day before, we still do not know exactly what his judgment was on Monday afternoon. Buell on his part wrote the next day of the "superior numbers" of the enemy.[96] Both Federal generals had plenty to think about of an administrative nature: Grant had his many stragglers to get back to their units, and his trains to straighten out; Buell had still to bring his wagons forward in addition to much of his artillery; both had their wounded. Pittsburg Landing must have been a confused, congested place that rainy night, with traffic hard to handle on the steep, miry roads that led from the river to the dark and dripping woods.

Pursuit with fresh troops being impossible, Grant turned at once to other plans, which he sketched to Buell, adding, "Under the instructions which I have previously received, and a dispatch also of to-day from Major General Halleck, it will not then do to advance beyond Pea Ridge, or some point which we can reach and return [from] in a day. General Halleck will probably be here himself tomorrow." [97] Instructions had, he explained, already been sent to his own division commanders "to be ready in the morning either to find if an enemy was in front or to advance." In view of his recent removal from command and Halleck's later sharp censure, Grant was hardly in position to depart from instructions.

After a night of tribulations of a weary general retreating in the dark through rain and deep mud, Braxton Bragg's morale hit a new low; and at 7:30 on April 8, still ten miles from the food and comfort of Corinth, he wrote to Beauregard: "Our condition is horrible. Troops utterly disorganized and demoralized. Road almost impassable. No provisions and no forage; consequently everything is feeble. Straggling parties may get in tonight." He had ordered Breckinridge to hold on with the rear guard until pressed by the enemy, and he asked if fresh troops with five days' rations could not be sent to his relief. "It is most lamentable to see the state of affairs," said the discouraged general, "but I am powerless and almost exhausted." Wood with his two brigades and Sherman with two—including Hildebrand's—and some cavalry did do some pressing. Clear evidence of the haste of the Confederates was found: hospitals with wounded, artillery ammunition, abandoned equipment of all sorts, including Johnston's field desk with its interesting papers. Sherman was satisfied that the enemy's artillery and infantry had crossed Lick Creek—nearly five miles from Shiloh Church—during the night and early morning. That there was still fight in the cavalry covering the enemy's retreat Sherman learned when a sharp charge caused one of his infantry regiments to break, though it later re-formed and advanced again. Wood's third brigade, just off the boats, came puffing up through the mud, got fired at a little, and evinced an eagerness—according to Wood—"to engage the enemy." [98] But the Battle of Shiloh was over.

Were the Federals taken by surprise at Shiloh? In a narrow, tactical sense they were not: the men of Prentiss's and Sherman's divisions were in ranks before they were struck. Hardee confirmed the statements of Bragg and Hardcastle by saying that "at early dawn" the Federals attacked his pickets. Though Peabody deserves credit for this, Prentiss referred to instructions he had received with regard to outposting when he took command of his division, and he spoke of strengthening his picket on the Corinth road on account of the events of Saturday; he also mentioned sending a company to the left after a conference with Stuart.[99]

It is notable that the dispatch to the *New York Herald* which seems to have been the earliest from Pittsburg about the battle, stated that it was begun by three hundred men of the Twenty-fifth Missouri attacking "the advance guard of the rebels," and also that the Federal forces were soon formed.[100] But this excellent piece of reporting gave way to the long and colorful account written by no other person than Whitelaw Reid, a twenty-five-year-old correspondent of the *Cincinnati Daily Gazette,* who used the pen name "Agate." Reid was sick, spent the night at Crumps with Wallace, went up to Pittsburg the next morning, and must have picked up many of his "facts" from refugees from the firing line. Although he dated his story at Pittsburg the 9th, much of it was written on a hospital boat at Cairo and the train thence to Cincinnati, where the flamboyant account appeared on the 14th. He was rewarded with an increase of salary, and plaudits for his courage in telling the unpleasant "truth" about how the surprised Federal camps were overrun at the first rush of the enemy.[101]

Psychologically, however, the Northern army was badly surprised. Grant's troops, well imbued with the thought of marching against the enemy, were taken aback when the enemy struck them, even though they had time to form their ranks. The morale of the Confederates was greatly strengthened by merely marching against the invaders, and every one of Johnston's soldiers, as he lay in the cheerless line of battle on Saturday night, perhaps with an empty stomach, knew he would be fighting the next morning. Few Northern soldiers were mentally prepared. Even though they formed ranks before the blow, it still had an awful suddenness, and the moral advantage of striking over parrying is shown by the greater number of men who fled from the Union ranks. Johnston's regimental and company officers were also better prepared mentally than Grant's for the task of battle leadership.

What would have happened had Lew Wallace been allowed to

follow his route of march? Though Grant could not have done otherwise than send his second and third couriers after him, Wallace himself took conflicting positions in the matter. In his official complaint a year after the battle about the criticism he had received, he sought to explain Grant's recalling him by the fact that Sherman had been driven from the position he had occupied in the morning: if he had been allowed to continue his march, he would, he said, in all probability have been "cut to pieces by the enemy's reserves and detachments" Grant, that is, had saved him. Later, Wallace seems to have fancied that he might have delivered a staggering blow to the Confederates, as Stonewall Jackson did to Hooker at Chancellorsville; and he sought to make it appear that his recall was a mistake. But when he went over his route of march with the battlefield historian in November, 1901, he had to concede that the point at which he had turned around was four miles short of where, for forty years, he had believed it was. He also learned that his march had been carefully watched by an enemy cavalry patrol, a part no doubt of the two companies that the Official Records show were sent by Polk on Saturday night to Adamsville to observe his movements. More than that, Wallace discovered that the narrow corduroy road that led to the bridge over Owl Creek ran for half a mile across an otherwise impassable swamp. And that was not all. The bridge was defended by two full regiments of infantry and a battery of artillery. Wallace still, however, wished to make it appear that a great stroke had been within his grasp, and in his *Autobiography* he stated that he *"was actually in rear of the whole Confederate army"* and if Grant's third order had not *"unfortunately"* arrived he would have gone on.[102] Though the creek and the swamp would have saved him from the fate of which he had once written in a tone akin to horror, they would also have kept him from being even a threat to the Confederates.

Another very pertinent question is: What if Buell had not come? If the general himself had tarried at Waynesboro, Nelson would have been on hand by noon, for there is no reason to doubt that he would have executed Grant's first order promptly and wholeheartedly. Even without Nelson's troops, the advantage in the situation had passed to Grant with the arrival of Wallace. The stubborn defense that the Confederates put up on Monday must raise doubt as to how successful he would have been on passing to the offensive, even though he had been strengthened by the Third Division, the Fourteenth Wisconsin, and the Fifteenth Michigan. But boasts that Beauregard would have made an end of Grant and then "liberated" Tennessee and Kentucky are absurd. Beauregard could not have destroyed Grant without destroying himself; and, on the other side of the Tennessee River, Buell would still have had the only large force at the time in either army that was well disciplined and conditioned to the road.

It has been asserted that, throughout the fighting on Monday, Beauregard was hopeful that Van Dorn would arrive with 20,000 men to restore a balance in the battle. Johnston's telegram to Davis on the 3rd did not refer to the troops across the Mississippi as an anticipated component in his venture, and Beauregard's long report did not mention Van Dorn. The battlefield was a hard day's march from Corinth, and there had been no telegram announcing that Van Dorn's men had entrained at Memphis—a message that would certainly have been sent. How then could Beauregard have even hoped for the arrival of Van Dorn? On the 9th he telegraphed to Van Dorn at Des Arc, Arkansas, eighty miles west of Memphis and thirty from a railroad: "Hurry your forces as rapidly as possible. I believe we can whip them again." Then he briefly described the battle and affirmed that it had always been intended to return to Corinth after the offensive stroke. There is no indication that Van Dorn had disappointed him; Beauregard was complaining only because he had not been able to bring home more loot.[103]

The performance of the Confederates was magnificent. But they were not the victims of undue ill luck. It is true that they wanted to attack on the 5th instead of the 6th; but the delay of an entire day was due to a late start, the inexperience of commanders, and poor march discipline, as much as to the storm on Friday night. Furthermore Nelson was in Savannah by midafternoon of the 5th and he could have been at Pittsburg that night, with Crittenden arriving sometime Sunday morning. If Wallace had strayed on Saturday as he did on Sunday, he still would have been on hand by evening. Thus Monday's battle would have been fought on Sunday. If bad luck contributed to the upset of the calculations of the Confederates, it was compensated for by the nonarrival of Wallace and Nelson, whom Grant had every reason to expect would be on hand by early afternoon. Fortune held steady in her favors, as was proper in a battle marked by the valorous defensive and offensive fighting of both armies, a battle whose final outcome left the situation about as it had been before.

Grant's dispatch to Halleck on the evening of the 7th began, "Yesterday the rebels attacked us here with an overwhelming force, driving our troops in from their advanced positions to near the Landing." The arrival of three divisions of Buell's army and the success of the second day were noted, the message ending with the statement that he intended to follow far enough the next day to see that "no immediate renewal of the attack" was contemplated. In a shorter message of the 8th he stated that the enemy had been badly routed and was fleeing toward Corinth, and that the Federal cavalry and infantry were following with instructions to go as far as Pea Ridge. He wanted "transports sent here for our wounded." The congratulatory orders which Grant and Buell issued on Tuesday both spoke of the enemy as numerically superior. But the report Grant wrote on the 9th, which began with sentences designed to bring a little cheer to homes throughout the North where anxious people would be reading the dreaded casualty lists, made no reference to the enemy strength. The arrival of Nelson was described, but magnanimously Grant said nothing about the very important order he had sent Nelson at an early hour on Sunday. Wallace's absence was attributed solely to his taking a "circuitous route." Many were praised, but Sherman was especially commended: "Although severely wounded in the hand the first day his place was never vacant. He was again wounded, and had three horses killed under him." The number of killed reported was quite accurate and it was stated that the two days of fighting had precluded immediate pursuit, while the rain on Monday night made the roads impractical for artillery the next morning.[104]

Shiloh was one of the bloodiest battles of the war. Of the 42,682 effectives that Livermore gives for Grant's army, 1,513 were killed and 6,601 wounded—only 292 being from Lew Wallace's division. In Buell's force of about 20,000 there were 241 killed and 1,907 wounded. Of the 2,885 reported as captured or missing, more than four-fifths were from Grant's Second and Fourth Divisions. One Confederate return puts their effective total at 38,773; an earlier one gives 40,335. There were 1,723 killed and 8,012 wounded; only 959 were reported missing. Though most of the guns captured on Sunday were retaken by the Federals the next day, the Southerners took back five regimental colors and twenty-one flags of the United States.[105]

The woods of Shiloh are a nation's shrine. The spot where Albert Sidney Johnston fell; the place where William Wallace was wounded and was found unconscious on the 7th; Beauregard Road, Peabody Road, Gladden Road, McClernand Road, the Sunken Road; the old landing where Grant rode off the *Tigress* and up the river bank; Bloody Pond, where men in blue and men in gray crawled painfully to drink and die; the Hornets' Nest; the somber cannon marking the positions of the batteries; the river where the smoke-enshrouded *Tyler* and *Lexington* blasted with their guns in the culminating hours of Sunday; the place where stood the little church that gave its hallowed name; the monuments of regiments and states; the countless tablets that record the ebb and flow of battle. The hundreds of graves, row on row, are mostly of men unknown; but named are those of two Confederates buried with the Federals. And also those of six Wisconsin color bearers who died when Prentiss stood fast and fought.

CHAPTER XV

SPRING CHANGES INTO SULTRY SUMMER

> Major-generalships in the Regular Army are not as plenty
> as blackberries.   *Lincoln to Governor Yates*

W HILE Beauregard's tired men were trudging back through the night
and mud toward Corinth, and the weary Federals were seeking food
and shelter from the heavy rain, John Pope was closing in on the
Confederates who had garrisoned the great stronghold at Island No.
10. Before morning came on April 8 he had made them prisoners.
It was the climax of an operation lasting three weeks, which had
elements of distinction or even brilliance which set it off as one of
the finest achievements of the war.

Though the guns of Island No. 10 could fire effectively both up
and down the river, there was a fatal element in the position. To
the east and not far from the river lay Reelfoot Lake, which touched
the marshes that ran northward to near Hickman, and thirty miles
to the south discharged its waters into the Mississippi after they had
flowed through a swamp-bordered stream.* Thus the promontory that
thrust northward toward New Madrid was almost an island. Only
a small flatboat plied the waters of the lake, and consequently the
only route of escape for the men manning the batteries of the island,
as well as those at the guns on the river bank in Tennessee, was
southward across the narrow neck of land to Tiptonville.[1]

* See map, page 294.

It was an unhappy situation in which the Confederates were placed by Pope's capture of New Madrid. Comprehending fully his opportunity to isolate the enemy completely, Pope at once began moving the New Madrid guns southward to new positions on the river. The enemy saw what he intended, and promptly responded with an attack by five light gunboats on one of his new batteries, an attack which was, however, successfully beaten off. Soon the 23,000 Federals were masters of the west bank of the Mississippi for a distance of seventeen miles. Though Pope had the supply line of the enemy cut by gunfire, the garrison at Island No. 10 had plenty of provisions on hand. There was also the possibility that the larger and stronger gunboats that the Confederates were reported building might suddenly appear and destroy or damage Pope's batteries.[2] In only one way could the operation be brought to a successful conclusion, and that was by putting infantry across the river with as little delay as possible.

On March 17 Pope suggested to Flag Officer Foote that he have a gunboat run the batteries, to carry troops across the river; but the sailor declined on account of the risk involved. Two days later Pope submitted to Halleck a plan to construct a canal eastward from New Madrid to a point on the Mississippi above Island No. 10, in order to by-pass the batteries. Without delay the department commander enthusiastically approved the idea, told Pope to impress all the Negroes he could find to help with the work, and stimulated him with the remark, "If you can in this way turn and capture the enemy, it will be one of the most brilliant feats of the war." [3]

The difficult undertaking was turned over to Colonel Josiah W. Bissell and his Engineer Regiment of the West, an organization of selected workmen, skillful mechanics, and officers capable of doing the seemingly impossible. Wrote Pope in his report: "The canal is 12 [9] miles long, 6 [3] of which are through very heavy timber. An avenue 50 feet wide was made through it by sawing off trees of large size 4½ feet under water. For nineteen days the work was prosecuted with untiring energy and determination, under exposures and privations very unusual even in the history of warfare." The flooded land on the promontory north of Island No. 10 as well as bayous made the achievement possible, but there is no doubting its extraordinary character.[4]

As Bissell's men worked with their ingenious sawing contrivances and dragged great trees from the bayous, the gunboats and mortars thundered at the island. No damage of any consequence was done, and a rather contemptuous Federal army officer when asked what the flotilla was doing, replied, "Oh! it is still bombarding the State of Tennessee at long range." Although four light-draught steamers were promptly taken through the canal, the gunboats drew too much water to pass. Believing he would have to work unaided by the Navy, Pope began the construction of heavy protected barges to carry guns to cover his landing. However, though Foote remained firm in the belief that it would be fatal to attempt to run the enemy batteries, Henry Walke thought otherwise: the man who had played so important a part for Grant from Belmont days to Donelson was not one to stand back when the odds looked hopeless to others.

So Foote gave the order, and on April 4 the *Carondelet* made ready to run the gantlet. Heavy chains were put over vulnerable spots, and a barge laden with hay and coal was lashed to her side; she looked, said someone, like "a farmer's wagon prepared for market." But she had a grim crew, ready to dare and to fight; nineteen volunteer sharpshooters came aboard; pistols, cutlasses, boarding pikes, and hand grenades were made ready for use in case of mishap and an enemy attempt at boarding. As the moon went down at ten o'clock the sky darkened with heavy clouds. At full speed, with the skillful hand of First Master William R. Hoel at the wheel, the *Carondelet* started, to be guided in her course by flashes of lightning, like General Grant that same night as he rode into the woods near Pittsburg Landing. The vessel almost grazed the island, coming so close that commands could be heard from within the batteries; though heavily fired upon, she was not hit. Walke thought her escape might have been due to the fact that the enemy guns had been depressed to keep out the rain, giving her the chance to get past the most dangerous fort before the hostile guns were properly elevated for direct fire.

But the enemy cannonading brought anguish to the responsible sailor who had written the order. If the *Carondelet* got through she was to fire her guns in a prearranged way. Anxiously Foote listened. He thought he heard the signal; but the thunder was crashing so heavily that he could not be sure. So he sent Pope a message at New Madrid: "I beg you will immediately inform me by bearer if Commander Walke has arrived with his vessel and the condition in which you find her and her officers and men." However great the relief that came with the news of the safety of his vessel, Foote was not eager for a repetition of the danger, and on the 6th he informed Halleck that he thought "it injudicious to hazard another boat in attempting to reach New Madrid." Then Thomas Scott reported from New Madrid to Stanton by telegraph that although Pope was progressing well he needed another gunboat; but they could not prevail on Foote to run the forts again. "It can be done with comparative safety any night, and might save the lives of thousands of our soldiers. The risk of the boat is trifling compared with that of Pope's army," said the Assistant Secretary. He asked if it would not be possible to have an order come from the Secretary of the Navy, so as to relieve the Flag Officer of the responsibility of the decision. But at 5:15 in the afternoon Stanton received another telegram stating that a message had just arrived from Foote saying he would send a second boat if the night were dark. At 2:00 A.M. of the 7th the *Pittsburg* slipped her moorings in a heavy thunderstorm and started on her run past the seventy-three guns of the Confederates. Once more the enemy gunnery was not what it might have been, and presently Pope telegraphed Foote that the gunboat had arrived safely. The expression of his appreciation was unstinted: "With the aid of the two boats you have sent, and of the gallant officers who command them, I shall be able to effect the passage of the river with the necessary force and without increasing the tremendous hazard which must otherwise have attended such an operation." [5]

In spite of the storm there was no delaying, and Walke, who Pope said was "prompt, gallant, cheerful," attacked the enemy batteries with the two gunboats and signaled at noon that he had silenced them. Then Pope threw forward the division that had been concealed on the four steamers; after it had landed on the east shore other troops were ferried over. By nine o'clock at night the small enemy force left in the island batteries as the main body sought to escape southward, signaled its capitulation to Foote. The main body found itself cut off at Tiptonville, and about 4:00 A.M. of the 8th it too surrendered.

The fruits of victory were great: 3 generals, 273 field and company officers, 6,700 men; 123 pieces of heavy artillery, 35 field guns, 7,000 small arms; tents for 12,000 men; horses and mules by the hundreds, other equipage, and several boatloads of provisions. Halleck sped the news of the great capture to Stanton, and was more than generous in his telegram to Pope: "I congratulate you and your command on your splendid achievement. It excels in boldness and brilliancy all other operations of the war. It will be memorable in military history and will be admired by future generations. You deserve well of your country." Thrilled by the exploit, Governor Yates and William Butler (at whose house Lincoln had boarded when he first came to Springfield) wired the President urging that Pope be made a major general in the regular army. But their good friend was not to be stampeded and the message that came back on the 10th read: "I fully appreciate General Pope's splendid achievements, with their invaluable results, but you must know that major-generalships in the Regular Army are not as plenty as blackberries." [6]

Buell's Third Division, commanded by Mitchel, had not accompanied his army to Savannah, but had been sent to Murfreesboro to rebuild the railroad bridge over Stones River while the track back to the Tennessee capital was being repaired. "General Mitchel returned from Nashville on a hand car," was Colonel Beatty's sole diary comment for March 28, perhaps because he had exhausted himself the day before in recording some thoughts about army life and a description of a lively cotillion on the lawn in front of his tent. In Mitchel's pocket was a letter of instructions that Buell had given him the day before near Columbia. As soon as the Murfreesboro bridge was finished Mitchel was to move the bulk of his three-brigade division of 9,000 men to Shelbyville, throwing out a brigade and some cavalry to Fayetteville, twenty-two miles to the south; an advance to Huntsville, Alabama, or to Decatur was indicated as a possibility, but was not prescribed.[7]

Mitchel was at Shelbyville on April 5, and it was probably the next day that there reported to him a leading Federal spy, James J. Andrews, who planned, and came near to carrying to a successful conclusion, one of the most dramatic episodes of the war. A native of Flemingsburg, Kentucky, and a man of impressive appearance and winning manners, Andrews had maintained good repute with the Confederates by carrying valuable items such as quinine through the Federal lines. At Nashville he met Buell and told him that he could induce an engineer on the railroad between Chattanooga and Atlanta to run his engine westward from Chattanooga. They could then, said Andrews, if provided with a small group of men to meet emergencies, burn the important bridge over the Tennessee at Bridgeport. Buell approved the idea, and eight men from the Second Ohio volunteered for the undertaking; they all returned safely to their regiment, but the expedition failed because the engineer did not appear.[8]

THE TENNESSEE–ALABAMA THEATER

Mitchel and Andrews then devised a bold and hazardous operation: Andrews would take some twenty men, including three locomotive engineers and some firemen, and after assembling at Marietta, Georgia, would steal a train, run northward, and burn some ten bridges so as to isolate Chattanooga against reenforcement from the south. Turning westward, he would not destroy the bridge at Bridgeport but would meet Mitchel, who, under a wide interpretation of Buell's order, would seize Huntsville and move troops eastward by the railroad. The objective of the plan, according to the historian of the Andrews party, was the capture of Chattanooga. Mitchel may well have thought that if the road to the south of the town were cut he could seize and hold it until more troops were given him. Under his instructions from Buell he had command of forces in Columbia and Nashville only in case of an enemy move against the Tennessee capital. But Mitchel may have thought that if he could report that he had Chattanooga the proviso would be relaxed.

In late twilight of Monday, April 7, Andrews met on the roadside east of Shelbyville twenty-three men from three Ohio regiments. All had volunteered for an enterprise which had been described to them merely as hazardous; and all were dressed in newly purchased civilian clothes, with revolvers as well as money in their pockets. The project was fully explained, and the men were directed to say that they were from Fleming County, Kentucky, and that, shocked at the oppression and the outrages of the Lincoln government, they were new but hearty converts to secession on their way to join the Confederate army and fight for freedom. There were, Andrews assured them, no men in the Southern army from that county, so no one would challenge them as residents there. If really cornered, a man was actually to enlist. After a warm handshake with their inspiring leader and instructions to be in Marietta on Thursday night, the Buckeye men in small groups turned their faces eastward into the rainy darkness of that historic night.

In stormy weather Mitchel's leading troops broke camp at noon on Tuesday and started southward over heavy roads. Fayetteville was reached on Thursday, and under a sunny sky one brigade and two batteries pressed on to camp that night within ten miles of Huntsville. Quietly they took the road again at 2:00 A.M., preceded by cavalry that had been taking into custody all persons that might give an alarm. As daylight came one party of horsemen dashed west of Huntsville to cut the railroad and the telegraph line; another rode toward the east for the same purpose, while a third party with Mitchel himself in charge made for the town itself. The surprise was complete, and for the "forced march of incredible difficulty" which Mitchel reported he found himself rewarded with 200 prisoners, 15 locomotives, a large number of passenger, box, and flat cars, and two Southern mails. In the uptown telegraph office was found a copy of the message that Beauregard had sent to Adjutant General Cooper two days before. When deciphered it revealed that there were 35,000 effectives at Corinth, with Van Dorn's 15,000 presently expected, and asked that the command of Major General John C. Pemberton be brought from Savannah, Georgia, to Corinth, on the ground that the loss of Savannah, as well as Charleston, could be better afforded than the possible fall of the entire Mississippi valley.[9]

Three regiments and a battalion of Confederate troops en route for Corinth had passed through Huntsville the day before Mitchel rode in; but an eastbound train, that just eluded the Federal horse-men and gun sent to block the line, carried a warning to three more enemy regiments that were following. Mitchel, however, had only begun his operation; and, his infantry having arrived promptly, he pushed a regiment westward by rail to Decatur, where it arrived in time to save the bridge that had just been set afire. Some time during the night a train with about 2,000 men of the brigade that had fur-nished the volunteers to Andrews, with the car next the engine mounting two field pieces, moved slowly eastward under the com-mand of Mitchel himself. Boldness paid off: the enemy regiments that had been held up at Stevenson retired eastward, and five more loco-motives were acquired at the important railroad junction. Afraid that the enemy would destroy the bridge over the Tennessee, Mitchel went only a short distance beyond Stevenson to Widden's Creek, where he destroyed the bridge. The ruse worked perfectly, for though Mitchel said he could rebuild the structure in a day, Kirby Smith at Knoxville told General Leadbetter, commanding at Chattanooga, that the destruction of the bridge over the creek showed that Mitchel had no designs against Chattanooga.[10]

And what about Andrews, who should have appeared west of Chattanooga on Friday if everything had gone according to plan? Believing that the heavy rains would delay Mitchel's march on Hunts-ville, Andrews passed word to some of his groups to delay a day; thus it was near midnight Friday when most of his men got off a train at Marietta, though two men who had not received the message arrived the night before. Early on Saturday morning twenty men of the total number boarded a train northward; and when it stopped for breakfast at Big Shanty (present Kennesaw), where it was known there was no telegraph office, the engine and four empty boxcars at the head were stolen as the crew was eating, the theft being made under the eyes of a nearby sentinel. A telegraph wire was immediately cut; but lack of proper tools prevented the raiders from doing really effective damage to the track. It was necessary to run on the sixteen-mile-an-hour schedule of the stolen train in order to pass a regular freight and two passenger trains that were known to be approaching. The conductor of the stolen train and a companion pursued it on foot, found a handcar, then procured an engine that belonged to a mining company a few miles from the railroad and which, as luck would have it, was this morning at the station in Etowah. When this engine had to be abandoned because a rail had been removed, though at the expense of considerable time, the pursuers resumed on foot, to obtain presently the engine of the first train that Andrews had passed.

All would probably have gone well if the run had been made the day before; but on Saturday several extra trains were evacuating valuables from Chattanooga precisely because of Mitchel's approach. Unexpected delays resulted, with Andrews calmly explaining to wondering railroad men that he was taking ammunition to Beauregard, while the soldiers lay quietly within one of the cars, ready to fight at any moment if their leader's story and manner did not allay suspicion. It had also begun to rain hard, and the burning cars that were left in the covered bridges to ignite them were pushed ahead by the pursuers before this occurred. Eventually, when out of fuel, the intrepid raiders abandoned the engine which was all that was left of their train, and took to the woods some seventeen miles south of Chattanooga. All were captured: eight, including Andrews, were hanged; six escaped; and six, recaptured after one escape, were exchanged.[11]

Mitchel made an error in not putting the soldiers under the command of an officer, who would have persuaded or compelled Andrews to let them stop and ambush their pursuers. Although the telegraph line had been broken after each station, the energetic conductor, William A. Fuller, by skillfully using a boy sent south from Chattanooga to find the cause of the interruption of messages, succeeded in sending a dispatch ahead. The chance of escape westward through the town had thus vanished; but bridges over Chickamauga Creek might still have been burned if the pursuing engine had been halted.

There is no more impressive memento of the war than the engine the raiders stole, an engine whose cab carried the name "General," and which now stands in the Union Station at Chattanooga with a tablet that briefly narrates the story. Brave men handled the throttle of the General that day, and brave men rode behind her. No less stirring is the story of the undaunted pursuers, with whom the Union survivors in later years would recount in a friendly manner the incidents of the day and seek to make an accurate record of what transpired.

"Gen. Halleck passed Cairo to-day, *en route* for Pittsburg Landing." Such was an April 10 dispatch which was read the next day while the general himself was establishing his headquarters on the bluff overlooking the landing. From St. Louis on the 8th he had sent a two-sentence telegram to Washington about the battle at Pittsburg Landing; this he supplemented on the 13th with a message saying that it was the unanimous opinion at Pittsburg that Sherman had saved the day on the 6th "and contributed largely to the glorious victory of the 7th." He requested that Sherman be made a major general of volunteers to date from the 6th. On the same day Halleck issued a General Order thanking Grant and Buell, and their officers and men, for the bravery and endurance with which they had met the general attacks of the enemy on the 6th, and had defeated and routed him the next day. "The soldiers of the great West have added new laurels to those which they have already won on numerous fields," was a compliment, followed by the admonition that greater discipline and order were needed. The next day he continued his feud with Grant in a note that told him: "Your army is not now in condition to resist an attack. It must be made so without delay." Grant responded with an order that stressed the instruction of sentinels, prescribed drill for as many hours a day as was consistent with health, and enjoined company commanders against excusing anyone.[12]

Though sniping at Grant, Halleck stood firmly behind him when the real test came. Stanton telegraphed sharply on the 23rd that the President wanted to know why he had made no official report about the late battle. Rumors were evidently spreading, and Lincoln wished to be informed "whether any neglect or misconduct of General Grant or any other officer contributed to the sad casualties that befell our forces on Sunday." In his reply Halleck said nothing about any failure to fortify the position and attributed the losses "in part to the bad conduct of officers who were utterly unfit for their places, and in part to the numbers and bravery of the enemy." He preferred, he said, to express no opinion about individuals until he received the reports of division commanders, and he was as abrupt as Stanton in his ending: "A great battle cannot be fought or a victory gained without many casualties. In this instance the enemy suffered more than we did." A few days later, when forwarding reports, Halleck still talked sharply: "The newspaper accounts that our divisions were surprised are utterly false. Every division had notice of the enemy's approach hours before the battle commenced." [13]

When he took over the role of field commander, Halleck's position was not an easy one. He had been only a lieutenant of engineers in the Mexican War and had had little combat service—in Lower California at the war's end. The frequent charge that he was habitually and unduly cautious is an exaggeration; in that regard as in others his record is spotty. Attention has been called to the remarkable building that he erected in San Francisco, for which he raised a great deal of money, and which was a monument both to imagination and audacity. It should also be recalled that Buell said the move up the Tennessee had been made without proper preparation and was "hazardous." Thus neither Halleck's civilian record nor his war record to the moment warrants calling him an overly cautious man.

But only when he reached Pittsburg could Halleck feel the presence of the enemy, still, however, a few miles away. Not many weeks before, McClellan, taking the field at last, had broken down at Yorktown as soon as his columns were fired upon. Having been an engineer, he began to dig. Picks, shovels, and axes were equally the implements of Halleck, and it is to his credit that his first order said nothing about fortifying; discipline and order were pronounced requisite to marching "forward to new fields of honor and glory." He talked like a good, stout-hearted infantryman; but there was, of course, no telling when the engineer in him would come to the surface.

General Frederick Steele, whose advance into eastern Arkansas had been halted, and who was now back in St. Louis, informed Halleck on the 13th that Van Dorn was reliably reported as having reached Memphis, and that Price was following. This could hardly have been a surprise, even without the intercepted and deciphered message of Beauregard; for on the 5th Halleck had told Curtis, then at Cassville, Missouri, and starting to move eastward, "The great battle of the war is to be fought on the Tennessee River. If we succeed, Price and Van Dorn will soon leave your front." But it was not easy to keep accurate information of the moves of the two elusive Confederates or of their strength, and Curtis had put their combined forces as high as 30,000 or even 40,000 men. With all the enemy troops in Arkansas seemingly going to Beauregard, while the captured dispatch revealed his request for men from Georgia, it was not strange that Halleck changed his plan to have Pope move against Fort Pillow, and instead sent him an order on the 15th to come up the Tennessee. Pope's regiments were already afloat. Leaving a small force with

Foote and the gunboats, which was to occupy Fort Pillow if it should be abandoned, he started without delay to join the main field army.[14]

"All quiet here to-night. Roads in terrible condition." So ended Scott's short dispatch of the 21st to Stanton reporting the arrival of Pope's troops at Pittsburg. As if to make it more convincing, a co-operative telegrapher added, "It has rained incessantly for four days." Stanton was in touch with all parts of the far-flung front, but he had to tell General Morgan, facing Cumberland Gap with a ninety-mile supply line "washed into deep chasms or belly-deep in mud," that he had no ordnance officer to send him. He would, however, keep the request high on the list of priorities; and he cheered the general by saying, "We have taken New Orleans, and hope soon to have Yorktown and Corinth." [15]

On the 26th Grant wrote to Mrs. C. F. Smith that her husband had died the afternoon before; though the letter was not long, it said much:

> In his death the nation has lost one of its most gallant and most able defenders. It was my fortune to have gone through West Point with the general (then captain and commander of cadets) and to have served with him in all his battles in Mexico and in this rebellion, and I can bear honest testimony to his great worth as a soldier and friend. Where an entire nation condoles with you in your bereavement no one can do so with more heartfelt grief than myself.[16]

Every post and every armed vessel throughout Halleck's great department was ordered to fire a salute for the lamented general, with flags lowered to half-mast from noon to evening. But as he waited for some of his transportation to arrive, Old Brains thought not only of tributes to fine officers; he gave heed to the stomachs of his men. He tasted their food and found it not to his liking. He ordered that a company officer inspect the food at each meal and see that it was properly cooked; general and field officers were to give the matter attention, and medical officers were to instruct in the culinary art when they found a want of knowledge. There would be fewer sick men if there were less defective cooking, said the order. Careful regulations about the use of wagons were issued; instructions for the supply of ammunition contained the admonition: "When the cartridge boxes of the men are found unfilled, the commanding officer of the company will be arrested for neglect of duty." [17]

While Halleck was preparing to advance with his army of more than 100,000 men, Mitchel with his one division was holding a front of one hundred and twenty-five miles deeper in enemy territory than anyone had previously penetrated. Communication with Buell was uncertain because the telegraph line was frequently broken, though two cavalry regiments were patrolling between Columbia and Savannah. Not having heard from his superior, Mitchel on April 17 wrote directly to the Secretary of War; but before the letter arrived, Secretary Chase, who had written to the general on the 6th (his letter seems to have been lost), showed Stanton an answering telegram of the 19th. In it Mitchel told of his operations and said: "I spared the Tennessee bridges near Stevenson in the hope I might be permitted to march on Chattanooga and Knoxville, but am now ordered to burn the bridges. I do not comprehend the order, but must obey it as early as I can. This entire line ought to be occupied, in my opinion, and yet I fear it will be abandoned." Without delay Stanton went into action; a telegram to Mitchel on the 21st expressed much interest in his operations, directed him to make daily reports, and stated that Halleck was being asked to explain the meaning of the bridge-burning order. The reply that came the next day from Halleck was directed to the "Hon. A. Lincoln": "No orders, to my knowledge, have been given to General Mitchel to destroy railroad bridges. On the contrary, he has saved some which were fired by the enemy." [18]

Buell, however, had definitely given such an order, for Mitchel began a long letter to him on the 20th, "Your order to burn the Bridgeport Bridge is received." After explaining his situation, his accomplishments, and his difficulties, he wrote: "I wish it were possible to give me force enough to strike a blow at Chattanooga. It was in hope that this might be done that I spared the Tennessee bridge." The letter reached Buell on the night of the day that Halleck telegraphed to Lincoln, and in his reply of the 23rd Buell stressed "the importance of destroying the Bridgeport Bridge" and said, "The railroad would hardly be a proper line of communication for us against Chattanooga at any rate." Apparently Buell did not want Morgan, who he said would attack Cumberland Gap very soon, to be assisted by a threat against Chattanooga; and he even told Mitchel that the force near Murfreesboro "should only be reduced when the enemy has fully developed his plans." [19] In other words, the enemy should be allowed to call the tune.

Mitchel's situation was difficult. Heavy rains and bad roads made supply from Shelbyville practically impossible. He had the railroad open from Decatur to Athens, Alabama, and engineers were trying to connect with the pike to Columbia. A delegation of citizens from Athens had told him they would raise the Federal flag when assured of adequate protection and would aid in rebuilding the bridges between their town and Columbia. But in the meantime his men had to eat; and 100,000 rations that were sent by boat from Pittsburg and unloaded in an inconvenient place near Florence were at length moved in hired wagons to the railroad, which delivered them safely. An enemy force of possibly 1,500 infantry with some cavalry had seized and was protecting the bridge at Bridgeport, but it had destroyed a bridge at Stevenson and one to the west of it. Another force of 1,000 Confederates was reported to be in Chattanooga. Mitchel himself put cavalry patrols into Stevenson and infantry at Bellefonte, fifteen miles away, to which point he maintained telegraphic communication. He was on the move day and night, and he told Stanton it was almost too much for him physically, adding, "But for the fact that I have sixteen engines, and cars in proportion, it would be madness to attempt to hold my position a single day." [20]

Mitchel kept imploring Buell to have the main army reach out and occupy Tuscumbia, saying that, if that were not done, he would have to shorten his line and fall back to the north bank of the Tennessee. As early as the 20th Halleck told Buell he thought Tuscumbia should be held as an outpost if Mitchel could withdraw its garrison in case of an attack; but he agreed with Buell in thinking Mitchel should keep his main force north of the river—which Mitchel had done from the first. Six days later Halleck turned over to Buell the complete direction of troops beyond the Tennessee, and on the 27th Mitchel reported that he had abandoned the line from Tuscumbia to Decatur, had destroyed the bridge at the latter place, and now had his right flank at Athens. No longer anxious about the small force he had had south of the river, Mitchel turned his attention toward occupying Stevenson in force with the view of securing Bridgeport. Two bridges, each three hundred feet long, had to be built. One was begun at 4:00 P.M. on the 26th; and by 4:20 the next afternoon two regiments of infantry, a company of cavalry, and one field gun had crossed. It was, Mitchel explained to Stanton, "a floating bridge, built on cotton bales captured from the enemy." [21]

Presently the builder of floating bridges learned he had been made a major general.

On the last day of April Halleck reorganized his command. The Second, Fourth, Fifth, and Sixth Divisions of Grant's old Army of the Tennessee, and the division of George H. Thomas, which had reached Savannah on April 8, were made into the right wing. Thomas, now a major general, was given the command; his own division went to Brigadier General Thomas J. McKean, while Grant's Second and Sixth Divisions were given to Brigadier Generals Thomas A. Davies and Thomas W. Sherman, respectively. McKean and Davies were West Point graduates with about thirty years' experience in civil life, while T. W. Sherman was a member of the class of 1836 who had remained in military service. Buell's Army of the Ohio, reduced to the divisions of Nelson, McCook, and Wood, became the center. Pope's Army of the Mississippi, which was camped at Hamburg and consisted of four infantry divisions and one of cavalry, became the left wing. A reserve was formed under McClernand; it consisted of his own old division, now under Brigadier General Henry M. Judah (a classmate of Grant's), and the divisions of Lew Wallace and Crittenden.[22]

Grant was made second in command, and Halleck immediately sent him a note saying that the new arrangement made it necessary for him to have his headquarters near those of the army. This seemed to indicate that Grant, with his field experience, was to be used as a real deputy commander; and there was indeed plenty to keep such an officer well employed. Grant, however, soon found himself virtually idle and made some sort of protest, only to receive a harsh letter from Halleck. Though there was truth in the latter's statement that Grant's new position recognized his seniority in a way that no other assignment would, the fact meant little when it was clear that he had in effect been shelved. He would far rather have had the command of the four divisions of his old army that remained in the right wing than occupy a position with a high-sounding name which was actually humiliating. The unhappy side of Halleck's nature was starkly revealed in his closing sentences: "For the last three months I have done everything in my power to ward off the attacks which were made upon you. If you believe me your friend you will not require explanations; if not, explanations on my part would be of little avail." [23]

Buell quickly complained of the organization which left him with only three divisions, one of which was composed almost entirely of new regiments, while Thomas, his former subordinate, had five. "You must excuse me," he wrote to Halleck, "for saying that, as it seems to me, you have saved the feelings of others very much to my injury." So far as the feelings of McClernand were concerned, Buell could have spared himself, for that general would discover that the reserve he commanded was merely a pool from which Halleck would assign divisions here and there as he saw fit; it was not a force kept in hand to deliver the final knockout blow. After Corinth was taken McClernand wrote to Halleck recounting fully his services "in the present unhappy drama" and saying he had been badly treated since in fact he had been subordinated to men he ranked. It was lawyer against lawyer, and Halleck argued the case in his reply to the offended McClernand, but without the harshness he had shown toward Grant.[24]

May came in clear and pleasant; but messages from Scott warned Washington that the enemy was concentrating heavy forces, and a postscript said, "The evidences are that Beauregard will fight at Corinth." Then Halleck took over; and a telegram he sent on the 3rd, which was in the Capital at 2:00 P.M., must have fairly put Stanton on the edge of his chair in nervous expectancy and suspense: "I leave here to-morrow morning, and our army will be before Corinth to-morrow night. There may be no telegraphic communication for the next two or three days." [25]

Pope did indeed make good progress on the 4th and reported at nightfall that he was occupying a strong position one and one-half miles from Farmington, with a bad creek in his front and an impenetrable jungle and swamp on his left. But he was a little shaky about his other flank: "I hope Buell's force will keep pace on our right." Buell, however, was sounding a warning and holding back: "We have now reached that proximity to the enemy that our movements should be conducted with the greatest caution and combined methods. I shall therefore make no further advance until I receive your orders." Pope thereupon received the instruction: "Don't advance your main body at present; we must wait till Buell gets up." Thomas got the right wing forward until three divisions were on a line running somewhere near Monterey, with W. T. Sherman on the right. In his report the wing commander said, "General Sherman's right flank being much exposed, was intrenched immediately." [26]

All in all, it was quite a day in the military experience of Henry Halleck, as April 4 had been for McClellan.

Washington, which must have been waiting for word that Halleck's guns had opened on Corinth, received a dreary telegram sent by Scott on the 5th from Monterey: "Heavy rains for the last twenty hours. Roads bad. Movement progressing slowly. Enemy still concentrating forces at Corinth." But there was a cheerful touch: Sherman's nomination for promotion "nobly gained upon the field of Shiloh" was giving "great satisfaction." Watching the ominous downpour, Sherman himself took up his fluent pen and wrote a circular that said: "Every ounce of food and forage must be regarded as precious as diamonds. Roads will be impassable and our bridges swept away." [27]

The next day the sky had cleared but the roads were still deep with mud and water. A dispatch had come from Washington about the taking of Yorktown. But new deserters told of the strong intrenchments at Corinth and of the arrival of additional troops. Beauregard was certain, said the ex-Confederates, that he could repulse any attack. Such was the gloomy word that Halleck passed on to Stanton in a message ending, "This country is almost a wilderness and very difficult to operate in." Assistant Secretary Scott was no more cheering. By using the railroads and drawing only on New Orleans, Mobile, Memphis, Fort Pillow, and intermediate points, he said, Beauregard could add 60,000 men to the force he had had ten days before; he raised the question of sending 40,000 to 50,000 men from the East and added impressively, "I submit the case as now understood by all parties here." Halleck, he explained, would continue to advance and "in a few days invest Corinth, then be governed by circumstances." Just who was included in "all parties here" cannot be said; but Buell at least seemed disturbed, for presently he reported to Halleck, "The ground everywhere is intersected by creeks and marsh bottoms, over which corduroy roads have to be made, forming perfect defiles." Defiles have an evil name in military circles; holding the specter of them in front of a commander who was already disturbed was a good way to slow him down. A little more encouraging was Pope's brave report from the left: "I am not likely to be taken at a disadvantage and trust you will not be uneasy about us." [28]

In a leisurely way the forward movement continued, with intrenchments thrown up after each advance, a procedure that Buell protested against a little as not being needed in the center. On the 9th Pope, who was somewhat exposed near Farmington, was sharply attacked. His covering force was driven in; but his main line held, and the enemy retired to his works. "Weather clear and very hot," said Scott in reporting the affair to Washington. On the 17th Sherman took a position at some cost but found his left exposed because of Buell's failure to advance. He held on, and rather sharp notes went from Halleck to the commander of the center, who pleaded misunderstanding of orders. On the 23rd Scott departed, to be back in civil life within a few days. His last dispatch, sent the day before, reported the Tennessee River was getting low. This could give the High Command concern about the future supply of the army, at the very time when Governor Morton of Indiana, visiting his troops at the front, telegraphed that Halleck's command had been greatly reduced by sickness. "In the opinion of many officers our forces are at present outnumbered," said the governor. It was fearful, he said, to contemplate the consequences of a defeat at Corinth and he earnestly asked that ten more regiments, if possible, be sent up the Tennessee without delay. The reply was written by Lincoln to Halleck the day after Stonewall Jackson's unexpected attack at Front Royal, when the Capital was still uncertain about the fate of General Banks. It ended: "My dear general, I feel justified to rely very much on you. I believe you and the brave officers and men with you will get the victory at Corinth." [29]

On the 23rd Beauregard again made aggressive moves but was unable to strike any of the Federal forces in an exposed position. On the 28th Sherman, supported by Hurlbut and to a less extent by Davies and Judah, made an advance that brought the Federal right within a mile of the enemy's main line. Wrote Thomas in his report: "Every inch of ground was obstinately contested until we had gained our position, and soon after a strong effort was made by the enemy to drive us from it, which was met by our men with so much coolness and determination that it terminated in a complete withdrawal from our immediate front." [30]

Since Pope by this time was in advance of Farmington and Buell was up in the center, the army after four weeks was where Halleck had rashly asserted it would be in a single day. Sherman later called the movement "a magnificent drill, as it served for the instruction of our men in guard and picket duty, and in habituating them to outdoor life"; and Conger has pointed out that persons who have criticized Grant severely for not intrenching at Pittsburg have often ridiculed Halleck for his excessive digging. But certainly there was nothing bold or interesting about the advance, except occasionally on the left; and on May 9, the day after Buell had cautioned about the defiles, Halleck actually appealed to Thomas Scott to restrain the commander of the left wing: "Don't let Pope go too far ahead; it is dangerous and effects no good." [31]

Pope seems also to have been responsible for a final incident that gave some color to the slow, methodical movement. It has added interest because of an officer who had an important part in it. Philip H. Sheridan returned to St. Louis from a horse-purchasing expedition just after Halleck had left; and Captain Kelton, who was winding up matters there, yielded to Sheridan's eager wish for active service by sending him up the Tennessee to report to Halleck. Grant may not have been especially impressed with the diminutive officer who was sent to him on April 18 to repair the road to his headquarters —just another captain, he may have thought. But the Ohio graduate of the West Point class of 1853 was very army-wise for his years, for he had had good service in the Northwest before proving his efficiency as quartermaster for Curtis. In addition to helping with some engineering work, Sheridan became a camp manager or housekeeper for Halleck, who knew little about living in the field and appreciated the order and efficiency that soon manifested themselves. The fresh beef that came to the headquarters table after Sheridan took on the duties of commissary of subsistence may have been responsible for some of Halleck's moments of good humor. On the morning of April 26 a Michigan captain brought Sheridan a telegraphic order from Governor Blair making him colonel of the Second Michigan Cavalry, a regiment run down by sickness and split into factions. Halleck at first said that War Department approval must be secured before he would recognize the order; but Sheridan persuaded him to issue an order that relieved him from duty at headquarters and started him on his upward rise.[32] When a high-ranking major general gives up a resourceful, thirty-year-old headquarters mess officer, his heart is really in the cause.

The next evening, after he had settled his property accounts, Sheridan went to Farmington. With his infantry blouse adorned with a pair of well worn eagles given him by General Gordon Granger, and a haversack with coffee, sugar, bacon, and hard bread, he did what would thrill any soldier—rode to the headquarters of Colonel Washington Elliott and reported his regiment ready for duty. Then as midnight came, Elliott's own Second Iowa Cavalry and the Second Michigan set out together to cut the railroad south of Corinth in accordance with Pope's order.

The enemy position at Corinth was a strong one. To the east of the town the Confederate works ran along a ridge, in front of which flowed two parallel streams less than a mile apart. After uniting, the combined waters turned westward and gave protection on the south. Only to the north of the town did the fortified ridge lack a protecting creek in its front. While there were no works to the west, it was only four miles to the Tuscumbia River, into which flowed some swampy streams.

Beauregard, in spite of the fact that his lines were well laid out and strong, issued preliminary orders as early as May 9 for retirement; but he continued to send "deserters" with stories of his increasing strength and his firm intention to defend Corinth. Along with the frauds there were of course genuine cases, and the man who informed Pope that the enemy had about a hundred regiments was probably telling something very near the truth. It was, however, not until the 26th, following a conference the day before at which Hardee had presented a written "estimate of the situation," that the final preparations for removal began. The orders were detailed and careful, with elaborate provisions to cause the Federals to believe that instead of being abandoned the town was being newly reenforced. Quaker guns, whose efficacy Beauregard had learned while in the East, took the place of real ones; a single band played here and there along the front; a bugler or two blew loudly at different places. Finally it was directed, "Whenever the railroad engine whistles during the night near the intrenchments the troops in the vicinity will cheer repeatedly, as though re-enforcements had been received." It was a clever ruse, for on May 13 Scott had reported to Stanton that the officer in charge of advance pickets stated that trains arriving the night before in Corinth had been greeted with cheers, and he said, "The enemy are concentrating a powerful army." [33]

Everything did not work perfectly, of course, and Bragg, in charge of the railroad station, inserted a characteristic wail in a note to Beauregard on the 29th: "I find trunks enough here to load all trains for a day. They are being piled for burning and great is the consternation." But the sick and wounded were successfully evacuated, as well as the heavy guns and much in the way of valuable stores. During the night of May 29–30 the rest of Beauregard's army of some 53,000 effectives out of an aggregate present of 75,000 marched away.[34]

The picture within the Federal lines is interesting. At 10:00 A.M. of the 29th Pope had opened his heavy guns on the enemy works, and during the day Sherman pushed a heavy battery to within a thousand yards on the right.[35] Then came the night and the noises from across no man's land. Pope, who on May 6 and 7 had reported that the enemy was evacuating, and had sent in evidence of such a move on the 27th, was completely deceived. At 1:20 A.M. he telegraphed Halleck:

The enemy is re-enforcing heavily, by trains, in my front and on my left. The cars are running constantly, and the cheering is immense every time they unload in front of me. I have no doubt, from all appearances, that I shall be attacked in heavy force at daylight.[36]

Ten minutes later Halleck told Buell: "There is every appearance that Pope will be attacked this morning. Be prepared to re-enforce him, if necessary." As dawn came Sherman saw dense smoke in Corinth and queried headquarters as to what it meant. Halleck could not tell, but he spoke of the telegram from Pope and said, "It is the impression that Corinth is to be given up, and a stand made in the angle between the railroads." At six o'clock a dispatch from Pope cleared everything up:

All very quiet since 4 o'clock. Twenty-six trains left during the night. A succession of loud explosions, followed by dense black smoke in clouds. Everything indicates evacuation and retreat. I am pushing forward my skirmishers in several directions toward Corinth. Will telegraph you again in a few minutes.

Though at first deluded by the lusty cheering, John Pope was not too long in divining the truth; and he was as good as his word in the matter of telegraphing again, for at 7:15 he reported:

I am in possession of the enemy's intrenched position, an embrasured work of seven guns. Four regiments are feeling their way into Corinth, and are now within three-quarters of a mile of the town. The whole country here seems to be fortified.[37]

The three dispatches that Halleck sent to Stanton on the 30th showed no great elation, but perhaps disappointment or even chagrin, masked by the inference that Beauregard had acted unwisely. While he could not himself have been in the deserted town—deserted by civilians as well as the military—he reported the enemy's positions as "exceedingly strong," and said, "He cannot occupy stronger positions." After speaking of the destroyed property, equipment left by "flying troops," and prisoners and deserters estimated by Pope to number 2,000, he commented: "General Beauregard evidently distrusts his army, or he would have defended so strong a position. His troops are generally much discouraged and demoralized. In all their engagements the last days their resistance has been weak." [38]

Halleck was now to pay for his harsh treatment of correspondents, whom he had classified as "unauthorized hangers-on" and had virtually barred from his army. A dispatch to the *Chicago Tribune* from Pittsburg Landing on the 30th recited certain facts about the evacuation and continued: "General Halleck has thus achieved one of the most barren triumphs of the war. In fact, it is tantamount to a defeat." A reporter for the *Cincinnati Commercial,* under a Corinth date line, played up the skillful deceptions of the enemy and said that in the evacuation "Beauregard had achieved another triumph." [39] Neither reporter took pains to note that it was within Beauregard's power to withdraw any time he wished to, though perhaps not with so much of his equipment and supplies. Sherman's view, influenced doubtless by the high regard in which he held Halleck, was certainly different from that of the reporters. In an undesirably long order to his troops issued on the 31st he said:

It is a victory as brilliant and important as any recorded in history, and every officer and soldier who has lent his aid has just reason to be proud of his part. No amount of sophistry or words from the leaders of the rebellion can succeed in giving the evacuation of Corinth under the circumstances any other title than that of a signal defeat, more humiliating to them and to their cause than if we had entered the place over the dead and mangled bodies of their soldiers.[40]

It is safe to say that many of Sherman's officers and men thought their commander was being a little too emphatic; but the questions that Jefferson Davis presently sent for Beauregard to answer showed clearly that he thought a major loss had been suffered by the Confederates, even though a field army had been saved. Copies of the dispatches of the two Northern correspondents who had said that Halleck had achieved little if anything were made a part of Beauregard's reply to the Richmond President. Grant's statement in his *Memoirs* that he was satisfied that Corinth could have been captured in a two days' campaign commenced promptly on the arrival of reenforcements after the battle of Shiloh, very definitely expressed his view at the time of writing, rather than at the time in question.[41] But one can say with confidence that, with his different temperament and his greater field experience, Grant would not have moved against Corinth in the way that Halleck did.

Though Halleck had been completely deceived, was not a pursuit possible? The Federals were well in hand and could take the road promptly, though not with cooked rations in their haversacks. The order that went without delay to the commanders of the wings and the center ended, however, very weakly: "General Pope, with his reenforcements from the right wing, will proceed to feel the enemy on the left." A dispatch to Washington the next day stated that the main body of the Confederates had headed for Okolona, a town sixty-seven miles away, which was not a bad guess, seeing that Beauregard stopped presently at Tupelo, fifty miles away. Pope, Halleck said, was following with 50,000 men; but it was not intended to have him go far, for the enemy had the railroad. The next day, when Halleck learned of the damage done to the railroad at Booneville and of the destruction of a train full of arms and ammunition by the cavalry expedition, he became more enthusiastic and telegraphed Pope: "Colonel Elliott's operation was splendid, and he shall be rewarded. Press the enemy as hard as you deem it safe and advisable. . . . If you want any re-enforcements, say so, and you shall have them." A second dispatch told Pope that if he pressed vigorously he might demoralize the enemy greatly and make some captures.[42]

Close pursuit was by no means easy, for some of the roads ran through swamps, and bridges had been destroyed; supply became difficult, and Pope himself fell sick and stopped at Danville, only ten miles from Corinth. A telegraph line was run to him so that he could keep Halleck constantly informed as news came from his subordinates. For the purposes of control his army had already been divided into wings. Brigadier General William S. Rosecrans, whose work in West Virginia had been notable, and who had been ordered to the West in mid-May, had the right wing, while Schuyler Hamilton had the left. A pursuit, however, should be directed from the field, and not from a sickbed.

Halleck himself was giving major attention to opening up railroad communications, which was proper, for the Tennessee River was falling, and its use for supply might soon be difficult. Buell was sending troops eastward to rebuild bridges and try to connect with Mitchel; Sherman was working to get the railroad to Memphis in condition; McClernand was rebuilding bridges on the line to Columbus, Kentucky, which Halleck saw as his main supply route. The multitude of streams gave the enemy the chance to hamper the Federals; and without hesitation he destroyed cotton, supplies, and equipment in addition to bridges. Though Halleck had no railroad maintenance units such as an army now has, there were many mechanics in the Union army; and they were put to repairing locomotives and rebuilding cars. Foreseeing the future, Thomas Scott, an expert railroader, had described by telegraph a railroad organization that should be made ready by June 1; Halleck followed up by asking that cars and locomotives be sent to Columbus.[43]

On June 2 Pope telegraphed that he would attack the enemy at Baldwyn, a place where roads united thirty miles from Corinth, but he did not think it advisable to push the pursuit farther on account of the great difficulty of supply. There was an actual touch of vigor in Halleck's reply the next day: "Push on your forces to Baldwyn and ascertain position and force of the enemy. Keep me advised." Pope, putting together reports from various commanders, and with his optimistic turn of mind stimulated by the captures at Island No. 10, ended a dispatch to Halleck: "The roads for miles are full of stragglers from the enemy, who are coming in in squads. Not less than 10,000 are scattered about, who will come in within a day or two." It was certainly counting chickens before they were hatched, and that on a colossal scale. Stanton likewise was optimistic and terminated a message that congratulated Halleck and told him of McClellan's repulse of Joe Johnston's attack at Fair Oaks, with the sentence,

"He is not yet in Richmond, but we hope he soon will be." [44]

If Halleck had not changed the telegram that McClellan had sent him in late January about the deserter's story, and told Grant that Beauregard was actually on the way west with fifteen regiments, one might think that he now sought merely to keep ahead of the eastern general, who seemed about to march into Richmond. Again he turned a mere forecast into an actuality and telegraphed Stanton that Pope reported taking 10,000 prisoners and deserters, and that thousands of the enemy were throwing away their arms. This naturally elated the Secretary, who replied the same day (June 4): "Your glorious dispatch has just been received, and I have sent it into every State. The whole land will soon ring with applause at the achievement of your gallant army and its able and victorious commander." [45]

The Confederates did not obligingly come in as Pope had predicted; but the general himself recovered from his illness and on the evening of the 4th was at Booneville, with worse swamps and roads in his rear than he had previously encountered. He reported that the enemy was in position at Baldwyn, but said he thought it uncertain whether Beauregard would stand for a battle. The Confederates were indeed where Pope said, and an order issued the next morning placed Bragg, Polk, and Hardee in line of battle with Breckinridge behind one flank and Van Dorn behind the other. "We will hold our present positions," said the directive, "and prepare vigorously for the move to Tupelo. No time is to be lost. In the mean time our front must be well protected." Polk was instructed to send one of his best brigades to the front to drive back Federal parties and hold an important road junction. An order to Van Dorn spoke of the possibility of assuming the offensive against the pursuing Unionists, but took the precaution of directing him, in case of further retirement, to take along all civilians, whether friends or not, who might give information to the enemy. It was not, however, to be a case of permanent resettling, for the order said, "Whenever the danger is past, they can be allowed to return to their homes." [46]

The covering operations of the enemy made it appear that he might stand and fight, and so Pope suggested that two more divisions be advanced in his direction. With them Halleck sent Buell, with explicit instructions to take the general command since he was senior to Pope—standing just above him in the March 21 list of major generals. "I am satisfied that the enemy will retreat in a day or two,

which will satisfy us about as well as if he were defeated in a battle,"
was the strange ending of a note that Halleck sent Buell on the 6th,
in which he said he wished no risk to be run, as the rest of the army
was distant and occupied. Buell at Booneville reported that a reconnaissance the night before revealed the enemy's pickets just where
they had been, but said reassuringly, "I shall not run any improper
risk." During the night of June 7–8 he prepared a rather comprehensive order for an advance at 5:00 A.M.; but word came of the
enemy's retreat, which, said Buell, "superseded the necessity of the
movement." At midnight on the 8th Pope reported that the battalion
of cavalry he had sent toward Baldwyn in the morning had just returned, having passed through and gone three miles beyond; a regiment sent out at sunset was to go to Guntown, ten miles south of
Baldwyn.[47]

In accordance with a careful order issued at 5:00 P.M. of the 6th
Beauregard had begun his retreat at 3:00 A.M. of the 7th, Hardee's
corps, the last to withdraw, being directed to take up the march at
4:00 P.M. There must have been some apprehension of further pursuit, for the order ended, "All finger-boards and mile-posts should be
taken down by the cavalry of the rear guards." By the 10th Beauregard's army of 60,235, of whom 45,365 were classed as effectives—
that is, men ready to stand in an actual line of battle—was in camp
at Tupelo. Three days later he would be writing to the Confederate
Adjutant General a report claiming that his evacuation of Corinth
had foiled the Federal plan of cutting his supply railroads behind
him. He had, he said, "confidently anticipated an opportunity for
resumption of the offensive with chances for signal success." Ten
days later he would pick up his pen again to answer the questions
asked by President Davis, which were brought to him by no less a
courier than the son of Sidney Johnston.[48]

On June 9 Halleck ordered Pope to fall back to some suitable
position between Corinth and Baldwyn where good water could be
procured, keeping outposts in Baldwyn and perhaps a picket at Guntown. Buell was ordered eastward with four divisions to make a
junction with Mitchel. Sherman, now a major general, was pushed
farther toward Memphis with his own division and that of Hurlbut;
his mission was to repair not only destroyed bridges but the wrecked
economy: "Assure all country people that they will be permitted to
take their cotton freely to market and that the ordinary channels of

trade will be immediately reopened." Washington was informed that the enemy had fallen back to Saltillo, fifty miles from Corinth by rail and nearly seventy by road; and Halleck reported the statement of an Englishman who had been in the Confederate commissary that they had had 120,000 men at Corinth but could not now muster over 80,000.[49]

With the issuance the next day of an order returning Thomas to his division and restoring Grant to the command of his army, the Campaign of Corinth came to an end. Halleck's fundamental error lay in the neglect of the proven ability and aggressiveness of his second in command. When Pope fell sick Grant should have been sent to command the pursuing forces, unhampered of course by instructions except to destroy as much of the enemy as he could. What might have been accomplished, no one can say; but it would have saved the sending of the slow and cautious Buell to conduct the last gesture of shooing the enemy away. It is interesting that Sheridan got as far as Guntown and later commented upon what was lacking to make a pursuit that might have netted some results.[50] On June 9, 1862, Sheridan, a regimental commander for just two weeks, could not have foreseen that near the end of the war he would have the lead in another pursuit and would write to Grant, "I wish you were here yourself."

On June 6 the Forty-third and the Forty-seventh Indiana, the two regiments that Pope had left with Foote, went ashore at Memphis and took possession of the town. Foote had been relieved on May 9 by Flag Officer Charles H. Davis because of his Fort Donelson wound; and from the next day there had been lively action on the great river. At that time the gunboats were anchored five miles above Fort Pillow, while one of the mortar boats, screened by a point of land, was engaged in throwing periodically a large, discommoding shell into the Confederate work. Standing guard over the engineless craft was the *Cincinnati,* tied up to a tree, with steam down. Early on the morning of the 10th she was attacked by six Confederate vessels which took her completely by surprise. Though her guns did considerable damage she was rammed and sunk—fortunately in shallow water. Before the action was over the remaining Federal boats were able to get steam up sufficiently to enter the fight; but victory in the battle of Plum Run Bend—and it was a real fleet action—was definitely with the Confederates. Well pleased with the result, the successful commander wrote to Beauregard that, if he could get sufficient fuel and the enemy force was not greatly increased, "they will never penetrate farther down the Mississippi." [51]

It was the second time the Confederates had given the United States Navy a surprise, having done so the previous October in a defeat at the head of the passes that lead to the river's mouths.[52] That humiliation had been well atoned for by Farragut's brilliant action against the forts below New Orleans and the capture of the key city in late April. And soon the disgrace of Plum Run Bend was wiped out, though with Ellet's army rams playing a major part.

On June 5, the day after Fort Pillow and Fort Randolph, nearer to Memphis, were abandoned, Davis anchored his five remaining gunboats a little above the city, with four of the new rams farther up the river. At daybreak he dropped down the stream and discovered eight enemy craft, gunboats and rams, lying close in front of the city. Though the Confederate rams, unlike Ellet's, carried guns, they had only twenty-eight guns against sixty-eight on the Federal vessels. This did not hold them back, and after opening fire they moved slowly to meet the attackers. The battle had gone on at a distance for some twenty minutes, when two Federal rams, the *Queen of the West* under the command of Colonel Ellet himself, and the *Monarch* commanded by his brother, dashed out from the Arkansas shore, passed in front of Davis's flotilla, and at full speed made for the enemy vessels. Then things began to happen in earnest. For an hour and a half the battle lasted in front of thousands of spectators, who beheld a far greater spectacle than the inhabitants of Charleston had witnessed when Beauregard's guns hammered Fort Sumter into submission. But this time there were no shouts of jubilation, for the battle ended with all the Confederate boats sunk, captured, or grounded, save the *Van Dorn,* which escaped. The only casualty on the Federal side was Colonel Ellet, who received a revolver shot in the leg, not thought serious at the time, but from which he died within a fortnight. It was the colonel's son, who, with three others, went ashore with a flag of truce and demanded the surrender of the city. There being no option, the mayor yielded; and young Ellet took down the Confederate flag from above the post office, and raised a Union flag, such as had flown there only a year before.[53]

Meanwhile Mitchel, with his 9,000 men and his sixteen active locomotives, had been maintaining his long front in northern Alabama, with such displays of aggressiveness as he found possible. On May 1 he reported to Stanton that he had personally headed an expedition the day before against Bridgeport, from which the enemy had recently made an attack against one of his brigades. By using some deception he succeeded in placing troops in position on a wooded hill within five hundred yards of the works the enemy had constructed to defend the west end of the great bridge. At the first volley the Confederate guards ran; and their efforts to blow the bridge failed. Volunteers who answered Mitchel's call put out a fire at the far end of the main span; but they were unable to save the span beyond, which led to the left bank of the Tennessee. "It is of small moment," said Mitchel, "its length being only 450 feet." Such enterprise as he had shown never went long uncommended, and the same day Stanton sent him a telegram that began, "Your spirited operations afford great satisfaction to the President." [54]

Although Mitchel indicated that his campaign was over, some of his troops crossed the river at Bridgeport on May 1 and advanced twelve miles in the direction of Chattanooga. Some stores were captured as well as a Southern mail, and Mitchel reported that panic prevailed in the town, which he said was garrisoned by not more than 2,000 troops. Another expedition penetrated to Jasper, ten miles north of Bridgeport and brought back word of strong Union sentiment. The message informing Washington of these reconnaissances ended, "As there is no [hope] of an immediate advance upon Chattanooga, I will now contract my line." [55]

Toward the west Mitchel was having trouble. Two weeks previously he had told Buell that the Confederates, unable to subsist their cavalry at Corinth, would send it into Tennessee to conduct guerrilla warfare; he had urged that Tuscumbia be occupied in sufficient force by the main army at Pittsburg to prevent or hamper such moves, and he had "begged" Brigadier General James S. Negley at Columbia to put a regiment at Pulaski, only to have the request disapproved by Buell. While Mitchel was busy at Bridgeport, Colonel John H. Morgan, who had already harassed the Federals in his native Kentucky, and Colonel John S. Scott, crossed the Tennessee at Florence, the latter striking at Athens with some 200 men, the former at Pulaski with 400. Scott was easily turned back; but Morgan captured 15 officers and 250 enlisted men at Pulaski, mostly convalescents returning to the army. Among the officers was Mitchel's son, a prize balanced by Morgan's brother, a first lieutenant, who was in Mitchel's hands. "I believe this is the first instance in the history of war where a general has been deprived of his own lines of supply and communication," said Mitchel to the War Secretary. Whether his history was correct or not, he had a point, which seems to have occurred to Buell also, for three days later Colonel Fry, Buell's chief of staff, informed Mitchel that in the future he would have command of all troops on the railroads to both Decatur and Stevenson. But Fry gave a strong hint that there should be no thought of offensive action: "As matters now stand you can do nothing more than render secure Nashville and Middle Tennessee." [56]

Guerrilla warfare increased, and Mitchel had difficulty keeping the many bridges on his railroads from being destroyed. But he apparently continued to harbor offensive aspirations until he returned on the evening of May 27 from a conference with the officers at Nashville. The next day he requested assignment to the Army of the Potomac, saying, "My advance beyond the Tennessee River seems impossible, and others are here abundantly qualified to do all that is required." Stanton replied that although the President would be glad to have Mitchel on the Potomac he did not think it advisable to remove him from a command where he had rendered such distinguished service, and where his abilities could not be replaced.[57]

Having been thus assured of the continued confidence of Washington, Mitchel presently sent Negley toward Chattanooga, to be joined in the vicinity of Jasper by a supporting column from Stevenson. This gave a force of about 6,000 infantry, cavalry, and artillery, with which Mitchel intended to drive back enemy troops that he had heard had crossed the river near Chattanooga for the purpose of seizing Winchester. Negley surprised and routed the Confederates, their commander, Brigadier General John Adams, escaping without sword, hat, or horse. While Unionists turned out to meet Negley along the road with demonstrations of their joy, alarm spread among the Confederates beyond the Tennessee. On June 6 General Kirby Smith at Knoxville telegraphed the governor of Georgia that the evacuation of Chattanooga seemed to be inevitable, adding that General Leadbetter, if unable to hold the town, was to retire to Knoxville. The possibility of even giving up all East Tennessee was suggested in a dispatch to an officer at Clinton, who was cautioned, "You will, of course, keep this communication strictly to yourself." [58]

On the afternoon of the 7th Negley reached the Tennessee opposite Chattanooga and shelled the enemy batteries in position across the river for three hours. Mitchel had authorized him to take the town if he deemed it prudent; and, though he did not think it "very difficult or hazardous" to do so, he reported the next morning that it was almost impossible to construct enough pontoons to cross the river in force. He put the enemy garrison at 3,000 men and ten guns, but spoke in a note a few days later as if the Confederates had not exhibited much stamina under his shelling. The question of supply disturbed Negley, and after shelling the town and the rifle pits for another six hours he withdrew, feeling that he had accomplished his mission. With him he took some eighty prisoners, a drove of beef cattle, and a number of horses intended for the Confederate army, as well as a special present for Andrew Johnson, the military governor of the state, in the shape of the principal prosecutors of the Unionists in the vicinity.[59]

When the echo of Negley's guns died out the quiet of nature descended upon Chattanooga, which was not to be disturbed again by the sound of battle for many months. But Mitchel had clearly won the respect of Kirby Smith, who described him as "an energetic commander"—a compliment from an enemy that is to be prized. However, Smith thought that past success might lead Mitchel to some "daring and hazardous undertaking"; and he told Leadbetter to be watchful for some misstep by his adversary while at the same time he gave "vigilant and unremitting attention to every movement" that Mitchel made. Leaving a few boats near Chattanooga to tempt the Yankees into a crossing would have been more in accord with such an admonition than the order Smith issued on June 6 to send a steamer up the river to burn or otherwise destroy all craft between Chattanooga and Kingston.[60]

As Negley retired northwestward over the poor mountain roads word came to Mitchel from the officer commanding at Murfreesboro that the enemy was threatening that place. Although the force for such a threat must have come very suddenly into being, Mitchel at first credited its existence, and even expressed to Buell the conviction that the enemy would follow Negley from Chattanooga; but on the tenth he informed Buell, "From later intelligence I am led to believe that the large force reported does not exist." There were, however, clear indications of increased hostile activity, and he urged that an adequate force should promptly occupy Middle Tennessee and northern Alabama, saying, "Since the fall of Corinth we surely have forces sufficient." [61] Already Halleck had ordered Buell's road-hardened divisions to turn their faces eastward.

A year later Joseph Holt, Judge Advocate General of the Army, published a report upon the Andrews railroad raid in which he said, "The expedition itself, in the daring of its conception, had the wildness of a romance, while in the gigantic and overwhelming results which it sought, and was likely to accomplish, it was absolutely sublime." He quoted from an editorial in the *Southern Confederacy* which said, "The mind and heart shrink back appalled at the bare contemplation of the awful consequences which would have followed the success of this one act." In the meantime Mitchel had died; and Buell, who had been removed from active command and was at Saratoga, New York, wrote to the Adjutant General that the enterprise, which Holt credited to Mitchel, had been "set on foot" by himself. Years later Fry, who had been Buell's chief of staff, set the matter right by distinguishing between the first and second attempts by Andrews. However, he expressed the view that, even if the bridges south of Chattanooga had been burned, Mitchel "would not have taken, certainly would not have held Chattanooga"; and he even suggested that Mitchel's threats against the town were unfortunate because they attracted the attention of the enemy to it—a weak contention indeed, for the Confederates themselves soon launched an offensive through the place whose virtues they well understood. [62]

Chattanooga was without question a hard place to capture, for the river and the mountains conspired to defend it; when taken, it could be difficult to supply from the north, as the Union army would discover later. But soon after the Andrews raid Morgan telegraphed from before Cumberland Gap, "East Tennessee in an uproar." If at that moment Chattanooga had had no rail connection with Atlanta and the seaboard, and especially if Mitchel had been given command over Negley, there would have been possibilities for a bold commander. Neither Buell nor Fry could understand Mitchel, who had too much of a spirit of blitzkrieg. One cannot imagine Buell moving boldly into Huntsville as Mitchel did after hearing, the night before, that 5,000 enemy troops had arrived there; [63] nor can one picture him moving east on a railroad train without previous reconnaissance and in the face of a possible ambush.

What next to do—that was Halleck's problem. When Corinth fell he had an army of 120,000 present for duty out of an aggregate present of 150,000; and it is a temptation to make use of exact knowledge about the enemy that he did not have and neglect realities that he had to face and then say what he should have done.

Halleck was deep in enemy territory, and the Southerners were beginning to develop a harassing warfare calculated to plague even a more experienced commander. At the same time they were applying their new conscription policy in a thorough manner. Pope informed Halleck that the enemy in falling back carried everything away for miles around, leaving even well-to-do families nearly destitute of food, while all males were "forced into the army." Presently Grant, habitually cautious about rumors, reported that the "whole State of Mississippi, capable of bearing arms," seemed to be entering the army. Halleck himself would say that the surrender of any territory which the Federals had occupied would mean the "certain death" of every Union man therein—a very grim and controlling thought for a commander. Perhaps the generals were mistaken, but that is what they believed. A hot summer was approaching, and in that day the army did not have summer uniforms; men sweltered in clothes made for winter wear. A year later, Grant, well seasoned then by hard field service and commanding a toughened army, would contemplate a summer campaign with some dismay, and would speak of the difficulty of finding water for a marching army, as well as of the dust and heat to be encountered. [64]

Halleck's thinking was clearly set forth in a long dispatch to Stanton on June 25, in which he put down the "sanitary condition" of his command as his controlling consideration. Since the capture of Corinth the health of the army had been comparatively good, but, said he: "The question now arises, can it be kept so during the summer? Or, in other words, can we carry on any summer campaign without having a large proportion of our men on the sick list?" Following the enemy into the swamps of Mississippi would result, he claimed, in disease. But he was not for complete inaction and put the case against it clearly: "And yet to lie still, doing nothing, will not be satisfactory to the country nor conducive to the health of the army." He then outlined his program. Pope was in observation south of Corinth "on high timbered ridges in the vicinity of clear streams and springs of water." Grant's army had been occupied mainly along the railroads to Memphis and to Columbus, "and driving guerrilla parties out of West Tennessee." When this work was completed he was to take position where he could guard the railroads and at the same time be "on a plateau which is said to be the most healthy part of Tennessee." Some reenforcements had been sent to Curtis for his operations in Arkansas, and more would follow. Buell's army was "moving east through a healthy region via Decatur, Huntsville, and Stevenson to Chattanooga and East Tennessee." There were possibilities beyond Chattanooga and "should he be able to penetrate into Georgia as far as Atlanta he will still be in a dry and mountainous country." The entire plan he told the Secretary was based on consultation with medical officers and the assumption that the enemy would conduct no active operations during the summer.[65]

Consultation with medical officers was certainly proper; but Halleck should also have advised with Grant and Pope, the two among his army commanders who had fine accomplishments to their credit and who knew much about the endurance of soldiers. In spite of what he said against lying still, that was virtually the program he mapped out for those two generals, except for a possibility presently mentioned. In view of what was to take place, Halleck's basic assumption that the enemy would remain inactive looks a little naïve; and one must condemn a program that surrenders the initiative to the foe unless there is no alternative. (However, since Halleck's time great general staffs have gambled in more crucial ways than he upon the enemy's not taking the offensive.) Within a short time, as will be seen, Halleck wrote to Sherman that he knew how to complete the campaign in the West. He did not divulge the plan, so that his ideas cannot be appraised; but there is no reason to doubt that he had given thought to the future. Naturally what Grant wrote in his *Memoirs* about the possibilities that were open in June, 1862, carries considerable weight.[66] But his intimation that 80,000 men from the great army that compelled the evacuation of Corinth might have moved against Vicksburg or some point in the interior of Mississippi ignores the fact that when he tried such an operation some months later, he found his communications cut, saw a great depot of supplies go up in flames, and had to abandon a move on which much effort had been expended.

It has generally been asserted that that highly important position could have been taken in the early summer of 1862 if the full Federal strength had been properly and opportunely employed. Situated on a high bluff at a bend in the Mississippi, with swampy land across the river, and the bayous and lagoons of the Yazoo River hampering access from the north, Vicksburg was equaled by few places in defensive virtues. So long as Vicksburg was held, the Confederates could maintain contact with the three states west of the river, upon which they depended extensively for supplies. In April the fortification of the place began to be pushed, and a move against it by Farragut in late May was turned back without much trouble, though some of the lighter Federal vessels remained in the vicinity for blockade purposes. Just a few days before Halleck set down his program, an additional force of 15,000 men was ordered by the Confederates to the defense of Vicksburg; and, on the day he wrote, Farragut on explicit orders from Secretary Welles, and very much against his own inclination, appeared a second time before the city, this time with a brigade of 3,200 troops from New Orleans.[67]

Halleck did not ignore Vicksburg, although it can be argued that his treatment of the possibility of an immediate move against the stronghold was inadequate. He wrote:

In this arrangement I have not provided for a movement on Vicksburg. It is hoped that the two flotillas [Farragut's blue-water ships and Davis's gunboats] united will be able to reduce the place. If not, it will probably be necessary to fit out an expedition from the army.

Here was more wishful thinking. Halleck must have had Grant's army in mind when he intimated taking over if the sailors failed. But he was ignoring the important element of time, and that at a moment when it might have been suspected that time was of the essence. Halleck, however, did not regard his proposals as flawless, for his letter ended: "If the War Department has any suggestions or instructions to give in the matter under consideration I shall be most happy to receive them." Actually on the 23rd Stanton had sent him a short telegram about a "cut-off" move in the rear of Vicksburg that General Butler, who was in command of the troops occupying New Orleans, had just suggested as a possibility, but which

Stanton thought Butler might not be able to carry out on account of insufficiency of men. It was all very vague, and the message did not reach Halleck until five days after it was sent—three days, that is, after he had set forth his own proposals. There was no hint of urgency in the Secretary's dispatch, and Halleck replied, "It is impossible to send forces to Vicksburg at present, but I will give the matter very full attention as soon as circumstances will permit." [68]

It certainly was apparent to Halleck that the fall of Fort Pillow would follow that of Corinth; and if he had at once sent some 15,000 men down the Tennessee and Mississippi, they would have reached Memphis soon after the destruction of the Confederate fleet. They then could have followed the Union gunboats to Vicksburg and might have successfully carried out the attack that Sherman attempted in December, for until the middle of June there seems to have been only a few regiments at Vicksburg for land defense. If successful, the force would, however, have been very much isolated, and the Confederates had railroads by which they could have concentrated against it. Busy as he was in the vicinity of Corinth, and knowing that Vicksburg was on the Navy's agenda, Halleck should not be blamed too severely for failing to attempt such a venture. Criticism must also be placed on the High Command and the absence of a sufficient land force at New Orleans to give proper support to Farragut's operation. The brigade he brought was put to work constructing with the aid of Negroes a canal that it was hoped would divert the Mississippi from its course in front of Vicksburg. Before long three-fourths of them were dead or ill with fever, and the project was abandoned.[69]

One day in early June, Sherman, while gossiping with Halleck, was told casually that Grant was going on a leave of absence. Sensing what was back of the action, he at once rode to Grant's headquarters, where he found office equipment being packed while the general himself was busy in his tent sorting letters and papers. When asked what it meant, Grant replied, "Sherman, you know. You know I am in the way here. I have stood it as long as I can, and can endure it no longer." Sherman, being then in what he called "high feather," turned on his persuasive eloquence and logic, telling Grant that if he went events would go right along and he would be left out, "whereas, if he remained, some happy accident might restore him to favor and his true place." Grant promised to reconsider, and on

June 6 Sherman received word that he was not going away; whereupon Sherman wrote expressing his gladness and saying, "You could
not be quiet at home for a week when armies were moving, and rest
could not relieve your mind of the gnawing sensation that injustice
had been done you." [70]

Though his own estate was low Grant sent Lincoln a plea the next
day in behalf of another officer—and apparently it was the first time
he addressed the President. He "most respectfully" recommended
that Major J. N. Cook, a paymaster, be transferred from the volunteer
to the regular service. It was due to Cook that the Western troops
had been paid, and "but for his energy and perseverance some suffering of families and much discontent" would have resulted. The
note [71] must have revealed to Lincoln something of the character of
the general about whom he had heard malicious talk; and within a
few days he performed the final act in righting an old injustice to
Grant.

While Grant was serving as regimental quartermaster in Mexico,
$1,000 of government funds for which he was responsible had been
stolen. A board had promptly found him not guilty of neglect or
carelessness; nevertheless, the full amount had been restored to the
government. The claim that he had made to Congress for repayment
had never been acted upon, probably because no influential person
was interested in pressing the case. But now on June 17, 1862,
Lincoln signed a bill providing for the reimbursement of "Lieutenant
Ulysses S. Grant." [72]

Four days later Grant, with his staff and an escort of twelve cavalrymen, set out for Memphis, where he had received permission to
establish the headquarters of his army as well as those of the District
of West Tennessee, which he still commanded. Twenty miles from his
destination he narrowly escaped capture by Confederate cavalry
under a General Jackson who had been informed that Grant would
pass a certain road junction a few miles north of his location. On
arriving at the place after a hard ride, Jackson learned that the well-
mounted Federals had passed three-quarters of an hour before; and
he never imagined that the little party had stopped only a mile to
the west and was passing the hot hours of midday in the shade of
a little grove. Grant did not know of his narrow escape until a man
who had been in Jackson's custody reported it some days later; and
so, when he informed Halleck of his "warm ride of three days," all he

could say was that the road was very fine and in good condition. But matters in Memphis, he said, were "in bad order, secessionists governing much in their own way." Presently he learned that the M. Jeff Thompson whose irregular operations had been an annoyance when he was in Cairo was carrying on in the vicinity of his new headquarters. On the very day that Halleck told Stanton he could not help with Butler's "cut-off," Grant reported news had just come up the river from Farragut. The gunboats had left Memphis to cooperate at Vicksburg, and Grant said, "A land force of 13,000 is said to be up from New Orleans." [73] Some one had exaggerated badly but Grant did right in passing the report to Corinth.

Buell arrived personally in Huntsville on June 28, and presently the divisions of McCook, Nelson, Crittenden, and Wood were thereabout, while Thomas remained at Iuka on Halleck's order. Mitchel evidently expected that Buell would move by rail toward Stevenson without delay, for on the 24th he concluded a dispatch, "Please give me all the notice you can, that we may be ready to transport your troops." But Buell stayed at Huntsville and worked on questions of supply, ordering at the same time that all bridges and culverts on the railroad be protected by guards and stockades. He also built pontoons, as he should have done at Nashville. Forage was his main problem, and was the subject of many dispatches. In all, he needed three hundred tons of supplies a day; and because of destroyed bridges he had to use wagons on a twenty-two-mile stretch of the road from Decatur to Columbia. Thomas sought to aid him; but the river was so low that it was impossible to get a locomotive to Florence, and the lack of a dependable one on the restored line between Decatur and Tuscumbia prevented sending supplies to Buell from the rear. Another commander might have found a different solution of the problem of subsisting and making progress toward Chattanooga, though Fry would later say that everything possible was done.[74]

On July 2 Mitchel departed, with Buell complaining of poor discipline in his command and the general himself under criticism for cotton buying that he had allowed to take place. His division was presently under the command of Rousseau, who had led a brigade in McCook's division the second day at Shiloh. Beatty in his diary appraised the new commander as larger and handsomer than Mitchel, but not up to him in culture, energy, system, and industry. He described Buell's policy as that of a dancing master: "By your leave, my dear sir, we will have a fight; that is, if you are sufficiently fortified; no hurry; take your time." [75]

The last day of June had come when Halleck received a telegram that must have given him a start. One can imagine Old Brains—by this time a little habituated to a soldier's life but still far from looking like a toughened, sophisticated campaigner—cogitating in his hot headquarters without the benefit of cold drinks upon knotty problems of military occupation, with an occasional thought as to what Washington was thinking about the program he had recently submitted. Then there arrived a message from Stanton, sent two days before, which had not only been delayed but garbled in transmission. Enough of the dispatch could be read to indicate that McClellan was not in Richmond but was in trouble, and that Washington wanted 25,000 men from the West and wanted them in a hurry.[76]

Never in history had a commander been unexpectedly faced with such a logistical problem.

Halleck thought that Washington had been stampeded, and said so in a message to McClernand; but he set himself to carrying out the order expeditiously and without complaining in his reply. He explained that the condition of the railroads and the river would "render the movement very slow," and continued: "I think under the circumstances the Chattanooga expedition better be abandoned or at least be diminished. If not, I doubt our ability to hold West Tennessee after detaching so large a force as that called for." He would telegraph more in detail after the Secretary's message had been repeated so that all of it could be read.[77]

In midafternoon Stanton had Halleck's dispatch, and wired much more optimistically about the situation in front of Richmond: "If the advantage is not on our side it is balanced." But the Secretary said that the Chattanooga move was not to be given up on any account—on that the President was adamant. Furthermore, Lincoln was "not pleased with the tardiness of the movement" then going on in that direction. The demand for troops was not immediately canceled, though it was presently, after Halleck had arranged for sending some units to Columbus by rail, and others by river from Pittsburg Landing and Hamburg. McClernand was to be in charge of the movement, and Halleck's directive to him ended: "You go to a new theater; success attend you." [78]

When a corrected copy of Stanton's telegram of the 28th arrived Halleck sent his current estimate of the situation:

Because of the departure of Buell and the dispatch of reenforcements to Curtis in Arkansas, he had only 65,000 effectives; if he sent the number of men requested for the East, he would have only 40,000 left. All spies, scouts, deserters, and prisoners reported that not an enemy soldier had been sent to the defense of Richmond, as Washington had from time to time intimated. The Confederate force in the state, commanded by Bragg since June 20, was not less than 75,000 or 80,000, with conscripts being added daily. Furthermore, the enemy required no guards for his depots or bridges, had plenty of rolling stock, and could concentrate rapidly.

The figure for the Confederate strength was not badly in error, for Bragg's return of July 1 showed 61,561 men present from a total of 96,549 present and absent, with some cavalry not included in the count. [79]

Instead of reducing friction, Grant's separation from Halleck brought about a new outburst, due once more to a flaw in communications. He had not been in Memphis a week when Old Brains wired him:

You say 30,000 men are at Shelbyville to attack La Grange. Where is Shelbyville? I can't find it on any map. Don't believe a word about an attack in large force on La Grange or Memphis. Why not send out a strong reconnaissance and ascertain the *facts*? It looks very much like a mere stampede. Floating rumors must never be received as facts. . . .[80]

Grant replied, "I did not say 30,000 troops at Shelbyville, but at Abbeville, which is south of Holly Springs on the road to Grenada." After describing what he had done in the way of reconnaissance, he said, "I heed as little of the floating rumors about the city as any one," and he cited a strong Union man from Okolona as the source of his report, adding that, although he did not accept the precise figure, he believed there was a considerable force of Confederates at Abbeville and that the bridge over the Tallahatchie River was being repaired. "I have asked," said Grant, "for the Eleventh

Illinois Cavalry, now at Corinth, that I might do effectually what you now ask why I have not done." Then, after remarking "Stampeding is not my weakness," he struck hard by telling Halleck that he had been giving orders directly to troops of the Army of the Tennessee. He cited an instance of this and said, "Your orders have countermanded mine." [81]

The flurry over the call for troops by Washington worked as a diversion in favor of Grant. After passing through a threatened loss of 25,000 men Halleck may well have considered the futile search for non-existent Shelbyville as a trifling matter even on a hot day. He apparently attempted to be just to Grant in his delayed reply, though the imperious strain in his nature made him yield little as to the rightness of his position. After claiming that he had not intended to reflect on Grant, he said, "Nor did I suppose for a moment that you were stampeded; for I know that is not in your nature; but I believed there was a stampede about the enemy threatening our line to Memphis with 30,000 men, and I now have good evidence that he did not have one-tenth of that number." He had given orders directly to Grant's troops mainly because of Grant's having removed himself to Memphis, remote from much of his command; when promptness was essential he would have to continue to do the same. In the ending another little compliment struggled to manifest itself, but it was spoiled by a claim now grown very old:

I must confess that I was very much surprised at the tone of your dispatch and the ill-feeling manifested in it, so contrary to your usual style, and especially toward one who has so often befriended you when you were attacked by others.[82]

Still there seemed to be an eagerness to find fault and to be harsh in dealing with his subordinate. It was Whitelaw Reid's newspaper that stirred Halleck into telegraphing Grant curtly on July 8: "The Cincinnati Gazette contains the substance of your demanding reenforcements and my refusing them. You either have a newspaper correspondent on your staff or your staff is very leaky. This publication did not come from these headquarters." Three days later the telegraph instrument in Memphis rattled with twelve blunt, fateful words: "You will immediately repair to this place and report to these headquarters." [83]

Behind this message there was something very momentous, that could never have occurred to Grant as he pondered what was now in store for him. To Halleck there had just come a telegram from Stanton transmitting the order which Lincoln had that day issued making Halleck General in Chief and directing him to report at Washington as soon as he could do so "with safety to the positions and operations within the department under his charge." Halleck's reply went directly to the President: Grant, next in command, had been summoned from Memphis; Halleck would start for Washington as soon as he had had a personal interview with him.[84]

As Grant rode back to Corinth, past the road junction where he had escaped being captured, past the house whence word had gone to General Jackson about his presence, through La Grange and other towns with which he would later become better acquainted, a new phase of the war in the West was beginning in deadly earnest. Early on the morning of Sunday, July 13, Colonel Nathan B. Forrest, who a few days before had set out from Chattanooga with a force of cavalry presently augmented to three regiments numbering about 1,400 men, attacked the unsuspecting Federal garrison at Murfreesboro. Brigadier General Thomas T. Crittenden (cousin of the Thomas L. Crittenden who had a division in Buell's army) had assumed command of the two infantry regiments, a little cavalry, and a four-gun battery at that place only two days before; and the new commander was soon a prisoner in the hands of the party that Forrest sent into the town after the manner of Mitchel at Huntsville. Having been informed as to the positions of the Federal garrison, about equal in numbers or a little superior to his own command, Forrest planned his attack skillfully.

A part of the Confederate force immobilized the Third Minnesota and the Kentucky battery that were camped northwest of Murfreesboro, while the rest struck at the Ninth Michigan and the detachment of Pennsylvania cavalry located just east of the town. Early in the fight Colonel Duffield of the Michigan regiment was wounded; but Lieutenant Colonel John G. Parkhurst rallied his men, counterattacked, and occupied a good defensive position with flanks protected by baggage wagons and baled forage. Until noon the fight went on, and some of Forrest's officers advised withdrawal; but their leader, not to be dissuaded from success on his forty-first birthday, resorted to very unchivalrous warfare by sending to Parkhurst under a flag of truce a note that began, "I must demand an unconditional surrender of your force as prisoners of war or I will have every man put to the sword." After advising with Duffield, Parkhurst yielded, believing that Forrest had, as he said in his note, an "overpowering force," and that he would execute his threat. Concentrating then against the Minnesota regiment, Forrest soon secured it also, after its colonel had been allowed to confer with the wounded Duffield.[85]

On the very day that Forrest supplemented his adroit and proper tactics with a threat condemned by modern codes of warfare [86]—without which he might not have succeeded—the first railroad train was to have passed to Stevenson over the line which only the day before had been put in operating order. It was to have received a guard of forty men at Murfreesboro to protect it and the shoes, socks, and pants that Colonel Fry had told the quartermaster at Nashville should be the first shipment to the part of Buell's army that had now reached Stevenson.[87] It would have been appropriate finery to use in a parade to flaunt the high standard of living of the Yankees before the unbelieving Chattanoogans; but Forrest destroyed bridges again, and when Buell's men got new clothes they would have to wear them out chasing into Kentucky after Braxton Bragg.

While Forrest was striking at Middle Tennessee, John Morgan, who left Knoxville on July 4 at the head of 867 officers and men, began another raid into Kentucky. When he had ridden into the state after his attack on Pulaski he had been driven away from Bowling Green. Foiled once more in his efforts to destroy the bridge there as well as the one over Green River, Morgan turned eastward to harry and destroy, and to bring new enthusiasm and hopes to Kentucky secessionists. He threatened the long and difficult line of communications of General George Morgan, who at last on June 18 had found Cumberland Gap evacuated by the Confederates after he had crossed the mountains by paths deemed untraversable by an army with guns.[88] The much-coveted pass had been immediately fortified against an advance from the east, and since the Federal Morgan had accumulated ample supplies, his men were not in immediate danger of meager rations when the bold and fast horsemen of the Confederate Morgan moved into their rear.

The new situation in Tennessee and Kentucky heightened the deep concern that Lincoln felt after McClellan's retreat to Harrison's Landing on the James River. He became anxious, "almost impatient," to have Halleck in Washington. "Having due regard to what you leave behind, when can you reach here?" he asked. Halleck answered that Grant had just arrived from Memphis and he expected to leave in two days—July 17. A confidential note to Sherman revealed an aspect of Halleck's character that was habitually concealed: "Good-by, and may God bless you. I am more than satisfied with everything you have done. You have always had my respect, but recently you have won my highest admiration. I deeply regret to part from you." Toward his successor there was no unbending; and Grant indicated in his *Memoirs* that little was said to him about his future operations.[89] Yet Halleck had given him a helpful appraisal when he acknowledged that it was not in Grant's nature to be stampeded. In a list of nice things to tell a general, that would certainly be near the top.

So Halleck left, after telling Sherman that he had studied out and could finish the campaign in the West, but did not understand and could not manage affairs in the East and had no desire to be involved in the quarrels of Stanton and McClellan.[90] But no appointment to high place that had been made up to that time stood more clearly upon past accomplishments than Halleck's, though it has been condemned by cheap criticism based solely on the move against Corinth. Sherman told Halleck of being impressed by his "comprehensive knowledge of things gathered, God knows how," and added that his success had "attracted the world's attention."[91] Said the *New York Times,* "Gen. Halleck comes to Washington with the prestige of unmistakable success." Radical-minded Horace Greeley, still complaining bitterly of Halleck's order of the preceding November that barred escaped slaves from Army camps, conceded: "But Gen. Halleck is a thoroughly educated soldier; he has large natural capacity; he has brains enough to detect and profit by his own errors." James Gordon Bennett's *New York Herald* took much satisfaction in calling Halleck a conservative, while *Harper's Weekly,* once a strong defender of McClellan, listed the impressive accomplishments in the West and gave Halleck credit as the responsible commander.[92] Halleck's place, however, was not in the field. He could not have met the rigors of hard campaigning or the ordeal of battle. A real field soldier was required from now on in the West, and it was a "happy accident" indeed that took Halleck from the scene. But Grant still had to prove his fitness, for even in the mind of Sherman, who admired what Grant had done at Belmont and at Donelson, and had witnessed his calmness and his will to fight in the revealing hours of

Shiloh, the departure of Halleck seemed unfortunate. Sherman knew Grant had been unfairly treated; but he did not yet suspect his great stature as a general. He feared, he would later say, that Grant lacked breadth of knowledge and an understanding of grand strategy. Vicksburg would be the test. A final decision about that place Halleck made just before his departure; for on the day that Grant arrived from Memphis there came a telegram from Stanton asking, for the Secretary of the Navy, whether it was intended to have a land force cooperate with Farragut. The answer was in the negative: Curtis had just reached Helena and wanted more troops; Buell would probably need to be helped in Tennessee and Kentucky. This could not have pleased Gideon Welles, though Farragut, fearing his ocean vessels would stick on mud bars, and eager to have the sniff of healing salt water in the nostrils of his ailing crews, would be much pleased to get away and leave the problem of Vicksburg to the river gunboats and the pleasure of the Army. But he was not to leave without a great humiliation, for on the very day—July 15—that Halleck telegraphed, the new Confederate ram *Arkansas,* well armored, well gunned, and fast, suddenly emerged from the Yazoo where she had been built, and after smashing her way through the combined Federal flotillas, came to rest defiantly beneath the Vicksburg batteries.[93] It was bad enough when six Confederate boats surprised the *Cincinnati* at Plum Run Bend, but it was almost unthinkable that a single enemy craft could get the best of two Federal fleets. When Welles received the news and read the headlines in the papers he was in no position to be critical of the Army.

Such was the aspect of the situation when Grant on July 17 issued an order assuming command of his own old army and the Army of the Mississippi—under Rosecrans since Pope's departure for the East in late June—as well as the District of Mississippi and Cairo.[94] A scant year had passed since he had issued the order taking command at Ironton. After using a few days to discipline his troops, he was on the march against Hardee when an order called him away. Then there had come the quick seizure of strategically situated Paducah, as a response to the Confederate occupation of Hickman. Then Belmont, Fort Henry, Fort Donelson, Shiloh. It was an ascending sequence, leading to a climax: Vicksburg, at whose leering batteries the unhappy, humiliated Farragut now gazed, while sickening soldiers toiled futilely in the heat and mud.

APPENDIX

I. GRANT'S REPORT ON BELMONT

Coppée stated that Grant submitted to the Secretary of War on June 26, 1865, a fresh report on the Battle of Belmont "to take the place of the old one." Conger observed that the report in the *Official Records,* which is headed "Cairo, Ill., November 17, 1861," is doubtless the substituted report, and he asserted that it is consequently to be received with "double caution." Although late reports are often to be viewed with care, Conger apparently did not make a comparison of Grant's first and second reports to observe in what they differed. The first report, which was dated Nov. 12, 1861, was given considerable newspaper attention and was reprinted by Moore in his contemporary documents of the War.[1]

In the first report Grant put his force at 2,850, in the second one at 3,114. In the second version McClernand—with whom Grant had a break in 1863—was given the same commendation for coolness and judgment, and the sentence about his having his horse shot three times was strengthened by the words "under him"—as if that might not be taken for granted. Both changes indicate revision in the way of greater accuracy.

The first report began with the statement that Grant left Cairo on Nov. 6 for the purpose of a "reconnaissance towards Columbus," but the inadequacy of that description was corrected by the next sentence, which stated carefully the twofold purpose of the expedition. The document was, however, faulty as a complete record mainly through the lack of background material. This deficiency the final report remedied; in it the statement about leaving Cairo on the 6th with such and such a force was preceded by nearly two pages of dispatches from Capt. McKeever (Frémont's adjutant at St. Louis) and the orders Grant gave Cols. Oglesby and W. H. L. Wallace on Nov. 6.

Although Conger accepted the implication of Coppée that the final report on Belmont was written in 1865, it was actually completed a year before (and perhaps was started on Nov. 17, 1861), for on Apr. 27, 1864, Rawlins wrote to his wife that he and Col. Bowers had finished Grant's Belmont report the day before.[2] It may have been held after completion in the hope that copies of one dispatch from McKeever and one from Wallace that are referred to but not given, might be found.

Rawlins's own statement as to the care which was used in writing the document is corroborated by what Gen. Wilson said with regard to Grant's reports. As he was on Grant's staff for a considerable period, Wilson knew from personal observation how matters were handled, and he wrote that no instance was known where Grant over-ruled Rawlins or changed what Rawlins wrote about a disputed point after he had made a full investigation. For this reason, said Wilson, no reports, whether referring to the Civil War or any other war, were probably ever framed with a more scrupulous regard for truth, than were those of Grant.[3] Conger seems to have been unfamiliar with Wilson's comments.

The only report Grant submitted on Fort Donelson was the short one written the day of the surrender, and the only one on Shiloh was that of Apr. 9, 1862.

II. THE CASE OF GEORGE H. THOMAS

It is frequently stated that Gen. George H. Thomas was discriminated against because of his Virginia birth. Those who press the charge commonly use remarks that Lincoln supposedly made in the summer of 1861 at a meeting with Sherman and Gen. Robert Anderson in the Willard Hotel. Sherman wrote that although it was hardly "probable" that Lincoln would have come to the hotel to meet them, it was his "impression that he did," and he said that he and Anderson had some difficulty in prevailing upon Lincoln to promote Thomas to a brigadier generalship.[4]

Actual facts about Thomas's promotions do not support a charge of unfair treatment. In March of 1861 he was a major in the 2nd Cavalry; in April, when Lee was made a colonel and assigned to the 1st Cavalry, Thomas was promoted and took the vacated place of lieutenant colonel; on May 3 he was made colonel and given command of the regiment (renumbered the 5th in the summer), when A. S. Johnston resigned (while commanding the Pacific Department Johnston was only a brevet brigadier and was still the official commander of the 2nd Cavalry). With two promotions in a month it does not look as if there was discrimination against Thomas, and Van Horne said specifically: "The promotion of Thomas was rapid, but entirely regular, though indicating the extensive defection of the ranking cavalry officers." [5]

A total of fifty-six brigadier generals of volunteers ranked Thomas, of whom three declined the appointment. Many of them were men who had graduated from West Point before Thomas, and he was promoted before the following Northern-born officers who had preceded him at the Academy: John Sedgwick (Conn.), C. F. Smith (Penn.), Silas Casey (R.I.), George G. Meade (born in Spain to Pennsylvania parents). He was likewise promoted before Col. John J. Abercrombie of Tennessee, who had graduated eighteen years before Thomas and who had served with distinction in Indian wars and had an excellent Mexican War record.[6] But it does not seem to have been charged that Abercrombie was held back because of his Southern birth while Northern officers were passed around him.

Thomas was made a brigadier on Aug. 17, 1861, and on the 25th he wrote a letter in which he said he thought Gen. Robert Patterson should demand a court of inquiry if he could not otherwise obtain justice in regard to his recent ill-starred operations in the Shenandoah Valley in which Thomas had taken part. The claim that this action brought Thomas into disfavor conflicts with the fact that Lincoln shared Thomas's view, for he indicated in a letter that he believed Patterson had been too harshly criticized.[7]

On Aug. 24 Sherman and Thomas were assigned by the order of Gen. Scott to the Department of the Cumberland, which had been formed out of Kentucky and Tennessee and placed under the command of Anderson by a War Department order of Aug. 15.[8] It has been said that Thomas submitted a plan for cutting through Cumberland Gap, a claim that may go back to Don Piatt, journalist and poet, as well as a soldier, who in addition was a contentious figure and a detractor of Winfield Scott, Grant, and Sherman. Piatt stated that Thomas submitted the plan to the War Department,[9] which would have been a strange procedure, since a department commander and a General in Chief of the Army intervened between Thomas and the Secretary of War. Thomas was not in the habit of doing business in that irregular way.

As a matter of fact, Thomas wrote Anderson on Sept. 22 about being "constantly beset with importunities from citizens near the [Kentucky-Tennessee] border to advance to their relief," a move which he said would lead to certain disaster unless he could have 4,000 well-drilled men and a battery of artillery. Reports indicated that the enemy intended to invade Kentucky in force, and Thomas concluded, "I beg that the Government will place me in a condition to defend this part of the State." [10] Thus at the time that Lincoln was writing the previously considered memorandum that described a thrust toward Knoxville, the future "Rock of Chickamauga" was thinking primarily of defense.

A clash over command arose presently between Thomas and Ormsby Mitchel, who had been made a brigadier on Aug. 9 and had assumed command of the Department of the Ohio with headquarters at Cincinnati on Sept. 21.[11] Since Mitchel had been born in Kentucky and had brought renown to Cincinnati for his scientific work, and was known throughout the region for his energy, he had a prestige that Thomas lacked. While Thomas had had more military service than the popular and inspiring astronomer, Mitchel was a West Point graduate, and Union men could well regard him as better qualified than Thomas to advance the cause of the North in Kentucky, where there was a struggle for minds as well as territory. In answer to a telegram from Gen. Scott's adjutant, Mitchel wrote a long and newsy letter on Sept. 26. He said that in reply to his telegram to the Kentucky legislature, asking to be placed in their state within fifteen miles of Cincinnati, there had come an earnest appeal to send 5,000 troops to drive back Zollicoffer. Larz Anderson, brother of Robert and a resident of Cincinnati, had also brought a request for assistance from the general, who had his headquarters in Louisville. In accordance with his energetic nature, Mitchel had already been acting. He reported that he had control of the near end of the Covington-Lexington railroad; a regiment was to go that day to make the entire line secure; in the evening another would move to the Lexington-Louisville line.

"These," said Mitchel, "will be followed by a force sufficient to render it possible (when combined with the troops under General Thomas at Camp Dick Robinson, 130 miles from this) to commence active immediate operations to drive Zollicoffer and Breckinridge out of the State or to capture them." After explaining his own ideas, Mitchel said, "I have no knowledge of the views of General Anderson further than he begs me to aid Lexington and Frankfort and General Thomas." He stated that the immediate occupancy of Kentucky was of the greatest importance and that the fall of Louisville would be a disaster producing consequences that could not be estimated. He concluded, "I therefore urge the necessity of placing in supreme command of this expedition to Kentucky and Tennessee an experienced general, who will command the entire confidence of the Government." [12]

The final words should not be taken as a veiled implication that there was any lack of confidence in Thomas's loyalty. Mitchel, a Kentuckian, would hardly have suggested to Winfield Scott, a Virginian, that one should question the oath that another Virginian had recently taken no less than three times (with each promotion). Though Thomas, while still a colonel, had had a little experience commanding a brigade under Patterson, he had directed no operation. No more than Mitchel himself was he at that moment "an experienced general."

On Oct. 10 Secretary Cameron and Adj. Gen. Lorenzo Thomas were in Cincinnati on their way to St. Louis to investigate the Frémont situation. The Adjutant General wrote to Sherman, who had just come into command of the Cumberland department on account of Anderson's poor health, and inclosed a copy of a directive given to Mitchel, which assigned the latter to duty in Sherman's department and instructed him to go to Camp Dick Robinson to prepare the troops for a forward movement, "the object being to take possession of Cumberland Ford and Cumberland Gap, and ultimately seize the East Tennessee and Virginia Railroad and attack and drive the rebels from that region of country." [13]

The letter that Mitchel wrote to George Thomas the same day, informing him of the assignment he had received and asking Thomas to do certain things, must have been a surprise to the latter. He replied the next day, in good temper and very respectfully, but after saying that he would do everything he could until Mitchel arrived, he stated that justice to himself required that he "ask to be relieved from duty with these troops, since the Secretary has thought it necessary to supersede me in the command, without, as I conceive, any just cause for so doing." He added that he was doing everything possible to prepare for a move such as Mitchel described, but did not claim he had submitted any plan of operation, nor indeed that he was under any orders for an advance.[14] Mitchel had said nothing about bringing troops from Ohio, though it is possible that Thomas conjectured that he would do so. If such were the case, he was being unduly touchy, for Mitchel ranked him, and if Mitchel arrived with reenforcements it would not have been a case of merely superseding Thomas, but of a junction of commands.

The case was straightened out on the 13th when Sherman wrote to Thomas, "General Mitchel is subject to my orders, and I will, if possible, give you the opportunity of completing what you have begun." [15] Sherman's statement as to his apprehension over the posture of events in Kentucky indicates that no vigorous forward movement was intended.

Because of his untimely death, Mitchel never had the opportunity to demonstrate battlefield ability, and one may doubt whether he would have made a record equal to that of Thomas. The latter, however, in four years of war never showed the dash and audacity that Mitchel revealed in his operations in northern Alabama. When Cameron picked him in place of Thomas to lead an advance on Cumberland Gap there is no reason to believe he was actuated by a lingering distrust of Thomas, and there are reasons for thinking that in addition to selecting the senior officer he was picking the one best fitted for that operation.

Soon after the capture of Fort Donelson had given the occasion for quickly rewarding an outstanding performance by promoting Grant,[16] Lincoln moved to reward other officers whose service had been meritorious but much less striking. Though Thomas's name was not on the list of brigadiers recommended for promotion on Mar. 3, 1862, it was submitted to the Senate three days later, when the four Mill Springs colonels were recommended for promotion to brigadiers. On the 6th the Senate military committee reported favorably on the nine names submitted on the 3rd. On the 14th Irvin McDowell, the senior on the list, was confirmed as a major general; on the 18th Ambrose Burnside, named second by Lincoln, but not second in seniority as a brigadier, was approved. Thus two Easterners were placed next after Grant, the Westerner, as major generals of volunteers. On the 17th the military committee reported favorably on Thomas and three of his colonels. On the 21st the remaining seven men recommended as major generals on the 3rd—all from the West— were confirmed, and at the same time the three Mill Springs colonels who had been favorably reported were approved as brigadier generals. Though the remaining colonel was favorably reported on and confirmed on the 24th, Thomas was not given confirmation until Apr. 25. The Senate, not the President, was responsible for the fact that he did not date from Mar. 21. It may be recalled that there were no senators from Virginia to interest themselves in his case.

It was, however, an act of the administration, inadvertent or deliberate, that resulted in Thomas being promoted ahead of Sherman. Though Stanton recommended that Mitchel be promoted "to date from April 11, 1862, for gallant and meritorious conduct in the capture of Huntsville, Alabama," [17] he did not follow Halleck's suggestion that Sherman's promotion be dated Apr. 6. The Secretary's recommendation was written on Apr. 17, but it lay either on his desk or on Lincoln's, for it did not receive the President's signature until the 29th. It reached the Senate on May 1 and was immediately approved. Thus Sherman, who had ranked Thomas as a brigadier and had taken his part in his little clash with Mitchel, became Thomas's junior as well as Mitchel's.[18]

It was not Virginia-born Thomas who for awhile had a right to feel that he was discriminated against by the administration, but Ohio-born William S. Rosecrans. A high-ranking graduate of West Point in the class of 1842, he had been an instructor there and had also had a very successful career after resigning from the Army in 1854. He was colonel of an Ohio regiment when made a brigadier general in the *regular army,* dating from May 16, 1861. It was well known that it was his turning movement that won the Battle of Rich Mountain on July 11, and after succeeding to the command in western Virginia when McClellan went to Washington, he defeated efforts of the Confederates to regain that region. His service won a vote of thanks from the legislature of West Virginia and can be deemed as significant as the victory of Thomas at Mill Springs. Yet when good work was being rewarded in March, 1862, Rosecrans was passed over, and it was not until September that Lincoln gave him an interim promotion, dating it back to Mar. 21. His name appears at the head of the major generals of that day because he decisively ranked all of them as a brigadier.

In considering the case of George Thomas it is hard to forget his record in the later years of the war and view him as he was in 1861 and early 1862. But to say he suffered injustice in the matter of promotion because of Lincoln's prejudice against him, without more positive evidence than has been given, and without looking at the entire promotion question and record, is to use little except suspicion to accuse another of suspicion.

III. THE CASE OF ANNA ELLA CARROLL

For twenty years Anna Ella Carroll had petitions and memorials before Congress which sought to establish that she deserved the credit for the campaign up the Tennessee River that began with the capture of Fort Henry on Feb. 6, 1862. She also set forth her case in a magazine article in 1886, from which a brief quotation was taken in Chap. IV. Though one committee of the House accepted her claim and recommended that she be given the pay of a major general dating back to 1861, she in the end was not rewarded or given the credit she sought. Historians have passed over her in silence, but recent endorsements of her case in books and magazines make it necessary to examine it.[19]

While in St. Louis in the fall of 1861, Miss Carroll, daughter of a governor of Maryland, talked with Capt. Charles M. Scott, the pilot of one of Grant's transports at the Battle of Belmont. Although she praised Scott for a number of years, and spoke broadly in her first petition to Congress in 1870 of "information elicited from steamboat pilots, and other practical men," she later showed great hostility to Scott and claimed that the only information she obtained from him was about the navigability of the Tennessee. Scott on the other hand wrote as early as Mar. 17, 1862, about his "suggestions to Miss Carroll" being the "first ever made to the administration that the Tennessee River was the best point to attack the enemy and shorten the war," and he later strongly denounced Miss Carroll for her efforts to secure recognition and recompense from Congress.[20]

Miss Carroll claimed that after returning to Washington, she submitted to Thomas A. Scott, Assistant Secretary of War, on Nov. 30, a paper setting forth the proposal to use the Tennessee River. It has generally been accepted that she did this, and that the paper was identical with the one she submitted with her petitions to Congress. The actual paper given Scott seems not to have been located, and the only real support for the claim is in letters that he wrote eight and ten years later. It will be seen that his memory was very inaccurate about the move up the Tennessee, so one cannot have unqualified confidence in what he said about receiving a paper from Miss Carroll.

The contradictory nature of Miss Carroll's own statements discredits her own case. In January, 1867, she wrote a letter to Grant, and said with regard to using the Tennessee, "The suggestion having occurred to your mind, you think it must naturally have done so to every military mind." She claimed only that no one in Washington had thought of the plan until she proposed it. Virtually admitting that she deserved no credit for the actual movement Grant made, she was reduced to asserting priority in putting the plan on paper, for at that time she seems to have been acknowledging her indebtedness to Capt. Scott for the general idea. She asked Grant to record "the date when the Tennessee became in your mind the plan of conducting the campaign in the Southwest, and to whom you communicated it, verbally or otherwise." In her first petition, dated Mar. 25, 1870, she stated with reference to the letter she said she had given Thomas Scott, a copy of which she submitted, "Your memorialist is not advised as to how the paper was used by the War Department, but she does believe that it caused the Tennessee River to be adopted as the strategical line in 1862, and thereby influenced most materially the destinies of the war." In spite of this clear admission that she had no *knowledge* on the subject, she wrote to Dr. J. W. Draper that the Tennessee expedition was executed "in pursuance of a direct order of President Lincoln" to Halleck. Miss Carroll's recollection increased with the passage of years, until she said in 1878 that she had urged Scott to press her plan upon the attention of the President and left her paper with him "fully convinced that her suggestions would be executed as they were, triumphantly and victoriously to the salvation of the Union." [21]

The supporting material that Miss Carroll submitted to Congress came for the most part from persons who had no first-hand knowledge whatever of military planning and can be at once dismissed. Even Ben Wade, chairman of the Congressional Committee on the Conduct of the War, did not have the information to which he afterward pretended. His committee was not a board of strategy, nor even an advisory body. Its members were well posted only with regard to battles and operations into which they formally probed; and in such cases they presented reports containing dispatches and orders as well as sworn testimony. Wade himself was a very controversial figure; in listing the minor possibilities for the Republican presidential nomination in 1860, Nevins includes the "ignorant, profane Ben Wade," and refers to his "blustering egotism." [22] As a leader of the radicals, Wade opposed Lincoln's reconstruction policy, and was in conflict with him on other matters, including conscription. During the summer of 1864, when Lincoln's reelection was uncertain, he joined with Henry Winter Davis in a newspaper denunciation of the President for not signing a bill by Davis that Wade had championed in the Senate.[23] There is something grotesque in his later pretention to having been an influential advisor of Lincoln. Wade's wife was an intimate friend of Miss Carroll and he wrote several letters strongly supporting her claim. It is significant that in them he did not refer to any investigation that his committee had made; the most he could do was allude vaguely to questions he had asked some officers—and these he did not name. Some of his statements doubtless arose from confusion between Miss Carroll's claim and Lincoln's War Order of Jan. 27, 1862, about which Stanton cautiously informed him the same day, in order to get passage of legislation pending in Congress.

Thomas Scott was in an embarrassing position with regard to Miss Carroll, for he had been largely responsible for her printing and distributing a political pamphlet in the summer of 1861, which he thought would aid the Union cause. Though he had assured her that she would be compensated, she had received only $1,250 of the $6,750 she claimed was due her, at the time Scott gave up his War Department position in the late spring of 1862, and his efforts to get his successor to complete the payments were unsuccessful. In 1870 and again in 1872 Scott wrote the chairman of the Senate Military Committee supporting Miss Carroll's claim. According to some versions of his first letter in the Congressional documents, Miss Carroll's paper of Nov. 30, 1861, went only to the Secretary of War, who at the time was Simon Cameron. According to all versions of the 1872 letter Scott submitted it not only to Cameron but to Lincoln.[24]

In the second letter Scott stated that after Stanton was appointed

Secretary of War (in mid-January, 1862) he himself "was directed to go to the western armies and arrange to increase their effective force as rapidly as possible," for the purpose of carrying through the Tennessee River campaign "then inaugurated." This statement and the concluding sentence of the letter seem like a complete indorsement of the Carroll case. But what Scott wrote in 1872 is completely refuted by the letter of instructions Stanton gave him on Jan. 29, 1862, as well as by the letters he himself wrote from the West.

As noted in the text, Halleck, thinking Scott was still in St. Louis, wrote on Feb. 9 a letter addressed to Stanton, which he expected Scott to copy and send forward, as if he had written it. It began, "I have conversed with Gen'l Halleck and agree with him that the Tennessee and Cumberland constitute the proper line for an early spring campaign," and then discussed what could be done and the force required.[25] Scott having departed, the letter was sent to him at Cairo, with a note of explanation from Halleck, and Scott sent it to Stanton. It will also be recalled that on Feb. 17 Scott, who had returned to St. Louis, sent a special courier to Washington with a letter and a map explaining the operation Halleck desired to carry out, and urging that it be given full support. Such contemporary documents from an unquestionable source make clear that Scott's memory was in error when in 1872 he wrote that he was sent westward to start the Tennessee River operation. He was sent to make general reports on the situation, and the operations that Stanton was looking forward to were the vague ones that Lincoln's War Order of Jan. 27 had set for Feb. 22. Scott merely supported an operation that he found already begun.[26]

In a letter that Miss Carroll wrote to Lincoln on Aug. 14, 1862, and which became available when the Robert Todd Lincoln Collection was opened in July, 1947, she indirectly but completely demolished her entire case. She had recently had an interview with the President, in which she had proposed that she be given $50,000 to go abroad and write in support of the Union cause, and her letter reveals that Lincoln said to her that he thought the proposition "the most outrageous one ever made to any government, upon earth." In this long letter, in which Miss Carroll lectured Lincoln and sought to exhibit both her ability and the service she had rendered through her political pamphlets, there is no reference to her Tennessee plan, nor a statement that can be taken as a veiled allusion to it. If in the interview referred to, Lincoln had had before him the person he believed responsible for the February successes, he would not have made the harsh remark that Miss Carroll herself put into the record.[27] Miss Carroll knew that no paper she had written had had anything to do with the movement up the Tennessee, but she probably later forgot about the letter she had written to Lincoln on Aug. 14, 1862.

In view of the indubitable facts, how is it possible to endorse the claim of Miss Carroll? It can be done only by saying that orders were issued by Lincoln of which there is now no trace in the *Official Records* or elsewhere, and by ignoring official dispatches he actually sent to Halleck and Buell, as well as his order of Jan. 27, 1862. It is also necessary to pay no heed to the telegrams exchanged by Grant, Foote, Halleck, and McClellan on Jan. 28–30, and likewise Stanton's instructions to Thomas Scott, and the latter's letters from the West. Finally one must disregard some of Miss Carroll's own statements, especially that to Grant and the one in her first petition to Congress. Such things have been and still are done.[28]

IV. THE CLAIMS OF THAYER, EMERSON, AND WASHBURNE

Matching the claim made for Anna Ella Carroll is one equally untenable that Grant planned the Tennessee River campaign during the ten days he was at Ironton in August, 1861, and even submitted the proposal to the President through Congressman Washburne. He indicated nothing of the sort in his *Memoirs,* but the claim was put into the literature of the war by men of unimpeachable integrity who were acquainted with him and who seemed to speak from first-hand knowledge.

Gen. John M. Thayer, who after the war was governor of Nebraska and a United States Senator, seems to have first published the claim in 1895 in a magazine article entitled "Grant at Pilot Knob." He stated that he was sent by Frémont with his regiment, the 1st Nebraska, to report to Grant at Ironton, and the records indeed show that he was ordered there from St. Louis on Aug. 14 and that Grant reported his arrival the next day.[29] He correctly noted that, at the time Prentiss unexpectedly arrived and relieved Grant, an expedition had been started toward Greenville where Hardee was located with a Confederate force. But one cannot accept Thayer's statement that it was Grant's intention, after disposing of Hardee, to move to Cape Girardeau, cross the Mississippi and make Cairo his base for future operations. Such a move would not have been in accordance with the written instructions Frémont had given Grant and Grant knew that Cairo was under another commander.

Thayer stated that Grant invited him to go to St. Louis on the one-car train in which he left the night after Prentiss's arrival. After the two had breakfasted, Grant reported to Frémont and was soon back at the hotel in a very unhappy frame of mind. Frémont wished to send him to Jefferson City, while he wished to go no farther into Missouri but wanted a leave of absence for five days to visit Galena. Thayer thereupon persuaded Grant to return to headquarters and request a leave, and he recorded that the general came back presently "with a much more cheerful expression on his countenance." The leave had been granted—said Thayer. Though at the time the Nebraska colonel thought Grant merely wished to see his family, he wrote that he later learned that while at Galena Grant saw or wrote to Washburne, saying he wished to be sent to Cairo. The appeal, according to Thayer, brought results, for within ten days Grant was recalled from Jefferson City and was given command of the District of Southeastern Missouri.

The Thayer story is completely nullified by the fact that Grant did not go to Galena. He did ask for a leave, but received from Frémont's adjutant the following note, dated Aug. 19, "The general desires me to say that urgent service requires that your leave be postponed for the present. He will be glad to give you leave to visit Galena in a short time." As Grant sent his last dispatch from Jefferson City on Aug. 28 and received the same day from Frémont in person an order to go to Cape Girardeau "forthwith," it is clear that he did not receive a leave upon returning to St. Louis. He in fact sent a report from Cape Girardeau on the 30th.[30]

Thayer compounded his own inaccurate recollection by adding— with possible embellishment—a story told him by Montgomery Blair. The former Postmaster General said that one day at a cabinet meeting Lincoln remarked to Secretary Cameron: "Did we not receive a communication some time last spring from a man by the name of Grant, out at Springfield, Illinois, forwarded by Governor Yates, laying out a plan of campaign down the Mississippi." The Secretary answered in the affirmative and when Grant's plan was put before the cabinet, Lincoln explained that it had made a great impression on him at the time, but the press of many matters had forced it from his mind until Washburne called attention to Grant and suggested that he be sent to Cairo. Lincoln—so Blair stated—then directed Cameron to order Frémont to put Grant in command of the District of Southeastern Missouri.

The story is completely out of character for Grant, who would hardly have intruded into the domain of Winfield Scott. It is also out of character for Lincoln, for the memorandum he wrote in September about possible operations in the West was properly sent to Army Headquarters. The *Official Records* do not give an order from Cameron to Frémont about Grant, and the lengthy instructions that Frémont gave Grant when he sent him to Cape Girardeau can only be regarded as originating with himself, as well as the choice of Grant for the position.

A story still more amazing than Thayer's was told by John W. Emerson in a series of articles entitled "Grant's Life in the West and his Mississippi Valley Campaign," that began to appear in October, 1896.[31] Emerson, a lawyer, lived in Ironton and had met Grant in 1859 when the latter was in St. Louis, and he stated that during Grant's ten days at Ironton he observed him carefully. Although Emerson evidently used the *Official Records* he made some errors that are significant in weighing the reliability of his story. He stated that the order which Grant received on Aug. 7 at Mexico, Mo., directed him to go to Ironton, and that he passed through St. Louis during the night without calling on Frémont.[32] Actually, however, Grant was originally ordered only to St. Louis and probably received the order on the 6th, while it was a letter of instructions given to him on the morning of the 8th that sent him to Ironton.[33] Although Grant said clearly enough in his *Memoirs* that he was in Mexico when he read in a St. Louis paper about first being recommended and then confirmed as a brigadier, Emerson stated that Grant learned of all this after he reached Ironton. Going into particulars, Emerson said that Grant was recommended for promotion on Aug. 7 and was confirmed on the 9th,[34] when in fact he was recommended on July 31 and confirmed on Aug. 5,[35] the day before Congress adjourned. The loyal Ironton citizen certainly wished everything possible to happen to Grant while in the Pilot Knob region.

On the third day after he reached Ironton, Grant—according to Emerson—asked Emerson for a better map than the one he had, and the next evening on going to the general's headquarters, Emerson found him working on the map, which was well marked up. In addition to marks at New Madrid and Columbus and some on the Tennessee and the Cumberland, the sharp-eyed Irontonian discovered —and remembered thirty-five years later—that "there were also dotted lines overland from the point opposite Cairo to the rear of Columbus and from Paducah and Smithland in the direction of Forts Henry and Donelson." When he wrote this Emerson probably did not bother to check whether the forts in question existed on Aug. 12, 1861. Donelson certainly did not, and although work may have started on Fort Henry, it could not have been far advanced, and it is doubtful whether either Grant or Emerson had heard of it. Emerson also recorded that after Grant had been superseded by Prentiss, the adjutant at Ironton had told him that he "had copied a great plan of campaign which General Grant sent to Congressman Washburne to lay before the President." [36]

Emerson completed his story by giving a letter that Washburne wrote him on Feb. 7, 1881, confirming or supplementing a recent conversation. Washburne asserted that Grant soon after his promotion sent him a plan for "breaking the Confederate lines on the rivers and advancing through Kentucky and Tennessee." Struck by its boldness he at once "submitted" it to the President. Two weeks later he became indignant when a letter from Grant told of his transfer to Jefferson City. He hastened to Lincoln in protest, with the result that the President directed Cameron to order Frémont to recall Grant. This was done immediately and Grant was "sent south." [37]

Chronology also shatters Washburne's story, for at the time referred to the Confederate line of defense from Columbus through Forts Henry and Donelson to Bowling Green did not exist. It was not until September that Confederate troops moved into Kentucky.

Two letters that Grant wrote to Washburne confirm the conclusion that Washburne was remembering badly in 1881. The one from Cairo, dated Sept. 3, 1861, which is the first in the little volume of published letters to Washburne,[38] reads as if it were the first letter Grant had written to the congressman. He said he was certain that Washburne had played a part in giving him his "present position," and thanked him for his "kind office in the matter." Since Grant specifically said that "General Fremont has seen fit to intrust me with an important command here," one must conclude that Grant was referring to his promotion and not to his assignment to Cairo. Thanks for his advancement would certainly have been included in the first letter he wrote Washburne after being made a brigadier. Furthermore, if he had previously submitted a plan for an operation based on Cairo, some remark about the prospect of carrying it out would have been in order—the congressman would have wanted to know how matters stood.

In a letter to Washburne from Savannah, Tenn., dated Mar. 22, 1862, Grant said: "I see the credit for attacking the enemy by the way of the Tennessee and Cumberland is variously attributed. It is little to talk about it being the great wisdom of any general that first brought forth this plan of attack. Our gunboats were running up the Tennessee and Cumberland all fall and winter watching the progress of the rebels on these works [Forts Henry and Donelson]. General Halleck no doubt thought of this route long ago, and I am sure I did." [39] If Grant had written to Washburne about the matter the preceding August, he would certainly have alluded to the fact.

At one and the same time Grant not only disposed of the unsound claim that would in the future be made about himself, but gave the perfect answer to the entire Tennessee River question. The idea was nothing to claim credit for, because as he later told Miss Carroll, and as the son of Sidney Johnston wrote, it was obvious. Colonel Henderson brushed aside the oft-argued question whether it was Lee or Jackson who suggested the march to Pope's rear at Manassas with the remark, "It is easy to conceive. It is less easy to execute." Recently, Gen. Sir Archibald Wavell has emphasized the same enduring military truth: "Marlborough's most admired stratagem, the forcing of the Ne Plus Ultra lines in 1711, was one that a child could have thought of but probably no other general could have executed." [40]

NOTES

References to the *Official Records* are given in such a way as to show the number of dispatches supporting a paragraph, as well as their proper order. Thus, *O.R., 7*, 562–563 indicates a single message running from p. 562 to p. 563, while *O.R., 7*, 562, 562–563, 563 indicates additional dispatches on pp. 562 and 563. The repetition of a page number may also appear, as in *O.R., 8*, 530, 532, 540, 532.

NOTES TO CHAPTER I

1. The chief sources for this chapter are Lewis's *Captain Sam Grant* and, to a lesser degree, Grant's *Memoirs*.

2. Church, *Grant*, p. 53. A brief and sympathetic discussion, subsequent to the one found in Lewis, has been given by Jones in *Ark of Empire*, p. 112.

3. This and the next paragraph are built largely on an unsigned article "Galena and Its Lead Mines," in *Harper's New Monthly Magazine*, XXXII, 682–696 (May, 1866). The census reported a population of 8,196 for "Galena City," and 1,045 for "East Galena."

The statement in *Harper's* about Dent opening the first trading post in Galena is supported in an article in the *Journal of the Illinois Historical Society*, XXV, 108–118 (1932), entitled "Galena, Looking Back," by Alice L. Snyder, whose father came to Galena in 1835, and whose mother came three years later. The account is based upon personal recollection of events and local traditions.

4. Woodward, who says that Grant appears to have been a "Douglas Democrat," asserts (*Meet General Grant*, p. 164): "During the campaign Grant heard Lincoln speak, and seems to have been converted to the Republican view of things. I say 'seems,' for his statement of the matter is so loose and vague that it is difficult to grasp what he meant. At any rate, Lincoln, whom he saw and heard from a distance—as a spectator in a crowd—made a great impression on him." It would be interesting to know Woodward's source

for this statement. Nicolay and Hay state (*Lincoln*, II, 286–287) that Lincoln spent the long summer days of the campaign in Springfield and say specifically, "He made no addresses, wrote no public letters, held no conferences." Many writers have emphasized that he did no speaking during the campaign.

In electoral votes the four candidates stood in the order, Lincoln, Breckinridge, Bell (Constitutional Union Party), Douglas; in popular votes the order was, Lincoln, Douglas, Breckinridge, Bell.

5. Woodward (*op. cit.*, p. 136) states that Grant's position at Galena was "humiliating," and adds, "He was at the bottom of his pit, a forlorn figure, a man who dared not think of the future, and who had lost the bright pictures of his day-dreams." This view is not in harmony with a statement Grant made in a letter to his father on Oct. 1, 1858. Saying that he preferred his father's "offer to any one of mere salary that could be offered," he continued: "I do not want any place for permanent stipulated pay, but want the prospect of one day doing business for myself. There is a pleasure in knowing that one's income depends somewhat upon his exertions and business capacity, that cannot be felt when so much and no more is coming in, regardless of the success of the business engaged in or the manner in which it is done." (Cramer, *Letters of Grant*, p. 12.) There is no reason to believe that Grant's agreement with his father was not in accord with what he had written. Garland (*Grant*, p. 149) quotes a nephew-in-law of Jesse Grant as saying that everyone connected with the store looked up to Ulysses as an older man and former soldier, and explains that, although the three Grant brothers had guaranteed salaries of only $600 a year, they were working for a common fund and had what they needed.

NOTES TO CHAPTER II

1. Lewis, *Captain Sam Grant*, p. 395. Lewis is the chief source for the first part of the chapter. Some of Grant's statements in his *Memoirs* are incorrect, both as to what occurred locally—reported by Lewis from other sources—and nationally. For instance, he says (I, 229) that eleven states had seceded by the date of Lincoln's inauguration, while only seven had; he also describes the President's first call as one for "75,000 volunteers for ninety days' service," when in reality it was a call for militia—and the distinction is important. He states further that the second call was for 300,000 (*ibid.*, p. 242). The second call and the troops actually raised under it was considered *supra*, I, 114–118. Wilson's discussion in his *The Life of Rawlins* of matters covered in the first pages of this chapter cannot always be accepted as accurate; he even places the Battle of Bull Run in mid-June, 1861 (p. 51). The *Life* was written in fulfillment of a promise made to Rawlins in 1869 to be his literary executor; but it was not published until 1916, when Wilson was 79 years old.

2. Lewis gives much of the letter (*op. cit.*, pp. 403–404), quoting from Burr's work on Grant (1885). The original is in a private collection; a copy is in the author's possession.

3. Cramer, *Letters of Grant*, pp. 24–26. The letter also appears in facsimile form.

4. Lewis, *op. cit.*, pp. 409–410.

5. Grant, *op. cit.*, I, 239; Lewis, *op. cit.*, pp. 410–413; Cramer, *op. cit.*, pp. 27–30.

6. Cramer, *loc. cit.* Grant's Aunt Rachel, a Mrs. Tompkins, lived in Virginia on a large plantation with many slaves, and was completely loyal to the South. In this letter to Mary, Grant said he would like to see a copy of a letter from their aunt to their sister Clara. Cramer gives "as a historical curiosity" a letter written June 5 from Chestnut Hill, Va. by Mrs. Tompkins's secretary and directed to "Miss Grant." It argues the case of the South at length and with much underlining of words. Near the end of the letter is the passage: "Mrs. Tompkins says that if *you* can justify your Bro. Ulysses in drawing his sword against those connected by the ties of blood, and even boast of it, you are at liberty to do so, *but she can not.* And should one of those kindred be stricken down by his sword the awful judgment of God will be meted out to him, &, if not repented of, the hot thunderbolts of His wrath will blaze round his soul through eternity."

7. Lewis, *op. cit.*, pp. 414–415, 418–419; Cramer, *op. cit.*, p. 32.

8. Cramer, *op. cit.*, pp. 34–37.

9. Lyons's report, *O.R., 3,* 4–7; Lyon to Cameron, June 29, *ibid.*, pp. 386–387.

10. *Ibid.*, pp. 7–9, 369–370.

11. Grant, *op. cit.*, I, 234–238; Lewis, *op. cit.*, pp. 421–422.

12. Lewis gives the letter as taken from the original in the National Archives (*op. cit.*, p. 424). As given by Grant, *op. cit.*, I, 239–240, and in *O.R., 122,* 234, some editing has been done.

13. Cramer, *op. cit.*, pp. 38–39.

14. Grant, *op. cit.*, I, 240.

15. Lewis, *op. cit.*, pp. 317, 319.

16. Young, *Around the World with General Grant*, II, 213–215; Lewis, *op. cit.*, pp. 425–426; McClellan, *Own Story*, p. 47.

17. Lewis, *op. cit.*, p. 426. Lewis states that Jesse Grant later recalled that he forwarded the governor's telegram to Terre Haute, where Reynolds had temporarily gone. Tradition in Lafayette, however, says that Grant stopped there to see Reynolds.

18. *Ibid.*, pp. 427–428.

19. *Ibid.*, pp. 428–430.

20. Grant's *Memoirs*, I, 246–254, are the source for his service through Mexico, Mo. He incorrectly stated, however, that Col. Palmer commanded the 13th instead of the 14th Illinois.

21. The two changes of orders, alluded to in the *O.R.*, were due to McClellan, who first meant to send Grant to Bloomfield, Mo., and then countermanded the order (Harding to Frémont, July 19, and Harding to Lyon, July 21, *O.R., 3,* 399–403).

22. Phisterer, *Statistical Record*, pp. 267–269. Phisterer shows the date of promotion to major general or the date and cause of termination of service. Of the 37 officers, 22 were promoted, 4 were mustered out, 3 declined the appointment, 1 was killed in action, 5 resigned, and 2 died.

Appointments were dated back to May 17 probably to do justice to seniority, a few of the officers on the list ranking some who had been promoted several weeks before on account of special situations. For instance, Lyon was appointed in May, but he appears twelfth in order of rank on the completed list.

23. Sherman, *Memoirs,* I, 171–172. Sherman, whose letter was headed, "Office of St. Louis Railroad Company," said he would not volunteer because he did not think he should be a private, and did not believe he had the chance of being elected to a suitable office because the men would not know him. Grant on the other hand in his letter gave no explanation as to why he was not volunteering.

24. Cramer, *op. cit.,* pp. 43–46.

25. *O.R., 3,* 390; Nicolay and Hay, *Lincoln,* IV, 402–403, quoting Montgomery Blair about Frémont's delay; *O.R., 3,* 406.

Harney was removed as commander of the old Department of the West on May 16, but there was apparently delay in the receipt of the order. On the 21st he published to the people of Missouri a proclamation to which was joined a copy of his agreement made the day before with Sterling Price for the pacification of the state. On the 24th Frank Blair said in a letter to Cameron, "The agreement between Harney and General Price gives me great disgust and dissatisfaction to the Union men; but I am in hopes we can get along with it, and think that Harney will insist on its execution to the fullest extent, in which case it will be satisfactory." On the 27th Adj. Gen. Thomas wrote to Harney expressing the President's doubt about the arrangement with Price, and saying, "The authority of the United States is paramount, and whenever it is apparent that a movement, whether by color of State authority or not, is hostile, you will not hesitate to put it down." Although Harney professed faith in Price, he wrote him several notes indicating he had information that arms were coming into the state and that organizations were threatening it. (*O.R., 3,* 374–381.)

Five days after relinquishing command to Lyon on May 31, Harney reiterated his belief in Price and said his own removal was an unmerited disgrace. On June 6 Missouri was added to McClellan's Department of the Ohio, the headquarters of the Department of the West being moved to Fort Leavenworth. With Lyon presently departing on an expedition, there was considerable confusion in St. Louis, which continued after Missouri was put into the revised Western Department on July 3, on account of Frémont's absence. As agent for the United States Frémont had purchased arms in Europe, about which Secretary of State Seward wired him on July 27, asking where the arms were and saying, "Send an invoice of the articles." The next day Frémont replied that the arms (of amount he did not mention) had been shipped to New York to his order, as he thought they would go to his department; and he added, "I trust you will confirm this disposition of them. The rebels are advancing in force from the South upon our lines. We have plenty of men, but absolutely no arms, and the condition of the State is critical." On July 28 Frémont importuned Montgomery Blair for three times the $353,761 that his quartermaster had requisitioned. On July 30 he wrote to Lincoln that there were $300,000 in unappropriated treasury funds in St. Louis, but the paymaster had refused to give him $100,000. He indicated he was going to seize it, ending his message, "I will hazard everything for the defense of the department you have confided to me, and I trust to you for support." (*Ibid.,* pp. 381, 383, 384, 409, 410, 416, 417.)

26. *Ibid.,* pp. 428–429, 430–431.

27. Letter to Grant's sister, Cramer, *op. cit.,* p. 38; *O.R., 3,* 431. Because reports appear ahead of correspondence in the *Official Records,* some of Grant's messages occur on earlier pages than the one just cited, but the pertinent dates are later. There are three or four references to him of date earlier than Aug. 8.

28. Lincoln to Burnside, July 27, 1863, *O.R., 35,* 461.

29. *O.R., 3,* 432.

30. *Ibid.,* pp. 432–433.

31. *Ibid.,* pp. 598, 612, 433.

32. *Ibid.,* pp. 130–131.

33. *Ibid.,* p. 438.

34. Cramer, *op. cit.,* pp. 47–49.

35. *O.R., 3,* 437–438.

36. *Ibid.,* pp. 440–441.

37. *Ibid.,* pp. 442–443.

38. Harding to L. Thomas, July 7, *ibid.,* pp. 391–392; Schofield to Harding, July 15, *ibid.,* pp. 395–396; Harding to Lyon, July 21, *ibid.,* pp. 400–403; Lyon to Harding, July 17, *ibid.,* p. 397; Schofield to Harding, July 26, *ibid.,* pp. 407–408.

Col. Chester Harding, Jr., was an adjutant general of Missouri volunteers and was virtually in command at St. Louis after Lyon's departure. The long letter he wrote to Lyon on July 21 gave a full explanation of the situation at Cairo and in Missouri. He spoke of "mismanagement of transportation at Rolla," and of equipment and supplies lying there when he supposed they had gone forward. On July 17 Lyon wrote at length to Scott's adjutant, describing his difficulties and saying, "But for the immense interests at stake I could never have undertaken the great work in which I am engaged under such discouraging circumstances" (*ibid.,* pp. 397–398).

39. *Ibid.,* pp. 47–48.

40. Schofield's report, *ibid.,* pp. 61–62. Presumably on account of Lyon's death Schofield submitted a report covering everything from the time of arrival at Springfield from Rolla to the time of his return to regimental command on the retreat after the battle. In reference to the meeting between Lyon and Sigel, he wrote, "I was not present at the conference, having spent the morning in going the rounds of the camp to see if any improvement could be made in our dispositions for defense, thinking all intention of making an attack had been abandoned." He also gave emphasis to the fact that "the enemy showed no indication of an intention to advance in force."

Lyon had, as his dispatch of the 4th indicated, called for reenforcements. A telegram from headquarters that was sent to Frémont while the latter was inspecting Cairo on the 6th said: "General Lyon wants soldiers—soldiers—soldiers. So says General Hammer, who has just arrived from Springfield."

(*Ibid.*, p. 419.) Frémont has been blamed for not properly supporting Lyon, but it is hard to see the full justice of this. Lyon had accepted the necessity of retirement, and Schofield makes it abundantly clear that a battle was not forced upon him.

41. *Ibid.*, pp. 61–62.

42. Sturgis gives in his report the composition of the two columns and speaks of being confronted by an enemy force of 20,000 when he assumed command (*ibid.*, pp. 64–71). He also states, "Our ammunition was well-nigh exhausted, and should the enemy make this discovery through a slackening of our fire, total annihilation was all we could expect." He was undoubtedly in a very difficult position, and one can understand his saying, "The great question in my mind was, 'Where is Sigel?'" Sturgis's promotion to a brigadier generalcy was dated back to Aug. 10, 1861. His service in the East has been described in Vols. I and II of this work.

In his report Sigel stated that an enemy regiment that was thought to be from Lyon's column got to within ten paces of his battery, killed all the horses, turned the flanks of his infantry and forced them to retire (*ibid.*, pp. 86–88). An incident of the same sort had taken place at Bull Run. The enlistment time of the 5th Missouri had already expired, but Sigel had induced them, "company by company," to remain for eight days; this period had terminated on the 9th. In his other infantry regiment, 400 three-month men had been discharged, their places having been taken by recruits who had had little drill. About two-thirds of his officers had left, some companies having no officers at all.

43. Livermore, *Numbers and Losses*, p. 78, puts the Federal killed at 223, wounded at 721, and missing at 291, giving total casualties of 1235. For the Confederates he gives: killed, 257; wounded, 900; missing, 27; total, 1184. He puts Lyon's force at about 5,400, and McCulloch's "effectives" at about 11,600. Price commanded the Missouri troops but put them under the orders of Mc-Culloch (*O.R.*, *3*, 99).

44. *O.R.*, *3*, 439. At noon on Aug. 12, Cols. J. B. Wyman and J. D. Stevenson at Rolla with the 13th and 7th Missouri Volunteers, wrote to Frémont a dispatch based on the report of a messenger who had just arrived from Springfield (*ibid.*, *111*, 500). It stated that McCulloch and Price as well as Lyon had been killed, and said, "The force of the enemy, by their muster-rolls captured, was 23,000, with rifled cannon . . . . Major-General [sic] Lyon's aide, Major Farrar, will bear this dispatch, and give you all information."

45. *Ibid.*, *3*, 440. Sigel was one of the brigadiers dating from May 17. His appointment was confirmed by the Senate on Aug. 3.

46. *Ibid.*

47. *Ibid.*, p. 54. All other messages were signed "J. C. Frémont," and had his rank added. This was signed "John C. Fremont," without any rank. The dispatch repeats information in that from Cols. Wyman and Stevenson.

48. *Ibid.*, p. 441.

49. *N.Y. Tribune*, Aug. 15.

50. *O.R.*, *3*, 439, 441–442.

51. Order to Col. Lauman (7th Iowa) and five other colonels, *ibid.*, p. 440. Lauman's order was afterward changed and he was sent to Ironton (*ibid.*, p. 442). See also orders *ibid.*, *111*, 500–501.

52. Order to Col. Thayer (1st Nebraska), *ibid.*, *3*, 442.

53. *Ibid.*

54. Schofield's report, *ibid.*, p. 64; report of Lieut. John V. DuBois, *ibid.*, p. 80.

The next February, Schofield wrote (*ibid.*, pp. 94–95) to Halleck, then commanding the Department of the Missouri, about Sigel, who was being considered for promotion. He said that Sigel's technical military knowledge was far superior to that of most officers in the army, and that he was conversant with military history. But he pronounced him "greatly deficient" in "tactics, great and small logistics, and discipline." He added that he did not condemn Sigel "in the unmeasured terms common among many," and on the contrary saw many fine qualities in him. He said, however, that he *knew* Sigel could not create "confidence in the troops he is to command." As basis for his remarks Schofield repeated some of his observations on the retreat from Springfield.

55. *Ibid.*, p. 443.

56. Lincoln Papers, LIII, 11226. On the 17th Frémont wrote the President a letter in which he put the entire force that had entered the state at 60,000 and that of McCulloch at 35,000 (*ibid.*, pp. 11257–11258).

57. *Ibid.*, p. 444.

58. *Ibid.*, pp. 444–445, 444.

59. *Ibid.*, p. 445.

60. *Ibid.*

61. *Ibid.*

62. Grant, *op. cit.*, I, 257; Frémont's directive to Prentiss, Aug. 15, *O.R.*, *3*, 443–444.

NOTES TO CHAPTER III

1. Young, *Around the World with General Grant*, II, 214–215; *Harper's Weekly*, V, 555, 604 (Aug. 31 and Sept. 21, 1861), with a picture of the camp on p. 596.

2. *O.R.*, *111*, 499. The date Aug. 9 is obviously incorrect. It should probably be Aug. 19, which is that on a note refusing Grant a leave of absence "for the present" (*ibid.*, p. 501).

3. *O.R.*, *3*, 452.

4. Report of Grover to Grant, *ibid.*, p. 140. There were a few casualties. The train was stopped, the men detrained, and the assailants dispersed.

5. *Ibid.*, pp. 452–453.

6. *Ibid.*, p. 454.

7. *Ibid.*, p. 463.

8. *Ibid.*, p. 465; Grant, *Memoirs*, I, 260. Grant's last dispatch from Jefferson City was dated Aug. 28. A message from Frémont to Davis (*O.R.*, *3*,

461), dated Aug. 27, and addressed to Davis at Jefferson City, speaks of not having heard from him. If all dates are correct, it looks as if Davis was slow in going to his assignment.

9. *O.R., 3,* 463.

10. *Ibid.,* p. 109.

11. *Ibid.,* pp. 141–142. The order is addressed "Brigadier-General Grant, present," and is dated Aug. 28.

12. On June 3, Gen. Scott telegraphed to McClellan at Cincinnati that Anderson was sick, and asked if a Col. Guthrie of the Kentucky Volunteers would be suitable for his place; if so, McClellan was to put him in command. McClellan replied the next day that Guthrie, instead of being a Kentuckian, was a native of Urbana, O., and was entirely unsuited for the Kentucky situation; he recommended that no one be put in Anderson's place; he could take care of it himself. (*Ibid., 109,* 156, 156–157.) The order of Aug. 15 creating the new Department of the Cumberland is *ibid., 4,* 254.

13. *O.R., 3,* 143.

14. Cramer, *Letters of Grant,* pp. 53–55.

15. *O.R., 4,* 255.

16. *Ibid.,* pp. 255–256. On Aug. 29, Thomas Scott telegraphed to Gov. Morton a request to meet Anderson the next day at noon at the Burnett House, Cincinnati, to communicate all the information he had about Kentucky; if he could not go he was to send a confidential messenger (*ibid., 109,* 187). Anderson's departure from Washington was evidently delayed.

17. *O.R., 3,* 144, 144–145. Grant informed Frémont about his communication to McClernand.

18. Grant, *op. cit.,* p. 262; *O.R., 3,* 453–454, 146. From Frémont's instructions, Grant must have believed that Prentiss had stopped at Jackson. In his first dispatch to Frémont on Sept. 1 he spoke of not hearing from Prentiss; in a later message he said, "General Prentiss has just arrived" (*ibid.,* pp. 144, 145).

19. *Ibid.,* pp. 144, 145–146. On Aug. 5 John Nicolay, at Lincoln's direction, wired Frémont for a report about Cairo. The next day Nicolay sent Gen. Scott a note telling of the President's action and enclosing a copy of Frémont's reply (*ibid.,* p. 427). On the 2nd Frémont had reported to Scott from Birds Point, stating he had just arrived with eight transports. He said that the day before Pillow had at New Madrid 11,000 men, including 2,000 well appointed cavalry, and had been "further re-enforced today" (*ibid.,* p. 420).

20. *Ibid.,* pp. 142, 147.

21. Wilson, *Grant's Letters to a Friend,* pp. 1–2; Wilson, *Rawlins,* p. 53. Grant had written to Rawlins from St. Louis on Aug. 7, the day before he went to Ironton.

22. *O.R., 3,* 146–147, 154–155.

23. Grant to Frémont, *ibid.,* p. 149.

24. *Ibid.,* pp. 151–152; Grant to Frémont, *ibid.,* p. 148.

25. *Ibid.,* pp. 147–148.

26. *Ibid.,* p. 142. Grant's telegram does not seem to be in the records, but it is referred to in a letter (*ibid.,* p. 149) written later in the day. Whether

the telegram alluded to New Madrid and said the operation should be made the next night, is uncertain; the letter did.

27. *Ibid.,* pp. 152, 141, 470. Cameron said that the governor of Indiana had telegraphed several days before about the serious aspect of matters in Kentucky, and he had been advised, with the President's consent, to hold "four regiments in camp for the emergency he feared." The dispatch ended: "If this Department was more fully advised by you of the wants of your department, we might be able to serve you more promptly. It certainly is my desire to give you every possible assistance."

28. *O.R.,* 4, 399, 179, 180, 181.

29. Nicolay and Hay, *Lincoln,* IV, 240; *O.R., 109,* 188; *3,* 166, 150. Just what orders had been given about fortifications in Kentucky is not clear. Frémont's initial letter to Grant spoke only of works already commenced in Illinois and Missouri. A dispatch that McClernand sent Frémont at midnight on the 5th described "the engineering party" that had spent the day in Kentucky (*O.R., 4,* 196). See also *infra,* n. 36. Grant's words, "I am now nearly ready for Paducah," clearly imply a previous dispatch, and the one in the records must be the second message Grant alludes to in *Memoirs,* I, 265.

30. Grant's report, *O.R., 4,* 197; McClernand to Frémont, *ibid.,* p. 196.

31. *O.R., 109,* 189; *4,* 198. The directions to Paine stressed discipline and the restraining of men from entering private houses.

32. *Ibid., 3,* 149–150. The message is dated Sept. 5, but Grant's *Memoirs,* I, 267, state that he got it on his return to Cairo. Rather elaborate directions for fortifications in Kentucky opposite Cairo imply previous instructions. In an article written twenty-five years after the events ("In Command in Missouri," *B. and L.,* I, 278–288), Frémont ignores messages received from Grant on Sept. 5, speaks in a way that gives the impression that his own directive about Paducah reached Grant that day, states that an officer he had sent within the Confederate lines stopped at Cairo, informed Grant that the enemy was moving on Paducah, and urged him to take that place without delay; he furthermore asserts that this was in accordance with his instructions to Grant on Aug. 28. Grant had his own spies, and the claim that an officer returning to Frémont told him the Confederates had started to Paducah is contradicted by Grant's statement in his report that he learned of this after reaching Paducah—he does not speak of the word as corroboration. Furthermore Paducah is not mentioned in Frémont's instructions of Aug. 28.

33. *O.R., 4,* 196–197, for telegram and letter; Grant to Paine and Hillyer (Grant's aide) to Paine, *ibid.,* pp. 198, 256.

34. *Ibid., 3,* 471; *107,* 320, 335. The instructions to Smith were communicated through Grant (*ibid., 4,* 257). The order putting Smith in command, dated Sept. 7, is *ibid., 109,* 190.

35. *Ibid.,* p. 189.

36. It is entirely unlikely that Grant had told McClernand to make the report about the Paducah expedition that McClernand wrote at midnight, Sept. 5 (*ibid., 4,* 196). It contained the serious error that Grant had taken "six 64-pounders, four 32-pounders, and six 6-pounders," when in reality he had "four pieces of light artillery." Though reporting on the outcome of the

expedition was Grant's prerogative and duty, McClernand said, "I anticipate the pleasure of being able to announce to you the entire success of this movement."

McClernand's report to Frémont on the 7th about the situation at Paducah (*ibid., 3, 475*) may have been somewhat justified by Grant's absence. But dispatches from Hillyer to Paine and to McClernand (*ibid., 4, 256*) show that Grant's headquarters were in touch with Frémont on that day and were transmitting instructions to subordinates in Grant's absence. Frémont encouraged McClernand's irregular procedure when he said in a telegram on the 8th, "Keep up frequent communication with Paducah, and keep me minutely advised" (*ibid., 3, 480*).

When Grant turned over command at Cape Girardeau to Col. M. L. Smith, he specifically instructed him to make reports directly to Frémont, unless he received instructions to the contrary (*ibid., 3, 144*). In that case there was a saving of time. Grant's order to Paine at Paducah concluded, "Make frequent reports to me at district headquarters, and also to the Department of the West at Saint Louis, sending me copies of such reports" (*ibid., 4, 198*).

37. *O.R., 3, 479.*

38. *Ibid., 4, 256, 402.*

39. A Frankfort dispatch of Sept. 7 to the *Cincinnati Commercial Tribune* said: "The stirring event of today was the arrival of Gen. Anderson, the hero of Fort Sumter. He was accompanied by his brother Larz Anderson of your city, and Capt. Prime, a member of his staff. We understand that his visit is not in his official character, but purely social."

40. The legislature overrode Magoffin's veto and he signed the proclamation on Sept. 13. Gen. Smith published it on Oct. 1 in a general order (*ibid., pp. 287–289*).

41. *O.R., 3, 466–467.*

42. *Ibid., pp. 469–470.*

43. *Ibid., pp. 477–478.*

44. *Ibid., pp. 478–479.* The letter begins, "I send by another hand what I ask you to consider in respect to the subject of the note by your special messenger."

45. Stone, *Immortal Wife,* p. 396; Nicolay and Hay, *op. cit.,* IV, 414–415.

46. Nicolay and Hay, *op. cit.,* IX, 333–334.

47. *Ibid.* Nicolay and Hay comment, "No man can be sufficiently sure of friends to write them such letters as this."

48. *O.R., 3, 463–465.* Statements in the first part of the letter suggest that Meigs was not concerned about cost; but in the latter part he speaks of how he had brought prices down on horses and wagons.

49. Stone, *op. cit.,* p. 404; Nicolay and Hay, *op. cit.,* IV, 414.

50. *O.R., 3, 485–486;* Nicolay and Hay, *op. cit.,* pp. 421–423.

51. *O.R., 3, 470;* Hendrick, *Lincoln's War Cabinet,* p. 387; *N.Y. Tribune,* Sept. 18, 20, Oct. 9, 1861. On the competency of Frémont to arrest Blair, the *Tribune* quoted the *St. Louis Democrat* of Sept. 17.

52. *O.R., 3, 502, 185, 503, 504.*

53. *Ibid., pp. 540–549.* The report appeared in the newspapers, e.g. in the

N.Y. Tribune of Oct. 30. After commenting upon the report, *Harper's Weekly* said on Nov. 16 (V, 722), "But nothing can justify its publication." For a short but judicious discussion of the charges against Frémont, see Goodwin, *John Charles Frémont,* pp. 234–237.

54. *O.R., 3,* 553.

55. *Ibid.,* pp. 251–252, 252–253.

56. Springfield dispatch of Oct. 29 in *N.Y. Tribune* of Nov. 6; *O.R., 3,* 557, 558, 559, 560. Stone, discussing sources in his *Immortal Wife,* asserts on p. 473 that, with the exception of a few enumerated technical liberties, the book is true. The treatment on pp. 412–420 of Frémont's removal, however, fails in important ways to agree with the official records. Stone describes Frémont as intending to attack at dawn, with promise of a great victory, when he received at midnight—with Jessie in his tent—a messenger *from Hunter* bearing the order relieving him of command. No mention is made of the fact that Lincoln had given explicit instructions that the order was not to be delivered if a battle was imminent. Stone claims that the order was sent by a courier to Hunter in St. Louis.

Stone states that he portrayed only one or two incidents that he could not document, and mentions one. Mrs. Frémont's hurried trip to Springfield to warn her husband, which is graphically set forth at some length, is not easily reconciled with news dispatches. One from Springfield on the 3rd, published by the *N.Y. Tribune* on the 7th, read: "Gen. Fremont and staff left here for St. Louis this morning. He is accompanied by his Body Guard, and will reach St. Louis on Wednesday." It is not likely that the reporter included the general's wife as part of his staff or bodyguard. Stone has the Frémonts reach St. Louis together by train. A dispatch of the 8th (*ibid.,* Nov. 9) said: "Gen. Fremont arrived here in a special train this evening, and was met at the depot by an immense and enthusiastic crowd of citizens. Large delegations of Germans from the various Wards in the city escorted the General to his quarters in a torchlight procession."

Though Frémont had nothing to do with Grant's promotion to a brigadiership, Stone says on p. 405 that Frémont "appointed" him, explaining to his wife that he did so because Grant had qualities he could not find combined in any other man—dogged persistence and iron will. These characteristics had not yet been demonstrated, and in the article referred to in note 32 Frémont did not claim he had appraised Grant highly.

57. *O.R., 3,* 561, 560. A Springfield dispatch of Nov. 3 stated that small bodies of the enemy had the day before come within twelve miles and preparations were being made by Frémont to attack them when the order relieving him was received. A message the next day said a scout reported the enemy as slowly advancing, and added that a battle was imminent at any moment. But a dispatch of the 5th announced that Hunter had made a reconnaissance on the 4th with 1,400 cavalry and a section of guns; the country near Wilson's Creek had been explored, but no enemy had been found, having reportedly left on the 3rd. The main hostile body was said to be at Cassville and Hunter was represented as having little faith that the enemy would attack. A dispatch of the 6th said that information received by Hunter indicated that Price, if

pursued further, would scatter his army or retire to Ft. Smith, Ark. (*N.Y. Tribune*, Nov. 7, 9).

On Nov. 6 Price issued an order at Cassville to continue his retreat toward Pineville the next morning. The following day he wrote to Gen. A. S. Johnston from west of Cassville saying he was falling back toward Arkansas before Frémont, who had halted at Springfield, apparently to rest and await the arrival of the remainder of his forces. In a letter of the 8th to the Confederate Secretary of War, Gen. McCulloch said his scouts had been "near and around" Springfield for the last eight or ten days, and he reported the continuous arrival of Federal troops, estimated at near 50,000 men with 120 guns. (*O.R.*, 3, 731–732, 733–734.)

It seems certain that Frémont did little if anything in the way of reconnoitering at a distance and mistook enemy patrolling and reconnaissance as an indication of an intended advance.

58. *O.R.*, *3*, 553–554.

59. *Ibid.*, p. 569. A Springfield dispatch of Nov. 4 spoke of the great gloom caused in the army by the removal of Frémont and of the possibility that the Germans would resist Hunter. The next day a reporter wrote: "The troops are now as apparently enthusiastic as ever, and the more they learn of their new commander the better they are satisfied with him. This feeling is also strengthened by the high opinion entertained of Gen. Hunter by all the old regular army officers. The reports that officers, many companies and regiments threw down their arms upon the announcement of the removal of Gen. Fremont, cannot be traced to any trustworthy source." (*N.Y. Tribune*, Nov. 8, 9.)

60. *Ibid.*, pp. 484–485, 536–537, 511, 168–169. The order Grant promised he would execute is not in the records. On Sept. 22 he made a reconnaissance in force toward Columbus, and in reporting about it (*ibid.*, *4*, 199–200) he stated that the health of his command was improving, though the number of sick was still large.

61. Cramer, *op. cit.*, p. 57.

62. *Ibid.*, pp. 57–58.

63. *O.R.*, *3*, 511, 536–537.

64. *Ibid.*, pp. 509, 401, 536–537, 556–557.

65. *Ibid.*, pp. 536–537, 537, 556.

66. Cramer, *op. cit.*, pp. 61–63. Grant states in *Memoirs*, I, 264, that he was in civilian clothes when he arrived at Cairo.

67. *O.R.*, *3*, 501–502, 511, 536–537; *4*, 306–307; *3*, 536, 556. Some of these references show that Grant and Smith received instructions directly from Frémont, though the dispatches are not in the records. Grant told Capt. McKeever that he was inclosing Sherman's dispatch, but a note by the editors of the *O.R.* indicates they did not find it.

Anderson issued at Cincinnati on Sept. 7 a special order removing his headquarters from that city to Louisville, and on Sept. 24 he issued belatedly at the latter place General Order No. 1 taking command of his department. Sherman assumed command on Oct. 8. (*O.R.*, *4*, 257, 273 with editorial note, 297.)

68. Lewis, *Captain Sam Grant*, p. 174.

69. W. P. Johnston, *Life of Gen. A. S. Johnston*, p. 247.

70. *Ibid.*, p. 291.

71. *O.R.*, *3*, 501; Johnston, *op. cit.*, pp. 308–309, 311–312. Gen. Johnston did not actually speak of the United States except in the opening of his proclamation, which began, "The armed occupation of a part of Kentucky by the United States. . . ." Then after referring to the Confederate States of America and the people of Kentucky, he said, "It is for them to say whether they will join either Confederacy, or . . . ." Like some other Southern leaders did, Johnston seemed to believe the right of secession was strengthened if the United States was described as a Confederacy. His son and biographer was inaccurate in saying that the Confederates occupied Hickman on Sept. 5 and Columbus on the 7th (*op. cit.*, p. 305), thus making the movement into Columbus the day after Grant took Paducah. The facts were of course readily available in 1878 when the *Life* was published. On Sept. 4, 1861, Gov. I. G. Harris of Tennessee protested to Polk about the movement of Pillow's forces into Hickman, of which he had just been informed, saying that both he and Davis were "pledged to respect the neutrality of Kentucky," and he hoped the troops would be withdrawn unless their presence was an "absolute necessity." Polk replied, "I had never received official information that the President and yourself had determined upon any particular course in reference to the State of Kentucky." (*O.R.*, *4*, 180.)

72. Grant had included his Aunt Rachel in the list of four persons to whom he wished his sister to send photographs (Cramer, *op. cit.*, p. 63).

73. Confederate insignia of rank were on the stand-up collar and not on the shoulders as in the U. S. Army (*O.R.*, *Atlas*, II, Plate CLXXII). Rather strangely, all generals, from brigadier to full general, had the same collar badge—a wreath enclosing one large and two small stars. In the first volumes of this work the error was made of assuming that the number of stars a Confederate general officer wore varied from one to four, and in some cases the stars were put on the shoulder. In spite of the uniformity of the Confederate insignia, Southern officers will on occasion be referred to as one-, two-, three-, or four-star generals.

74. Henderson, *Science of War*, p. 256.

NOTES TO CHAPTER IV

1. *O.R.*, *3*, 558, 556. Grant's brigades were very unequal in strength, McClernand having 4,515 officers and men, and Wallace only 726. His order of Oct. 14, brigading his troops, gave Wallace three infantry regiments, four companies of cavalry, and a battery (*ibid.*, pp. 533–534); but on the 27th he thought it "prudent and humane" to send the 2nd Iowa to St. Louis to recuperate its health (*ibid.*, p. 556).

2. *Anna Ella Carroll*, "Plan of the Tennessee Campaign," *North American Review*, CXLII, 342–347 (Apr., 1886).

3. Grant's report on Belmont, *O.R.*, *3*, 267.

4. *Ibid.*, p. 268.

5. *Ibid.*, pp. 259, 268.

6. *Ibid.*, pp. 268, 273, 269. McKeever's order is not in the records, but Grant describes it.

7. Conger, *The Rise of Grant*, Appendix, p. 371. Grant's order to Oglesby was: "On receipt of this turn your column towards New Madrid. When you arrive at the nearest point to Columbus from which there is a road to that place, communicate with me at Belmont." The words "arrive at" and "communicate with," leave no doubt that a halt was intended. The order to Wallace began, "Herewith I send you an order to Colonel Oglesby to change the direction of his column towards New Madrid, halting to communicate with me at Belmont from the nearest point on his road." Actually Conger is contradictory, for he states on p. 85 that Oglesby was to halt and communicate with Grant at Belmont.

8. *O.R.*, *3*, 273.

9. Grant's report, *ibid.*, pp. 267–273. The report is drawn upon for details of the operation without specific reference. For a discussion of the report and Conger's comment thereon, see Appendix I.

10. Dougherty's report, *ibid.*, p. 291.

11. *O.R.*, *3*, 270.

12. *Ibid.*, p. 259. The dispatch is headed, "On board transport near Columbus, Ky., November 7, 1861." Without stating the hour, it begins, "Yours of yesterday just received."

13. Col. Perczel's report, *ibid.*, pp. 258–259.

14. Walke's report, *ibid.*, pp. 275–276.

15. *Ibid.*, pp. 308, 363. Capt. Butler of the *Prince* spoke of the *H. R. W. Hill* as also taking reenforcements across the river (*ibid.*, p. 362).

16. Report of Surgeon J. H. Britton, *ibid.*, pp. 274–275; Grant, *Memoirs*, I, 278–279; Force, *From Fort Henry to Corinth*, p. 23. Conger states the boarding incident should not be taken seriously because it lacks corroboration (*op. cit.*, p. 376). One must doubt that he had read the statement in Force's book, a work of much merit that will be cited frequently. Personal experiences such as a ride across a narrow plank, and the narrow escape from a bullet that Grant said soon followed are likely to remain vivid in the memory. Conger makes no comment about the second incident.

17. *O.R.*, *3*, 271, 281. Buford spoke of being intercepted before taking the new route (*ibid.*, pp. 284–285).

18. Smith to Paine, *ibid.*, p. 301. Smith sent a regiment to cover Paine's left flank (order to Col. Sanderson, *ibid.*, p. 302).

19. *Ibid.*, p. 299.

20. *Ibid.*, *III*, 506; Walke's, Grant's, and Oglesby's reports, *ibid.*, *3*, 376, 272, 256–257; Grant to Smith, *ibid.*, *4*, 346. Conger's description (*op. cit.*, p. 366) of the message to Smith is brief and rather misleading. His implication that Grant's dispatch to McKeever differs essentially from that to Smith is not warranted, for the two messages are essentially the same in what they say of the battle.

21. *O.R., 111,* 507; *4,* 346.

22. *Ibid., 3,* 274.

23. Conger, *loc. cit.* Conger states that Grant had an "altered point of view" the day after the battle and forgot the dark hours of the enemy counterattack and the pursuit. Doubtless he may have appraised things differently on the 8th; but nothing in the dispatches he sent on the night of the 7th supports Conger's assertion.

24. Grant to Polk, *O.R., 114,* 515. On Oct. 14 Polk had written to Grant proposing exchange of some prisoners on the basis of terms agreed upon Sept. 5 by Gen. Pillow and Col. Wallace. The same day Grant replied, saying: "In regard to the exchange of prisoners proposed I can of my own accord make none. I recognize no Southern Confederacy myself but will communicate with higher authority for their views. Should I not be sustained I will find means of communicating with you." (*Ibid.,* p. 511.) It was, as Conger notes (*op. cit.,* p. 102), a rather brusque reply; but Conger gives no support for his statement that Grant was not "sustained." The letter that he says Grant "caused" McClernand to write to Polk on Oct. 22 did not propose "exchange" but spoke of releasing some prisoners "unconditionally" (*O.R., 114,* 512). Polk replied, ". . . and although your mode of accomplishing it waives the recognition of our claims as belligerents I am not disposed to insist on an unimportant technicality when the interests of humanity are at stake" (*ibid.,* p. 513), and made good his word by giving up sixteen Federals for three Confederates.

Polk wrote to Grant on Dec. 6, in a letter that seems to have terminated the Belmont incident and gives a breakdown of figures, "I have released 114 against 124 released by you" (*ibid.,* p. 529). He spoke as if in the future men would be "exchanged" man-for-man and grade-for-grade. The figure he gave indicated that six men Grant offered to release declined to return and Polk gave credit for only those who did.

25. Polk to Grant, *ibid.,* pp. 515–516. That Polk had received recent instructions from his superiors was revealed to Webster by the officer who represented him. From the full report that Webster wrote on the 9th (*ibid.,* pp. 516–517) it appears that all the 64 prisoners that Grant offered were wounded or sick; but they could not have been serious cases, or Grant could not have taken them to his transports.

26. Cramer, *Letters of Grant,* pp. 64–67.

27. The *Chicago Tribune* referred on Nov. 14 to the copying of the *Journal's* account by the *Cleveland Herald.* Then it charged the *Journal* had no special correspondent at Cairo but had manufactured its story from dispatches sent to the *Tribune,* having probably learned the trick from the *Chicago Times,* which it pronounced adept at "stealing special dispatches and manufacturing correspondence."

28. Sandburg, *Lincoln,* II, 536.

29. The letter, which was signed "C," began, "Croaking has become the order of the times," and continued: "Our late descent on Belmont has been characterized as 'marching up the hill, and marching down again,' with great loss; and nothing more; as if there had been no object in view, or as if the

ridiculous idea had been entertained by Generals Grant and McClernand, of taking and holding Belmont."

30. The dispatch, which is reprinted in Moore, *Rebellion Record*, II, 287–288, gave correctly Grant's object in attacking and said: "It might be well to notice here the underhanded antagonism evident in many of our prominent journals to the Union cause, in pronouncing—even in the face of positive evidence to the contrary—every action in which our troops are engaged, and as must necessarily be, a few of our numbers are slain, to be positive defeats and repulses."

In replying to his father on Nov. 28 about a newspaper attack upon himself and McClernand, Grant said, "All who were on the battlefield know where General McClernand and myself were, and there is no need of resort to the public press for our vindication" (Cramer, *op. cit.*, pp. 72–73).

31. Fiske, *The Mississippi Valley in the Civil War*, p. 50.

32. *O.R.*, *3*, 277, 277–283; *111*, 506. The dispatch of Nov. 8 refers to the one of the 6th.

33. *Ibid.*, *3*, 566–567, 567; *111*, 507. The dispatch that Curtis allowed to go forward is not in the records but is described in his message of the 8th. His telegram of 3:00 P.M., Nov. 9, stated: "Yesterday Colonel Fiala sent report of General Grant's movement on Belmont, as ordered by General Frémont today." Fiala was one of Frémont's officers.

34. *Ibid.*, *111*, 507. For Grant's reply, see *ibid.*, *3*, 570–571.

35. The supplementary volume of the records containing McKeever's dispatch was not published until 1898; the volume with Curtis's telegram and most of the documents on Belmont appeared in 1881, four years before Grant's death.

36. War Department General Order No. 99, 1861.

37. Mearns, *Lincoln Papers*, I, 160; Nicolay and Hay, *Lincoln*, IV, 114–115.

38. *O.R.*, *3*, 548.

39. Lewis says (*Sherman*, p. 194) that Sherman had said 60,000 men were needed for defense and "for offense, before we are done, 200,000." It is difficult to believe that Sherman had ever made a careful estimate of man power needed for general offensive operations in the West; and his actions a short time later—described in Chapter VI—make it doubtful that he thought 60,000 men sufficient for defense.

R. M. Kelly in his twenty-page article "Holding Kentucky for the Union," *B. and L.*, Vol. I, states (p. 385): "In explaining the needs of his department to the Secretary, Sherman expressed the opinion that two hundred thousand men would be required for successful operations on his line. This estimate, which, as events showed, evinced remarkable foresight, then discredited his judgment." What is meant by "on his line" is not clear. The Department of the Cumberland, which Sherman commanded, consisted of Kentucky and Tennessee; except for East Tennessee, the Federals had secured most of this region by the end of March, 1862, with far fewer than 200,000 troops.

40. *O.R.*, *4*, 340–341; Sherman, "An Address on Grant," in Wilson and Coan, *Personal Recollections*, pp. 109–110; Dana and Wilson, *Life of Grant*, pp. 52–53.

41. Conger, *op. cit.*, pp. 95, 68, 372.

42. *Ibid.*, p. 367; Cramer, *op. cit.*, p. 65; Detrich's report, *O.R.*, *3*, 294–295; *O.R.*, Atlas, I, Plate IV–3; Conger, *op. cit.*, p. 375; McClernand's report, *O.R.*, *3*, 280; Grant, *Memoirs*, I, 274.

43. Taylor's report, *O.R.*, *3*, 290.

44. Oglesby's report, *ibid.*, pp. 256–257; Thompson to Polk, *ibid.*, p. 261; Perczel's report, *ibid.*, pp. 258–259.

45. Paine's report, *ibid.*, pp. 302–303; Smith's order, *ibid.*, p. 303.

46. *Ibid.*, *4*, 522. For cancellation of request see *ibid.*, *7*, 746.

47. Polk's report, *ibid.*, *3*, 306–310.

48. Paine's report, *ibid.*, pp. 302–303.

49. A dispatch to Polk from Col. C. Wickliffe on Nov. 7 said word had just been received confirming a report he had previously sent by a Maj. Milburn about "the advance of a column from Paducah in the direction of Columbus, or rather southeasterly from Paducah" (*ibid.*, p. 733). "Southwesterly" must have been meant, for Paine camped for the night on Mayfield Creek on the Clinton road (*ibid.*, p. 302).

50. *Ibid.*, pp. 304, 311. Polk's telegram of the 8th ended, "Enemy at Milburn last night 7,000 strong." Paine's command of four regiments, a battery, and some dragoons, was certainly not half that strength. Johnston replied to Polk on the 8th; he said he had awaited dispatches with more details (*ibid.*, pp. 310–311).

51. Polk's report, *ibid.*, p. 310.

52. Grant, in a short report which he wrote on Nov. 20 when forwarding those of his subordinates, stated that persons coming from the South put the enemy loss at 600 and added, "My own impression is, their loss was much greater" (*ibid.*, pp. 272–273). What led him to his new view when the figure he quoted confirmed the one he gave on the 8th, is difficult to see.

53. Brinton's report, *ibid.*, pp. 274–275; *B. and L.*, I, 355 n., where the killed are put at 120, the wounded at 383, and the captured at 104.

54. *O.R.*, *3*, 310.

55. *Ibid.*, p. 312.

56. *Ibid.*, pp. 313–316, 317.

57. William M. Polk, "General Polk and the Battle of Belmont," *B. and L.*, I, 348–357. A subsequent account by the same writer appears in *Leonidas Polk*, II, Chap. II.

58. *B. and L.*, I, 356–357. On Nov. 11 Polk was injured by the bursting of a large gun, two officers and about ten men being instantly killed in the accident (W. M. Polk, *Leonidas Polk*, II, 44–46). Pillow commanded at Columbus for about two weeks, and Polk's report of the 10th was apparently not forwarded at once (*O.R.*, *7*, 705). On the 13th Pillow sent Davis a short report on the recent battle; he put the Confederate loss at 632 and the Federal at about 2,000; he also spoke of the certainty of a heavy attack upon Columbus within eight days (*ibid.*, *3*, 739).

NOTES TO CHAPTER V

1. Dyer, *Compendium*, pp. 254–257; Phisterer, *Statistical Record*, pp. 24–29; *O.R.*, Atlas, II, Plates CLXII–CLXXI; Halleck to Schenck, July 22, 1863, *O.R.*, *45*, 748.

2. *O.R.*, *3*, 567; *4*, 349.

3. *Ibid.*, *3*, 570, has the order about Sherman. An unsigned letter from McClellan to Buell dated Nov. 7 (*ibid.*, *4*, 342), makes it seem certain that Sherman's letter of Nov. 6 to the Adjutant General (*ibid.*, pp. 340–341), which concluded with the sentence suggesting that he be relieved, had not been received at the time it had been determined to supersede him with Buell. The statements he had made to the Secretary of War and Col. Thomas when they were in Louisville were probably responsible. The order that McClellan as commander of the Army of the Potomac issued to Buell to report to the General in Chief (himself) for orders, was dated Nov. 9 (*ibid.*, *107*, 503).

4. *Ibid.*, *3*, 567. It is doubtful if Frémont would ever have been returned to duty if it had not been for the agitation in his favor on account of his stand on slavery. He received an assignment in West Virginia the following March, with results already described.

5. Mearns, *Lincoln Papers*, I, 295–296; II, 343–344, 346–347, 457–458; Nicolay and Hay, *Lincoln*, III, 309; Cramer, *Letters of Grant*, p. 54.

Hunter tarnished his reputation somewhat by writing Lincoln a "private and confidential" note on the day of his inauguration, applying for the brigadiership in the regular army made vacant "by the treason of Gen. Twiggs." He spoke of Sumner as being an applicant and said, "I am as old if not a better soldier than Col. Sumner" (Mearns, *op. cit.*, II, 457–458). Sumner received the appointment.

6. Halleck, *Elements*, pp. 326 n., 404 n.

7. In *Ark of Empire* Jones shows Halleck's essential part in the building of the Montgomery Block, and gives a portrayal of his achievements in California previously lacking.

8. *Harper's Weekly*, V, 754 (Nov. 30, 1861); *O.R.*, *107*, 491–493.

9. Halleck to McClellan, Nov. 28, 1861, *O.R.*, *8*, 389–390, refers to personal talks; *ibid.*, *3*, 568–569, gives letter of instructions.

10. *O.R.*, *111*, 507; *122*, 519; McClellan, *Own Story*, p. 173; *O.R.*, *3*, 570–571; *7*, 442.

11. *O.R.*, *107*, 369–370.

12. *Ibid.*, pp. 386–387.

13. *Ibid.*, *122*, 167–170.

14. *Ibid.*, *4*, 385–387.

15. Sandburg, *Lincoln*, I, 424–425.

16. *O.R.*, *109*, 191–192.

17. Greeley, *The American Conflict*, I, 483. The figures are those published by Governor Harris on June 24. Greeley quotes at length from the proclamation by a convention held in June at Greeneville, East Tennessee, in which it was said that the vote of June 8 was "free, with but few exceptions, in no

part of the State, other than East Tennessee." The proceedings of the convention, including the names of delegates and an address to the legislature, is given in *O.R., 109,* 168–179. See also Patton, *Unionism and Reconstruction in Tennessee,* Chap. I.

18. Brownlow, *Sketches of Secession,* p. 277.

19. *O.R., 8,* 369, 370.

20. Halleck to Blair, in Raymond, *Life of Lincoln,* p. 330 n.; Nicolay and Hay, *op. cit.,* V, 94–95; Halleck to Asboth, *O.R., 8,* 465. On Dec. 4 the *N.Y. Tribune* reprinted and commended an attack on Halleck's order by the *St. Louis Democrat.*

21. *O.R., 8,* 817, 377, 818, 817, 395.

22. *Ibid.,* pp. 410, 468. On Dec. 7 Halleck directed the mayor of St. Louis to require all municipal officers to subscribe immediately to the oath of allegiance prescribed by the Convention of the state on Oct. 16, and he instructed the provost marshal to arrest all state civil officers who failed to take the oath within the prescribed time (*ibid.,* p. 414).

On Nov. 26 Governor H. R. Gamble issued General Order No. 1 from the Headquarters of the Missouri State Militia at St. Louis (*ibid.,* p. 378). The order described the arrangements made with the War Department about this new state force, prescribed its organization, and appointed and commissioned Halleck major general. The next day Halleck turned over command to Brig. Gen. John M. Schofield, who had also been commissioned in the new militia (*ibid.,* p. 389); on Dec. 26 Schofield was given command of Federal troops about Warrenton, Mo. (*ibid.,* p. 468).

23. *N.Y. Times,* Nov. 18; McCulloch to Cooper and to Benjamin, *O.R., 3,* 742–743, 743 (the latter essentially duplicated, *ibid., 8,* 686). McCulloch put the Federals at 30,000 with an abundance of artillery and reported considerable disaffection in their ranks as well as quarreling among officers. He stated that Brig. Gen. Lane had returned to Kansas, carrying off 500 to 600 Negroes belonging to Union men as well as secessionists, and that most Unionists had fled with the retiring Federal army, leaving Springfield nearly deserted.

24. Steele to Halleck, Halleck to Steele, Sigel, and Asboth, *O.R., 8,* 374–376; Special Order No. 8, *ibid.,* p. 374; Sherman to Halleck, Halleck to Sherman, *ibid.,* pp. 374–382. Another dispatch from Halleck to Sherman on the 27th read, "Unless telegraph lines are interrupted make no movement without orders" (*ibid., 111,* 507).

25. *Ibid., 8,* 382.

26. *Ibid.,* pp. 382, 391. For a dispatch from Pope on the 29th, and for one to Hunter from Halleck relaying reports about Price and McCulloch, see *ibid.,* pp. 393, 392.

27. Lewis, *Sherman,* p. 189.

28. *O.R., 109,* 198.

29. On Dec. 12 Sherman wrote to Halleck from Lancaster, O., beginning his letter: "I believe you will be frank enough to answer me if you deem the steps I took at Sedalia as evidence of a want of mind." In reference to a bitter attack by the *Cincinnati Commercial Tribune,* whose reporter he had disciplined while in Kentucky, he said: "These newspapers have us in their power,

and can destroy us as they please, and this one can destroy my usefulness by depriving me of the confidence of officers and men." (*O.R., 8,* 819.) The next day his foster brother, who was also his brother-in-law, wrote to Halleck, inclosing a copy of a letter he had just written to the editors of the *Commercial* (*ibid., 109,* 200–201). Halleck answered Ewing on the 17th and on the 18th he wrote to Sherman: "The newspaper attacks are certainly shameless and scandalous, but I cannot agree with you that they have us in their power 'to destroy us as they please.' I certainly get my share of abuse, but it will not disturb me." Halleck may have gone too far in explaining away his countermanding of Sherman's Sedalia order; but he did not whitewash Sherman, and referred to the troubled general's tactless remarks at St. Louis and at Sedalia. Certainly Sherman, recuperating at a home where he was surrounded by an affectionate and understanding family, should have felt that his superior was well disposed toward him and was carrying out his own hard work with confidence when he read the fine ending: "I hope to see you well enough for duty soon. Our reorganization goes slowly, but we will effect it in time." (*Ibid., 8,* 441–442, 445–446.)

30. *Ibid.,* pp. 695–697.

31. *Ibid.,* pp. 429, 436, 435, 436; Halleck's and Pope's reports, *ibid.,* pp. 37, 38–40; *ibid.,* p. 452. One of Pope's dispatches mentioned no cavalry and put the infantry at 1,600. For earlier thanks to a commander by Halleck, see, *ibid., 111,* 510.

32. Report of Maj. George C. Marshall, *O.R., 8,* 34–36; Halleck to McClellan, Dec. 20, *ibid.,* p. 37; Pope to Halleck, Dec. 12, *ibid.,* p. 429; Davis to W. P. Harris, *ibid.,* p. 701.

On Nov. 30 Secretary Benjamin wired McCulloch: "I cannot understand why you withdrew your troops instead of pursuing the enemy when his leaders were quarreling and his army separated into parts under different commanders. Send an explanation." (*Ibid.,* p. 699.) McCulloch answered that it was impossible to explain the matter by telegraph and asked permission to come to Richmond at once; his request was granted on condition it was safe to leave his command (*ibid.,* pp. 701–702). In his long report on his operations, written at Richmond on Dec. 22 (*ibid., 3,* 743–749), he stated that he and Price had been on friendly terms personally, but "never could agree as to the proper time for marching to the Missouri River." He advised fortifying Springfield and holding it with infantry and artillery, while Price's mounted men gave "protection against jayhawkers from Kansas."

Price wrote to McCulloch on Dec. 6, from a camp on the Sac River, that the condition of affairs in Missouri made it necessary for him to move his command to the Missouri River "at the earliest practicable day" (*ibid., 8,* 702–703). Roads, he said, were being closed against thousands of recruits who wished to join him. He begged McCulloch for instant and effective cooperation in a movement upon the Missouri River and also into Kansas. He stated that he was transferring the state troops as rapidly as possible "and very successfully" into the Confederate service.

33. *Ibid.,* pp. 408–410. Halleck expressed very candid views about the conditions in his command, and after saying it was not an army "but rather

a military rabble," and praising McClellan for what he had done for the Army of the Potomac, he said, "I hope, with your assistance, to do the same here. You are aware that I am almost destitute of regular officers, and those of the volunteers are, with some exceptions, entirely ignorant of their duties. It is said, General, that you have nearly as many regular officers on your personal staff as I have in this whole department. I was very sorry to receive your orders to-day taking away four or five of the very few I now have. I will, however, do the best I can without them." In his reply on Dec. 10, McClellan claimed this was an exaggeration (*ibid.*, p. 419).

34. *Ibid.*, p. 419.

35. *Ibid.*, p. 450.

36. *Ibid.*, pp. 448–450. On Dec. 6 Halleck had reported to McClellan, "The enemy is in possession of nearly one-half of the State, and a majority of 60,000 or 80,000 of the inhabitants are secessionists" (*ibid.*, p. 408). In a letter of the 10th, after referring to the behavior of troops under Lane and Col. C. R. Jennison, he said: "A few more such raids in connection with the ultra speeches made by leading men in Congress, will make this State as unanimous against us as is Eastern Virginia." He stated that the number of Union regiments from Missouri was misleading, because they were composed largely of foreigners or men from other states. A dispassionate examination of the whole matter based on talks with leading men from different parts of the state led him to believe that the majority of Missourians were against the Union; a single false step or a defeat would ruin the Federal cause. He saw action as the only way to deal with the situation and closed his letter; "Can't we get some arms soon? I cannot move without them. Winter is already upon us, and I fear much longer delay will render it exceedingly difficult to operate, and yet a winter campaign seems absolutely necessary to restore our lost ascendency and the quiet of the State." (*Ibid.*, pp. 818–819.)

37. Stephenson, *The Political Career of General James H. Lane*, pp. 22–25. Stephenson suggests that Gen. Taylor's report of the battle was biased in favor of Davis and against Lane by the fact that Davis's first wife was Taylor's daughter. Lane's regiment came to be known as the "Steadfast Third."

38. Nicolay and Hay, *op. cit.*, V, 83.

39. See Stephenson, *op. cit.*, Chap. XI, for a highly documented account of Lane's career from the breaking out of war until Feb. 16, 1862, when he wrote Lincoln declining the offered brigadiership. Something of Lane's character is revealed by his attitude with regard to his birthplace. Stephenson writes (p. 16): "Lane himself made conflicting statements. When it gave him political advantage, he was a native of Kentucky, but when it served his purpose better, he was a native of Indiana."

40. Nicolay and Hay, *op. cit.*, VI, 381.

41. Beveridge, *Lincoln*, III, 324.

42. *O.R., 4,* 308–309.

43. W. M. Polk, *Leonidas Polk,* II, 36. Nov. 28 is the date tentatively assigned by the editors of the *O.R.* to Polk's report on the state of the Tennessee and Cumberland river defenses, written in compliance with an order from Johnston when he took command in the West (*O.R., 7,* 710–711). Polk

stated that the forts were not in the region he commanded until Johnston arrived—in mid-September. An engineer officer had reported that Fort Henry was almost completed, and Polk said a Negro force furnished by planters in Tennessee and northern Alabama had been used to push it to completion, and to build another work across the river from it. He also said that the "service of a considerable slave force was obtained" to construct "additional outworks" for the fort on the Cumberland River. Heiman, commanding at Fort Henry, made a long report to Polk on Oct. 18, describing both his own work and Fort Donelson, which he said was inadequate unless outworks were built (*O.R.*, *4*, 459–462).

44. *Ibid.*, pp. 345–346. A tablet at the Fort Donelson Military Park states that work on the fort was started on May 10, 1861. Progress must have been slow.

45. *Ibid.*, pp. 453–454. On Sept. 15 Henry wrote to Davis about Polk's seizure of Columbus, saying there was some dissatisfaction in Nashville, but adding, "Whether it was altogether politic to take possession I need not say, but it will be ruinous to order him back." He believed Kentucky was not acting sincerely and made the strong statement: "The neutrality of Kentucky has been all the time a cloak to enable the Lincoln party there to hide their design to arm the friends of Lincoln and disarm the Southern Rights party. We ought to strike now. A step backward would be fatal, in my opinion. We cannot long avoid a conflict with the paid and bought friends of Lincoln in Kentucky, and the fight might as well come off now as at any other time. If it is to be done, it should be done quickly." (*Ibid.*, pp. 192–193.)

46. Henry wrote on Oct. 17 to Polk about four 32-pounder guns which he had obtained three weeks before at Memphis for Fort Donelson, and which had just been taken to the fort from Clarksville. At his solicitation Governor Harris had ordered an artillery company to Donelson from Nashville. (*Ibid.*, p. 458. See also Henry to Johnston, *ibid.*, pp. 453–454.)

47. *Ibid.*, pp. 496–497. Henry reported to Johnston that Fort Henry was "in fine condition for defense," the work being "admirably done." He stated that the 10th Tennessee, which was garrisoning it, was healthy and well disciplined, and was one of the very best regiments he had seen in service. It is clear from Henry's letter that not much had as yet been done at Fort Donelson, though an energetic officer was then in charge.

48. *Ibid.*, pp. 526, 528–529, 345–346.

49. *Ibid.*, *7*, 444.

50. *Ibid.*, pp. 445–446. The message was repeated in the letter of the same date.

51. *Ibid.*, pp. 461–462. On Nov. 21 Governor Yates of Illinois wrote to Halleck that he had received pressing applications from both Grant and McClernand for an armed regiment at Cave in Rock and asked for instructions. The next day Halleck directed him to make no troop movements until he received orders. (*Ibid.*, *8*, 372, 373.)

52. *Ibid.*, *7*, 440. After graduating from West Point in 1831, Whittlesey resigned from the army after a year of service, and he was living in Ohio at the outbreak of the war. He was appointed to the staff of Brig. Gen. O. M.

Mitchel, when that officer was put in command at Cincinnati in September.

53. W. P. Johnston, "Albert Sidney Johnston at Shiloh," *B. and L.*, I, 547; appendix, *supra*, p. 456; Polk to Johnston, *O.R.*, 7, 710–711; Henry to Johnston, Nov. 1, *ibid.*, 4, 496–497; Johnston to Benjamin, *ibid.*, pp. 528–529. Henry spoke of Donelson being poorly located on the river. Actually, a bend gave its guns effective fire down the stream.

54. *Ibid.*, 7, 694–696. For a letter to President Davis from the chairman and the secretary of the committee, see *ibid.*, pp. 692–693.

55. *Ibid.*, p. 758.

56. *Ibid.*, p. 442. Conflicting returns for Nov. 30 (*ibid.*, pp. 727–728) do not seem to indicate more than 20 regiments at Columbus. But a return of Johnston's entire command for Dec. 12 (*ibid.*, p. 762) puts Polk's force at 24,968, present and absent. This would indicate 30 to 35 regiments.

57. *Ibid.*, 8, 383; 7, 462–463; 8, 416; 7, 482, 460. On Dec. 6 Grant informed Oglesby it was reported that the enemy was placing guns in position near Belmont, and that the working party was not well guarded. He directed Oglesby to send all his cavalry that night to make a reconnaissance; if the Confederates were not too strong Oglesby was to make a dash and spike their guns, observing "great caution not to be drawn into ambush or engage a superior force of the enemy." A cooperating detachment was to be sent from Cairo. (*Ibid.*, 8, 410.)

The Mississippi call was made on Nov. 21. On the same day Johnston addressed letters to the governors of Mississippi and Alabama, requesting more troops. On Nov. 22 Polk reported to Johnston about available reenforcements: the governor of Louisiana had promised several regiments; the governor of Mississippi could give an armed battalion or two regiments if he had arms, and he was sending heavy guns and cannon powder; Commodore Hollins had arrived with one gunboat and all six vessels of his force were expected in two or three days. (*Ibid.*, 7, 688–689, 687–688, 692.)

58. Grant to Kelton, Dec. 8, *ibid.*, p. 482; same, Dec. 13, *ibid.*, 8, 432. For orders alerting troops, see *ibid.*, 8, 430, 433.

59. *Ibid.*, 7, 731. On Nov. 28 Pillow forwarded to Johnston reports of an impending attack by 75,000 to 100,000 Federals (*ibid.*, p. 708). Though still nominally in command on Dec. 2, he wrote to Polk that he hesitated to undertake anything without consulting him, because Polk was able to "resume at pleasure." After referring to Hollins's gunboats and asserting that an attack on the Federal gunboats and batteries was impossible without the support of land forces, he concluded, "I ask your approval of the movement."

60. *O.R.*, 110, 224–226. People in Memphis were disturbed by Pillow's being temporarily in command at Columbus. "His daily sensation dispatches keep the country in alarm and commotion," was the report that came to Johnston's headquarters from the office of the Memphis and Charleston Railroad (*ibid.*, p. 222).

61. Johnston's return of Dec. 12 gave Polk 17,802 present for duty out of 21,831 present, all at Columbus. On Dec. 31 Grant had 14,374 present for duty at six stations. (*O.R.*, 7, 762, 525.)

62. Conger finds (*Rise of Grant*, p. 119) the cause of Grant's alert a matter

of "surmise," but suggests a connection with a report (*O.R., 8,* 711) that Jeff Thompson sent Polk from New Madrid on Dec. 13. Thompson said the Federals near Charleston had paid him back the night before for his recent attack on them (which had netted two prisoners and some equipment). He was on his part planning a reprisal for that night. Minor affairs at Charleston would hardly have caused Grant to prepare for a heavy attack. Time also seems to rule the Thompson message out as in any way pertinent, for it was sent at 10:00 A.M., and Grant spoke of receiving information from Columbus in the afternoon. Care and some hours must have been necessary for a messenger to reach Cairo; Grant began his dispatch of the 8th, "I have just got in a man who spent yesterday in Columbus."

63. *O.R., 8,* 373–374, 375, 464–465; *8,* 404; *7,* 507.

64. *Ibid., 109,* 198; *8,* 402–403. In the message of the 2nd Halleck asked if McClellan could not send him a brigadier of high rank to take command of three or four divisions, and suggested four possibilities. In addition to not being able to move Grant to a new assignment, he could not remove Curtis from St. Louis "for the present." It is safe to assume he also regarded Smith to be essential at Paducah. He ended his letter picturesquely, "I dare not intrust the 'mustangs' with high command in the face of the enemy."

65. *Ibid., 8,* 369–370, 404.

66. *Ibid., 8,* 440; *114,* 120, 121.

67. *Ibid.,* p. 122.

68. *Ibid.,* p. 149.

NOTES TO CHAPTER VI

1. *O.R., 4,* 342, 355–356.

2. *Ibid., 107,* 338–339.

3. *Ibid., 4,* 205–210, 211, 487, 502, 509, 502, 516, 516–517.

4. Zollicoffer to Cooper and to Wood, *ibid.,* p. 524. His reference to Wartburg was by its older name, Montgomery. For strength return of Nov. 20, see *ibid., 7,* 687. Zollicoffer's command consisted of Tennessee troops except for a battalion from Alabama and a regiment from Mississippi. His strength present and absent was 4,857.

5. *Ibid., 4,* 530. The message does not show to whom it was sent. For a message from Jacksboro to Cooper on the 7th, see *ibid.,* p. 527.

6. *Ibid.,* pp. 530–531.

7. *Ibid.,* p. 527. The message is dated Nov. 7, and refers to telegrams from Zollicoffer of the 5th and 6th that do not seem to be in the records. Johnston thought the Federals were moving on Jamestown, and believed their fortifying London consistent with such an operation.

Zollicoffer wrote on the 8th that the direct roads from Jacksboro to Huntsville, Montgomery, and Jamestown were poor and broken, the mountain being generally 30 or 40 miles wide. When he later moved he went through Wartburg (*ibid., 7,* 686–687).

8. *Ibid., 4,* 207, 319, 318.

9. *Ibid.,* pp. 302–303, 324–325. In the second dispatch Sherman made the comment, "If General Lee assumes the command at Cumberland Ford, he will occupy all your time, and I cannot pretend to control your movements," in answer to Thomas's statement (*ibid.,* p. 206) of the 23rd, "I find a rumor in the papers that General Lee will supersede Zollicoffer. If he does, I should wish to be prepared for him fully."

10. *Ibid.,* p. 356.

11. *Ibid.,* pp. 350–351, 353–354.

12. *Ibid.,* pp. 528–529.

13. *Ibid.,* pp. 354, 357, 356–357, 358, 354, 359.

14. *Ibid.,* p. 320. The message was received Nov. 4, but Thomas's action is not indicated. On Oct. 20, E. L. Van Winkle wrote Gen. Carter from Somerset, saying his brother had left "fully equipped" the night before, and giving a detailed description of roads in East Tennessee (*ibid., 109,* 195–196).

15. *Ibid., 4,* 359–360. The message was received Nov. 17. For "Revolt of the Unionists in East Tennessee," see *ibid.,* pp. 230–251. The subject is treated very objectively by Patton, *Unionism and Reconstruction in Tennessee,* Chap. III.

16. *O.R., 4,* 531–532.

17. *Ibid.,* pp. 358–359.

18. *Ibid.,* pp. 360–361, 362 (repeated, *7,* 439).

19. *Ibid., 7,* 442–443, 445.

20. *Ibid.,* p. 446.

21. *Ibid.,* p. 448.

22. *Ibid.,* p. 454; *4,* 361–362.

23. *Ibid., 7,* 443–444.

24. *Ibid.,* p. 445.

25. *Ibid.,* p. 447. In a letter of the 27th (*ibid.,* pp. 450–452), Buell spoke of his plans for seven regiments at Indianapolis.

26. *Ibid.,* p. 450.

27. *Ibid.,* pp. 450–452.

28. *Ibid.,* p. 457.

29. *Ibid.,* pp. 457–458. The letter bore no date but had the heading "Monday night," the editors adding "November 29, 1861." As the 29th was a Friday, there is some error. McClellan spoke in his letter of having telegraphed Buell his satisfaction over the letter just received. The telegram carried the date Nov. 29, and Buell's letter was dated the 27th. Two days for the delivery of Buell's letter was a little rapid, but not impossible. The 28th, Thanksgiving Day, may have seemed like Sunday to McClellan, with the result that he automatically dated his letter "Monday."

30. *Ibid.,* pp. 468–470.

31. *Ibid.,* pp. 473–474, 925.

32. *Ibid.,* pp. 487–488.

33. *Ibid.,* pp. 480, 483, 487–488.

34. *Ibid.,* p. 456; *4,* 244; *7,* 697, 707. Zollicoffer spoke of pack saddles as "often needed to fit up dashing movements in a mountainous country im-

passable to wagon trains." He had requisitioned them two weeks before—Nov. 10.

35. *O.R., 7,* 485–486, 686, 697, 753, 495, 500, 501, 511. In speaking of his move to Somerset, Carter said the road from London was impassable for wagons, and that on account of steep and rough hills, artillery might find a longer road more suitable.

There were some inconsistencies in Carter's statements. On Nov. 19 he reported to Thomas that he might be attacked by a strong force and be compelled to fall back after destroying most of his stores; the next day he said it had been a false alarm, and added that recruits were arriving every day. On Nov. 24 he sent word of the results of a reconnaissance to Cumberland Ford and said that subsistence "in large quantities" could be obtained in Knox County, where Barbourville was located. On the 28th he said reports indicated considerable corn and wheat in that county—he estimated the bushels—as well as horses, cattle, and hogs belonging to secessionists who had gone south. Also in Clay County, east of London, 100 barrels of flour were about ready for hauling away by "the rebels." He reported only two infantry regiments and some 200 cavalry at Cumberland Gap. A Confederate return shows that Carter correctly identified the force by regiments, and gives the strength as 1,824, but puts the cavalry at 300. (*Ibid,* pp. 439–441, 446–447, 456, 705.)

On Dec. 6 Carter believed Barbourville was threatened and thought he could not do much to resist the force the enemy was building up. On the 4th he had seemed anxious to move to Somerset on account of the chance of engaging Zollicoffer and because of sickness at London. On the 12th he seemed eager to return to his old position, but said he had received an order detaching him from Thomas's command. (*Ibid.,* pp. 478–479, 472–473, 495.) For the latter's divisional organization as of Dec. 6, see *ibid.,* p. 479.

36. *Ibid.,* p. 754; Leadbetter to Benjamin, *ibid.,* p. 726; Brownlow, *Sketches of Secession,* Chap. XX. Col. Danville Leadbetter, who had been hastily sent from Richmond to see about rebuilding bridges, wired from Greeneville on Nov. 30, "Two insurgents have to-day been tried for bridge-burning, found guilty, and hanged" (*O.R.,* 7, 726). On Nov. 25 Benjamin wrote to Col. Wood at Knoxville respecting prisoners taken among the "traitors" in East Tennessee: "All such as can be identified as having been engaged in bridge-burning are to be tried summarily by drum-head court-martial, and, if found guilty, executed on the spot by hanging. It would be well to leave their bodies hanging in the vicinity of the burned bridges." All persons in jail were to be held, but those who came in voluntarily, gave up their arms, and took the oath of allegiance, were to be treated with leniency. (*Ibid.,* p. 701.)

37. *Ibid.,* pp. 484–485.

38. *Ibid., 8,* 724–725, 725–726.

39. Johnston to Benjamin and to Governor Harris, *ibid., 7,* 779; Benjamin to Johnston, *ibid.,* pp. 783–784; *ibid.,* pp. 781–782, 783–784. The ordnance officer reporting the Nashville fire had no doubt about its incendiary origin

(ibid., pp. 785–786). For his report to Col. Gorgas, Confederate chief of ordnance, see *ibid., 110,* 242.

40. *Ibid., 7,* 788–789, 794–795, 792–793, 782. An editorial note to the strength return *(ibid.,* pp. 813–814) observes that the original was not dated and was imperfect, but gives the date as "about December 31, 1861." It was reported to Buell on Dec. 24 that Floyd had arrived with his brigade *(ibid.,* p. 715).

41. Crittenden to Johnston, Dec. 28, *ibid.,* pp. 800–801; *ibid.,* p. 791; Wallace to Benjamin, *ibid.,* p. 768; Young to Currin, *ibid.,* pp. 777–779; Austin to Davis (from Richmond), *ibid.,* p. 799; Benjamin to Ramsay, Dec. 22, *ibid.,* p. 785; *ibid.,* pp. 804–807.

Crittenden said that 1,500 men were present for duty in the two regiments at the gap. J. C. Ramsay was Confederate District Attorney for Tennessee and was at Knoxville. Benjamin said to him: "Better that any, the most dangerous enemy, however criminal, should escape, than that the honor and good faith of the Government be impugned or even suspected. General Crittenden gave his word only that Brownlow would not be tried by the court-martial, and I gave authority to promise him protection if he would surrender, to be conveyed across the border." Brownlow was subsequently allowed to go North. Much about the Brownlow case is found in *O.R., 114,* 823–931, under the caption "Confederate Policy of Repression in East Tennessee." Brownlow, *loc. cit.,* gives diary entries about his imprisonment.

When informed by Ramsay that the military authorities intended to try bridge burners for treason, Benjamin approved the action and said he hoped to hear that all the bridge burners had been hanged "at the end of the burned bridge" *(ibid., 7,* 700, 700–701). It will be seen that Halleck, in dealing with sabotage, held that treason was a civil offense, and persons charged with it must be tried by civil courts.

42. *Ibid.,* pp. 511–513, 787.

43. *Ibid.,* pp. 926, 520–521.

44. *Ibid.,* pp. 509–510, 518, 522. For the map in question, see *O.R.,* Atlas, I, Plate IX–2.

45. *O.R., 8,* 461, 462–463.

46. *Ibid.,* p. 459; Binmore to Kelton, *ibid.,* p. 465. For the order appointing the commission, and its proceedings, see *ibid., 114,* 374–406; and for the records of other commissions that dealt with saboteurs, pp. 406–514.

47. *Ibid.,* pp. 464–465.

48. Halleck, in a letter of Jan. 15, 1862, to Adj. Gen. Thomas *(ibid., 7,* 929), referred to instructions from McClellan, and to a direction with regard to Gen. Smith that he had not carried out. One can assume that he would not have put Grant in command of an enlarged district without taking the matter up further with McClellan, if two general officers he had sent recently to Cairo had not reported favorably. For Halleck's order and those of Grant assuming command and naming his staff, and for his December strength return, see *ibid., 109,* 201; *7,* 515, 525. There seems to be no return by Smith.

49. *Ibid.,* pp. 515–517, 523–524.

50. Wilson, *The Life of Rawlins,* pp. 68–71.

51. *Ibid.,* p. 71. The fact that Wilson obtained the letter from Washburne's papers in the Library of Congress suggests that Rawlins probably discussed the entire Cairo situation with him. He writes that army contractors resented Grant's efforts to make them deliver supplies of full weight and proper quality, and complained of him to reporters, that incidents connected with Grant's retirement from the regular army were circulated at an early date, and that the prejudicial rumors based on these reached Washburne in Washington (*ibid.,* pp. 67–68).

Lew Wallace in his *Autobiography,* I, 351–353, describes an inspection visit by Grant and Rawlins to Paducah in October. They stayed in the house where he was quartered, and during a sociable evening, at which cigars and liquor were available, Smith and Grant talked much about the Mexican War. Wallace said that Grant was "a fine talker, and particularly excellent in description." In a few days newspapers arrived with lurid descriptions of the meeting as an orgy and drunken revel, though there was no intoxication at all. Some blame was put upon Wallace for the reports, and in self-defense he traced the offensive articles to a regimental chaplain, whom he induced to resign.

52. Carpenter, *Six Months in the White House,* p. 135.

53. *N.Y. Tribune,* Dec. 4, 1861. Hendrick gives the deleted paragraph in *Lincoln's War Cabinet,* p. 230.

54. A *Tribune* correspondent reported Lincoln as saying, when asked if he would attend a Washington lecture by Greeley: "Yes, I will. I never heard Greeley, but I want to hear him. In print every one of his words seems to weigh about a ton; I want to see what he has to say about us" (Sandburg, *Lincoln,* I, 401).

55. *N.Y. Tribune,* Dec. 4, 1861.

56. *Ibid.,* Dec. 6. Greeley stated that the majority of Republicans were in accord with the sentiment of his paper, which was that the sole purpose of the war was "preserving the integrity of the Union and vindicating the rightful authority of the Government." After speaking of· the "antagonist falsehood," he said, "What we *do* demand and insist on is that, as the efforts and sacrifices of the Nation are not to be perverted to the overthrow of Slavery, so *they shall not to be rendered ineffective or fruitless by anxiety to uphold and perpetuate Slavery.*" Greeley admitted that his position was one of expediency, but he emphatically did not believe that there were "true and hearty Unionists" who would refuse to fight for the Union if Negroes were allowed and invited to do so.

57. Hendrick, *op. cit.,* pp. 200–205; Nicolay and Hay, *Lincoln,* V, 39–41.

58. *O.R., 8,* 725–726.

59. *Ibid., 7,* 524.

60. *Ibid.,* pp. 773, 773–774. Polk stated that he had been about to call upon Johnston for 3,000 troops when the latter's telegram arrived. Johnston revoked his order (*ibid.,* p. 774). On the 24th Polk asked him if he still wished troops, and Johnston replied that he wanted 10,000 or more men if possible, without the loss of a day. Polk sent 5,000 infantry. (*Ibid.,* pp. 790, 808; *110,* 243.)

61. Lincoln Papers, LXIII, 13531–13532.

62. *O.R., 111,* 511. A letter from Cameron of Jan. 3, 1862, is of interest in connection with Hunter's complaints (*ibid.,* pp. 512–513).

63. McClellan's statement to Halleck about an expedition by Hunter into Arkansas and northern Texas has been mentioned. Hunter pronounced the project impractical, but McClellan argued for it (*ibid., 8,* 428–429). McClellan as General in Chief thought Hunter could move 500 miles with a weak force, although as commander of the large and well equipped Army of the Potomac he would not venture even fifteen miles to Fairfax.

NOTES TO CHAPTER VII

1. *O.R., 7,* 526, 926. The editors state that the letter to Buell was "not found"; it probably resembled closely the one to Halleck.

2. *Ibid.,* p. 526. Buell's telegram to Halleck does not seem to be in the records.

3. *Ibid.,* pp. 527, 530 (Smith to Cullum with editorial note, and Cullum to Buell). Also see Buell to Cullum, *ibid.,* p. 528.

4. *Ibid.,* pp. 528–529. Buell said that if the expedition up the rivers could not reach the bridges it should establish itself ashore under the protection of the gunboats.

Though not yet back in his office, McClellan wrote to Halleck at length on the 3rd (*ibid.,* pp. 527–528). He said the enemy must be prevented from shifting troops from western Kentucky, and that a force should be sent up the Cumberland of sufficient strength to defeat anything sent to repel it, while a demonstration should be made against Columbus, with a possible feint up the Tennessee. No time was to be lost, and Halleck was asked to send his views on the subject, and report the nature and strength of the force he could send and the time required to prepare it.

5. *O.R., 8,* 476–478; Halleck to Whittlesey, Jan. 2, 1862, *ibid.,* p. 481.

6. *Ibid.,* pp. 484–487.

7. *Ibid., 7,* 530, 530–531.

8. *Ibid.,* pp. 927–928.

9. *Ibid.,* p. 531. In noting that Halleck could not properly support a movement for some time, McClellan showed a certain inconsistency with the position he had taken in his letter to Halleck on Jan. 3.

10. Halleck to Buell, *ibid.,* p. 533; Foote to Meigs, Nov. 30, 1861, and Jan. 4, 1862, *ibid., 8,* 397, 488; James B. Eads, "Recollections of Foote and the Gunboats," *B. and L.,* I, 338–346. (An editorial note to the article by Eads describes the great labors necessary in the construction of the gunboats, which were supposed to be completed Oct. 10, 1861, but were not finished until Jan. 15, 1862. Funds were short, and Eads, the contractor, drew heavily on his own resources and those of friends.) For efforts toward providing Navy crews, see Foote to Meigs, with inclosures from W. A. Howard, *O.R., 8,* 397.

On Jan. 6 Halleck also wrote the President (*ibid., 7,* 532–533), describing at length the difficulties under which he was working in Missouri. It drew from Lincoln the indorsement dated Jan. 10: "The within is a copy of a letter just received from General Halleck. It is exceedingly discouraging. As everywhere else, nothing can be done." As Lincoln had in the meantime received Halleck's telegram of the 7th speaking of the demonstration he had ordered, the comment should not be considered a questioning of Halleck's efforts. In his letters both to Buell and to Lincoln, Halleck spoke of the danger of operating on exterior lines, which usually led to disaster.

11. *Ibid.*, p. 534; Grant, *Memoirs*, I, 286–287. In a long letter of Nov. 21, 1861, to Gen. Polk (*O.R., 110*, 214–216), J. T. Trezevant, acting ordnance officer at Memphis, spoke of "submarine batteries" which Polk had ordered to be rapidly constructed. He said, "If fifty batteries will do good, 500 to 1,000 will do more good still, and we are not in a position to count the cost now. If you need aid in finishing 100 in a day instead of twenty our men say you shall have it; and with such assurance, the force now at work upon them can be readily doubled." Trezevant said he was "preparing some of them to go off by electricity," and asked about the advisability of making tests.

12. *O.R., 7*, 533–534; *109*, 203.

13. Lincoln to Buell, and Halleck to Lincoln, *ibid., 7, 535*.

14. *Ibid.*, pp. 537–538.

15. *Ibid.*, pp. 540, 543, 544.

16. *Ibid.*, pp. 547, 548–549. Six days seem excessive for the transmission of McClellan's letter of the 6th; but Lincoln's letters of the 1st to Halleck and Buell were received on the 6th, and thus took five days.

17. *Ibid.*, pp. 545–546; *8*, 503–504, and *109*, 204 (Halleck to McClellan, and to Sherman about ice in river); *7*, 551–552. Grant believed the Columbus garrison was weaker than it had been for several months, and remarked, "It is also probable that the best-armed and best-drilled troops have been taken."

18. *Ibid., 7*, 928–929. Lincoln suggested that Halleck threaten Columbus and "'down-river' generally," thinking that "Columbus and East Tennessee, one or both," might be taken if a heavy concentration were made at Bowling Green. By way of illustration he said, "Suppose last summer, when Winchester ran away to re-enforce Manassas, we had foreborne to attack Manassas, but had seized and held Winchester." He added that he realized the greatest difficulty in applying his principle would "be the want of perfect knowledge of the enemy's movements."

19. *Ibid.*, p. 547.

20. *Ibid.*, pp. 545, 551–552. Buell wrote to McClellan on Jan. 13 that his strength had been suddenly increased from 70,000 to 90,000 men by regiments which, though not fit for active operations, would "answer a certain purpose" (*ibid.*, p. 548).

21. *Ibid.*, pp. 458, 473, 487–488, 929.

22. *Ibid., 114*, 402–406. Halleck mildly reproved the commission for its release of six men after administering the oath of allegiance, and said it should have remanded them to prison until the department commander could act on their cases.

23. *Ibid., 8*, 500–502, 503–504. The first letter dealt with a great variety of

matters: want of arms, the sending of two regiments of Illinois cavalry to Kansas without Halleck's knowledge, the mustering out of illegal and unreliable organizations, etc. Of the cavalry regiments he wrote, "I am unwilling to believe that this measure was either advised or approved by you." After speaking of his inability to prevent waste of public property because of poor officers, a new leak developing as soon as one was stopped, he concluded, "If the Government will commission such officers, the country must pay for their incompetency and rascality."

Included with the letter was a copy of one that Schofield had written from Wellsville on the 2nd, relating the depredations of Reserve Corps cavalry. Five of its men were now in irons, and Schofield wrote, "No doubt there are some good men in this battalion, but as a class they are well-mounted and well-armed barbarians." He understood there was at Benton Barracks "a considerable force of good mounted men without arms"; and he asked that some of them be sent to him without weapons or horses, and that he be authorized to give them the mounts and arms of "Major Hollan's battalion." He added, "If something of this kind is not done soon there will be very few Union men in this part of the State."

The second letter gave some information about Grant's demonstration.

24. *Ibid.*, 7, 522, 536–537. Another letter of Dec. 29 from Buell to Thomas, with more explicit instructions, is *ibid.*, p. 78. For the map that accompanied this letter see *ibid.*, Atlas, I, Plate IX–2. Schoepf said the operation he described could be carried out by 10,000 men. For his sketch, see *ibid.*, 7, 946.

25. *Ibid.*, pp. 535–536.

26. *Ibid.*, p. 550.

27. *Ibid.*, pp. 556, 558. Buell wrote, "I am sure that the roads are in a horrible condition," but he also stated that he had been assured that an abundance of forage could be derived from the country in the direction of Liberty. If possible, he wanted Thomas to buy meal rather than haul flour.

28. Thomas's report, *ibid.*, pp. 79–82.

29. On the 18th Crittenden reported to Johnston that he was threatened by a superior force in front and would have to fight where he was because he could not cross the river, and he requested a diversion in his favor. In his final report he told of a council of war with brigade, regimental, and cavalry commanders. (*Ibid.*, pp. 103, 105–110.) For his march order, a copy of which fell later into Thomas's hands, see *ibid.*, p. 82.

30. Carroll's report, *ibid.*, p. 111.

31. Wolford's, Thomas's, Manson's, and Kise's reports (*ibid.*, pp. 100, 79, 84, 90). Page references will not in general be given for reports referred to in the text.

Thomas said "pickets from Wolford's cavalry encountered the enemy advancing on our camp," which implies motion. Wolford explicitly stated that pickets were sent in the direction of Mill Springs at daylight in obedience to Thomas's order. He reported the enemy's advance to Manson and proceeded with his command to the relief of his pickets. He met the enemy less than two miles from the Federal camp and fired on it, and he claimed it "constantly retreated." It was after he found the enemy in force that Wolford fell back.

O'Connor gives Thomas credit for virtually devising a new method of out-posting (*Thomas,* p. 148). His description of the usual system of the time does not agree with instructions in Army Regulations of 1861; and his unsup-ported statement, "Thomas junked this picketing system, and threw out strong patrols," conflicts with Kise's report, which indicates no moving bodies—move-ment distinguishing a patrol from a picket. Although Wolford refers to the groups he sent toward the river in the morning as "pickets," they evidently were patrols. What Thomas did was quite in accord with paragraph 633 of Army Regulations, which said, "Cavalry patrols should examine the country to a greater distance than infantry, and report to the infantry guard every thing they observe. The morning patrols and scouts do not return until broad daylight; and when they return, the night sentinels are withdrawn, and the posts for the day resumed."

O'Connor states that Thomas realized Crittenden would attempt to attack him before he concentrated, that word came at midnight that the Confederates were on the march, and that he received exact knowledge of the composition of the enemy column (*op. cit.,* pp. 148, 149). If true, this would be a severe criticism of Thomas, for his report does not mention it and he did not inform even the outpost commander. O'Connor states that Manson was a brigadier, and makes a major background error in saying (p. 147) that Halleck "quickly politicked" his way into command of all Union armies in the West.

32. O'Connor, *op. cit.,* p. 150.

33. Van Horne states that when Thomas had eight infantry regiments and two batteries on hand "he pressed the enemy in a brilliant charge" (*The Life of Thomas,* p. 52). Piatt asserts that Thomas "ordered the Ninth Ohio In-fantry to charge" (*General Thomas,* p. 123). Pratt says that Thomas brought the 9th Ohio around behind his line of battle and threw it with the bayonet into the Confederate left flank (*Eleven Generals,* p. 181). Cleaves states that after Thomas ordered a bayonet charge, the entire enemy line gave way and retreated in the utmost confusion (*Rock of Chickamauga,* p. 98).

McCook wrote in his report, "Seeing the superior number of the enemy and their bravery, I concluded the best mode of settling the contest was to order the Ninth Ohio Regiment to charge the enemy's position with the bayonet and turn his left flank. The order was given the regiment to empty their guns and fix bayonets; this done, it was ordered to charge." Thomas's statement is, "The Second Minnesota kept up a most galling fire in front, and the Ninth Ohio charged the enemy on the right with bayonets fixed, turned their flank, and drove them from the field, the whole line giving way and retreating in the utmost disorder and confusion." (*O.R., 7,* 94, 80.) Col. R. M. Kelly writes on p. 389 of his article "Holding Kentucky for the Union," in *B. and L.,* I, 373–392, that "the 9th Ohio, on the right, was forcing back the enemy through open ground, when, slightly changing direction, it made a bayonet charge against the enemy's left."

34. Carter's report, *O.R., 7,* 97.

35. Thomas says that Zollicoffer fell from a shot from Fry's pistol (*ibid.,* p. 81); Manson that his body was pierced by three bullets (*ibid.,* p. 86); Kelly that Fry fired on Zollicoffer who fell "pierced by a pistol-shot in the breast

and by two musket-balls" (*loc. cit.*); *D.A.B.* has him shot through the breast by Fry. Pratt says that a regiment of "Minnesota lumbermen" came up to sustain the Union center and that their fire killed Zollicoffer (*op. cit.*, p. 181). For the confusion in identification of units that led to Zollicoffer's death, see Kelly, *op. cit.*, pp. 388–389.

36. Thomas's report, *O.R.*, 7, 80–81; Crittenden to Johnston's headquarters, *ibid.*, p. 103.

37. Thomas's, Manson's, and Crittenden's reports, *ibid.*, pp. 81–82, 86, 108; Kelly, *op. cit.*, p. 390.

38. *Ibid.*, p. 83. Though Thomas exaggerated relative strengths, the Federal force actually engaged probably did not number much over 2,500, against something like 4,000 of the enemy.

39. *Ibid.*, p. 76. A second dispatch is given *ibid.*, *109*, 205.

40. *Ibid.*, 7, 102. Though over Stanton's name, the proclamation was "By order of the President."

41. O'Connor asserts, "At no other time did such an instance occur" (*op. cit.*, p. 155). Cleaves calls the failure to give Thomas's name a galling omission (*op. cit.*, p. 100).

42. Cleaves suggests that promotion was due (*loc. cit.*). O'Connor says that Lincoln is reported—by whom he does not reveal—to have said, "Let the Virginian wait" (*op. cit.*, p. 156). He also states that Thomas was "obviously" still viewed with suspicion, and refers to "intriguing parties in Washington." He even asserts that the promotion of Thomas (to a rank above Buell and Grant) "would undoubtedly have saved the Union much blood and treasure lost by the blunderings of men who passed ahead of him in favor." This very strong statement is not surprising alongside assertions that Thomas scrapped usual methods of outposting and accordingly "fooled the Confederate command," that his staff officers brought him reports of the enemy advance—in spite of Thomas's own statement that he learned of it from Manson—and (p. 154) that the Confederate forces at Bowling Green "evaporated without a fight" because their flank was uncovered by Thomas's victory, as if more important factors were not the subsequent capture of Fort Henry and the investment of Fort Donelson.

Thomas's promotion is discussed in Appendix II.

43. *O.R.*, 7, 102.

44. *Ibid.*, p. 110.

45. Crittenden to Johnston, Feb. 1, *ibid.*, p. 855. Crittenden said he was satisfied that an investigation would "establish that the battle of Fishing Creek and the subsequent movement were military necessities, for which I am not responsible."

46. On Jan. 30 Benjamin wrote to Johnston (*ibid.*, p. 850) about the "painful rumors" that President Davis could hardly believe, since such reports are frequent in case of disaster. He thought, however, that the morale of the army would be utterly destroyed if Crittenden remained in command, and directed that he be relieved, further orders in the case being left to Johnston's judgment. Presently the Richmond authorities changed their views, and on Feb. 8 Benjamin wrote to Johnston, "General Crittenden has demanded a court of inquiry,

and it has been ordered; but for all the accounts which now reach us we have no reason to doubt his skill or conduct in his recent movements, and feel convinced that it is not to any fault of his that the disaster at Somerset is to be attributed" (*ibid.*, pp. 862–863). Within a short time Johnston had Crittenden in command of a division in his reorganized army.

47. The order appointing the court of inquiry was issued by Gen. Braxton Bragg on July 24, 1862, by direction of President Davis. On Aug. 8 Bragg wrote to the Secretary of War, then G. W. Randolph, saying he thought Crittenden was not fit for a responsible position. (*Ibid.*, *25*, 658, 673.) An order of May 31, 1864, assigned "General George B. Crittenden (colonel C. S. Army)" to the command of the Department of Western Virginia and East Tennessee (*ibid.*, *51*, 750). He is subsequently mentioned several times in a commendatory way, always as a colonel. *D.A.B.* says that after the Battle of Mill Springs, Crittenden was put in arrest and censured, after which he resigned, to reenter the Confederate service and serve without rank on the staff of Gen. J. S. Williams.

NOTES TO CHAPTER VIII

1. *O.R.*, *8*, 508–511. On Jan. 22 Halleck reported that the paper strength of his department was probably 105,000; several irregular corps had been mustered out since the 1st, and more would be when money was received to pay them; a large percentage of his command was sick (*ibid.*, p. 513).

2. Wilson, *The Life of Rawlins*, p. 70.

3. *O.R.*, *8*, 826.

4. *Ibid.*, p. 827.

5. *Ibid.*, pp. 512–513.

6. *Ibid.*, pp. 496–497, 514–515, 528–529. After listing his grievances Price had said, *"We must understand each other."* Halleck's answers to his questions should have been clear enough.

7. Steele to Halleck, *ibid.*, pp. 478–479.

8. *Ibid.*, p. 514.

9. The date Jan. 25 on the dispatch as printed in *O.R.*, *7*, 565–566, is certainly incorrect. It does not harmonize with dates of messages to Paine and Porter (*ibid.*, pp. 560–561). On that date the *N.Y. Tribune* published a Cairo dispatch of the 21st which said the last of the expedition had returned. Grant wrote to his sister on the 23rd of being back a few days. Force says that Grant wrote to St. Louis on the 20th (*From Fort Henry to Corinth*, p. 27).

10. *O.R.*, *7*, 561.

11. *N.Y. Tribune*, Jan. 18, 1862; *N.Y. Times*, Jan. 24.

12. *O.R.*, *7*, 838, 839, 75 (several interesting dispatches from Tilghman to Polk, covering the period Jan. 18–25), 847.

13. *Ibid.*, p. 561.

14. *Ibid.*, pp. 561–562.

15. Cramer, *Letters of Grant*, pp. 77–79.

16. Wilson, *Grant's Letters to a Friend*, p. 3.

17. Grant, *Memoirs,* I, 287.

18. *O.R., 7,* 930.

19. Smith closed his dispatch of the 22nd, written from near Calloway, 17 miles north of Fort Henry, with the statement that he planned to start for Paducah at 8 o'clock the next morning, when a boat would leave with his sick and the mail (*ibid.,* p. 561). In *Memoirs,* I, 287, Grant spoke as if he had received Smith's statement before renewing his request to visit St. Louis. This seems to be definitely incorrect and detracts a little from the credit due himself. Force states that Grant received Smith's report on the 22nd (*loc. cit.*).

20. *N.Y. Tribune,* Jan. 25, 1862.

21. *O.R., 7,* 68–72. On Jan. 28 McClernand wrote a letter to Lincoln about what he had done during the demonstration. He stated that if he had been supported by the gunboats and the columns of Paine and Smith, he had no doubt that he could have taken Columbus. Then he said, "If you will give me 25,000 men and the co-operation of the Gunboats, I will take Columbus." He raised the question of foreign intervention if there were not a significant Federal success and spoke of possible financial disaster. He recalled that he had told Lincoln that there was no necromancy in war; it was merely a matter of common sense. The letter ended, "It would be indelicate for me to say more." (Lincoln Papers, LXVII, 14198–14201.)

22. *O.R., 5,* 41. The original is in the Stanton Papers, II, 50507. The text of the order is not in Lincoln's hand.

23. Stanton Papers, II, 50508.

24. *Ibid.,* p. 50276.

25. *O.R., 7,* 568. See also Thomas to Buell, Jan. 26, on p. 567.

26. *Ibid.,* p. 566. See also Buell to Thomas, and Thomas's reply, on p. 567.

27. *Ibid.,* p. 580.

28. *Ibid.,* p. 121.

29. *Ibid.,* p. 120. For different versions, see *O.R. Navies,* Ser. I, XXII, 524. Although the dispatch is described as a letter, an indorsement on one of the versions refers to the office copy in the telegraph office. A merit of the Navy over the Army records is that they indicate whether a message was a telegram or a letter. In the *O.R.* there are cases where one cannot be certain.

30. Conger rejects the intimation by Grant in his *Memoirs*—by no means definite—that he "instigated Foote to telegraph," as if it were "going over the head or forcing the hand of his immediate commander," a thing which "the well-disciplined and perfectly subordinate Grant" would not have done (*The Rise of Grant,* p. 153). To clear him, Conger repudiates as unreliable the sentences Grant wrote years after the event, and himself manufactures out of nothing the actual words that Halleck used when he talked with Grant: "Go back and consult with Foote and let me know by telegraph what you and he both think about it after your consultation." This renders Grant meekly and colorlessly subordinate—and not sufficiently imaginative to consult with Foote until directed to do so. Conger also imagines a "retort" by Halleck under which Grant was "smarting" when he got back to Cairo, although the only evidence that Grant felt rebuffed and humiliated is what he wrote (*Memoirs,* I, 287) on the very page to which Conger takes so much exception.

Conger has Grant return from his demonstration on Jan. 25 and places him in St. Louis on the 26th or 27th (*op. cit.,* p. 151). In doing this he overlooks the reasons given above, in n. 9, for not accepting the date on Grant's dispatch announcing his return, and he also does not observe that that message repeated a request to visit headquarters. He accordingly takes Halleck's message of the 22nd as a reply to Grant's original request of Jan. 6.

31. *O.R., 7,* 121. Conger states (*op. cit.,* p. 154) that the interesting thing about Grant's message is its failure even to hint at such strategic consequences of the capture of Henry and Donelson as the abandonment of Bowling Green and Columbus—which Grant asserts in his *Memoirs* that he foresaw; but he is far from critical, and after pointing out that Grant was not yet even commander in the West, he says: "As a district commander, he saw an enemy fort in his front which his gunboats could silence and his men could take and hold. It would raise morale and be an advantage for further operations. He so reported. What more can one ask of a district commander? That he be a prophet?" This is much to the point, but one can still be sure that the last sentence of Grant's dispatch indicated that he had things in mind he did not set down.

32. *O.R. Navies,* Ser. I, XXII, 525, 525–526.

33. *O.R., 7,* 571.

34. Buell to McClellan, Jan. 30, *ibid.,* pp. 572–573; Halleck to McClellan, *ibid.,* p. 572 (quoted presently in full); Halleck to Buell, Feb. 7, *ibid.,* p. 592.

35. *N.Y. Tribune,* Jan. 23, 1862. John Tucker, as second assistant secretary, was to have charge of transportation by sea, while P. H. Watson, third assistant, was to deal with personnel and business connected with troops in the field.

36. Sipes, *The Pennsylvania Railroad,* pp. 15–16.

37. On Jan. 7 Cameron telegraphed to Buell: "A gentleman called yesterday from Kentucky, stating he had been sent by one of your officers to ask more troops. How many more do you want and of what kind? We are exceedingly anxious to have some results in Kentucky, especially towards East Tennessee." Buell replied that no person had been sent to ask for more troops, though there should be more, and better artillery and cavalry. "Concert of action," he said, "by which the enemy may be prevented from concentrating his whole force from Columbus to Bowling Green on one point of attack, would have the same and a better effect than more troops immediately here." (*O.R., 7,* 535.)

References in several of Scott's letters to a possible movement of troops from the East indicate that the subject had been discussed; and he went into the subject of rail and water transportation in his report from Pittsburgh. It will be seen that both Halleck and Buell later urged that troops be sent from the Army of the Potomac to take part in western operations.

38. *O.R., 7,* 572.

39. *Ibid.,* pp. 930–931. After indicating that he had doubts about the new mortar boats, McClellan ended his letter, "It is very desirable to move all along the line by the 22d February, if possible." This enigmatic sentence seems to be the only way in which Lincoln's War Order reached Halleck. Foote received an intimation that something was planned for Washington's Birthday

in a telegram from H. A. Wise, Assistant Inspector of Ordnance: "The President authorizes you to make the change you require on the *Benton* on the terms you have submitted to General Meigs, if the work can positively be executed by the 22d February next" (*O.R. Navies,* Ser. I, XXII, 523).

40. The original of McClellan's letter to Stanton is in the Lincoln Papers, LXVII, 14262–14272. As given in *O.R., 5,* 42–45, it carries the date Feb. 3, McClellan saying it had not been submitted at the time he received Lincoln's note of Feb. 3, whose questions he said it "substantially answered." See *supra,* I, 138–142. McClellan's note to Lincoln was headed "Saturday," which was Feb. 1, and is in the Lincoln Papers. It did not state when Halleck's message arrived, but said, "I gave dispatch to the Secy of War."

41. *O.R., 8,* 513, for indorsement on Baxter's letter. In his letter to Stanton from Cairo on Feb. 12 (Stanton Papers, III, 50752–50765), Scott said he understood that Baxter had received $150,000 from Washington; some of it had been expended at Cairo, and $10,000 had been taken up the Tennessee River. See also Kamm, *The Civil War Career of Thomas A. Scott,* pp. 103–104.

42. Letter of Jan. 30, Washburne Papers, XXII, 4340–4341.

43. *O.R., 7,* 121.

44. *Ibid.,* pp. 121–122.

45. *Ibid.,* p. 572.

46. *Ibid.,* pp. 571–572. Halleck must have had a report about roads from Smith, that differed from what Foote had said, for he closed his letter, "The roads south of the Tennessee River are almost impassable. General Smith reported on his recent reconnaissance up the river 'that the road was horrible, and new tracks had to be cut through the woods. It took an entire day for one brigade to move 3 miles.'"

47. *Ibid.,* p. 574.

48. *Ibid.* The next day, when replying to some brief details that Halleck had telegraphed, Buell asked if active cooperation were necessary to his success (*ibid.*). He also said, "The operation which was suggested in my letter yesterday would be an important preliminary to the next step." His earlier letter (*ibid.,* pp. 573–574) contained an extract from a report of an intelligence agent in Paducah. (Probably because he might seem to be trespassing, Buell began, "I venture to enclose . . . .") The intelligence agent had written: "Two new gunboats, one old one, and 500 troops on one transport up Tennessee River can shell out Fort Henry, destroy the bridge, run up the river to Tuscumbia, and the troops can land and destroy two or three bridges near the river along there." That may have gone beyond what Smith, referred to in the report, had said. Irrespective of what the gunboats might do, one transport would hardly induce the Confederates to give up the position at Fort Henry, and the 500 troops might have had trouble on their return. The prediction that was made about the Cumberland proved in the end to be inaccurate. Buell also sent the extracts to McClellan.

49. Buell to McClellan, Feb. 1, *ibid.,* pp. 931–933. The original letter is in the Stanton Papers, II, 50553–50556, the envelope with it being postmarked Louisville, Feb. 6. Stanton noted the discrepancy in dates when he replied on Feb. 9.

50. Stanton Papers, II, 56277–56280.

51. *O.R., 7,* 575. The letter to Halleck began, "Inclosed herewith I send you a communication from General Smith containing the latest and most reliable information I have from the Upper Tennessee." The editors of the *O.R.* state the inclosure was not found; but Grant's statement shows that his thoughts were going farther up the river than Fort Henry. Numerous instructions were necessary for a force scattered as Grant's was, and for the organization and general conduct of the movement. These and other dispatches of Grant and Halleck appear on pp. 576–580.

52. *Ibid., 8,* 538, 534.

53. *Ibid.,* pp. 828–829; *7,* 578–579.

54. *Ibid.,* p. 579.

55. *Ibid.,* p. 581.

56. Foote to Welles, Paducah, Feb. 3, *O.R. Navies,* Ser. I, XXII, 534–535; Benjamin to Johnson, *O.R., 7,* 857. Foote said he had arrived the night before in the *Tyler,* the four ironclads having preceded him. He stated, "The transports have not yet arrived, although expected last night from Cairo, which causes detention, while, in the meantime, unfortunately, the river is falling." He said he would change his flag to the *Cincinnati,* and added the postscript: "Several transports with troops have just arrived."

Davis's proclamation (*O. R. Navies,* Ser. I, XXII, 818) may have been the result of a Dec. 28 letter to him from W. Preston of Bowling Green, forwarded by Johnson. Preston said, "Since the report of Mr. Cameron and the message of Mr. Lincoln great discontents have been manifested among the Union men in Kentucky." In his judgment a judicious presidential proclamation would cause many Kentuckians in Federal service to change allegiance to the Confederacy, "or engender such distrust between the Southern and Northern troops and officers as to paralyze their confidence and impair fatally their efficiency." (*Ibid.,* pp. 801–802.)

NOTES TO CHAPTER IX

1. McClernand's report, *O.R., 7,* 126–130. The date of arrival at Paducah is incorrectly given as Feb. 2.

2. Grant to Halleck, Feb. 4, *ibid.,* p. 581. See also Grant, *Memoirs,* I, 290, and Henry Walke, "The Gun-Boats at Belmont and Fort Henry," *B. and L.,* I, 358–367.

3. McCormick states that the quarrel that later developed between Grant and McClernand may have been started by this incident (*Ulysses S. Grant,* p. 34). McClernand's report touched on the matter without any indication of irritation. As previously noted, he had already engaged in rather insubordinate proceedings. McCormick's statement on p. 33 that through the summer and fall, as well as the winter, McClellan, Buell, and Halleck wrote one another "grandiloquently," does not harmonize with the fact that Buell and Halleck came to the command of their department in mid-November, and apparently did not correspond with each other until January.

4. *O.R., 7,* 581.

5. Gosnell, *Guns on the Western Waters,* p. 47, quoting from a paper by Eliot Callender. Walke speaks of the large number of torpedoes loosened by the strong current and gives a diagram and description of one of them (*op. cit.,* pp. 362, 364).

6. Gosnell, *op. cit.,* pp. 47–48.

7. Halleck's dispatches are not in the records but are referred to in Grant's report (*ibid.,* pp. 124–125).

8. *Ibid.,* pp. 125–126 (repeated pp. 585–586). Smith apparently made no report; but Tilghman said that five transports with troops of Smith's command arrived during the night of the 5th (*ibid.,* p. 139).

9. Stanton Papers, III, 50588–50592; *O.R., 7,* 585. The Stanton Papers include many letters from Scott. *O.R., 122,* 875, 876, gives one dated Columbus, Feb. 1, and a telegram from Stanton the same day directing Scott to go from Columbus to Detroit, which was not on his original itinerary. Actually, however, Scott reported on the 2nd from Pittsburgh. Scott reported from Columbus that two fully equipped batteries would leave Cincinnati in three days for Kansas.

Kamm covers Scott's western trip in considerable detail in Chaps. IV and V of *The Civil War Career of Thomas A. Scott.*

10. *O.R., 7,* 583–585, 936–937. Buell's statement to Halleck was, "I will re-enforce your column by a brigade from Green River if you find you absolutely require it; otherwise I have use for it." In a midnight message to McClellan he said, "I will send him a brigade."

11. *Ibid.,* pp. 584–585; *109,* 205.

12. Tilghman's report, *ibid.,* pp. 136–144; Tilghman to Polk and to Mackay, *ibid.,* p. 858.

13. Walke, *op. cit.,* pp. 362–365. This account is drawn upon elsewhere without specific reference. See also Jesse Taylor, "The Defense of Fort Henry," *B. and L.,* I, 368–372.

14. *O.R. Navies,* S . I, XXII, 535–536.

15. Foote's report, *O.R., 7,* 122–124. Tilghman's adjutant and another officer came to the flagship after the Confederate flag was lowered, with word that Tilghman would like to see the flag officer. Foote makes it clear that he regarded the fort as having surrendered, for he said the officers he sent ashore had "orders to hoist the American flag where the secession ensign had been flying."

16. Tilghman's report; additional reports, *ibid.,* pp. 131–135, 145–147, 148–152.

17. Walke, *op. cit.,* p. 367.

18. Tilghman had apparently changed his plan to concentrate close under Fort Henry. He wrote in his report (*O.R., 7,* 140): "I argued thus: Fort Donelson might possibly be held, if properly re-enforced, even though Fort Henry should fall; but the reverse of this proposition was not true." As to concentrating, he said, "I hesitated not a moment." He seems to have moved his main body outside the works of Fort Henry fairly early on the 6th. He said it was 10:15 when he received a messenger "stating that our pickets re-

ported General Grant approaching rapidly and within half a mile of the advance work, and movements on the west bank indicated that General Smith was fast approaching also." The hour must be incorrect.

19. The correspondent of the *Boston Journal* wrote, "Gen. Grant did not accompany the column but remained by the river" (Moore, *Rebellion Record,* IV, 75).

20. *O.R. Navies,* Ser. I, XXII, 537, 540; *O.R., 7,* 123; Cullum to Halleck, *ibid., 109,* 207.

21. *O.R., 7,* 124.

22. *Ibid.,* pp. 124–125. Grant said, "The gunboats have proved themselves able to resist a heavy cannonading."

23. *Ibid.,* p. 586.

24. *Ibid.,* pp. 588, 590, 590–591.

25. *Ibid.,* pp. 933–936, 590–591, 587–588. Buell said the move "would have to be made in the face of 50,000 if not 60,000 men." His dispatch—sent at 12:00 P.M., Feb. 6—may have been an answer to one McClellan had sent that day in which he said, after noting that Halleck had telegraphed that Fort Henry had been reenforced from Columbus and Bowling Green, "If road so bad in your front, had we not better throw all available force on Forts Henry and Donelson? What think you of making that the main line of operations? Answer quick." In a second message he asked, "If it becomes necessary to detach largely from your command to support Grant, ought you not to go in person?" (*Ibid.,* p. 587.) Receipt of the news of the capture of Fort Henry probably caused McClellan to reconsider his ideas.

26. *Ibid.,* p. 591; *8,* 547.

27. *Ibid., 7,* 591 (repeated p. 601 under date of Feb. 10), 125, 594, 937; *109,* 207 (general report by Cullum to Halleck).

28. *Ibid., 7,* 591, 592.

29. *Ibid.,* p. 593. Halleck said the badly damaged gunboats would be repaired as soon as possible, and added, "In the mean time we must push on with infantry and artillery on transports." He had no train, most regiments being without land transport. He hoped Buell would help all he could, and he deemed the "holding of Fort Henry of vital importance" to them both.

30. Stanton Papers, III, 50615, 50622–50623.

31. *Ibid.,* 50624–50628; *N.Y. Tribune,* Feb. 7, 1862. Scott's "private" letter also spoke in a highly complimentary way of Buell and discussed the moving of 30,000 to 50,000 troops from the East to the West, a plan he said Buell favored.

As late as the 6th McClellan thought the move into East Tennessee could be made, for he telegraphed Buell, probably in the morning (*O.R., 7,* 586), "I need not urge you to delay the move on East Tennessee as little as possible. I fully appreciate the obstacles. Same thing here."

32. Moore, *op. cit.,* pp. 75–76. Walke, who was with Foote soon after the surrender, wrote later (*op. cit.,* p. 366) that he did not believe the latter had made the unchivalrous statement to Tilghman attributed to him by correspondents; he was too much of a gentleman.

33. Harris to Benjamin, *O.R., 7,* 860–861.

34. Benjamin to Beauregard, Jan. 26, 1862; Roman, *Military Operations of General Beauregard*, I, 491; Beauregard to Benjamin, Jan. 29, *ibid.*, p. 492. See also Basso, *Beauregard*, pp. 68–70.

35. Roman, *op. cit.*, p. 231; W. P. Johnston, *Life of Gen. A. S. Johnston*, p. 486.

36. W. P. Johnston indicates that Gen. Johnston received word of the impending attack on Fort Henry on the 5th but probably not on the 4th (*op. cit.*, p. 429); Roman in general agrees (*op. cit.*, pp. 213, 216).

On Feb. 8 Col. Heiman wrote in his report (*O.R.*, 7, 151) that Grant landed 12,000 men on the east bank of the Tennessee and Smith 6,000 on the west. Thus he made an accurate estimate of the Federal strength. Because of his capture at Fort Donelson, Heiman's report was not forwarded to Gen. Cooper until Aug. 11. One cannot say with certainty the strength that Johnston thought Grant had, but it seems probable that he knew Heiman's estimate.

37. *O.R.*, 7, 852–855. The strength of the force at Bowling Green is taken as the average of the two figures noted by the editors as given in conflicting returns; some consolidation of battalions into regiments has been made.

38. Roman, *op. cit.*, pp. 216–219, 226–228.

39. There was an abundance of supplies at Fort Donelson and Clarksville, so that there would have been no difficulty in subsistence for the 27,000 men Roman mentioned. But wagon transportation would have been necessary for an attack against Grant at Fort Henry, unless the operation were completed in three or four days with cooked rations carried by the men. The country was difficult, and one can question the ability of the Confederate commanders and staffs to mount the operation successfully in a short time. The argument between Johnston and Beauregard as set down by Roman on pp. 218–219 is certainly open to question; but his assertion that transportation was available is borne out by the records (Buckner to Pickett, *O.R.*, 7, 864–865, with regard to rolling stock; Johnston to Benjamin, *ibid.*, pp. 130–131, with regard to steamers).

40. *O.R.*, 7, 861–862; Roman, *op. cit.*, pp. 220–221; W. P. Johnston, *op. cit.*, p. 487. Roman and Johnston give Hardee's name below that of Beauregard as a signer; in the *O.R.* version, it is addressed to him. If Beauregard had recorded the decisions of the meeting at Johnston's request, it would have been addressed to him or to his adjutant, not to Hardee.

41. *O.R.*, 7, 130–131 (repeated pp. 863–864).

42. The version given by Roman and Johnston speaks of Donelson as "not being tenable," while the *O.R.* reading is "not long tenable."

43. *Ibid.*, p. 136; Taylor, *op. cit.*, p. 372. Tilghman's report was published in the Northern press; see Moore, *op. cit.*, p. 79. A longer report (*O.R.*, 7, 136–144) that Tilghman wrote on Feb. 12 did not reach the Confederate authorities, but he furnished a copy upon his exchange as a prisoner of war in Aug., 1862.

44. *O.R. Navies*, Ser. I, XXII, 544; *O.R.*, 7, 130. Mrs. John Trotwood Moore, Tennessee State Librarian and Archivist, writes in a letter dated Apr. 26, 1949, "We have always understood that Fort Donelson was named to

honor Daniel S. Donelson, but we have never seen any record of why Fort Henry was so named."

45. *O.R., 7,* 596–597.

46. Johnston's report, *ibid.,* p. 358; Floyd to Johnston, *ibid.,* p. 865; Johnston to Benjamin, *ibid.,* pp. 130–131; Buckner to Pickett, *ibid.,* pp. 864–865. Johnston stated that the movement of the enemy on his right (Thomas's capture of Mill Springs) would have made a retrograde movement necessary in a short time. Buckner reported that a messenger just in from Louisville said that opinion there—based on the view of one of Buell's staff—was that the movement up the river was "chiefly a diversion"; he also said a clerk on a Cairo-Evansville boat put the strength of the expedition at 12,000.

47. Grant to Walke, *O.R. Navies,* Ser. I, XXII, 574–575. About the bridge see also: Walke to Foote, *ibid.,* p. 575; Cullum to Halleck, *O.R., 7,* 595; Grant to Wallace, *ibid.,* pp. 618–619 (the date should probably be Feb. 13, not 15).

48. *O.R., 7,* 594; *109,* 208.

49. *Ibid., 7,* 594.

50. *Ibid.,* p. 595. With regard to Buell's coming to take command on the Cumberland, Halleck said that Sherman ranked him, and therefore was entitled to the command "in that direction." He asserted his plan would give "greater concert of action," put Hunter in a position "more agreeable to him," economize labor for McClellan, and "avoid any clashing of interests or difference of plans and policy."

51. Hitchcock, *Fifty Years in Camp and Field,* p. 434. Hitchcock, now 63 years old, had resigned from the Army in 1855, because of a quarrel with Secretary of War Jefferson Davis over the extension of a leave of absence. Winfield Scott, whom Hitchcock had served well in Mexico as Inspector General, took up his case so vigorously that Hitchcock feared the services of Scott were threatened if he did not eliminate himself. A brevet brigadier general and stationed in St. Louis at the time of his resignation, Hitchcock continued to live there, indulging his scholarly tastes in writing. He recorded in his diary on May 6, 1861, that he had packed 27 boxes of books and was off for New York "to get out of the secession fever which now agitates this city and State." Though the recall of Hitchcock was one of the first things Scott desired, such action was not taken, presumably because some years earlier he had exposed Cameron's fraudulent treatment of the Winnebago Indians. Just when Halleck began to ask for Hitchcock, now again in St. Louis, is not clear; but McClellan wrote on Jan. 29, 1862, "I have also recommended General Hitchcock, as you desire," and telegraphed on Feb. 6, "I will push Hitchcock's case" (*O.R., 7,* 930–931, 587).

52. *O.R., 7,* 595–596, 600, 604.

53. *N.Y. Tribune,* Feb. 14, 1862; James B. Eads, "Recollections of Foote and the Gun-Boats," *B. and L.,* I, 338–346.

54. *O.R., 7,* 598. Cullum telegraphed to Halleck: "I have already consulted with Foote, anticipating your orders. He can't send gunboats up the Cumberland. Will see him again."

55. *Ibid.,* pp. 598–599. Grant gave up the simple designation "Field Orders"

which he had begun on the 5th, and which anticipated modern practice, and initiated "General Field Orders" and "Special Field Orders."

56. *Ibid.*, pp. 597, 598. The K.G.C. was formed about 1854 for conducting filibustering operations along the Gulf of Mexico, and was later changed into an aid to secession. See Gray, *The Hidden Civil War*, pp. 70–71, 225 (for the order's oath).

57. *Ibid.*, pp. 278, 867–868.

58. Cramer, *Letters of Grant*, pp. 80–82; *O.R.*, 7, 937 (received at 9:00 P.M.). A copy of Buell's message went to McClellan.

59. *O.R.*, 7, 153–156. For numerous references to completing the *Eastport* as a Federal boat, see *O.R. Navies*, Ser. I, XXII.

60. *Ibid.*, pp. 821–822, 578–579.

61. *O.R.*, 7, 599, 600. Buell inquired of Halleck, "May I ask what force you leave at Paducah? It is exposed to Columbus, is it not? How many gunboats have you? It may affect my movement."

62. Buell to McClellan, *ibid.*, 109, 208. McClellan replied on the 14th to Halleck's proposal of the 8th, and Halleck received the message—evidently a letter—on the 19th (*ibid.*, 7, 636).

63. *Ibid.*, p. 600. Halleck said picks and shovels were being sent to strengthen the land side of Fort Henry, and again directed Grant to transfer guns so as to resist an attack.

64. *O.R.*, 7, 600; Washburne Papers, XXII; Jour. of Senate Exec. Proceedings, XII. On Dec. 21, 1861, Lincoln sent the Senate a long list of interim appointments for confirmation. On Jan. 17, 1862, the military committee reported most of those recommended as brigadiers, but Smith's name was not on the list. He was reported and confirmed on the 14th. McClernand telegraphed Washburne supporting Grant's plea.

65. *O.R. Navies*, Ser. I, XXII, 583. Walke indicates on p. 430 of "Western Flotilla at Fort Donelson, Island Number Ten, Fort Pillow and Memphis," *B. and L.*, I, 430–452, that on Feb. 8 Grant "requested" him "to hasten to Fort Donelson with the *Carondelet*, *Tyler*, and *Lexington*." This does not agree entirely with his message to Foote of Feb. 10, in which he spoke of receiving "instructions" from Grant to go to the Cumberland. While Grant had no authority over a Navy officer, it seems likely that Foote had directed Walke to do what Grant wished unless it involved too much hazard to his vessels.

66. *O.R.*, 7, 601.

67. *Ibid.*, pp. 603, 604, 608; 109, 209; 7, 604. Foote ended his message to Assistant Secretary of the Navy G. V. Fox, "We suffer for want of men." Fox transmitted it to Stanton the next day. The lack of provision of crews for the gunboats seems to point to inadequate foresight by the Navy. On Jan. 22 Foote telegraphed Secretary Welles: "The seven contract gunboats are in commission and will be ready for service when manned. We will endeavor to make these efficient with 600 men. These are wanted immediately. Will you send them? Please telegraph reply." The next day Welles answered: "Orders have gone to General Halleck to provide men. Copy sent to you yesterday. The ships on the Atlantic are waiting for men."

The steps Grant took to procure men and which he reported to Halleck on the 20th, could not have seemed promising, for Foote telegraphed Welles on the 23rd, "Can we have 600 men? Army officers object to their men shipping. Boats, except the *Benton,* are in commission waiting for men." Four days later Fox told Foote in a "semiofficial" letter that he advised Halleck to furnish men as ordered, and said in a postscript, "You can not expect men from the Navy." On Feb. 4, A. H. Kilty, speaking for Foote, informed Halleck that permanent, not temporary crews, were required, and reported to the Navy Department, "Men volunteer, but the captains and colonels object." They were trying to get men from Chicago, but up to the moment had had little success. On the same day Fox informed Foote that 600 men who had been seamen would be sent from Massachusetts regiments, in detachments of 100, the first to start on the 10th. (*O.R. Navies,* Ser. I, XXII, 515, 516, 517, 522, 532.) Thomas Scott wrote Stanton from Cairo on the 11th that the Navy was sending 600 seamen from Boston and that 600 more were needed; he did not seem to think the procurement of floating personnel an Army responsibility, for he said, "It is very important, and the Navy should respond at once" (*O.R., 109,* 208–209). In a message to Halleck on Feb. 25 (*O.R., 7,* 665) Foote referred to the "new and bad men sent from the East."

See Charles B. Hirsch, "Gunboat Personnel on the Western Waters," *Mid-America,* XXXIV, 75–86 (Apr., 1952).

68. *O.R., 8,* 553; *7,* 605.

69. Trollope, *North America,* p. 405; *O.R., 7,* 604–605. Halleck's reply of the next day is *ibid.,* p. 607.

70. *Ibid.,* pp. 66–68; McKee, *"Ben-Hur" Wallace,* p. 42.

71. Lew Wallace, "The Capture of Fort Donelson," *B. and L.,* I, 398–428.

72. *O.R., 7,* 605.

NOTES TO CHAPTER X

1. Lew Wallace, "The Capture of Fort Donelson," *B. and L.,* I, 406; Conger, *The Rise of Grant,* p. 167; *O.R., 7,* 612.

2. Conger, *op. cit.,* p. 165; McPherson's report, *O.R., 7,* 161–164; *N.Y. Times,* quoting *Cincinnati Times,* Feb. 20, 1862; Walke to Foote, Feb. 12, *O.R. Navies,* Ser. I, XXII, 588; Henry Walke, "The Western Flotilla at Fort Donelson, Island Number Ten, Fort Pillow and Memphis," *B. and L.,* I, 431.

3. *O.R., 7,* 607–608, 608.

4. *Ibid.,* pp. 933, 153. Foote sent Welles from Paducah on Feb. 12 the report that Phelps had written on the 10th, with a covering note that ended, "I am now, with three ironclad steamers, ascending the Cumberland River to cooperate with General Grant in an attack on Fort Donelson. Lieutenant Commanding Phelps, with his division accompanies me." (*O.R. Navies,* Ser. I, XXII, 571.)

5. *N.Y. Tribune,* Feb. 13, 1862.

6. *O.R., 7,* 869, 870; *110,* 269.

7. *O.R., 110,* 271–272, 271.

8. *O.R. Navies,* Ser. I, XXII, 587–588, 594.

9. Walke to Foote, Feb. 15, *ibid.*, pp. 587–588.

10. Grant's and McClernand's reports, *O.R.*, 7, 159–160, 172–174; Smith's and Lauman's reports, *ibid.*, 109, 7–9, 9–11; Walke to Foote, *O.R. Navies,* Ser. I, XXII, 587–588.

11. McPherson's report, *O.R.*, 7, 162; Wallace, *B. and L.*, I, 409; *O.R.*, 7, 609.

12. *O.R.*, 7, 609, 603, 609; 8, 555.

13. *O.R.*, 7, 608–609; 8, 555; *O.R. Navies*, Ser. I, XXII, 595.

14. *O.R.*, 110, 272; 7, 878–879, 613. The last two messages from Grant to Halleck on p. 113 should evidently be dated the 13th, not the 14th.

15. *Ibid.*, p. 613.

16. Foote's report, *O.R. Navies*, Ser. I, XXII, 585–586; McPherson's report, *O.R.*, 7, 163.

17. Wallace, *B. and L.*, I, 409; Wallace's, McClernand's, and McArthur's reports, *O.R.*, 7, 236, 174, 215.

18. Bidwell's report, *ibid.*, pp. 394–395; 110, 274.

19. Bidwell's report, *loc. cit.;* Foote's report, *O.R.*, 7, 166–167; 110, 274. Gosnell writes in *Guns on the Western Waters*, pp. 67–68: "The excellent preliminary shooting of the *Carondelet* demonstrated what could be done while lying out of range of all but two of the enemy guns. With deliberate shooting, it would not have required a very long time for the four boats together to put out of action practically every gun opposed to them, meanwhile undergoing the shelling of only two guns even at the start. And it will be remembered that the Confederates' rifle, by rarest chance, was accidentally spiked after firing only three rounds on the big day; thus there remained only one gun with a long range—the Columbiad." Bidwell's statement (*loc. cit.*) that his men could whip the gunboats always if they would "only stand to their guns" assumes that the Federals would close the range, as Foote—influenced by his success at Fort Henry—did.

20. *O.R.*, 7, 613–614.

21. Wilkins, *Diary.*

22. *O.R.*, 7, 255.

23. *Ibid.*, pp. 615, 612.

24. *Ibid.*, p. 881.

25. Stanton Papers, III, 50765–50766, 50757–50758, 50646–50647, 50774–50775. With regard to the movement up the Tennessee and the Cumberland, Halleck said in his letter to Scott, "McClellan approves if Buell is willing, Buell is 'willin' but hesitates & asks questions."

26. *O.R.*, 7, 614. On Feb. 13 Curtis sent Halleck the dispatch (*ibid., 8, 59*): "The flag of the Union floats over the court-house in Springfield, Mo. . . . I entered the city at 10 a.m. My cavalry is in full pursuit. They say the enemy is making a stand at Wilson's Creek. Forage, flour, and other stores in large quantities taken. Shall pursue as fast as the strength of the men will allow."

27. *Ibid., 7,* 612.

28. *Ibid.*, p. 880.

29. *Ibid.*, pp. 268, 360.

30. Beauregard to Pryor, *ibid.*, p. 880.

31. The note seems to be missing, but Grant refers to it in his report written the next day (*ibid.*, p. 160).

32. Grant, *Memoirs*, I, 305; Force, *From Fort Henry to Corinth*, p. 48.

33. Foote to Welles, *O.R. Navies*, Ser. I, XXII, 585–586; Bidwell to Benjamin, *O.R.*, 7, 394–395. Bidwell gives a description of the defending batteries as well as the action, and says: "Our gunners were inexperienced and knew very little of the firing of heavy guns. They, however, did some excellent shooting."

34. Grant, *op. cit.*, p. 305; McClernand's, Wallace's, and Pillow's reports, *O.R.*, 7, 177–179, 237, 282.

The time of Grant's arrival and departure should have been recorded in the log of Foote's flagship, the *St. Louis*, "officially known as the Baron de Kalb" (*O.R. Navies*, Ser. I, XXII, 938). This boat struck a torpedo in the Yazoo River on July 13, 1863, and sank in fifteen minutes. A report by Acting Rear Admiral David G. Porter said the officers and men lost everything, but that small arms were saved, as well as the paymaster's books and government funds (*ibid.*, XXV, 284). Presumably the log was lost. At least the War Records in the National Archives do not contain a log for a river gunboat *St. Louis* (there was a deep water vessel with that name) or *Baron de Kalb*.

In his *Memoirs* Grant says nothing about the hour of his departure but states the condition of the road rendered it impossible to make good time. Badeau has him return about nine o'clock (*Military History of U. S. Grant*, I, 44); Conger says his return "must have been toward noon" (*op. cit.*, p. 174); Force has him learn of the serious state of affairs on reaching his line about one o'clock (*op. cit.*, p. 54); Shotwell gives 1:30 as the time (*The Civil War in America*, I, 173); a correspondent of the *St. Louis Democrat*, quoted by *Harper's Weekly* on Mar. 15, 1862 (VI, 166), had him back just before noon.

Horn is critical of the length of Grant's conference with Foote and says, "That he would remain within sound of the firing for several hours and do nothing about it is as hard to understand" (*The Army of Tennessee*, pp. 443–444). After his conference with Grant, Foote wrote Welles that it had been decided he was not needed in the vicinity of Fort Donelson so much as at Cairo in getting boats ready, and he was therefore returning to that place (*O.R. Navies*, Ser. I, XXII, 585–586). Even then there would seem to have been no noise of heavy battle. Force, who was with the 20th Ohio when Grant met it on his way to the conference, wrote afterward that, although the enemy sally had been made, "there was nothing in the sound that came through several miles of intervening forest to indicate anything more serious than McClernand's previous assaults" (*op. cit.*, p. 48). After commenting only on Badeau's statement, Horn says that "the truth is" that Grant did not arrive on the scene until three o'clock. The receipt by Dove at 2:30 of the note from Grant presently quoted alone disproves this unsupported claim.

35. *O.R.*, 7, 618.

36. *O.R. Navies*, Ser. I, XXII, 588.

37. Conger observes that it would be interesting to know where Grant

went, what he saw, and with whom he spoke, but does not attempt to straighten out the contradictory evidence (*op. cit.*, p. 175).

38. Conger, *op. cit.*, pp. 174–175; Wallace, *B. and L.*, I, 422. One of Grant's strong detractors, Augustus W. Alexander "of the St. Louis bar," published privately in 1887 a small book, *Grant as a Soldier,* which criticizes harshly nearly everything Grant did, from Belmont to Lee's surrender. He said, "It was an error in Grant not to make an attack himself on the 15th," and that he should have been expecting to be attacked, since, "in the presence of a hostile army, a general must always be expecting an attack." Foote receives heavy censure for requesting Grant to come to see him—"a request quite impertinent . . . that would be proper only if Foote was dying, or some sudden and serious fact had sprung up forbidding delay." (Alexander said Foote "remained the next day,"—so there was no hurry—although Foote left soon after the conference.) The discussion of Fort Donelson—for which all credit is given to McClernand and "only discredit" to Grant—ends with the statement, "For his conduct in quitting his headquarters for the gunboat and absenting himself till after 4 p.m. he should have been sent before a court-martial."

39. Smith's report, *O.R., 109,* 7–9; report of Col. Tuttle, who commanded 2nd Iowa, *ibid.,* pp. 229–230; Buckner's report, *ibid.,* p. 333; Force, *op. cit.,* p. 56. Tuttle says that the advanced position was held for about an hour. McPherson states that the position actually occupied had "about as great an elevation as any portion" of the enemy works (*O.R., 7,* 163); Smith says the rest of the works were "some 400 yards distant and the ground more or less favorable." Col. John Smith states that orders to attack came from Gen. Smith at 2:00 P.M. (*ibid.,* p. 221); and a tablet in the Fort Donelson Military Park states that it was "about 2 P.M." that Lauman's brigade received orders to assault.

40. After describing the battle of the morning McClernand says (*O.R., 7,* 179): "We rested upon our arms until about 1:30 o'clock p.m., when your [Grant's] arrival gave promise that the general wish to advance would soon be gratified. In reply to my suggestion, urging a simultaneous assault at all points, I was gratified to receive an order to that effect." This would look as if Grant had seen McClernand before he wrote to Foote. But Wallace says (*ibid.,* p. 238), "About 3 o'clock General Grant rode up the hill and ordered an advance and attack on the enemy's left, while General Smith attacked their right. At General McClernand's request I undertook the proposed assault." In an indorsement on McClernand's report, Grant said, "No suggestions were made by McClernand at the time spoken of" (*ibid.,* p. 170).

As Wallace tells it in *B. and L.,* I, 421–422, Grant, at an hour not given, rode up to him and McClernand and directed that their commands be retired and throw up works to await reenforcements. Then, being informed of the mishap to the First Division, Grant crumpled some papers in his hand, his face flushed, and after saying "in his ordinary quiet voice . . . 'Gentlemen, the position on the right must be retaken,' he turned and galloped off." This not only has Grant reach the right of his army without knowing it has been badly handled, but disagrees with Wallace's report. In his *The Story of the Civil War,* II, 29–30, Ropes seemingly accepts the *B. and L.* account.

41.. Wilkins, *Diary,* entries for Feb. 15 and 16. The first entry states: "Gen'l Smith has just captured a line of works and [is] doing fine. . . . It is now 11:00 a.m. and [we] have just received orders to reenforce the shattered right." Though the hour fits well with that given by Badeau, it is irreconcilable with what Smith and others wrote.

42. Reports of Cols. M. L. Smith and George F. McGinnis, *O.R., 7,* 233–234; Wallace's report, *ibid.,* pp. 240, 239; McClernand's report, *ibid.,* p. 180; Wilkins, *Diary.*

43. Grant, *Memoirs,* I, 307. It is often stated that Grant examined the haversacks of some Confederate casualties and, finding them filled, deduced that the enemy was trying to escape. In his *Memoirs* he says he heard some of his men say the enemy had rations and seemed intent on staying out and fighting as long as their provisions held out. The question is of little import. More significant are the statements in the note to Foote about enemy demoralization and the chance of victory, and the attack Grant definitely ordered.

44. Dove to Foote, *O.R. Navies,* Ser. I, XXII, 588–589.

45. *O.R., 7,* 396.

46. *O.R. Navies,* Ser. I, XXII, 589–590. The date was not given, but Wallace signed himself as commanding the Middle Department, a position he held from Mar. 22, 1864, to Feb. 1, 1865. He apparently knew nothing of Grant's request and thought the gunboat attack was a voluntary act by Dove.

47. Conger, *op. cit.,* p. 138 n.

48. Pillow's, Buckner's, and Floyd's reports, *O.R., 7,* 284, 332–333, 269.

49. *Ibid.,* pp. 612, 600, 616.

50. Trollope, *North America,* p. 408; *O.R. Navies,* Ser. I, XXII, 523; Sherman to Halleck, *O.R., 7,* 618.

51. *O.R., 7,* 616, 621–622. At 5:30 Buell telegraphed Halleck (*ibid.,* p. 622) that steamers were leaving Louisville that evening to take on one brigade at Green River, the rest of Nelson's division to embark the next day 25 miles below Louisville. He asked to have the brigade "instructed at Smithland which river to ascend and where to land."

52. *Ibid.,* p. 617.

53. *Ibid.,* pp. 620, 617–618; *109,* 212. At 1:00 P.M. McClellan had telegraphed Halleck that Buell would move in force on Nashville as rapidly as circumstances permitted. While a division would be sent to Grant if necessary, McClellan thought it would be better employed in the direct advance on Nashville (*ibid., 7,* 617).

54. *O.R., 109,* 212. At 10:00 P.M., T. T. Eckert telegraphed A. Stanger in Cleveland that McClellan wanted to talk directly with Buell that night or at 11:00 in the morning and asked him to make the arrangement, adding, "Buell can cross the Ohio. Will you make the arrangements?" (*ibid.*). Nothing was said about bringing Halleck into the conversation. McClellan's message to Halleck is in the same place. Grant's *Memoirs,* I, 325, state that McClellan's dispatch did not reach him until Mar. 3. He apparently made no acknowledgment. Events had disposed of the question.

55. *Ibid.*, 7, 620.

56. *Ibid.*, pp. 619–620, 939–940, 883–885. On Jan. 10 Garfield had an engagement with Marshall near Prestonsburg, Ky. He reported on the 14th that 25 enemy dead were found and that the Confederates admitted 125 killed (*ibid.*, pp. 30–32). He said further, "Our loss was 1 killed and 20 wounded, 2 of whom have since died. We took 25 prisoners, among whom was a rebel captain. Not more than 900 of my force were actually engaged, and the enemy had not less than 3,500." Marshall wrote the same day to Johnston (*ibid.*, pp. 46–50): "The loss of the enemy was very severe. I understand he will report 1 killed and 10 or 12 wounded; his usual practice. We suppose his loss to be over 250 killed and about 300 wounded. . . . The field itself bears unerring testimony to his severe loss. I can only say to you, general, that my troops acted firmly and enthusiastically during the whole fight; and, though the enemy numbered 5,000 to our 1,500, they were well whipped." As to his own casualties, Marshall said, "I think our loss will amount to 11 killed and 15 wounded; not more." Both sides withdrew from the battlefield, and Marshall wrote, ". . . but an enemy greater than the Lincolnites (starvation) summoned me to reach a point where we might obtain food for man and horse."

57. *Ibid.*, p. 619. The order for the new districts is *ibid.*, 8, 555–556. In it Halleck reverted to his General Order No. 3 of Nov. 20, 1861, which had caused so much criticism, saying it would be strictly enforced and that officers who had permitted it to be violated would "be arrested and tried for neglect of duty and disobedience of orders."

58. *Ibid.*, 7, 618.

59. *N.Y. Tribune*, Feb. 12, 1862; Helen Nicolay, *Lincoln's Secretary*, p. 130; *O.R.*, 7, 624.

60. *O.R.*, 7, 255. Johnston indicated that the battle had been renewed by the Federals as a continuation of the attack of the day before.

61. Dove to Foote, *O.R. Navies*, Ser. I, XXII, 588–589. Though the note is not given, its contents are indicated by Dove's actions.

62. Lauman's report, *O.R.*, 109, 10.

63. *Ibid.*, 7, 255–256. The message was sent at 11:00 P.M., Feb. 15, and was forwarded to Richmond the next day by Johnston. Floyd made the rather peculiar statement, "The enemy maintained a successful struggle, which continued for nine hours, and resulted in driving him from the field . . . ." He made no mention of his own force being back within their lines, or of the loss of an important section of his works.

64. *Ibid.*, pp. 296–297.

65. Statements by Floyd and Pillow, *ibid.*, pp. 275, 302; Forrest's and Buckner's reports, *ibid.*, pp. 295–296, 335. The three artillery companies Floyd had brought from Virginia, which he described as "so remarkable for their efficiency and real gallantry," were lost.

66. *Ibid.*, pp. 160–161.

67. Lewis, *Captain Sam Grant*, pp. 336–338. The story that Grant's want of funds on reaching New York was partly due to his having lent money at Panama to a sick discharged soldier who was returning home is well supported

by Emerson in "Grant's Life in the West and His Mississippi Valley Campaigns," *Midland Monthly,* 210–211 (Sept., 1897). Emerson got the story from the former soldier, named Babcock, who was working as a carpenter for him at Ironton. The money—$40 with $10 interest—was repaid to Grant at St. Louis in 1859 through Emerson as agent. Babcock said the loan had saved his life.

68. *O.R., 7,* 161.

69. Dove to Foote, *O.R. Navies,* Ser. I, XXII, 588–589; Wallace's report, *O.R., 7,* 239; Wallace's testimony, *O.R. Navies,* Ser. I, XXII, 590; Wallace, *B. and L.,* I, 428; Johnson's report, *O.R., 7,* 363. Wallace did not say explicitly in his report, though he implied, that the Confederate major he mentioned had said the fort had surrendered. In the Dove case he testified that the major had been sent by Buckner with word that he "had capitulated during the night." According to the first two accounts Wallace sent the major to Grant; but in the *B. and L.* story he said, "I joined the officer bearing the flag, and with my staff rode across the trench and into the town." Any directions Grant may have sent out after he replied to Buckner are apparently unrecorded; an orderly would have had a hard time to find Wallace or any of his staff, according to his last account.

70. *O.R., 7,* 624–625. Halleck said that four gunboats were badly disabled and that Foote would not be able to return "for some days." It had been necessary to break up two artillery companies to furnish personnel for the gunboats and the mortar boats; it was almost impossible to get the mortars up the river and not much aid could be expected from the Navy for several days. The sentence, "Have constructed a battery above Fort Donelson on the river to cut off communications with Clarksville and Nashville," seems inexplicable.

At 11:00 A.M. of the 16th McClellan telegraphed Buell, "Give me in detail your situation and that of the enemy. Whither did he go from Bowling Green? I wish the position of things in full." In an undated dispatch that the editors of the *O.R.* ascribe provisionally to the same day, he was more exuberant: "Time is now everything. If Nashville is open the men could carry their small rations and bread, driving meat on the hoof. Leave tents and all baggage. If you can occupy Nashville at once it will end the war in Tennessee." (*Ibid.,* p. 626.)

Buell replied that the enemy was supposed to have gone to Nashville; he had had no report from Mitchel the night before, but wires would soon be up to him. In a second dispatch he said he had no definite information about Grant, except that he had Donelson invested with, he estimated, at least 30,000 men. He had repeatedly inquired of Halleck for the very information McClellan wanted, "but with little or no success." (*Ibid.,* p. 627.)

71. General Field Orders, No. 13, and Special Field Orders, No. 10, *ibid.,* pp. 625–626; Buckner's report, *ibid.,* p. 327–328; Cullum to Halleck, *ibid.,* p. 944.

72. *Ibid.,* p. 625.

73. *Ibid.,* pp. 159–160.

74. Livermore, *Numbers and Losses,* p. 78. Livermore puts the number of

Confederate "missing" at 14,623, referring to Grant's *Memoirs,* I, 314, which state, "The commissary general of prisoners reported having issued rations to 14,623 Fort Donelson prisoners at Cairo, as they passed that point." See also Badeau, *op. cit.,* I, 51 n. Without noticing Grant's figures, Horn writes (*op. cit.,* p. 97): "The exact number of prisoners was never officially announced. Estimates run all the way from 5,000 to 12,000; it was probably near 7,000 or 8,000." The latter figures cannot be accepted without completely disregarding statements of responsible officers at the time. On Feb. 18, Brig. Gen. Paine, commanding at Cairo, said in a telegram to Halleck, "There are 11,000 prisoners here now," and on the same day Cullum reported that 4,000 to 5,000 had already been sent to St. Louis on four steamers that he named; 3,000 more would be sent to Indiana directly from Donelson. The next day Rawlins informed Buckner that transportation was ready for 6,000 men and Grant wanted that number embarked that evening. "The remainder," Rawlins added, "will be allowed to remain in their camps until morning." (*O.R., 116,* 278, 277, 283.)

Paine's figure may have been too high, for it would put the total prisoners at about 18,000—a number, however, in agreement with 14,623 going through Cairo and 3,000 directly to Indiana. If one accepts 4,500 as the figure for those already sent to St. Louis and 2,500 as that for those left at Cairo, and 7,000 as the number yet at Donelson, he has a total of 14,000, in harmony with the bounding figures Grant gave in his telegram announcing the surrender of the fort, sent after he had talked with Buckner. On the other hand, Johnston on Mar. 17 wrote to Benjamin that the force within the fort on Feb. 13, "the first day of the conflict there," was 17,000 (*ibid., 7,* 922). He made no claim as to how many escaped. After discussing available returns, Livermore concluded that it was probably safe to accept Grant's estimate of 21,000 for the total Confederates engaged.

It is interesting that Governor Yates and two other men telegraphed Halleck from Cairo on the 18th, "We think it unsafe to send prisoners to Springfield, Ill.; there are so many secessionists at that place" (*ibid., 116,* 277).

75. Johnson's report, *O.R., 7,* 364–365; Brewster to Pillow and reply, *ibid.,* pp. 301–304.

76. Porter, *Campaigning with Grant* (quoting from an address by Buckner), p. 382; Green, *Grant's Last Stand,* p. 312.

NOTES TO CHAPTER XI

1. *O.R., 7,* 627–628. Halleck wired Cullum, "Stop all forces required to resist Beauregard" (*ibid.,* p. 628).

2. Cullum to McClellan, Cairo, Monday, Feb. 17, *N.Y. Tribune,* Feb. 18, 1862; *O.R., 7,* 628; *ibid., 116,* 270, 271. Cullum's message does not seem to be in the *O.R.*

In the dispatch that Commander Dove sent Foote on Feb. 16 reporting the fall of Fort Donelson, he said, "The *Carondelet,* being most disabled of the gunboats, will go down this afternoon" (*O.R. Navies,* Ser. I, XXII, 588–589).

Walke wrote that the fog at Cairo was so dense that the boat had difficulty finding the landing, and a recent rumor of an enemy attack caused some people to believe her whistle was that of a Confederate vessel ("The Western Flotilla . . . ," *B. and L.*, I, 437). The logs of the *Carondelet* and *Conestoga* in the National Archives do not go back as far as Feb., 1862.

At 10:00 A.M. of the 17th McClellan wired Halleck (*ibid., 7*, 628): "Please give me your reasons more fully for objecting to Buell's plan. Give facts on which your opinion is based." This looks as if he had not heard of the surrender of Donelson; but a message headed "Monday morning," addressed by J. J. Astor, an aide of McClellan's, to "My dear Schuyler," ends, "We are jubilant here to-day over the capture of Fort Donelson" (*ibid., 116*, 270).

3. Helen Nicolay, *Lincoln's Secretary*, p. 131.

4. *O.R., 7*, 629; *8, 559*. The message to Sherman ended, "You will not be forgotten in this."

5. Stanton Papers, III, 50765–50766, 50795–50799.

6. *O.R. Navies*, Ser. I, XXII, 584; Hendrick, *Lincoln's War Cabinet*, p. 237.

7. *O.R., 7*, 629.

8. *Ibid.*, p. 889.

9. *Ibid.*, p. 632.

10. *Ibid.*, pp. 632–633. Halleck said that Hunter had acted "nobly, generously, bravely." In *Memoirs*, I, 296, Grant spoke of Hunter sending "men freely from Kansas."

11. *Ibid.*, p. 634.

12. *Ibid.*, p. 940. On Feb. 18 Cullum informed Halleck that the telegraph had reached Fort Henry and that he would order its continuance to Fort Donelson (*ibid., 116*, 277).

13. *Ibid., 7*, 633.

14. *Ibid., 7*, 633; *8, 560*. The mortar boats were also to be returned as soon as possible. Halleck said Curtis had driven Price out of Missouri and was capturing prisoners and supplies.

15. *Ibid., 7*, 890, 891. Governor Harris telegraphed from Memphis to President Davis that a stand could not be made at Nashville; he asked for plans and said he would rally all Tennesseans possible and would go with them himself to the army (*ibid., 110*, 275).

16. Grant was ranked by McClellan, Frémont, and Halleck, whose commissions were in the regular army, and by Dix, Banks, Butler, Hunter, Morgan, and Hitchcock, commissioned in the volunteers (Phisterer, *Statistical Record*, pp. 247, 251). The appointment of Governor Morgan of New York had not yet been confirmed. See Appendix II.

17. *O.R., 109*, 214, 213.

18. *Ibid., 7*, 890. On the 16th Beatty recorded that it was said Beauregard had been dangerously sick in Hardee's house in Bowling Green, "and that under cover of this report he left town dressed in citizen's clothes and visited our camps on Green River" (*Memoirs of a Volunteer*, p. 85).

19. On the 15th Polk wrote to his wife: "I send out toward Paducah to-morrow a strong column under the direction of General Cheatham, for the

purpose of checking reinforcements to the enemy at Donelson. The weather is wretched for such a march, and the roads worse; but it is necessary, and must be done. I shall also make a demonstration on Bird's Point." The next day he added, "I have just received a dispatch from General Johnston instructing me to withhold the movement on Paducah." Beauregard's staff had already arrived, and the general, though sick at Jackson, was expected the next day. (W. N. Polk, *Leonidas Polk,* II, 74.)

20. *O.R.,* 7, 636, 636–637, 637, 636. Halleck's message to Cullum stated that he had the authority of the Secretary of War for the direction he gave. Benjamin ordered that a fleet of vessels be sent from Memphis or some other point to aid in the evacuation of Columbus.

21. *Ibid.,* pp. 638–639, 636, 635, 637, 124. In telegraphing about the 2nd Iowa, Halleck may have remembered that the regiment had left St. Louis under a cloud on account of a theft in a building under its charge—see *Harper's Weekly,* Mar. 15, 1862 (VI, 166).

22. *O.R.,* 7, 638.

23. *Ibid.,* pp. 637–638.

24. *Ibid.,* pp. 635, 639. On the 18th Scott wrote to Halleck at length (*ibid.,* pp. 941–942), explaining Buell's situation and saying he had about 40,000 men for the operation against Nashville.

25. Mitchel to Buell—a fine report—*ibid.,* pp. 634–635; Beatty, *loc. cit.*

26. *O.R.,* 110, 275–276.

27. *Ibid.,* 7, 640, 642.

28. *Ibid.,* pp. 640–641, 640, 641.

29. *Ibid.,* p. 642; 8, 561; 7, 641; 8, 560–561.

30. *N.Y. Tribune,* Feb. 21, for quotation from the *Times* and Greeley's comment.

31. *N.Y. Tribune,* Feb. 19, 1862.

32. *O.R.,* 7, 643–644.

33. *Ibid.,* p. 645.

34. *Ibid.*

35. *Ibid.,* p. 646. In a "strictly private" dispatch, one of McClellan's adjutants told Fry that it would be better for all concerned if Washington were "fully advised about matters in Kentucky" (*ibid.,* p. 650). On the 20th Halleck telegraphed McClellan that he could not give details because the telegraph line across the Ohio had been down; but he estimated that there were 15,000 men at Cairo, Fort Holt, and Bird's Point, "and at Forts Henry and Donelson, from 20,000 to 25,000" (*O.R.,* 109, 214). Grant had about 27,000 men. In a dispatch to Halleck on the 27th Sherman said he estimated Grant's force at 25,000 (*ibid.,* 7, 670).

36. *Ibid.,* p. 647.

37. *Ibid.,* p. 648. From Paducah, Foote telegraphed Cullum (*ibid.*): "General Grant and myself consider this a good time to move on Nashville. Six mortar boats and two iron-clad steamers can precede the troops and shell the forts. . . . The Cumberland is in a good stage of water, and General Grant and I believe that we can take Nashville. Please ask General Halleck if we shall do it."

38. On Feb. 6 Scott telegraphed Stanton from Louisville: "I have your message of censure. I have not given order to any General—nor did not dream of doing so. . . ." In a "private and confidential" note the next day, he said, "Your message of yesterday *hurt me*. It is all past now." (Stanton Papers, III, 50631, 50622–50623.)

39. *O.R., 7,* 648.

40. *Ibid.,* p. 655. The dispatch is actually dated the 23rd, which harmonizes with the words "one whole week," for the capture of Fort Donelson was on the 16th. The editors of the *O.R.* suggest that the correct date was the 21st, probably because in a dispatch on the 22nd—presently cited—Stanton said Halleck's telegram of "yesterday" had been received and submitted to the President.

41. *Ibid.,* pp. 645–646, 645. See also McClellan to Cullum (p. 641) and Cullum to McClellan (p. 644), both of Feb. 20. Cullum said four gunboats were watching for movement from Columbus, and he concluded, "Had spy there Tuesday night, and have scouts near to-night."

42. Stanton Papers, IV, 50820; also earlier letter of same date, *ibid.,* pp. 50821–50827.

43. *O.R., 7,* 649–650. Another order was also issued on the subject of discipline, which said, "All depredations committed upon citizens must be summarily punished" (*ibid.,* p. 650).

44. *Ibid.,* p. 649.

45. *Ibid.,* pp. 423–424. For Foote's proclamation to the inhabitants of Clarksville, see p. 423.

46. *N.Y. Tribune,* Feb. 20, 24, 1862. Quoting the *N.Y. Evening Post, Harper's Weekly* said on Mar. 8 (VI, 151), "General M'Clellan was the most observed of observers."

47. *O.R., 7,* 652.

48. *O.R. Navies,* Ser. I, XXII, 624.

49. *O.R., 7,* 656; Beatty, *op. cit.,* p. 86. On the 22nd Thomas wrote to Fry (*O.R., 7,* 653–654): "It rained two days ago as I never saw it rain before. It has done the same today."

50. Grant to Cullum, *O.R., 7,* 662.

51. Extracts from Ammen's diary, *ibid.,* pp. 659–660. In Buell's army there was a continuous sequence of numbers for brigades, and a brigade number had no reference to the division to which it belonged. Ammen commanded the 10th Brigade.

52. *Ibid.,* pp. 662–663.

53. Ammen's diary, *loc. cit.*

54. Nicolay and Hay, *Lincoln,* IV, 235; Beatty, *op. cit.,* pp. 86–87; *O.R., 7,* 425.

55. *Ibid.,* pp. 944–945; Grant, *Memoirs,* I, 320.

56. *O.R., 7,* 425, 657. On the 28th Buell reported that he thought Thomas's division would begin to arrive the next night (*ibid.,* p. 671).

57. *Ibid.,* pp. 666, 667. Grant said in *Memoirs,* I, 319–320, that he informed department headquarters he would go to Nashville on the 28th. Actually he set no date in the message to Cullum.

58. *O.R., 7,* 670–671.
59. Grant, *op. cit.,* p. 321; Coppée, *Grant and his Campaigns,* p. 26 n.; *N.Y. Tribune,* Mar. 6, 1862 (a two-column dispatch dated Nashville, Feb. 27); Bill, *Rehearsal for Conflict,* pp. 36–38.

NOTES TO CHAPTER XII

1. *O.R., 7,* 660.
2. *Ibid.,* p. 661. In a dispatch to Sherman and Foote on the 23rd (*ibid.,* p. 655), Halleck spoke as if he expected a decisive contest near the Cumberland. When he learned of the evacuation of Nashville, his idea naturally changed. Col. D. Stuart, commanding at Paducah during Sherman's absence in Cairo, revealed that there was still a shortage of weapons when he reported to Halleck on the 25th the presence of eight unarmed Ohio regiments (*ibid.,* p. 665).
3. *Ibid.,* pp. 661, 660. The dispatches to both Buell and Halleck enjoined them to communicate frequently.
4. *Ibid.,* pp. 664, 678.
5. *O.R., 7,* 663–664, 678, 679, 680–681. Carter said that if his command were large enough he could send part of it through Big Creek Gap to take the enemy in the rear, and probably capture the entire opposing force. The gap mentioned was near Jacksboro, and the chance of capturing the Confederates looks very fanciful. Carter said nothing about the enemy strength at Cumberland Gap or Knoxville. On Feb. 16 Cooper directed Col. Leadbetter at Knoxville to reenforce Cumberland Gap with all men not needed to guard the railroad, and informed him that "forces" were on the way to Knoxville from Richmond (*ibid.,* p. 888). Thus the threat was accomplishing something.
6. *Ibid.,* pp. 879, 908 (order of Feb. 25).
7. *Ibid.,* pp. 899–901, 904–905, 426–427. Johnston's reorganized force was called the "Central Army" in his order, and consisted of three divisions and a reserve, embracing about 40 infantry regiments, nine batteries, and some cavalry. Hardee had the first division; Crittenden, the second; Pillow, the third. In a dispatch to Richmond, Johnston referred to his force as a "corps of the army."
8. *Ibid.,* pp. 421–422, 906–907, 907; *8,* 754–755.
9. *Ibid., 109,* 215–216. The line from Donelson to Nashville was also to be repaired, or a new one constructed.
10. *Ibid., 8,* 562; Sheridan, *Memoirs,* I, 131; *O.R., 8,* 567–568, 568, 574. See also Franz Sigel, "The Pea Ridge Campaign," *B. and L.,* I, 314, 334.
11. *O.R., 8,* 734; Lewis, *Captain Sam Grant,* p. 81 (on Van Dorn); *O.R., 8,* 748–749, 750–752.
12. *Ibid., 8,* 755, 764, 283. On Feb. 23 Curtis had written to Halleck (*ibid.,* pp. 567–568), "It is said Van Dorn will move a force by Roaring Creek to cut off my line of communication. It is also said he has joined the main army

at Boston Mountains and arrested McCulloch. All accounts agree in saying the main army is distracted with internal feuds among their forces."

13. *Ibid.,* pp. 577–578, 588–589, 592, 283, 197. In his message of the 4th Curtis said he would expect Hunter on his right soon.

14. Curtis's report, *ibid.,* pp. 199–201.

15. *Ibid.,* pp. 239, 201.

16. *Ibid.,* p. 284.

17. *Ibid.,* pp. 202–203, 215, 206, 285, 194, 195. The casualties that Livermore gives (*Numbers and Losses,* p. 79), Federal, 1,384, Confederate, 800, are the accurate figures for the former and Van Dorn's estimate for the latter.

18. *Ibid.,* pp. 191–193, 281, 193, 190–191, 611. Curtis's longer report (*ibid.,* pp. 191–204) was dated Apr. 1; and Van Dorn's (*ibid.,* pp. 283–286), Mar. 27.

On the 13th Curtis sent a dispatch (*ibid.,* pp. 610–611) to the "Commanding Officer U.S. Forces en route for [from] Kansas," informing him of the recent engagement, saying that there was a good place to camp two and a half miles west of Bentonville, and adding, "I desire to secure an early junction of our forces, if your orders are consistent with such a movement." The next day Halleck informed Curtis that reenforcements and ammunition were on the way and told him to hold his position (*ibid.,* p. 617).

19. *O.R., 8,* 559; *7,* 942–944; *8,* 560–561, 564–565, 566, 571–572.

20. *Ibid.,* pp. 571–572, 570, 573; Lewis, *op. cit.,* p. 87 (on Granger).

21. *O.R., 8,* 578–580.

22. *Ibid.,* p. 581; *7,* 437, 677–678; *8,* 583; *7,* 437; *N.Y. Tribune,* Mar. 10 and 17, 1862.

23. *O.R., 7,* 436–437; *Harper's Weekly,* VI, 198, 202–203 (Mar. 29, 1862); *O.R., 7,* 437–438; W. M. Polk, *Leonidas Polk,* II, 80–81.

24. *O.R., 8,* 757, 757–758.

25. Pope to Cullum, *ibid.,* pp. 580–581. Confederate Maj. Gen. J. P. McCown identified the men as Thompson's (*ibid.,* p. 127).

26. *Ibid.,* pp. 582–583, 587–588.

27. *O.R., 7,* 437; *8,* 590–591 (Cullum to Halleck), 609 (Foote to G. V. Fox), 595 (Halleck to Cullum). Foote's dispatch mentioned the difficulty in holding the gunboats in position for an attack downstream, and described structural defects. Cullum told of the bad condition of the hulls and machinery of the gunboats, and prophesied failure if the enemy made a resistance equal to that he had made on all former occasions. Halleck discussed the probable effectiveness of the fire of the mortars and said, "I repeat, I do not want the gunboats to fight till they are ready." For some of Foote's difficulties with personnel and pay, see Foote to Meigs, *ibid.,* pp. 576, 600–601.

28. *Ibid.,* pp. 597–598, 82–83, 613, 613–614. On Mar. 13 Halleck definitely ordered Foote to attack Island No. 10. He thought the main work should be done by the mortar boats, and he did not want to have the gunboats injured, because they would be required immediately for other operations (*ibid.,* p. 608). Foote telegraphed the same day (*ibid.*), "Your instructions to attack Island No. 10 are received, and I shall move for that purpose to-morrow morning." (The attack was not made because of the fall of New Madrid.) He commented: "Generally, in all our attacks down the river I will bear in mind

the effect on this place [Cairo] and the other rivers which a serious disaster to the gunboats would involve."

Welles's enmity and jealousy of Stanton had been communicated to Fox, who feared the Navy was not getting proper credit. On Mar. 1, he wrote to Foote: "J. W. Grimes, of the Senate, is your strong friend; perhaps a note to him, giving a narrative (not complaining), would be agreeable. Your reputation is that of the Navy and the cause, and well you have sustained it under difficulties that place the entire credit on your head, and none here, or with the Western general. I understand him. . . . I wish some trophy of your noble fight at Fort Henry. Can you send any little flag or old swords for distribution to the naval committees?" (*O.R. Navies,* Ser. I, XXII, 648–649.)

29. *Ibid.,* pp. 598–599, 599–600; *3,* 209.

30. *Ibid., 8,* 618, 614.

31. *Ibid.,* pp. 563–564, 568–569, 570–571. In the order referring to Paine, Halleck took occasion to refer to the habit some officers had of giving information to the press. "The law and Army Regulations afford a remedy for all personal grievances," he said, "no matter by whom they have been caused, and when military officers carry their complaints to newspapers the inference is that they are without foundation." He threatened arrest and court martial for publishing without proper authority "any information respecting the movements of our armies, even of battles won or any official papers," and said, "the Secretary of War has directed that the whole edition of the newspaper publishing such information be seized and destroyed." He evidently considered removing Paine, for Cullum wrote him on Feb. 19: "I do not think it wise to supersede Paine in command; though he is somewhat of a politician, and not always discreet, he is energetic, full of zeal, has pluck, and knows localities" (*ibid., 7,* 944).

In his report to McClellan on Feb. 27 about Curtis's entry into Fayetteville (*ibid., 8,* 68), Halleck gave the name of the captain who had died of poisoned food at Mud Town and of two officers who had recovered.

32. *Ibid., 8,* 582, 604, 611–612.

33. On Feb. 26 Thompson wrote to Van Dorn from New Madrid, "The Legislature is to meet here on Monday if we are not driven away before then" (*ibid.,* pp. 758–759).

34. *O.R., 7,* 942–943.

35. Grant, *Memoirs,* I, 325; *O.R., 7,* 674, 677. Grant wrote: "My dispatches were all sent to Cairo by boat, but many of those addressed to me were sent to the operator at the end of the advancing wire and he failed to forward them. This operator afterwards proved to be a rebel; he deserted his post after a short time and went south taking his dispatches with him."

36. *O.R., 7,* 679–680.

37. *Ibid., 109,* 217.

38. *Ibid., 7,* 680.

39. *Ibid., 7,* 682; *11,* 3.

40. *Ibid., 11,* 3–22 *passim; 109,* 222.

41. In his order (*O.R., 7,* 674) to Grant of Mar. 1, directing the move up the Tennessee, Halleck said: "Avoid any general engagement with strong

forces. It will be better to retreat than risk a general battle. This should be strongly impressed upon the officers sent with the expedition from the river [that is, to strike the railroad]. General C. F. Smith, or some very discreet officer, should be selected for such command." Having accomplished his missions "or such of them as may be practicable," Grant was to return to the vicinity of Fort Henry "and move on Paris."

42. Halleck to Grant, Mar. 10, *O.R.*, *11*, 27; same with enclosure, Mar. 6, *ibid.*, pp. 13–14; Grant to Halleck, Mar. 11, *ibid.*, p. 30. Halleck stated that the writer of the anonymous letter was known to Davis as "a man of integrity and perfectly reliable." In his reply Grant said, "I refer you to my orders to suppress marauding as the only reply necessary." (Orders alone could not clear him, and it will be seen that he later voluntarily admitted there had been irregularities.) In an earlier dispatch on the 11th (*ibid.*, p. 29) Grant acknowledged Halleck's message of the day before and said, "The people of Tennessee are much in want of protection to-day against the Governor's conscriptions orders. I wish we were in condition to afford them the protection they require."

43. *Ibid.*, p. 32.

44. Washburne Papers, XXIII, 4587; *O.R.*, *11*, 39, 40. Grant made an interesting comment about the security of the force he would leave behind. Although Fort Heiman was the dominating point and commanded the river effectually, it was accessible by good roads from the interior. A small garrison might not be secure there, though it would be perfectly so at Henry.

45. *O.R.*, *7*, 683–684. Halleck said categorically, "There never has been any want of military subordination on the part of General Grant." He sent Grant copies of the letter of the Adjutant General and his reply, and on Mar. 24 Grant wrote in a rather long letter reviewing the matter (*ibid.*, *11*, 62–63), "I most fully appreciate your justness, general, in the part you have taken, and you may rely upon me to the utmost of my capacity for carrying out all your orders." Badeau points out (*Military History of U. S. Grant*, I, 64, 65 n.) that Halleck did not furnish Grant with a copy of his message of Mar. 2 to McClellan, which "was not left on file in the War Department," but was obtained by Badeau "after long research and repeated efforts." He was unable to find McClellan's reply, and Stanton assured him that he never heard that Halleck had been authorized to place Grant in arrest. As given in *O.R.*, *7*, 680—published after Badeau's work—McClellan's reply has written below it: "Approved: Edwin M. Stanton, Secretary of War."

Thomas's communication of Mar. 10 to Halleck began, "It has been reported that soon after the battle of Fort Donelson Brigadier-General Grant left his command without leave." This does not connect Halleck with the report; and it is not strange that Grant, upon receiving from Halleck a copy of the letter, believed him in no way responsible for what had happened, and viewed him solely as one whose good offices had rescued him from disfavor in Washington. Badeau's discovery of Halleck's first telegram to McClellan naturally caused Grant to change his view on the subject. The incident was very regrettable; but in the end it has strengthened Grant's historical position, for it shows how little he owed to the favor of superiors. It also makes less impressive the claims that suspicion and prejudice kept the merits of other officers from being appreciated.

Although the basic facts are clear enough, the incident is still inaccurately portrayed. Horn states, "After the capture of Fort Donelson, Grant through some vagary went off on an unauthorized and unnecessary trip to Nashville" (*The Army of Tennessee*, p. 115). This disregards Grant's natural desire to see Buell about the return of Smith and overlooks the fact that he had notified Cullum of his intended trip. He was never in arrest, yet Horn says he was "relieved of his arrest" on Mar. 17. As has been seen, Halleck informed him on the 10th that he was to command the expedition up the river in person; what happened on Mar. 17 will be explained presently. In Seitz's *Braxton Bragg* it is said (p. 97) that Lincoln actively intervened: "By this time President Lincoln had reached the bottom of Halleck's action in removing Grant and on March 17th restored him to his command." In Davidson's *The Tennessee* it is stated that Lincoln saved Grant by promoting him to a major generalship, and it is indicated that command passed again to him because of the injury to Smith (pp. 25, 31).

46. *N.Y. Tribune*, Mar. 4, 1862; *O.R., 8,* 596.

47. *Ibid.*, pp. 831–832.

48. *Ibid., 11,* 11, 10, 16.

49. *Ibid.*, p. 19. It was presumably at an earlier hour of the same day—Mar. 8—that Halleck informed Buell: "I have encouraged steamers here to take goods to Nashville. This will enable you to use them when they arrive there without exposing my plan by sending them up empty." He requested Buell to inform him when and how many troops he would send, if he so decided. (*Ibid.*, p. 18.)

50. *Ibid.*, pp. 24–25. The dispatch began: "Reserves intended to support General Curtis will now be drawn in as rapidly as possible and sent to the Tennessee," and it ended, "I shall soon fight a great battle on the Tennessee unsupported, as it seems, but if successful, it will settle the campaign in the West."

The account of the move up the Tennessee given on pp. 25–31 of Davidson's *The Tennessee* is very critical of the Federals for slowness. Halleck is pictured as having command over Buell from the start, and is said to have held his generals in check, whereas it has been seen that he complained of delay because of not getting aid from Buell, over whom he initially had no authority. The criticism is somewhat nullified by the statement that it was a considerable feat to assemble the necessary steamers at the right place and time. (There was also a fuel problem.) Johnston's retirement is in contrast praised, though it is not noted that he was in friendly territory and encountered no destroyed bridges, as did Buell. It is indicated that Johnston and Beauregard had the wisdom to decide to concentrate at Corinth even before the withdrawal from Kentucky began. Actually in the memorandum written at Bowling Green on Feb. 7 (*supra*, p. 215) Corinth was not mentioned, and it was expressly said that if withdrawal beyond Nashville was necessary, it would be to Stevenson. It has been seen here that in the last of February Beauregard thought Confederate forces west of the Tennessee sufficient to warrant an offensive against Paducah, and even wrote of the possibility of taking St. Louis.

51. McClellan, *Own Story*, p. 137; *O.R., 7*, 930–931.

52. *O.R., 8*, 605–606; *11*, 33, 33–34; *8*, 611; Stephenson, *The Political Career of General James H. Lane*, p. 32; *O.R., 11*, 20.

NOTES TO CHAPTER XIII

1. *O.R., 11*, 43. Grant informed St. Louis on the 18th (*ibid.*, pp. 45–46) that he had arrived "last evening."

2. In *Memoirs*, I, 329, Grant spoke of his cordial reception by Smith and said, "He was on a sick bed at the time, from which he never came away alive." Grant's reports to St. Louis seem to ignore Smith's illness; on Mar. 26 he referred to him as the senior officer at Pittsburg and assigned him to command at that place (*O.R., 11*, 67).

3. *Ibid.*, pp. 42–43; *10*, 22–24.

4. *Ibid., 11*, 45–46. Grant said he would go to Crumps Landing and Pittsburg the next day.

5. *Ibid.*, p. 41.

6. *Ibid.*, p. 35. At the same time Grant recommended Cols. W. H. L. Wallace and John A. Logan, saying they were from civil pursuits but were fully qualified, and had earned promotion on the field of battle. Wallace and Logan were promoted as of Mar. 21, and Morgan Smith and Webster later in the year.

7. Conger, *The Rise of Grant*, pp. 233–234.

8. *O.R., 11*, 46–47.

9. *Ibid.*, p. 41.

10. Sherman, *Memoirs*, I, 232. A dispatch from Sherman to Rawlins dated Mar. 17 in *O.R., 10*, 27, begins: "I have just returned from reconnaissance towards Corinth and Purdy, and am strongly impressed with the importance of the position, both for its land advantages and its strategic position. The ground itself admits of easy defense by a small command, and yet affords admirable camping ground for a hundred thousand men." The message is printed, with a few minor differences, in his *Memoirs*, I, 233, but with the date Mar. 19. It seems to be the report that Sherman promised in the postscript to his adjutant's message to write "this evening"—but that message is dated Mar. 18.

11. *O.R., 11*, 50. The order of the 17th for the debarkation of Hurlbut's division (*ibid., 109*, 225) stated, "General Sherman's division will remain on board transports, and hold themselves in readiness to move promptly in any direction by land or water." No citizens were to be allowed within the lines of Hurlbut's camp, and guards were to be carefully instructed "to make prisoners of all found lurking in the neighboring country unless they are on their own farms and at their own work, when they must be encouraged and protected." An order of Sherman's of the 13th, which was to be read "immediately" to every company, stated that "the laws of Congress make pillage punishable

by death," and it spoke of the disgrace that attached to conduct preventing "that respect with which it should be our aim to impress our enemies now, who must become our friends before peace can be hoped for" (*O.R.*, *11*, 34–35). These are notable words in view of the bitter condemnation heaped on Sherman for his method of conducting war in 1864–1865.

12. *Ibid.*, *10*, 24–25. Enclosed were copies of his instructions to the commander of the cavalry detachment and the order for his own division. Sherman instructed the cavalry: "Don't hesitate to make the attempt at the railroad unless you have strong evidence of its too hazardous character. The object is worth a desperate effort. I send with you a good guide, and herewith a good sketch of the intervening country." A report of what seems to be the same effort, addressed to Rawlins, is given on pp. 26–27. It bears the date Mar. 17, which may be wrong because it is doubtful that Sherman knew on the 17th of Grant's arrival at Savannah; one recalls also the discrepancy in the dates on the two versions of the message previously described. His report to Smith seems to put responsibility for the cavalry's failure upon the fact that the chief guide was wounded. In the one to Grant he said the enemy's utter confusion was attested by "horses loose and mired in the bottoms, saddles, sabres, shotguns scattered through the woods and along the several roads and by-paths by which they retreated toward Purdy."

In his "Record of Events" for March Sherman wrote (*ibid.*, *10*, 28): "On the 16th dropped down to Pittsburg Landing, and disembarked and attempted destruction of railroad. Cavalry encountered a force, which was routed, but failed in the undertaking. Division went into camp, extending from the Purdy to the Hamburg road, 2½ miles back from the landing, on 19th."

13. *O.R.*, *11*, 48–49.

14. Cullum to Halleck, Mar. 3, *O.R.*, *7*, 435; Gwin to Foote, Savannah, Mar. 1, *O.R. Navies*, Ser. I, XXII, 643–645; Shirk to Foote, Mar. 1, *ibid.*, pp. 645–646. In transmitting the reports to Welles (*ibid.*, p. 643), Foote wrote, "The Union sentiment is predominant on the borders of the Tennessee, but is repressed from apprehension that it will not receive support from Union troops."

15. Gwin to Foote, Cairo, Mar. 5, *ibid.*, pp. 647–648; order by Brig. Gen. Daniel Ruggles, *O.R.*, *7*, 435. After saying that recent elections showed the strength of the Unionists in two counties in southern Tennessee, Gwin wrote, "The constant cry from them to me is, 'Send us arms and a sufficient force to protect us in organizing and we will drive the secessionists out of Tennessee ourselves.'" The same Gwin had reported his gunboat as "riddled" at Pittsburg! Doubtless Thomas Scott saw the report, for Foote said in his letter to Welles that Scott was in his office.

16. Force gives in *From Fort Henry to Corinth*, pp. 99–100, a description of the area based on notes made by Col. Charles Whittlesey, "who made a study of the field every day for two weeks succeeding the battle." The names he gives to some of the streams are not those found on the Battlefield Commission Map made by Maj. D. W. Reed in 1900. The Reed map is the basis for maps in the present work.

17. Grant to Halleck, Mar. 19, *O.R.*, *11*, 49. The vessel that Grant located

at "Duck Creek" was the *Dunbar,* which Shirk described as a "rebel gunboat" (*O.R. Navies,* Ser. I, XXII, 520).

18. Reports by Smith, Wallace, and Hayes, *O.R., 10,* 10–13.

19. *O.R., 10,* 11; *7,* 912; Horn, *The Army of Tennessee,* p. 114.

20. Grant, *Memoirs,* II, 86; *O.R., 10,* 11–12.

21. Horn, *op. cit.,* p. 115 (on Ruggles); *O.R., 11,* 332, 339–340.

22. *Ibid.,* p. 297.

23. *Ibid.*

24. *Ibid.,* pp. 302, 310.

25. Horn, *op. cit.,* p. 104.

26. *O.R., 11,* 314.

27. *Ibid., 7,* 258–261; *11,* 365–366. In his letter to President Davis, Johnston said, "I determined to fight for Nashville at Donelson, and gave the best part of my army to do it, retaining only 14,000 men to cover my front, and giving 16,000 to defend Donelson." (Here is further confirmation of Grant's figure of about 21,000 as the total enemy force at Donelson, for Johnston certainly did not mean his 16,000 to include the original garrison.) The decision, clearly admitted, was of course a repudiation of the conclusions of the conference between himself, Beauregard, and Hardee recorded in the memorandum of Feb. 7, previously described. Johnston also made the interesting and significant statement, "I had made every disposition for the defense of the fort my means allowed, and the troops were among the best of my forces, and the generals— Floyd, Pillow, and Buckner—were high in the opinion of officers and men for skill and courage, and among the best officers of my command. They were popular with the volunteers, and all had seen much service. No re-enforcements were asked."

28. Johnston to Col. Helm, Mar. 18, *ibid., 11,* 338.

29. *Ibid.,* p. 47.

30. *Ibid.,* pp. 27, 33, 33–34, 37–38.

31. *Ibid.,* pp. 66, 42, 44.

32. Don Carlos Buell, "Shiloh Reviewed," *B. and L.,* I, 487–536 (specifically p. 491); *O.R., 7,* 615.

33. *O.R., 11,* 60–61.

34. On Mar. 31 Halleck wrote Grant, "A pontoon train will probably be shipped to-morrow or the day after." On Apr. 2 he told Buell: "I have sent twenty pontoons to General Grant. Will send more if required." (*Ibid.,* pp. 82, 86.)

35. *Ibid.,* p. 46; on Johnson, pp. 25, 612; on Brownlow, p. 39; on diving boats, pp. 34, 38. On Mar. 6 Buell said in a dispatch to McClellan (*ibid.,* p. 11): "I have been concerned to hear that it is proposed to organize a provisional government for Tennessee. I think it would be injudicious at this time. It may not be necessary at all." In his reply the next day McClellan said (*ibid.,* p. 611): "The subject of provisional governor was arranged for by the President, and the decision is final. I think your dispatch advising against it arrived too late." To Johnson's message from Cincinnati that he would be in Louisville the next day, Buell replied (*ibid.,* p. 612), "You must not expect to

be received with enthusiasm, but rather the reverse, and I would suggest to you to enter without any display."

36. *Ibid.,* p. 48. See also Buell to Halleck, Mar. 18, *ibid.,* p. 613, which puts the force moving toward Savannah at 26,000.

37. On Mar. 20 Halleck told Buell a telegraph party had been sent to Savannah; on the 27th Grant reported to headquarters that the wire had arrived and the line had been started, and that he had called up three companies of cavalry from Fort Henry to protect it (*ibid.,* pp. 51–52, 70).

38. Buell to Brig. Gen. Ebenezer Dumont, letter of instructions, Mar. 20, *ibid.,* pp. 54–55 (also order of Mar. 21, *ibid., 109,* 228); *ibid., 11,* 612, 39, 59. In a long letter of the 23rd (*ibid.,* pp. 60–61) Buell gave considerable information about the enemy, speaking of a concentration of force and rolling stock at Atlanta, and stating that Floyd had left Chattanooga for Knoxville. He remarked, "We are working somewhat in the dark as regards Middle and East Tennessee at least, for we do not know yet what is being done with the Virginia army."

39. *Ibid.,* pp. 46, 49.

40. *Ibid.,* pp. 51–53 *passim.*

41. *Ibid.,* pp. 50–51.

42. *Ibid.,* pp. 55, 55–56, 37. In his longer message Grant gave a basis for the statement in his *Memoirs* about messages that had not reached him previously, telling Halleck: "I have just learned to-day that your dispatches to me after the taking of Fort Donelson reached Fort Henry—some of them, at least —but were never sent to me. What has become of the operator, then, at Fort Henry? I don't know. At present a soldier detailed from the rank is filling the station."

43. *Ibid.,* pp. 57, 62.

44. Sherman to Cols. Hildebrand and Stuart, *ibid.,* p. 61; Johnston to Davis, p. 361; *ibid., 10,* 28. Johnston said, "My force is now united, holding Burnsville, Iuka, and Tuscumbia, with one division here." He added that he had ordered Van Dorn, then at Jacksonport, intending to attack the enemy at New Madrid, to move to Memphis.

45. *O.R.,* Atlas, I, Plate LXXVIII–3, 6.

46. *O.R., 109,* 230.

47. Fuller, *The Generalship of Grant,* pp. 103–104; Liddell Hart, *Sherman,* p. 125.

48. Conger, *op. cit.,* p. 265. Sidney Johnston's son wrote in *B. and L.,* I, 252, that Grant "did not fortify his camps, it is true; but he was not there for defense, but for attack." He added some discerning comments.

49. *O.R., 3,* 511.

50. Halleck, *Elements of Military Art and Science,* p. 344.

51. Freeman, *George Washington,* IV, 141–142. Freeman states that Washington would probably have approved of Adams's statement, and he quotes (*ibid.,* p. 445, n. 26) from a letter by Washington to Gen. Schuyler: "I begin to consider lines as a kind of trap, and not to answer the valuable purposes expected of them, unless they are passes that cannot be avoided by the enemy."

One can recall what Grant wrote from Jefferson City: "Drill and discipline are more necessary for the men than fortifications" (*supra*, p. 43).

52. Wilson, *Grant's Letters to a Friend*, pp. 6–9; Washburne Papers, XXIII, 4658–4659; W. M. Polk, *Leonidas Polk*, II, 78.

53. Wilson, *loc. cit.* Grant wrote to his father on Nov. 27, 1861 (Cramer, *Letters of Grant*, pp. 68–71): "If it is necessary that slavery should fall that the Republic may continue its existence, let slavery go. But that portion of the press that advocates the beginning of such a war now, are as great enemies to their country as if they were open and avowed secessionists." Cramer points to the similarity between this statement and one in Lincoln's well known letter to Greeley of Aug. 3 (22), 1862 (Greeley, *The American Conflict*, II, 250).

54. *O.R., 10*, 28; *11*, 65.

55. *Ibid.*, pp. 63–64, 70, 67, 74. Buell wrote from Nashville on Mar. 23 in the letter (*ibid.*, p. 58) that the scouts brought to Grant that the Columbia bridge probably would not be finished for three or four days and that he deemed it unsafe to give detailed information. Grant informed Halleck, "Rebel cavalry are scattered through from here to Nashville gathering supplies" (*ibid.*, p. 67).

56. *Ibid.*, pp. 67, 70. The fact of the nominations could be learned from the newspapers. On the 20th Grant addressed Smith as major general, avoided the issue by addressing McClernand as general, but addressed Wallace as brigadier general (*ibid.*, p. 52). Buell signed himself to Halleck in one dispatch on the 24th as a brigadier general, in another the same day as a major general; the next day he was again a brigadier, as also in an order on the 26th; but on the 27th and continuously thereafter he was a major general.

57. *Ibid.*, p. 80.

58. *Ibid.*, p. 63.

59. *Ibid.*, pp. 73, 73–74. Halleck's dispatch of Feb. 17 to Grant (*supra*, p. 261) was evidently one of those not received.

60. *Ibid.*, pp. 80, 84.

61. *Ibid.*, pp. 83, 82.

62. *Ibid.*, pp. 70–71, 75; Force, *op. cit.*, p. 105.

63. *O.R., 11*, 361, 370–371; W. P. Johnston, *Life of Gen. A. S. Johnston*, p. 549; Roman, *op. cit.*, I, 266; *O.R., 10*, 382–384 (for Confederate organization) and 100–105 (for Federal organization). Some of the Union regiments included had not yet arrived. With the general officers at his disposal Grant cannot be criticized for not initiating a corps organization; his ranking generals were McClernand and Lew Wallace, who Conger states (*op. cit.*, p. 233) "were far from being ripe" for corps command.

64. *O.R., 8*, 633–634; *11*, 76, 79, 81, 81–82. In a dispatch to Buell on the 29th (*ibid.*, p. 77) Halleck said: "There is no danger of the enemy's moving from the direction of Decatur to Stevenson. I wish he would." It can be assumed that he meant a major move, not a raid. Stanton's care in not interfering with commanders is shown by a statement in a dispatch of Mar. 23 to Buell (*ibid.*, p. 59), after Frémont's assignment to command the new Mountain Department: "General Frémont asks to have General Garfield directed to report to him. I refused to give the direction, because it may delay or frustrate

judicious movements in progress under your direction." Then Stanton asked to be informed about Garfield's force and the operations he was intended to conduct.

65. Gosnell, *Guns on the Western Waters*, p. 21.

66. *O.R.*, *11*, 69, 76, 68–69, 77.

67. *Ibid.*, pp. 78, 83–84.

68. For the procedure by which the Navy got possession of the rams see Gosnell, *op. cit.*, p. 24, and West, *Gideon Welles*, p. 205. West does not give Stanton credit for the construction of the ram fleet but says he supported the Ellets in their desire to be a part of the Army; he states that the fleet was built by the Ellet family "personally."

69. George H. Pettis, "The Confederate Invasion of New Mexico and Arizona," and Latham Anderson, "Canby's Services in the New Mexico Campaign," and A. W. Evans, "Canby at Valverde," *B. and L.*, I, 103–111, 697–699, 699–700. Anderson and Evans take issue with Pettis's assertion that Canby's personally taking over command was responsible for the Union defeat.

70. Carter's report, *O.R.*, *10*, 19–20. In his report to Richmond (*ibid.*, pp. 20–21) Gen. Kirby Smith spoke of the unreliability of his own Tennessee regiments and recommended that they be sent elsewhere and be replaced by other troops.

71. Mar. 21, 1862.

72. *Harper's Weekly*, VI, 194 (Mar. 29, 1862); *N.Y. Tribune*, Mar. 13, 1862.

73. *N.Y. Tribune*, Mar. 20; *N.Y. Times*, Mar. 12, 13, 15.

74. *N.Y. Times*, Mar. 20, 21, 22; Nevins, *The Emergence of Lincoln*, II, 217; *N.Y. Times*, Mar. 22. The *Times* credited "a Philadelphia contemporary" for first reporting the capture of Yancey.

75. Dispatch of Mar. 29 in *N.Y. Tribune* of Apr. 7, 1862.

76. Phisterer, *Statistical Record*, p. 62.

77. By combining fourteen different returns, Livermore arrived at a Confederate strength of 401,395 for April, 1862, the figure ignoring four commands for which returns could not be found (*Numbers and Losses*, pp. 43–44). He states that on Mar. 1, 1862, the Confederate Adjutant General reported 340,250 men plus 20 to 25 unreported regiments.

NOTES TO CHAPTER XIV

1. *O.R.*, *11*, 87. Sherman wrote at the same time to Col. David Stuart, commanding his 2nd Brigade, camped near the mouth of Lick Creek: "I wish you to send Colonel Smith's regiment to-night, under cover of darkness, along up Lick Creek to the vicinity of Greer's; to keep well under cover, and to take prisoners all they encounter, especially all who would give notice of them being there. Let them be careful to take a good guide, and not return by the road they go." The instructions to the cavalry were explained.

2. *Ibid.*, *10*, 83–84.

3. *Ibid.*, *11*, 88–89.

4. *Ibid.*, *10*, 84–85. Grant stated that some men were still in gray uniforms and were reluctant to draw new ones on account of their poor quality.

5. Report by Taylor, *ibid.*, p. 86; by Sherman, *ibid.*, *11*, 90.

6. Webster to Grant, Apr. 3, *ibid.*, *10*, 85–87; Grant to Halleck's adjutant, *ibid.*, pp. 84–85; Grant to Nelson, *ibid.*, *11*, 89.

7. *B. and L.*, I, 581 n.

8. *O.R.*, *11*, 387. As given in *B. and L.*, I, 581–582 n. the positions of Hardee and Bragg are reversed; in the *O.R.* version "On Pittsburg" begins the following sentence.

9. *O.R.*, *109*, 232; *11*, 90–91, 87–88. Sherman lost the 5th Ohio Cavalry but received two battalions of the 4th Illinois; changes were to "be immediately made."

10. *Ibid.*, p. 91.

11. *Ibid.*

12. Grant's message of the 4th to Halleck's adjutant is not in the records but is mentioned in that of the 5th to Halleck (*ibid.*, *10*, 89). Conger believed it was doubtful if the missing message contained any additional information (*The Rise of Grant*, p. 227). Full reports of the skirmish were given by Sherman and Col. Ralph B. Buckland (*O.R.*, *10*, 89–92).

13. Grant, *Memoirs*, I, 334–335.

14. *O.R.*, *11*, 92.

15. Report of Col. Jacob Thompson, *ibid.*, *10*, 400–403; Sherman to Grant, *ibid.*, *11*, 93–94, 93. There is no way to tell which note Sherman wrote first. In the second one described he said, "We are in the act of exchanging cavalry, according to your order."

16. *Ibid.*, *10*, 330.

17. *Ibid.*, *11*, 91–92. Ammen wrote in his diary under date of Mar. 31, "General Nelson directs me to conduct the march so as to reach Savannah, Tenn., Monday, April 7, as we are not wanted there before that time" (*ibid.*, *10*, 330). It is not evident on what Nelson could have based his statement. Buell's postwar article "Shiloh Reviewed," *B. and L.*, I, 487–536, states (p. 491): "On the 4th General Nelson received notification from General Grant that he need not hasten his march, as he could not be put across the river before the following Tuesday; but the rate of march was not changed." This is so completely contradicted by the previously quoted message that Grant sent Nelson on the 3rd that it cannot be accepted merely on Buell's word.

Ammen's diary shows the average rate of march for the last seven days was 11 miles a day—not excessive, but not bad because of the nature of the roads. On the 29th Buell informed Halleck that he would waste no time and was taking only enough forage and provisions to last him until he reached the river (*O.R.*, *11*, 77).

18. *Ibid.*, pp. 59, 58.

19. *Ibid.*, pp. 94–95. Though Halleck told Grant on Mar. 20 that Buell was marching "on Waynesboro" Grant had certainly been expecting him to come to Savannah.

20. Halleck to Buell, Mar. 29, *ibid.*, p. 77; Buell to Halleck, Mar. 24, *ibid.*, pp. 64–65; Halleck to Stanton, *ibid.*, p. 93. Halleck told Buell to concentrate

all his available forces at Savannah or Pittsburg. Buell said the Confederates had much rolling stock, could concentrate rapidly, and were expecting a battle at Corinth.

21. *N.Y. Tribune*, Apr. 7, 1862; a dispatch of Mar. 29.

22. Conger, *op. cit.*, p. 277; *O.R., 11*, 93. Conger does not refer to the sentence "General Buell will be here himself to-day" in one of Grant's telegrams (*ibid.*, p. 84) to Halleck on the 5th, which needs explaining if we are to believe that Grant thought Buell would not arrive until the 6th, and not believe merely that Grant intended to defer seeing him, knowing that a thirty-mile ride past a column of troops would cause him to arrive late on the 5th. The dispatch in question also contained the sentence, "One division of Buell's army arrived yesterday"—an erroneous statement, due perhaps to Grant's thinking Nelson had camped not far away. Nelson arrived at noon, and another telegram by Grant said he had "just arrived," so there can be little doubt that the first message described was sent during the morning. When did Buell's dispatch arrive? The terminating word "to-day" in Grant's acknowledgment suggests some hour after noon; and he wrote just after receiving Buell's message. Thus Grant's statement to Halleck about Buell's expected arrival on the 5th may have been based on previous information rather than on the message from Buell. Another reason for thinking Grant did not expect Buell to arrive until Sunday lies in action he took Sunday morning, which will be noted later.

23. *Ibid., 10*, 89. The first telegram described in note 22 said, "Some skirmishing took place with [between] our outguards and the enemy's yesterday and the day before." The second gave the casualties on both sides, which supports the view that it was the later message. The enemy strength in and about Corinth was put at 80,000 men, and it was added that "deserters place their force West at 200,000." Grant said there were small garrisons at Bethel, Jackson, and Humboldt, and added, "The numbers at these places seem to constantly change"—a remark that shows the need of an intelligence officer.

24. Buell, *op. cit.*, p. 492.

25. *Ibid.*, p. 519.

26. Thomas Jordan, "Notes of a Confederate Staff-Officer at Shiloh," *B. and L.*, I, 594–603.

27. *O.R., 10*, 392–395. The organization of Johnston's army down to regiments and batteries is given *ibid.*, pp. 382–384.

28. *Ibid.*, pp. 396–397.

29. *Ibid.*, pp. 385, 463–464, 386, 400, 464.

30. *B. and L.*, I, 583, 555 (statements by Johnston's son based on monograph prepared for him by Bragg); *O.R., 10*, 464.

31. Rich, *The Battle of Shiloh*, pp. 38–45; *O.R., 109*, 228. Rich makes a good case for believing that Peabody acted upon his own initiative rather than upon explicit directions from Prentiss.

32. Rich, *op. cit.*, p. 53; *O.R., 10*, 401.

33. Hardcastle's report, *O.R., 10*, 603; Rich, *op. cit.*, p. 54; Moore's report, *O.R., 10*, 282.

34. *Ibid.*, p. 184.

35. *Ibid., 11,* 95. The message was written by Rawlins and authenticated as by Grant's order.

36. *Ibid., 109,* 232. The words about meeting Buell give no clue as to the hour when Grant thought he might see him. But one notices that he said "to-day" and not "this morning," which would harmonize with the belief that Buell was still a few hours away from Savannah.

On p. 107 of Seitz's *Braxton Bragg* it is said that Grant left no word for Buell when he was "summoned" to Pittsburg on the morning of the 6th. The discussion of incidents previous to the battle is rather full, but Grant's prompt dispatches to Nelson and Buell were apparently missed. (The criticism on p. 33 of Davidson's *The Tennessee* also takes no account of them.) Seitz gives (p. 105) a brief account of a warning that Lew Wallace sent Grant on the evening of the 4th, revealed by him for the first time in his *Autobiography,* I, 454 ff. The message certainly did not reach Grant, and the incident was passed over in this work because of doubt about it. Wallace placed the event on Thursday the 4th, when the 4th was Friday. He blamed himself for the way in which he had handled the information brought him by two scouts about the Confederates being on the march from Corinth. Seitz is critical but says the message for Grant was delivered to the postmaster at Pittsburg to forward to Savannah, though Wallace states it was to be held for his return. Rich describes the incident and says that it would have been better for Wallace's reputation if the revelation had never been made (*op. cit.,* p. 46).

37. *Ibid., 11,* 95.

38. *Ibid.,* 10, 185, 170, 174, 175; Wallace, *op. cit.,* p. 461. Grant could well have described 8:15 as "about 8," while Wallace could have called 8:45 "about 9." Rawlins put the time as "not far from 7 or 7:30 o'clock a.m." (*O.R., 10,* 185).

39. Conger, *op. cit.,* p. 241; *O.R., 10,* 178.

40. Force, *From Fort Henry to Corinth,* p. 131.

41. *O.R., 10,* 286–287, 278, 288.

42. *Ibid.,* pp. 185, 175; Wallace, *op. cit.,* p. 464; statement in a letter of 1868 by Wallace's former adjutant, Gen. Frederick Knefler, *B. and L,* I, 607, *O.R., 10,* 175. In his *Autobiography* Wallace attempted a verbatim reconstruction of the order, which he had not done when he opened the case officially in 1863. Knefler said the order was to join the right of the army. Two other former officers of Wallace's staff wrote in 1868 (*B. and L.,* I, 607) that it was to join "Sherman's right." Wallace submitted the letters to Grant, who replied on Mar. 10, 1868 (*ibid.,* p. 609). Grant noted that his initial order had been oral, but added that he had always understood a memorandum, which he had never seen, had been made by Baxter and left with Wallace. After commending some of Wallace's service later in the war, he concluded, "I think it due to you that you should publish what your own staff and other subordinate officers have to say in exoneration of your course."

In the indorsement that Grant wrote on Apr. 25, 1862, upon Wallace's report of the battle, he said, "Certainly not later than 11 a.m. the order reached General Wallace to march by a flank movement to Pittsburg Landing." Grant of course thought of the 3rd Division as facing west toward Purdy and a march toward Pittsburg Landing would accordingly be a flank movement.

43. *O.R., 11,* 95–96.

44. Polk's report, *ibid., 10,* 408.

45. Report of Col. Thomas Morton, *ibid.,* p. 161.

46. Sherman to Prof. Henry Coppée, dated "In the Field, near Kenesaw, Ga., June 13, 1864," *O.R., 109,* 559–561. Coppée, a native of Georgia, was a West Point graduate of the class of 1845, was brevetted in Mexico, and resigned from the Army in 1855 to become a distinguished educator. He also was the author of books on Grant and Thomas. Sherman's long letter about the battle of Shiloh protested against current accounts, one of them Coppée's, which he said Grant would probably not think sufficiently important to correct. By way of general introduction, Sherman wrote: "Like General Taylor is said in his late days to have doubted whether he was at the battle of Buena Vista at all on account of the many things having transpired there, according to the historians, which he did not see, so I begin to doubt whether I was in the battle of Pittsburg Landing of modern description."

47. Sherman's report, *O.R., 10,* 248; Force, *op. cit.,* p. 248.

48. Cleburne's report, *O.R., 10,* 581; Hardee's report, *ibid.,* p. 568.

49. Force, *loc. cit.;* Polk's report, *O.R., 10,* 407; Johnson's report, *ibid.,* p. 445; Rich, *op. cit.,* p. 60.

50. Sherman's report, *O.R., 10,* 249–250; Force, *op. cit.,* p. 131.

51. Col. Reid's report, *O.R., 10,* 288.

52. Shaver's report, *ibid.,* p. 573; Force, *op. cit.,* p. 141; Maj. James T. Martin's report, *O.R., 10,* 577–578. Both the colonel and the lieutenant colonel of the Arkansas regiment (the 7th) were killed.

53. Force, *op. cit.,* p. 142.

54. Prentiss's report, *O.R., 10,* 277–280.

55. Grant, *Memoirs,* I, 340; McPherson to Rawlins, Mar. 26, 1863, *O.R., 10,* 181; Rawlins to Grant, Apr. 1, 1863, *ibid.,* pp. 185–186.

56. *Ibid., 109,* 232–233, from the original as received by Buell. The message as taken from Grant's letter book is *ibid., 11,* 95. The two or three differences are trivial.

57. Horn, *The Army of Tennessee,* p. 131. Alexander's extremely critical work on Grant is given in Horn's bibliography. Though Horn seemingly cites it only once, with reference to Halleck and not Grant, the book may have contributed to his judgment about both. On the other hand, Horn's bibliography does not list the recent works on Grant by Col. Conger and Gen. Fuller—two of the most outstanding works on the Civil War of recent years.

58. *O.R., 10,* 396, 112.

59. Buell, *op. cit.,* pp. 492–493; Nelson's report, *O.R., 10,* 323; Ammen's report, *ibid.,* pp. 331–332; Wood's report, *ibid.,* p. 377. Orders such as Wood describes, written at Buell's direction but signed by an aide, and addressed to Gen. George Thomas, whose division was following Wood's are *ibid., 11,* 96. The "intimation" of which Wood spoke must have been communicated verbally.

Buell's official report does not give the hour he reached Pittsburg. A correspondent with his army—though not a reliable one—put the time as between five and six (Rich, *op. cit.*, p. 84); but this would seem to be definitely too late.

In view of the order Grant gave Nelson it is hard to see why it was thought boats might be sent for his division. Ammen referred to a guide being procured but said nothing about difficulty in finding one; Nelson was silent on the subject. It has been said by some that Grant should have sent boats for Nelson; but no one has pointed out how many boats he knew were empty at Pittsburg with steam up at the time he wrote the order for Nelson. In having Nelson march and boats go for Wood (Crittenden), Grant probably thought he was planning the most prompt movement possible.

60. *O.R.,* 10, 614, 621, 624; Roman, *Military Operations of General Beauregard,* I, 293, 294; Beauregard, "The Campaign of Shiloh," *B. and L.,* I, 288; Horn, *op. cit.,* p. 134.

61. *O.R., 10,* 181; Force, *op. cit.,* p. 146; Grant, *Memoirs,* I, 340; *O.R., 10,* 250. Of a position Stuart had taken up, Roman writes that "here, without artillery, he maintained a creditable resistance against greatly superior numbers" (*op. cit.,* p. 292).

62. Force, *op. cit.,* p. 146.

63. *Ibid.,* p. 145.

64. *O.R., 10,* 86, 84–85, 274.

65. Force, *op. cit.,* p. 155; Rich, *op. cit.,* p. 78.

66. Hurlbut's report, *O.R., 10,* 204; Stuart's report, *ibid.,* p. 259; Force, *op. cit.,* p. 156. Sherman wrote to Coppée: "I remember the fact the better from General Grant's anecdote of his Donelson battle, which he told me then for the first time, that at a certain period of the battle he saw that either side was ready to give way if the other showed a bold front, and he determined to do that very thing, to advance on the enemy, when as he prognosticated the enemy surrendered. At 4 p.m. of April 6 he thought the appearances the same, and he judged, with Lew Wallace's fresh division and such of our startled troops as had recovered their equilibrium, we would be justified in dropping the defensive and assuming the offensive in the morning, and I repeat I received such orders before I knew General Buell's troops were at the river."

67. *O.R. Navies,* Ser. I, XXII, 762–765. That ground commanders helped the Navy officers is shown by Stuart's statement (*O.R., 10,* 259) that the major of the 71st Ohio led about 150 men to the bank of the river, "where he hailed the gunboats, informing them of the approach of the enemy."

Grant's reply to Gwin's officer was the only practical one under the circumstances. World War II led to the development of units in the Marine Corps that can be attached to divisions for directing naval gunfire support. See Lieut. Col. R. D. Heinl, USMC, "What the Army Should Know about Naval Gunfire," *Combat Forces Journal,* II, 34–38 (Oct., 1951).

For the return of the gunboat *Cairo* to Cairo, see *O.R., 8,* 122.

68. *O.R., 10,* 208, 205; Foote to Welles, Apr. 11, 1862, *O.R. Navies,* Ser. I, XXII, 762; Welles to Foote, Apr. 10, *ibid.,* p. 765.

69. *O.R., 10,* 551, 555.

70. The charge was formerly rather common and was supported by Jeffer-

son Davis (Roman, *op. cit.*, pp. 341–351 *passim*). Basso says on p. 183 of his recent biography that Beauregard failed in one of the great crises of the war, and makes the extravagant claim that if he had continued his attack Grant would have been driven into the river, annihilated, or forced to surrender. On the other hand Horn pictures the situation by writing, "Surely the Confederate army at this hour was at a minimum of competence" (*op. cit.*, p. 137).

Conger, although Grant is his hero, writes as a professional American soldier proud of fine Southern generalship as well as Northern; and his appreciation of the leadership of the attackers at Shiloh bears great weight precisely because he can comprehendingly and sympathetically put himself in their places and feel their difficulties. He states that no other possibility was open to Beauregard than "to break off combat and assemble his troops for the night" (*op. cit.*, p. 259).

71. Ammen's diary, *O.R.*, *10*, 332; *O.R. Navies*, Ser. I, XXII, 344–345; Grant, *Memoirs*, I, 345. Buell's report (*O.R.*, *10*, 292) put the number of fugitives when he arrived at 5,000 and said they increased toward evening. Nelson stated they amounted to 10,000, and added the strong statement, "They were insensible to shame or sarcasm—for I tried both on them—and, indignant at such poltroonery, I asked permission to open fire on the knaves" (*ibid.*, p. 324). Ammen—a former professor of mathematics at Indiana University but nonetheless a vivid diarist—put the figure at 15,000 (*ibid.*, p. 328).

72. Reports of Col. Grose, Lieut. Col. Anderson, Lieut. Col. Jones, *O.R.*, *10*, 337, 339; Buell's report, *ibid.*, p. 292; Buell, *B. and L.* I, 506; Grose, *The Story of the 36th Indiana*, pp. 104–105.

Ammen stated clearly enough (*O.R.*, *10*, 328) that only the 36th Indiana was engaged; it had two killed, one wounded. Nelson said (*ibid.*, p. 323) that the left of the Federal "artillery was completely turned by the enemy" when the 36th Indiana, supported by the 6th Ohio "drove back the enemy and restored the line of battle." Stone's battery, which the 36th Indiana supported, was by no means on the left of Webster's mass of guns. Buell's report made an unnecessary insinuation when he spoke of the fire of a battery which "happened" to be on the ground. His *B. and L.* article admitted (p. 507) that there was a space of only 400 yards from the river to Hurlbut's left, and also that only a few of Chalmer's skirmishers got within 100 yards of Stone's battery; but called the situation "critical." It is certainly appropriate to recall that when Buell reached Nashville he thought the situation so critical that he ordered up Smith and revealed his anxiety in a letter to McClellan, although there was no good reason for alarm, as Grant indicated in the note he wrote Buell the day he was in Nashville.

Buell also described the fire of the gunboats as "harmless," apparently regarding as worthless the contrary testimony of Hurlbut (*O.R.*, *10*, 205) as to his own observation "and the statement of prisoners."

73. Statements by Rowley, McPherson, and Rawlins, *O.R.*, *10*, 178–188; Wallace, *Autobiography*, p. 468; *B. and L.*, I, 607–609.

Wallace's statement in his *Autobiography* (p. 457) that he was well acquainted with the river road to Pittsburg Landing and knew the bridge over

Snake Creek had been rebuilt might have caused Grant to modify the position he took in the note in his *Memoirs* (I, 350–351) when, after finishing his chapter on Shiloh, he was furnished with a message (*B. and L.*, I, 609) Lew Wallace wrote to W. H. L. Wallace on Apr. 5, 1862. The note has been regarded by some as a tardy exoneration by Grant of Lew Wallace.

74. Col. Hovey's report, *O.R.*, *10*, 191. The 14th Missouri had been organized as "Birge's Western Sharpshooters."

75. Hurlbut's report, *ibid.*, p. 205; Jones's report, *ibid.*, p. 339; Buell, *B. and L.*, I, 519; Sherman's report, *O.R.*, *10*, 251. Sherman gave Buell a map which was to become the basis of some of the latter's criticisms. Buell's own revised map (*B. and L.*, I, 502–503) gives positions for McClernand and Sherman on the night of Apr. 6 different from those shown on the Thom, or "official," map (*ibid.*, p. 508, and *O.R.*, Atlas, I, Plate XII–4), which in turn do not agree with those of the Battlefield Commission Map of Maj. Reed. On the other hand the revised map in Grant's *Memoirs*, I, 341, shows Sherman practically in the position given by Reed.

76. *O.R. Navies*, Ser. I, XXII, 786, 763.

77. Grant, *Memoirs*, I, 349.

78. *B. and L.*, *I*, 593, 602; *O.R.*, *10*, 384. A communication that Jefferson Davis sent to the Confederate Congress on Apr. 8 is given *ibid.*, *110*, 298–299.

79. Pond's report, *O.R.*, *10*, 518.

80. *O.R. Navies*, Ser. I, XXII, 763.

81. Buell's article in *B. and L.*, I, states (p. 535) that friends advised him "to write an *impersonal* account of the battle," but that this was impossible although it would have been in harmony with his disposition. He certainly studied the battle carefully; but so did Manning Force, who was not swayed by strong personal interests. Force was to see more and harder fighting than Buell, was seriously wounded, and ultimately became a brevet major general. His rich experience combined with his natural qualities to make him a competent military analyst.

82. Sherman's, Wallace's, and Pond's reports, *O.R.*, *10*, 251, 170, 518; McClernand's, Crittenden's, and McCook's reports; *ibid.*, pp. 119, 256, 305–306; reports of Col. Wood (14th Wisconsin), *ibid.*, pp. 371, 372–373.

83. Ammen's, Nelson's, and Buell's reports, *O.R.*, *10*, 327, 324, 293; Force, *op. cit.*, pp. 164–166.

84. *O.R.*, *10*, 251.

85. *Ibid.*, p. 205.

86. *Ibid.*, p. 318, 252.

87. McClernand's, Veatch's, and Tuttle's reports, *ibid.*, pp. 120, 221, 149; Force, *loc. cit.*; casualty report, *O.R.*, *10*, 105–107; Ammen's diary, *ibid.*, p. 336.

88. Thompson's report, *ibid.*, p. 402.

89. *Ibid.*, pp. 388, 579, 441, 584, 519, 402. It is not clear why Hardee was shifted from the left and given the right, where the terrain was new to him, or why Bragg took his place; the change may have given each general more of his own troops.

90. *O.R. Navies*, Ser. I, XXII, 786, 764; *O.R.*, *10*, 377, 380.

91. Force, *op. cit.*, p. 175; Buell, *B. and L.*, I, 551; Rousseau's and Veatch's reports, *O.R.*, *10*, 309, 221. Buell said that what took place did not fulfill "the definition of a charge," and added that Grant did not come under the enemy fire. Rousseau saw the 1st Ohio moving forward and went to stop it, but learned the movement was on Grant's direction and thereupon confirmed it. He stated that Grant and his staff were in rear of the line. Buell argued that no colonel of a regiment would have overlooked commenting on a charge "led by the commander of the army"; but he failed to note that there are no reports from either the 1st Ohio or the 5th Kentucky of Rousseau's brigade. Badeau went into some detail about the charge, presumably obtaining his information from members of Grant's staff; but he did not identify the second regiment, which he asserted had begun to break (*Military History of U.S. Grant*, I, 89–90).

92. Fuller, *Generalship of Grant*, p. 111. Fuller agrees with John Codman Ropes in thinking that Grant should be criticized for not arranging for a pursuit; but he may not have looked at everything that bears on the question. Conger on the other hand writes that, in view of the situation and the knowledge Grant actually had of the enemy, there was nothing to justify his pushing troops beyond the line they had gained (*op. cit.*, p. 261).

Fuller disagrees sharply with Ropes's criticisms of Grant on Apr. 6 and expresses the opinion (*op. cit.*, p. 110) that they are "gross calumny," adding that Ropes would probably not have committed the calumny if he had ever himself experienced the chaos of war. He analyzes Grant's actions and pronounces his generalship on Sunday "quite wonderful." Woodward in *Meet General Grant* not only accepts Ropes's pronouncement but declares (pp. 251–252) that Ropes knew more about war than most generals. His own qualifications for making such a statement are not discernible.

It is possible that Ropes based his ideas partly on Buell's "Shiloh Reviewed" and also on Gen. W. F. Smith's article "Shiloh" in the *Magazine of American History*, XV (1886), 292–304, 470–482. Smith made much of the fact that Buell's flanks were not turned as were those of some of Grant's divisions on the 6th. It has been noted in the text that units of Grant's army helped Buell in this particular; and it is farfetched to compare local counterattacks that Beauregard's tired men made on Monday with the systematic Confederate offensive of Sunday. Smith was critical of Grant's taking the two regiments into a charge, saying that, if a charge had been called for, Rousseau would have ordered it! (It was Rousseau's first battle since he had fought as a captain in the 2nd Indiana at Buena Vista.) Smith's views may have been influenced by the fact that Grant removed him from corps command in 1864.

93. *O.R.*, *10*, 377–378.

94. *Ibid.*, *109*, 233–234 (as received by Buell); *11*, 96–97 (as taken from Grant's letter book). The differences are trivial.

95. "A Soldier's Letter from Shiloh," *Harper's Weekly*, LVII, 9–10 (Apr. 5, 1913). This previously unpublished letter by Capt. Robert Peabody Barry, who was in the 16th U.S. Infantry of McCook's division, gives a graphic description of the last days of the march to Savannah, the bad roads and difficult country, the crowded condition in Savannah, etc.

96. *O.R., 109,* 338; *11,* 400; *10,* 381, 297.

97. There is no message in the records from Halleck to Grant dated Apr. 6, and the previously quoted dispatch of the 5th said nothing about Halleck's departure from St. Louis (though the one he sent to Buell did). Grant must have picked up some news from officers on arriving boats.

98. Bragg to Beauregard, *ibid., 11,* 398–399; Sherman to Grant, *ibid., 10,* 639–641; Wood's report, *ibid.,* p. 378. Bragg complained that his artillery was "being left all along the road by its officers." On the other hand Sherman said, "The enemy has succeeded in carrying off the guns, but has crippled his batteries by abandoning the hind limber-boxes of at least twenty guns." Wood said that it was "determined satisfactorily" that the main body of the enemy "repassed Lick Creek, distant several miles from the battlefield, on Monday night." Sherman's high quality as a subordinate is shown by the fact that he made the reconnaissance the subject of a long letter to Grant on the 8th and did not wait, like Wood, to make it a part of his battle report.

99. Hardee's and Prentiss's reports, *ibid.,* pp. 568, 277–278.

100. The dispatch appeared on Apr. 10 not only in the *Herald* but also in the *N.Y. Times,* the *Cincinnati Daily Commercial,* the *Cincinnati Daily Gazette,* and doubtless other papers. Under the dateline, "Pittsburg, Apr. 9, 3:20 A.M.," it stated that the correspondent had arrived on the field at nine o'clock on Sunday. Speaking of Maj. Powell in the highest terms, it said that he was especially detailed by Halleck to accompany the 25th Missouri. Peabody also was specially cited. The Confederates were credited with "remarkably good generalship." Wallace was said to have taken the wrong road from Crumps Landing. Of Webster's battery the reporter wrote, "Such a roar of artillery was never heard on this continent." The *Lexington* and the *Tyler* were credited with an important part; but no credit was given to Buell for Sunday's battle, though his late arrival was noted. Johnston's death was reported, and it was stated that the enemy resistance on Monday was "terrific." The correspondent was lyrical in describing the charge on Monday of *five* regiments that Grant himself led "as he brandished his sword and waved them on to the crowning victory, while cannon balls were falling like hail around him." One can discount this considerably and still have a charge.

The *Times* printed the dispatch in a late extra of the 9th, on which day news of the battle became known, causing according to the *Herald* "intense excitement, enthusiasm and jubilation." On the 10th a Cairo dispatch in the *Herald* stated that Grant had been slightly wounded in the ankle.

101. Reid's story was reprinted in Moore's *Rebellion Record* (IV, 385–400) and thus got wide circulation and permanency. Extracts are given by Conger, *op. cit.,* pp. 257–258, 262–263. For facts about the writing of the dispatch see Cortissoz, *The Life of Whitelaw Reid,* I, 85–86. Its statements that Grant had thought there was great possibility of an attack on Pittsburg, and that he stopped at Crumps Landing on the evening of the 5th and warned of an attack at that place, cannot be accepted.

102. Letter of Maj. D. W. Reed to Maj. P. W. Rich, Feb. 13, 1909, *Iowa Journal of History and Politics,* XVIII (Apr., 1920), 305–308; Brewer's report,

O.R., 10, 461; Wallace, *Autobiography,* I, 467–468. Reed was historian at Shiloh and his letter is an important document.

103. Horn, *op. cit.,* pp. 140–141; *O.R., 11,* 405. Roman states (*op. cit.,* I, 319) that during the battle of the 7th Beauregard dispatched couriers to Corinth "to hurry forward General Van Dorn's army of about twenty thousand men, daily expected there from Van Buren, Arkansas." This is fantastic, so far as service at Shiloh was concerned; yet other statements by Roman indicate that is what he meant. Even if Beauregard had been able to hold a position near Shiloh Church he could not have remained, because he was out of food and his men were already hungry.

104. *O.R., 10,* 108, 111–112, 297, 108–111. Grant's indorsement on Wallace's report about sending some of his staff officers to hurry Wallace was not at all harsh. The newspaper statements that Wallace had taken the wrong road were sufficient to raise a question about his action, and in the summer he was relieved of active duty. On Mar. 13, 1862, he defended himself in a letter to Halleck, then General in Chief (*ibid.,* pp. 174–176). He made no reference to anything Grant had said or been quoted as saying, and spoke solely of a prejudice against himself that existed in Halleck's headquarters because of his absence from the first day's battle at Shiloh, which he understood Halleck himself entertained. The letter was referred to Grant, who obtained the statements from Rowley, McPherson, and Rawlins that have already been cited.

Wallace's report was not the only one about which Grant commented. The favorable remark about Hurlbut's has been quoted. At the head of McClernand's he wrote that it was in error in saying that Prentiss was surprised and captured in the morning; he also stated that the report had too much to say about divisions other than the 1st.

On Apr. 14, ten days before he submitted his report to Grant, McClernand wrote a letter to Lincoln (*ibid.,* pp. 113–114), perhaps in reply to a personal letter (one sentence seems to suggest it), and to thank him for his promotion. His brief description of the battle included the statement, "My division, as usual, has borne or shared in bearing the brunt," and a seemingly sly criticism of the army commander: "It was a great mistake that we did not pursue him [the enemy] Monday night and Tuesday." All divisions bore the brunt on Sunday, and while the 1st had more killed than the 2nd or 6th (the latter having only seven regiments compared with McClernand's twelve), it had fewer than the 4th or 5th. In his report McClernand actually spoke of the enemy being "further pursued" beyond where the battle stopped, and he said the Federal strength was "probably less than one-half of the enemy's" on Sunday, which would have meant it was still inferior after the advent of Buell. There is not the slightest reason to believe that McClernand believed on Monday night that more could have been accomplished, or even on Tuesday morning.

105. Livermore, *Numbers and Losses,* pp. 79–80; *O.R., 10,* 105–108, 398, 396.

The earlier Confederate return that gives an "effective total before the battle" of 40,335 was signed and forwarded by Beauregard on Apr. 21, 1862. The second was signed on June 30 by Bragg, who had recently taken command of the army. It gives 38,773 as the "effective total" that marched from Corinth. The editors of the *O.R.* noted the discrepancy but did not try to explain it. Livermore assumes that the four regiments, two battalions, and one battery left to guard Corinth were not included in the first return. By adding to the present for duty in the 3rd corps and the cavalry as given in the second return he obtains 44,233 as the total present for duty. Taking 93 per cent to give the effectives he gets 41,136, which he accepts as justifying using the figure 40,335. The procedure is not convincing, for the second return gives the 1st corps, 2nd corps, and reserve greater strength than does the first return, so some adjustment would seem to be needed there. Reconciliation of the difference in the two returns seems impossible.

Horn accepts 38,773 as the number of Confederate effectives without noting the first return (*op. cit.*, p. 143). He puts Grant's present for duty the first day at 39,895, a figure he evidently arrived at by subtracting 5,000 for Wallace from the total 44,895 present for duty in Grant's six divisions (*O.R., 10,* 112). While Wallace probably reached the field with about 6,000 men (he had to leave guards in his camps), the number present for duty in the 3rd division is given in the return cited as 7,564. Thus the present for duty figure in the five divisions engaged on the 6th was 37,331, which, however, omits two regiments and a battery from the 6th Division. If, following Livermore, we take 93 per cent of the Federal present for duty figure, in order to get a number comparable with the Confederate effectives, and then add 1,000 to include the omitted organizations, we get 35,718. Although the two forces were very nearly equal on Sunday, there is good reason for saying that Johnston was superior by at least 3,000 men.

NOTES TO CHAPTER XV

1. The chief sources for the capture of Island No. 10 are Pope's reports, *O.R., 8,* 78–79, 85–90, and Walke's article, "The Western Flotilla at Fort Donelson, Island Number Ten, Fort Pillow and Memphis," *B. and L.,* I, 430–459. These are used without specific citation.

2. Return of Mar. 31, *O.R., 8, 94.* On Mar. 30 Scott said in a dispatch to Stanton from Cairo, "We have information here that the rebels are finishing some heavy gunboats to ascend the river" (*ibid.,* p. 649).

3. *Ibid.,* p. 629.

4. See J. W. Bissell, "Sawing Out the Channel Above Island Number Ten," *B. and L.,* I, 460–462, and the annexed "Comment by General Schuyler," *ibid.,* p. 462. Pope gave credit to Schuyler for suggesting the canal; Bissell claimed he himself suggested it; Schuyler gave support for his own priority. Who first thought of the plan seems immaterial; it was a question of execution before the water over the submerged area went down.

The correction of the distances given by Pope is based upon the map *ibid.,* p. 461.

5. *O.R., 8,* 122–123, 120, 666; *111,* 520; *O.R. Navies,* Ser. I, XXII, 715–719 *passim.*

6. *O.R.*, *8*, 677, 681; *111*, 521.

7. Beatty, *Memoirs of a Volunteer*, pp. 95–96; *O.R.*, *11*, 71–72, 85. Mitchel had twelve regiments of infantry, one of cavalry, three batteries, and two companies of engineers.

8. Beatty, *op. cit.*, p. 98; Pittenger, *Daring and Suffering*, Chap. I. William Pittenger was a member of the second Andrews expedition, which is the only one generally referred to. His book is a well written—though long— account of the enterprise and the subsequent experiences of the raiders. He also wrote an article, "The Locomotive Chase in Georgia," *B. and L.*, II, 709– 716. Both book and article are in general used as sources without specific references.

9. Mitchel to Fry (Buell's chief of staff), Apr. 11, *O.R.*, *10*, 641; Beauregard to Cooper, Apr. 9, *ibid.*, 403, 618 (as deciphered and sent to Buell), 104 (as sent to Washington from Nashville); Lee to Beauregard with inclosures and report of investigation, *ibid.*, pp. 439–442. Except for a semicolon in place of a comma, Mitchel's reading was identical with the original.

Pittenger used the *O.R.* wherever possible for his eighth chapter, "The Bloodless Victories of Mitchel," but probably based it largely on what friends in the division told him. His account of the march to Huntsville agrees in general with that of Beatty (*op. cit.*, p. 101), who was in the rear brigade.

10. E. Kirby Smith to Richmond, Apr. 13, *O.R.*, *10*, 643; Mitchel to Buell, Apr. 11 [12?], *ibid.*, pp. 641–642; Smith to Leadbetter, *ibid.*, *11*, 416–417. Pittenger (*op. cit.*, p. 93 n.) observed that there was disagreement as to the time of Mitchel's move to Stevenson, some accounts putting it on the 11th, others on the 12th. He believed Mitchel probably started near midnight Friday, or early on Saturday morning. The date of Mitchel's dispatch to Buell is certainly incorrect, for work started "yesterday" is described as being completed "to-day." It mentions his going to Stevenson but does not tell when he returned. In a dispatch to Stanton on Apr. 17 (*O.R.*, *11*, 111) Mitchel said he moved both east and west on the 12th.

11. For the names and fates of the various men, see *B. and L.*, II, 715.

12. *N.Y. Times*, Apr. 11, 1862; *O.R.*, *10*, 98; *11*, 105, 105–106, 109. At 1:00 P.M. of the 8th Halleck informed Grant of Pope's victory and said, "I leave to join you to-morrow" (*ibid.*, p. 98); a similar dispatch was sent to Buell. At 11:00 A.M. the next day he telegraphed (*ibid.*, p. 99) that he had the night before received Grant's dispatch about the battle at Pittsburg. Hospital boats were being sent, and preparations were being made at Cincinnati to care for 10,000 sick and wounded. He was leaving with reenforcements immediately and told Grant, "Avoid another battle, if you can, till all arrive. We then shall be able to beat them without fail." Stanton telegraphed Halleck on the 9th (*ibid.*) that he had no instructions for him, adding, "Go ahead, and all success attend you." He also stated that an order of thanks had been issued.

13. *Ibid.*, *10*, 98–99.

14. *Ibid.*, *11*, 105; *8*, 661, 664; *11*, 107–108.

15. *Ibid.*, *11*, 116, 133.

16. *Ibid.*, p. 130.

17. *Ibid.*, pp. 621, 117, 138–139. Halleck issued his order with regard to Smith on the 25th before the arrival of a telegram from Stanton (*ibid.*, p. 132) requesting that proper military honors be paid.

18. *Ibid.*, pp. 104, 118–119, 111, 115, 116–117, 117. The promptness with which news was reaching the Capital is shown by the dispatch that A. Stager, who was in charge of the Washington telegraph office, sent Stanton at 11:30 A.M., Apr. 12. He quoted a message transmitted to him that morning by the telegraph superintendent at Nashville, which told of Mitchel's occupation of Huntsville, and continued: "The Savannah line got O.K. to Columbia this morning. It had been cut in several places and wire destroyed. The line is now interrupted south of Columbia. We are doing our best to keep it up, but the roads are nearly impassable south of Columbia, and the wire is cut down as fast as we put it up."

19. *Ibid.*, pp. 618–619, 118–119. Mitchel spoke of rumors that Kirby Smith was about to cross the river at Chattanooga to drive him back to Nashville, and concluded, "I shall await your orders with anxiety." His actions indicated he feared being ordered back rather than forward.

20. *Ibid.*, pp. 618–619, 124, 125.

21. *Ibid.*, pp. 115, 128, 134, 137–138.

22. *Ibid.*, p. 144. An order of the 28th (*ibid.*, pp. 138–139) spoke of the commands of Grant, Buell, and Pope as army corps. Considerable confusion in designation followed.

23. Halleck to Grant, Apr. 30, *ibid.*, *109*, 245; same, May 12, *ibid.*, *11*, 182–183. Grant's complaint may have been verbal, for there is nothing in the records from him, and Halleck's communication does not refer to any note.

24. *Ibid.*, pp. 144, 240–241, 256–257.

25. *Ibid.*, *11*, 154; *109*, 246; *10*, 665.

26. *Ibid.*, *11*, 160–161, 623–624; *109*, 247; *10*, 739. Logistics were giving difficulty, for Halleck said to Pope: "It is impossible to entirely supply Buell from Pittsburg. A double road, if necessary, must be made to Hamburg."

27. *Ibid.*, *11*, 164, 164–165.

28. *Ibid.*, *10*, 665; *11*, 166, 172, 176.

29. *Ibid.*, pp. 173–177 *passim; 109*, 248; *11*, 197–201 *passim*, 207–208, 209–210; *10*, 666–667. Lincoln stated that the line of the upper Potomac had been thinned "until yesterday it was broken at heavy loss to us, and General Banks put in great peril, out of which he is not yet extricated, and may be actually captured."

30. *Ibid.*, *10*, 776, 740.

31. Sherman, *Memoirs*, I, 254; Conger, *The Rise of U. S. Grant*, p. 264; *O.R.*, *11*, 177.

32. Sheridan, *Memoirs*, I, 136–141; *O.R.*, *109*, 252. Sheridan states that he received Governor Blair's order, which was dated May 25, on the 27th; but Halleck's order is dated May 26.

33. *O.R.*, *11*, 506, 545–546; *10*, 770; *11*, 184. On May 5 Pope reported (*ibid.*, *11*, 164) that all deserters said the enemy was badly fed and that there was much dissatisfaction.

34. *Ibid.*, *11*, 557; *10*, 791 (field return for May 28).

35. Halleck to Stanton, May 30, *ibid.*, *10*, 667.

36. *Ibid.*, *11*, 167, 168, 217, 225. On May 20 Pope reported that officers' baggage was at the Corinth railroad station, the information having come from the Negro servant of a Federal officer, who had been captured at Shiloh and had escaped (*ibid.*, p. 192).

37. *Ibid.*, pp. 228, 225, 225–226. Halleck alerted Grant as to the possibility of an attack against the left (*ibid.*, p. 228), saying, "It will be well to make preparation to send as many of the reserves as can be spared of [from] the right wing in that direction as soon as an attack is made in force. At any rate, be prepared for an order to that effect." Grant wrote in *Memoirs*, I, 379–380, that it was probably on the 28th that Brig. Gen. John A. Logan, then commanding a brigade in McClernand's old division, told him that the enemy was evacuating Corinth, basing his assertion on the statements of railroad men who claimed that by putting their ears to the rails they could distinguish loaded from empty trains and tell the direction in which they were running.

38. *O.R.*, *10*, 667–668.

39. Cortissoz, *The Life of Whitelaw Reid*, I, 89–90; *O.R.*, *10*, 771–773, for dispatches to the *Tribune* and the *Commercial*. Reid returned to Pittsburg Landing after writing his account of the Battle of Shiloh for the *Cincinnati Gazette;* and after Halleck issued his order about "unauthorized hangers-on," he was selected by the correspondents to make a protest. The letter he wrote to Halleck—which is given by Cortissoz—had the tone of an injured person and ill became anyone who had done so much to cause incorrect beliefs about the battle. In the absence of censorship laws a general had no recourse except to order a correspondent away. Though Reid may have deserved such summary treatment, Halleck was both unreasonable and unwise in applying the remedy indiscriminately. Cortissoz states that every legitimate, accredited correspondent left, save three, one of whom was too sick to go, while the other two resolved to try to skulk through the camps in fictitious positions.

40. *O.R.*, *11*, 234.

41. Grant, *Memoirs*, I, 381. Grant wrote, "I am satisfied," not "I was satisfied." Horn states that if Halleck had shown the confidence and alacrity justified by his greater force he might have surrounded and captured Beauregard's army. (*The Army of Tennessee*, p. 148.) This ignores the nature of the terrain and the facilities Beauregard had, and also the fact that Halleck did not believe himself superior in strength to Beauregard after early May.

42. *O.R.*, *11*, 230–231; *10*, 668, 862–865 (reports of Elliott, Hatch, and Sheridan); *11*, 237. Horn states (*op. cit.*, p. 152) that when Beauregard's destination was finally discovered, a brigade of Pope's cavalry was sent "after him." Elliott stated clearly that he left at midnight on the 27th and struck Booneville at 2:00 A.M. of the 30th, at which hour Pope and Halleck were expecting Beauregard to attack.

43. *O.R.*, *11*, 244, 247, 251–252, 207–208, 263. On June 5 Lincoln forwarded to Halleck by telegraph the dispatch he had just received from McClellan inviting his "excellency's attention to the great importance of occupying Chattanooga and Dalton" by the western forces (*ibid.*, *10*, 670). Halleck

replied that preparations for a move on Chattanooga had begun on the 2nd and troops had been started in that direction. He added that he was embarrassed by "Mitchel's foolish destruction of bridges," referring to those at Decatur and west thereof. This was unfair, for the enemy could have destroyed the bridges at will after Mitchel withdrew to the north bank of the Tennessee. Since Mitchel did not have sufficient force to hold a bridgehead at Decatur, it is hard to blame him for destroying the bridge for security reasons.

44. *Ibid.*, *11*, 245, 249, 242. In one of his dispatches Pope said he thought he could prevent the enemy from concentrating at Baldwyn, and that he was satisfied the Confederates would scatter. But on the 3rd he told Rosecrans to press the enemy at least as far as Baldwyn, where a heavy force might be found since the roads from Corinth united at that place (*ibid.*, p. 249).

45. *Ibid.*, *10*, 669. Lincoln also telegraphed. Halleck may have been impelled into his unfortunate telegram in part by Stanton's statement in his message of the 2nd (*ibid.*, *11*, 242), "Every one is anxious to hear the latest news, and I hope you will telegraph frequently. The President would be glad to have the news every hour." In this dispatch Stanton said that Halleck could handle his railroad transportation better than it could be managed from Washington.

On July 3 (*ibid.*, *10*, 671) Halleck telegraphed to Stanton: "I have seen a published statement of General Beauregard that my telegram respecting the capture of locomotives, prisoners, and arms contained as many lies as lines. The number of locomotives captured was reported to be nine, and I so telegraphed you. General Beauregard says only seven. It turns out on a full investigation that we captured eleven. In regard to the number of prisoners and arms taken I telegraphed the exact language of General Pope. If it was erroneous, the responsibility is his, not mine." Whether or not Halleck checked on Pope's actual words before making his positive statement cannot be said. Three years later, after the war, some sharp letters were exchanged between Pope and Halleck on the subject (*ibid.*, *11*, 635–637).

46. *Ibid.*, pp. 255–256, 587, 586.

47. *Ibid.*, pp. 258, 264, 263–264, 273–274, 274. Though Halleck authorized Buell to make an attack if he was confident the enemy was retiring (*ibid.*, p. 264) he still adhered to what he had told Pope on the 4th (*ibid.*, p. 252), "The main object now is to get the enemy far enough south to relieve our railroads from danger of an immediate attack. There is no object in bringing on a battle if this object can be obtained without one. I think by showing a bold front for a day or two the enemy will continue his retreat, which is all I desire."

48. *Ibid.*, *10*, 770–771; *11*, 604; *10*, 763, 774–777. Although Beauregard spoke in his letter to Cooper about the "extraordinary preparations, expense, labor, and timidity" that the Federals had used in their approach, he said nothing, however, about the expense and labor consumed in constructing the works at Corinth, nor anything about the feelings of the inhabitants who abandoned the place when the army left.

49. *Ibid.*, *11*, 278, 280–281, 279; *10*, 670–671. Halleck stated in his dispatch to Stanton, "General Pope estimated rebel loss from casualties, prisoners, and

desertion at over 20,000, and General Buell at between 20,000 and 30,000."
But all that Buell had said in his message that day (*ibid., 11*, 279) was: "The
loss of the enemy in the retreat has been undoubtedly very great, from
disasters, sickness, etc. The deserters all estimate it as from 20,000 to
30,000."

50. *O.R., 11*, 288; Sheridan, *op. cit.*, I, 152.

51. Gosnell, *Guns on the Western Waters*, Chap. VII; *O.R., 10*, 888–889.
Gen. Strong, commanding at Cairo, reported to Halleck on May 11 that two
of the Confederate boats were blown up and one was sunk. In a dispatch of
May 19 Halleck told Stanton that he had "urged our flotilla to risk running
past Fort Pillow," but that the attempt had not been made. (*O.R., 10*, 888; *11*,
202.)

52. Gosnell, *op. cit.*, Chap. III.

53. *Ibid.*, Chap. VIII; Greene, *The Mississippi*, pp. 15–17; Alfred W. Ellet,
"Ellet and His Steam-Rams at Memphis," *B. and L.*, I, 453–459. Alfred Ellet,
who as a lieutenant colonel commanded the *Monarch*, was put in command
of the ram fleet after his brother's death and was subsequently made a brigadier
general. On the naval engagement and the occupation of Memphis see also
O.R., 10, 906–914.

54. *O.R., 11*, 155–156, 156. See also Mitchel's report to Buell, *ibid., 10*,
655–656.

55. *Ibid., 11*, 161–162.

56. Mitchel to Stanton, May 4, *ibid.*, pp. 162–163; Fry to Mitchel, May 7,
ibid., p. 624. Mitchel's communication was a letter; but on the same day he
telegraphed Stanton that he had written of three important matters: protection of slaves who furnished information; his lack of command of his own line
of communication; and the desirability of holding the part of Alabama north
of the Tennessee. There seems to be no message from Stanton to Buell directing that Mitchel be given charge of his communication line.

On May 6 Mitchel wrote to Stanton, "The failure to occupy Tuscumbia,
I fear, is to become a frightful source of trouble" (*ibid.*, p. 167). He added
that he had not heard from Halleck or Buell for two weeks, and that if guerrilla
warfare were waged by the enemy, it would be necessary for him to have a
large force of cavalry.

Although there might have been considerable hazard in occupying Tuscumbia, a brigade at Florence would have been in little if any danger; and it would
have been a great deterrent to Confederate crossing of the Tennessee. When
informed that Andrew Johnson protested the removal of a regiment from
Nashville because secessionists were thereby encouraged, Halleck told Stanton
that it was no time to hunt disloyalists, and added, "We are now at the
enemy's throat, and cannot release our great grasp to pare his toe-nails" (*ibid.*,
pp. 128–129). A detachment of troops that could have prevented enemy raids
across the Tennessee would have been quite a different matter.

57. *Ibid.*, pp. 180, 222. In the first dispatch (May 10) Mitchel reported
guerrilla warfare and informed Stanton that he had just been placed in command of troops north of his position as far as Nashville, inclusive.

58. *Ibid.*, pp. 257, 271; *10*, 919–921; *11*, 596, 593. Smith telegraphed to

Lee in Richmond that he feared Chattanooga would fall, and that he had directed the removal of all stores (*ibid.*, p. 596).

59. *Ibid.*, p. 271 (statement to Buell by Mitchel about Negley being authorized to take Chattanooga if he thought it prudent); *10*, 919–921. Mitchel had fitted up some kind of gunboat which was to join Negley at Chattanooga but did not. Though Negley overestimated the enemy force he seemed to have little fear of it.

60. *Ibid.*, *11*, 595, 593.

61. *Ibid.*, pp. 282, 282–283, 287. Upon receipt of the report about Murfreesboro, Mitchel directed Negley to stop his threat against Chattanooga, not having yet received word that he was retiring. On the 10th he reported to Buell that Negley had not been able to cross the river (*ibid.*, p. 288).

62. *Ibid.*, *10*, 630–634 (Holt's report), 634–635 (Buell's letter); James B. Fry, "Notes on the Locomotive Chase," *B. and L.*, II, 716; Fry, *Operations of the Army Under Buell*, p. 21. Gen. Morgan claimed later that it was his suggestion to Buell and orders by the latter that led to the demonstration opposite Chattanooga (George W. Morgan, "Cumberland Gap," *B. and L.*, III, 62–69). On June 9 Buell informed Morgan that though Negley was opposite Chattanooga his stay there could not be counted on. It was not until two days later that he told Mitchel that Morgan was advancing on Cumberland Gap and directed, "Endeavor as much as possible to keep your force in an attitude to threaten Chattanooga and occupy the attention of Kirby Smith." (*O.R.*, *10*, 53; *23*, 9.) Thus Morgan's postwar statement is incorrect.

63. *Ibid.*, *11*, 114; Pittenger, *op. cit.*, 89.

In *B. and L.*, II, 701–707, there appears an article, "Operations in North Alabama," written by Buell, in which he emphasizes certain inconsistencies in Mitchel's dispatches; and in a long note appended to the article, occasioned by the publication of Pittenger's book and Frederick A. Mitchel's biography of his father, he speaks of Pittenger's claim that the Andrews raid was "a part of a comprehensive plan of invasion devised by Mitchel" and adds "it rests on no evidence whatever." Pittenger really claimed no *comprehensive* plan but merely a move on Chattanooga and possibly Knoxville. Since Andrews was hanged soon after his exploit while Mitchel died in the fall of 1862, absence of documentary evidence about their plan is not surprising. Pittenger talked with Andrews during their imprisonment, and what he wrote should carry much weight. It is incontestable that Mitchel had 2,000 men on a train at Stevenson while Andrews was racing for Chattanooga. Pittenger's book comments several times on Buell's slowness and caution, while it strongly praises Mitchel for vigor and boldness.

64. *O.R.*, *11*, 253, 278; *25*, 87; *23*, 81–82; Cramer, *Letters of Grant*, p. 99.

65. *O.R.*, *23*, 62–63.

66. Grant, *Memoirs*, I, 383–384.

67. Greene, *op. cit.*, pp. 19–21; Lewis, *Farragut*, II, Chaps. IX, X. In addition to his sloops and seagoing gunboats, Farragut had a number of mortars under Commander David Dixon Porter.

68. *O.R.*, *25*, 26, 43.

69. Greene, *op. cit.*, pp. 21–23; Lewis, *op. cit.*, p. 121.

70. Sherman, *op. cit.*, I, 255–256.

71. The original is in a private collection; photostatic copy in the author's possession.

72. Church, *Grant*, p. 42, gives Grant's sworn statement of June 27, 1848, concerning the theft. *Congressional Globe*, 37th Congress (1861–1862), 2nd Session, Part 3, 2658–2659, 2674, 2717, 2871 gives the course of the bill through the Senate and its signing by the President.

On Jan. 4, 1853, Grant wrote to the Secretary of War from Fort Vancouver explaining that he had been unable to submit his reports ending June 30, 1852, because he had gone from "Governor's Island on the 30th of June, on a leave of absence for a few days to attend to some business in Washington City before sailing for this coast," and on returning on the night of July 4 he had learned to his surprise that his regiment was to embark so as to be ready to sail the next day at 2:00 P.M. Although he had forwarded his accounts by the first mail after his arrival on the West Coast, a report of the case had been made to the President. Presumably Grant's business in Washington was a claim for reimbursement, for on Sept. 8, 1853, he wrote from Fort Vancouver to both the Quartermaster General and the Commissary General for orders to go to Washington to settle his accounts, because he had resigned as regimental quartermaster: "I am particularly anxious to be present in Washington for the reason that I had public funds stolen from me during the Mexican War, and for which I have been petitioning Congress ever since, but without being able to get any action on my claim." (Originals in a private collection; copies in author's possession.)

73. Grant, *op. cit.*, I, 385–390; *O.R.*, 25, 29–30, 41–42, 43. Grant reported a probable effort to burn Memphis, which he said would be partially successful, but would "operate more against the rebels than ourselves." He urged the importance of having an entire division of his army in the city.

74. *O.R.*, 23, 29, 58, 122–123 (about pontoons), 73–165 *passim*.

In *Memoirs*, I, 410, Grant put the responsibility for Buell's slow progress upon the orders he had received to repair the railroad, but said nothing about a large part of the road being in operation under Mitchel. He stated that the road from Nashville to Chattanooga could easily have been put in order by troops other than Buell's. In a long letter to Halleck dated July 11 (*O.R.*, 23, 122–123) Buell did not mention rebuilding the railroad as a cause of delay, but told of the long march with a large train in hot weather, as well as the crossing of a wide river by ferry (at Decatur). Without censuring Mitchel he stated that the latter's report had caused him to believe the road from Nashville to Stevenson would be open by July 1. On the 8th Fry spoke of a regiment as having advanced from Stevenson to assist the engineers at work on the railroad from Nashville (*ibid.*, p. 105); and Buell told Halleck in his letter of the 11th that he had about doubled the force at work.

75. *Ibid.*, 11, 290–296 (a letter with inclosures to Stanton about the trade question); Beatty, *op. cit.*, pp. 121, 117. Some of Mitchel's first reports to Stanton explained what he was doing with regard to trade; and Beatty wrote

that he was satisfied that Mitchel had been strictly honest and had done nothing that would "cast the slightest shadow upon his good name." There was much in the newspapers on the question.

The charges of lack of discipline were based largely upon the conduct of the brigade commanded by Col. John B. Turchin, a Russian who had formed his ideas of warfare in the Crimea, and whom Buell put before a court (Beatty, *op. cit.*, p. 120). Beatty called Turchin's policy that of the devil, but strongly condemned Buell's opposed mild policy toward secessionists. Ammen greatly amused Beatty, who described him as a strange combination of qualities, talking incessantly and always having the floor. (*Ibid.*, pp. 117, 120–125 *passim.*)

76. *O.R., 23,* 69–70.

77. *Ibid.,* pp. 74–75. Halleck said it would be impossible to send cavalry and exceedingly difficult to transport artillery with horses or guns. He asked if infantry would suffice.

78. *Ibid.,* pp. 75, 76. Lincoln telegraphed Halleck on the 30th that they would be very glad to have 25,000 infantry, but not to send a man if it would endanger any point he regarded as important or would weaken the move on Chattanooga, which was an objective Lincoln ranked with Richmond. On July 1 Halleck wired both Lincoln and Stanton that the countermanding of the order had saved the situation in the West. The next day the President stated that they would still like to have some troops if possible. (*Ibid.,* pp. 75, 82, 88.)

79. *Ibid., 23,* 81–82; *25,* 631.

80. *Ibid., 25,* 46.

81. *Ibid.,* pp. 46–47.

82. *Ibid.,* pp. 67–68.

83. *Ibid.,* pp. 83, 90.

84. *Ibid.,* p. 90.

85. Henry, *Forrest,* pp. 85–90. Henry states that Crittenden took over command on the morning of the 12th, but a dispatch Crittenden sent to Col. Fry indicates he was present and issuing orders on the 11th (*O.R., 23,* 125). Forrest left Murfreesboro on the evening of the 13th and paroled all prisoners when he reached McMinnville. Horn puts the "stores" captured by Forrest as worth "almost" a million dollars (*The Army of Tennessee,* p. 161), while Henry says the total value of captured property—wagons, guns, cavalry equipment, etc.—was "perhaps" a quarter-million. Probably to strengthen his claim of having a very strong force, Forrest signed his note demanding surrender as a brigadier general, though he was still only a colonel.

In a long dispatch of July 12, O. R. Greene, adjutant in Nashville, said to Col. Fry, "I do not usually believe startling information, but I am convinced that I am reliably informed that a heavy movement is taking place upon Murfreesborough via McMinnville from Chattanooga" (*O.R., 23,* 132–133). Apparently Crittenden was not alerted.

86. The first instructions for the conduct of armies issued by any government were those promulgated by the United States as War Department General Order No. 100 for 1863, which appeared on Apr. 24. This historic document was written by Francis Lieber, a distinguished German who received a

severe wound in the battle of Ligny and had come to the United States in 1827. While professor of international law at Columbia College he drew up in the summer of 1862 a report on the subject of guerrilla warfare. His second paper was revised by a board of officers of which Maj. Gen. Hitchcock was president, before it was submitted to and approved by the President. (Holland, *The Laws of War on Land*, pp. 71–72; G.O. 100, 1863, p. 1.) Paragraph 60 stated: "It is against the usage of modern war to resolve, in hatred and revenge, to give no quarter. No body of troops has the right to declare that it will not give, and therefore will not expect quarter. . . ." The Geneva Conventions of 1907 state: "It is especially forbidden . . . to declare that no quarter will be given." (Holland, *op. cit.*, 4, 43; War Department, *Rules of Land Warfare*, pp. 58, 161.)

87. *O.R.*, 23, 125, 129, 130, 137.

88. Holland, *Morgan and His Raiders*, pp. 116, 104; *O.R.*, 23, 132–133; George W. Morgan, "Cumberland Gap," *B. and L.*, III, 62–69.

89. *O.R.*, 23, 143, 150–151; 25, 100; Grant, *op. cit.*, p. 393. Halleck explained to Lincoln that he was in touch with Buell and Governor Johnson and was arranging reenforcements for Curtis.

90. *O.R.*, 25, 100. Lincoln terminated a dispatch to Halleck on July 2 with the question, "Please tell me, could you make me a flying visit for consultation, without endangering the service in your department?" Halleck replied the same day, saying that under the circumstances he did not believe he could leave, though the state of his health and his weariness would make a trip to Washington "exceedingly desirable." (*Ibid.*, pp. 63, 64.)

On July 6 Lincoln gave Gov. Sprague of Rhode Island a letter of introduction to Halleck in which he wrote: "I know the object of his visit to you. He has my cheerful consent to go, but not my direction. He wishes to get you and part of your force, one or both, to come here." After repeating what he had previously said about sending troops, Lincoln concluded, "Still, please give my friend Governor Sprague a full and fair hearing." At 5:00 P.M. of the 10th Lincoln received a dispatch sent that day by Halleck, which read: "Governor Sprague is here. If I were to go to Washington I could advise but one thing: to place all the forces in North Carolina, Virginia, and Washington under one head, and hold that head responsible for results." (*Ibid.*, pp. 76, 88.) With no one available for such a position, Lincoln took the natural step of ordering Halleck to Washington as General in Chief.

91. *Ibid.*, pp. 100–101.

92. *N.Y. Times*, July 19, 1862; *N.Y. Tribune*, July 26; *N.Y. Herald*, July 26; *Harper's Weekly*, VI, 508–509 (Aug. 9, 1862).

In the chapter "Not Wanted—Victory in the West," in Eisenschiml's *Why Was Lincoln Murdered?* one finds it stated (p. 353) that it is hard to fathom the reasons for Halleck's promotion, since he had demonstrated merely that he was good at intriguing and poor at campaigning. (Incredible though it may seem, it is also asserted that Halleck held the position of General in Chief to the end of the war. Grant's tenure of that position for the final year can surely be regarded as one of the basic and elementary facts of the war.) In the same author's *The Story of Shiloh* (a book which claims that Buell ranked

Grant at Shiloh and makes no mention of Grant's very important order early on Apr. 6 to Nelson to march to a point opposite Pittsburg) one finds it stated that the removal of McClellan and the appointment of Halleck were "extraordinary acts" which no one has "ever satisfactorily explained" (pp. 51, 56). It is indicated that McClellan battled "hard-hitting armies led by the best Southern military talent" all the way up the "vicious terrain" of the Peninsula, and that Halleck moved "without encountering any resistance whatever" (p. 50). No one should discount Joe Johnston and his subordinates, who opposed McClellan's march. But are we to understand that Beauregard, Bragg, Hardee, and Polk were not among the best Confederate generals? The statement that Halleck encountered no resistance does not accord with the record. Dyer's *Compendium* gives one battle (Williamsburg), one engagement, one action, and eleven skirmishes during McClellan's movement; and it lists one engagement, one action, and nine skirmishes during Halleck's advance. The balance is notable.

Horn seems in general to support Eisenschiml, for he quotes (*The Army of Tennessee*, p. 160) Alexander's assertion that Halleck, unable to command one army successfully, was ordered to Washington to command all the armies. Such a view conforms to the general pattern of Alexander's book of condemnation.

Thomas L. Snead, a Confederate colonel, in his article "With Price East of the Mississippi," *B. and L.*, II, 714–734, lists the Southern losses in the West subsequent to Halleck's taking command in Nov. 1861, and says that it was "no wonder the Government was so well pleased with him that on the 8th of June, 1862," it extended his command over the whole of Kentucky and Tennessee. Jefferson Davis regarded the capture of Corinth as a severe blow, and it is hard to criticize Lincoln for viewing it as another achievement in Halleck's favor. The basic question is simple enough: What other Federal general had at the time secured as many and as significant victories through the operations of troops under his command?

93. *O.R., 25,* 97; *23,* 143 (Halleck to Buell, saying Curtis was at Helena calling for reenforcements); Gosnell, *op. cit.,* Chap. X; Lewis, *op. cit.,* pp. 111–115; Shotwell, *The Civil War in America,* I, 259–261.

94. *O.R., 25,* 102.

NOTES TO THE APPENDIX

1. Coppée, *Grant and His Campaigns,* p. 24 n.; Conger, *The Rise of Grant,* pp. 367–368; Moore, *Rebellion Record,* III, 278–279.

2. Wilson, *The Life of Rawlins,* p. 425.

3. *Ibid.,* p. 176.

4. Sherman, *Memoirs,* I, 192–193.

5. Van Horne, *The Life of Thomas,* p. 31.

6. Phisterer, *Statistical Record,* pp. 267–269; *Register of Graduates and Former Cadets, United States Military Academy.*

7. Van Horne, *op. cit.,* p. 34; *supra,* II, 397, n. 117.

8. Van Horne, *op. cit.,* p. 39; *O.R., 4,* 254.

9. Piatt, *General Thomas*, p. 110.

10. *O.R., 4*, 268.

11. In the spring of 1860 Mitchel had left Cincinnati to be director of the new Dudley Observatory at Albany, and he was accordingly commissioned as from New York. A brief account of his heroic efforts in building the Cincinnati Observatory is found in Black's address "The Cincinnati Telescope," delivered on its centenary. On money raised locally Mitchel went abroad to consult astronomers about his project, securing letters of introduction in Washington from John Quincy Adams. Though the crotchety Adams wrote in his diary about the "braggart vanity" of Mitchel, he came to Cincinnati by stagecoach at the age of seventy-five to lay the corner-stone of the observatory.

12. *O.R. 4*, 275–276.

13. *Ibid.*, pp. 299–300.

14. *Ibid.*, p. 303.

15. *Ibid.*, p. 306.

16. Hitchcock was recommended and approved as a major general a week before Grant was promoted. His age and long prior service as a general officer made him a special case. On Dec. 23, 1861, Lincoln recommended the appointment of Governor Edwin D. Morgan of New York as a major general. The Senate postponed action on two different occasions because of reluctance to commission a governor, but confirmed it on Apr. 15, 1862, the appointment dating from Sept. 28, 1861, in accordance with Lincoln's original recommendation. Morgan never served in the field, but he did excellent work in raising troops as commander of the Department of New York.

On Jan. 20, 1862, Lincoln recommended that Cassius M. Clay, an ardent antislavery Kentuckian who was soon to return from Russia, where he was minister, be made a major general. The Senate committee reported favorably on the 24th, but confirmation was not given until Apr. 11. It was purely a political appointment to satisfy an influential person hard to deal with. Though Clay, who differed with Lincoln on fundamental policy, sought command of a department, he received no assignment; and an order of Sept. 11, 1862, for him to report to Gen. Butler for duty in the Department of the Gulf, was canceled orally by Lincoln, who sent him on a secret political mission to the legislature of Kentucky. (Halleck to Schofield, Sept. 20, 1862, *O.R.*, *107*, 331; *21*, 568, especially note.) Clay resigned his commission on Mar. 11, 1863, and returned to St. Petersburg, replacing Simon Cameron, who had succeeded him as minister.

The source for dates of recommendations and confirmations in this and the next paragraph of the text is the *Journal of Senate Executive Proceedings*, Vol. XII (1861–1862).

17. After recommending on Apr. 15 that Mitchel be made brevet major general, Lincoln requested on the 30th that the recommendation be returned to him. This was done on May 2, the day the Senate received and acted upon the recommendation of May 1 that Mitchel be made a full major general.

18. Between the names of Thomas and Sherman in the list of major generals of volunteers is that of George C. Cadwalader (Phisterer, *Statistical Record*, p. 252). Cadwalader had been a volunteer officer in the Mexican War,

and had reached the rank of brevet major general. He has been seen in this work (I, 70) as a major general of Pennsylvania troops under Gen. Patterson, but disappeared with the discharge of the three-month men. At Lincoln's direction Stanton nominated him on Mar. 28, 1862, for appointment as a major general of volunteers; and he was confirmed on Apr. 25. Being a lawyer by profession, he was assigned to the board revising military laws and regulations.

19. The *Indiana Magazine of History* published in Sept. 1950 (XLVI, 221–248) my article "The Tennessee River Campaign and Anna Ella Carroll." In it were criticisms of Marjorie Barstow Greenbie's *My Dear Lady,* a book accepting the Carroll claim. Complaining letters came to me from Mrs. Greenbie and to the editor of the magazine from her husband, Sydney Greenbie. Some comments on the Greenbies' joint work, *Anna Ella Carroll and Abraham Lincoln,* are made in following notes.

20. Senate Misc. Doc. 100, 41st Cong., 2nd Sess.; House Misc. Doc. 179, 44th Cong., 1st Sess., p. 20.

For a full and careful analysis of the dispute between Miss Carroll and Capt. Scott, see F. Lauriston Bullard, "Anna Ella Carroll and Her 'Modest' Claim," *Lincoln Herald,* Oct., 1948, pp. 2–10. Bullard states, "There can be no doubt that Miss Carroll did an artistic job wheedling the pilot," and "On the basis of the Congressional documents we think Captain Scott wins his case." He lists the different Congressional documents bearing on the case.

21. Carroll to Grant, Jan., 1867, and Carroll to Draper, n.d., House Misc. Doc. 179, 44th Cong., 1st Sess., pp. 120–121, 118–119; Senate Misc. Doc. 100, 41st Cong., 2nd Sess.; Carroll's 1878 statement, House Misc. Doc. 58, 45th Cong., 2nd Sess., p. 10.

Mrs. Greenbie's *My Dear Lady* states (pp. 145, 153, 165) that Miss Carroll was at the Battle of Belmont, and quotes her as saying, "When I saw the dead and dying as they lay upon the field, and witnessed the sad sight of the ambulance wagons bearing the wounded to the hospitals, my heart sank within me." In my paper in the *Indiana Magazine of History* I said (p. 245), "To anyone familiar with the facts about the battle of Belmont, Miss Carroll's claim that she was present must be utterly fantastic." This specific challenge of Miss Carroll's veracity seems not to have been met by the Greenbies in their new book, for it is not claimed there that she was at the battle, and the quotation from her does not appear.

22. Nevins, *The Emergence of Lincoln,* II, 237.

23. Sandburg, *Lincoln,* III, 174–175; Nicolay and Hay, *Lincoln,* IX, Chap. V.

24. See p. 236 of my paper.

25. Stanton Papers, III, 50646–50647.

26. Professor Kamm made a thorough study of Scott's letters, in preparing his monograph *The Civil War Career of Thomas A. Scott,* and I have his permission to quote a statement attached to a letter of Mar. 24, 1952. He writes: "I believe that your contention concerning the inaccuracy of Scott's statement made in 1872 is abundantly verified by the materials in the *Official Records,* and in the Stanton Papers. . . . Stanton's note to Halleck of Feb. 21 [*supra,* p. 273] indicates that Stanton looked upon the campaign as originating with

Halleck. Statements of this type fully support your contention that Scott first learned of the operation up the Tennessee when he arrived in Indianapolis, thus changing the nature of his mission. . . . The relatively leisurely nature of his inspection trip is indicated by the instructions [in Stanton's directive of Jan. 29], 'You will remain at each point until directed to proceed.' "

27. The letter is given in full in *Anna Ella Carroll and Abraham Lincoln*, pp. 351–354. The Preface to the book admits that it is very damaging to Miss Carroll's character, but makes an effort to mitigate the fact by saying that there can be no doubt about the (sinister?) intent of the "preserver" of this letter, who did not keep other letters, of which it is said there is evidence that Miss Carroll wrote to Lincoln. The statement that the three remaining letters from her in the Robert Todd Lincoln Collection are inconsequential is not warranted. In that of July 14 she strongly urged Lincoln to veto the Confiscation Bill just passed by Congress. In spite of his own objections to the act, he, however, signed it. Miss Carroll's letter of Oct. 21 requesting an interview shows that she did not have free and easy access to Lincoln, as is sometimes stated or implied.

28. The Greenbies' new book states (p. 311) that the War Department overrode Halleck and placed Anna's plan in Grant's hands for execution. The claim is not documented, and is in direct conflict with Mrs. Greenbie's thesis in *My Dear Lady*. There it is said (p. 156) that Grant knew nothing of the move up the Tennessee until ordered by Halleck to make it. The later statement is less tenable than the former one, for Halleck did order Grant to make the move. Stanton evidently was unconscious of any "overriding," for he said to Halleck in his message of congratulations on the taking of Fort Henry, "You have my perfect confidence and may rely upon the utmost support in your undertakings." (*Supra*, p. 209. See also Kamm's statement, above.) Since Halleck's department soon was greatly extended, and he received command over Buell, the overriding claim makes both Stanton and Lincoln look a little foolish.

There is also a significant shift relative to Thomas Scott in the new book. In *My Dear Lady*, p. 172, a reference is made to his letters to Stanton, though their actual contents are not indicated—a fact on which I commented in my paper. When Scott's trip is described in the new book (p. 305), no mention is made of letters that give an "almost daily record of his activities." The new work, however, asserts (p. 305) that Scott carried with him from the East Miss Carroll's maps, plan, and data. Even Scott did not say this in his letter of 1872; and, had it been true, it is hard to see how the material could have had any influence on Grant, who started up the Tennessee on the evening of Feb. 3, when Scott was in Detroit, having been ordered there from Columbus by a telegram from Stanton (Stanton Papers, III, 50579–50582; *O.R., 122,* 876). The meeting between Miss Carroll and Lincoln (described on p. 319) soon after the capture of Fort Donelson, in which the President is reported to have said that the armies were moving under the directing hand of a woman, is completely refuted by Miss Carroll's subsequent statement about lack of knowledge of the use made of her paper.

The Greenbies emphasize in their latest work (pp. 304–305) that Miss Carroll's plan contemplated going all the way to Mobile, and say it was only a short distance overland from the Tennessee to the headwaters of the Tombigbee and Alabama rivers, so that there was an "easy route" all the way to the Gulf. To build a canal miles long, or alternatively to move gunboats and transports overland, is not easy. They give Miss Carroll credit (pp. 329–330) for Buell's move to reenforce Grant, on the basis of her statement in a letter to the War Department on Mar. 26, 1862, wherein she said she was convinced that Halleck's true policy was to strengthen Grant. In Chap. XIII, preceding, it has been seen that Buell started for Savannah eleven days before Miss Carroll wrote her letter and would already have been there but for the destroyed bridge at Columbia.

The preface of the new work begins and ends with a quotation from a strong endorsement of Miss Carroll that Cassius M. Clay wrote for a newspaper in 1886. When Grant started up the Tennessee, Clay was still farther away than Thomas Scott—he was in Russia. Though he returned to the United States soon afterward, he went back to St. Petersburg as minister a year later (Clay to Seward, St. Petersburg, Jan. 24, 1862, *O.R., 115,* 1191–1193; *D.A.B.*). Sandburg refers to him as a "fearless strutter" (*Lincoln*, II, 45), and quotes Senator Orville Browning's diary entry that Lincoln—his intimate friend —told him that Clay "had a great deal of conceit and very little sense."

29. *McClure's Magazine*, V, 433–436 (Oct., 1895); *O.R., 3,* 443, 444.

30. *Ibid., 111,* 501; *3,* 465, 141–142, 143–144.

31. *Midland Monthly,* beginning with Vol. VI, No. 4.

32. *Ibid.,* IX, 54.

33. *O.R., 3,* 428–429, 430–431.

34. *Midland Monthly,* IX, 109.

35. Senate Executive Journal, XI, 487, 554.

36. *Midland Monthly,* IX, 118.

37. *Ibid.,* pp. 220–221.

38. Wilson, *Grant's Letters to a Friend,* pp. 1–2.

39. *Ibid.,* pp. 7–8.

40. Johnston's statement, *supra,* p. 123; Henderson's, *supra,* I, 257; Wavell's in his *Generals and Generalship,* p. 11.

BIBLIOGRAPHY

(Only works quoted or cited as authority)

Alexander, Augustus W., *Grant As a Soldier*. St. Louis, Author, 1887.

B. and L. See *Battles*.

Badeau, Adam, *Military History of Ulysses S. Grant, from April, 1861, to April, 1865* (3 vols.). New York, Appleton, 1881.

Basso, Hamilton, *Beauregard: The Great Creole*. New York, Scribner, 1933.

Battles and Leaders of the Civil War, eds. Robert V. Johnson and C. C. Buel. New York, Century, 1884–1888.

Beatty, John, *Memoirs of a Volunteer, 1861–1863*, ed. Harvey S. Ford. New York, Norton, 1946.

Beveridge, Albert J., *Abraham Lincoln, 1809–1858* (4 vols.). Boston, Houghton Mifflin, 1928.

Bill, Alfred Hoyt, *Rehearsal for Conflict: The War with Mexico, 1846–1848*. New York, Knopf, 1947.

Black, Robert L., "The Cincinnati Telescope," *Publications of the Philosophical Society of Ohio*, 1944, pp. 19–46.

Brownlow, William C., *Sketches of the Rise, Progress, and Decline of Secession, with a Narrative of Personal Adventures Among the Rebels*. Philadelphia, Childs, 1862.

Bullard, F. Lauriston, "Anna Ella Carroll and Her 'Modest' Claim," *Lincoln Herald*, L, No. 3, pp. 2–10 (Oct., 1948).

Carpenter, Francis B., *Six Months at the White House with Abraham Lincoln: The Story of a Picture*. New York, Hurd and Houghton, 1866.

Carroll, Anna Ella, "Plan of the Tennessee Campaign," *North American Review*, CXLII, 342–347 (Apr., 1886).

Chicago Tribune.

Church, William Conant, *Ulysses S. Grant and the Period of National Preservation and Reconstruction*. New York, Putnam, 1897.

Cincinnati Commercial.

Cincinnati Daily Gazette.

Cleaves, Freeman, *Rock of Chickamauga: The Life of General George H. Thomas.* Norman, Univ. of Oklahoma Press, 1948.

Conger, Arthur L., *The Rise of U. S. Grant.* New York, Century, 1931.

Coppée, Henry, *Grant and His Campaigns: A Military Biography.* New York, Richardson, 1866.

Cortissoz, Royal, *The Life of Whitelaw Reid* (2 vols.). New York, Scribner, 1921.

Cramer, Jesse Grant, ed. See Grant.

D.A.B. See *Dictionary.*

Dana, Charles A., and James H. Wilson, *The Life of Ulysses S. Grant, General of the Armies of the United States.* Springfield, Mass., Bill, 1868.

Davidson, Donald, *The Tennessee* (2 vols.). New York, Rinehart, 1946–1948.

Dictionary of American Biography. New York, Scribner, 1928–1936, 1943.

Dyer, Frederick H., *A Compendium of the War of the Rebellion,* Des Moines, Dyer, 1908.

Eisenschiml, Otto, *The Story of Shiloh.* Chicago, The Civil War Round Table, 1946.

——, *Why Was Lincoln Murdered?* Boston, Little, Brown, 1937.

Emerson, John W., "Grant's Life in the West and His Mississippi Valley Campaigns," serial in *Midland Monthly* (Des Moines), Vols. VI–XI (1896–1899).

Fiske, John, *The Mississippi Valley in the Civil War.* Boston, Houghton, Mifflin, 1900.

Force, Manning F., *From Fort Henry to Corinth* (Vol. II of *Campaigns of the Civil War*). New York, Scribner, 1882.

Freeman, Douglas Southall, *George Washington: A Biography* (4 vols.). New York, Scribner, 1948–1951.

Fry, James B., *Operations of the Army Under Buell, from June 10th to October 30th, 1862, and the "Buell Commission."* New York, Van Nostrand, 1884.

Fuller, J. F. C., *The Generalship of Ulysses S. Grant.* New York, Dodd, Mead, 1929.

Garland, Hamlin, *Ulysses S. Grant: His Life and Character.* New York, Doubleday & McClure, 1898.

Goodwin, Cardinal, *John Charles Frémont: An Explanation of his Career.* Stanford University, Stanford University Press, 1930.

Gosnell, H. Allen, *Guns on the Western Waters: The Story of the River Gunboats in the Civil War.* Baton Rouge, Louisiana State Univ. Press, 1949.

Grant, Ulysses S., *General Grant's Letters to a Friend, 1861–1880,* ed. James Grant Wilson. New York, Crowell, 1897.

——, *Letters of Ulysses S. Grant to His Father and His Youngest Sister, 1857–78,* ed. Jesse Grant Cramer. New York, Putnam, 1912.

——, *Personal Memoirs of U. S. Grant* (2 vols.). New York, Webster, 1885.

Gray, Wood, *The Hidden Civil War: The Story of the Copperheads.* New York, Viking, 1942.

Greeley, Horace, *The American Conflict: A History,* Hartford, Case, 1864–1866.

Green, Horace, *General Grant's Last Stand: A Biography.* New York, Scribner, 1936.

Greenbie, Marjorie Barstow, *My Dear Lady: The Story of Anna Ella Carroll, the "Great Unrecognized Member of Lincoln's Cabinet."* New York, Whittlesey House, 1940.

Greenbie, Sydney, and Marjorie Barstow Greenbie, *Anna Ella Carroll and Abraham Lincoln.* Tampa, Univ. of Tampa Press, 1952.

Greene, Francis Vinton, *The Mississippi* (Vol. VIII of *The Campaigns of the Civil War*). New York, Scribner, 1884.

Grose, William, *The Story of the Marches, Battles and Incidents of the 36th Regiment Indiana Volunteer Infantry.* New Castle, Courier Press, 1891.

Halleck, Henry Wager, *Elements of Military Art and Science; or, Course of Instruction in Strategy, Fortification, Tactics of Battles, etc.* New York, Appleton, 1846.

Harper's New Monthly Magazine, unsigned article "Galena and Its Lead Mines," XXXII, 682–696 (May, 1866).

Harper's Weekly.

Heinl, R. D., "What the Army Should Know About Naval Gunfire," *United States Army Combat Forces Journal,* II, 34–38 (Oct., 1951).

Henderson, G. F. R., *The Science of War: A Collection of Essays and Lectures, 1892–1903.* London, Longmans, Green, 1905.

Hendrick, Burton J., *Lincoln's War Cabinet.* Boston, Little, Brown, 1946.

Henry, Robert Selph, *"First with the Most" Forrest.* Indianapolis, Bobbs-Merrill, 1944.

Hirsch, Charles B., "Gunboat Personnel on the Western Waters," *Mid-America,* XXXIV, 75–86 (Apr., 1952).

Hitchcock, Ethan Allen, *Fifty Years in Camp and Field: Diary of Major-General Ethan Allen Hitchcock,* ed. W. A. Croffut. New York, Putnam, 1909.

Holland, Cecil Fletcher, *Morgan and His Raiders: A Biography of the Confederate General.* New York, Macmillan, 1942.

Holland, Thomas Erskine, *The Laws of War on Land (Written and Unwritten)*. Oxford, Clarendon Press, 1908.

Horn, Stanley F., *The Army of Tennessee: A Military History*. Indianapolis, Bobbs-Merrill, 1941.

House Miscellaneous Documents.

Johnston, William Preston, *The Life of Gen. Albert Sidney Johnston*. New York, Appleton, 1879.

Jones, Idwal, *Ark of Empire: San Francisco's Montgomery Block*. Garden City, Doubleday, 1951.

Journal of Senate Executive Proceedings.

Kamm, Samuel R., *The Civil War Career of Thomas A. Scott*. Philadelphia, privately printed, 1940.

Lewis, Charles Lee, *David Glasgow Farragut: Our First Admiral*. Annapolis, United States Naval Institute, 1943.

Lewis, Lloyd, *Captain Sam Grant*. Boston, Little, Brown, 1950.

——, *Sherman, Fighting Prophet*. New York, Harcourt, Brace, 1932.

Liddell Hart, B. H., *Sherman: Soldier, Realist, American*. New York, Dodd, Mead, 1929.

Lincoln Papers. Robert Todd Lincoln MS. Collection in the Library of Congress.

Livermore, Thomas L., *Numbers and Losses in the Civil War in America, 1861–65*. Boston, Houghton, Mifflin, 1901.

McClellan, George Brinton, *McClellan's Own Story: The War for the Union*. New York, Webster, 1887.

McCormick, Robert R., *Ulysses S. Grant: The Great Soldier of America*. New York, Appleton-Century, 1934.

McKee, Irving, *"Ben-Hur" Wallace: The Life of General Lew Wallace*. Berkeley, Univ. of California Press, 1947.

Mearns, David C., ed., *The Lincoln Papers* (2 vols.). Garden City, Doubleday, 1948.

Moore, Frank, ed., *Rebellion Record: A Diary of American Events with Documents, Narratives, Illustrative Incidents, Poetry. . . .* New York, Putnam, 1861–1863; Van Nostrand, 1864–1868.

Nevins, Allan, *The Emergence of Lincoln* (2 vols.). New York, Scribner, 1950.

New York Herald.

New York Times.

New York Tribune.

Nicolay, Helen, *Lincoln's Secretary: A Biography of John G. Nicolay*. New York, Longmans, Green, 1949.

Nicolay, John G., and John Hay, *Abraham Lincoln: A History* (10 vols.). New York, Century, 1890.

O'Connor, Richard, *Thomas: Rock of Chickamauga*. New York, Prentice-Hall, 1948.

O.R. See *War of the Rebellion.*

O.R. Navies. See next entry.

Official Records of the Union and Confederate Navies in the War of the Rebellion. Washington, Government Printing Office, 1894–1927.

Patton, James Welch, *Unionism and Reconstruction in Tennessee, 1860–1869.* Chapel Hill, Univ. of North Carolina Press, 1934.

Phisterer, Frederick, *Statistical Record of the Armies of the United States* (supplementary volume of *Campaigns of the Civil War*). New York, Scribner, 1883.

Piatt, Donn, *General George H. Thomas: A Critical Biography,* with concluding chapters by Henry V. Boynton. Cincinnati, Clarke, 1893.

Pittenger, William, *Daring and Suffering: A History of the Andrews Railroad Raid into Georgia in 1862.* New York, War Publishing Co., 1887.

Polk, William M., *Leonidas Polk, Bishop and General* (2 vols.). New ed. New York, Longmans, Green, 1915.

Porter, Horace, *Campaigning with Grant.* New York, Century, 1907.

Pratt, Fletcher, *Eleven Generals: Studies in American Command.* New York, William Sloane Associates, 1949.

Raymond, Henry J., *Life, Public Services, and State Papers of Abraham Lincoln.* London, Stevens, 1865.

Reed, D. W., Letter on Lew Wallace at Shiloh, *Iowa Journal of History and Politics,* XVIII, 305–308 (Apr., 1920).

Register of Graduates and Former Cadets. West Point, U. S. Military Academy, 1948.

Revised Regulations for the Army of the United States, 1861. Philadelphia (J. G. L. Brown, printer), 1861.

Rich, Joseph W., *The Battle of Shiloh.* Iowa City, State Historical Society of Iowa, 1911.

Richmond Daily Enquirer.

Roman, Alfred, *The Military Operations of General Beauregard in the War Between the States, 1861–1865* (2 vols.). New York, Harper, 1884.

Ropes, John Codman, *The Story of the Civil War: A Concise Account of the War in the United States of America Between 1861 and 1865* (4 vols.). New York, Putnam, 1891.

Rules of Land Warfare. Washington, Government Printing Office, 1914.

Sandburg, Carl, *Abraham Lincoln: The War Years* (4 vols.). New York, Harcourt, Brace, 1939.

Seitz, Don C., *Braxton Bragg: General of the Confederacy.* Columbia, S.C., The State Co., 1924.

Senate Miscellaneous Documents.

Sheridan, Philip H., *Personal Memoirs of P. H. Sheridan, General United States Army* (2 vols.). New York, Webster, 1888.

Sherman, William T., *Memoirs of William T. Sherman* (2 vols.). New York, Appleton, 1875.

Shotwell, William Gaston, *The Civil War in America* (2 vols.). New York, Longmans, Green, 1923.

Sipes, William B., *The Pennsylvania Railroad: Its Origin, Construction, Condition, and Connections*. Philadelphia, 1875.

Smith, William F., "Shiloh," *Magazine of American History*, XV, 292–304, 470–482 (1886).

Snyder, Alice L., "Galena, Looking Back," *Journal of the Illinois Historical Society*, XXV, 108–118 (1932).

Stanton Papers. MS. collection in the Library of Congress.

Stephenson, Wendell Holmes, *The Political Career of General James H. Lane*. Topeka, Kansas State Historical Society, 1930.

Stone, Irving, *Immortal Wife*. Garden City, Doubleday, 1944.

Thayer, John M., "Grant at Pilot Knob," *McClure's Magazine*, V, 433–436 (Oct., 1895).

Trollope, Anthony, *North America*, eds. Donald Smalley and Bradford Allen Booth. New York, Knopf, 1951.

Van Horne, Thomas B., *The Life of Major-General George H. Thomas*. New York, Scribner, 1882.

Wallace, Lew, *An Autobiography* (2 vols.). New York, Harper, 1906.

War of the Rebellion: Official Records of the Union and Confederate Armies. Washington, Government Printing Office, 1882–1900.

References are by Serial number in italic, and page, following the abbreviation *O.R.:* e.g., *O.R., 3,* 432. A key transferring serial numbers into series, volumes, and parts, is given in the index volume of the complete work. For an explanatory note, see *supra*, p. 457.

Washburne Papers. MS. collection in the Library of Congress.

Wavell, General Sir Archibald, *Generals and Generalship*. New York, Macmillan, 1941.

West, Richard S., Jr., *Gideon Welles: Lincoln's Navy Department*. Indianapolis, Bobbs-Merrill, 1943.

Wilkins, John E., typescript diary, lent by D. G. Wilkins of Corpus Christi, Texas.

Williams, Kenneth P., "The Tennessee River Campaign and Anna Ella Carroll," *Indiana Magazine of History*, XLVI, 221–248 (Sept., 1950).

Wilson, James Grant, ed. See *Grant*.

Wilson, James Harrison, *The Life of John A. Rawlins*. New York, Neale, 1916.

Woodward, William E., *Meet General Grant*. New York, Liveright, 1928.

Young, John Russell, *Around the World with General Grant* (2 vols.). New York, American News Co., 1879.

INDEX

Ranks shown are the highest held in connection with mention in this volume. The abbreviation C.S. denotes civil as well as military officers of the Confederate States. A hyphen is used between nonconsecutive page numbers to indicate scattered references to a subject as well as continuous treatment. Only a few references are made to the notes.

Abbeville, Miss., 435
Abingdon, Va., 284, 286
Adams, Brig. Gen. John, C.S., 425
Adams, John, cited, 329
Adamsville, Tenn., 360, 392
Alabama, invasion fear in northern part, 124; Beauregard writes to governor, 286
Albany, Mo., 115
Albuquerque, N. Mex., 341
Alexander, Col. J. W. S., at Ironton, 39, 40
Ammen, Col. Jacob, 12, 279; reaches Clarksville, 278; arrives at Savannah and sees Grant, 350–351; his statement about Nelson's delay, 370–371; at Battle of Shiloh, 378–379, 385
Anderson, Brig. Gen. Patton, C.S., at Battle of Shiloh, 366
Anderson, Brig. Gen. Robert, 188; goes to Cincinnati as Department commander, 47; reports to Secretary Chase, 50; visits Frankfort, 59; gives up command because of ill health, 72
Andrews, James J., Federal spy, conducts railroad raid, 400–404; Holt's report on and Buell's reply, 427
Arkansas, 28, 55, 65, 76, 102, 107, 114, 118, 269, 338, 409; Curtis invades, 287; he asks people to return to Federal allegiance, 289–290
Arkansas, Confederate ram, its exploit at Vicksburg, 440
Armies, Confederate: Army of the Mississippi, 388. *See also* Johnston and Beauregard; for forces operating in southwest Missouri, *see* McCulloch, Price, and Van Dorn
Armies, Federal: Army under Halleck, 410, 422, *see also* Halleck; Army of the Mississippi, 410, 440, *see also* Pope; Army of the Ohio, 410, *see also* Buell; Army of the Potomac, 102, 141, 158, 178, 188, 224, 253, 259, 272, 326, 338; Army of the Tennessee, 410, 422, 440, *see also* Grant; for forces operating in southwest Missouri, *see* Lyon, Frémont, and Curtis
Arms, shortage of (North and South), 14, 23, 109, 148, 165, 511 n. 2
Army Regulations, cited, 40, 71, 313, 353
Arthur, Chester A., ex-President, at Grant's funeral, 259
Asboth, Brig. Gen. Alexander, 113, 282; at Battle of Pea Ridge, 291

Associated Press, 88

Athens, Tenn., 409, 424

Atlanta, Ga., 400

Aunt Rachel (Mrs. Rachel Grant Tompkins), Grant's secessionist aunt living in Virginia, 74, 459 n. 6

Baldwyn, Miss., 419–421

Baltimore, Md., 7

Banks, Maj. General Nathaniel P., 413

Barbourville, Ky., 110, 133

Bardstown, Ky., 170, 269, 272, 328

Barren River, Ky., 148, 239, 325, 326

Batesville, Ark., 295

Baton Rouge, La., 16

Baxter, Capt. A. S., Grant's quartermaster, reports to St. Louis of serious lack of funds, 181–182; sent to Washington by Grant, 185–186; secures funds, 193; carries order to Lew Wallace, 362

Beatty, Col. John, 279; cited, 268, 277–279, 433–434

Beauregard, Gen. P. G. T., C.S., 197, 264, 281, 289, 315–325, 333, 338, 344, 350, 396, 406, 423; his expected move westward with reenforcements reported by McClellan to Buell and Halleck, 190; Halleck reports him to Grant as on the way, 194; he reaches Bowling Green and confers with Johnston, 213–216; advises an attack on Grant, 214–215; reports gloomily about Fort Donelson, 242; reports illness at Jackson, Tenn., 265–266; writes about an elaborate offensive, 286–287; awakens to realities and orders evacuation of Columbus, 287; stresses importance of New Madrid, 297; his order to his troops, 322; at Battle of Shiloh (assumes command on Johnston's death), 354–393; his message to Cooper captured by Mitchel, 402; actions in front of Corinth, 412, 413, 415; abandons Corinth, 416; replies to Davis, 418; conduct of his retirement, 420, 421; relieved by Bragg, 435

Beauregard Road, at Shiloh Park, 395

Beech Grove, Ky., 169, 171, 175

Beecher, Henry Ward, 103

Belknap, Maj. William W., at Battle of Shiloh, 379

Belle Memphis, Grant's headquarters boat, 81–83

Bellefonte, Ala., 409

Belleville, Ill., Grant at, 16

Belmont, Mo., 50, 53–55, 78, 82, 93, 96, 106, 127, 205, 361, 439, 440; operation against and battle of, 80–86; press reports about, 88–90; critique of the battle, 93–95; casualties, 98; Grant's report on the battle, 441–442

Benjamin, Judah P., Sec. of War, C.S., 121, 124, 132, 137, 146, 148, 286, 321; insists that promise to Brownlow be kept, 149; comments on reports of Crittenden's intemperance, 177; allots Kentucky's new quota of troops, 198; receives report from Johnston about abandonment of Bowling Green, 216; directs abandonment of Columbus, 286; Johnston reports his command in good spirits, 322

Bennett, James Gordon, 439

Benton, Mo., 47

Benton, gunboat, 243

Benton Barracks, Mo., 64

Bentonville, Ark., 274, 291, 298; captured by Curtis, 274

Bethel, Tenn., 319, 320, 348

Beveridge, Albert J., cited, 119

Beverly, W. Va., 272

Bidwell, Capt. B. G., C.S., at Fort Donelson, 237, 247

Big Creek Gap, 341

Big Sandy River, Ky.–W. Va., 325

Big Shanty (Kennesaw), Ga., 403

Birds Point, Mo., 49, 50, 75–78, 85, 96, 109, 126, 266

Bissell, Col. Josiah W., cuts canal at Island No. 10, 397

Black Hawk War, 6

Blair, Austin, governor of Michigan, appoints Sheridan a colonel, 414

Blair, Francis P., Jr., congressman, 31; aids Lyon in capturing Camp

Jackson, 16; urges appointment of Frémont, 23; his quarrel with Frémont, 62–64

Blair, Francis P., Sr., 62

Blair, Montgomery, Postmaster General, 154; urges appointment of Frémont, 23; Frémont's telegram to, 35; his tactless letter to Frémont and his trip to St. Louis, 62

Bland, Col. P. E., at Ironton, 39

Blandville, Ky., 62

Bloody Pond, at Battle of Shiloh, 374

Bloomfield, Mo., 77, 80, 82, 95

Bodyguards (Frémont's), 42–43, 66

Booneville, Miss., 418, 420

Bowling Green, Ky., 120, 132, 138, 142, 147, 160, 162, 171, 184, 231, 253, 264, 269, 274, 326, 438; Johnston reports Confederate occupation of, 74; Halleck asks that Buell's move toward be delayed, 163; Buell gives up move in favor of East Tennessee, 166–167, 169; Confederate troops reported as leaving to reenforce Fort Henry, 202; Confederate strength at, 308; its fall predicted by Halleck, 209; Johnston decides to abandon, 216; Hardee reports his withdrawal from, 239; Mitchel arrives at, 239; situation in, 268

Boyle, Brig. Gen. Jeremiah T., 147, 170

Bragg, Gen. Braxton, C.S., 321, 323, 325, 338, 420; his peculiarities and his first activities near Corinth, 319–321; complains of demoralization, 320–321; at Battle of Shiloh, 354–356, 363, 376, 377, 386, 390, 391; in withdrawal from Corinth, 416; replaces Beauregard, 435; strength of his command, 435

Bramlette, Col. Thomas E., 137

Brand, Robert, mayor of Galena, addresses meeting, 10–11

Breckinridge, Brig. Gen. John C., C.S., 7, 10, 323; at Battle of Shiloh, 354, 363, 371, 376, 386, 389, 390

Bridgeburners, executed by Confederates in East Tennessee, 147;

Halleck approves but defers shooting of, 168–169; commutes sentences, 270

Bridgeport, Ala., 401, 409; controversy about destruction of bridge at, 408; Mitchel saves part of the bridge, 424

Brigadier generals, appointment of, 22

Brownlow, William G. (Parson), 149; reaches Nashville, 327–328

Brownsville, Tex., 8

Bruce, E. M., congressman, C.S., severely critical of Johnston, 323

Brunot, Mo., 27, 28

Brunson, Boss, deputizes Grant to recover property, 8

Buchanan, James, Grant votes for, 7

Buchanan, Col. Robert C., 4

Buckland, Col. Ralph P., at Battle of Shiloh, 366, 367

Buckner, Brig. Gen. Simon B., C.S., 110, 111, 132, 133, 142, 218, 230, 234, 242; in Confederate sortie at Fort Donelson, 248; accepts the command and asks terms of surrender, 255–256; his former favor to Grant, 256; accepts but criticizes Grant's terms, 256; reports pillaging by Federals, 257; becomes a prisoner, 258; his last meeting with Grant, 258–259

Buel, Col. W. H., an imposter, 128

Buell, Maj. Gen. Don Carlos, 112, 136, 159, 167, 168, 179, 186, 219, 239, 241, 242, 278, 314, 329, 338, 339, 344, 350, 378, 382, 385, 405, 409, 419, 435; receives command of the Department of the Ohio, 102; McClellan's instructions, 130–132; Sherman informs Thomas of his arrival, 137; urged by McClellan to move into East Tennessee, 139; recommends movement on Bowling Green and Nashville, with use of the Cumberland and Tennessee, 141–144; receives sharp telegram, then approval from McClellan, 142–143; wants Halleck to threaten Columbus, 142; actions with regard to move on Cumberland Gap, 139–146; receives from McClellan letters of Carter to Maynard, 144; his equivocal position, 145–146; reports he is leaving Zollicoffer alone, 146–147; reports engagement near Mundfordville, 147; reports strong Union sentiment in Kentucky, 149–150; strength of his command, 150; describes his intentions differently to the Adjutant General and to McClellan, 150; urged by Lincoln to cooperate with Halleck, 160; answers that McClellan will make plan, 160; gives Halleck an estimate of the situation, 161; urges a stroke at the Bowling Green-Columbus line, 162; informs Lincoln he never favored move toward East Tennessee, 162; informed of Halleck's demonstration, 164; wins his case for advance on Bowling Green but repents, 166–167; directs Thomas to move against Zollicoffer, 169; orders road construction, 170–171; reports victory at Mill Springs, 176; says it is impractical to continue toward East Tennessee, 188; queries Thomas about the situation, 188; his reaction to Halleck's order for a forward move, 195; stresses importance of the Fort Henry operation, 202; tells McClellan it is hazardous, 208; congratulates Halleck and promises a brigade, 210; is praised by Ass't Sec. Scott but criticized by press, 212; undecided as to his actions, 218; telegraphs about rescuing Halleck's column, 221; fears attack on Paducah, 224, 230; decides to use land and water to advance, 231; telegraphs McClellan about Fort Donelson, 248; promises Halleck a division, 250; reports about his advances on Bowling Green and East Tennessee, 251; Halleck wants him sent to Clarksville, 260; suggests meeting Halleck at Smithland, 264; informs Halleck enemy is concentrating at Nashville, 268; location of his divisions, 269; approaches Nashville, 277–278; his alarm upon arriving, 279–281; Grant's trip to Nashville to see him, 281; McClellan proposes he operate against Chattanooga, 284; informs McClellan about Garfield, 285–286; Lincoln's characterization, 308; comes under command of Halleck, 308; expected by the Confederates at Corinth, 315; his march from Nashville to Savannah, 324–328; his effective strength, 325; reports about destroyed bridge, 327; made major general, 334; Grant reports his approach, 337; he wishes to stop at Waynesboro, 351; informs Grant of time of his arrival, 351; reaches Savannah, 353; his post-war statement and comments about him, 353, 383; informed by Grant of his order to Nelson, 356; holds Nelson back, 370; his statement about Ammen's contribution at Shiloh, 379; in Battle of Shiloh, 381–393; his congratulatory order, 394; authorizes Andrew's first raid, 400–401; his instructions to Mitchel, 400, 408, 422, 425; assigned the center in Halleck's army and protests, 411; in advance on Corinth, 411–416; takes over pursuit of Beauregard, 420, 421; his attitude toward the Andrews raid and Mitchel, 427; comment on, 427–428, 433; his part in Halleck's plan, 429; reaches Huntsville and has supply problem, 433

Buffalo, N. Y., 103
Buford, Col. Napoleon Bonaparte, at Battle of Belmont, 84–85
Bull Run, Battle of (First), 31, 103, 258, 286, 382
Burkesville, Ky., 170, 171
Burnside, Maj. Gen. Ambrose, 252, 341
Butler, Maj. Gen. Benjamin, 339;

makes suggestion about Vicksburg, 430
Butler, William, 400

Cabinet, 105; meeting on Trent case, 154–155
Cairo, Ill., 14, 41, 49, 52, 56, 58, 70, 71, 75, 82, 85, 96, 102, 109, 114, 119, 126, 152, 165, 179, 184, 190, 191, 193, 206, 212, 240, 257, 269, 272, 274, 433; Lincoln's concern about, 51; Grant opens headquarters at, 51; Cullum sent to, 210; Trollope's view of, 226; Ass't Sec. Scott considers it vulnerable, 240; word arrives about Ft. Donelson, 260; gunboats ordered back for its protection, 265; Beauregard plans attacking, 286
Cairo, gunboat, 345–346, 376
California, Grant's service in, 4
California, Mo., 43
Callender, Eliot, quoted, 200
Cameron, Simon, Sec. of War, 105, 159; telegraphs Frémont, 35; replies to Frémont's statement about western Ky., 54; his inspection trip to the West, 64–65; makes issue with Lincoln by his report, 153; sent to Russia as minister, 191
Camp Beauregard, Ky., 227
Camp Dick Robinson, Ky., 110
Camp Douglas, Chicago, 257
Camp Halleck, Tenn., 220
Camp Jackson, St. Louis, 128; captured by Lyon and Blair, 16
Camp Yates, Ill., 13, 18; Grant made mustering officer at, 14
Canal at Island No. 10, 398
Canby, Brig. Gen. Edward R. S., at Battle of Valverde, 341
Cape Girardeau, Mo., 47, 57, 59, 75–77, 80, 82, 85, 299, 334; Grant at, 48–51
Captures. See Casualties
Carondelet, gunboat, at Fort Henry, 203, 205, 218; at Fort Donelson, 225, 230, 238, 256; reaches Cairo with word about Fort Donelson,

260; runs guns of Island No. 10, 398
Carr, Col. Eugene A., 288; at Battle of Pea Ridge, 291
Carroll, Anna Ella, comments on the Frémonts, 76; her claim to have originated Tennessee River campaign, 76, 448–452
Carroll, Brig. Gen. William H., C.S., 147, 149
Carter, Col. James, penetrates gap in East Tenn., 341–343
Carter, Brig. Gen. Samuel P., 139, 143, 144, 251, 325, 328; urges move on Cumberland Gap, 136; asks for ammunition, money, and regimental flags, 140; expresses pleasure over prospect of forward move, 140; reports to Congressman Maynard about the situation, 144; desires to return to vicinity of Cumberland Gap, 146; at Battle of Mill Springs, 174; operations in Eastern Ky., 286
Carter, Capt. William B., destroys bridges in East Tennessee, 138–139
Caseyville, Ky., 122
Cassville, Mo., 68, 288, 292
Casualties (including captures), at Belmont, 84; near Lexington, Mo., 117; at Mill Springs, 175; at Fort Henry, 205; at Fort Donelson, 258, 506–507; at New Madrid, 299; at Shiloh, 394; at Island No. 10, 399; at Wilson's Creek, 462; at Pea Ridge, 512
Cavanaugh, Col. T. H., 168
Cave in Rocks, Ill., 122
Centerville, Va., 208
Cerro Gordo, Tenn., 222
Chalmers, Brig. Gen. James R., C.S., at Battle of Shiloh, 376–378
Chancellorsville, Battle of, 392
Charleston, Mo., 55, 78, 82, 84, 85, 96
Charleston, S. C., 7, 275, 402, 423
Charm, Confederate transport, 83
Chase, Salmon P., Sec. of Treas., 307; receives report from Anderson, 50; shows Stanton telegram from Mitchel, 408

Chattanooga, Tenn., 138, 213, 222, 261, 286, 321, 322, 400–404, 408, 409, 437; McClellan suggests operation against, 284; Mitchel advances toward, 424; Negley's attack on, 425–426

Cheatham, Brig. Gen. B. Franklin, C.S., at Battle of Belmont, 99

Chetlain, Augustus L., elected captain of the Galena company, 11–12

Chicago, Ill., 6, 87, 103

Chicago Evening Journal, cited, 88

Chicago Tribune, cited, 88–90, 344, 417

Chickamauga Creek, Ga., 404

Chickasaw, Ala., 312, 337, 345–347

Chillicothe, Mo., 115

Choctaws. *See* Indians

Church, Col. William, cited, 4

Cincinnati, O., 2, 4, 109, 111, 142, 191, 305, 336; Anderson goes to as point of observation, 47, 50; Stanton appeals to Board of Trade in, 340

Cincinnati, gunboat, 220, 240; at Fort Henry, 206; at Plum Run Bend, 422

Cincinnati Commercial Tribune, cited, 47, 417

Cincinnati Daily Gazette, cited, 391

Clarksville, Tenn., 120, 218, 220, 224, 231, 253, 278, 280; Halleck wants Buell sent to, 260; taken by Foote, 273; occupied by Smith, 275–276

Cleburne, Brig. Gen. P. R., C.S., at Battle of Shiloh, 366, 386

Cleveland, O., 201, 220

Cleveland Herald, cited, 89

Cleveland, Grover, President, at Grant's funeral, 259

Clifton, Tenn., 287, 334

Clinton, Tenn., 133, 426

Columbia, Ky., 139, 146, 170

Columbia, Tenn., 273, 325, 352, 400, 402, 408, 409, 424, 433; Buell delayed by destroyed bridge, 326; new bridge completed, 337

Columbia River, 4

Columbus, Ky., 61, 75, 77, 83, 85, 86, 124, 125, 160, 162, 190, 231, 240, 241, 281, 321, 419; Frémont in-

forms Washington enemy may occupy, 48; Grant reports he can take the position, 54; seized by the Confederates, 55; Grant's demonstration against, 78–86; Buell wants it threatened by Halleck, 142; described by Halleck as very strong, 179; abandonment of provided for by Johnston, 216; Halleck fears an attack from, 260, 264; Beauregard predicts it will meet the fate of Fort Donelson, 266; its abandonment ordered, 286, 287; evacuation and Federal occupation, 296; strength of, 296–297, 340

Columbus, O., 191, 201

Columbus-Bowling Green R.R., strategical value of, 156

Comanches. *See* Indians

Commerce, Mo., 48, 77, 92, 261; selected as base for Pope, 270, 293

Committee from Alabama and Mississippi, 124

Conestoga, gunboat, 122, 159, 164, 277; reconnoiters Fort Henry and Fort Donelson, 119–121; at Fort Henry, 200; on raid up the Tennessee, 209, 221, 225; at Fort Donelson, 237, 257

Conger, Col. Arthur L., cited, 78, 87, 94, 245, 247, 313, 331, 352, 414, 441

Congress, Confederate, votes Missouri and Kentucky into the Confederacy, 150; Federal, 28, 59, 112, 113, 276

Cook, Maj. J. N., commended by Grant to Lincoln, 432

Cook, Col. John, 51, 53, 75, 183, 359

Cooper, Gen. Samuel, Adjutant General, C.S., 58, 98–99, 148, 213, 251, 286, 402

Coppée, Henry, cited, 441

Corinth, Miss., 284, 287, 314, 315, 318–320, 325, 334, 347, 354, 362, 382, 393–396, 402, 408, 413, 419, 421, 424; Halleck predicts strong fortification of, 306; Grant reports enemy strength, 311, 337, 352; he prepares to move against the position, 328–329; stopped by

Halleck, 329; he reports enemy reenforcements arriving, 330; Johnston's conference, 335; Beauregard advises return to Corinth from before Shiloh, 356; his retreat to, 390; Halleck's advance against, 411–416; Federal reports of enemy strength, 412, 422; position abandoned by Beauregard, 416–417; the Federal pursuit, 418–422

Corpus Christi, Tex., 3

Correspondents, puzzled by Grant's demonstration, 184

Cotton, Grant sends consignment to Louisville, 335

Councils of War by Confederate generals, at Bowling Green, 213–216; at Fort Donelson, 242, 254; at Corinth, 415

Courts. Martial, 161

Covington, Ky., 111; residence of Jesse R. Grant, 1; Ulysses visits, 18

Crab Orchard, Ky., 135, 137, 139

Creeks. See Indians

Crisp house, Grant's headquarters at Fort Donelson, 243

Crittenden, Maj. Gen. George B., C.S., 146; takes over Zollicoffer's command, 171; attacks Thomas at Logan's Crossroads, 171–176; his reports about the battle, 177; charges of intemperance and later career, 177

Crittenden, Brig. Gen. Thomas L., 360; at Battle of Shiloh, 381–385, 393

Cropper, Mr., Federal guide, 77

Cross Hollow, Ark., 288, 289

Crumps Landing, Tenn., 314, 315, 318, 328, 360, 362, 376; Grant prepares for enemy attack on, 348–349

Cullum, Brig. Gen. George W., Halleck's chief of staff, 218, 220, 225, 226, 233, 238, 257, 261, 271, 276, 277, 304; sent to Cairo, 210; directed to stop regiments if necessary, 233; compliments and cautions Grant, 252; telegraphs McClellan about Fort Donelson,

260; not alarmed over danger of attack, 264; receives progress report from Grant, 267; receives instructions from McClellan, 275; reports about New Madrid, 293; enters Columbus, 296; urges Foote to attack Island No. 10, 298; his devotion to duty, 301; Halleck queries him about neglect of orders, 302

Cumberland Ford, Ky., 132, 325

Cumberland Gap, Ky.–Tenn., 131, 132, 133, 134, 135, 137, 139, 142, 269, 286, 328, 408; Lincoln's plan to enter, 109; Carter desires to return to vicinity of, 146; Confederate strength, 149; Gen. George Morgan reports from vicinity of, 407; seized by Morgan, 438

Cumberland Iron Works, Tenn., 126

Cumberland River, 61, 102, 118, 122, 142, 152, 156, 158, 186, 243, 286, 287, 325, 361; Confederate efforts to block as invasion route, 120–121; recommended to Halleck by Whittlesey, 123; to McClellan by Buell, 142; favored by Halleck, 179–180

Curtis, Gen. Samuel R., 127, 128, 179, 218, 250, 274, 340, 414, 435, 440; gives report about Frémont, 64–65; transmits order for removal of Frémont, 65; receives directions from McClellan to take charge in St. Louis, 67; telegraphs Washington about Frémont and McKeever's report on Grant, 91; upbraided by "Naomi," 129; ordered to move against Price, 169; moves against Price and Van Dorn, 287–291; at Battle of Pea Ridge, 291–293; given command of Kansas troops, 308; he reports about Van Dorn and Price, 406; his part in Halleck's plan, 429

Dan, Julia Grant's houseman, 5

Dana and Wilson, cited, 93

Danville, Ky., 133, 137, 170

Danville, Miss., 418

Davies, Brig. Gen. Thomas A., given command of Smith's old division, 410; in advance on Corinth, 413

Davis, Flag Officer Charles H., 430; at Plum Run Bend, 422; at Battle of Memphis, 423

Davis, Judge David, 304

Davis, Jefferson, President, C.S., 6, 118, 148, 149, 194, 215, 258, 265, 354, 393; reluctantly approves seizure of Columbus and Hickman, 55; his regard for A. S. Johnston, 73; congratulates Polk on Battle of Belmont, 98; approves hanging of bridgeburners, 147; issues proclamation offering amnesty to Kentuckians, 198; assures Johnston of his confidence in him, 323–324; notified of Johnston's move against Pittsburg Landing, 347–348; asks Beauregard to explain about Corinth, 418

Davis, Col. Jefferson C., 288; relieves Grant at Jefferson City, 46

Decatur, Ala., 222, 250, 284, 321, 322, 325, 382, 400, 409, 425, 433; occupied by Mitchel, 403

Democratic Conventions of 1860, 7

Demonstrations, ordered by McKeever, 75–78; ordered by Halleck, 164–165

Dennison, William, governor of Ohio, sends regiments to Frémont, 35–36

Dent, Emma, sister of Julia Dent Grant, 3

Dent, Col. Frederick, father of Julia Dent Grant, Grant's letter to, 12

Dent, Mrs. Frederick, 3

Dent, Frederick, Jr., classmate of Grant, 3; Grant quotes from his letter, 12–13

Dent, Julia. See Grant, Julia Dent

Departments: of the Cumberland, 47, 102; of Kansas, 102, 119, 308; of Kentucky, 47; Middle Department, 101; of the Mississippi, 219, 308; of the Missouri, 102, 103, 219; of the Monongahela, 101; of the Ohio, 102, 130, 219; of the Susquehanna, 101; of the

West, 13; Western Department, 23, 65, 67, 75, 102

Des Arc, Ark., 393

Detrick, Capt. John E., at Belmont, 94

Detroit, Mich., 4, 201

Dickey, Col. T. Lyle, 357

Districts: of Cairo, 252; of Mississippi and Cairo, 440; of North Missouri, 24; of Southeastern Missouri, 47; of West Tennessee, 252

Dogtooth Bend, 165

Doniphan, Mo., 274; capture of, 224

Dougherty, Col. Henry, at Belmont, 81

Douglas, Stephen A., 7, 10

Dove, Commander Benjamin M., at Fort Donelson, 244, 253, 256

Dover, Tenn., 121, 145, 161, 165, 205

Duck River, Tenn., 318, 325, 337, 344

Duffield, Col. William W., 437–438

East Tennesseans, 111; their uprising, 137–139; pay severe penalty, 147; Lincoln describes their plight, 163; McClellan's sympathy for, 167

East Tennessee, 131, 132, 135, 136, 138, 145, 146, 158; Lincoln's plan for, 109–112; move toward, 132–144; called a powder key by Col. Leadbetter, 149; Lincoln asks Buell about move to, 162; operation stressed by Lincoln and McClellan, 162–163; changed decisions about, 166–167

Eastport, Miss., 287, 337, 347

Eastport, captured Confederate gunboat, 227

Eddyville, Ky., 72

Elkhorn Tavern, Ark., 340

Ellet, Col. Charles, Jr., ordered to construct ram fleet, 339–340; at Battle of Memphis (fatally wounded), 423

Elliott, Aaron, comments on Grant, 18

Elliott, Col. Washington L., 415; makes successful raid, 418

Elliott's Mill, Ky., 78

Emerson, John W., his claim about the Tennessee River campaign, 454–455

England, danger of war with, 153

Essex, gunboat, 198, 199, 206, 221; at Fort Henry, 205

Eureka, Cal., 4

Fair Oaks, Battle of, 419

Fairfax, Va., 342

Falling Waters, W. Va., 111

Farmington, Mo., 29

Farmington, Tenn., 411, 413, 415

Farragut, Rear Admiral David G., captures New Orleans, 423; his efforts to take Vicksburg, 430, 431, 440

Fayetteville, Ark., 31, 274, 288, 292

Fayetteville, Tenn., 400, 402

Fishing Creek, Ky., 171, 174

Fleming County, Ky., 402

Flemingsburg, Ky., 400

Florence, Ala., 222, 230, 287, 316, 409, 424, 433; Buell queries about bridges at, 351

Florida, 319; Federal successes in, 341

Florida, Mo., 20, 21

Floyd, Brig. Gen. John B., C.S., 73, 149, 218, 230, 231; ordered into Fort Donelson, 232; takes command and reports optimistically to Johnston, 234; reports on Federal gunboat attack, 237–238; makes plan of abandonment, 242; his frustrated sortie, 244–248; turns over command and escapes, 254–255; sent to Chattanooga, 321

Foote, Flag Officer (Commodore) Andrew H., 159, 198, 224, 238, 245, 267, 370; to cooperate in Grant's demonstration, 165; reports four ironclads about ready, 190; sends dispatch to Halleck supporting Grant's proposal about Fort Henry, 189; at Fort Henry, 200–206; returns to Cairo, 206; comments about in press, 212; his courtesy mentioned by Tilghman, 217; preaches at Cairo, 220; declines to run Fort Donelson's guns, 220; has trouble with personnel, 226; reports gunboats going to the Cumberland, 226; prepares to attack Fort Donelson, 235; the attack fails, 237; wounded, 243; his statement about the naval battle, 243; Grant informs him of the enemy sortie, 244; his report to Welles about Fort Donelson, 262; congratulates Grant, 277; hesitant to attack Island No. 10, 298; in capture of Island No. 10, 397–399; relieved of command because of wound, 422

Force, Col. Manning F., cited, 337–338, 373, 378, 388

Forney, John W., 276

Forrest, Col. Nathan B., C.S., escaped from Fort Donelson, 255; captures Murfreesboro, 437–438

Fort Craig, N. Mex., 341

Fort Crawford, Wis., 6

Fort Donelson, Tenn., 120, 123, 142, 159, 184, 188, 205, 216, 227, 248, 275, 302, 303, 313, 331, 361, 365, 370, 439, 440; reconnoitered by *Conestoga,* 121; Johnston's view about its defensibility, 124; Grant reports he will move against it, 207; Bushrod Johnson takes command at, 217–218; is reenforced by Johnston, 218; Pillow takes command, 221; Grant's march to, 229–230; investment of, 232–233, 235–237; gunboat attack fails, 238; Confederate plan to abandon, 242; defeated sortie, 244–248; Lincoln's great concern about success at, 253; surrender of, 254–258; pillaging at, 257; casualties, 258

Fort Heiman, Tenn., 227

Fort Henry, Tenn., 123, 142, 145, 159, 161, 164, 183, 184, 188, 190, 194, 287, 302, 313, 334, 440; described by Smith, 119; its armament reported, 122; Grant's move against, 199–200; Tilghman's comment about, 203; capture of, 203–205; comment on the operation, 206; McClernand attempts to change name to Fort Foote, 217

Fort Holt, Ky., 75, 78, 126, 127, 190

Fort Humboldt, Ore., Grant at, 4

Fort Leavenworth, Kans., 59, 288; headquarters, Department of Kansas, 102

Fort Moultrie, S. C., 188

Fort Pillow, Tenn., 216, 321, 406, 407, 412, 422; abandoned, 423

Fort Randolph, Tenn., abandoned, 423

Fort Sumter, S. C., 1, 10, 103, 188, 423

Fort Vancouver, Grant at, 4, 303

Fort Warren, Mass., 155

Fort Winnebago, Wis., 6

France, 153

Frankfort, Ky., 55, 58, 59

Franklin, Ky., 239

Franklin, Tenn., 325, 326

Franklin, Brig. Gen. William B., 208

Fredericktown, Mo., 28, 29, 40, 299

Frémont, Mrs. Jessie Benton, 23, 76; goes to Washington as husband's emissary, 60–62

Frémont, Maj. Gen. John C., 25, 31, 40, 41, 43, 56, 57, 72, 75–78, 106, 112, 114, 128, 273; presidential candidate in 1856, 7; appointed major general and assigned to Western Department, 23; his delay annoys Lincoln, 23; difficulties confronting him, 23–24; sends Grant to Ironton, 24, 29; reports to Cameron about Battle of Wilson's Creek, 34; telegraphs Montgomery Blair, 35; reports falsely that Grant is attacked, 35; declares martial law in St. Louis, 36; Lincoln's message to, 37; recalls Grant from Ironton, 41; his St. Louis headquarters, 42–43; sends Grant to Jefferson City, 43; assigns him to District of Southeastern Missouri, 47–48, 50; informs Lincoln Confederates may seize Columbus, Ky., 54; admonishes Grant, 58; requests irregular reports from McClernand, 58; his proclamation about Missouri and Lincoln's

reaction, 59–61; sends his wife to Washington to defend him, 60–62; suggests operation against Nashville, 61; quarrels with Frank Blair, 61–64; quarrels with Gov. Gamble, 63; his irregular appointments, 64; reports the enemy capture of Lexington, 64; takes the field, 64–65; advances on Springfield, fears an attack, relieved of command, 66–67; reaches St. Louis and has report made about Battle of Belmont, 91; not given a new assignment, 103

Front Royal, Va., 413

Frost, Brig. Gen. Daniel M., C.S., 16

Fry, Col. James B., Buell's chief of staff, 139, 281, 425, 438; reports to McClellan for Buell, 269; his criticism of Mitchel and Andrews, 427

Fry, Brig. Gen. Speed S., 176; at Battle of Mill Springs, 172–174

Fuller, Maj. Gen. J. F. C., cited, 331, 529

Fuller, Capt. William A., C.S., 404

Galena, Ill., 1, 5–7, 30; receives word of Lincoln's call for troops, 10; offers company, 12

Gamble, Hamilton R., governor of Missouri, 46; Frémont's quarrel with, 63

Gantt, Col. E. W., C.S., commander at New Madrid, 297

Garfield, Brig. Gen. James A., 284, 325, 328, 342; operations in Eastern Kentucky, 251–252, 285–286; ordered to Buell's main army, 339; at Battle of Shiloh, 387–388

"General," locomotive stolen by Andrews' raiders, 404

Georgetown, O., 278; Grant's boyhood home, 1

Georgia, 263, 406; governor of, 425

Germans, in Missouri, attitude of, 24; Hunter asks that slander about German regiments be corrected, 68; Halleck comments on their attitude and behavior, 181, 197;

accused by Confederates of atrocities, 292

Gettysburg Campaign, 101; Lincoln's Gettysburg announcement, 176

Gladden Road, at Shiloh Park, 395

Gladesville (Glade Spring), Va., 251

Goldsborough, Commodore L. M., 252–253

Governors, of western states promise war support, 107–108

Governors Island, N. Y., 4

Grand Junction, Tenn., 216, 319

Granger, Brig. Gen. Gordon, in advance on New Madrid, 295; before Corinth, 415

Grant, Hannah Simpson, mother of Ulysses, 4

Grant, Jesse R., father of Ulysses, 1, 7, 13, 23; interested in sending Ulysses to West Point, 2; moves to Bethel and becomes mayor, 4; enters business at Galena, Ill., 5; letters from Ulysses, 13, 15, 17, 22, 49

Grant, Julia Dent, meets and marries Ulysses, 3–4; her children, 4–5; her attitude on the war, 15; Grant's letter to her after Belmont, 88

Grant, Mary Francis, sister of Ulysses, 14; letters from Ulysses, 14, 28–29, 69, 71–72, 185, 221

Grant, Orvil, brother of Ulysses, 1, 7; in father's Galena store, 5

Grant, Samuel Simpson, brother of Ulysses, 1, 7, 8, 14; in father's Galena store, 5

Grant, Maj. Gen. Ulysses S., 1, 88, 96, 102, 106, 123, 159, 180, 194, 206, 218, 273, 280, 289, 295, 301–302, 321, 338, 344, 374, 414, 422, 428, 439; his life through West Point, 1–3; assigned to 4th Infantry, 3; becomes engaged to Julia Dent, 3; Mexican War record, 3–4, 8–9; his marriage and children, 4–5; service in U. S. and on Pacific Coast, 4–5; resigns from the Army, 5; farming and business ventures in Missouri, 5; enters father's business at Galena, Ill., 5–8; expects war, 7; helps organize Galena company and goes to Springfield, 11–13; writes Col. Dent about Northern feeling, 12–13; writes father about the crisis, 13, 15, 17; writes sister of the situation, 14; appointed mustering officer at Camp Yates, 14; observes move against Camp Jackson, 16–17; offers services to government but letter is lost, 17; calls on McClellan at Cincinnati, early acquaintance with, 17–18; stops to see Joseph J. Reynolds, 18; takes command of 21st Illinois, 18–19; moves to Quincy and Palmyra, 19–20; his "trepidation" over responsibility of command, 19–20, 21; moves against Harris, 20–21; at Mexico, Mo., 21–22; promoted to brigadier general, 22; pleased with progress of his regiment, 23; ordered to Ironton and activities at, 24–30; prepares to move against Hardee, 37–40; relieved by Prentiss, 41; comments on his service at Ironton, 37–38, 39–40, 41; Grant's remarks about McClellan's headquarters, 42; sent to Jefferson City, service there, 43–47; sent to District of Southeastern Missouri, 47; Frémont's instructions, 47–48, 50; at Cape Girardeau, 48–49; difficulty with Prentiss, 50–52; goes to Cairo, 51; suppresses dispatch, 52; writes to Washburne, mentioning offer to Rawlins, 52; reports about Sikeston and New Madrid, 52–53; orders Col. Waagner back from Belmont, 53; informs Frémont he could take Columbus, Ky., 54; reports seizure of Columbus and Hickman by the Confederates, 55–56; seizes Paducah, 56–58; reproved by Frémont, 58; reports about Columbus, 58, 69, 70, 71; contrasted with Frémont, 59; his part in Frémont's Nashville plan, 61; tells sister the war is formidable, 69; appoints Rawlins his adjutant, 70; seeks to stop river commerce with the enemy, 70, 127; preparations for winter and care of sick, 70–71; visits Gov. Yates to obtain equipment, 71; gets uniform and sends picture to his sister, 71; writes father with regard to appointments, 71; sends expedition toward Ironton, 72; his first dispatch from Sherman, 72; suggests expedition to Gen. Smith, 72–73; organization of his command, 75; reports he could take Columbus but for deficiency in transportation, 75; directed to make demonstrations, and his orders, 76–78; complexity of his mission, 80; receives new report and decides to attack Belmont, 81; the Battle of Belmont, 83–85; his reports, 85–86; solicitude for wounded and congratulatory orders to troops, 87; communications with Polk, 87–88, 100; his letter to his wife about the battle, 88; McKeever reports he disobeyed orders, 91; receives telegram from McClellan, 91; congratulated by McClellan in orders, 92; his action at Belmont analyzed, 93–95; reported by Polk as killed, 98; his comment on Hunter, 103; action on McClellan's order to report direct, 106–107; reports about Columbus garrison and condition of his command, 124–125; his alert against attack, 125–126; justifies shooting marauders, 127; admonished by Halleck, 128–129; his district enlarged, 151–152; Rawlins' report to Washburne, 152; strength of Grant's command, 152, 166; writes Buell about suppressing smuggling across the Ohio, 152; reports he has map of Columbus defenses, 152; asks permission to visit St. Louis to explain desired move, 164; makes demonstration ordered by Halleck, 164–166, 169; takes Smith's part in a controversy, 168; reports

about his demonstration and renews request to visit headquarters, 183; seeks to get crews for the new gunboats, 184; his demonstrations as viewed by the Confederates, 184; his report to his sister, 185; sends Baxter to Washington with letter to Washburne, 185–186; received coldly by Halleck at St. Louis, 186; telegraphs Halleck he can take and hold Fort Henry, 189; his preparations and departure, 196–198; reconnoiters Fort Henry, 199–200; examines mine, 200; issues order for attack, 201; reports capture of Fort Henry and says he will take Fort Donelson, 206–207; his courtesy mentioned by Tilghman, 217; move on Donelson prevented by high water, 217; issues strong order on discipline, 220; reconnoiters Fort Donelson, 221; asks cooperation of Foote, 224–225; issues warning order, 225; sends Walke to the Cumberland, 225; wires Washburne, urging confirmation of Smith, 225; issues order for move on Fort Donelson, 227–228; his march to Fort Donelson, 229–230; investment of, 232–233, 235–237; calls Lew Wallace from Fort Henry, 233; informs Halleck of arrival of Floyd and reenforcements in the fort, 234; persuades Foote to attack, 235; reports severe fall in temperature and arrival of reenforcements, 235; informs Cullum a siege will be necessary but assures him of success, 238; confers with Foote on his flagship, 243; finds Confederates have made a sortie, 244; orders a counterattack, 245–246, 248; is given command of the District of West Tennessee, 252; plans assault on Fort Donelson, 253–254; receives Buckner's note about capitulation, 254; stipulates unconditional surrender, 255;

Buckner's former favor to him, 256; reports surrender of Fort Donelson, 257; offers financial aid to Buckner and his last meeting with him, 258–259; reports about plundering and prisoners, 261; recommended for promotion, 261; issues congratulatory order to his troops, 263; confirmed by Senate as major general, 265; acknowledges Sherman's cordial note, 267; tells Cullum he can take Nashville, 267; reorganizes his command into four divisions, 275; reports readiness to move, 276; orders Nelson to continue to Nashville, 278; reports about Nashville, 278; gets command in shape for move, 281; visits Nashville and sees Buell, 281; reports information from Memphis, 281; calls on Mrs. James K. Polk, 281–282; actions during suspension from command, 303–305; his first acts at Savannah, Tenn., 310–311, 313–315; his reorganized staff, 312–313; his message to Buell, 324; stretching Halleck's orders, he prepares to move on Corinth, 328–329; restrained by Halleck, 329; reports reenforcements arriving at Corinth, 330; indicates to Smith an eagerness to attack, 330; sends maps of his position to Halleck, 331; his failure to intrench, 331–332; writes with confidence to Washburne, 333; reports Buell's bridge building, 334; informs Halleck about shipping cotton, 335; has new dispute with him, 335–336; reports Confederate discontent as told by deserters, 337; reports Buell's approach, 337; his army organization compared with Johnston's, 338; reviews Sherman's division, 346; reports approach of Nelson and sends him message, 347; injured by fall of horse, 348; prepares against attack on Crumps Landing, 348–349; called to Pittsburg Landing by sharp skirmish, 349; receives reports from Sherman on enemy activity, 350; receives message from Buell and replies, 351–352; sends estimate of the situation to Halleck, 352–353; his seniority to Buell, 353; hears gunfire and orders Nelson to march, 359; writes Buell of order to Nelson and sends order to Wood, 359–360; gives warning order to Lew Wallace, 360; at Battle of Shiloh, 361–393; his reports and congratulatory order on Shiloh, 394; responds to Halleck's criticism, 405; writes Mrs. C. F. Smith about her husband's death, 407; made second in command and receives sharp explanation from Halleck, 410–411; his later comment on the Corinth operation, 418; returned to command of his army, 422; his part in Halleck's summer plan, 429; commends a paymaster to Lincoln, 432; repaid for funds stolen from him in Mexico, 432; persuaded by Sherman not to go on leave, 432; narrowly escapes capture on road to Memphis, 432; forwards report about Vicksburg, 433; a new misunderstanding with Halleck, 436; issues order taking command after Halleck's departure, 440; his report on Belmont, 441–442; claims for Grant regarding the Tennessee River campaign, 452–456

Greeley, Horace, editor N. Y. Tribune, 34, 35, 89, 103, 276, 439; contrasts Davis and Lincoln, 154; comments on capture of Fort Henry, 212–213; writes of Union sentiment in the South and predicts end of war, 231; replies to N. Y. Times, 270
Green River, Ky., 148, 210, 325, 438
Greenfield, Mo., 116
Greenville, Mo., 27, 29, 76; Grant plans move on, 37–41
Greer, a farmer near Shiloh church, 345

Grenada, Miss., 216

Groesbeck, Col. John, 35–36

Grose, Col. William, cited, 379

Guerilla Warfare, begins anew in Missouri, 300; in Tennessee, 425

Guerillas, their punishment prescribed by Halleck, 161

Gunboats, Confederate, reconnoiter Cairo, 58, 125; reported building in Tennessee River, 123; at Columbus, 125; at New Madrid, 297–298; fear of at Island No. 10, 397; at Plum Run Bend, 422–423; at Memphis, 423; at Vicksburg, 440

Gunboats, Federal, respected by River people, 53; at Battle of Belmont, 83–85; work on new ironclads pushed, 163–164; crews lacking, 164, 499–500; four ironclads reported about ready, 190; reduce Fort Henry, 203–205; raid up Tennessee, 206, 221–223, 287; attack at Fort Donelson, 237, 247; recalled for protection of Cairo, 265; difficulty in attacking downstream, 298; at Battle of Shiloh, 376–377, 379; at Island No. 10, 398–399; at Plum Run Bend, 422–423; at Memphis, 423; at Vicksburg, 440. *See also Benton, Cairo, Carondelet, Cincinnati, Conestoga, Essex, Lexington, Louisville, Pittsburg, St. Louis, Tyler*

Guntown, Miss., 421, 422

Gwin, Lieut. William, naval officer, 287, 316; at Battle of Shiloh, 376, 377, 382

Halleck, Maj. Gen. Henry W., 24, 112, 114, 118, 126, 127, 152, 159, 163, 176, 200, 220, 243, 269, 296, 334, 337, 374, 399, 409, 413, 432; receives command of Department of Missouri, 102, 109; his previous career, 104–105; meets President and cabinet, 105; his instructions from McClellan, 105–107; reaches St. Louis, 112; his G.O. No. 3 and its condemnation, 112–113; requests and receives authority to declare martial law, 113–114; informed that Price is moving north, his actions, 115; reports to McClellan about the situation and his countermeasures, 115–116; recalls Sherman from Sedalia and gives him leave, 116; commends Pope, 117; reports to McClellan that he cannot spare troops, 118; expresses unfavorable view of Lane, 118–119; asks Smith about Hardee's reported move, 122; receives suggestion for operation up the Cumberland and Tennessee from Col. Whittlesey, 123; approves exchange of prisoners, 127; reports Grant as essential at Cairo, 127; shows ill temper toward him, 128–129; McClellan wishes to draw from Halleck to strengthen Buell, 142; informed Price is in retreat, 150; directs Sigel to prepare to take the field, 151; states he will be able to act up the Cumberland and Tennessee by early February, 1862, 151; issues orders about punishing saboteurs, 151–152; appoints a military commission, 151; urged by Lincoln to support Buell's move on Bowling Green, 160; replies that he hopes to cooperate in a few weeks, 160; informs Buell of his situation and requests he write, 160; issues order about military justice, 161; asks Buell to postpone movement toward Bowling Green, 163; orders demonstration, 164–165; informs Buell of his action, 165–166; declines to remove Smith, 168; acts on sentences of military commission, 168–169; reports that Price's retreat was a ruse, 169; his illness with the measles, 169, 178; outlines plan that uses the Cumberland and Tennessee, 178–180; replies to Lincoln's suggestions about Koerner, 180–181; forwards Baxter's report to McClellan, 182; reports Sherman's health improved, 183; receives Grant brusquely, 186; asks Smith for report about roads, 186; receives telegrams from Grant and Foote urging capture of Fort Henry, 189; elements that entered his decision, 189–191; tells Foote to make preparations, 190; telegraphs McClellan he will order an advance, 192; orders Grant to take Fort Henry, 193–194; gives him full authority about organizing his force, 194; asks that Tennessee be added to his department, 194; reports his actions to Buell, 195; informs McClellan of discontent in German units, 197; has doubts about the new gunboats and the mortars, 197; his actions during the Fort Henry operation, 201–202; reports its capture to McClellan, 207–208; expects counterattack on Fort Henry, 208; urges Buell to support the Tennessee operation, 208; predicts abandonment of Bowling Green, 209; receives congratulations from Stanton, 209; congratulates Foote but overlooks Grant, 210; sends Cullum to Cairo, 210; reports to McClellan about Columbus and Fort Donelson, 210; summarizes the situation to Buell, 210; wants Hitchcock appointed so as to take command on the Tennessee, 218; says he will go to the Tennessee himself, 219; urges that Buell advance by the rivers, 219; recommends new command arrangement for the West, 219; gives instructions to Grant about Clarksville and Fort Henry, 219–220; reports success in Missouri and continues to urge support from Buell, 223–224; urges attack on Clarksville, 224; puts pressure on Foote, 225–226; renews his pleas to Buell, 226, 230–231; continues to send reenforcements to Grant, 226; reports on Union sentiment up the Tennessee, 231; hears rumors of an attack on Cairo, 233; urges Foote and Buell to exert themselves, 233; still regards Grant as temporary commander, 234; requests troops from the East, 241; telegraphs McClellan about Fort Donelson, 249; again urges Buell to come to the Tennessee, 250; reports Curtis's victory, 250; condemns Buell's advance on Nashville and predicts its abandonment, 250; argues with McClellan, 250; cautions Sherman at Paducah, 252; reports hard fighting at Fort Donelson, 257; fears an attack on Grant from Columbus and Nashville, 260; gives order about sick and wounded, 261; recommends promotions and asks for the West, 261; refers to further operations, 261; sees letter to Stanton carried by Ass't Sec. Scott's courier, 262; becomes unsettled over fear of attack and begs Buell for aid, 264, 266; reports success in Arkansas, 265; answers McClellan on question of rank, 266; issues congratulatory order, 266–267; recommends Smith's promotion, 267; recovers from his panic, 269; commutes sentences of bridgeburners, 270; repeats request for unified command, 270, 274; selects Commerce as base for Pope, 270, 293; explains situation to McClellan, 272–273; urges Scott share responsibility, 273; reports about Curtis, 274; answers Stanton on command arrangement, 283; questions Cullum sharply, 283; desires rapid move up the Tennessee, 284; provides for extension of telegraph, 287; plans reenforcement for Curtis, 288; congratulates him for victory at Pea Ridge, and reports on the battle, 292; actions in New Madrid operation, 293, 295, 298; sends Steele into Arkansas, 295; orders attack on Columbus, 296;

congratulates Pope for New Madrid and reports Missouri free of Confederate flags, 299; seeks to win Southerners over, 300; condemns reprisals, 300; denounces Price's authorization of guerillas, 300; comment on Halleck, 301–302; he asks Cullum about neglect of his orders, 302; his removal and restoration of Grant, 303–306; enlarges objective of the Tennessee move, 304; replies to Stanton about command desired, 306; predicts enemy will strongly fortify Corinth, 306; indicts McClellan for his friendship for Buell, 307; criticizes Buell to Scott, 307; opens trade as a ruse, 307; is given the Department of the Mississippi, 308; his instructions to Grant at Pittsburg Landing, 314; Halleck contrasted with McClellan, 325; orders Buell to move to Savannah, 325; sends pontoons up the Tennessee, 326; gives contingent instructions for move on Corinth, 328; holds Grant back, 329; his *Elements* cited, 332; has new dispute with Grant, 335–336; not interfered with by Washington, 338; gives Buell permission to stop at Waynesboro, 351; Grant writes Buell of expecting Halleck, 390; approves Pope's suggestion of a canal at Island No. 10, 397; congratulates him for capture of the island, 400; arrives at Pittsburg Landing, 405; issues congratulatory order and recommends Sherman's promotion, 405; snipes at Grant but stands firmly behind him, 405; calls Pope up the Tennessee, 406; predicts move by Van Dorn and Price, 406; issues order about administrative matters, 407; replies to Lincoln about the Bridgeport bridge, 408; reorganizes his army, 410; explains Grant's position to him in sharp manner, 410–411; answers complaints of

Buell and McClernand, 411; predicts he will be before Corinth in a day, 411; his advance on Corinth, 412–416; reports possession of Corinth, 417; his treatment of and by the press, 417; comment on his Corinth operation, 418, 422; his pursuit of Beauregard, 418–422; makes inaccurate report about Pope's captures, 420; his plan for the summer, 428–431; ordered to send troops to McClellan, cancelled, 434–435; a new misunderstanding with Grant, 435–436; called to Washington to be General in Chief, 437; his endorsement by Sherman and the press, 439; reluctant to go East, 439; bids Sherman cordial farewell, formal toward Grant, 439

Halleck, Mrs. Henry, 105

Hamburg (Hamburg Landing), Tenn., 287, 318, 347, 353, 434

Hamilton, Alexander, 6

Hamilton, Brig. Gen. Schuyler, 419; in New Madrid operation, 294

Hamilton, William S., at Galena, 6

Hampton Roads, Va., 340

Hancock, Brig. Gen. Winfield Scott, 105

Hardcastle, Maj. A. B., C.S., at Battle of Shiloh, 357, 391

Hardee, Maj. Gen. William J., C.S., 41, 74, 321, 420, 421, 440; commands Confederates in northern Arkansas, 26–30, 37–39; Grant prepares to move against, 37; reported by Grant as in Kentucky, 69; Halleck queries Smith about, 122; attends conference at Johnston's headquarters, 213–216; informs Johnston of evacuation of Bowling Green, 239; reports retreat to Murfreesboro, 265; at Battle of Shiloh, 354–356, 363, 366, 386, 391; recommends withdrawal from Corinth, 415

Harney, Brig. Gen. William, 16, 460

Harper's Weekly, cited, 42, 439

Harris, Col. Thomas, C.S., 20–21

Harrison's Landing, Va., 438

Hawkins, Capt. J. P., staff officer to Grant, 313

Hay, John, secretary to Lincoln, 61, 196–197, 301

Hayes, Maj. Charles S., makes raid against railroad, 319

Hayes, Rutherford B., ex-President, at Grant's funeral, 259

Hazen, Col. William B., at Battle of Shiloh, 384

Heiman, Col. A., C.S., 119

Helena, Ark., 295, 440

Henderson, Ky., 281

Henderson, Col. G. F. R., cited, 74, 456

Henry, Gustavus G., senator, C.S., fears invasion up the Cumberland, 120–121; reports favorably about Fort Donelson, 123

Henry County, Mo., 300

Heth, Maj. Gen. Henry, C.S., 118, 148

Hickenlooper, Capt. A., at Battle of Shiloh, 373

Hickman, Ky., 127, 440; seized by the Confederates, 55

High Command, Federal, 130, 159, 176, 277, 413. *See also* Lincoln, Stanton, McClellan

Hildebrand, Col. Jesse, 346; at Battle of Shiloh, 363, 367, 390

Hillyer, Capt. William S., aide to Grant, at Battle of Shiloh, 359, 360

Hitchcock, Maj. Gen. Ethan A., 219; Halleck wants him appointed to take command on the Tennessee, 218; he declines the assignment, 219

Hoel, William R., pilot at Island No. 10, 398

Hollins, Commodore George N., C.S., 126, 216

Holt, Joseph, judge advocate general, makes report about the Andrews raid, 427

Home Guards of Missouri, 16, 17, 27, 43–45, 114

Hooker, Maj. Gen. Joseph, 319, 392

Horn, Stanley F., cited, 323, 502, 507, 515, 532, 542

Hornets' Nest, at Battle of Shiloh, 372, 377, 395

Humansville, Mo., 150

Humboldt, Tenn., 216, 319, 320, 325

Hunt, Capt. William R., C.S., reports about the ordnance situation, 108–109

Hunter, Maj. Gen. David, 91, 118, 176, 197, 219, 234, 241; selected to replace Frémont, 65; relieves him and reports on the situation, 67–68; falls back on Rolla and Sedalia, 68–69; receives command of the Department of Kansas, 102; his past record, 103–104; writes complaining letter to Lincoln, 156–157; thanked by Halleck for sending troops to Fort Donelson, 267; to cooperate with Curtis, 288; retired from Western command, 308

Huntsville, Ala., 321, 322, 400, 401, 402, 403; Mitchel's capture of, 402

Huntsville, Ark., 288

Hurlbut, Brig. Gen. Stephen A., 314, 348, 421; given command of 4th Div. of Grant's army, 275; at Battle of Shiloh, 365–369, 372–377, 381, 384, 385; in advance on Corinth, 413

Illinois, 23, 36, 96, 102, 142, 152, 344

Illinois Central R.R., president of, 152

Illinois River, 19

Indian Territory, operation into mentioned by McClellan, 118

Indiana, 35, 54, 61, 102, 142, 344

Indianapolis, Ind., 191; Ass't Sec. Scott arrives at, 201

Indians, 292; Choctaws, reported atrocities at Battle of Pea Ridge, 282, 340; Comanches, 289; Creeks, chief of, 196; Seminoles, chief of, 196

Iowa, 102, 344; Grant's trips to, 8

Irish Dragoons, 66

Iron Mountain R.R., 72

Ironton, Mo., 48, 59, 274, 299, 334, 440; Grant's service at, 24–30, 37–41

Island No. 10, 216, 297, 298, 299, 318, 321, 419; defense of ordered

by Beauregard, 287; capture of, 396–400
Itra Landing, Tenn., 199
Iuka, Miss., 265, 346

Jacksboro, Tenn., 132, 133, 136, 341–342
Jackson, Miss., 216
Jackson, Mo., 48–51, 53, 57
Jackson, Tenn., 286, 318, 325, 328
Jackson, Claiborne F., governor of Missouri, 117; secession attitude and acts, 15–16; writes Price from New Orleans, 147–148, 156
Jackson, Gen., C.S., almost captures Grant, 432, 437
Jackson, Brig. Gen. John K., C.S., at Battle of Shiloh, 377
Jackson, Lieut. Gen. Thomas J. (Stonewall), C.S., 59, 111, 326, 343, 392, 413
Jacksonport, Ark., 289, 295
James River, 438
Jamestown, Tenn., 132–134
Jasper, Tenn., 425
Jefferson, Thomas, 155
Jefferson Barracks, Mo., 27; Grant assigned to duty at, 3
Jefferson City, Mo., 49, 52, 59, 65, 115, 300; Grant's service at, 43–47
Jennings, Maj., C.S., 224
John Paine, steamer, 335
Johnson, Andrew, Senator, 145, 426; urges move toward Cumberland Gap, 135, 163; appointed military governor of Tennessee, 327; fears Nashville inadequately defended, 339
Johnson, Brig. Gen. Bushrod, C.S., 230, 234, 242, 256; takes command at Fort Donelson, 218; his escape, 258; at Battle of Shiloh, 367
Johnson, George W., Confederate governor of Kentucky, receives quota of new regiments from Benjamin, 198
Johnson County, Mo., 300
Johnston, Gen. Albert Sidney, C.S., 134, 146, 153, 170, 234, 242, 280, 289, 292, 311, 320, 333, 390,

393; previous record and assignment to western command, 73–74; issues proclamation, 74; reports Confederate moves on Paducah and Bowling Green, 74; writes Benjamin about the Cumberland River, 121; informs him that he believes Fort Donelson is defensible, 124; Sherman believes he intends an offensive, 136; asks for secret service money, 137, 148; informs Polk of destruction of bridges in East Tennessee, 138; discerns Buell's intention, 146; writes about the situation hopefully, 148–149; receives report about defeat at Mill Springs, 177; reports to Benjamin about Grant's demonstration, 184; Halleck expects him to try to retake Fort Henry, 208; his strength after fall of Fort Henry, 214; holds conference with Beauregard and Hardee, 213–216; expects Federal gunboats to take Fort Donelson, 218; recovers hopefulness about its defense, 232; reports optimistically to Richmond, 239; reports about battle at Fort Donelson, 253; his prestige damaged by defeats, 265, 322; asks for commander for East Tennessee, 286; recognizes Beauregard as independent commander, 287; his march toward Corinth and comments on, 321–323; President Davis's loyalty to him, 323; he reaches Corinth, 330; organizes Army of the Mississippi, 338; holds conference at Corinth, 338; notifies Davis of his move against Pittsburg Landing, 347–348; his order for attack at Shiloh, and deployment of his army, 354–355; his address to his army, 355; rejects Beauregard's advice to return to Corinth, 356; at Battle of Shiloh (killed), 363, 368, 371
Johnston, Gen. Joseph E., C.S., 147, 191, 213, 259, 419
Johnston, Col. William Preston, C.S.,

son of Gen. A. J. Johnston, 421; cited, 123

Jordan, Col. Thomas, C.S., writes about Johnston's attack order, 354–355; in Battle of Shiloh, 382

Judah, Brig. Gen. Henry M., given command of McClernand's division, 410; in advance on Corinth, 413

Kansas, 31

Kansas-Nebraska Act, 7

Kelton, Capt. John C., adjutant at St. Louis headquarters, 25, 38, 40, 43, 124, 164, 414

Kentucky, 61, 102, 109, 111, 120, 130, 131, 142, 144, 147, 151–152, 159, 319, 344, 393, 438; maintains position of neutrality, 47; Gov. Morton's fear about, 49–50; neutrality violated by Confederates under Polk, 54–55; Union sentiment in eastern part, 132; question of supplies in eastern part, 133, 135; voted into the Confederacy by Confederate Congress, 150

Kentucky River, 325

Kernstown, Battle of, 343

Kingston, Tenn., 426

Kise, Lieut. Col. William C., at Battle of Mill Springs, 172–174

Knights of the Golden Circle, 221

Knoxville, Tenn., 111, 133, 136, 147, 149, 212, 213, 286, 308, 339, 403, 425, 438: Kirby Smith reported at, 328

Knoxville Whig, 149

Koerner, Gustave P., 180–181

Lafayette, Ind., 15

Lagow, Capt. Clark B., Grant's aide, 43; writes 2nd order for Nelson, 362

LaGrange, Tenn., 437

Lake Ontario, 4

Lancaster, O., 129

Lane, James H., senator, 179, 308; his previous record, 119; Lincoln's commitments to, 196; chiefs of Creeks and Seminoles

urge he be sent to lead expedition, 196

Lauman, Brig. Gen. Jacob G., at Fort Donelson, 245, 248

Leadbetter, Col. Danville, C.S., 403, 425; reports East Tennessee a powder keg, 149

Leavenworth, Kans. See Fort Leavenworth

Lebanon, Ky., 139, 142, 143, 150, 170

Lebanon, Mo., 45, 300

Lee, Gen. Robert E., C.S., 101, 102, 213

Lexington, Ky., 110, 111, 117, 136, 142, 318

Lexington, Mo., 45; Confederate capture of, 64

Lexington, gunboat, 159, 225, 316, 346; at Battle of Belmont, 80; on raid up Tennessee River, 209, 221–223; at Battle of Shiloh, 376–378, 381, 395

Liberty, Mo., 45, 139

Lick Creek, Tenn., 316, 347, 355, 390

Liddell Hart, Basil H., cited, 331

Lincoln, Abraham, President, 30, 59, 61, 76, 77, 80, 104, 105, 131, 132, 145, 160, 192, 209, 229, 263, 275, 277, 283, 338; nominated for presidency, 7; his election, 8; calls for troops, 10; appoints general officers, 22; appoints Frémont major general and gives him Western Department, annoyed at his delay, 23; his later comment about Grant, 24; Frémont's alarming telegram, 34; his reply, 37; solicitous about Cairo, 51; informed by Frémont of enemy intention to seize western Kentucky, 54; his reaction to Frémont's proclamation, 60–61; his remark about Mrs. Frémont's visit, 61; apprehensive about Kentucky because of Frémont's act, 63; receives reports about Frémont from Secretary Cameron and Adj. Gen. Thomas, 65; instructions to Curtis as to order for Frémont's removal, 65–

66; his recommendations to Hunter, 67–68; receives disturbing telegram from Sherman, 72; writes McClernand about Battle of Belmont, 92; his discouragement recorded by Nicolay, 109; outlines movement into East Tennessee, 109–112; gives Halleck authority to declare martial law, 114; regrets Halleck's unfavorable opinion of Lane, 118; his involvement with Lane, 119; his action on Cameron's report, 153; his message to Congress, 154; his attitude in *Trent* case, 154–155; because of McClellan's illness he telegraphs Halleck and Buell, 156; replies to Hunter's complaints, 157; urges Halleck to support Buell's forward movement and their full concert of action, 160; asks Buell categorically about move to East Tennessee, 162; displeased by Buell's reply, elaborates reason for East Tennessee move, 162; distressed over general inaction, 164–165; reference to his Gettysburg announcement, 176; proposes Koerner as an aide for Halleck, 180–181; issues his War Order No. 1, 187; his commitments to Lane, 196; his son's illness, 252; greatly concerned about Fort Donelson, 253; approves Stanton's recommendation of Grant's promotion, 261; death of his son, 276; his appraisal of Buell, 308; informs Buell and Halleck of Confederate withdrawal from Centerville, 327; releases his War Order to the press, 342; declines to appoint Pope major general in regular army, 400; assures Halleck he believes he will take Corinth, 413; approves bill reimbursing Grant for loss in Mexico, 432; insists on move toward Chattanooga and criticizes its slowness, 434; impatient for Halleck's arrival, 438–439

Lincoln, William, son of Abraham, illness and death of, 252, 276

Linn Creek, Mo., 45

Little Rock, Ark., 28

Logan, Brig. Gen. John A., 535; as congressman addresses 21st Illinois and introduces Grant, 19

Logan's Crossroads, Thomas arrives at, 171; Battle of, see Battle of Mill Springs

London, England, news from, 343

London, Ky., 135, 139, 144

London Times, cited, 343

Longstreet, Lieut. Gen. James, C.S., cited about Grant, 9

Lookout Mountain, Tenn., 284

Louis Philippe, 272

Louisiana, 3

Louisville, Ky., 47, 110, 111, 130, 137, 160, 191, 335; Sherman in command at, 72; Buell takes command, 137; Ass't Sec. Scott arrives at, 211

Louisville, gunboat, at Fort Donelson, 238, 247, 256

Louisville Journal, cited, 90

Lovelaceville, Ky., 61

Lower California, 406

Lyford, Lieut. Stephen C., naval officer, 249

Lynchburg, Va., 138

Lyon, Brig. Gen. Nathaniel, 22, 65; sends arms to Springfield, 14; captures Camp Jackson, 16; leads expedition to southwest Missouri, 31–32; at Battle of Wilson's Creek (killed), 32–33

Lyons, Lord, British minister, 276

MacGavock, Lieut. Col. R. W., C.S., 121

Madison, James, 155

Maginot Line, 332

Magoffin, Beriah, secessionist governor of Kentucky, 55; compelled to sign Unionist proclamation, 59

Manassas, Va., 253, 286, 327, 328, 342

Manson, Brig. Gen. Mahlon D., 176; at Battle of Mill Springs, 172–174

Marble Creek, Mo., 39

Marietta, Ga., 401–403

Markland, A. H., mail agent, 207

Marsh, Col. C. C., at Ironton, 50

Marshall, Brig. Gen. Humphrey, C.S., 328; commands in eastern Kentucky, 251–252

Martial Law, declared by Frémont, 36; Halleck gets presidential authority for, 114

Mason, James M., Confederate commissioner to Europe, 153

Massachusetts, 162

Matamoros, Mexico, 19; Grant writes Julia about living in Galena, 5

Mattoon, Ill., 18

Mayfield, Ky., 56, 61, 164, 165

Mayfield Creek, Ky., 183

Maynard, Horace, congressman, 145; urges move toward Cumberland Gap, 135, 163; gives letter from Carter to Lincoln, 144; denounces inaction toward East Tennessee, 147

McAllister, Capt. Edward, at Battle of Shiloh, 378

McArthur, Brig. Gen. John, at Fort Donelson, 236–237

McClellan, Maj. Gen. George B., 113, 127, 136, 145–147, 150, 152, 159, 169, 186, 196, 202, 224, 242, 276–278, 325, 326, 338, 406; commands Department of the Ohio, 17; absent when Grant calls, 18; Grant's description of his headquarters, 42; acts to insure order in St. Louis, 67; becomes General in Chief, 77, 102; informed by Smith of firing at Columbus, Ky., 85; telegraphs Grant, 91; congratulates him, 92; his instructions to Halleck, 105–107; plans received from Scott in May, 1861, 107; asks Halleck to support Buell or attack Columbus, 118; speaks of operation into Indian Territory and Texas by Hunter, 118; his instructions to Buell, 130–132; urges move into East Tennessee, 139; sends Buell a sharp telegram, 142; continues to urge move into East Tennessee but gives approval to one toward Nashville and up the rivers, 141–147; speaks of his own intended moves, 143, 163; enjoins Buell to keep East Tennesseans hopeful, 143; inquires as to the depth of the Cumberland and Tennessee, 145; Halleck gives him an important appraisal, 151; his illness, 156; distressed over Buell's attitude and stresses East Tennessee, 163–167; influenced by his own intended operations, 167; contradictory attitude toward Smith, 168; receives comprehensive appraisal from Halleck, 178–180; sends Buell and Halleck telegram about spy's report, 190; action on Halleck's telegram about ordering an advance, 192; told by Buell the Tennessee operation is hazardous, 208; his reaction to capture of Fort Henry, 209; alarmed about Fort Donelson, 234; authorizes diversion of troops from Hunter, 234; rejects Halleck's plan for the West, 241; defends Buell's move on Nashville, and argues with Halleck, 250–251; receives dispatch from Halleck, 260; makes correct appraisal, 268–269; forecasts operations of the Army of the Potomac, 269; telegraphs sharply to Halleck, 271; makes unreasonable demands, 271–272; agrees with Halleck about Curtis, 274; gives instructions directly to Cullum, 275; suggests Halleck aid Buell, 283–284; queries Buell about Garfield, 284; directs Buell to aid Halleck, 284; comment about McClellan, 286; his earlier contact with Grant, 303; authorizes arrest of Grant, 303; removed as General in Chief, 306–307; his post-war comment on Halleck, 307–308; his order to his troops, 342; press dispute about him, 342–343; Stanton reports to Halleck optimistically about his prospects at Richmond, 419–420; Stanton reports his defeat and retreat, 434, 438–439

McClernand, Maj. Gen. John A., 57, 75, 81, 85, 88, 92, 100, 106, 125, 205, 218, 225, 328, 349, 419, 434; as congressman he addresses 21st Illinois, 19; Grant writes him as commander at Cairo, 50; his communications with Frémont, 58, 465–466; at Battle of Belmont, 81, 85; he writes to McClellan, 90; his report and congratulatory order, 90–91; uses Grant's absence to make report about recent demonstration, 187; leads advance against Fort Henry, 199–200; at Fort Henry, 201–203; seeks to change its name to Fort Foote, 217; in investment of Fort Donelson, 230, 233, 236, 237; in the battle at, 244–246; at Savannah, 310; made major general, 334; at Battle of Shiloh, 365, 367, 369, 372, 375, 383–385; given command of the reserve in Halleck's army and protests, 411

McClernand Road, at Shiloh Park, 395

McCook, Brig. Gen. Alexander McD., 269, 337, 410; leads Buell's advance toward Savannah, 326–327; at Battle of Shiloh, 383–388

McCook, Brig. Gen. Robert L., 176; at Battle of Mill Springs, 173–174

McCulloch, Brig. Gen. Ben, C.S., 45, 47, 68, 115, 118, 289, 340; in Battle of Wilson's Creek, 32–33; reports to Richmond about his plans and those of Price, 114; at Battle of Pea Ridge (killed), 291

McDowell, Maj. Gen. Irvin, 57, 215, 258, 382

McDowell, Col. John A., at Battle of Shiloh, 366, 367

McIntosh, Col. James, C.S., at Battle of Pea Ridge (killed), 291

McKean, Brig. Gen. Thomas A., receives command of Thomas's division, 410

McKeever, Capt. Chauncey, 70, 72, 75, 76, 78, 86, 87, 124; directs demonstrations by Grant and Smith, 76; Grant's reports to after Belmont, 85–86; he reports that Grant disobeyed orders, 91

McKinstry, Brig. Gen. Justus, 112

McPherson, Col. James B., 206, 229, 313, 349, 353; assigned to Grant for Fort Henry operation, 194; at Fort Henry, 201; examines Hamburg Landing, 350; at Battle of Shiloh, 360, 361, 369, 372, 379, 380

Meade, Maj. Gen. George G., 101, 176

Meigs, Brig. Gen. Montgomery C., quartermaster general, accompanies Montgomery Blair to St. Louis, 62

Memorandum of Beauregard and Hardee, 215–216

Memphis, Tenn., 28, 53, 107, 108, 120, 147, 190, 216, 220, 263, 274, 281, 287, 313, 319, 325, 393, 412; Sherman moves toward, 421; battle and capture of, 422–423; Grant moves headquarters to, 432

Memphis and Charleston Railroad, Sherman's efforts to cut, 311

Merrimac, Confederate ironclad, 340

Mexican War, 3–4, 8, 13, 14, 22, 28, 76, 102, 104, 119, 289, 332, 374, 406, 432; Scott's treatment of guerillas in, 161; Taylor's and Scott's treatment of prisoners, 255

Mexico, Mo., Grant sent to, 21; secession attitude in, 22–23

Mexico City, Mexico, 3, 9

Michigan, 102, 344; governor of, 414

Milburn, Ky., 97

Military Commission, appointed by Halleck, 151; he approves sabotage sentences, but nullifies those on treason, 169

Mill Springs, Ky., 169; Zollicoffer takes position at, 146; Battle of, 171–176, 265

Mines, reported by Grant near Columbus, 164; taken from Tennessee River, 200

Minnesota, 102, 344

Mississippi, 53, 344; invasion fear in

northern part, 124; governor of, 148, 286

Mississippi River, 50, 78, 107, 109, 158, 180, 361, 396, 397; Scott's early plans for, 107; its importance realized in the South, 108; Grant reports it mined at Columbus with a chain across, 164; rejected by Halleck as proper invasion route, 178–179

Mississippi Valley, 141

Missouri, 54, 55, 67, 78, 102, 114, 142, 273, 344; secession sentiment in, 15–16; in near rebellion, 23–24; voted into the Confederacy by the Confederate Congress, 150; Halleck says withdrawal of troops from is impossible, 160; he reports no more Confederate flags flying in, 200; new guerilla outbreaks, 300; Confederate legislature of, 301

Missouri Compromise, 7

Missouri River, 45, 53, 114, 116

Mitchel, Maj. Gen. Ormsby M., 264, 268, 277, 324, 326, 419, 421, 427, 442–447; reaches Bowling Green with Buell's advance, 239; his operations from Murfreesboro to capture of Huntsville, 400–403; protests about destroying bridge, 408; his operations in northern Alabama, 408–409, 424–428; promoted to major general, 410; asks transfer to Army of the Potomac, 427; leaves Buell's army, 433

Mobile, Ala., 319, 325, 412

Mobile and Ohio R.R., 318

Monarch, ram, at Battle of Memphis, 340

Monitor, armored vessel, 340

Monterey, Tenn., 318, 347, 412; secured by the Confederates, 331

Monterrey, Mexico, 5, 9, 255; Battle of, 3, 319

Montgomery Block, Halleck's connection with its construction, 105

Monticello, Ky., 133

Moore, Col. David, in Battle of Shiloh, 357, 363, 368

Morgan, Brig. Gen. George W., 408; takes over Garfield's command, 339; reports conditions in East Tennessee, 407, 427; takes Cumberland Gap, 438

Morgan, Col. John H., C.S., makes raid on Pulaski, 424–425; makes raid into Kentucky, 438

"Mormon War," The, 73

Morristown, Tenn., 146

Mortar boats, value doubted by Halleck, 197; being tested, 221; Trollope's comment about, 249; their slow advance to the Cumberland, 249

Morton, Oliver P., governor of Indiana, his fear concerning Kentucky, 49–50, 58; shows Halleck's telegram to Ass't Sec. Scott, 201–202; reports pessimistically from before Corinth, 413

Mound City, Ill., 56

Mt. McGregor, N. Y., Buckner's visit to Grant, 258

Mud Town, Ark., poisoning of Federals in, 300

Muldraugh Hill, Ky., 109

Munfordville, Ky., 147

Munson's Hill, Va., 147, 213

Murfreesboro, Tenn., 278, 284, 287, 408, 426; Hardee reports retreat to, 265; Mitchel rebuilds bridge at, 400; captured by the Confederates, 437–438

Murray, Ky., 164, 165

"Naomi," upbraids Curtis, 129

Napoleon, 355; cited, 81, 286; Halleck refers to his treatment of guerillas, 161; used as model by Col. Jordan in preparing order, 354

Nashville, Tenn., 74, 120, 131, 138, 142, 148, 179, 216, 239, 253, 263, 284, 307, 327, 400, 401; ordnance storehouse burned, 148; Lincoln urges Halleck to support Buell's move on, 160; Halleck condemns Buell's move and predicts the city's abandonment, 250; the move defended by McClellan, 250–251; the city reported evacuated, 273, 278; Nelson arrives at,

279; Grant's trip to see Buell, 281
Nassau, Bahama Islands, Federal gunboat at, 148
Nebraska, 344
Negley, Brig. Gen. James S., 424; shells Chattanooga, 425–426
Negroes, 49, 125; Halleck's order regarding escaped slaves, 112–113; use as soldiers recommended by Cameron, 153; Greeley's comment about, 154
Nelson, Brig. Gen. William, 269, 353, 385, 410; arrives at Clarksville and order to Nashville by Grant, 278; reaches Nashville, 279; takes over lead of Buell's march, 338; receives message from Grant, 347; reaches Savannah, 350; ordered by Grant to march to opposite Pittsburg, 359; Grant's 2nd message, 362–363; his 3rd message, 369–370; Nelson's failure to march as ordered, 370; at Battle of Shiloh, 381–385, 392–394
Nevins, Allan, cited, 450
New Albany, Ind., 335, 336
New Bern, N. C., 341
New Madrid, Mo., 52–54, 78, 82, 95, 125, 127, 179, 261, 301, 318, 321, 396–398; defense of ordered by Beauregard, 287; Pope's operations against and capture of, 293–295, 297–299, 340
New Orleans, La., 147, 183, 241, 320, 412, 430; capture of, 423
New York, N. Y., 103, 104
New York Herald, cited, 89, 391, 439
New York Times, cited, 184, 270, 341–343, 439
New York Tribune, cited, 33–34, 49, 63, 103, 138, 212
Nicolay and Hay, cited, 119, 279
Nicolay, John, secretary to Lincoln, cited, 109, 112, 261
Norfolk, Mo., 53
North Carolina, 107
North Missouri R.R., 115

Officers, promotion of, 176, 443, 446–448
Oglesby, Col. Richard, 75, 78, 80, 81,

85, 127, 331; instructed by Grant about defense of Birds Point, 72; Grant's instructions to him for the Belmont operation, 76–77, 78, 82; his report on Belmont, 95–96
Ohio, 102, 141, 344
Ohio River, 47, 53, 102, 152, 158
Okolona, Miss., 418, 435
Osage River, Mo., 65, 115
Osceola, Mo., 300
Osterhaus, Col. Peter J., at Battle of Pea Ridge, 291
Otterville, Mo., 117, 150
Owl Creek, Tenn., 316, 318, 355, 362, 392

Pacific R.R., 43
Padgett, Capt., C.S., 203
Paducah, Ky., 61, 74, 85, 96, 97, 102, 114, 119, 120, 122, 164, 165, 168, 179, 191, 202, 240, 272, 284, 304, 365, 440; seized by Grant, 56–57; C. F. Smith sent to, 57; Buell fears attack on, 224–231; Polk's intended demonstration against, 265–266; Beauregard plans attacking, 286
Paine, Brig. Gen. E. A., 80, 86, 97; in temporary command at Paducah, 56–57; in Columbus demonstration, 96; orders reprisals, 300
Palmer, Brig. Gen. John M., 20; in New Madrid operation, 294
Palmyra, Mo., 19, 20, 151
Palo Alto, Battle of, 3, 319
Panther Creek, Tenn., 199, 203
Parkhurst, Lieut. Col. John G., 437–438
Parrott guns, 182
Patterson, Maj. Gen. Robert, 110
Pea Ridge, Ark., 288; Battle of, 291–292, 340, 342
Pea Ridge, Tenn., 330, 333, 390, 394
Peabody, Col. Everett, at Battle of Shiloh (killed), 357, 368, 391
Peabody Road, at Shiloh Park, 395
Pemberton, Maj. Gen. John C., C.S., 402
Peninsular Campaign, 101
Pensacola, Fla., 319, 320, 325
Perry, steamboat, 127
Phelps, Lieut. S. Ledyard, naval of-

ficer, 190, 231, 316; leads wooden gunboats up the Tennessee, 206, 221–222; enters Columbus, 296

Pike, Brig. Gen. Albert, C.S., 289

Pikeville, Ky., 251, 285

Pillow, Brig. Gen. Gideon J., C.S., 52, 54, 98, 100, 230, 234, 258; his Mexican War record, 15; criticizes Polk's conduct of Battle of Belmont, 99; receives thanks of Confederate Congress for his own conduct there, 99; predicts Federal move up the Tennessee, 124; suggests attack on Cairo, 126; takes command at Fort Donelson, 221; hopeful of successful defense, 231–232; in the sortie from, 244, 247–248; passes the command and escapes, 255

Pilot Knob, Mo., 41, 76

Pitman's Ferry, Ark., 27, 295

Pittsburg, gunboat, at Fort Donelson, 238, 247; runs batteries of Island No. 10, 399

Pittsburg Landing, 328, 334, 344, 386, 393, 406, 409, 434; Grant's concentration at, 310–315; first action at, 315–316; description of, 316–318; Halleck arrives at, 405; for battle, *see* Shiloh

Pittsburgh, Pa., 58, 201, 344

Plum Run Bend, Federals surprised at, 422

Plummer, Brig. Gen. Joseph B., 75, 80, 83, 85; in Belmont operation, 77, 82; in New Madrid operation, 299

Pocahontas, Ark., 274, 289, 295

Point Pleasant, Mo., 298, 299

Point Pleasant, O., Grant's birthplace, 4

Polk, James K., President, 15

Polk, Mrs. James K., Grant calls on, 281–282

Polk, Maj. Gen. Leonidas, C.S., 74, 83, 86, 126, 129, 138, 184, 197, 338, 392, 420; occupies Columbus and Hickman, 55; attitude on exchange of prisoners, 87–88; deceived by Federals and his actions in Battle of Belmont, 96–98; reports victory and is complimented by Davis, 97–98; receives thanks of Confederate Congress, 99; defends himself against Pillow's attack, 99; his comment on Grant, 100; recommendations received from Capt. Hunt, 108; his intended demonstration against Paducah, 265–266; ordered to evacuate Columbus, 287; reports evacuation of, 296; stresses importance of New Madrid, 297; at Battle of Shiloh, 354, 355, 363, 366, 386

Polk, William M., cited, 99–100, 333

Pomme de Terre River, Mo., 66

Pond, Col. Preston, Jr., C.S., in Battle of Shiloh, 382, 383, 386

Pontoons, 326, 352, 378, 433

Pope, Maj. Gen. John, 22, 128, 208, 209, 218, 226, 296, 301, 340, 417, 422; mustering officer at Camp Yates, 13; returns to St. Louis, 14; commands North Missouri District, 24; reports about situation near Sedalia, 115–116; intercepts numerous bands moving to Price, 117; informs Halleck that Price is retreating, 150; his operation against New Madrid, 293–295, 297–299; made major general, 334; captures Island No. 10, 396–400; sent up the Tennessee, 406; in advance on Corinth, 411–416; reports reenforcement of, then evacuation of Corinth, 416–417; in pursuit of the Confederates from Corinth, 418–421; his part in Halleck's plan, 429; called East, 440

Poplar Bluff, Mo., capture of, 224

Porter, Capt. David D., naval officer, 183, 199

Potomac River, 327, 342

Potosi, Mo., attack on, 27

Pound Gap, Ky., 342

Powell, Maj. James E., at Battle of Shiloh (killed), 357, 363

Prairie du Chien, Wis., 6; Grant recovers property at, 8

Prentiss, Brig. Gen. Benj. M., 48, 50, 115, 348, 395; sent to Cairo with Illinois regiments, 14; relieves

Grant at Ironton, 41; declines to obey Grant, 51–52; receives command of Grant's 6th Division, 334; at Battle of Shiloh (captured), 357, 358, 365, 368, 369, 372, 376, 382, 391

Price, Maj. Gen. Sterling, C.S., 78, 81, 86, 114, 116, 118, 128, 148, 161, 250, 289; made commander of Missouri forces, 16; captures Lexington, Mo., 64; retires toward Springfield, 65; Frémont's correspondence with, 67; reported falling back to Arkansas, 68–69; moves toward Missouri River, 115; conflicting reports about, 116; issues proclamation for 50,-000 Missourians, 116–117; reported by Pope to be retreating, 150; his retreat a ruse, 169; correspondence with Halleck, 182; poor discipline in his camp, 182–183; at Battle of Pea Ridge, 291–292; organizes guerillas, 300; reports about his moves and strength, 406

Price's Landing, Mo., 127

Pride, Col. G. G., volunteer aide to Grant, at Battle of Shiloh, 361

Prince, Confederate transport, 83

Princeton, Ky., 72

Prisoners, exchange of, 87–88, 100; Halleck justifies, 127

Proclamations, by Gamble, 46; by McCulloch, 47; by Grant, 56; by Frémont, 59–61, 65; by Johnston, 74; by Price, 116–117; by Zollicoffer, 150; by Davis, offering amnesty to Kentuckians, 198

Pulaski, Tenn., 424, 438

Purdy, Tenn., 314, 318, 319, 348

Queen of the West, ram, in Battle of Memphis, 423

Quincy, Ill., 19

Radicals, approve Frémont's proclamation, 63, pleased by Cameron's recommending Negro troops, 154

Ram Fleet, construction of, 339–340; at Battle of Memphis, 423

Randolph County, Ill., 221

Rappahannock River, Va., 215

Rawlins, Lieut. Col. John Aaron, 41, 180; early life and character, 7–8; at Galena meetings, 10–12; Grant offers position to, 52; joins Grant at Cairo and is appointed adjutant, 70; writes the Belmont order, 81; writes Washburne about reports concerning Grant, 152; in Battle of Shiloh, 359, 362, 372, 379, 380

Reelfoot Lake, Tenn., 396

Regiments, Confederate
Alabama: 1st Cav., 346; Arkansas: 7th, 386; Louisiana: 18th, 316, 377; Mississippi: 3rd, 357; 6th, 366; Tennessee: 23rd, 366

Regiments, Federal
Illinois: 8th, 77; 11th, 77; 12th, 56; 14th, 20; 18th, 77; 21st, 21, 28, 47; 22nd, 81; 27th, 84; 29th, 77; 32nd, 316; 40th, 385; 2nd Cav., 296; 4th Cav., 357; 7th Cav., 297; 11th Cav., 435; 1st Art., 95 (Btry B), 374; Indiana: 10th, 172–174; 11th, 227, 238, 246; 22nd, 384; 24th, 380; 25th, 246; 32nd, 147, 344; 36th, 378, 379; 43rd, 422; 47th, 422; 52nd, 246; Iowa: 2nd, 245, 385; 7th, 81, 248; 10th, 77, 80, 82, 95; 13th, 385; 15th, 361, 367; 16th, 361, 367; 2nd Cav., 415; Kentucky: 1st, 135; 4th, 172–174; 10th, 172, 175; 12th, 171, 174; 1st Cav., 172–174; Michigan: 15th, 383, 385, 393; 2nd Cav., 414, 415; Minnesota: 2nd, 173–174; 3rd, 437; Missouri: 2nd, 21; 6th, 39; 8th, 51, 59, 246, 281, 337; 9th, 28, 40; 14th, 365; 21st, 336, 358; 23rd, 368; 25th, 357; 33rd, 361; 2nd Cav., 117; Ohio: 2nd, 401; 9th, 56, 173–175; 20th, 243, 338; 24th, 381; 49th, 344, 365; 5th Cav., 319, 336, 345, 357; Tennessee: 1st, 171, 174; 2nd, 171, 174, 341; Wisconsin: 14th, 383, 385, 393; Engineer Regiment of the West, 397

Regiments, Mexican War, etc., 3rd Indiana, 119; Mississippi Rifles,

119; 4th U. S. Infantry, 3, 388; 2nd U. S. Cavalry, 73

Reid, Col. Hugh T., at Battle of Shiloh, 364

Reid, Whitelaw, 436; writes account of Battle of Shiloh, 391

Republicans, Convention of 1860, 6; position on slavery, 11

Resaca de la Palma, Battle of, 3, 319

Revolutionary War, 332

Reynolds, Brig. Gen. Joseph J., 22; commands Indiana regiment, 18

Rhea, farmer, near Shiloh church, 357

Richmond, Va., 58, 114, 132, 138, 149, 213, 239, 253, 263, 286, 324, 434

Richmond Daily Enquirer, cited, 22

Rio Grande River, 3, 341

Roberts, Col. Benjamin S., at Battle of Valverde, 341

Rockcastle River, Battle of, 132, 169

Rogers, Commander John, 53, 54

Rolla, Mo., 31, 37, 67, 115, 169

Roman, Lieut. Col. Alfred, C.S., cited, 214–215, 371

Ropes, John Codman, criticism of by Conger, 247; sustained and criticized by Fuller, 529

Rosecrans, Brig. Gen. William S., joins Halleck's army, 419; succeeds to command of the Army of the Mississippi, 440

Ross, Col. Leonard F., 127

Rost, Pierre A., Confederate commissioner to Europe, 343

Rousseau, Brig. Gen. Lovell H., 433; at Battle of Shiloh, 385, 388

Rowletts Station, Ky., action at, 147

Rowley, Maj. William R., seeks to influence Grant politically, 7; writes to Washburne, 193, 305, 333; joins Grant's staff, 305; at Battle of Shiloh, 360, 361, 379, 384

Ruggles, Brig. Gen. Daniel, C.S., 320, 330; in command at Corinth, 287

Rundstedt, Field Marshal Karl Gerd von, 223

Russell, Earl (Lord John), 343

Russell, Col. R. M., C.S., at Battle of Shiloh, 366

Russellville, Ky., 218

Russia, Cameron sent to as minister, 191

Sackets Harbor, N. Y., Grant at, 4

Saint. *See* St.

Saline County, Mo., 117

Salt River, Mo., 20, 47

Saltillo, Miss., 422

San Antonio, Tex., 73

San Francisco, Cal., 4, 105, 406

Sanitary Commission, report of, 161–162

Santa Anna, Antonio López de, Mexican president and general, 255

Saratoga, N.Y., 427

Savannah, Ga., 402

Savannah, Tenn., 328, 344, 353, 378, 387, 393, 408; Grant arrives at, 310

Schoepf, Brig. Gen. Albin, 150; at Battle of Rockcastle River, 132; makes forward move, 134–135; at Somerset, 146; in operation against Mill Springs, 169–171

Schofield, Brig. Gen. John M., reports on Lyon's expedition and Battle of Wilson's Creek, 31, 33; reports on retreat from Springfield, 36

Scott, Col. John S., C.S., 424

Scott, Thomas A., Ass't Sec. of War, 219, 306, 308, 414, 415, 419; telegraphs Gov. Morton about Kentucky, 49–50; sent West by Stanton on inspection trip, 191; reaches Indianapolis and learns of move up the Tennessee, 201–202; requests instructions from Stanton, 202; goes to Louisville and reports, 211–212; reaches Cairo and queries Halleck about attack on Fort Donelson, 226–227; reports Halleck's plans to Stanton, 240; disturbed over the situation, 241; sends a courier to Stanton with Halleck's plans, 261–262; reprimanded by Stanton, 273; reports to Stanton about Foote and Island No. 10, 399; reports arrival at Pittsburg Landing, 407; dispatches during advance on Corinth, 411–413; returns to Washington and resigns,

413; analysis of his support of the Carroll claim, 450–451

Scott, Lieut. Gen. Winfield, 3, 6, 57, 64, 73, 77, 87, 109, 130, 161, 185, 255, 267, 332; issues order for relief of Frémont, 65; comments about Halleck, 105; his letters of May, 1861, to McClellan outlining plans, 107

Seay, farmer, near Shiloh church, 357

Sedalia, Mo., 43, 115, 117

Sedgwick, Maj. Gen. John, 319

Seminoles. See Indians

Senate, 225, 276, 334; confirms Grant's promotion as major general of volunteers, 265

Seward, William H., Sec. of State, 7, 114; announces surrender of Mason and Slidell, 155

Shaver, Col. R. G., C.S., at Battle of Shiloh, 368

Shawneetown, Ill., 168

Shelbyville, Tenn., 321, 400, 402, 409

Sheridan, Col. Philip H., 259; quartermaster for Curtis, 288; joins Halleck and given a cavalry regiment, 414–415; reaches Guntown, 422

Sherman, Brig. Gen. Thomas W., 338; given command of Prentiss's division, 410

Sherman, Maj. Gen. William Tecumseh, 22, 83, 102, 111, 127, 129, 218, 219, 259, 267, 281, 330–334, 349, 357, 364; his comment on Grant, 40; in command in Kentucky, 72, 92–93, 135–137; in Missouri, given leave by Halleck because of his health, 115–116; returns to duty, 151, 183; given District of Cairo, reports from Paducah, 252; enters Columbus, 296; at Pittsburg Landing with Grant's 5th Division, 310, 315; reconnoiters Pea Ridge, 330–331; sent to liquidate batteries at Chickasaw, 337; conducts reconnaissance and reviews his division, 345–346; instructed to reenforce Lew Wallace if attacked, 348; issues alert order, 349–350; reports to Grant on enemy activity, 350; at Battle of Shiloh, 365–385, 390; especially commended by Grant, 394; in advance on Corinth, 412, 413, 416; calls Corinth a brilliant victory, 417; promoted to major general, 421; persuades Grant not to go on leave, 431–432; eulogizes Halleck, 439; his view of Grant, 439–440

Sherman, Mrs. W. T., 116

Shields, Brig. Gen. James, 343; submits plan of operations at Stanton's request, 195–196

Shiloh, Battle of, Johnston's attack order and approach march, 355–356; Federals attack Confederate pickets, 356–357; the first day, 363–382; the second day, 382–388; the pursuit dispute, 388–390; the question of surprise, 390–391; the march of Lew Wallace, 391–392; other comments about, 392–394; forces engaged and losses, 394–395; Halleck's reports on and congratulatory order, 405

Shiloh Church, Tenn., 315, 382, 384, 390

Shiloh Creek, Tenn., 357, 366

Shirk, Lieut. James W., naval officer, 316; at Battle of Shiloh, 376, 377, 386

Sibley, Brig. Gen. Henry H., C.S., at Battle of Valverde, 341

Siegfried Line, 332

Sigel, Brig. Gen. Franz, 34, 151, 218, 287; at Battle of Wilson's Creek, 32–34; in the retreat from, 36–37; as an element of discord, 181, 197; in Battle of Pea Ridge, 290–292

Sikeston, Mo., 50–53, 77, 299

Simpson, Hannah. See Grant, Hannah Simpson

Simpson, John, Grant's grandfather, 2

Slack, Col. James R., in New Madrid operation, 293

Slidell, John, Confederate commissioner to Europe, 152

Smith, Maj. Gen. Charles F., 61, 75, 76, 86, 87, 161, 188, 206, 225,

227, 248, 275, 319, 332, 353, 383; previous career and assignment to Paducah, 57; Grant suggests expedition to him, 72–73; telegraphs McClellan about firing at Columbus, 85; issues order condemning plundering, 96; reports to McClellan about Forts Henry and Donelson, 120, 121; refers to Confederate threats against Paducah, 120; replies to Halleck's queries as to enemy activity, 122–123; McClellan proposes to put him under Buell, 143; unfavorably reported about, saved by Halleck, 168; reconnoiters Fort Henry and states it can be reduced, 183–185; in attack on Fort Henry, 200–201; Grant urges Washburne to secure his confirmation, 225; in investment of Fort Donelson, 230, 233, 236; leads assault, 245–246; recommended by Halleck for promotion, 267; occupies Clarksville, 275–276; called to Nashville by Buell, 280; Halleck queries about the move, 302; placed in command of Tennessee River expedition, 303; is injured, 310; made major general, 334; death of and tributes to, 407

Smith, Mrs. C. F., Grant's letter to, 407

Smith, Maj. Gen. E. Kirby, C.S., sent to East Tennessee, 286; reported at Knoxville by Brownlow, 328; deceived by Mitchel's ruse, 403; alarmed by threat to Chattanooga, 425–426

Smith, George H., directed to install telegraph lines, 287

Smith, John E., opens Galena meeting, 11

Smith, Col. Morgan L., 313; at Fort Donelson, 246–247; at Battle of Shiloh, 381

Smithland, Ky., 61, 269

Snake Creek, Tenn., 316, 318, 348, 379

Somerset, Ky., 137, 142, 146, 170, 171

Southern Confederacy, cited, 427

Spain, 161, 181

Sprague, William, governor of Rhode Island, 22, 541

Springfield, Ill., 12–14, 18, 46, 103, 168, 191, 261

Springfield, Mo., 31, 34, 45, 46, 77, 78, 116, 150, 179

St. Francis River, Mo., 76

St. Louis, Mo., 4, 13, 14, 25, 31, 38, 40–43, 46, 47, 64, 75, 91, 103, 109, 114, 129, 160, 184, 191, 248, 261, 281, 287, 288, 292, 311; Frémont's headquarters at, 42; Halleck opens headquarters, 112; Beauregard and Van Dorn write about attacking the city, 286, 289

St. Louis, gunboat, at Fort Henry, 206; at Fort Donelson, 235, 243, 247, 248, 256

St. Louis and Iron Mountain R.R., 24

Stanton, Edwin M., Sec. of War, 192, 193, 202, 218, 219, 273, 307, 313, 377, 409, 412, 424, 425, 439, 440; his appointment and congratulatory order after Battle of Mill Springs, 176; informs Senator Wade of Lincoln's War Order, 187; sends Ass't Sec. Scott on inspection trip to the West, 191; receives requested plan of operations from James Shields, 195; congratulates Halleck for Forts Henry and Donelson, 209, 273; recommends Grant's promotion, 261; acts to get gunboat personnel, 265; writes Greeley about Fort Donelson, 270–271; replies to Scott's courier message, 275; telegraphs Halleck about his organization plan, 277, 306; queries Buell about plans for Gen. Morgan, 399; orders construction of ram fleet, 339–340; disseminates information, 407; inquires of Halleck about destruction of bridges, 408; reports optimistically to Halleck about McClellan, 419–420; issues an extravagant statement, 420; informs Mitchel of Lincoln's satisfaction with his operations, 424; receives Halleck's summer plan,

428; telegraphs him about Vicksburg, 430–431; reports McClellan's defeat and makes call on Halleck for troops, later cancelled, 434

Steele, Brig. Gen. Frederick, leads expedition toward Arkansas, 295; reports about Van Dorn and Price, 406

Stembel, Commander Roger N., 69

Stevenson, Ala., 216, 250, 409, 425, 438; seized by Mitchel, 402

Stone's battery, at Battle of Shiloh, 378

Stones River, Tenn., 400

Stoney Lonesome, Tenn., 360

Strength of Confederates, 83, 99–100, 132, 138, 149, 208, 214, 297, 344, 352, 394, 416, 421, 435, 479, 521, 531–532

Strength of Federals, 31, 65, 75, 80, 132, 149, 150, 152, 161, 166, 325, 344, 394, 479, 509, 532

Strong, Brig. Gen. William, 333

Stuart, Col. David, at Battle of Shiloh, 369, 372, 374, 383, 391

Sturgis, Brig. Gen. Samuel D., 462; at Battle of Wilson's Creek, 33; takes over command from Sigel, 36

Sugar Creek, Ark., 289, 291

Sumner, Maj. Gen. Edwin V., 103, 208

Sunken Road, at Battle of Shiloh, 368, 395

Tallahatche River, Ala., 435

Taylor, D. G., steamboat, 128

Taylor, Maj. Ezra, at Battle of Belmont, 95; at Battle of Shiloh, 374, 384

Taylor, Col. William H. H., 345–347

Taylor, Maj. Gen. Zachary, 3, 6, 75, 255, 333

Telegraph lines, extension of, 252, 287, 335, 408

Tennessee, 47, 61, 102, 107, 147, 194, 393, 438; governor of, 148, 286

Tennessee and Georgia R.R., 158

Tennessee River and operation up, 56, 102, 122, 142, 156, 158, 159, 186, 207, 243, 284, 287, 361,

401, 403, 406, 409, 413, 419, Grant's seizure of mouth of, 56–57; McClellan queries Halleck about, 118; an obvious invasion route, 119, 123; gunboat *Conestoga* reconnoiters Fort Henry, 119–120; Col. Whittlesey makes specific proposal to Halleck, 123; Buell's proposal sanctioned by McClellan, 143; Lincoln does not mention the route, 167; Halleck strongly endorses it, 179–180; Smith reports gunboats can reduce Fort Henry, 189; Grant and Foote inform Halleck they can take Fort Henry, 189; Halleck orders the operation, 190, 193; movement begins, 199; operation called hazardous by Buell, 208; ascent of river by gunboats, 206, 221–223, 287; Halleck desires rapid move up, 284; the Carroll claim, 448–452; the claims of Thayer, Emerson, and Washburne, 452–456. *See also* Fort Henry, Grant, Halleck, Shiloh

Texas, annexation of, 3; operation into mentioned by McClellan, 118

Thayer, Col. John M., at Fort Donelson, 244; at Battle of Shiloh, 381; his claim about Grant and the Tennessee campaign, 452–454

Thomas, Maj. Gen. George H., 110, 132, 136, 137, 139, 147, 150, 159, 191, 269, 280–281, 331, 411; his operations in Eastern Kentucky, 135–146; moves against Mill Springs, 169–171; at Battle of Mill Springs, 172–176; comment on his conduct of the battle, 174–175, 177; question of suspicion about, 176, 442–448; given command of the right wing of Halleck's army, 410; in advance on Corinth, 411, 413; is detached from Buell, 434; returned to his division, 442

Thomas, Brig. Gen. Lorenzo, Adjutant General, 113, 150, 168; makes inspection trip to the West with Cameron, 64–65; receives pessimistic report from Sherman, 92–93; inquires about Grant's absence from his command, 305

Thompson, Col. Jacob, C.S., at Battle of Shiloh, 356, 382, 385, 386

Thompson, Brig. Gen. M. Jeff, C.S., 52, 53, 95–96, 297, 433

Tigress, Grant's headquarters boat, 359–361, 370, 381, 395

Tilghman, Brig. Gen. Lloyd, C.S., 184, 212; leaves Paducah on Grant's approach, 56; his actions at Fort Henry, 200–205; capture of, 205; reports courtesy of Grant and Foote, 207

Tilghman Creek, Tenn., 383

Tipton, Mo., 65

Tiptonville, Tenn., 396, 399

Trabue, Col. Robert P., C.S., at Battle of Shiloh, 371

Trembly, Pvt. Edward N., reports gunfire at Pittsburg Landing, 359

Trent affair, 153–156

Trollope, Anthony, cited, 226, 249

Troops, calls for, 10, 18

Trumbull, Lyman, senator, offers to write in Grant's behalf, 23

Tupelo, Miss., 418, 420, 421

Tuscaloosa, Ala., 147

Tuscumbia, Ala., 222, 322, 409, 424, 433

Tuttle, Col. James M., at Battle of Shiloh, 385

Tyler, gunboat, 159, 225, 316, 318, 345, 395; at Belmont, 80; in Tennessee River Raid, 221, 222; at Fort Donelson, 237; at Battle of Shiloh, 376, 377, 381

Union College, N.Y., 104

Unionists, reported in large numbers by Phelps, 223

United States Military Academy. *See* West Point

Valverde, Battle of, 341

Vance, Lieut. Joseph, 28

Van Dorn, Maj. Gen. Earl, C.S., 402, 420; Beauregard asks his cooperation in an offensive, 286; past career of, 288–289; writes about an attack on St. Louis, 289; moves against Curtis, 289–291; in Battle of Pea Ridge, 291–292; Halleck cautions Curtis about him, 293; ordered to Memphis, 338; question of his absence from Shiloh, 393; reports about his movements, 406

Van Dorn, Confederate ram, in Battle of Memphis, 423

Veatch, Col. James C., at Battle of Shiloh, 374, 385, 388

Vera Cruz, Mexico, 3, 255

Vicksburg, Miss., Grant's post-war statement about possibilities of its capture in 1862, 429; Halleck's allusion to it in his plan, 430; its situation and fortification, 430; early efforts to take, 430; Butler's suggestion about, 430–431; comment on a possibility, 431; its challenge to Grant, 440; situation when Halleck left, 440

Virginia, 101–103, 107, 149, 334

Virginia and Tennessee R.R., 109, 284, 339

Waagner, Col. G., 50–54

Wade, Benjamin, Senator, informed by Stanton of Lincoln's War Order, 188; his support of the Carroll claim, 450

Wagner, Col. George D., at Battle of Shiloh, 387, 388

Walke, Commander Henry, at Belmont, 80, 81, 83, 85; at Fort Henry, 203, 205, 225; at Fort Donelson, 230, 232–234; at Island No. 10, 398–399

Walker, Leroy P., former Sec. of War, C.S., reports discouragingly to Richmond, 263; expresses confidence in Beauregard, 268

Walker's Gap, 131

Wallace, Maj. Gen. Lew, 247, 303, 328, 354, 367, 369, 372, 376; describes Grant's meeting with officers at Fort Henry, 227; called from Fort Henry to Fort Donelson, 233; given command of Grant's 3rd Division, 236–237; in battle at Fort Donelson, 244–246; his statement about Grant,

245; surrender incident, 256; sent back to Fort Henry, 257; strikes from Crumps Landing at Mobile and Ohio R.R., 318–319; made major general, 334; hears of threats from direction of Purdy, 348; receives warning order from Grant, 360; receives Grant's order from Baxter, the dispute, 362; at Battle of Shiloh, 379–385, 392–394; his different stories of his march, 392

Wallace, Brig. Gen. William H. L., 50, 75, 81, 83, 349, 364, 395; instructions from Grant in Belmont operation, 78; in command of Grant's 2nd division, 348; at Battle of Shiloh (mortally wounded), 365–372

Warner, steamboat, 360

Warsaw, Mo., 68

Wartburg, Tenn., 133

Washburne, Elihu B., congressman, 123, 180; addresses Galena meeting, 11; Grant writes to, 52; Rawlins writes to, 152, 185–186, 333; Rowley writes to, 193, 305, 333; Grant telegraphs him about securing confirmation for Smith, 225; supports Emerson's Tennessee River claim for Grant, 455–456

Washington, D.C., 10, 37, 57, 77, 91, 147, 160, 248, 299, 326, 405

Washington's Birthday, 229; Congress observes, 276

Wavell, Gen. Sir Archibald, cited, 456

Waynesboro, Tenn., 353, 392; Halleck gives permission to Buell to stop there, 351

Webster, Col. Joseph D., Grant's chief of staff, 313; carries Grant's note to Polk, 87–88; at Fort Donelson, 246; reconnoiters near Hamburg, 347; at Battle of Shiloh, 373–379

Welles, Gideon, Sec. of Navy, 340, 377, 399; Foote's report to about Fort Donelson, 243, 262; orders Farragut to return to Vicksburg, 430

West, Capt., C.S., 169

West Point, 2, 5, 12–14, 28, 55, 73, 239, 258, 274, 289, 311, 319, 354, 410, 414

West Virginia, 139, 141, 419

"Western Division," organization of urged by Halleck, 219

Western Investigating Commission, 304

White, Capt., C.S., Grant reports about, 28

White Haven, home of Dent family, 3, 5

White House, The, 103, 104, 167, 277

White River, Ark., 70

Whittlesey, Col. Charles, 142, 180; suggests operation up Cumberland and Tennessee to Halleck, 123; at Fort Donelson, 243; at Battle of Shiloh, 381

Wilkes, Capt. Charles, takes Confederate commissioners from the *Trent,* 153

Wilkins, Lieut. John, diary of cited, 238, 336–337

Williamsburg, Ky., 146

Willich, Col. August, at Battle of Shiloh, 384–385

Wilson, Brig. Gen. James H., cited, 152, 442

Wilson's Creek, Battle of, 3, 32–33, 46, 65; retreat from, 36–37

Winchester, Tenn., 425

Wisconsin, 36, 102, 344; Grant's trips to, 8; color bearers killed at Shiloh, 395

Wolford, Col. Frank, at Battle of Mill Springs, 172–174

Wood, Brig. Gen. Thomas J., 170–171, 269, 410; ordered by Grant to Savannah, 360; his march, 370–371; at Battle of Shiloh, 387–390

Woodburn, Ky., 239

Wool, Maj. Gen. John E., 101

World War II, 159

Yancey, William L., Confederate commissioner to Europe, 343–344

Yankee, Confederate gunboat, 69

Yates, Richard, governor of Illinois, 11, 23; makes Grant mustering officer, 14; appoints him to command of 21st Ill., 18; promises him a rifled battery, 71; urges Pope be made a major general in the regular army, 400

Yazoo River, Miss., 440

Yorktown, Va., 412, 416

Zagonyi, Maj. Charles, 64, 66

Zollicoffer, Brig. Gen. Felix, C.S., 58, 110, 111, 134, 135, 138, 150, 159, 170; at Battle of Rockcastle River, 132; reports his intentions and operations to Johnston, 132–134; reported by Buell as on the Cumberland, 141; goes into winter quarters at Mill Springs, Ky., 146; issues proclamation to Kentuckians, 150; Thomas ordered to move against him, 169; superseded by Crittenden, 171; at Battle of Mill Springs (killed), 175